AUDITING
CONCEPTS•STANDARDS•PROCEDURES

AUDITING
CONCEPTS•STANDARDS•PROCEDURES

Edited by Thomas D. Hubbard, Johnny R. Johnson & Ann B. Pushkin

CONTRIBUTING AUTHORS:

Wesley T. Andrews
Florida Atlantic University

Jerry Bullington
Smith Elliott & Company
Certified Public Accountants

Donna Lynn Welker
Texas A&M University

Louis G. Gutberlet
Kenneth Leventhal & Company
Certified Public Accountant

Thomas D. Hubbard
University of Nebraska

Johnny R. Johnson
University of Georgia

Joyce C. Lambert
University of Nebraska

Thomas E. McKee
East Tennessee State University

Ann B. Pushkin
West Virginia University

© DAME PUBLICATIONS, INC.   1983

ISBN 0-931920-44-2

Library of Congress Catalog Card No. 82-72439

Printed in the United States of America

PREFACE

This text is designed for use by undergraduate or graduate auditing students. The material in the text is arranged so that it can be used as the primary text for the undergraduate auditing course or along with supplementary readings, in a graduate auditing course. The text material can be easily understood by students who have completed a one quarter or one semester course in financial accounting. Also, the text is easily adapted to a quarter or a semester system. Finally, since the text is comprehensive in nature, it provides students with an excellent background for the auditing sections of the CPA Examination and other professional examinations.

EIGHT UNIQUE FEATURES

Auditing contains eight features not found in traditional auditing texts. First, it is comprehensive in the technical topics that students will encounter frequently throughout their professional careers. For example, two chapters, 5 and 8, are devoted to a discussion of internal control; and the importance of internal control as well as the relationship between internal control and substantive tests are discussed throughout the text. Likewise, Chapter 3 presents an in-depth discussion of professional ethics as well as the auditor's responsibilities in tax practice and management advisory services. Chapter 6 also presents an in-depth discussion of audit evidence including a theoretical discussion of minimum audit procedures for balance sheet and income statement accounts. This theoretical discussion is then used in other chapters to improve the students' understanding of the reasons for various audit program steps. Thus, audit program steps for specific accounts are not presented within a vacuum, as in many texts, but instead the audit program steps are related to the theoretical discussion of minimum audit procedures and audit evidence which are presented in Chapter 6. Chapter 7 also presents a comprehensive, but understandable, discussion of the impact of EDP on auditing procedures, and the impact of EDP on the auditor's work is integrated throughout the text.

A second unique feature of this text is that theory and logic is used throughout the text in explaining auditing issues. For example, audit program steps are discussed in terms of theoretical aspects of audit evidence and minimum audit procedures which are developed in Chapter 6. Likewise, simply quoting an official pronouncement as support for an auditing standard or procedure has been avoided. Instead, auditing standards and procedures have been evaluated in view of current auditing theory, including current findings from auditing research projects.

A third unique feature of this text is that it presents the topics in a manner that is understandable to students with little or no business background. For example, internal control concepts and principles, as well as the relationship between internal control and substantive tests, are illustrated in Chapters 5 and 8 by using a comprehensive example of internal control which might be found in a restaurant and which all students should be able to relate to. After these illustrations with a familiar, but comprehensive example, subsequent chapters then discuss internal control concepts and principles as they apply to more complex systems which the students may not be as familiar with. A similar form of presentation, i.e., moving from the familiar to the less familiar, is also employed in discussing other difficult topics, such as statistical sampling and EDP.

A fourth unique feature is that each chapter contains a comprehensive summary. These summaries will be especially helpful to students as they review the text material.

A fifth unique feature of this text is that each chapter contains a wide variety of AICPA adapted multiple-choice questions, over 650 in total. In view of the trend towards more objective questions on the professional examinations, exposure to multiple-choice questions is now a necessary part of a student's auditing education.

A sixth unique feature of this text is the comprehensive nature of the *Solution Manual*. Each solution is supported with detailed explanations. For example, each multiple-choice solution is supported by a narrative explanation which details why a given answer is the best of the four alternative answers presented in the question.

A seventh unique feature of this text is the way in which we have used contributing authors to ensure that the text reflects a wide variety of experience and education. For example, contributing authors represent both academicians and practitioners. Also, contributing authors have experience in public accounting, both large and small firms, industry, and government. However, the work of all contributing authors has been carefully edited to avoid duplication and to ensure consistency in the writing style which is used throughout the text.

An eighth feature that is unique for a first edition is that every chapter in the text has been extensively class tested. This classroom testing was done both at West Virginia University and the University of Nebraska at Lincoln.

ORGANIZATION

The text is organized into 18 chapters. These chapters are grouped into six parts.

The first three chapters of the book constitute Part One of the text. These chapters emphasize auditing theory, concepts, and standards as well as the nature of the auditing profession.

Part Two of the text begins with Chapter 4 which discusses the planning of audit engagements. Next, Chapter 5 discusses internal control principles and standards. Part Two concludes with a discussion on the nature of evidential matter and quality control for CPA firms.

Part Three of the text discusses compliance tests. This part begins with Chapter 7 which discusses internal control review for manual and EDP systems. Next, Chapter 8 discusses tests of compliance and the evaluation of internal control systems. Part Three concludes with a discussion of attribute sampling and compliance testing.

Part Four of the text discusses substantive tests. This part begins with Chapter 10 which discusses substantive tests and sampling for variables. Part Four then continues with chapters which discuss the audit of the revenue cycle; the audit of the expense and production cycle; and the audit of the financing and investing cycle. This part concludes with Chapter 14 which discusses completing the audit engagement.

Part Five of the text discusses the auditor's reporting responsibilities. This part contains chapters on audit reports, other types of reports, and the auditor's legal liability.

The text concludes with Part Six which presents a discussion of accounting services.

REVIEW QUESTIONS, PROBLEMS, AND MULTIPLE-CHOICE QUESTIONS

Each chapter contains a variety of review questions, problems, and multiple-choice questions. End-of-chapter material is provided for every major issue discussed in the chapter, and these materials, as indicated earlier, contain a wide variety of CPA exam adapted questions. In adapting questions from professional exams, however, care was taken to modify the data so as not to ask a question or problem which had not been covered at that point in the text.

ACKNOWLEDGE-MENTS

We are indebted to J.B. Dresselhaus, a partner in the firm of Johnson Grant & Co., CPAs, for reviewing the manuscript from the practitioners' viewpoint. Also, the following other individuals in public accounting or industry made valuable suggestions: Samuel Johnson, Barry Wabler, and Marc Pinto.

We are also indebted to Claire Arevalo, a writing consultant at the University of Georgia, for editing the text. Ms. Arevalos' input on the drafts of each chapter resulted in a more readable text.

We are also indebted to the students at the University of Nebraska at Lincoln and West Virginia University for class testing the text.

Finally, we would like to thank Anna Hubbard and Judy Hunter for their editorial assistance, Jan Tiefel for typesetting the text and Stephen Emry for all art work.

We will appreciate comments from the readers of this text.

1983

Thomas D. Hubbard
Johnny R. Johnson
Ann B. Pushkin

CONTENTS

The Auditing Profession

Introduction. Auditing from the Internal, Governmental, and External Perspectives. Reasons for an Audit. Importance of the Attest Function. Relationship of Auditing to Accounting. Public Accounting Firms. Qualifications of the Auditor. Overview of the Audit Process. Summary. Review Questions. Discussion Questions and Problems. Objective Questions.

Introduction. Postulates. Postulates of Auditing. Auditing Concepts. *Evidence. Due Audit Care. Fair Presentation. Independence.* Generally Accepted Auditing Standards (GAAS). *General Standards. Field Work Standards. Reporting Standards. Standards versus Procedures.* Standard Audit Report and Other Reports. *Modifications of the Standard Audit Report.* Summary. Review Questions. Discussion Questions and Problems. Objective Questions.

Introduction. The Nature of the AICPA's Code of Professional Ethics. Rules of Conduct. *Applicability of Rules of Conduct. Rule 101 — Independence. Rule 102 — Integrity and Objectivity. Rule 201 — General Standards. Rule 202 — Auditing Standards. Rule 203 — Accounting Principles. Rule 204 — Other Technical Standards. Rule 301 — Confidential Client Information. Rule 302 — Contingent Fees. Rule 501 — Acts Discreditable. Rule 502 — Advertising and Other*

Forms of Solicitation. Rule 503 — Commissions. Rule 504 — Incompatible Occupations. Rule 505 — Form of Practice and Name. Other Codes of Professional Ethics. Statements on Responsibility in Tax Practice. *Signature of Preparer. Signature of Reviewer: Assumption of Preparer's Responsibility. Answer to Questions on Returns. Recognition of Administrative Proceeding of a Prior Year. Use of Estimates. Knowledge of Error: Return Preparation. Knowledge of an Error: Administrative Proceedings. Advice to Clients. Certain Procedural Aspects of Preparing Returns. Positions Contrary to Treasury Department or Internal Revenue Service Interpretations of the Code.* Statement on Standards for Management Advisory Services. *Definitions. Standards for MAS Practice.* Summary. Review Questions. Discussion Questions and Problems. Objective Questions.

Beginning the Audit Engagement

Introduction. The Audit Process. Client Solicitation Process. *Community Visibility. Referrals. Prospective Clients Soliciting Bids for Audit Services. Advertising.* Client Evaluation, Acceptance and Continuance Procedures. *Evaluation of Prospective Clients. Communication with Predecessor Auditor. Engagement Letters. Client Continuance.* Understanding the Client and Industry. Evaluating Current Economic Conditions. Obtain Knowledge of Client's Industry. Refine Knowledge of Client. Analytical Review Procedures. Development of Overall Audit Plan. *Developing an Overall Audit Strategy. Scheduling the Audit Work. Using the Work of a Specialist. Considering and Coordinating Work with Internal Auditors. Audit Programs. Audit Working Papers. Audit Symbols (Tick Marks).* Summary. Review Questions. Discussion Questions and Problems. Objective Questions.

Introduction. A Simple System of Internal Control. The Nature of Internal Control. *Accounting Versus Administrative Control. Compensating Controls. Internal Control and Firm Size.* Basic Concepts of Internal Accounting

Control. *Management Responsibility. Reasonable Assurance. Methods of Data Processing. Limitations. Personnel. Segregation of Functions. Execution of Transactions. Recording of Transactions. Access to Assets. Comparison of Recorded Accountability with Assets.* Foreign Corrupt Practices Act. Summary. Review Questions. Discussion Questions and Problems. Objective Questions.

Introduction. Evidential Matter. Nature of Assertions. Use of Assertions in Developing Audit Objectives and Designing Substantive Tests. Minimum Substantive Audit Procedures for Income Statement Balances. Minimum Substantive Audit Procedures for Balance Sheet Balances. Relationship Between Minimum Substantive Audit Procedures for Balance Sheet and Income Statement Accounts. Nature of Evidential Matter. Competence of Evidential Matter. Sufficiency of Evidential Matter. Evaluation of Evidential Matter. Quality Control for CPA Firms. Nature of Quality Control for a CPA Firm. Elements of Quality Control for a CPA Firm. Summary. Review Questions. Discussion Questions and Problems. Objective Questions.

Field Work — Compliance Tests

Introduction. Review Responsibility. Reporting Material Control Weaknesses. Internal Control Review and Documentation Procedures. *Review of the System. Data Gathering Techniques. Documentation.* EDP Systems and Controls. General Controls. *Organization and Operation of EDP Department. Applications or Systems Approval and Documentation. EDP Hardware Controls. Access Controls. Data or Procedural Controls.* Application Controls. *Input Controls. Processing Controls. Output Controls.* Review and Reporting Responsibilities for EDP Systems. Auditing Techniques for EDP Systems. *Audit Compliance Testing Without Utilizing the Computer. Techniques for Computer Audit Compliance Testing. Substantive Audit Testing Techniques Using the Computer.* Summary. Review Questions. Discussion Questions and Problems. Objective Questions.

Sampling Risks. Nonsampling Risks. Ultimate Risk. Audit Objectives and Financial Statement Assertions. *Defining Audit Objectives. Nature of Financial Statement Assertions. Evidence-Gathering Procedures.* Designing and Evaluating Substantive Tests. *Types of Substantive Tests. Analytical Review Techniques. Tests of Details of Transactions or Balances. Sampling and Substantive Tests. Identifying Audit Populations. Factors Influencing Sample Size. Selecting Sample Items. Evaluation of Sample Results. The Audit Decision.* Variables Sampling Plans. *Descriptions of Different Variables Sampling Plans. Advantages and Disadvantages of Variables Sampling. Control of Sampling Risks in Statistical Plans.* Illustrative Case. *Same Size Determination. Assumed Data for Illustrative Case. Point Estimates. Standard Error of Sample Means. Precision Limits and Confidence Levels.* Summary. **Appendix A. Appendix B.** Derivation of Sample Size Formula and Control of the Beta Risk. *Derivation of Sample Size Formula. Control of the Beta Risk.* Review Questions. Discussion Questions and Problems. Objective Questions.

Introduction. Overview of the Revenue Cycle. Audit Objectives and the Revenue Cycle. Planning the Audit of the Revenue Cycle. Developing Audit Programs Related to the Revenue Cycle. *Audit Program for Preliminary Evaluation of Controls. Developing Substantive Tests of Balances of the Accounts Affected by the Revenue Cycle. Sales, Sales Returns and Allowances, Accounts Receivable, and Notes Receivable. Allowance for Doubtful Accounts and Bad Debts Expense.* Summary. Review Questions. Discussion Questions and Problems. Objective Questions.

Introduction. *Overview General Voucher Segment. Overview of General Cash Disbursements Segment. Overview of Petty Cash Disbursement Segment. Overview of Payroll Segment.* Audit Objectives of the Expense and Production Cycle. *Overall Objectives. Specific Objectives of the Audit of the Expense and Production Cycle.* Developing Audit Programs Related to the Expense and Production Cycle. *Substantive Audit Programs. Substantive Audit Program for Imprest Petty*

Another Auditor. Reporting a Departure from a Promulgated Accounting Principle. Predecessor Auditor—Reporting Responsibilities of Successor Auditor. Reporting on Unaudited Statements in Comparative Form. Continuing Auditor and Updating. Reports Based in Part on the Work of a Specialist. Dating the Audit Report. Discovery of Information After Releasing the Financial Statements and Audit Report. Other Information in Documents Containing Audited Statements. Segment Information. Summary. Review Questions. Discussion Questions and Problems. Objective Questions.

Introduction. Financial Statements Prepared in Accordance with a Comprehensive Basis of Accounting Other Than GAAP. *Non-GAAP Criteria. Disclosure in Non-GAAP Financial Statements. Reporting Under OCBOA. Auditing Standards in OCBOA Engagements. Cash Basis Financial Statements. Reports on Other Types to OCBOA Statements.* Reports on Compliance with Contractual and Regulatory Requirements. *Nature of Restrictions. Reporting on Compliance. Reporting on Financial Statements Prepared Pursuant to a Contractual Agreement.* Examination of Financial Statement Elements and Reporting. *Expressing an Opinion on Specified Elements, Accounts or Items of a Financial Statement. Reporting on Agreed-Upon Procedures with Respect to Specified Elements, Accounts or Items of a Financial Statement.* Prescribed Form Reports. *Prescribed Auditor's Opinion. Prescribed Financial Statement Format.* Reporting on Internal Accounting Control. *Expression of an Opinion on a Client's System of Accounting Control. Planning the Audit of Internal Control. Reviewing the Design of the Control System. Testing Compliance with Prescribed Procedures. The CPA's Report. Report on Accounting Control Based on a Study and Evaluation Made as Part of an Audit. Special-Purpose Reports on Internal Accounting Control at Service Organizations. Reports Based on Criteria Established by Regulatory Agencies.* Letters for Underwriters. *The Auditor's Responsibility. Content of Comfort Letters.* Summary. Review Questions. Discussion Questions and Problems. Objective Questions.

Services

☐ THE AUDITING PROFESSION

FAIR PRESENTATION ETHICAL CONDUCT INDEPENDENCE EVIDENCE DUE CARE FAIR PRESENTATION ETHICAL CONDUCT INDEPENDENCE EVIDENCE DUE CARE FAIR PRESENTAT
ARE FAIR PRESENTATION ETHICAL CONDUCT INDEPENDENCE EVIDENCE DUE CARE FAIR PRESENTATION ETHICAL CONDUCT INDEPENDENCE EVIDENCE DUE CARE FAIR PRESEN
JE CARE FAIR PRESENTATION ETHICAL CONDUCT INDEPENDENCE EVIDENCE DUE CARE FAIR PRESENTATION ETHICAL CONDUCT INDEPENDENCE EVIDENCE DUE CARE FAIR PRE
E DUE CARE FAIR PRESENTATION ETHICAL CONDUCT INDEPENDENCE EVIDENCE DUE CARE FAIR PRESENTATION ETHICAL CONDUCT INDEPENDENCE EVIDENCE DUE CARE FAIR
ENCE DUE CARE FAIR PRESENTATION ETHICAL CONDUCT INDEPENDENCE EVIDENCE DUE CARE FAIR PRESENTATION ETHICAL CONDUCT INDEPENDENCE EVIDENCE DUE CARE
EVIDENCE DUE CARE FAIR PRESENTATION ETHICAL CONDUCT INDEPENDENCE EVIDENCE DUE CARE FAIR PRESENTATION ETHICAL CONDUCT INDEPENDENCE EVIDENCE DUE CA
CE EVIDENCE DUE CARE FAIR PRESENTATION ETHICAL CONDUCT INDEPENDENCE EVIDENCE DUE CARE FAIR PRESENTATION ETHICAL CONDUCT INDEPENDENCE EVIDENCE DU
DENCE EVIDENCE DUE CARE FAIR PRESENTATION ETHICAL CONDUCT INDEPENDENCE EVIDENCE DUE CARE FAIR PRESENTATION ETHICAL CONDUCT INDEPENDENCE EVIDENCE

LEARNING OBJECTIVES

CT INDEPENDENCE EVIDENCE DUE CARE FAIR PRESENTATION ETHICAL CONDUCT INDEPENDENCE EVIDENCE DUE CARE FAIR PRESENTATION ETHICAL CONDUCT INDEPENDENC
NDUCT INDEPENDENCE EVIDENCE DUE CARE FAIR PRESENTATION ETHICAL CONDUCT INDEPENDENCE EVIDENCE DUE CARE FAIR PRESENTATION ETHICAL CONDUCT INDEPENI
L CONDUCT INDEPENDENCE EVIDENCE DUE CARE FAIR PRESENTATION ETHICAL CONDUCT INDEPENDENCE EVIDENCE DUE CARE FAIR PRESENTATION ETHICAL CONDUCT INDE
ICAL CONDUCT INDEPENDENCE EVIDENCE DUE CARE FAIR PRESENTATION ETHICAL CONDUCT INDEPENDENCE EVIDENCE DUE CARE FAIR PRESENTATION ETHICAL CONDUCT IN

After studying this chapter, students should understand

1. The definition of auditing.
2. The differences between internal auditors, governmental auditors, and external auditors.
3. The nature of the attest function and the importance of independence.
4. The reasons for an audit.
5. The relationship between accounting and auditing.
6. The nature of CPA firms, including the services they provide.
7. The nature of the CPA exam and the general requirements to become a CPA.
8. The nature of the audit process, including the importance of an engagement letter.

PENDENCE EVIDENCE DUE CARE FAIR PRESENTATION ETHICAL CONDUCT INDEPENDENCE EVIDENCE DUE CARE FAIR PRESENTATION ETHICAL CONDUCT INDEPENDENCE EVIDEN
NDEPENDENCE EVIDENCE DUE CARE FAIR PRESENTATION ETHICAL CONDUCT INDEPENDENCE EVIDENCE DUE CARE FAIR PRESENTATION ETHICAL CONDUCT INDEPENDENCE EW
T INDEPENDENCE EVIDENCE DUE CARE FAIR PRESENTATION ETHICAL CONDUCT INDEPENDENCE EVIDENCE DUE CARE FAIR PRESENTATION ETHICAL CONDUCT INDEPENDENCE
DUCT INDEPENDENCE EVIDENCE DUE CARE FAIR PRESENTATION ETHICAL CONDUCT INDEPENDENCE EVIDENCE DUE CARE FAIR PRESENTATION ETHICAL CONDUCT INDEPENDE
CONDUCT INDEPENDENCE EVIDENCE DUE CARE FAIR PRESENTATION ETHICAL CONDUCT INDEPENDENCE EVIDENCE DUE CARE FAIR PRESENTATION ETHICAL CONDUCT INDEPE
CAL CONDUCT INDEPENDENCE EVIDENCE DUE CARE FAIR PRESENTATION ETHICAL CONDUCT INDEPENDENCE EVIDENCE DUE CARE FAIR PRESENTATION ETHICAL CONDUCT IN
ETHICAL CONDUCT INDEPENDENCE EVIDENCE DUE CARE FAIR PRESENTATION ETHICAL CONDUCT INDEPENDENCE EVIDENCE DUE CARE FAIR PRESENTATION ETHICAL CONDUCT
ON ETHICAL CONDUCT INDEPENDENCE EVIDENCE DUE CARE FAIR PRESENTATION ETHICAL CONDUCT INDEPENDENCE EVIDENCE DUE CARE FAIR PRESENTATION ETHICAL COND
TATION ETHICAL CONDUCT INDEPENDENCE EVIDENCE DUE CARE FAIR PRESENTATION ETHICAL CONDUCT INDEPENDENCE EVIDENCE DUE CARE FAIR PRESENTATION ETHICAL C
SENTATION ETHICAL CONDUCT INDEPENDENCE EVIDENCE DUE CARE FAIR PRESENTATION ETHICAL CONDUCT INDEPENDENCE EVIDENCE DUE CARE FAIR PRESENTATION E
PRESENTATION ETHICAL CONDUCT INDEPENDENCE EVIDENCE DUE CARE FAIR PRESENTATION ETHICAL CONDUCT INDEPENDENCE EVIDENCE DUE CARE FAIR PRESENTATION E
FAIR PRESENTATION ETHICAL CONDUCT INDEPENDENCE EVIDENCE DUE CARE FAIR PRESENTATION ETHICAL CONDUCT INDEPENDENCE EVIDENCE DUE CARE FAIR PRESENTATIO
RE FAIR PRESENTATION ETHICAL CONDUCT INDEPENDENCE EVIDENCE DUE CARE FAIR PRESENTATION ETHICAL CONDUCT INDEPENDENCE EVIDENCE DUE CARE FAIR PRESENTA
E CARE FAIR PRESENTATION ETHICAL CONDUCT INDEPENDENCE EVIDENCE DUE CARE FAIR PRESENTATION ETHICAL CONDUCT INDEPENDENCE EVIDENCE DUE CARE FAIR PRES
DUE CARE FAIR PRESENTATION ETHICAL CONDUCT INDEPENDENCE EVIDENCE DUE CARE FAIR PRESENTATION ETHICAL CONDUCT INDEPENDENCE EVIDENCE DUE CARE FAIR P
NCE DUE CARE FAIR PRESENTATION ETHICAL CONDUCT INDEPENDENCE EVIDENCE DUE CARE FAIR PRESENTATION ETHICAL CONDUCT INDEPENDENCE EVIDENCE DUE CARE FA
IDENCE DUE CARE FAIR PRESENTATION ETHICAL CONDUCT INDEPENDENCE EVIDENCE DUE CARE FAIR PRESENTATION ETHICAL CONDUCT INDEPENDENCE EVIDENCE DUE CAR
E EVIDENCE DUE CARE FAIR PRESENTATION ETHICAL CONDUCT INDEPENDENCE EVIDENCE DUE CARE FAIR PRESENTATION ETHICAL CONDUCT INDEPENDENCE EVIDENCE DUE
ENCE EVIDENCE DUE CARE FAIR PRESENTATION ETHICAL CONDUCT INDEPENDENCE EVIDENCE DUE CARE FAIR PRESENTATION ETHICAL CONDUCT INDEPENDENCE EVIDENCE C

Chapter 1

Introduction to Auditing

This chapter was written by
Joyce C. Lambert, Ph.D., C.P.A.,
Associate Professor of Accounting,
University of Nebraska, Lincoln

INTRODUCTION

"In God we trust, all others we audit." This quote sums up a basic viewpoint of some professionals towards auditing. Auditing has existed in one form or another since ancient times. Records show that auditing activity was part of early life in Babylonia, China, Greece, and Rome. One ancient meaning for the word "auditor" was a "hearer or listener." In Rome, auditors heard transactions as they took place. They observed the events as they happened and were able to recount the responsibilities and obligations to which each party was bound. Modern auditing, as defined by the American Accounting Association, is

> . . . a systematic process of objectively obtaining and evaluating evidence regarding assertions about economic actions and events to ascertain the degree of correspondence between those assertions and established criteria and communicating the results to interested users.[1]

An examination of the definition of auditing reveals that there are three key aspects of the definition. First, auditing is not an activity which can be performed in a haphazard manner, it is a systematic process based on logic and reasoning.

Second, during an examination of financial statements the auditor objectively obtains and evaluates evidence regarding assertions about economic actions and events embodied in the financial statements to ascertain the degree of correspondence between those assertions and established criteria. In the audit of financial statements prepared by a company, the established criteria are generally accepted accounting principles (GAAP). That is, the financial statements must be prepared in accordance with GAAP. Consequently, the auditor must obtain and evaluate evidence to determine whether the assertions (the elements of the financial statements) meet the established criteria (GAAP).

The third and final key aspect of the definition is that auditing involves communicating the results of the audit to interested users. The auditor communicates the findings of the audit process by issuing an audit report. In the audit report, the auditor gives an opinion as to whether the assertions are reported in accordance with the established criteria. For example, in the audit of financial statements the auditor issues an audit report which describes the scope of the examination in the first paragraph and states in the last paragraph whether in his or her opinion the financial statements are fairly presented in accordance with

---

[1] *A Statement of Basic Auditing Concepts*, (Sarasota, Florida: American Accounting Association, 1971), p. 2.

generally accepted accounting principles applied on a consistent basis. This communication function is illustrated in the Mobile Corporation report:

February 17, 1985

Board of Directors and Shareholders
Mobile Corporation

We have examined the balance sheets of Mobile Corporation as of December 31, 1984 and 1983, and the related statements of income, retained earnings, and changes in financial position for the years then ended. Our examinations were made in accordance with generally accepted auditing standards and, accordingly, included such tests of the accounting records and such other auditing procedures as we considered necessary in the circumstances.

In our opinion, the financial statements referred to above present fairly the financial position of Mobile Corporation as of December 31, 1984 and 1983, and the results of its operations and the changes in its financial position for the years then ended, in conformity with generally accepted accounting principles applied on a consistent basis.

BRIDGES, GEISERT & VICKERY

Certified Public Accountants

The audit report for Mobile Corporation is a standard unqualified audit report that identifies the financial statements examined, describes the scope of the examination—"Our examinations were made in accordance with generally accepted auditing standards and, accordingly, included such tests of the accounting records and such other auditing procedures as we considered necessary . . ." and expresses the auditor's opinion that the statements are presented fairly in conformity with GAAP applied on a consistent basis.

The opinion fulfills the attest function of certified public accountants. That is, the standard audit report of a CPA attests to the fairness, or lack of fairness, of the audited financial statements. The date of the audit report (February 17, 1985) is the date that the auditors completed all of the important aspects of their audit field work—the date they completed the evidence gathering process. The audit report should be addressed to the "Board of Directors and Shareholders" or to the group of individuals responsible for engaging the CPA firm rather than to the management of Mobile Corporation. Addressing the report in this manner tends to emphasize the independence of the auditors from the management of the company. The audit report is discussed in Chapters 2 and 15.

AUDITING FROM THE INTERNAL, GOVERNMENTAL, AND EXTERNAL PERSPECTIVES

Although the audit process of obtaining and evaluating evidence and communicating the results to interested users applies to all audit applications, the objectives of auditing vary depending on the needs of users of the audit report. Internal auditing, governmental auditing, and external auditing all serve different objectives.

Internal auditing is defined as:

> . . . an independent appraisal function established within an organization to examine and evaluate its activities as a service to the organization. The objective of internal auditing is to assist members of the organization in the effective discharge of their responsibilities. To this end, internal auditing furnishes them with analyses, appraisals, recommendations, counsel, and information concerning the activities reviewed.[2]

A comparison of the definition of internal auditing with the general definition of auditing by the American Accounting Association reveals that internal auditing is broader in scope than external auditing. Specifically, internal auditors are concerned with more than the correspondence between assertions about economic events captured in financial statements and the established criteria for reporting the assertions. Internal auditors require a broader definition of auditing because they are employed by the company that they audit. Consequently, internal auditors must define their function in such a way that the function will include any activity that is helpful to their employer.

Governmental auditing covers a wide range of activities on the federal, state, and local levels and numerous regulatory agencies. Governmental auditors not only examine financial statements but also determine whether government program objectives are met and whether certain government agencies and private enterprises comply with applicable laws and regulations. For example, Congress authorized the General Accounting Office (GAO) to oversee various government programs such as welfare and various Defense Department contracts. The Cost Accounting Standards Board (CASB) was also created by Congress to develop cost accounting standards which must be followed on large federal government defense contracts.

---

[2] *Standards for the Professional Practice of Internal Auditing*, The Institute of Internal Auditors, Inc., Altamonte Springs, Florida, 1981, p. 1.

External auditing, which is the emphasis of this text, involves reporting on financial statements prepared by management for external users or third parties. Third parties include stockholders, creditors, bankers, potential investors, and federal, state, and local regulatory agencies. External audits are performed by independent CPA firms. Although the audit fee for an external audit is paid by the company being audited, external auditors, unlike internal auditors, are not employees of the company being audited—they must be independent of the company and its management. If external auditors do not maintain personal integrity and objectivity regarding the audit client, the audit report will lack credence from the viewpoint of third party users. Independence is, therefore, the backbone of external auditing.

External auditors must be independent in fact and in the appearance they present to third parties. So in addition to being objective and unbiased, they must free themselves of any impediments which, in the eye of third party users, would impair their *appearance* of independence. Independent auditors cannot own stock in the companies they audit nor have a direct or material indirect financial interest in their clients. Independent auditors cannot perform duties equivalent to that of employees or members of management for the companies they audit.

The attest function refers to the independent auditor's expression of an opinion on the fairness of a firm's financial statements. As illustrated, the auditor's opinion states whether the statements are fairly presented in accordance with generally accepted accounting principles applied on a consistent basis (attests to the fairness or lack of fairness of the audited statements). Unless otherwise indicated, the term "auditor" in this text will refer to the independent external auditor, the CPA who is acting in the role of independent auditor performing the attest function.

REASONS FOR AN AUDIT

Entities are audited by independent CPAs for numerous reasons. Some audits are needed because they are required by law. Companies regulated by the Securities and Exchange Commission are required to have annual independent audits. Various governmental units are also required by law to have audits at specified intervals.

Absentee ownership is another reason why audits are needed. Stockholders desire audits to determine management's stewardship of their assets. Some banks also require audited financial statements before granting loans. Likewise, when business firms are under consideration for mergers or sale, audits are desirable to properly ascertain the business's financial condition. Termination or death of a partner usually necessitates an audit to allocate assets in accordance with the partnership agreement. Finally, some suppliers require audited financial statements before they will grant a large amount of credit for sales of their products.

Audits can also have a preventive effect. If employees or management know they will be audited, this fact may help prevent and detect errors or irregularities.

IMPORTANCE OF THE ATTEST FUNCTION

As indicated earlier, the attest function refers to the auditor's expression of an opinion on a company's financial statements. This section explains why the attest function is important.

A company's financial statements, which summarize the financial activities of the past accounting periods, are prepared internally by management. The company's vice president of finance or the controller, who is responsible for the actual financial data accumulation, is usually technically competent to prepare statements in accordance with generally accepted accounting principles, but he or she is not independent. A company's own personnel may be biased or under pressure to present information in a more favorable light than actually exists. Thus, external users of the financial statements—creditors, stockholders, and potential investors—are not satisfied with management's reporting on its own stewardship.

As a result, an independent, objective "referee," the CPA is brought in to audit the financial statements and render an opinion on their fairness. This attest function plays a critical part in our economy. By rendering an objective, unbiased opinion on a company's financial statements, the auditor adds credibility to those statements, thus permitting the capital markets to operate efficiently.

Financial data is necessary for decision making by many interested parties. Financial statements facilitate the flow of funds in the money markets. Audited financial statements correct earlier misinformation in the market place created by earnings projections or other management statements which have proven to be incorrect.

A by-product of the attest function is to provide suggestions to the management of the audited company on improvements in the company's accounting system and controls. These suggestions may lead to management advisory services engagements. Strengthening the client's internal accounting control system and suggestions for improving the efficiency and effectiveness of the firm can be valuable aids to management.

RELATIONSHIP OF AUDITING TO ACCOUNTING

An external auditor renders an opinion on an entity's financial statements by stating whether or not they are fairly presented in accordance with generally accepted accounting principles applied on a consistent basis. In order to express an opinion, the auditor must fully know and understand generally accepted accounting principles. So an auditor must also be an accountant.

An auditor can be compared to a referee of a football game. The players are comparable to the accountants. Referees perform an objective role, making sure that the players keep to the generally accepted rules of the game. If the players violate the rules, the referee blows the whistle and imposes a penalty. Auditors make sure an entity reports its financial activities in accordance with generally accepted accounting principles applied on a consistent basis. If there is a departure from GAAP which the firm will not correct, the auditor will disclose the violation in the audit report. Depending on the circumstances, the auditor may issue a qualified opinion, an adverse opinion, or withdraw from the engagement if necessary.[3] Of course, the football game is not a perfect comparison. For example, the auditor is not performing concurrent or continuous reviewing, as a referee does.

The auditor/accountant relationship can also be compared to the judge/lawyer relationship. A judge is also a lawyer with a thorough knowledge of the law. A judge is not an advocate for a client, but is an impartial, objective administrator of the law. Likewise an auditor is an accountant with a thorough knowledge of generally accepted accounting principles. The auditor, like a judge, is not an advocate of the client, but rather is an impartial, objective person who determines whether the client has prepared the financial statements in accordance with generally accepted accounting principles applied on a consistent basis.

PUBLIC ACCOUNTING FIRMS

As indicated earlier, external audits are performed by public accounting firms. These firms may be organized as sole practitioners, partnerships, or professional corportions.[4] Different levels of professional

---

[3] The various types of audit reports which may be issued are discussed in detail in Chapters 2, 15, and 16.

[4] The ethical requirements to practice as a professional corporation are discussed in detail in Chapter 3.

personnel within a CPA firm include partners, principals, managers, seniors, semi-seniors, and juniors.

Several international CPA firms are termed the "Big 8." These are

- Arthur Andersen & Co.
- Arthur Young & Co.
- Coopers & Lybrand
- Deloitte, Haskins & Sells
- Ernst & Whinney
- Peat, Marwick, Mitchell & Co.
- Price Waterhouse & Co.
- Touche Ross & Co.

These firms have offices all over the world serving a variety of clients. In addition to serving clients, they are able to provide many personnel services such as training and continuing education sessions for their own professional staff.

Smaller CPA firms may group together to form "associations of local CPA firms." Because of pooled resources, the associations are able to provide for their own members services similar to those provided by Big 8 firms.

Services offered by public accounting firms are varied. Generally, these services may be classified as accounting and auditing, taxes, and management advisory services. Individual practitioners and small firms may specialize in one or more of these types of services. Accounting and auditing include such services as audits of publicly held firms and non-public entities, SEC registrations, SEC annual reports, compliance reports with various government agencies, reports to credit rating bureaus such as Dun and Bradstreet, and other types of special reports. Other accounting services for small businesses include compiling and reviewing unaudited financial statements and bookkeeping services (frequently called write-up work).

Tax services include federal, state, and local income tax returns for corporations, partnerships, individuals, cooperatives, estates, trusts, and informational returns for tax-exempt organizations. Other tax services include preparing returns for gift taxes, excise taxes, franchise taxes, payroll taxes, property taxes, and sale and use taxes. Tax planning, estate planning, and business planning comprise other areas for which CPA firms provide assistance along with assistance in specialized problems such as reorganizations, mergers, foreign operations, liquidations, specialized industries, and numerous other areas.

Management advisory services (MAS) cover many areas such as consulting on cost accounting systems, EDP systems, management information systems, budgetary systems, actuarial calculations, insurance coverage, lease or buy analyses, and inventory control systems. MAS is defined in *Statement on Standards for Management Advisory Services No. 1, Definitions and Standards for MAS Practice*, as:

> The management consulting function of providing advice and technical assistance where the primary purpose is to help the client improve the use of its capabilities and resources to achieve its objectives. For the purpose of illustration, "helping the client improve the use of its capabilities and resources" may involve activities such as
>
> > Counseling management in its analysis, planning, organizing, operating, and controlling functions.
> >
> > Conducting special studies, preparing recommendations, proposing plans and programs, and providing advice and technical assistance in their implementation.
> >
> > Reviewing and suggesting improvements of policies, procedures, systems, methods, and organization relationships.
> >
> > Introducing new ideas, concepts, and methods to management.
> >
> > Recommendations and comments prepared as a direct result of observations made while performing an audit or providing other accounting services, including tax consultations, are not MAS as herein defined.

Some firms, as previously stated, specialize in one or more activities or the firm is organized into the three functional categories—accounting and auditing, tax, and MAS. Other firms add a fourth, a small business division which specializes in serving the particular accounting and auditing, tax, and MAS needs of closely held companies and small public corporations.

QUALIFICATIONS OF THE AUDITOR

Professional qualifications required of an independent auditor consist of a formal education and relevant experience. The AICPA has recently interpreted this requirement to mean a college degree that includes a five-year professional accounting education embodying the common body of knowledge for accountants. An individual can demonstrate that he or she has obtained the common body of knowledge required of accountants by passing the CPA examination. It is currently recognized that a four-year college accounting education, passing the CPA exam, and obtaining two-years' experience in public accounting is sufficient training and experience to begin the practice of public accounting.[5] Of course, continuing professional education is required to maintain and expand one's professional knowledge.

Becoming a CPA represents the highest achievement of the accounting professional, and the designation of CPA is viewed by the public as representing professional competence. To become a licensed CPA, an individual must not only pass the CPA examination, but he or she must also meet individual state requirements as to residency, education, and experience.

The Certified Public Accountants' examination is a national exam given twice a year (May and November). It is a two-and-one-half day exam covering accounting practice, accounting theory, auditing, and business law. A grade of 75 on each part is necessary to pass the examination. Although the CPA exam is a national exam prepared and graded by the AICPA, State Boards of Accountancy administer the exam in each state for the AICPA. Each state, however, has its own requirements to sit for the exam, and if all four parts of the exam are not passed at one sitting, states will vary as to the length of time allowed to pass the remaining parts. In addition to passing the CPA exam, some states require passing additional exams such as an ethics exam before granting a CPA certificate to a qualified individual.

State Boards of Accountancy also regulate renewal of CPA licenses for a fixed fee. Some states have a mandatory continuing education requirement that must be fulfilled before a permit to practice is renewed.[6] State CPE requirements usually involve obtaining 120 hours of continuing education over a three-year period. Some states require that a specific percentage of the required hours relate to accounting and auditing subjects—as opposed to courses in income tax and MAS.

---

[5] *Report of the Committee on Education and Experience Requirements for CPAs*, American Institute of Certified Public Accountants, New York, 1969, p. 6.

[6] In many states the state societies, and not the state boards of accountancy, specify the continuing education requirements for membership in the state society.

OVERVIEW OF THE AUDIT PROCESS

Now that some basic aspects of the auditing profession have been discussed, this chapter concludes with an overview of the audit process.

When an entity desires an audit, it will approach a CPA firm. The CPA firm will examine the entity's accounting records, its system of internal control, and the previous year's audit report, if any. If there was a previous audit, inquiries must be made of the predecessor auditor in accordance with *Statement on Auditing Standards No. 7*[7]. These inquiries are basically of two types. First, the successor auditor will make inquiries of the predecessor auditor to decide whether to accept the engagement. Thus, the successor auditor will make inquiries about the integrity of the entity's management and the reason for the change in auditors. Second, if the successor auditor decides to accept the engagement, he or she will make inquiries of the predecessor auditor about matters, such as beginning account balances, which will facilitate the current audit. In addition, because accountants have legal responsibility for their work, the CPA firm will inquire about the management through various sources other than the predecessor auditor to determine the reputation of the entity. Based on its preliminary findings, if the CPA firm decides to accept the new client, an estimate is prepared budgeting the total number of hours and the cost range for the audit.

Once the client has engaged the CPA firm to perform the audit, the CPA firm will send an engagement letter confirming the arrangements for the audit. Obtaining an engagement letter signed by the chief executive officer and chief financial officer of the client is very important as the letter becomes the audit contract that describes the responsibilities of the auditor and the client. The engagement letter should include the following information:

- Name of the client and its year-end date.
- Financial statements to be examined and other reports, if any, to be prepared—for example, income tax returns.
- Identification of any limitations imposed by the client or the timing of the engagement that may affect the auditor's ability to gather sufficient competent evidential matter in support of the financial statements.
- The type of opinion expected to be issued as a result of the audit work.

---

[7] Statements on Auditing Standards are issued by the Auditing Standards Board. The statements provide guidance to the auditor in establishing audit objectives and in carrying out auditing procedures. The statements are discussed in detail throughout this text.

- The auditor's responsibility for the detection of errors and irregularities.
- Obligations of the client's staff to prepare schedules and statements and assist in other aspects of the audit work—for example, collect and organize accounting data to be examined.
- Fee to be charged by the auditors and the method of billing (usually monthly for work performed during the month).

Following is an illustrative audit engagement letter:

SWIFT, MARCH & COMPANY   Certified Public Accountants

(Date)

Mr. Thomas Thorp, President
Anonymous Company, Inc.
Route 32
Nowhere, New York 10000

Dear Mr. Thorp:

This will confirm our understanding of the arrangements for our examination of the financial statements of Anonymous Company, Inc., for the year ending (Date).

We will examine the Company's balance sheet at (Date), and the related statements of income, retained earnings, and changes in financial position for the year then ended, for the purpose of expressing an opinion on them. Our examination will be made in accordance with generally accepted auditing standards and, accordingly, will include such tests of the accounting records and such other auditing procedures as we consider necessary in the circumstances.

Our procedures will include tests (by statistical sampling, if feasible) of documentary evidence supporting the transactions recorded in the accounts, tests of the physical existence of inventories, and direct confirmation of receivables and certain other assets and liabilities by correspondence with selected customers, creditors, legal counsel, and banks. At the conclusion of our examination, we will request certain written representations from you about the financial statements and matters related thereto.

Our engagement is subject to the inherent risk that material errors, irregularities, or illegal acts, including fraud or defalcations, if they exist, will not be detected. However, we will inform you of any such matters that come to our attention.

We will review the Company's federal and state (identify states) income tax returns for the fiscal year ended (Date). These returns, we understand, will be prepared by the controller.

Further, we will be available during the year to consult with you on the tax effects of any proposed transactions or contemplated changes in business policies.

Our fee for these services will be at our regular per diem rates, plus travel and other out-of-pocket costs. Invoices will be rendered every two weeks and are payable on presentation.

We are pleased to have this opportunity to serve you.

If this letter correctly expresses your understanding, please sign the enclosed copy where indicated and return it to us.[8]

Very truly yours,

SWIFT, MARCH & COMPANY

_____

Partner

APPROVED:
By _____
Date _____

After receiving the engagement letter, the auditor will start the process of gathering audit evidence by reviewing and evaluating the system of internal control to determine the extent, nature and timing of subsequent auditing procedures. The auditor will then develop an audit plan and assign staff and supervisory personnel to the audit engagement. An audit program is a list of audit procedures which are necessary to gather sufficient, competent, evidential matter. The evidence is then used to form an opinion on the overall fairness of the financial statements.

Once all auditing procedures are completed, the auditor will propose to the client adjusting entries, if necessary, on material items so that account balances in the financial statements will be fairly stated. If the client agrees to "book" the proposed adjusting entries, the final audited financial statements and footnotes will be prepared. If the client will not agree to recording the adjusting entries, the auditor must determine the effect of such rejection on the type of report to be rendered and upon

_____

[8] *AICPA Audit and Accounting Manual,* American Institute of Certified Public Accountants, New York, 1982, AAM 3361.2.

the financial statements and footnotes. Finally, the auditor will render the appropriate opinion in the audit report to accompany the financial statements.

SUMMARY

Auditing is a systematic process of objectively obtaining and evaluating evidence to ascertain the degree of correspondence between assertions about economic events and actions and the established criteria for reporting these assertions. The auditor's report is an expression of an opinion as to whether the assertions are reported in accordance with the established criteria.

There are three basic types of auditors: internal auditors, governmental auditors, and external auditors. The scope of an internal audit is broader than the scope of the external audit because the internal auditor is employed by the company he audits, and thus, internal auditors are concerned with any activity that is helpful to their employer. Governmental auditing covers a wide range of activities on the federal, state and local levels and numerous regulatory agencies. External auditing involves reporting on financial statements prepared by management for external users or third parties. External auditors must be independent in fact and in appearance.

The attest function of external auditing refers to the auditor's opinion on the fairness of the client's financial statements. The auditor's opinion states whether the statements are fairly presented in accordance with generally accepted accounting principles applied on a consistent basis.

Entities are audited for numerous reasons. Some of the reasons include laws, absentee ownership, and requirements of creditors and potential buyers of the business. Audits can also have a preventive effect for irregularities contemplated by employees of a client.

Since an auditor renders an opinion on an entity's financial statements, the auditor must fully know and understand generally accepted accounting principles. So an auditor must also be an accountant.

Public accounting firms are formed as sole practitioners, partnerships, and professional corporations. Services offered by public accounting firms are varied. Generally, they may be classified as accounting and auditing, taxes, and management advisory services.

The Certified Public Accountants' exam is a national exam given twice a year. It is a two-and-a-half day exam covering accounting practice, accounting theory, auditing, and business law. To become a CPA, a person must pass the CPA exam and satisfy the state requirements in terms of residency, education, and experience. Many states have a mandatory continuing education requirement that must be fulfilled before a renewal of a permit to practice is granted.

When an entity desires an audit, it will approach a CPA firm. The CPA firm will investigate the entity and give an estimate of the fee for the audit. Once the client has engaged the CPA firm to perform the audit, the CPA firm will send an engagement letter confirming the arrangements for the audit. Next, the auditor reviews and evaluates the system of internal control to determine the extent of testing necessary. At appropriate times, the auditor will perform the actual audit procedures. Once all procedures are completed, the auditor will propose adjusting entries if necessary. When all items are resolved, the final audited financial statements and footnotes will be completed. Finally, the auditor will render the appropriate opinion in the audit report to accompany the financial statements.

REVIEW QUESTIONS

1-1 Discuss three key aspects in the definition of auditing.

1-2 What is the nature of the first paragraph in an auditor's short-form report? Of the second paragraph?

1-3 What is the objective of an audit engagement by an independent external auditor? Discuss.

1-4 Differentiate between the scope of external auditing and the scope of internal auditing. Between external auditing and governmental auditing.

1-5 Why is independence the backbone of external auditing?

1-6 Distinguish between independence in fact and independence in appearance.

1-7 Why are external users of financial statements not satisfied with management's reporting on its own stewardship?

1-8 Explain the importance of auditing in the role of business today.

1-9 Contrast the differences between auditing and accounting.

1-10 Discuss three major types of services offered by CPA firms.

1-11   What are the professional qualifications required of an independent auditor?

1-12   How do State Boards of Accountancy regulate the practice of public accounting in their respective states?

1-13   There are two basic reasons why a successor auditor should communicate with the predecessor auditor. Discuss these reasons.

1-14   What is the purpose of an engagement letter?

1-15   Define an audit program.

1-16   Why does the auditor recommend adjusting entries on material items to the client? Briefly describe the nature of the decisions the auditor must make if the client refuses to "book" the recommended journal entries.

DISCUSSION QUESTIONS AND PROBLEMS

1-17   Dudley Dewright, CPA, has been employed for three years by Hardley, Rightly & Co., a regional CPA firm. For the past two years Dudley has been assigned to the financial audit of Neatless Bookkeeping Forms, Inc. The president of Neatless, Wayne Wise, is very impressed with Dudley's work and wants to offer Dudley a new position in Neatless' executive personnel structure—Director of Internal Auditing. Although Neatless is willing to pay Dudley an annual salary of $35,000, Wayne thinks that implementing a new internal audit function will save Neatless a "bundle" because audits by external auditors will no longer be needed. Furthermore, since Dudley has worked for two years on the external audit, he will not need any training at all. Wayne thinks this will be another cost savings for Neatless.

Wayne has an appointment with Dudley to discuss the proposition. As Dudley Dewright, how would you react to Mr. Wise's proposal? How would you explain to Mr. Wise the nature of your new position in relation to the annual audit by external auditors and the cost savings anticipated by Mr. Wise?

1-18   The following two statements are representative of attitudes and opinions sometimes encountered by CPAs in their professional practices:

1.   Today's audit consists of test checking. This is dangerous because test checking depends upon the auditor's judgment,

which may be defective. An audit can be relied upon only if every transaction is verified.

2. An audit by a CPA is essentially negative and contributes to neither the gross national product nor the general well-being of society. The auditor does not create; he merely checks what someone else has done.

Required:

Evaluate each of the above independent statements and indicate:

a. Areas of agreement with the statement, if any.
b. Areas of misconception, incompleteness or fallacious reasoning included in the statement, if any.

(AICPA adapted)

1-19 Feiler, the sole owner of a small hardware business, has been told that the business should have financial statements reported on by an independent CPA. Feiler, having some bookkeeping experience, has personally prepared the company's financial statements and does not understand why such statements should be examined by a CPA. Feiler discussed the matter with Farber, a CPA, and asked Farber to explain why an audit is considered important.

Required:

a. Describe the objectives of an independent audit.
b. Identify ten ways in which an independent audit may be beneficial to Feiler.

(AICPA adapted)

1-20 Three independent, unrelated statements follow regarding financial accounting. Each statement contains some unsound reasoning.

Statement I

One function of financial accounting is to measure a company's net earnings for a given period of time. An earnings statement will measure a company's true net earnings if it is prepared in accordance with generally accepted accounting principles. Other financial statements are basically unrelated to the earnings statement. Net earnings would be measured as the difference between revenues and expenses. Revenues are an inflow of cash to the enterprise and should be realized when recognized. This may be accomplished by using the sales basis or the production basis. Expenses should be matched with revenues to measure net earnings. Usually, variable expenses are assigned to the product, and fixed expenses are assigned to the period.

Statement II

One function of financial accounting is to accurately present a company's financial position at a given point in time. This is done with a statement of financial position, which is prepared using historical-cost valuations for all assets and liabilities except inventories. Inventories are stated at first-in, first-out (FIFO), last-in, first-out (LIFO), or average valuations. The statement of financial position must be prepared on a consistent basis with prior years' statements.

In addition to reflecting assets, liabilities, and stockholders' equity, a statement of financial position should, in a separate section, reflect a company's reserves. The section should include three different types of reserves: depreciation reserves, product warranty reserves, and retained earnings reserves. All three of these types of reserves are established by a credit to the reserve account.

Statement III

Financial statement analysis involves using ratios to test past performance of a given company. Past performance is compared to a predetermined standard, and the company is evaluated accordingly. One such ratio is the current ratio, which is computed as current assets divided by current liabilities, or as monetary assets divided by monetary liabilities. A current ratio of 2 to 1 is considered good for companies; but the higher the ratio, the better the company's financial position is assumed to be. The current ratio is dynamic because it helps to measure fund flows.

Required:

Identify the areas that are not in accordance with generally accepted accounting principles or are untrue with respect to the financial statement analysis discussed in each of the statements and explain why the reasoning is incorrect. Complete your identification and explanation of each statement before proceeding to the next statement.

(AICPA adapted)

OBJECTIVE QUESTIONS*

1-21 The independent auditor of 1900 differs from the auditor of today in that the 1900 auditor was more concerned with the

A. Validity of the income statement.
B. Determination of fair presentation of financial statements.
C. Improvement of accounting systems.
D. Detection of irregularities

---

* *Note:* Questions marked with an asterisk are not AICPA adapted questions; otherwise, questions in this section have been taken from prior CPA examinations.

1-22   When a CPA expresses an opinion on financial statements, his or her responsibilities extend to

A.   The underlying wisdom of the client's management decisions.
B.   Whether the results of the client's operating decisions are fairly presented in the financial statements.
C.   Active participation in the implementation of the advice given to the client.
D.   An ongoing responsibility for the client's solvency.

1-23*   When a CPA accepts an audit, which of the following will be sent to his or her client?

A.   A management letter.
B.   An engagement letter.
C.   A comfort letter.
D.   A confirmation letter.

1-24   Which of the following *best* describes why an independent auditor is asked to express an opinion on the fair presentation of financial statements?

A.   It is difficult to prepare financial statements that fairly present a company's financial position and changes in financial position and operations without the expertise of an independent auditor.
B.   It is management's responsibility to seek available independent aid in the appraisal of the financial information shown in its financial statements.
C.   The opinion of an independent party is needed because a company may not be objective with respect to its own financial statements.
D.   It is a customary courtesy that all stockholders of a company receive an independent report on management's stewardship in managing the affairs of the business.

1-25   The securities of Ralph Corporation are listed on a regional stock exchange and registered with the Securities and Exchange Commission. The management of Ralph engages a CPA to perform an independent audit of Ralph's financial statements. The primary objective of this audit is to provide assurance to the

A.   Regional Stock Exchange.
B.   Board of Directors of Ralph Corporation.
C.   Securities and Exchange Commission.
D.   Investors in Ralph securities.

1-26 The auditor's report may be addressed to the company whose financial statements are being examined or to that company's

  A. Chief operating officer.
  B. President.
  C. Board of Directors.
  D. Chief financial officer.

1-27 Which of the following *best* describes why publicly-traded corporations follow the practice of having the outside auditor appointed by the board of directors or elected by the stockholders?

  A. To comply with the regulations of the Financial Accounting Standards Board.
  B. To emphasize auditor independence from the management of the corporation.
  C. To encourage a policy of rotation of the independent auditors.
  D. To provide the corporate owners with an opportunity to voice their opinion concerning the quality of the auditing firm selected by the directors.

1-28 An opinion as to the "fairness" of financial statement presentation in accordance with generally accepted accounting principles is based on several judgments made by the auditor. One such judgment is whether accounting principles used

  A. Have general acceptance.
  B. Are promulgated by the AICPA Auditing Standards Board.
  C. Are the most conservative of those available for use.
  D. Emphasize the legal form of transactions.

1-29 Preliminary arrangements agreed to by the auditor and the client should be reduced to writing by the auditor. The *best* place to set forth these arrangements is in

  A. A memorandum to be placed in the permanent section of the auditing working papers.
  B. An engagement letter.
  C. A client representation letter.
  D. A confirmation letter attached to the constructive services letter.

1-30 The auditor's judgment concerning the overall fairness of the presentation of financial position, results of operations, and changes in financial position is applied within the framework of

    A.   Quality control.

    B.   Generally accepted auditing standards which include the concept of materiality.

    C.   The auditor's evaluation of the audited company's internal control.

    D.   Generally accepted accounting principles.

1-31   The auditor's opinion makes reference to generally accepted accounting principles (GAAP). Which of the following *best* describes GAAP?

    A.   The interpretations of accounting rules and procedures by certified public accountants on audit engagements.

    B.   The pronouncements made by the Financial Accounting Standards Board and its predecessor, the Accounting Principles Board.

    C.   The guidelines set forth by various governmental agencies that derive their authority from Congress.

    D.   The conventions, rules, and procedures which are necessary to define the accepted accounting practices at a particular time.

1-32   An independent auditor must be without bias with respect to the financial statements of a client in order to

    A.   Comply with the laws established by governmental agencies.

    B.   Maintain the appearance of separate interests on the part of the auditor and the client.

    C.   Protect against criticism and possible litigation from stockholders and creditors.

    D.   Insure the impartiality necessary for an expression of the auditor's opinion.

1-33   Audit programs are modified to suit the circumstances on particular engagements. A complete audit program for an engagement generally should be developed

    A.   Prior to beginning the actual audit work.

    B.   After the auditor has completed an evaluation of the existing internal accounting control.

    C.   After reviewing the client's accounting records and procedures.

    D.   When the audit engagement letter is prepared.

1-34   Which of the following ultimately determines the specific audit procedures necessary to provide an independent auditor with a reasonable basis for the expression of an opinion?

A. The audit program.
B. The auditor's judgment.
C. Generally accepted auditing standards.
D. The auditor's working papers.

1-35 Those procedures specifically outlined in an audit program are primarily designed to

A. Prevent litigations.
B. Detect errors or irregularities.
C. Test internal systems.
D. Gather evidence.

1-36 On February 13, 1983, Fox, CPA, met with the audit committee of the Gem Corporation to review the draft of Fox's report on the company's financial statements as of and for the year ended December 31, 1982. On February 16, 1983, Fox completed all remaining field work at the Gem Corporation's headquarters. On February 17, 1983, Fox typed and signed the final version of the auditor's report. On February 18, 1983, the final report was mailed to Gem's audit committee. What date should have been used on Fox's report?

A. February 13, 1983.
B. February 16, 1983.
C. February 17, 1983.
D. February 18, 1983.

After studying this chapter, students should understand

1. The nature of *The Philosophy of Auditing* by Mautry and Sharaf.
2. The ten generally accepted auditing standards.
3. The nature of the standard audit report, including the importance of the date and the way in which the audit report is addressed.
4. The definition of an uncertainty, and the nature of a subject to opinion or disclaimer of opinion which may arise because an uncertainty exists.
5. The definition of a limitation on the scope of the auditor's work, and the nature of the qualified opinion or disclaimer of opinion which may result from the scope limitation.
6. The nature of the qualified opinion or adverse opinion which may result when the financial statements are not prepared in accordance with GAAP applied on a consistent basis.

Chapter 2

Auditing Theory, Concepts, and Standards

This chapter was written by
Joyce C. Lambert, Ph.D., C.P.A.,
Associate Professor of Accounting,
University of Nebraska, Lincoln

INTRODUCTION

In accounting there have been numerous attempts to develop a general theory to aid the profession in developing new accounting principles and in applying existing principles. For example, the most recent effort has been the series of statements of financial accounting concepts which are issued by the Financial Accounting Standards Board. These concepts statements have dealt with topics such as the definition of assets, liabilities and equity and the objectives of financial statements. The idea behind the development of a conceptual theory is that once the concepts have been identified, accountants will be better equipped to develop new principles and apply existing principles. For example, once liabilities are defined accountants are better qualified to decide whether items, such as deferred income tax credits, should be recorded in the accounts.

Some auditors have argued that a conceptual base is not as important for auditing as it is for accounting. These auditors argue that auditing is primarily a process of gathering evidence about economic assertions, and it is fairly easy to decide what evidence to gather or not to gather without a conceptual basis. For example, if the auditor wants to determine whether a client's inventory exists, most auditors would agree that the best way to verify the existence of the inventory is to observe the inventory. Those auditors who minimize the importance of a conceptual base for auditing contend that the observation of inventory to determine its existence is more a matter of common sense than something that can be derived from a conceptual foundation. However, despite this reasoning, there have been several attempts in the profession to develop a theory of auditing which includes the basic postulates of auditing and the primary concepts in auditing.

This chapter begins with a discussion of a comprehensive attempt, by R.K. Mautz and Hussein A. Sharaf, to develop a theory of auditing. This discussion is followed by sections on current generally accepted auditing standards, auditing standards vs. auditing procedures, the standard audit report and other reports.

POSTULATES

Postulates are assumptions from which theory is derived. Since postulates cannot be proven, they must be accepted as true by those who rely on the theory. For example, a postulate that is encountered in everyday life is that all people are created equal. This postulate is accepted by most citizens as a basic truth and from this postulate several principles can be derived. For example, if all people are created equal, then it follows that people should not be discriminated against because of race, creed, sex or national origin.

Characteristics of postulates are consistency, independence, reproductiveness, and completeness. A set of basic assumptions should be consistent—that is, the postulates cannot contradict one another. Postulates must be independent, which means they cannot be derived from the other basic assumptions. Postulates are reproductive if a theory can be derived from the postulates. Finally, a set of basic postulates should be complete. The set should contain all the assumptions necessary to support the theory structure.

POSTULATES OF AUDITING

One of the landmark books on auditing theory is *The Philosophy of Auditing* by R.K. Mautz and Hussein A. Sharaf. In this book, the authors identify the following eight tentative postulates of auditing.[1]

1. *Financial statements and financial data are verifiable.* If this postulate is not true, it would be impossible for the auditor to draw conclusions regarding the economic assertions about the financial statements and financial data which are made by management. In general, most auditors agree that this first postulate is true for the amounts included in the basic financial statements. However, the postulate may not be true for certain supplemental information which is included in a corporation's annual report. Consequently, auditors have been reluctant to assume the same level of responsibility for supplemental data, such as data on price level adjusted financial statements, as they do for the information included in the basic financial statements.

2. *There is no necessary conflict of interest between the auditor and the management of the enterprise under audit.* This postulate is very important to the auditing profession because, if there is a conflict of interest between the auditor and management, the audit would have to be expanded substantially. For example, if management does not intend to present financial statements which are fairly presented in accordance with GAAP, the audit must be more extensive than would be required if management did intend to prepare financial statements on a GAAP basis. In most audits to-

---

[1] R.K. Mautz and Hussein A. Sharaf, *The Philosophy of Auditing* (Sarasota, Florida, 1961), p. 42.

day, this second postulate is probably true. However, there have been enough cases where management did intend to deceive the user of financial statements to cause auditors to carefully investigate their client's integrity. Procedures for making this investigation of management's integrity are discussed in Chapter 6 in the section which deals with quality control and CPA firms.

3.   *The financial statements and other information submitted for verification are free from collusive and other unusual irregularities.* This postulate, like the second postulate, is very important to the auditing profession. Most auditors agree that, if management is intent on deceiving the auditor and if enough people are involved, the client can be successful in their deceit. For example, if the client's inventory contains goods held on consignment, which should of course not be included in the inventory, and if the client's employees and the consignor take enough steps such as destroying documentation concerning the consignment and substituting documentation to indicate a purchase, it is very difficult for the auditor to catch the irregularity.

4.   *The existence of a satisfactory system of internal control eliminates the probability of irregularities.* This fourth postulate has been misunderstood by many auditors because of the manner in which it is worded. What Mautz and Sharaf intended to say is that as the system of internal control (broadly speaking a system of internal control may be defined as any technique or procedure which is implemented to prevent errors or irregularities or to detect any errors or irregularities that occur) is improved, the probability of undetected errors or irregularities occurring in the financial statements is decreased. This fourth postulate is generally accepted by the auditing profession, and it is discussed in detail in Chapters 5 and 7.

5.   *Consistent application of generally accepted principles of accounting results in the fair presentation of financial position and the results of operations.* This postulate is generally accepted by the auditing profession. In fact, in *SAS No. 5* the Auditing Standards Board states in effect that the primary criteria for fair presentation of financial statements is that the financial statements be prepared in accordance with generally accepted accounting principles applied on a consistent basis.

6. *In the absence of clear evidence to the contrary, what has held true in the past for the enterprise under examination will hold true in the future.* The key phrase in this postulate is "in the absence of clear evidence to the contrary." This postulate is generally accepted by the auditing profession. For example, in SAS No. 34, which deals with an entity's continued existence, the Auditing Standards Board states in paragraph 3 that ". . . in the absence of information to the contrary, an entity's continuation is usually assumed in financial accounting."

7. *When examining financial data for the purpose of expressing an independent opinion thereon, the auditor acts exclusively in the capacity of an auditor.* Auditors perform three basic types of services: (1) auditing services, (2) tax services, and (3) management advisory services. In performing tax services and management advisory services, the auditor's primary focus is on the interest of the client as long as the client's interests are not illegal and do not violate the basic principles of integrity. However, when the auditor performs audit services, the auditor's primary focus is on the interest of the users of the financial statements. Therefore, when the auditor examines financial statements, the auditor must be able to evaluate the financial statements in an objective manner. This requirement of objectivity means that the auditor must be independent of the client. As discussed further in Chapter 3, independence means more than an objective state of mind on behalf of the auditor. Specifically, for an auditor to be independent it is necessary for third parties, who have knowledge of all of the relationships between the auditor and the client, to believe that the auditor can examine the financial statements in an objective manner.

8. *The professional status of the independent auditor imposes commensurate professional obligations.* This postulate is widely accepted by both the auditing profession and the courts. In fact, courts have awarded millions of dollars to people who have suffered damages because auditors have allegedly not met their professional obligations. The auditor's legal liability is discussed further in Chapter 17.

AUDITING CONCEPTS

Auditing concepts are more narrow in scope than the postulates of auditing. They are not assumptions, but instead, are statements which can be derived from, and thus are consistent with the postulates of auditing. In addition to their eight postulates of auditing, Mautz and Sharaf identify five primary concepts of auditing: evidence, due audit care, fair presentation, independence, and ethical conduct.

Evidence

Evidence is the link between the financial statements and the auditor's opinion on them. Through evaluation of sufficient competent evidence, the auditor can reach a rational opinion on the fairness of presentation of the financial statements.

Mautz and Sharaf classify three types of evidence: *natural*, *created*, and *rational argumentation*. Natural evidence is the most convincing. For example, an item of inventory is its own evidence for existence. Some effort is necessary, however, to bring about created evidence. A scientist can create an experiment in order to ascertain certain evidence. For example, a chemist may take natural evidence, such as water, and analyze the water to determine that water is made up of hydrogen and oxygen. Thus, the experiment creates evidence by identifying the components of water. Finally, rational argumentation analyzes and arranges facts to arrive at a conclusion. For example, as a result of studying a number of samples of water, a chemist may conclude based on rational argumentation that it seems logical that all water is made up of two parts of hydrogen and one part of oxygen.

Audit evidence must be evaluated to determine its usefulness. In evaluating evidence, the auditor finds that some evidence is better than other evidence, and that the type of evidence which is needed to support various assertions differs depending on the type of assertion.

To illustrate this point, consider evidence which is obtained by physical observation. The physical observation can be performed by the auditor, the client or an independent third party. However, in terms of objectivity, observations made by the auditor or an independent third party are better (more objective) than observations which are made by the client because the client may be tempted, either consciously or unconsciously, to alter his or her perception of the evidence to support a particular management assertion in the financial statements.

As indicated, the type of evidence which is needed also depends upon the assertion which is being made. For example, physical observation may be very useful to determine the existence of an asset. However, physical observation may not be particularly useful in evaluating an assertion about the ownership of an asset.

Another aspect involved in evaluating evidence concerns the significance of the item about which an assertion is being made. Generally, the more significant an item, the stronger the evidence must be in its support. For example, more evidence is needed to support the cash balance in the main checking account than is needed to support the petty cash balance.

The auditor must also consider time and cost constraints in obtaining adequate evidence. He or she must perform audit work in a reasonable length of time and at a reasonable cost in order for the product of the work to be useful and affordable. However, the auditor must gather sufficient competent evidence to support the audit opinion. Exhibit 2-1 outlines the nature of evidence.

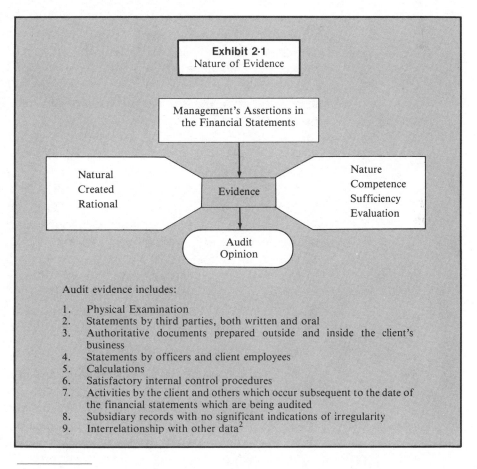

Exhibit 2-1
Nature of Evidence

Management's Assertions in the Financial Statements

Natural
Created
Rational

Evidence

Nature
Competence
Sufficiency
Evaluation

Audit
Opinion

Audit evidence includes:

1. Physical Examination
2. Statements by third parties, both written and oral
3. Authoritative documents prepared outside and inside the client's business
4. Statements by officers and client employees
5. Calculations
6. Satisfactory internal control procedures
7. Activities by the client and others which occur subsequent to the date of the financial statements which are being audited
8. Subsidiary records with no significant indications of irregularity
9. Interrelationship with other data[2]

---

[2] Mautz and Sharaf, p. 86.

**Due Audit
Care**

The concept of due audit care is the basis for judging an auditor's responsibility in performing professional services. Due audit care refers to the thoroughness and professionalism which the prudent auditor would apply in an audit situation. The "prudent auditor" concept is a legal concept that represents the average level of competence required of a professional. For example, due audit care in the preparation of working papers requires that they be complete in every respect. Working papers should include sufficient evidence to support the audit objective, show that the auditing standards, especially the standards of field work, were complied with, and show how all exceptions identified by the auditor were reconciled.

**Fair
Presentation**

According to Mautz and Sharaf, fair presentation consists of three subconcepts: *accounting propriety*, *adequate disclosure*, and *audit obligation*. The subconcept of accounting propriety, according to Mautz and Sharaf, is satisfied if the financial statements are fairly presented. They note that generally fair presentation results if the financial statements are prepared in accordance with GAAP. However, there may be cases in which the application of GAAP does not result in a fair presentation of the financial statements. In these cases, Mautz and Sharaf advocate that GAAP be replaced with a more appropriate principle, one which does result in the financial statements being fairly presented.

A second aspect of fair presentation identified by Mautz and Sharaf is adequate disclosure. Adequate disclosure refers to the extent, the kinds, and the amount of financial information reported. According to Mautz and Sharaf, financial information should be reported if the information is important to the average prudent investor.

A final aspect of fair presentation according to Mautz and Sharaf is audit obligation. Audit obligation recognizes that the auditor has a professional responsibility to perform an examination of financial information in accordance with generally accepted auditing standards.

Independence

As indicated earlier, independence means that when an auditor conducts an audit, he or she should be objective and unbiased. Moreover, the auditor should maintain the appearance of independence. Independence in fact is basically a state of mind which the auditor possesses. An independent auditor does not subordinate his or her judgment to the client or to others. The auditor should be free to select the audit procedures and the extent of their application with no restrictions placed on the auditor's reporting obligations.

In addition to independence in fact, Mautz and Sharaf emphasize the importance of independence in appearance since it is a necessary condition for the public to accept auditing as a profession. As indicated earlier, an auditor is independent in appearance only if a third party, who has full knowledge of the relationships between the client and the auditor, would be inclined to believe that the auditor is objective in evaluating the client's financial statements.

The last concept identified by Mautz and Sharaf is *ethical conduct*. This concept will be discussed in Chapter 3.

GENERALLY ACCEPTED AUDITING STANDARDS (GAAS)

Most auditing professionals do not believe that the work by Mautz and Sharaf, or other theoretical work, has had much impact on the development of generally accepted auditing standards. In fact, in 1947, fourteen years before *Philosophy of Auditing* was published, the AICPA's Committee on Auditing Procedure issued its *Tentative Statement of Auditing Standards — Their Generally Accepted Significance and Scope*. In this statement the Committee presented nine auditing standards, it added a tenth standard in 1948. The AICPA's *Code of Professional Ethics* requires compliance with the following ten GAAS in all audit engagements.

The ten GAAS are classified as the general standards, the field work standards, and the standards of reporting:

General Standards

1.   The examination is to be performed by a person or persons having adequate technical training and proficiency as an auditor.

2.   In all matters relating to the assignment, an independence in mental attitude is to be maintained by the auditor or auditors.

3.   Due professional care is to be exercised in the performance of the examination and the preparation of the report.

Standards of Field Work

1.   The work is to be adequately planned and assistants, if any, are to be properly supervised.

2.   There is to be a proper study and evaluation of the existing internal control as a basis for reliance thereon and for the determination of

the resultant extent of the tests to which auditing procedures are to be restricted.

3. Sufficient, competent, evidential matter is to be obtained through inspection, observation, inquiries, and confirmations to afford a reasonable basis for an opinion regarding the financial statements under examination.

Standards of Reporting

1. The report shall state whether the financial statements are presented in accordance with generally accepted accounting principles.

2. The report shall state whether such principles have been consistently observed in the current period in relation to the preceding period.

3. Informative disclosures in the financial statements are to be regarded as reasonably adequate unless otherwise stated in the report.

4. The report shall either contain an expression of opinion regarding the financial statements, taken as a whole, or an assertion to the effect that an opinion cannot be expressed. When an overall opinion cannot be expressed, the reasons therefore should be stated. In all cases where an auditor's name is associated with financial statements, the report should contain a clear-cut indication of the character of the auditor's examination, if any, and the degree of responsibility he is taking.

General Standards

The general standards concern the competence and independence of the auditor, and the professional manner in which an audit is conducted. The first general standard states that the auditor must be properly educated and trained. If an audit requires special expertise which the auditor does not possess, he or she must either acquire that expertise, employ or consult an independent third party who has the expertise, or decline the engagement. This first general standard is, in effect, a competency requirement for professional accountants. It measures the auditor's qualifications to participate in the profession.

The second general standard is independence. Independence is the backbone of auditing as it supports the attest function. As indicated earlier, an independent auditor maintains an objective and unbiased attitude toward the audit and does not subordinate his or her judgment to pressures from others. In addition to the second general standard, the professional code of ethics requires auditors to maintain the appearance of independence as viewed by third parties. Being independent in appearance means avoiding relations that would appear to others to create a conflict of interest. For example, the auditor cannot have a direct or material indirect financial interest in an audit client. The code of ethics of the profession, which defines independence, is the subject of the next chapter.

The third general standard, due professional care, emphasizes the professional attitude essential in performing an audit. Due professional care means that an auditor should not perform his or her work in a haphazard manner. Instead, auditors must work diligently and exercise caution in all aspects of their professional work. They are, after all, holding themselves out to the public as expert accountants and the public trust that has been placed in the profession must be protected. The auditor who bases an opinion on incomplete evidence or a haphazard approach to compliance with professional standards has, in effect, committed a fraud upon the public.

Field Work Standards

Planning and supervision is covered in the first standard of field work. For an audit to be effective, efficient, and timely, the auditor must plan all phases of the audit carefully. Planning includes staffing the audit and scheduling adequate supervisory personnel for the various audit areas.

As part of the audit planning process, the auditor must review the client's system of internal control as required by the second standard of field work. Since an adequate system of internal accounting control reduces the probability of material errors occurring and remaining undetected in the financial records, the auditor may base subsequent auditing procedures on the results of the internal control review.

The third standard of field work requires the auditor to gather sufficient, competent evidence. As discussed earlier, evidence is the basis of the audit opinion. As shown in Exhibit 2-1, evidence serves as the link between management's assertions in the financial statements and the auditor's expression of an opinion on the financial statements. Sufficient evidence refers to the quantity of evidence, "how much." Competent evidence refers to the quality of the evidence. Evidence which the auditor receives directly from a third party, such as an accounts receivable confirmation, is generally of a higher quality than evidence internally created in the client's firm, such as a sales invoice.

Reporting Standards

The first and second reporting standards require that the audit report explicitly state whether the financial statements are presented in accordance with GAAP applied on a consistent basis. Although consistency and conformance with GAAP are explicitly stated in the opinion paragraph of the audit report, adequate disclosure is not. It is assumed that disclosure is adequate unless otherwise stated. Any information which is deemed to be important to a prudent investor should be disclosed in the financial statements or the footnotes to the financial statements.

The fourth standard of reporting requires the auditor to issue a report to define the degree of responsibility he or she is assuming in conjunction with the financial statements. For example, if the auditor performed all tests necessary in the circumstances, he or she may assume the responsibility that all items in the financial statements follow generally accepted accounting principles. Modifications of full responsibility as well as disclaiming all responsibility are discussed in the subsequent section on audit reports. Finally, the audit report should include an opinion on the overall financial statements or a statement that such an opinion cannot be expressed. If an overall opinion cannot be expressed, the auditor must state the reasons why.

Standards Versus Procedures

Auditing standards refer to the ten GAAS and the Statements on Auditing Standards, which are considered interpretations of the the ten GAAS. Auditing standards are broad guidelines and they are the same for every audit. Auditing procedures, on the other hand, are the detailed steps performed in the audit to obtain specific evidence, such as counting cash, observing inventory, and reconciling bank statements. Auditing procedures differ according to the needs of each audit. They are the detailed procedures outlined in the audit programs developed for each audit engagement.

STANDARD AUDIT REPORT AND OTHER REPORTS

As indicated earlier, GAAS frequently make reference to the auditor's report. This section gives an overview of the standard audit report and other audit reports. These reports are discussed in more detail in Chapters 15 and 16. The standard audit report of Mobile Corporation from Chapter 1, is presented in Exhibit 2-2. As explained in Chapter 1, this report is an unqualified or "clean" opinion. It has also been termed the short-form report, though usage of this term is fading since the "long-form" report terminology has been replaced by the term "accompanying information," as discussed in Chapter 16.

The standard audit report should be addressed to the party who hires the CPA, usually the stockholders and/or board of directors of the audited business, if a corporation. For non-corporate business entities, the audit report would be addressed to the individual owner or owners, such as the partners in a partnership. However, if a third party engages a CPA to audit a business, the report is addressed to that party. For example, assume that the partners in a partnership engage a CPA to audit a corporation that the partnership may decide to purchase. In this case, the auditor's report should be addressed to the partners because they are the party who engaged the CPA (the client).

Exhibit 2-2
Standard Auditor's Report

February 17, 1985

Board of Directors and Shareholders
Mobile Corporation

We have examined the balance sheets of Mobile Corporation as of December 31, 1984 and 1983, and the related statements of income, retained earnings, and changes in financial position for the years then ended. Our examinations were made in accordance with generally accepted auditing standards and, accordingly, included such tests of the accounting records and such other auditing procedures as we considered necessary in the circumstances.

In our opinion, the financial statements referred to above present fairly the financial position of Mobile Corporation as of December 31, 1984 and 1983, and the results of its operations and the changes in its financial position for the years then ended, in conformity with generally accepted accounting principles applied on a consistent basis.

BRIDGES, GEISERT & VICKERY

Certified Public Accountants

The two-paragraph report consists of a scope and an opinion paragraph. The scope paragraph should contain the exact titles used by the business to describe its financial statements. For example, if the Mobile financial statements represented consolidated statements, the scope paragraph would begin: "We have examined the Consolidated Balance Sheet of . . ." A sole practitioner, as opposed to a CPA partnership or professional corporation, would begin the report: "I have examined the Consolidated Balance Sheet . . ." and use the first person throughout the report.

The scope paragraph of the Mobile report explicitly states that the audit was made in accordance with generally accepted auditing standards (GAAS). GAAS represents the ten standards discussed previously and the SASs which are interpretations of these standards. Note that there is no explicit reference to an evaluation of internal control. But since internal control is the second standard of field work, the reference to internal control is implicit. The assumption that there is adequate disclosure is also implicit since informative disclosure is the third reporting standard. The scope paragraph concludes by stating that the auditor has performed the tests and procedures he or she considered necessary for that particular audit.

The opinion paragraph states that the financial statements are presented fairly in accordance with generally accepted accounting principles (GAAP) applied on a consistent basis. Since Exhibit 2-2 is an unqualified opinion, it contains no language contrary to fair presentation. Finally, the auditor signs and dates the report. The date used is generally the last day of field work which is the last day the auditor spends in the client's office gathering evidence in support of the financial statements.

Modifications of the Standard Audit Report

Circumstances may prevent the auditor from issuing an unqualified opinion.

The auditor should not issue an unqualified opinion when any one of the following situations is present:

1. A material uncertainty exists which has a potential financial impact upon the company,

2. When there is a limitation on the scope of the auditor's work, or

3. When the financial statements are not prepared in accordance with GAAP applied on a consistent basis.

When one of the above circumstances exists, the auditor will have to modify the standard audit report as discussed below.

Existence of a material uncertainty. An uncertainty occurs when the impact of some current event is not subject to reasonable estimation. For example, the client and the CPA may not be able to arrive at a reasonable estimate of the financial impact, if any, of a pending lawsuit against the Company. In these cases, the scope paragraph should not be modified, but the auditor should add an explanatory middle paragraph, and in the last paragraph he or she may disclaim or qualify the opinion on the financial statements. The middle paragraph should explain the nature of the uncertainty and it might read as follows:

(Separate paragraph)

As discussed in Note X to the financial statements, the company is defendant in a lawsuit alleging infringement of certain patent rights and claiming royalties and punitive damages. The company has filed a counter action, and preliminary hearings and discovery proceedings on both actions are in progress. Company officers and counsel believe the company has a good chance of prevailing, but the ultimate outcome of the lawsuits cannot presently be determined, and no provision for any liability that may result has been made in the financial statements.

If the client explains the nature of the uncertainty in a footnote to the financial statements the auditor still needs a middle paragraph in the report. However, the auditor can shorten the paragraph by making reference to the client's explanation, as was done in the above illustration. In other words, there is no reason for the auditor to repeat detail information about the uncertainty which is already adequately explained by the client in the footnotes to the financial statements.

When an auditor disclaims an opinion because of an uncertainty, the auditor's opinion paragraph is modified to indicate that no opinion is being expressed on the financial statements because of the possible impact of adjustments to the financial statements had the outcome of the uncertainty been known. For example, if an auditor decides to disclaim an opinion because of an uncertainty, the auditor's opinion paragraph might read as follows:

(Opinion paragraph)

Because it is impossible to determine the effect of such adjustments, if any, as might have been required had the outcome of the uncertainty referred to in the preceding paragraph been known, we are unable to and do not express an opinion on the accompanying financial statements for the year ended December 31, 1984.

On the other hand, when the auditor qualifies the opinion because of an uncertainty, it should be made clear to the reader of the audit report that the qualification relates to any adjustments which might have been required had the outcome of the uncertainty been known. In the opinion paragraph of the auditor's qualified report, it is stated that the financial statements are fairly presented "subject to" the effects of such adjustments, if any, which might have been required had the outcome of the uncertainty been known. In other words, if the resolution of the uncertainty does not indicate that material adjustments should have been made to the current financial statements, these statements are fairly presented; otherwise the statements may not necessarily result in a fair presentation. An example of an auditor's opinion which is qualified because of an uncertainty follows:

> In our opinion, subject to the effects of such adjustments, if any, that might have been required had the outcome of the uncertainty referred to in the preceding paragraph been known, the financial statements referred to above present fairly the financial position of X Company as of December 31, 19____, and the results of its operations and the changes in its financial position for the year then ended, in conformity with generally accepted accounting principles applied on a basis consistent with that of the preceding year.

In deciding whether to qualify or disclaim an opinion because of an uncertainty, the auditor needs to carefully consider the nature of any adjustments which might have been needed had the outcome of the uncertainty been known. If the potential adjustments could have a pervasive affect on the financial statements, the auditor will most likely disclaim an opinion. On the other hand, if any adjustments would significantly affect only a few account balances, the auditor will likely use the "subject to" qualification. In the final analysis, the decision on the type of opinion to issue is very difficult to quantify, and substantial audit judgment is required in making the decision. The key factor in making the decision is that the reader of the audit report not be misled as to the quality of the financial statements.

Limitation on the scope of the auditor's work. As indicated earlier, the auditor states in the report that the examination was made in accordance with GAAS and included such tests of the accounting records and such other auditing procedures as the auditor considered necessary in the circumstances. In cases where the auditor does not follow generally accepted auditing standards or is unable to perform auditing procedures which he or she considers necessary, the standard report must be modified to reflect this limitation in the scope of the auditor's work.

Because of a scope limitation, the audit report should contain three paragraphs. The first paragraph would be similar to the standard scope paragraph except that it should make reference to the scope limitation. The second paragraph explains the nature of the limitation, and in the third paragraph the auditor may disclaim or qualify the opinion on the financial statements.

The middle paragraph should not be shortened by referring to a footnote for further explanation of the scope limitation because the footnotes and the financial statements are representations of management, and it is not appropriate for management to explain the nature of any limitations imposed on the auditor's work. Only the auditor is qualified to explain scope limitations including why the limitations occurred.

The auditor may issue a disclaimer or a qualified opinion depending on the nature and potential impact of the scope limitation. To illustrate a disclaimer of opinion because of a scope limitation assume that the client did not take a physical inventory of merchandise at year-end for 19x2 and that no evidence is available to support the cost of property and equipment acquired prior to December 31, 19x1. Given these facts, the auditor's disclaimer of opinion might read as follows:

(Scope paragraph)

We have examined the balance sheet of X Company as of December 31, 19x2, and the related statements of income, retained earnings and changes in financial position for the year then ended. Except as set forth in the following paragraph, our examination was made in accordance with generally accepted auditing standards and accordingly included such tests of the accounting records and such other auditing procedures as we considered necessary in the circumstances.

(Middle paragraph)

The company did not take a physical inventory of merchandise, stated at $1,350,000 in the accompanying financial statements. Further, evidence supporting the cost of property and equipment acquired prior to December 31, 19x1 is no longer available. The company's records do not permit the application of alternative procedures regarding the inventory or the cost of property and equipment.

(Disclaimer paragraph)

Since the company did not take a physical inventory and we were unable to apply adequate alternative procedures regarding inventory and the cost of property and equipment, as noted in the preceding paragraph, the scope of our work was not sufficient to enable us to express, and we do not express, an opinion on the financial statements referred to above.

When the auditor's scope is limited and the auditor decides not to disclaim an opinion, the auditor should issue a report which is qualified because of a scope limitation. In the third paragraph, the auditor expresses an opinion that the financial statements are fairly presented in accordance with GAAP applied on a consistent basis, *except for* any adjustments which may have been required had the auditor been able to complete the audit without any scope limitations. An auditor's report which is qualified because of a scope limitation would read as indicated below. In the example, only those parts of the auditor's report which would be modified are presented.

(Scope paragraph)

. . . Except as explained in the following paragraph, our examination . . . and such auditing procedures as we considered necessary in the circumstances . . . .

(Middle paragraph)

We did not observe the taking of the physical inventories as of December 31, 19xx (stated at $650,000), and December 31, 19x1 (stated at $492,000), since these dates were prior to the time we were initially engaged as auditors for the company. Due to the nature of the company's records, we were unable to satisfy ourselves as to the inventory quantities by means of other auditing procedures.

(Opinion paragraph)

In our opinion, except for the effects of such adjustments, if any, as might have determined to be necessary had we been able to observe the physical inventories . . . .

In deciding whether a scope limitation requires a disclaimer of opinion or a qualified opinion the auditor should consider the nature of the scope limitation. In general, if the potential adjustments which might occur had the audit work been performed been considered potentially pervasive in their effect on the financial statements, the auditor would likely issue a disclaimer of opinion; otherwise a qualified opinion may be appropriate. However, this is not a hard and fast rule, and, in the final analysis, the decision as to the type of audit report to issue depends on the auditor's judgment in the circumstances.

Departure from GAAP applied on a consistent basis. When the auditor discovers that the client has not followed GAAP in the preparation of the financial statements, which includes the violation of a measurement principle or a disclosure principle, the auditor requests that the client revise the financial statements to make them conform to GAAP. If the client refuses to revise the statements, the auditor must issue either an adverse opinion or a qualified opinion. The auditor must explain the reasons for the opinion and indicate the approximate effects of the departure from GAAP on the financial statements. In cases where the approximate effects of not following GAAP cannot be estimated, the auditor modifies the middle paragraph to state that the effects on the financial statements of not following GAAP are not subject to reasonable estimation.

An adverse opinion states that the financial statements are not fairly presented in accordance with GAAP. When the auditor issues an adverse opinion, no reference should be made to consistency in the *opinion paragraph* of the auditor's report because it is not meaningful to refer to the consistent application of accounting principles which are not generally accepted in the first place. However, if the lack of consistency is one factor which causes the auditor to issue an adverse opinion, the lack of consistency and the approximate effects on the financial statements should be stated as one of the reasons for the adverse opinion.

When the auditor issues an adverse opinion, the report should consist of three paragraphs. Assuming that the auditor's scope has not been limited, the scope paragraph is not affected by an adverse opinion. Consequently, in these cases the first paragraph is the same as the scope paragraph of the standard auditor's report. In the second paragraph, which may be shortened by referring to a footnote to financial statements, the auditor explains the reason(s) for issuing the adverse opinion and the approximate effect of not following GAAP on the financial statements. Finally, in the opinion paragraph the auditor states that the financial statements are not fairly presented in accordance with generally accepted accounting principles. The following example illustrates the third paragraph of an adverse opinion.

(Opinion paragraph)

> In our opinion, because of the effects of the matters discussed in the preceding paragraph, the financial statements referred to above do not present fairly, in conformity with generally accepted accounting principles, the financial position of X Company as of December 31, 19xx, or the results of its operations and changes in its financial position for the year then ended.

The issuance of an adverse opinion is an extreme step. An adverse opinion is not likely to be issued often in practice because the client is likely to either revise the financial statements to correct the reporting deficiency or fire the auditor who proposes the adverse opinion. Many times in practice a client's failure to follow GAAP applied on a consistent basis stems from a change in accounting principles or the failure to follow GAAP for a single transaction or a group of similar transactions. In these cases, the auditor will frequently issue a qualified opinion instead of an adverse opinion.

When the auditor issues a qualified opinion for a departure from GAAP other than for a lack of consistent application of accounting principles, the auditor's report consists of three paragraphs. Assuming there is no scope limitation, the scope paragraph is the same as the scope paragraph of the standard auditor's report. In the second paragraph, the auditor explains why the opinion paragraph is qualified and the approximate effects of not following GAAP on the financial statements. Finally, in the third paragraph, the auditor states that in the auditor's opinion, except for the effects of not applying some specific accounting principle or principles, the financial statements are otherwise fairly presented in accordance with GAAP applied on a consistent basis. An example of an auditor's report which is qualified because the company failed to follow GAAP and capitalize certain leases follows:

(Standard scope paragraph)

(Middle paragraph)

> The company has excluded from property and debt in the accompanying balance sheet certain lease obligations, which in our opinion, should be capitalized in order to conform with generally accepted accounting principles. If these lease obligations were capitalized, property would be increased by $652,000, long-term debt by $490,000, and retained earnings by $120,000, as of December 31, 19xx, and net income and earnings per share would be increased by $60,000 and $.06, respectively, for the year then ended.

(Opinion paragraph)

In our opinion, except for the effects of not capitalizing lease obligations, as discussed in the preceding paragraph, the financial statements present fairly . . . .

An audit report which is qualified due to a lack of consistent application of accounting principles differs from the general form of qualification which is used when the financial statements are not prepared in accordance with generally accepted accounting principles. A thorough discussion of what constitutes a change in an accounting principle and how the change should be reported by the auditor is provided in Chapter 15. For the time being it is sufficient to say that when there is a change in an accounting principle or principles, the auditor's report is qualified because of the change, and, in the report, the auditor explains how the accounting change affects the comparability of the financial statements.

In deciding whether to issue a qualified opinion or an adverse opinion, the auditor must consider the impact of the failure to follow GAAP on the financial statements taken as a whole. If the auditor believes that except for a specific departure or departures from GAAP, the financial statements are fairly presented in accordance with GAAP applied on a consistent basis, the auditor should issue a qualified opinion. On the other hand, if the departure from accepted accounting principles has a pervasive impact on the financial statements, the auditor must issue an adverse opinion.

Exhibit 2-3 summarizes the types of audit opinions which have been discussed in this chapter, and the types of deficiencies in the financial statements which would give rise to each type of opinion. These audit reports, as well as other types of audit reports, are considered in more detail in Chapters 15 and 16.

SUMMARY

Some auditors have argued that a conceptual base is not as important for auditing as it is for accounting. These auditors have argued that auditing is primarily a process of gathering evidence about economic assertions, and it is fairly easy to decide what evidence to gather or not to gather without a conceptual base. However, despite this argument,

Exhibit 2-3
Types of Audit Opinions

Types of Opinions	Types of Material Deficiencies in Financial Statements or Audits
UNQUALIFIED	No deficiencies in the financial statements or the audit
QUALIFIED (Financial statements taken as a whole present fairly but have a material deficiency)	
☐ "except for"	Accounting deficiency in financial statements or scope restriction in audit
☐ "subject to"	Uncertainty involving the financial statements
ADVERSE (Financial statements taken as a whole do not present fairly)	Accounting deficiency in financial statements
DISCLAIMER (No opinion is expressed on the financial statements)	Uncertainty involving the financial statements or scope restriction in audit
NO OPINION OR DISCLAIMER	Due to unusual circumstances, the auditor withdraws from the engagement

there have been several attempts to develop a theory of auditing. One of the most comprehensive attempts to develop a theory of auditing was *The Philosophy of Auditing* by R.K. Mautz and Hussein A. Sharaf.

Mautz and Sharaf identified eight tentative postulates of auditing:

1. Financial statements and financial data are verifiable.

2. There is no necessary conflict of interest between the auditor and the management of the enterprise under audit.

3. The financial statements and other information submitted for verification are free from collusion and other unusual irregularities.

4. The existence of a satisfactory system of internal control eliminates the probability of irregularities.

5. Consistent application of generally accepted principles of accounting results in the fair presentation of financial position and the results of operations.

6. In the absence of clear evidence to the contrary, what has held true in the past for the enterprise under examination will hold true in the future.

7. When examining financial data for purposes of expressing an independent opinion thereon, the auditor acts exclusively in the capacity of an auditor.

8. The professional status of the auditor imposes commensurate professional obligations.

In addition to their postulates, Mautz and Sharaf identify five primary concepts of auditing:

1. *Evidence* is the link between the financial statements and the auditor's opinion on them. Through adequate evidence, the auditor can reach a rational opinion on the fairness of the financial statements.

2. *Due audit care* is the basis for judging an auditor's responsibility in performing professional services. Due audit care refers to the care the prudent practitioner would exercise in an audit situation. The prudent auditor represents the average level of competence of the profession.

3. *Fair presentation* generally is achieved if the financial statements are prepared in accordance with generally accepted accounting principles. However, in cases where GAAP do not result in a fair presentation, GAAP should be replaced with principles that do result in a fair presentation.

4. *Independence* means that when an auditor conducts an audit, he or she should be objective and unbaised. An auditor must be independent in fact and in appearance.

5. The last concept identified by Mautz and Sharaf is *ethical conduct*, which will be discussed in Chapter 3.

Most auditing professionals do not believe that *The Philosophy of Auditing*, or other theoretical work, has had much impact on the development of generally accepted auditing standards. In fact, the AICPA's Committee on Auditing Procedure identified the ten generally accepted auditing standards well before the work by Mautz and Sharaf was published. The AICPA's *Code of Professional Ethics* requires compliance with GAAS in all audit engagements. The ten GAAS are classified as the general standards, the field work standards, and the standards of reporting.

The general standards include the competence, independence, and professional manner in which an audit is conducted. These standards relate to characteristics which the auditor must possess. Planning and supervision is covered in the first standard of field work. As part of audit planning, the auditor must review the client's system of internal control as required by the second standard of field work. This review will help the auditor determine how much testing will be necessary to evaluate the overall financial statements. The third standard of field work requires the auditor to obtain sufficient competent evidential matter to support the opinion on the financial statements.

The first and second reporting standards require that the audit report explicitly state whether the financial statements are presented in accordance with GAAP applied on a consistent basis. According to the third reporting standard, it is assumed that disclosure is adequate unless otherwise indicated. The fourth standard of reporting requires the auditor to define for the users of the audit report the degree of responsibility he or she is assuming with respect to the financial statements. The audit report should include an opinion on the overall financial statements or a statement that such an opinion cannot be expressed and the reasons why.

Auditing standards refer to the ten GAAS and to SASs which are interpretations of the standards. Auditing procedures are the detailed steps of the audit and they differ according to the needs of every audit.

The audit report is addressed to the party who hires the CPA. The *standard audit report* consists of two paragraphs: a scope paragraph and an opinion paragraph. The scope paragraph explicitly states that the audit was made in accordance with generally accepted auditing standards. The opinion paragraph states that the financial statements are presented fairly in accordance with generally accepted accounting principles applied on a consistent basis. The report is generally dated as of the last date of the auditor's field work.

Circumstances may prevent the auditor from issuing an unqualified opinion. An uncertainty occurs when the impact of some current event is not subject to reasonable estimation. In these cases, the CPA may disclaim an opinion or issue a qualified opinion. In either case, the CPA must include a middle paragraph in the report which explains the nature of the uncertainty. This paragraph may be shortened by referring to a footnote to the financial statements which includes the detailed disclosure information regarding the uncertainty. When an auditor disclaims an opinion or issues a qualified opinion because of an uncertainty, the auditor should make it clear that the qualification or disclaimer arises because of the possible impact that the resolution of the uncertainty might have on the financial statements. In the opinion paragraph the auditor should use the phrase, "subject to," when the qualification is due to an uncertainty.

An auditor may also need to modify the standard report when there is a limitation on the scope of the auditor's work. The auditor may issue a disclaimer of opinion or a qualified opinion depending on the nature of the scope limitation. In either case, the auditor's report should include a middle paragraph which explains the nature of the scope limitation as it is not appropriate for management to explain in a footnote a limitation imposed on the auditor's work. When the auditor disclaims an opinion or qualifies the opinion because of a scope limitation, the wording in the auditor's report should make it clear that the qualification or disclaimer is necessary because of adjustments which may have been required had the auditor been able to complete the audit without any scope limitation. When the qualification is due to a scope limitation, the auditor should qualify the opinion with an "except for" phrase.

In addition to report modifications which result from uncertainties or a scope limitation, the auditor may need to modify the report if the financial statements are not prepared in accordance with GAAP applied on a consistent basis, and the client refuses to revise the financial statements. In these cases, the auditor must issue either an adverse opinion or a qualified opinion, and explain his or her reasons for the opinion in a middle paragraph of the audit report. Also, the auditor must indicate the approximate effects on the financial statements of the departure from GAAP. In cases where the approximate effects of not following GAAP cannot be estimated, the auditor modifies the middle paragraph to state that the effects on the financial statements of not following GAAP are not subject to reasonable estimation.

REVIEW QUESTIONS

2-1   Define the nature of a postulate and discuss the relationship between postulates and theory.

2-2   Discuss the four characteristics of postulates.

2-3   Why is it important that financial statements and financial data be verifiable?

2-4   What would be the impact upon an audit engagement if there is a conflict of interest between the auditor and the client?

2-5   Briefly discuss the relationship between an adequate system of internal control and the probability of errors and irregularities in financial records.

2-6   What is the primary criteria accepted by the auditing profession to measure fair presentation of financial position and results of operations?

2-7   Why is it necessary for an auditor to act exclusively as an auditor when examining financial data for the purpose of expressing an independent opinion thereon?

2-8   Briefly state the relationship between auditing concepts and auditing postulates.

2-9   Why is evidence that is obtained directly by the auditor, or provided by an independent third party, more convincing than evidence supplied by the client?

2-10   Should the constraints of time/cost/benefit be considered in obtaining evidence in an audit engagement? Briefly discuss.

2-11   List the nine types of audit evidence identified by Mautz and Sharaf in *The Philosophy of Auditing*.

2-12   What is the basis for judging an auditor's responsibility in performing professional services? Define the "prudent auditor" concept.

2-13   Discuss the three subconcepts of fair presentation according to Mautz and Sharaf.

2-14   Does the competency requirement of the first general standard pertain to only entry level personnel or to all professional staff? Explain.

2-15   Identify the difference between independence in fact and independence in appearance. Is independence in appearance specifically mentioned in the second general standard?

2-16   Why is it important that the auditor exercise due audit care as required by the third general standard?

2-17   What is the purpose of the auditor's study and evaluation of the client's system of internal control?

2-18   Distinguish between competency and sufficiency of evidence.

2-19   What is the purpose of the generally accepted auditing standards? Contrast this purpose with the purpose of auditing procedures.

2-20   To whom should the audit report be addressed?

2-21   Discuss the nature and content of the scope paragraph in the standard audit report.

2-22   In the opinion paragraph of the standard audit report, what criteria are used to evaluate fairness of presentation of financial data?

2-23   What are the three basic circumstances that may prevent the auditor from issuing an unqualified opinion?

2-24   What types of reports may be issued when a material uncertainty exists?

2-25   Identify and discuss the differences in the types of audit reports that may be issued when a material uncertainty exists and when a limitation on the scope of the auditor's work exists.

2-26   What is the first step the auditor should take when the client has prepared financial statements that depart from GAAP applied on a consistent basis? If the client refuses to adhere to the CPA's recommendation, what types of reports may the auditor issue?

2-27   Explain why adverse opinions are not likely to be issued in practice.

DISCUSSION QUESTIONS AND PROBLEMS

2-28   Ray, the owner of a small company, asked Holmes, CPA, to conduct an audit of the company's records. Ray told Holmes that an audit is to be completed in time to submit audited financial statements to a bank as part of a loan application. Holmes immediately accepted the engagement and agreed to provide an auditor's report within three weeks. Ray agreed to pay Holmes a fixed fee plus a bonus if the loan was granted.

Holmes hired two accounting students to conduct the audit and spent several hours telling them exactly what to do. Holmes told the students not to spend time reviewing the controls, but instead to concentrate on proving the mathematical accuracy of the ledger accounts, and summarizing the data in the accounting records that support Ray's financial statements. The students followed Holmes' instructions and after two weeks gave Holmes the financial statements which did not include footnotes. Holmes reviewed the statements and prepared an unqualified auditor's report. The report, however, did not refer to generally accepted accounting principles nor to the year-to-year application of such principles.

Required:

Briefly describe each of the generally accepted auditing standards and indicate how the action(s) of Holmes resulted in a failure to comply with each standard.

Organize your answer as follows:

Brief Description of Generally Accepted Auditing Standards	Holmes' Actions Resulting in Failure to Comply With Generally Accepted Auditing Standards

(AICPA adapted)

2-29   Mountaineer Glass Manufacturers, Inc. maintains an advanced computer system not only for production but also for all information processing. The main-frame consists of a large high-speed Andahl computer with remote entry via 45 intelligent terminals. Sales transactions are captured on source documents before being keyed into terminals for processing of the data. As each sale is processed, the sales journal, subsidiary accounts receivable ledger, and general ledger balances are updated on disc. The journals and general ledger balances are printed on a weekly basis.

Mountaineer Glass offered the annual audit engagement to the CPA firm of Smith, Smith & Co. The partner-in-charge is having a difficult time deciding whether to accept the engagement since the CPA firm currently does not have professional staff with computer expertise.

Required:

Discuss whether Smith, Smith & Co. should accept the annual audit of Mountaineer Glass Manufacturers, Inc. Since the CPA firm does not have personnel with computer expertise, what alternative courses of action might Smith, Smith & Co. pursue regarding the client?

2-30 Upon completion of the examination of the client's financial statements, the CPA must issue a disclaimer of opinion or an opinion on the statements taken as a whole. His or her opinion may be unqualified, qualified, or adverse.

Required:

a. Under what general conditions may a CPA express an unqualified opinion on the financial statements of the client?
b. Define and distinguish among (1) a qualified opinion, (2) an adverse opinion, and (3) a disclaimer of opinion on the statements taken as a whole.

(AICPA adapted)

2-31 On completion of all field work on February 11, 19x2, the following report was rendered by Dale Shaw, CPA, to the directors of Pineview Country Club, Incorporated.

To the Directors of Pineview Country Club, Inc.

We have examined the balance sheet, the related statement of income and retained earnings of Pineview Country Club, Incorporated, and the statement of changes in financial position as of December 31, 19x1 and 19x0. Our examinations were made in accordance with the standards of the profession and included all tests of the statements that you considered appropriate in the circumstances.

In our opinion, with the exception of some minor errors that are considered immaterial, the aforementioned financial statements present fairly the financial position of Pineview Country Club, Incorporated, at December 31, 19x1 and 19x0, and the results of its operations for the years then ended, in conformity with pronouncements of the Financial Accounting Standards Board applied consistently throughout the period.

Dale Shaw, CPA
February 23, 19x2

Required:

List and explain deficiencies and omissions in the auditor's report. Organize your answer sheet by paragraph (scope and opinion) of the auditor's report.

(AICPA adapted)

OBJECTIVE QUESTIONS

2-32 An auditor who accepts an audit engagement and does not possess the industry expertise of the business entity, should

    A. Engage financial experts familiar with the nature of the business entity.

    B. Obtain a knowledge of matters that relate to the nature of the entity's business.

    C. Refer a substantial portion of the audit to another CPA who will act as the principal auditor.

    D. First inform management that an unqualified opinion cannot be issued.

2-33 The first general standard requires that the examination be performed by a person or persons having adequate technical training and proficiency as an auditor. This standard is met by

    A. An understanding of the field of business and finance.

    B. Education and experience in the field of auditing.

    C. Continuing Professional Education.

    D. A thorough knowledge of the Statements on Auditing Standards.

2-34 Which of the following is mandatory if the auditor is to comply with generally accepted auditing standards?

    A. Possession by the auditor of adequate technical training.

    B. Use of analytical review on audit engagements.

    C. Use of statistical sampling whenever feasible on an audit engagement.

    D. Confirmation by the auditor of material accounts receivable balances.

2-35 Which of the following *best* describes what is meant by generally accepted auditing standards?

A. Acts to be performed by the auditor.

B. Measures of the quality of the auditor's performance.

C. Procedures to be used to gather evidence to support financial statements.

D. Audit objectives generally determined on audit engagements.

2-36   Which of the following underlies the application of generally accepted auditing standards, particularly the standards of field work and reporting?

A. The elements of materiality and relative risk.

B. The element of internal control.

C. The element of corroborating evidence.

D. The element of reasonable assurance.

2-37   Audit evidence can come in different forms with different degrees of persuasiveness. Which of the following is the *least* persuasive type of evidence?

A. Documents mailed by outsiders to the auditor.

B. Correspondence between auditor and vendors.

C. Sales invoices inspected by the auditor.

D. Computations made by the auditor.

2-38   An investor is reading the financial statements of the Stankey Corporation and observes that the statements are accompanied by an auditor's unqualified report. From this the investor may conclude that

A. Any disputes over significant accounting issues have been settled to the auditor's satisfaction.

B. The auditor is satisfied that Stankey is financially sound.

C. The auditor has ascertained that Stankey's financial statements have been prepared accurately.

D. Informative disclosures in the financial statements but *not* necessarily in Stankey's footnotes are to be regarded as reasonably adequate.

2-39   When a client declines to make essential disclosures in the financial statements or in the footnotes, the independent auditor should

A. Provide the necessary disclosures in the auditor's report and appropriately modify the opinion.

B. Explain to the client that an adverse opinion must be issued.
C. Issue an unqualified report and inform the stockholders of the improper disclosure in an "unaudited" footnote.
D. Issue an opinion "subject to" the client's lack of disclosure of supplementary information as explained in a middle paragraph of the report.

2-40 Which of the following *best* describes the objective of the fourth standard of reporting, which requires that the auditor's report shall either contain an expression of opinion regarding the financial statements, taken as a whole, or an assertion to the effect that an opinion cannot be expressed?

A. To protect the auditor against allegations that some portion of the financial statements includes a material misstatement.
B. To prevent misinterpretation of the degree of responsibility the auditor is assuming when the auditor's name is associated with the financial statements.
C. To prevent the reader from assuming that an auditor will detect errors or irregularities that have a material effect on the financial statements.
D. To protect auditors who are not associated with financial statements and who do not lend their names to the financial statements.

2-41 Limitations on the scope of the auditor's examination may require the auditor to issue a qualified opinion or to disclaim an opinion. Which of the following would generally be a limitation on the scope of the auditor's examination?

A. The engagement of the auditor to report on only one basic financial statement.
B. The examination of a subsidiary's financial statements by an auditor other than the one who examines and reports on the consolidated financial statements.
C. The engagement of the auditor after year-end.
D. The unavailability of sufficient competent evidential matter.

2-42 If an auditor wishes to issue a qualified opinion because the financial statements include a departure from generally accepted accounting principles, the auditor's report should have an explanatory paragraph referring to a footnote that discloses the principal effects of the subject matter of the qualification. The qualification should be referred to in the opinion paragraph by using language such as

A. "With the exception of."
B. "When read in conjunction with the footnotes."
C. "With the foregoing explanation."
D. "Subject to the departure explained in the footnotes."

2-43 The sufficiency and competency of evidential matter ultimately is based on the

A. Availability of corroborating data.
B. Generally accepted auditing standards.
C. Pertinence of the evidence.
D. Judgment of the auditor.

2-44 When a CPA lacks independence in connection with an audit engagement, he or she should

A. State, in the audit report, the reason for the lack of independence.
B. Disclaim an opinion on the financial statements.
C. List, in the audit report, all the generally accepted auditing procedures actually performed by him or her.
D. Issue a piecemeal opinion.

2-45 Which of the following would be an *inappropriate* addressee for an auditor's report?

A. The corporation whose financial statements were examined.
B. A third party, even if the third party is a client who engaged the auditor for examination of a non-client corporation.
C. The president of the corporation whose financial statements were examined.
D. The stockholders of the corporation whose financial statements were examined.

2-46 In determining the type of opinion to express, an auditor assesses the nature of the reporting qualifications and the materiality of their effects. Materiality will be the primary factor considered in the choice between

A. An "except for" opinion and an adverse opinion.
B. An "except for" opinion and a "subject to" opinion.
C. An adverse opinion and a disclaimer of opinion.
D. A "subject to" opinion and a piecemeal opinion.

2-47   A CPA is most likely to refer to one or more of the three general auditing standards in determining

A. The nature of the CPA's report qualification.
B. The scope of the CPA's auditing procedures.
C. Requirements for the review of internal control.
D. Whether the CPA should undertake an audit engagement.

2-48   The fourth generally accepted auditing standard of reporting requires an auditor to render a report whenever an auditor's name is associated with financial statements. The overall purpose of the fourth standard of reporting is to require that reports

A. State that the examination of financial statements has been conducted in accordance with generally accepted auditing standards.
B. Indicate the character of the auditor's examination and the degree of responsibility assumed by the auditor.
C. Imply that the auditor is independent in fact as well as in appearance with respect to the financial statements under examination.
D. Express whether the accounting principles used in preparing the financial statements have been applied consistently in the period under examination.

2-49   The first general standard of generally accepted auditing standards, which states in part that the examination is to be performed by a person or persons having adequate technical training, requires that an auditor have

A. Education and experience in the field of auditing.
B. Ability in the planning and supervision of the audit work.
C. Proficiency in business and financial matters.
D. Knowledge in the areas of financial accounting.

2-50   Auditing standards differ from auditing procedures in that procedures relate to

A. Measures of performance.
B. Audit principles.
C. Acts to be performed.
D. Audit judgments.

2-51   What is the general character of the three generally accepted auditing standards classified as general standards?

A. Criteria for competence, independence, and professional care of individuals performing the audit.
B. Criteria for the content of the financial statements and related footnote disclosures.
C. Criteria for the content of the auditor's report on financial statements and related footnote disclosures.
D. The requirements for the planning of the audit and supervision of assistants, if any.

2-52   The general group of the generally accepted auditing standards includes a requirement that

A. The field work be adequately planned and supervised.
B. The auditor's report state whether or not the financial statements conform to generally accepted accounting principles.
C. Due professional care be exercised by the auditor.
D. Informative disclosures in the financial statements be reasonably adequate.

2-53   What is the general character of the three generally accepted auditing standards classified as standards of field work?

A. The competence, independence, and professional care of persons performing the audit.
B. Criteria for the content of the auditor's report on financial statements and related footnote disclosures.
C. The criteria of audit planning and evidence gathering.
D. The need to maintain an independence in mental attitude in all matters relating to the audit.

2-54   One of the generally accepted auditing standards specifies that the auditor

A. Inspect all the fixed assets acquired during the year.
B. Charge fair fees based on cost.

C. Make a proper study and evaluation of the existing internal control.

D. May not solicit clients.

2-55 An independent auditor must be without bias with respect to the financial statements of a client in order to

A. Comply with the laws established by governmental agencies.

B. Maintain the appearance of separate interests on the part of the auditor and the client.

C. Protect against criticism and possible litigation from stockholders and creditors.

D. Insure the impartiality necessary for an expression of the auditor's opinion.

2-56 What is the meaning of the generally accepted auditing standard which requires that the auditor be independent?

A. The auditor must be without bias with respect to the client under audit.

B. The auditor must adopt a critical attitude during the audit.

C. The auditor's sole obligation is to third parties.

D. The auditor may have a direct ownership interest in his client's business if it is not material.

2-57 No matter how competent a CPA may be, the opinion expressed on financial statements will be of little value to those who rely on it unless he or she

A. Issues an unqualified opinion.

B. Maintains a program of continuing education.

C. Serves his or her clients with professional concern for their best interests.

D. Maintains his or her independence.

2-58 The general group of the generally accepted auditing standards includes a requirement that

A. The auditor's report state whether or not the financial statements conform to generally accepted accounting principles.

B. The field work be adequately planned and supervised.

C. Due professional care be exercised by the auditor.

D. Informative disclosures in the financial statements be reasonably adequate.

2-59   The major reason an independent auditor gathers audit evidence is to

A.   Form an opinion on the financial statements.
B.   Detect fraud.
C.   Evaluate management.
D.   Evaluate internal control.

2-60   Evidential matter is generally considered sufficient when

A.   It is competent.
B.   There is enough of it to afford a reasonable basis for an opinion on the financial statements.
C.   It has the qualities of being relevant, objective, and free from unknown bias.
D.   It has been obtained by random selection.

2-61   The auditor's judgment concerning the overall fairness of the presentation of financial position, results of operations, and changes in financial position is applied within the framework of

A.   Quality control.
B.   Generally accepted auditing standards which include the concept of materiality.
C.   The auditor's evaluation of the audited company's internal control.
D.   Generally accepted accounting principles.

2-62   An opinion as to the "fairness" of financial statement presentation in accordance with generally accepted accounting principles is based on several judgments made by the auditor. One such judgment is whether the accounting principles used

A.   Have general acceptance.
B.   Are promulgated by the AICPA Auditing Standards Board.
C.   Are the most conservative of those available for use.
D.   Emphasize the legal form of transactions.

2-63   The auditor's report makes reference to the basic financial statements, which are customarily considered to be the balance sheet and the statements of

A.   Income and changes in financial position.
B.   Income, changes in retained earnings, and changes in financial position.

C.   Income, retained earnings, and changes in financial position.

D.   Income and retained earnings.

2-64   The standard auditor's report is generally considered to have a scope paragraph and an opinion paragraph. In the report the auditor refers to both generally accepted accounting principles (GAAP) and generally accepted auditing standards (GAAS). In which of the paragraphs are these terms used?

A.   GAAP in the scope paragraph and GAAS in the opinion paragraph.

B.   GAAS in the scope paragraph and GAAP in the opinion paragraph.

C.   GAAS in both paragraphs and GAAP in the scope paragraph.

D.   GAAP in both paragraphs and GAAS in the opinion paragraph.

2-65   An unqualified standard audit report by a CPA normally does not explicitly state

A.   The CPA's opinion that the financial statements comply with generally accepted accounting principles.

B.   That generally accepted auditing standards were followed in the conduct of the audit.

C.   That the internal control system of the client was found to be satisfactory.

D.   The subjects of the audit examination.

2-66   If the auditor believes that required disclosures of a significant nature are omitted from the financial statements under examination, the auditor should decide between issuing

A.   A qualified opinion or an adverse opinion.

B.   A disclaimer of opinion or a qualified opinion.

C.   An adverse opinion or a disclaimer of opinion.

D.   An unqualified opinion or a qualified opinion.

2-67   When an auditor issues a qualified opinion because of an uncertainty, the reader of the auditor's report should conclude that

A.   The auditor was not able to form an opinion on the financial statements taken as a whole.

B .   The uncertainty occurred after the balance-sheet date but prior to the audit-report date.

C. There were no audit procedures feasibly available to the auditor by which he could obtain satisfaction concerning the uncertainty.

D. The ability of the company to continue as a "going concern" is questionable.

2-68   If an auditor wishes to issue a qualified opinion because the financial statements include a departure from generally accepted accounting principles, the auditor's report should have an explanatory paragraph referring to a footnote that discloses the principal effects of the subject matter of the qualification. The qualification should be referred to in the opinion paragraph by using language such as

A. "With the exception of."
B. "When read in conjunction with the footnotes."
C. "With the foregoing explanation."
D. "Subject to the departure explained in the footnotes."

2-69   An auditor's "except for" report is a type of

A. Adverse opinion.
B. "Subject to" opinion.
C. Qualified opinion.
D. Disclaimer of opinion.

2-70   An auditor's "subject to" report is a type of

A. Disclaimer of opinion.
B. Qualified opinion.
C. Adverse opinion.
D. Standard opinion.

2-71   The use of the phrase "subject to" in an auditor's opinion is appropriate when the qualification pertains to

A. Nonadherence to generally accepted accounting principles.
B. Nonadherence to generally accepted auditing standards.
C. Lack of consistency with the preceding year.
D. Uncertainty as to the outcome of a material contingency.

2-72   The use of an adverse opinion generally indicates

A. Uncertainty with respect to an item that is so material that the auditor cannot form an opinion on the fairness of presentation of the financial statements as a whole.

  B. Uncertainty with respect to an item that is material but not so material that the auditor cannot form an opinion on the fairness of the financial statements as a whole.

  C. A violation of generally accepted accounting principles that has a material effect upon the fairness of presentation of the financial statements, but is not so material that a qualified opinion is unjustified.

  D. A violation of generally accepted accounting principles that is so material that a qualified opinion is not justified.

2-73 Once an auditor has determined that an exception is material enough to warrant qualification of his or her report, the auditor must then determine if the exception is sufficiently material to negate an overall opinion. If an auditor is applying this decision process to an exception based on a departure from generally accepted accounting principles, he or she is deciding

  A. Whether to issue an adverse opinion rather than a "subject to" opinion.

  B. Whether to issue a disclaimer of opinion rather than a "subject to" opinion.

  C. Whether to issue an adverse opinion rather than an "except for" opinion.

  D. Nothing because this decision process is not applicable to this type of exception.

2-74 The use of a disclaimer of opinion might indicate that the auditor

  A. Is so uncertain with respect to an item that he or she cannot form an opinion on the fairness of presentation of the financial statements as a whole.

  B. Is uncertain with respect to an item that is material but not so material that he or she cannot form an opinion on the fairness of presentation of the financial statements as a whole.

  C. Has observed a violation of generally accepted accounting principles that has a material effect upon the fairness of presentation of financial statements, but is not so material that a qualified report is unjustified.

  D. Has observed a violation of generally accepted accounting principles that is so material that a qualified opinion is not justified.

2-75 In which of the following situations must the CPA issue a disclaimer of opinion?

A. He or she owns stock in the company.
B. Some portion of the client's financial statements does not conform to generally accepted accounting principles.
C. He or she has omitted a normally required auditing procedure.
D. Generally accepted accounting principles have not been applied on a basis consistent with that of the preceding year.

2-76   Generally the auditor's opinion on financial statements should be dated to coincide with the

A. Balance sheet date.
B. Completion of all important audit procedures.
C. Closing of the client's books.
D. Transmittal of the report to the client.

2-77   During the year ended December 31, 19x10 Jolly Corporation had its fixed assets appraised and found that they had substantially appreciated in value since the date of their purchase. The appraised values have been reported in the balance sheet as of December 31, 19x10, respectively. The total appraisal increment has been included as an extraordinary item in the income statement for the year then ended; and the appraisal adjustment has been fully disclosed in the footnotes. If a CPA believes that the values reported in the financial statements are reasonable, what type of opinion should he or she issue?

A. An unqualified opinion.
B. A "subject to" qualified opinion.
C. An adverse opinion.
D. A disclaimer of opinion.

FAIR PRESENTATION ETHICAL CONDUCT INDEPENDENCE EVIDENCE DUE CARE FAIR PRESENTATION ETHICAL CONDUCT INDEPENDENCE EVIDENCE DUE CARE FAIR PRESENTA
ARE FAIR PRESENTATION ETHICAL CONDUCT INDEPENDENCE EVIDENCE DUE CARE FAIR PRESENTATION ETHICAL CONDUCT INDEPENDENCE EVIDENCE DUE CARE FAIR PRES
UE CARE FAIR PRESENTATION ETHICAL CONDUCT INDEPENDENCE EVIDENCE DUE CARE FAIR PRESENTATION ETHICAL CONDUCT INDEPENDENCE EVIDENCE DUE CARE FAIR P
E DUE CARE FAIR PRESENTATION ETHICAL CONDUCT INDEPENDENCE EVIDENCE DUE CARE FAIR PRESENTATION ETHICAL CONDUCT INDEPENDENCE EVIDENCE DUE CARE FA
ENCE DUE CARE FAIR PRESENTATION ETHICAL CONDUCT INDEPENDENCE EVIDENCE DUE CARE FAIR PRESENTATION ETHICAL CONDUCT INDEPENDENCE EVIDENCE DUE CARE
EVIDENCE DUE CARE FAIR PRESENTATION ETHICAL CONDUCT INDEPENDENCE EVIDENCE DUE CARE FAIR PRESENTATION ETHICAL CONDUCT INDEPENDENCE EVIDENCE DUE
CE EVIDENCE DUE CARE FAIR PRESENTATION ETHICAL CONDUCT INDEPENDENCE EVIDENCE DUE CARE FAIR PRESENTATION ETHICAL CONDUCT INDEPENDENCE EVIDENCE D
DENCE EVIDENCE DUE CARE FAIR PRESENTATION ETHICAL CONDUCT INDEPENDENCE EVIDENCE DUE CARE FAIR PRESENTATION ETHICAL CONDUCT INDEPENDENCE EVIDENC

LEARNING OBJECTIVES

JCT INDEPENDENCE EVIDENCE DUE CARE FAIR PRESENTATION ETHICAL CONDUCT INDEPENDENCE EVIDENCE DUE CARE FAIR PRESENTATION ETHICAL CONDUCT INDEPENDEN
NDUCT INDEPENDENCE EVIDENCE DUE CARE FAIR PRESENTATION ETHICAL CONDUCT INDEPENDENCE EVIDENCE DUE CARE FAIR PRESENTATION ETHICAL CONDUCT INDEPEN
L CONDUCT INDEPENDENCE EVIDENCE DUE CARE FAIR PRESENTATION ETHICAL CONDUCT INDEPENDENCE EVIDENCE DUE CARE FAIR PRESENTATION ETHICAL CONDUCT IND
HICAL CONDUCT INDEPENDENCE EVIDENCE DUE CARE FAIR PRESENTATION ETHICAL CONDUCT INDEPENDENCE EVIDENCE DUE CARE FAIR PRESENTATION ETHICAL CONDUCT

After studying this chapter, students should understand

1. The nature of four parts of the AICPA's *Code of Professional Ethics.*
2. The five concepts of professional ethics.
3. The thirteen *Rules of Conduct* from the AICPA's *Code of Professional Ethics.* Students should strive for an in-depth understanding of these rules, including the reasons for the rules, the types of services to which the rules apply, and the way in which the rules are applied.
4. The nature of other codes of professional ethics, such as codes established by state boards of accountancy and various professional organizations.
5. The ten *Statements on Responsibilities in Tax Practice.*
6. The Statements on Standards for Management Advisory Services.

INDEPENDENCE EVIDENCE DUE CARE FAIR PRESENTATION ETHICAL CONDUCT INDEPENDENCE EVIDENCE DUE CARE FAIR PRESENTATION ETHICAL CONDUCT INDEPENDENCE
CT INDEPENDENCE EVIDENCE DUE CARE FAIR PRESENTATION ETHICAL CONDUCT INDEPENDENCE EVIDENCE DUE CARE FAIR PRESENTATION ETHICAL CONDUCT INDEPENDENC
NDUCT INDEPENDENCE EVIDENCE DUE CARE FAIR PRESENTATION ETHICAL CONDUCT INDEPENDENCE EVIDENCE DUE CARE FAIR PRESENTATION ETHICAL CONDUCT INDEPEN
CONDUCT INDEPENDENCE EVIDENCE DUE CARE FAIR PRESENTATION ETHICAL CONDUCT INDEPENDENCE EVIDENCE DUE CARE FAIR PRESENTATION ETHICAL CONDUCT INDE
ICAL CONDUCT INDEPENDENCE EVIDENCE DUE CARE FAIR PRESENTATION ETHICAL CONDUCT INDEPENDENCE EVIDENCE DUE CARE FAIR PRESENTATION ETHICAL CONDUCT I
ETHICAL CONDUCT INDEPENDENCE EVIDENCE DUE CARE FAIR PRESENTATION ETHICAL CONDUCT INDEPENDENCE EVIDENCE DUE CARE FAIR PRESENTATION ETHICAL CONDU
ION ETHICAL CONDUCT INDEPENDENCE EVIDENCE DUE CARE FAIR PRESENTATION ETHICAL CONDUCT INDEPENDENCE EVIDENCE DUE CARE FAIR PRESENTATION ETHICAL CO
NTATION ETHICAL CONDUCT INDEPENDENCE EVIDENCE DUE CARE FAIR PRESENTATION ETHICAL CONDUCT INDEPENDENCE EVIDENCE DUE CARE FAIR PRESENTATION ETHICAL
ESENTATION ETHICAL CONDUCT INDEPENDENCE EVIDENCE DUE CARE FAIR PRESENTATION ETHICAL CONDUCT INDEPENDENCE EVIDENCE DUE CARE FAIR PRESENTATION ETH
PRESENTATION ETHICAL CONDUCT INDEPENDENCE EVIDENCE DUE CARE FAIR PRESENTATION ETHICAL CONDUCT INDEPENDENCE EVIDENCE DUE CARE FAIR PRESENTATION
FAIR PRESENTATION ETHICAL CONDUCT INDEPENDENCE EVIDENCE DUE CARE FAIR PRESENTATION ETHICAL CONDUCT INDEPENDENCE EVIDENCE DUE CARE FAIR PRESENTAT
ARE FAIR PRESENTATION ETHICAL CONDUCT INDEPENDENCE EVIDENCE DUE CARE FAIR PRESENTATION ETHICAL CONDUCT INDEPENDENCE EVIDENCE DUE CARE FAIR PRESEN
E CARE FAIR PRESENTATION ETHICAL CONDUCT INDEPENDENCE EVIDENCE DUE CARE FAIR PRESENTATION ETHICAL CONDUCT INDEPENDENCE EVIDENCE DUE CARE FAIR PRE
DUE CARE FAIR PRESENTATION ETHICAL CONDUCT INDEPENDENCE EVIDENCE DUE CARE FAIR PRESENTATION ETHICAL CONDUCT INDEPENDENCE EVIDENCE DUE CARE FAIR
NCE DUE CARE FAIR PRESENTATION ETHICAL CONDUCT INDEPENDENCE EVIDENCE DUE CARE FAIR PRESENTATION ETHICAL CONDUCT INDEPENDENCE EVIDENCE DUE CARE F
VIDENCE DUE CARE FAIR PRESENTATION ETHICAL CONDUCT INDEPENDENCE EVIDENCE DUE CARE FAIR PRESENTATION ETHICAL CONDUCT INDEPENDENCE EVIDENCE DUE CA
CE EVIDENCE DUE CARE FAIR PRESENTATION ETHICAL CONDUCT INDEPENDENCE EVIDENCE DUE CARE FAIR PRESENTATION ETHICAL CONDUCT INDEPENDENCE EVIDENCE DU
DENCE EVIDENCE DUE CARE FAIR PRESENTATION ETHICAL CONDUCT INDEPENDENCE EVIDENCE DUE CARE FAIR PRESENTATION ETHICAL CONDUCT INDEPENDENCE EVIDENCE

INTRODUCTION

Wisdom is knowing what to do;
virtue is doing it.

This quote sums up two aspects of any ethical question: What should I do? Will I do it? The concept of individual responsibility is of paramount importance in establishing a code of ethics. Individuals are responsible for their own actions and must bear some responsibility for what is allowed to happen around them.

A code of professional ethics is designed to assure acceptable professional behavior. Formulated by the members of a professional society, it sets minimum standards of conduct for the common good of the profession. A code of ethics is made known to its subjects through publications which are disseminated to the members of the profession and is available for public inspection.

A code of ethics helps to simplify decisions for its members. The approved behavior patterns are contained in the code. Members, therefore, know what is expected of them, and can achieve more uniform actions than if no guides were developed.

This chapter begins with a discussion of the nature of the AICPA's *Code of Professional Ethics*. The first section is followed by a discussion of the AICPA's *Rules of Conduct*, and other codes of professional ethics. The chapter concludes with a discussion of the CPA's responsibilities in tax practice and in providing management advisory services.

THE NATURE OF THE AICPA'S CODE OF PROFESSIONAL ETHICS

The AICPA's *Code of Professional Ethics* emphasizes the CPA's responsibility to the public, to clients, and to the CPA's colleagues. The CPA's responsibility to the public has increased as the number of investors and creditors have grown, as the relationship between company managers and investors (creditors and stockholders) has become more impersonal, and as the government makes increasing use of accounting information in reaching decisions which affect the general public. The *Code of Professional Ethics* also stresses the CPA's responsibilities to clients and colleagues, since these relationships cannot fail to affect the CPA's responsibilities to the public.

The AICPA's *Code of Professional Ethics* consists of four distinct parts:

- Concepts of Professional Ethics.

- Rules of Conduct.

- Interpretations of Rules of Conduct.

- Ethics Rulings.

There are five broad concepts of professional ethics. These concepts, as the name implies, are not intended to be detailed, enforceable rules, but rather, broad ethical goals which every CPA should strive to achieve. The five concepts of professional ethics are:

- A certified public accountant should maintain his (her) integrity and objectivity and, when engaged in the practice of public accounting, be independent of those he (she) serves.

- A certified public accountant should observe the profession's general and technical standards and strive continually to improve his (her) competence and the quality of his (her) services.

- A certified public accountant should be fair and candid with his (her) clients and serve them to the best of his (her) ability, with professional concern for their best interest consistent with his (her) responsibility to the public.

- A certified public accountant should conduct himself (herself) in a manner that will promote cooperation and good relations among members of the profession.

- A certified public accountant should conduct himself (herself) in a manner which will enhance the stature of the profession and its ability to serve the public.

After examining these concepts of professional ethics, most people would agree that they express the very essence of the conduct which a CPA should strive to achieve. However, the concepts leave unanswered specific questions about what a CPA may or may not do. For example, the first concept requires that a CPA, when engaged in the practice of public accounting, be independent of those he or she serves. However, the concept does not specify what conduct would impair or not impair the CPA's independence. For the actions which are prohibited or not prohibited, the CPA must look to the rules of conduct, the interpretations of the rules of conduct, and the ethics rulings.

The fact that the concepts of professional ethics may not provide specific answers to the conduct which is permitted or not permitted, however, does not diminish their importance. The concepts are very important because (1) they were and still are considered by the AICPA in establishing the *Rules of Conduct*, the *Interpretations of the Rules of Conduct*, and the *Ethics Rulings*, and (2) the *Concepts of Professional Ethics* provide guidance to the CPA in determining ethical conduct in areas where no specific *Rule of Conduct*, *Interpretation*, or *Ethics Ruling* has been issued.

In addition to the concepts of professional ethics, the AICPA's *Code of Professional Ethics* (the Code) includes *Rules of Conduct*, *Interpretations of Rules of Conduct*, and *Ethics Rulings*. The AICPA's *Rules of Conduct* is the primary list of actions by a CPA which are permitted or prohibited by the *Code*. The Institute's *Rules of Conduct* set forth the minimum levels of acceptable conduct and are mandatory and enforceable by the AICPA's Ethics Division. In addition to the *Rules of Conduct*, the AICPA's Ethics Division has also issued *Interpretations of the Rules of Conduct* and *Ethics Rulings*. *Interpretations of the Rules of Conduct* are issued to give the CPA more detailed guidance about a specific rule of conduct. *Ethics Rulings* are similar to the *Interpretations of the Rules of Conduct* in that the rulings also give detailed guidance about how to comply with a rule of conduct. However, the rulings differ from the *Rules of Conduct* in that *Ethics Rulings* are formal responses to a CPA's questions concerning how a specific rule of conduct or intepretation of a rule of conduct applies to a specific situation which the CPA faces. Thus, *Ethics Rulings* are generally more specific than the *Rules of Conduct* or *Interpretations* because they address circumstances which may be unique to the CPA who has posed the question. Also, they are not enforceable on the membership.

RULES OF CONDUCT

Now that the four basic parts of the AICPA's *Code of Professional Ethics* have been discussed, this section considers the *Rules of Conduct*, which is the primary listing of the actions by a CPA which are permitted or prohibited by the *Code*. In addition, a discussion of some of the most important *Interpretations of the Rules of Conduct* and *Ethics Rulings* are included. The rules of conduct, which are classified by ethical concept and are numbered, may be identified generally as:

Independence, Integrity, and Objectivity

101   Independence

102   Integrity and Objectivity

Competence and Technical Standards

201   General Standards

202   Auditing Standards

203   Accounting Standards

204   Other Technical Standards

Responsibilities to Clients

301   Confidential Client Information

302   Contingent Fees

Other Responsibilities and Practices[1]

501   Acts Discreditable

502   Advertising and Other Forms of Solicitation

503   Commissions

504   Incompatible Occupations

505   Form of Practice and Name

**Applicability
of Rules of
Conduct**

The AICPA's *Code of Professional Ethics* derives its authority from the bylaws of the AICPA. The rules apply to all services performed in the practice of public accounting, including tax and management advisory services, except (1) where the wording of a specific rule indicates that the rule applies only to a certain type of services, or (2) in certain cases, to members of the AICPA who are practicing outside the United States. These members of the AICPA are not subject to discipline for departing from the *Rules of Conduct* if the member is (1) practicing outside the United States and (2) his or her conduct is in accordance with the rules of conduct established by the country in which the CPA is practicing. However, in all cases where the user of the CPA's report would assume that U.S. standards were being followed, the CPA must comply with Rules 202 and 203 of the AICPA's *Rules of Conduct*. These rules deal with U.S. generally accepted auditing standards and accounting principles, respectively.

A member of the AICPA is also held accountable for the actions of his or her partners and accounting staff under the member's supervi-

---

[1] The 400 series rules have been suspended by the AICPA as they are related to encroaching on the practice of fellow accounting practitioners and were considered unconstitutional as being in restraint of trade. This series is being reserved for future use.

sion. Thus, a member of the AICPA cannot permit others, with which the member is associated, to violate the *Rules of Conduct*.

A member of the AICPA who is not engaged in the practice of public accounting is only required to abide by Rules 102 and 501. These rules deal with integrity and objectivity (Rule 102) and acts which are considered discreditable to the profession (Rule 501).

Rule 101 — Independence

The first rule of conduct deals with independence. As indicated earlier in this text, independence is the backbone of auditing because the CPA cannot add credibility to the financial statements through the attest function if the CPA is not independent of the client. Furthermore, there are two aspects of independence: independence in fact and independence in appearance. Independence in fact is a state of mind. If a CPA is independent in fact, the CPA can evaluate the client's financial statements in an objective and unbiased manner. Independence in appearance is concerned with how third parties view the relationships between the CPA and the client. If a third party (1) knew of all the relationships between a CPA and the CPA's client and (2) believed that the CPA could evaluate the client's financial statements in an objective and unbiased manner, then the CPA is independent in appearance.

Rule 101 reads as follows:

> A member or a firm of which he (she) is a partner or shareholder shall not express an opinion on financial statements of an enterprise unless he (she) and his firm (her firm) are independent with respect to such enterprise. Independence will be considered to be impaired if, for example:
>
> A. During the period of his (her) professional engagement, or at the time of expressing his (her) opinion, he (she) or his firm (her firm).
>
>   1.   a.   Had or was committed to acquire any direct or material indirect financial interest in the enterprise; or
>
>   b.   Was a trustee of any trust or executor or administrator of any estate if such trust or estate had or was committed to acquire any direct or material indirect financial interest in the enterprise; or
>
>   2.   Had any joint closely held business investment with the enterprise or any officer, director, or principal stockholder thereof which was material in relation to his (her) or his firm's (her firm's) net worth; or
>
>   3.   Had any loan to or from the enterprise or any officer, director, or principal stockholder thereof. This latter proscription does

not apply to the following loans from a financial institution when made under normal lending procedures, terms, and requirements:

a. Loans obtained by a member or his (her) firm which are not material in relation to the net worth of such borrower.

b. Home mortgages.

c. Other secured loans, except loans guaranteed by a member's firm which are otherwise unsecured.

B. During the period covered by the financial statements, during the period of the professional engagement, or at the time of expressing an opinion, he or his firm (her firm).

1. Was connected with the enterprise as a promoter, underwriter, or voting trustee, a director or officer or in any capacity equivalent to that of a member of management or of an employee; or

2. Was a trustee for any pension or profit-sharing trust of the enterprise.

The above examples are not intended to be all-inclusive.

There are eight key questions with respect to Rule 101. The first relates to the type of services which are covered by the rule. An examination of the first paragraph of the rule indicates that the rule applies only to cases where the CPA is expressing an opinion on the financial statements of an entity. Thus, independence, as required by Rule 101, is necessary when the CPA reports on (1) audited financial statements, (2) a review of financial statements, or (3) unaudited financial statements. Accordingly, where the CPA is not independent under Rule 101, the CPA's report on the client's financial statements must be limited to a statement which says that the CPA is not independent and therefore does not express any opinion on the financial statements. Furthermore, when the CPA disclaims an opinion on the client's financial statements because of a lack of independence, the CPA should not state why he or she is not independent since a detailed explanation for the lack of independence might tend to confuse the reader. Specifically, the reader of the CPA's report might reason that a lack of independence for one reason is better or worse than a lack of independence for another reason when in fact this is not the case. Instead, if the CPA is not independent, the CPA cannot conduct an examination in accordance with generally accepted auditing standards and the specific reason(s) for the lack of independence is not important.

A CPA may report on a compilation of financial statements (for a nonpublic client) even if the CPA is not independent. A compilation report is allowed when the CPA is not independent because the CPA is not expressing any opinion on the financial statements, but instead, the CPA is simply saying that he or she has compiled (prepared) the financial statements from the records of the company. Therefore, since a compilation report involves less judgment than other types of reports, it is unlikely that a CPA's compilation report will be influenced by the CPA's lack of independence. However, the standard compilation report must still be expanded to state that the CPA is not independent with respect to the client. Reports on a compilation of financial statements are discussed in detail in Chapter 18.

A second question which arises with respect to independence is the period of time for which independence is required. An examination of Rule 101 indicates that the period of time for which independence is required differs slightly depending upon whether one is considering Part A or Part B of the rule.

Part A of Rule 101 prohibits certain financial relationships with the client. These relationships are prohibited during the period of the CPA's professional engagement and at the time the CPA expresses his or her opinion on the financial statements, which is typically one to two months after the date of the financial statements. This rule means that, before the CPA accepts the engagement, the CPA must discontinue any of the prohibited relationships he or she may have with the new client. Furthermore, as long as the CPA continues with the engagement, the CPA cannot engage in any of the prohibited relationships.

To illustrate this point, assume that a CPA has a stock investment in IBM on March 2, 1984, and, on this date, the CPA is approached about performing the IBM audit for the calendar year ending December 31, 1984. Part A of Rule 101 says that the CPA can accept the audit engagement for 1984 as long as he or she disposes of the investment in IBM before accepting the engagement. Furthermore, as long as the CPA continues with the audit of IBM, the CPA cannot engage in any of the prohibited relationships with IBM. Notice specifically that the CPA is considered to be independent for the 1984 IBM audit even though the CPA held a stock investment in IBM for a portion of the year. The reason that the CPA is independent for the 1984 audit is that the CPA disposed of the investment before accepting the engagement. Therefore, after disposing of the investment, the CPA would have no further financial interest in IBM, and consequently, the CPA could objectively evaluate any transactions which IBM engaged in either before or after the CPA disposed of the investment and accepted the engagement.

As indicated earlier, the period of time for which independence is required under Part B of Rule 101 differs slightly from the independence period under Part A of the rule. Part B of the rule prohibits the CPA from engaging in any activities which are equivalent to management activities for the company. The activities are prohibited during the period covered by the financial statements, during the period of the professional engagement, and at the time the CPA expresses an opinion on the financial statements.

To illustrate Part B of the rule, assume that on March 2, 1984, Phillip Hodges, a CPA, leaves the employment of the Lane Company and establishes a CPA firm. Now the question is whether Mr. Hodges' CPA firm is independent of the Lane Company for the 1984 calendar-year audit. The answer is that Mr. Hodges' CPA firm is not independent because he was an employee of the Lane Company for the period covered by the financial statements. Mr. Hodges could do audit type work for the Lane Company for 1984, but his report on the financial statements would be limited to a statement that he was not independent and consequently expressed no opinion on the financial statements.

To continue this illustration further, now assume that (1) Mr. Hodges is a partner in the firm of Cole and Armbrister and the firm does the audit of the Lane Company's financial statements, (2) Mr. Hodges leaves the CPA firm on March 4, 1984, to become controller of the Lane Company. Now the question is whether or not Cole and Armbrister, the CPA firm, is independent of the Lane Company for 1984. The answer is that the CPA firm is independent of the Lane Company for 1984 because the firm did not engage in any of the prohibited activities for 1984. Specifically, once Mr. Hodges leaves Cole and Armbrister, his actions, e.g., being an employee of the Lane Company, is no longer attributable to the CPA firm.

A third question which arises in connection with Rule 101 concerns the meaning of the phrase, "any direct financial interest in the enterprise." On the surface this phrase seems very clear; the CPA cannot have *any direct* financial interest in the enterprise. However, with CPA firms which have many offices all over the world the phrase becomes a bit less clear.

The AICPA has interpreted the phrase "he and his firm" (her firm) in Rule 101 to refer to all partners or shareholders in the public accounting firm; the phrase refers also to full and part-time professional staff on the audit engagement or located in an office participating in a significant part of the engagement. Consequently, a non-partner CPA could own some shares of stock in an audit client of his or her firm as long as he or she did not participate in the audit engagement or was not employed in an office which performed a significant part of the audit. For example, a non-partner CPA employed at the Kansas City office of a CPA firm may own a few shares of XYZ Company of New Orleans, as long as he or she does not participate in the audit and the Kansas City office does not perform a significant part of the audit. However, despite this interpretation, many CPA firms still insist that no staff person have *any* investments in *any* client of the firm regardless of where the client is located.

Another question related to the phrase "direct financial interest" concerns financial interests which are owned by people, such as relatives, who have a close relationship with the CPA. More specifically, when should these holdings be considered a direct financial interest of the CPA? In general, the financial interests of a person who depends on the CPA for his or her support is considered a direct financial interest of the CPA, and the financial interests of a person who has a close relationship with the CPA, but who does not depend on the CPA for his or her support, is considered to be an indirect financial interest of the CPA. Finally, the financial interests of a person who does not depend on the CPA for his or her support and who does not have a close relationship with the CPA has no impact on the CPA's independence.

A question about relatives and independence also arises when a close relative is employed by the client in a responsible position. A CPA would not be independent if his or her brother, sister, parent, or child was employed by the client in a responsible position. However, unless there are special circumstances to indicate otherwise, other relatives which are employed by the client would not impair a CPA's independence.

A fourth question relating to independence arises when a CPA is asked to be a director or trustee of a charitable, religious, civic, or other non-profit organization which is an audit or review client or potential client. The CPA is allowed to serve as a director of such organizations under the following conditions:

- The CPA's position is purely honorary.

- The CPA's position in the organization is identified as honorary in all letterheads and other externally circulated materials in which the CPA is named as a director.

- The CPA restricts his (her) participation in the organization's activities to the use of his (her) name, and the CPA does not vote or otherwise participate in the management functions of the organization.

A fifth question relating to independence arises when the CPA performs bookkeeping services for a client. The question is whether the CPA can keep the books, prepare the financial statements, and still be independent for the purposes of conducting an audit or review engagement, or issuing a compilation report on the financial statements, which the CPA has prepared.

When this issue is analyzed from a conceptual viewpoint, it is very difficult to argue that a CPA can keep the books for a company and still be independent for purposes of examining the financial statements, which are prepared from the books. After all, when the CPA examines the financial statements, the CPA is in effect checking his or her own bookkeeping work. However, from a practical standpoint, a substantial portion of the fees which are earned by many CPA firms are earned from performing such bookkeeping services and reporting on the resulting financial statements. Consequently, if bookkeeping services for a client were considered to impair independence for that client, many CPA firms and their smaller nonpublic clients would suffer.

The AICPA considered the issue of bookkeeping and independence, and concluded, probably because of pressure from practicing CPAs, that performing bookkeeping services for a client does not impair independence as long as five conditions are met.

1. The CPA must not have any relationships with the client which would impair the CPA's integrity and objectivity.

2. The client must have sufficient knowledge of generally accepted accounting principles so that the client can accept responsibility for his or her own financial statements. In most cases, this condition will require that the CPA carefully review the financial statements with the client.

3. The CPA must not perform management functions for the client. For example, the CPA cannot sign checks or collect cash for the client or be involved in the management function.

4. When examining the financial statements of the client, the CPA must follow the applicable generally accepted auditing standards. The fact that the CPA has prepared the financial statements does not invalidate the CPA's need to gather and document evidence concerning the fairness of the financial statement balances.

5. When the client's securities come under the jurisdiction of the SEC or other federal or state regulatory body, the responsibility for maintaining the accounting records must be transferred from the CPA to the client.

A sixth question with respect to independence involves management advisory services (MAS) and independence. Specifically, the question is whether a CPA firm can do MAS work for a client and still be independent with respect to that client. For example, if a CPA advises the client about the type of computer equipment to purchase, can the CPA be unbiased in evaluating the computer system's controls and processing accuracy? Also, if the CPA serves as a close advisor of the client, does the advisory relationship between the CPA and the client make their goals so intertwined that the CPA cannot objectively evaluate the client's financial statements?

Management advisory services is one of the fastest growing areas of accounting practice, especially for larger CPA firms. Consequently, the lucrative nature of a MAS practice makes the issue of MAS and independence even more critical. Both the SEC and the AICPA have considered the issue of MAS and independence, and both groups have concluded that, as a general rule, MAS does not impair independence. However, the SEC Practice Section of the AICPA Division for CPA firms (discussed in Chapter 6 of this text) does prohibit its members from performing certain executive recruitment services for its audit clients. Also, the AICPA's Management Advisory Services Executive Committee has issued certain standards which CPAs should abide by in performing MAS. These standards are discussed later in this chapter.

A seventh question with respect to independence concerns tax services and independence. Specifically, the question is whether a CPA can advise a client on how to minimize income tax expense, and, at the same time, be objective in evaluating the tax expense and taxes payable balances which appear in the client's financial statements. Both the SEC and the AICPA have considered the issue of tax services and independence, and both groups have concluded that performing tax services for a client does not impair the CPA's independence. However, the AICPA has issued ten responsibilities in tax practice which CPAs are required to follow. These responsibilities are discussed later in this chapter.

An eighth question with respect to independence concerns the payment of the CPA's fee. Specifically, how can a CPA be independent of the client when the CPA depends on the client for his or her livelihood? Since the client does pay the CPA's fee, perfect independence between the CPA and the client probably will never be achieved. However, there are factors which encourage or help the CPA to be as independent as possible, given the fact that the CPA's fee is paid by the client.

The major factor which encourages a CPA to maintain his or her independence is the potential costs of sacrificing the independence. Not only would the CPA lose his or her license to practice accountancy, but also, the CPA, as indicated in Chapter 17, would be personally liable for damages which occurred because of his or her lack of independence. Three major conditions necessary in establishing a viable defense in a liability suit involving negligent audit work are (1) the CPA has carefully documented his or her work papers to show sufficient competent evidence in support of the financial statement assertions, (2) the CPA has not intentionally deceived the client or others relying on the financial statements and the CPA's report, and (3) the CPA is *independent* of the client. In addition, even if the CPA did not lose his or her license forever, the negative publicity surrounding the lawsuit and suspension of the CPA's license would severely damage the reputation of the CPA and his or her firm. Consequently, the cost of losing one's independence far outweighs any short-term gains from yielding to client pressures.

One major factor which helps a CPA maintain his or her independence is the corporate audit committee. An audit committee is a subcommittee of the corporation's board of directors which is established to work with the corporation's independent CPAs and the corporation's internal auditors. This committee is made up of outside directors. These outside directors are full members of the board of directors, but they are not otherwise employed by the corporation. That is, except for their membership on the board of directors, they do not serve in any other managerial capacity for the company.

Members of a corporation's board of directors have personal liability for their actions. Consequently, before they would attempt to put pressure on a CPA firm to agree to a questionable accounting principle, the members would have to weigh the costs and benefits of that action. However, members of the audit committee, since they do not participate in the day to day management of the company, have less to gain from the application of questionable practices than other members of the management team. Consequently, members of the audit committee are likely to be more objective than the day to day management team in dealing with the CPA.

The typical duties of an audit committee include the following:

- Appointing the independent CPA firm for the corporation. Generally, the CPA's appointment is required to be approved by the full board of directors and stockholders of the company.

- Discussing the audit scope with the internal and external auditors.

- Resolving conflicts which arise between the management of the company and the external auditors or the internal auditors.

- Reviewing the audit reports and discussing the audit findings with both the external and internal auditors.

- Assuming overall responsibility for specialized aspects of the corporation's accounting system, such as the adequacy of the system of internal accounting control and compliance with the Foreign Corrupt Practices Act (as discussed in Chapter 5).

Because of the objectivity of the audit committee and their overall responsibility for accounting matters, it is likely that audit committees do increase the CPA's independence. Consequently, both the AICPA and the SEC have recommended that corporations establish audit committees. Furthermore, the New York Stock Exchange now requires all companies listed on the exchange to have audit committees.

Two other major factors which help the CPA maintain his or her independence are Forms 10-Q and 8-K which are required by the SEC. Among other things, Form 10-Q requires a company's independent CPA to write a letter to the SEC concerning any changes in accounting principles other than a change in principle which is required by a new FASB standard. In his or her letter the CPA must state that the new principle is preferable to the old principle. Consequently, this requirement should discourage companies from making arbitrary changes in their accounting principles, just to make the company's financial statements look better. It should be noted that the requirements of Form 10-Q are greater than the requirements of APB *Opinion No. 20* because APB *Opinion No. 20* only requires the company to show that a change in principle was justified.

Form 8-K is used by a company under the SEC's jurisdiction to report significant corporate events, such as a change in auditors. Specifically, whenever there is a change in auditors the company is required to file Form 8-K with the SEC and state in the form whether there was any disagreement in the last two years between the client and its former auditor concerning (1) accounting principles, (2) financial statement disclosure, or (3) auditing procedures. Furthermore, if there was a disagreement, the company must state whether the disagreement was resolved to the auditor's satisfaction. Finally, the former auditor must examine the Form 8-K and write a letter to the SEC saying whether or not he or she agrees with the statements made by the former client.

**Rule 102 —
Integrity and
Objectivity**

The second rule in the *Rules of Conduct* deals with integrity and objectivity, and the rule reads as follows:

> A member shall not knowingly misrepresent facts and when engaged in the practice of public accounting, including the rendering of tax and management advisory services, shall not subordinate his (her) judgment to others. In tax practice, a member may resolve doubt in favor of his (her) client as long as there is reasonable support for his or her position.

Clearly, integrity and objectivity constitute the very essence of a profession, and, if CPAs did not have these characteristics the profession would not be beneficial to society.

**Rule 201 —
General
Standards**

The third rule in the AICPA's *Rules of Conduct* deals with the general standards. The rule reads as follows:

> A member shall comply with the following general standards as interpreted by bodies designated by Council and must justify any departures therefrom.
>
> A. **Professional competence.** A member shall undertake only those engagements which he or his (her) firm can reasonably expect to complete with professional competence.
>
> B. **Due professional care.** A member shall exercise due professional care in the performance of an engagement.
>
> C. **Planning and supervision.** A member shall adequately plan and supervise an engagement.

D. **Sufficient relevant data.**   A member shall obtain sufficient relevant data to afford a reasonable basis for conclusions or recommendations in relation to an engagement.

E. **Forecasts.**   A member shall not permit his (her) name to be used in conjunction with any forecast of future transactions in a manner which may lead to the belief that the member vouches for the achievability of the forecast.

Rule 201 is basically self-explanatory. However, a few comments are in order with respect to professional competence and forecasts. With respect to professional competence, notice that the rule does not require the member to be an expert in all types of engagements before the engagement is accepted. Instead, the rule requires the member to be able to obtain the necessary competence before the engagement is completed. CPAs have also recognized that every person assigned to an engagement cannot be expert in all aspects of the engagement. However, the audit team as a whole must have the necessary competence to complete the engagement.

With respect to forecasts, investors have long recognized that, if a person can predict earnings and the financial position of a company far enough in advance, the investor can earn superior returns in the market. Consequently, there has been pressure on companies to furnish forecasts and for the CPA to attest to the accuracy of these forecasts. However, forecasts of earnings and financial position simply have not been very accurate. For example, a number of studies in finance have shown that the various models which are used to forecast next year's earnings yield a predicted earnings figure which is no more accurate than a prediction which says that next year's earnings will be the same as this year's earnings.

Since there is a high demand for forecasts but the forecasts are generally very inaccurate, the CPA should use care when he or she is associated with forecasts. Consequently, the rule on forecasts prohibits a CPA from vouching for the achievability of the forecasts. A CPA may prepare or assist in preparing a financial forecast for a client provided there is full disclosure of (1) the sources of the information used, (2) the major assumptions, (3) the character of the work performed by the CPA, and (4) the degree of responsibility the CPA is taking. With respect to the degree of responsibility the CPA is taking, the CPA would never vouch for the achievability of the forecast. However, the CPA may take some responsibility for the sources of the information used and the assumptions made in the forecast. For example, the CPA might review the information which was input into the forecasting model and review the reasonableness of the assumptions which are made.

**Rule 202 —
Auditing Standards**

The fourth rule in the AICPA's *Rules of Conduct* deals with auditing standards. The rule reads as follows:

> A member shall not permit his (her) name to be associated with financial statements in such a manner as to imply that he (she) is acting as an independent public accountant unless he (she) has complied with the applicable generally accepted auditing standards promulgated by the Institute. Statements on auditing standards issued by the Institute's auditing standards executive committee (now the Auditing Standards Board) are, for purposes of this rule, considered to be interpretations of the generally accepted auditing standards, and departures from such statements must be justified by those who do not follow them.

The ten Generally Accepted Auditing Standards were presented in Chapter 2. These consisted of three general standards, three standards of field work, and four reporting standards. As indicated in Rule 202, the Statements on Auditing Standards which are issued by the Auditing Standards Board, formerly the Auditing Standards Executive Committee, are considered to be interpretations of the ten Generally Accepted Auditing Standards. The ten Generally Accepted Auditing Standards as well as the Statements on Auditing Standards are discussed throughout this text.

**Rule 203 —
Accounting
Principles**

The fifth rule in the AICPA's *Rules of Conduct* deals with generally accepted accounting principles, and the rule reads as follows:

> A member shall not express an opinion that financial statements are presented in conformity with generally accepted accounting principles if such statements contain any departure from an accounting principle promulgated by the body designated by Council to establish such principles which has a material effect on the statements taken as a whole, unless the member can demonstrate that due to unusual circumstances the financial statements would otherwise have been misleading. In such cases his (her) report must describe the departure, the approximate effects thereof, if practicable, and the reasons why compliance with the principle would result in a misleading statement.

There are three key aspects to Rule 203. The first is the body designated by Council to establish generally accepted accounting principles. The second key aspect of Rule 203 is the general rule itself, and the third key aspect is the exception to the general rule.

At the time Rule 203 was adopted the FASB was named as the body designated by Council to establish generally accepted accounting principles. However, the opinions of the Accounting Principles Board and the Accounting Research Bulletins, which were issued by the Committee on Accounting Procedure, are also covered by the rule until such time as these opinions or bulletins are superseded by an FASB pronouncement. Consequently, the promulgated principles to which Rule 203 applies are:

- Statements of Financial Accounting Standards which are issued by the FASB.

- Interpretations of Statements of Financial Accounting Standards which are issued by the FASB.

- Opinions of the Accounting Principles Board which have not been superseded.

- Accounting Research Bulletins of the Committee on Accounting Procedure which have not been superseded.

As indicated in Chapter 2, the pronouncements which are identified above are frequently referred to as the primary sources of generally accepted accounting principles. The principles are primary because these pronouncements are covered by Rule 203 of the *Rules of Conduct*. As indicated in Chapter 2, *SAS No. 5* states that CPAs agree on the existence of a body of GAAP, and they are considered to be experts by the public in identifying accounting principles that are appropriate for particular clients. Nevertheless, the determination that an accounting principle is generally accepted requires considerable judgment based on experience if the principle is not identified as GAAP by an accounting pronouncement. In judging the fairness of an accounting principle for a particular client application, the CPA generally looks to the following sources, which are presented in the order of their authority as specified in *SAS No. 43*.

- Pronouncements of an authoritative body designated by the AICPA to establish accounting principles, pursuant to Rule 203 (ARBs, APB Opinions, FASB Statements and Interpretations) of the AICPA *Code of Professional Ethics*. If an accounting practice is sanctioned by a promulgated accounting principle covered by Rule 203 no additional support is needed.

- Pronouncements of bodies composed of expert accountants that follow a due process procedure, including broad distribution of proposed accounting principles for public comment, for the intended purpose of establishing accounting principles or describing existing practices that are generally accepted.

- Practices or pronouncements that are widely recognized as being generally accepted because they represent prevalent practice in a particular industry or the knowledgeable application to specific circumstances of pronouncements that are generally accepted.

- Other accounting literature.

Many readers may also remember that the FASB also issues Statements of Financial Accounting Concepts. These concepts, however are not covered by Rule 203 because the Statements of Financial Accounting Concepts are more general in nature than the detailed accounting principles which are covered by Rule 203. However, in *SAS No. 43* the Auditing Standards Board decided that Statements of Financial Accounting Concepts should be considered as other accounting literature for the purpose of identifying GAAP. Furthermore, the Board reasoned that Statements of Financial Accounting Concepts would normally be more important than many other sources of other accounting literature, such as articles and textbooks.

The second important aspect of Rule 203 is the general rule itself. The rule says that in general a CPA cannot say that a client's financial statements are fairly presented in accordance with generally accepted accounting principles if (1) the statements contain any departure from the primary sources of GAAP and (2) that departure has a *material* impact on the financial statements taken as a whole. Thus, in general, if the financial statements contain a departure from the primary sources of GAAP and that departure has a material impact on the financial statements taken as a whole, the CPA must issue either a qualified opinion or an adverse opinion on the financial statements. The format of a qualified opinion or an adverse opinion was discussed in Chapter 2, and the topic is discussed further in Chapter 15.

The third important aspect of Rule 203 is the exception to the general rule. The exception clause in Rule 203 states that there may be cases where the application of a primary source of GAAP would result in misleading financial statements. In these cases, the CPA does not have to give a qualified opinion or an adverse opinion. Specifically, the CPA can state in the opinion paragraph of his or her report that the financial statements are fairly presented in conformity with generally accepted accounting principles applied on a consistent basis. However, in these cases the CPA must describe in the report (1) the departure from the primary source of GAAP, (2) the effects of the departure from the primary source of GAAP on the financial statements, if it is practical to determine the effects, and (3) the reasons why compliance with the primary source of GAAP would result in misleading financial statements. These three disclosures are usually provided in a middle paragraph which is added to the CPA's standard audit report.

Rule 204 — Other Technical Standards

The sixth rule in the AICPA's *Rules of Conduct* deals with other technical standards, and the rule reads as follows:

> A member shall comply with other technical standards promulgated by bodies designated by Council to establish such standards, and departures therefrom must be justified by those who do not follow them.

As indicated earlier, a CPA is in violation of the AICPA's *Code of Professional Ethics* if he or she does not abide by Rule 202, which deals with generally accepted auditing standards, and Rule 203, which deals with generally accepted accounting principles. Rule 204 states that a CPA is in violation of the AICPA's *Code of Ethics* if (1) he or she departs from other technical standards issued by bodies designated by Council of the AICPA to establish such standards and (2) he or she cannot justify the departure from the other technical standards. Thus, Rule 204 puts the burden of justifying the departure from other technical standards on the CPA.

Currently, there are three bodies which have been designated by Council of the AICPA to issue technical standards covered by Rule 204:

- The Management Advisory Services Executive Committee is designated to issue technical standards with respect to the offering of management advisory services. The standards which have been issued by this committee are discussed later in this chapter.

- The Accounting and Review Services Committee is designated to issue technical standards with respect to the compilation and review of financial statements (SSARSs). These standards are discussed in Chapter 18.

- The FASB is designated to issue technical standards with respect to disclosure of supplemental information which is not a part of the basic financial statements but which does appear in financial reports which contain the basic financial statements. For example, data on changing prices is not part of the basic financial statements, but disclosures on changing prices is required to be made in the annual reports of many companies. Consequently, the FASB has the responsibility for establishing the disclosure standards.

**Rule 301 —
Confidential
Client Information**

The seventh rule in the AICPA's *Rules of Conduct* deals with confidential client information, and the rule reads as follows:

> A member shall not disclose any confidential information obtained in the course of a professional engagement except with the consent of the client.
>
> This rule shall not be construed (a) to relieve a member of his or her obligation under Rules 202 and 203, (b) to affect in any way his or her compliance with a validly issued subpoena or summons enforceable by order of a court, (c) to prohibit review of a member's professional practices as a part of voluntary quality review under Institute authorization, or (d) to preclude a member from responding to any inquiry made by the ethics division or trial board of the Institute, by a duly constituted investigative or disciplinary body of a state CPA society, or under state statutes.
>
> .Members of the ethics division and trial board of the Institute and professional practice reviewers under Institute authorization shall not disclose any confidential client information which comes to their attention from members in disciplinary proceedings or otherwise in carrying out their official responsiblities. However, this prohibition shall not restrict the exchange of information with an aforementioned duly constituted investigative or disciplinary body.

In the course of performing professional services for a client, the CPA necessarily becomes aware of information that is confidential in nature, and the CPA must hold the information in strict confidence. Confidential information about the client should never be disclosed even to client employees or to other members of the CPA firm, unless the disclosure is necessary for the CPA to perform his or her professional services. Of course, confidential information should never be disclosed to third parties without the client's permission.

Although confidentiality is very important, there must be some exceptions to the general rule. For example, information which the CPA obtains about the client is not privileged under federal law, and in many cases the information is not privileged under state law. Consequently, in these cases, the CPA must testify in court; he or she cannot refuse to testify under a claim of privileged information. The other exceptions to the general rule on confidentiality are discussed in the second and third paragraphs of Rule 301.

**Rule 302 —
Contingent Fees**

The eighth rule in the AICPA's *Rules of Conduct* deals with contingent fees, and the rule reads as follows:

> Professional services shall not be offered or rendered under an arrangement whereby no fee will be charged unless a specified finding or result is attained, or where the fee is otherwise contingent upon the findings or results of such services. However, a member's fees may vary depending, for example, on the complexity of the service rendered.
>
> Fees are not regarded as being contingent if fixed by courts or other public authorities or, in tax matters, if determined based on the results of judicial proceedings or the finding of governmental agencies.

The rule on contingent fees is included in the *Rules of Conduct* so the CPA will not be tempted to bias his or her findings to increase the fee for professional services. For example, if the CPA's fee for an audit was based on a percentage of net income, the CPA might be tempted to accept accounting principles simply because the application of the principle resulted in a higher net income. Similarly, if a CPA's fee for the preparation of a tax return was based on the tax liability, the CPA might be tempted to take an illegal deduction to reduce the tax liability. Consequently, a CPA cannot make his or her fee for professional services contingent *i pon the CPA's findings*.

As indicated in Rule 302, fees are not considered to be contingent fees if the fees are fixed by a court or other public authority, or in tax matters, if determined based on the results of judicial proceedings or the findings of governmental agencies. The key point in these examples is that, while the fee may be contingent, the fee is contingent upon the findings of someone other than the CPA.

**Rule 501 —
Acts
Discreditable**

The ninth rule in the AICPA's *Rules of Conduct* deals with acts which are considered discreditable to the profession, and the rule reads as follows:

> A member shall not commit an act discreditable to the profession.

Rule 501 is a general rule prohibiting acts which are discreditable to the accounting profession. Evasion of income taxes and other felonies would be examples of violations of this rule. An interpretation of Rule

501 states that discrimination based on race, color, religion, sex, age, or national origin in hiring, promotion, or salary practices is considered an act discreditable to the profession. In addition, the retention of client records, after the client has demanded that the records be returned, is considered to be an act discreditable to the profession.

Rule 502 — Advertising and Other Forms of Solicitation

The tenth rule in the AICPA's *Rules of Conduct* deals with advertising and other forms of solicitation, and the rule reads as follows:

> A member shall not seek to obtain clients by advertising or other forms of solicitation in a manner that is false, misleading or deceptive.

Historically, the AICPA did not permit its members to advertise because the AICPA did not believe that advertising was in keeping with the dignity of the profession. However, due to consumerism, legal challenges of other professions' ban on advertising, and the threat of anti-trust action against the AICPA, the membership of the AICPA voted in 1978 to permit advertising as long as the advertising is not false, misleading, or deceptive.

Under the new rule on advertising, the AICPA permits advertising that is informative and objective as long as the advertising is in good taste and professionally dignified. There are no restrictions on the type of advertising media, frequency of placement, size, artwork or type style. For example, *Interpretation 502-1* of the *Rules of Conduct*, states that the following types of informational advertising are permited.

1. Information about the member and the member's firm, such as —

   a. Names, addresses, telephone numbers, number of partners, shareholders, or employees, office hours, foreign language competence, and date the firm was established.

   b. Services offered and fees for such services, including hourly rates and fixed fees.

   c. Educational and professional attainments, including date and place of certifications, schools attended, dates of graduation, degrees received, and memberships in professional associations.

2. Statements of policy or position made by a member or a member's firm related to the practice of public accounting or addressed to a subject of public interest.

However, advertising that is false, misleading, or deceptive, is prohibited. For example, *Interpretation 502-2* of the *Rules of Conduct* states that certain activities are prohibited. These prohibited activities include those that —

1.   Create false or unjustified expectations of favorable results.

2.   Imply the ability to influence any court, tribunal, regulatory agency, or similar body or official.

3.   Consist of self-laudatory statements that are not based on verifiable facts.

4.   Make comparisons with other CPAs.

5.   Contain testimonials or endorsements.

6.   Contain any other representations that would be likely to cause a reasonable person to misunderstand or be deceived.

Rule 503 — Commissions

The eleventh rule in the AICPA's *Rules of Conduct* deals with commissions, and the rule reads as follows:

> A member shall not pay a commission to obtain a client, nor shall he (she) accept a commission for a referral to a client of products or services of others. This rule shall not prohibit payments for the purchase of an accounting practice or retirement payments to individuals formerly engaged in the practice of public accounting or payments to their heirs or estates.

There are two key aspects to Rule 503. First, a CPA should not pay a commission to receive a client because a CPA should be selected based on his or her reputation and not on the amount of commission the CPA is willing to pay. Also, if a CPA paid a commission to receive a client, the CPA would likely add the amount of the commission to the client's bill, and thus the client would be paying for something other than professional services.

The second key aspect of Rule 503 deals with the prohibition against a CPA receiving a commission for a referral to a client of products or services of others. If such commissions were allowed, the client could never be sure whether he or she was getting the best product or service or whether the CPA was simply recommending the product or service of the vendor who paid the highest commission. Consequently, a CPA cannot accept a commission for referral of a product or service. Of course, a CPA may charge a client for any work the CPA performs in connection with recommending a product or service to a client. For example, a CPA could charge a fee for evaluating the various microcomputers on the market, and then advising the client on which computer to purchase.

It must be noted that Rule 503 does not prohibit a CPA from paying a fee to another CPA or accepting a fee from another CPA. This exception to the rule exists for situations where a CPA has performed a service for a potential client by evaluating that potential client's needs and then referring the client to another CPA more qualified to perform the service. Rule 502 would be violated, however, by a referring CPA's acceptance of a fee from another CPA if no service had been performed for the client.

**Rule 504 —
Incompatible
Occupations**

The twelfth rule in the AICPA's *Rules of Conduct* deals with incompatible occupations. The rule reads as follows:

> A member who is engaged in the practice of public accounting shall not concurrently engage in any business or occupation which would create a conflict of interest in rendering professional services.

The emphasis in Rule 504 is on prohibiting a CPA from *concurrently* practicing public accounting and any other business or profession which creates a *conflict of interest* with public accounting. Although there is no formal listing of businesses or professions which create a conflict of interest with the practice of public accounting, the authors believe that a CPA should not concurrently practice public accounting and any other business or profession which involves providing advice about financial matters. For example, a CPA should not practice law and public accounting at the same time because in the practice of law the attorney's primary responsibility is to the client whereas in the practice of public accounting the CPA has a joint responsibility to the client and to the public. Also, a CPA should not sell insurance and practice public accounting because in his or her role as a CPA, the accountant will evaluate the client's insurance coverage.

Students should realize that the CPA may have a license to practice public accounting and a license to practice another profession which involves advice about financial matters. However, the CPA cannot practice both professions at the same time for the same client. For example, a CPA may have a license to practice law, but the CPA cannot practice law and public accounting at the same time for the same client. In many states, the CPA may not concurrently engage in the practice by accountancy and law even if different clients are involved, as these two professions are considered to create a public conflict of interests.

Rule 505 — Form of Practice and Name

The thirteenth and final rule in the AICPA's *Rules of Conduct* deals with the form of a CPA's practice, and the name the CPA uses for his or her business. The rule reads as follows:

> A member may practice public accounting, whether as an owner or employee, only in the form of a proprietorship, a partnership, or a professional corporation whose characteristics conform to resolutions of Council.
>
> A member shall not practice under a firm name which includes any fictitious name, indicates specialization, or is misleading as to the type of organization (proprietorship, partnership, or corporation). However, names of one or more past partners or shareholders may be included in the firm name of a successor partnership or corporation. Also, a partner surviving the death or withdrawal of all other partners may continue to practice under the partnership name for up to two years after becoming a sole practitioner.
>
> A firm may not designate itself as "Members of the American Institute of Certified Public Accountants" unless all of its partners or shareholders are members of the Institute.

The rule on form of practice and name is basically self-explanatory. However, students sometimes have trouble understanding two parts of the rule: the part that prohibits any fictitious name and the part that prohibits any name which is misleading as to the type of organization.

The portion of the rule which prohibits use of a fictitious name means that the name of a CPA firm must be based on the name of a real person or persons. For a proprietorship, the name of the CPA firm must be based on the name of the present or former proprietor. For a partnership, the name of the CPA firm must be based on the names of one or more present or former partners in the firm. Finally, for a professional corporation, the name of the CPA firm must be based on the names of one or more of the present or former shareholders or of partners who were associated with a predecessor accounting firm.

The portion of the rule which prohibits any name that is misleading as to the type of organization means that a CPA firm cannot use a name which implies that the firm is a different type of organization than it is. For example, a sole proprietor cannot use a name that implies that the business is a partnership. Notice, however, that a partner who survives the death or withdrawal of all other partners may continue to use the partnership name for up to two years after becoming a sole practitioner. After two years, if the CPA is still a sole practitioner, he or she must change the name to a name that indicates the true nature of the business.

As indicated in Rule 505, a CPA firm can practice as a professional corporation. These corporations (which use the abbreviation P.C., such as in Jones & Smith, P.C.) can be organized under the laws of some states where the corporation enjoys the tax advantages of a regular corporation, but where the shareowners of the corporation are generally jointly and severally liable for the acts of the corporation. In other words, the shareowners are liable for the acts of the corporation as if the shareowners were partners in their firm.

If a CPA firm is organized as a professional corporation, the corporation must abide by seven resolutions which were adopted by the AICPA Council. These resolutions were designed to ensure that a CPA firm which is organized as a professional corporation has the same relationships with the public and its clients as it would if the firm were organized as a partnership or proprietorship. The resolutions are as follows:

1. **Name.** The name under which the professional corporation or association renders professional services shall contain only the names of one or more of the present or former shareholders or of partners who were associated with a predecessor accounting firm. Impersonal or fictitious names, as well as names which indicate a specialty, are prohibited.

2. **Purpose.** The professional corporation or association shall not provide services that are incompatible with the practice of public accounting.

3. **Ownership.** All shareholders of the corporation or association shall be persons engaged in the practice of public accounting as defined by the code of professional ethics. Shareholders shall at all times own their shares in their own right and shall be the beneficial owners of the equity capital ascribed to them.

4. **Transfer of Shares.** Provision shall be made requiring any shareholders who ceases to be eligible to be a shareholder to dispose of all of his (her) shares within a reasonable period to a person qualified to be a shareholder or to the corporation or association.

5. **Directors and Officers.** The principal executive officer shall be a shareholder and a director, and to the extent possible, all other direc-

tors and officers shall be certified public accountants. Lay directors and officers shall not exercise any authority whatsoever over professional matters.

6. **Conduct.** The right to practice as a corporation or association shall not change the obligation of its shareholders, directors, officers, and other employees to comply with the standards of professional conduct established by the American Institute of Certified Public Accountants.

7. **Liability.** The stockholders of professional corporations or associations shall be jointly and severally liable for the acts of a corporation or association, or its employees—except where professional liability insurance is carried, or capitalization is maintained, in amounts deemed sufficient to offer adequate protection to the public. Liability shall not be limited by the formation of subsidiary or affiliated corporations or associations each with its own limited and unrelated liability.

OTHER CODES OF PROFESSIONAL ETHICS

The code of ethics which has been discussed thus far is of course the *Code of Professional Ethics* of the AICPA. However, most state societies and state boards of accountancy have traditionally adopted the AICPA *Code* as their own code of ethics. Consequently, if a CPA violates the *Code* of the AICPA he or she is also generally in violation of the code of ethics of his or her state society and state board of accountancy. Therefore, a violation of the AICPA's *Code* may not only result in censure, suspension, or expulsion of the member by the AICPA, but also, the member may be penalized by his or her state society and state board of accountancy. Of course, the ultimate penalty that a CPA can receive is to have his or her license to practice revoked by a state board of accountancy.

As indicated earlier, most state societies and state boards of accountancy have traditionally adopted the AICPA's *Code* as their own code of ethics. However, recently some state societies and state boards of accountancy have been reluctant to accept some modifications in their ethics which were adopted by the AICPA. For example, the AICPA formally had a rule which prohibited one CPA from soliciting the client of another CPA, but this rule has been repealed. However, some state societies and state boards of accountancy have retained the rule prohibiting solicitation of clients. Consequently, since the AICPA rules and state rules are not always the same, it is imperative that CPAs also become aware of the code of ethics which is followed by their state society and state board of accountancy.

In addition to the codes of ethics which apply to CPAs who practice public accounting, several professional groups who represent accountants in industry have also developed their own codes of ethics. For example, the Institute of Internal Auditors and the Bank Administration Institute have developed codes of ethics for their members. Consequently, members of industry groups, such as the members of the Institute of Internal Auditors, must become aware of and abide by their own particular code of ethics.

STATEMENTS ON RESPONSIBILITY IN TAX PRACTICE

As indicated earlier, CPAs have certain responsibilities in tax practice. These responsibilities have been identified and published in the form of ten *Statements on Responsibilities in Tax Practice*. These statements are not covered by Rule 204 — Other Technical Standards. Their authority is, therefore, derived from their general acceptance by the membership of the AICPA. The ten *Statements of Responsibility on Tax Practice* are as follows.

Signature of Preparer

This statement requires a CPA to sign the preparer's declaration on any federal tax return that the CPA prepares whether or not a fee is charged for preparing the return. The preparer's declaration is a statement on the return which in essence says that to the best of the preparer's knowledge the return is true, correct and complete.

Signature of Reviewer: Assumption of Preparer's Responsibility

This statement says that a CPA does not have to sign a return if the CPA did not prepare the return. However, the CPA, at his or her discretion, may sign the return if the CPA obtains knowledge with respect to the return substantially equivalent to that which he or she would have had to acquire to prepare the return in the first place. Thus, if a client asks a CPA to review a return and sign the preparer's declaration, the CPA may do so if he or she obtains knowledge equivalent to that knowledge which would be necessary to actually prepare the return.

Answer to Questions on Returns

This statement says that before a CPA signs the preparer's declaration, he or she should make sure that all questions on the return have been answered. If a question is not answered, the CPA should attach an explanation to the return stating why the answer to a question was omitted. A CPA cannot omit an answer to a question because that answer might have an adverse impact on the client.

Recognition of Administrative Proceeding of a Prior Year

This statement says that the treatment of an item on a tax return should be based on the rules and facts as they are evaluated at the time the return is prepared. Consequently, a CPA is not necessarily bound by an administrative proceeding of a prior year. For example, a CPA may take a deduction on the client's 1984 tax return even if a similar deduction has been disallowed by the IRS on a return for a year prior to 1984 provided that the facts and rules which are in effect for 1984 justify the deduction.

Use of Estimates

This statement says that a CPA may make use of estimates in preparing a tax return if the use of estimates is generally acceptable, or it is impractical to obtain exact data. However, the CPA must make sure that (1) the estimates are reasonable and (2) the estimates are not presented in a manner which implies greater accuracy than exists. For example, a CPA frequently uses a table which is prepared by the IRS to estimate the client's deduction for sales taxes.

Knowledge of Error: Return Preparation

This statement says that once a CPA learns of an error in a previously filed return or of a client's failure to file a required return the CPA should advise the client as to what actions the client should take, e.g., amend the incorrect return or file the required return. However, the CPA has no obligation to inform the IRS. Furthermore, the CPA cannot inform the IRS without the client's permission. If the client fails to correct the error, or file a return which was not filed, the CPA may decide that he or she should not prepare the client's return for the current year. However, if the CPA does prepare the return for the current year, the CPA should take reasonable steps to ensure that the error is not repeated in the current year.

Knowledge of an Error: Administrative Proceedings

This statement deals with cases where a CPA is representing a client in an administrative proceeding and the CPA learns of an error in the return which is being examined. The statement says that in these cases the CPA should encourage the client to disclose the error to the IRS. Furthermore, if the client refuses to disclose the error, the CPA may be under a duty to withdraw from the engagement. For example, if the CPA thinks that the IRS believes that the CPA is corroborating information which the CPA knows to be false, the CPA is under a duty to withdraw from the engagement.

With respect to this point, there may be cases where the CPA's withdrawal may clearly constitute a violation of the CPA's confidential relationship with the client and be equivalent to telling the IRS that there is an error in the return. In these cases, the CPA need not withdraw from the engagement, but the CPA should inform his or her client that the CPA's inability to answer questions about the item which is in error may have a prejudicial effect on the client's case.

Advice to Clients

This statement says that, when a CPA gives tax advice to a client, the CPA cannot be expected to follow up on the advice and change the original advice each time that the tax law changes. However, the CPA should make it clear that any advice which is given is based on the tax laws which are presently in effect.

Certain Procedural Aspects of Preparing Returns

This statement deals with four procedural aspects of preparing a return. First, the statement says that the CPA may ordinarily rely on data which is furnished by the client; the CPA is not required to review evidence which supports the client's information. However, the CPA should encourage the client to provide supporting data where appropriate. For example, when a client makes a gift of property, the CPA is not required to audit the amount of the gift. However, the CPA would ask questions and gather supporting information to ensure that the client has all the information to support the gift in the case of an IRS examination.

Second, the statement says that the CPA should make use of the client's prior year's returns in preparing the current year's return whenever feasible. This review of the client's prior year's returns should help the CPA in (1) obtaining an overall understanding of the client's tax status, (2) avoiding the omission or duplication of items, and (3) affording a basis for the treatment of similar or related transactions.

Third, the statement says that the CPA cannot ignore the implication of information that the CPA knows about. Consequently, the CPA is required to make a reasonable investigation of information which is furnished by the client but which appears to be incorrect or incomplete.

Fourth, the statement says that if a CPA prepares a federal tax return the CPA should sign the preparer's declaration without modifying the declaration. For example, the CPA cannot insert phrases, such as "prepared from the books without audit," into the preparer's declaration.

Positions Contrary to Treasury Department or Internal Revenue Service Interpretations of the Code

This tenth *Statement of Responsibility in Tax Practice* discusses three issues. First, the statement says that a CPA may take a position contrary to a Treasury Department or Internal Revenue Service interpretation of the *Internal Revenue Code* provided there is reasonable support for his or her position. Furthermore, the CPA need not disclose the treatment of the item in the tax return. Second, the statement says that a CPA may, in rare cases, take a position that is contrary to the *Internal Revenue Code* provided there is support for the CPA's position. However, in these cases the CPA should disclose the treatment of the item in question. Finally, the statement says that in no case may a CPA take a position that lacks reasonable support, even if the position is disclosed in the return.

STATEMENT ON STANDARDS FOR MANAGEMENT ADVISORY SERVICES

Prior to December 31, 1981, a series of *Statements on Management Advisory Services* was issued by the AICPA. These standards dealt with the following topics:

- Personal Characteristics of the Management Advisory Services (MAS) Practitioner.
- Competence of the MAS Practitioner.
- Due Care.
- Client Benefit.
- Understanding with the Client.
- Planning, Supervision, and Control.
- Sufficient Relevant Data.
- Communication of Results.

These standards were not covered by Rule 204 — Other Technical Standards, and consequently, the standards depended on general acceptance by the membership for their support.

Due to the increasing importance of MAS, the Management Advisory Services Executive Committee was formed, and this committee issued *Statement on Standards for Management Advisory Services No. 1* (SSMAS No. 1) in December of 1981. This statement defines management advisory services and establishes certain standards for MAS practice. Many of the standards established in *SSMAS No. 1* are the same standards that were issued earlier. However, the standards in *SSMAS No. 1* differ from the earlier pronouncement in that these later standards are covered by Rule 204 of the AICPA's *Code*. The standards in *SSMAS No. 1* do not supersede the earlier MAS standards, and the Management Advisory Services Executive Committee (MASec) recognized that practitioners may have to consult the earlier standards for guidance, especially on the details of the standards, until the Committee issues further standards.

SSMAS No. 1 consists of two key parts. The first part of the statement gives certain definitions which apply to MAS, and the second part of the statement discusses the standards for MAS practice.

Definitions

MAS services are defined in *SSMAS No. 1* as "the management consulting function of providing advice and technical assistance where the primary purpose is to help the client improve the use of its capabilities and resources to achieve its objectives." However, MAS services do not include comments prepared as a direct result of observations made while performing an audit, review or compilation of financial statements or while providing tax services.

SSMAS No. 1 also makes a distinction between a MAS engagement and MAS consultation. A MAS engagement is defined as "that form of MAS in which an analytical approach and process is applied in a study or project." MAS consultation, on the other hand, is defined as "that form of MAS based mostly, if not entirely, on existing personal knowledge . . . ." Thus, a MAS engagement is more formal in nature than MAS consultation.

Standards for MAS Practice

In *SSMAS No. 1*, MASec states that the standards which are included in Rule 201 of the AICPA's *Rules of Conduct* apply to both MAS engagements and MAS consultations. These standards were discussed earlier in this chapter and cover professional competence, due professional care, planning and supervision, sufficient relevant data, and forecasts. In addition, the following technical standards apply to MAS engagements.

Role of MAS practitioner.   In performing a MAS engagement, a MAS practitioner should not assume the role of management or take any positions that might impair the MAS practitioner's objectivity.

Understanding with client.   An oral or written understanding should be reached with the client concerning the nature, scope, and limitations of the MAS engagement to be performed.

Client benefit.   Since the potential benefits to be derived by the client are a major consideration in MAS engagements, such potential benefits should be viewed objectively and the client should be notified of reservations regarding them. In offering and providing MAS engagements, results should not be explicitly or implicitly guaranteed. When estimates of quantifiable results are presented, they should be clearly identified as estimates and the support for such estimates should be disclosed.

Communication of results. Significant information pertinent to the results of a MAS engagement, together with any limitations, qualifications, or reservations needed to assist the client in making its decision, should be communicated to the client orally or in writing.

SUMMARY

The AICPA's *Code of Professional Ethics* consists of four distinct parts: *Concepts of Professional Ethics*, *Rules of Conduct*, *Interpretations of Rules of Conduct*, and *Ethics Rulings*. There are five concepts of professional ethics. These concepts are not intended to be detailed, enforceable rules, but rather, broad ethical guidelines which every CPA should strive to achieve. The concepts deal with (1) integrity, objectivity and independence, (2) general and technical standards, (3) relations with clients, (4) relations with other members of the profession, and (5) relations with the public. The concepts are important because (1) they were and still are considered by the AICPA in establishing the *Rules of Conduct*, the *Interpretations of the Rules of Conduct*, and the *Ethics Rulings*, and (2) the *Concepts of Professional Ethics* provide guidance to the CPA in determining ethical conduct in areas where no specific rule of conduct, interpretations of the rules of conduct, or ethics ruling has been issued.

The AICPA's *Code of Professional Ethics* derives its authority from the bylaws of the AICPA. These rules apply to all services performed in the practice of public accounting, including tax and management advisory services, except (1) where the wording of a specific rule indicates that the rule applies only to a certain type of service, or (2) in certain cases, to members of the AICPA who are practicing outside the United States. However, in all cases where the user of the CPA's report would assume that U.S. standards were being followed, the CPA must comply with Rules 202 (GAAS) and 203 (GAAP) of the AICPA's *Rules of Conduct*. A member of the AICPA is also held accountable for the actions of his or her partners and the accountants under the member's supervision. A member of the AICPA who is not engaged in the practice of public accounting is only required to abide by Rules 102 (integrity and objectivity) and 501 (acts discreditable).

Rule 101 deals with independence. There are two aspects of independence: independence in fact and independence in appearance. Independence in fact is a state of mind. Independence in appearance refers to what third parties would think if they had knowledge of all the relationships between the CPA and the client.

Rule 101 applies only to cases where the CPA is expressing an opinion on the financial statements of an entity. Thus, independence, as required by Rule 101, is necessary when the CPA reports on (1) audited financial statements, (2) a review of financial statements, or (3) unaudited financial statements. In cases where the CPA is not independent under Rule 101, the CPA's report on the client's financial statements is limited to a statement which says that the CPA is not independent and therefore does not express any opinion on the financial statements. When the CPA disclaims an opinion on the client's financial statements because of a lack of independence, the CPA should not state why he or she is not independent since an explanation of the specific reason(s) for the lack of independence might tend to confuse the reader. A CPA may report on a compilation of financial statements even if the CPA is not independent. A compilation report is allowed when the CPA is not independent because the CPA is not expressing any opinion on the financial statements, but instead, the CPA is simply saying that he or she has compiled (prepared) the financial statements from the records of the company. Therefore, since a compilation report involves less judgment than other types of reports, it is unlikely that a CPA's compilation report will be influenced by the CPA's lack of independence. However, when the independence is lacking, the standard compilation report must be expanded to state that the CPA is not independent with respect to the client.

The period of time for which independence is required differs slightly depending on whether one is considering Part A or Part B of Rule 101. Part A of Rule 101 prohibits certain financial relationships with the client. These relationships are prohibited during the period of the CPA's professional engagement and at the time the CPA expresses his or her opinion on the financial statements. Part B of the rule prohibits the CPA from engaging in any activities which are equivalent to management activities for the company. The activities are prohibited during the period covered by the financial statements, during the period of the professional engagement, and at the time the CPA expresses an opinion on the financial statements.

With respect to a direct financial interest in a client, the AICPA has interpreted the phrase "he and his (her) firm" in Rule 101 to refer to all partners or shareholders in the public accounting firm; the phrase refers also to all full and part-time professional staff on the audit engagement or located in an office participating in a significant part of the engagement. However, some CPA firms still insist that no staff person have any investment in any client of the firm regardless of where the client is located.

In general, the financial interests of a person who depends on the CPA for his or her financial support are considered direct financial interests of the CPA, and the financial interest of a person who has a close relationship with the CPA, but who does not depend on the CPA for his or her support, are considered to be an indirect financial interest of the CPA.

A CPA is allowed to be a director or trustee of a charitable, religious, civic, or other non-profit organization provided the CPA's position is purely honorary. In general, a CPA can perform bookkeeping services, tax services, and MAS for a client and still be independent. However, bookkeeping services are prohibited for SEC clients. Also, a CPA cannot offer executive recruitment services for the CPA's clients.

Since the client does pay the CPA's fee, perfect independence between the CPA and the client probably will never be achieved. The major factor which encourages the CPA to maintain his or her independence is the potential costs of sacrificing the independence. One major factor which helps a CPA maintain his or her independence is the corporate audit committee. Two other major factors which help the CPA maintain his or her independence are Forms 10-Q and 8-K which are required by the SEC. The requirements of these forms discourage a client from changing accounting principles or auditors without valid reasons.

Rule 102 deals with integrity and objectivity. These characteristics constitute the very essence of a profession.

Rule 201 deals with the general standards. The general standards include: professional competence, due professional care, planning and supervision, sufficient relevant data, and forecasts.

Rule 202 deals with auditing standards. A CPA shall not permit his or her name to be associated with financial statements in such a manner as to imply that the CPA is acting as an independent public accountant unless he or she has complied with the applicable generally accepted auditing standards. SASs are considered to be interpretations of the ten Generally Accepted Auditing Standards.

Rule 203 deals with generally accepted accounting principles. A CPA cannot express an opinion that the financial statements are presented in conformity with GAAP if such statements contain any departure from an accounting principle promulgated by a body designated by Council to establish such principles which has a material effect on the statements taken as a whole, unless the CPA can demonstrate that due to unusual circumstances the financial statements would otherwise have been misleading. In such cases, the CPA must describe the departure, the approximate effects thereof, if practical, and the reasons why compliance with the principle would result in misleading financial statements.

Rule 204 requires CPAs to comply with other technical standards. These other technical standards include pronouncements by the Management Advisory Services Executive Committee, the Accounting and Review Services Committee, and the FASB pronouncements on disclosures of supplemental information which is not a part of the basic financial statements but which does appear in financial reports which contain the basic financial statements.

Rule 301 deals with confidential client information. A CPA cannot disclose any confidential information about the client except with the consent of the client. However, this rule does not (a) relieve a CPA of his or her obligations under Rules 202 and 203, (b) affect the CPA's compliance with a validly issued subpoena or summons, (c) prohibit a quality control review of the CPA's practice, or (d) preclude the CPA from responding to an ethics investigation.

Rule 302 prohibits a CPA from charging a fee that is contingent upon his or her findings. However, fees are not considered contingent fees if fixed by courts or other public authorities, or, in tax matters, if determined based on the results of judicial proceedings or the findings of governmental agencies.

Rule 501 prohibits a CPA from committing an act which is discreditable to the profession. The retention of client records, after the client has demanded that the records be returned, is considered to be an act discreditable to the profession.

Rule 502 permits advertising that is informative and objective as long as the advertising is in good taste and professionally dignified. However, advertising that is false, misleading or deceptive is prohibited.

Rule 503 prohibits a CPA from paying a commission to obtain a client. The rule also prohibits a CPA from accepting a commission for referral to a client of products or services of others.

Rule 504 deals with incompatible occupations. The emphasis in Rule 504 is on prohibiting a CPA from concurrently practicing public accounting and any other business or profession which creates a conflict of interest with public accounting.

Under Rule 505, a member may practice public accounting only as a proprietorship, a partnership or a professional corporation whose characteristics conform to resolutions of Council. A CPA firm shall not use any fictitious name, a name which indicates specialization, or is misleading as to the type of organization. A member may not designate itself as "members of the American Institute of Certified Public Accountants" unless all of its partners or shareholders are members of the Institute.

Since the AICPA rules and state rules are not always the same, it is imperative that CPAs become aware of the AICPA's *Code of Professional Ethics* as well as the code of ethics which is followed by their state society and state board of accountancy. In addition, accountants who are members of industry groups, such as the members of the Institute of Internal Auditors, must become aware of and abide by their own particular code of ethics.

There are ten *Statements on Responsibilities in Tax Practice*. These statements deal with: the signature of the preparer, signature of reviewer, answers to questions on returns, recognition of administrative proceeding of a prior year, use of estimates, knowledge of error in return preparation, knowledge of error in an administrative proceeding, advice to clients, certain procedural aspects of preparing returns, and positions contrary to Treasury Department or Internal Revenue Service interpretations of the Internal Revenue Code.

In December 1981, the Management Advisory Services Executive Committee issued *SSMAS No. 1*. This statement defines MAS and establishes certain standards for MAS practice. In *SSMAS No. 1*, MASec states that the standards which are included in Rule 201 of the AICPA's *Rules of Conduct* apply to both MAS engagements and MAS consultations. In addition, certain other standards apply to MAS engagements: role of the MAS practitioner, understanding with client, client benefit, and communication of results.

REVIEW QUESTIONS

3-1   What are the four basic parts of the AICPA's *Code of Professional Ethics*?

3-2   What are the five concepts of professional ethics?

3-3   Would the concepts of professional ethics explain to a CPA those actions which are permitted or not permitted? Discuss.

3-4   Discuss two reasons why the concepts of professional ethics are important.

3-5   Which is more specific, ethics rulings or rules of conduct? Why?

3-6   From what source does the AICPA's *Code of Professional Ethics* derive its authority?

3-7   Besides his or her own actions, whose actions is a member of the AICPA responsible for?

3-8   What are the two aspects of independence, and how do they differ?

3-9   Can a CPA who is not independent issue a report expressing an opinion on a firm's financial statements? Can he or she issue a compilation report? Why?

3-10   Under what conditions can a CPA be a director or trustee of an organization which is an audit client? Is this not a conflict of interest?

3-11   Does performing bookkeeping services impair the independence of a CPA? Does performing managerial activities? Performing management advisory services? Performing tax services?

3-12   List the four duties of a typical audit committee.

3-13   What are the five general standards?

3-14   Should a CPA vouch for the achievability of a financial forecast? Why?

3-15   What are considered Generally Accepted Accounting Principles in accordance with Rule 203?

3-16   Can a CPA refuse to testify on confidential client information, asserting an "accountant-client privilege"?

3-17   When is it acceptable for a CPA to charge contingent fees?

3-18   Can a CPA advertise? If so, can he (she) call himself (herself) a specialist in a certain area?

3-19   List two occupations which are probably incompatible with public accounting.

3-20   What body of guidelines directs the rendering of tax services? From what source does it derive its authority?

3-21 When would it not be appropriate for a CPA to withdraw from a tax-return preparation engagement?

3-22 What is the difference between a MAS engagement and a MAS consultation?

DISCUSSION QUESTIONS AND PROBLEMS

3-23 *Part I:* Assume that you examined the financial statements of the Nelson Company in accordance with GAAS and were satisfied with your findings.

Required:

Would the fact that the company had a loan (of substantial amount to the Nelson Company) payable to a loan company of which your brother was principal stockholder have any effect on your auditor's opinion? Discuss.

Part II: Your son, aged 16, owns 100 shares of the 50,000 shares of the Nelson Company common stock outstanding at the balance sheet date.

Required:

Would this fact have any effect on your auditor's opinion? Discuss.

(AICPA adapted)

3-24 An auditor's report was appended to the financial statements of Worthmore, Inc. The statements consisted of a balance sheet as of November 30, 19x0 and statements of income and retained earnings for the year then ending. The first two paragraphs of the report contained the wording of the standard unqualified report, and a third paragraph read as follows:

> The wives of two partners of our firm owned a material investment in the outstanding common stock of Worthmore, Inc. during the fiscal year ending November 30, 19x0. The aforementioned individuals disposed of their holdings of Worthmore, Inc. on December 3, 19x0 in a transaction that did not result in a profit or a loss. This information is included in our report in order to comply with certain disclosure requirements of the Code of Professional Ethics of the American Institute of Certified Public Accountants.
>
> **Bell & Davis**
> *Certified Public Accountants*

Required:

a. Was the CPA firm of Bell & Davis independent with respect to the fiscal 19x0 examination of Worthmore, Inc.'s financial statements? Explain.

b. Do you find Bell & Davis' auditor's report satisfactory? Explain.

c. Assume that no members of Bell & Davis or any members of their families held any financial interests in Worthmore, Inc. during 19x0. For each of the following cases, indicate if independence would be lacking on behalf of Bell & Davis, assuming that Worthmore, Inc. is a profit-seeking enterprise. In each case, explain why independence would or would not be lacking.

   1. Two directors of Worthmore, Inc. became partners in the CPA firm of Bell & Davis on July 1, 19x0, resigning their directorships on that date.

   2. During 19x0, the former controller of Worthmore, now a Bell & Davis partner, was frequently called on for assistance by Worthmore. He made decisions for Worthmore's management regarding fixed asset acquisitions and the company's product marketing mix. In addition, he conducted a computer feasibility study for Worthmore.

(AICPA adapted)

3-25 The attribute of independence has been traditionally associated with the CPA's function of auditing and expressing opinions on financial statements.

Required:

a. What is meant by "independence" as applied to the CPA's function of auditing and expressing opinions on financial statements? Discuss.

b. CPAs have imposed upon themselves certain rules of professional conduct that induce their members to remain independent and to strengthen public confidence in their independence. Which of the rules of professional conduct are concerned with the CPA's independence? Discuss.

c. The Wallydrug Company is indebted to a CPA for unpaid fees and has offered to issue to him unsecured interest-bearing notes. Would the CPA's acceptance of these notes have any bearing upon his independence in his relations with the Wallydrug Company? Discuss.

d.   The Rocky Hill Corporation was formed on October 1, 19x0 and its fiscal year will end on September 30, 19x1. You audited the corporation's opening balance sheet and rendered an unqualified opinion on it. A month after rendering your report you are offered the position of secretary of the Company because of the need for a complete set of officers and for convenience in signing various documents. You will have no financial interest in the company through stock ownership or otherwise, will receive no salary, will not keep the books, and will not have any influence on its financial matters other than occasional advice on income tax matters and similar advice normally given a client by a CPA.

1.   Assume that you accept the offer but plan to resign the position prior to conducting your annual audit with the intention of again assuming the office after rendering an opinion on the statements. Can you render an independent opinion on the financial statements? Discuss.

2.   Assume that you accept the offer on a temporary basis until the corporation has gotten under way and can employ a secretary. In any event you would permanently resign the position before conducting your annual audit. Can you render an independent opinion on the financial statements? Discuss.

(AICPA adapted)

3-26   Gilbert and Bradley formed a corporation called Financial Services, Inc., each man taking 50 percent of the authorized common stock. Gilbert is a CPA and a member of the American Institute of CPAs. Bradley is a CPCU (Chartered Property Casualty Underwriter). The corporation performs auditing and tax services under Gilbert's direction and insurance services under Bradley's supervision. The opening of the corporation's office was announced by a three-inch, two-column "card" in the local newspaper.

One of the corporation's first audit clients was the Grandtime Company. Grandtime had total assets of $600,000 and total liabilities of $270,000. In the course of his examination, Gilbert found that Grandtime's building with a book value of $240,000 was pledged as security for a ten-year-term note in the amount of $200,000. The client's statements did not mention that the building was pledged as security for the ten-year-term note. However, since the failure to disclose the lien did not affect either the value of the assets or the amount of the liabilities and his examination was satisfactory in all other respects,

Gilbert rendered an unqualified opinion on Grandtime's financial statements. About two months after the date of his opinion, Gilbert learned that an insurance company was planning to loan Grandtime $150,000 in the form of a first-mortgage note on the building. Realizing that the insurance company was unaware of the existing lien on the building, Gilbert had Bradley notify the insurance company of the fact that Grandtime's building was pledged as security for the term note.

Shortly after the events described above, Gilbert was charged with a violation of professional ethics.

Required:

Identify and discuss the ethical implications of those acts by Gilbert that were in violation of the AICPA's Code of Professional Ethics.

(AICPA adapted)

3-27   For many years the financial and accounting community has recognized the importance of the use of audit committees and has endorsed their formation.

At this time the use of audit committees has become widespread. Independent auditors have become increasingly involved with audit committees and consequently have become familiar with their nature and function.

Required:

a.   Describe what an audit committee is.
b.   Identify the reasons why audit committees have been formed and are currently in operation.
c.   What are the functions of an audit committee?

(AICPA adapted)

3-28   The following case relates to the CPA's management of his accounting practice.

Judd Hanlon, CPA, was engaged to prepare the federal income tax return for the Guild Corporation for the year ended December 31, 1984. This is Mr. Hanlon's first engagement of any kind for the Guild Corporation.

In preparing the 1984 return, Mr. Hanlon finds an error on the 1983 return. The 1983 depreciation deduction was overstated significantly

—accumulated depreciation brought forward from 1982 to 1983 was understated, and thus the 1983 base for declining balance depreciation was overstated.

Mr. Hanlon reported the error to Guild's controller, the officer responsible for tax returns. The controller stated: "Let the revenue agent find the error." He further instructed Mr. Hanlon to carry forward the material overstatement of the depreciable base to the 1984 depreciation computation. The controller noted that this error also had been made in the financial records for 1983 and 1984 and offered to furnish Mr. Hanlon with a letter assuming full responsibility for this treatment.

Required:

a. Evaluate Mr. Hanlon's handling of this situation.
b. Discuss the additional action that Mr. Hanlon should now undertake.

(AICPA adapted)

3-29 An auditor must not only appear to be independent; he must also be independent in fact.

Required:

a. Explain the concept of an "auditor's independence" as it applies to third party reliance upon financial statements.

b. 1. What determines whether or not an auditor is independent in fact?
    2. What determines whether or not an auditor appears to be independent?

c. Explain how an auditor may be independent in fact but not appear to be independent.

d. Would a CPA be considered independent for an examination of the financial statements of a

    1. Church for which he is serving as treasurer without compensation? Explain.
    2. Women's club for which his wife is serving as treasurer-bookkeeper if he is not to receive a fee for the examination? Explain.

e. Write a disclaimer of opinion such as should accompany financial statements examined by a CPA who owns a material direct financial interest in his audit client.

(AICPA adapted)

3-30   Brown, CPA, received a telephone call from Calhoun, the sole owner and manager of a small corporation. Calhoun asked Brown to prepare the financial statements for the corporation and told Brown that the statements were needed in two weeks for external financing purposes. Calhoun was vague when Brown inquired about the intended use of the statements. Brown was convinced that Calhoun thought Brown's work would constitute an audit. To avoid confusion Brown decided not to explain to Calhoun that the engagement would only be to prepare the financial statements. Brown, with the understanding that a substantial fee would be paid if the work were completed in two weeks, accepted the engagement and started the work at once.

During the course of the work, Brown discovered an accrued expense account labeled "professional fees" and learned that the balance in the account represented an accrual for the cost of Brown's services. Brown suggested to Calhoun's bookkeeper that the account name be changed to "fees for limited audit engagement." Brown also reviewed several invoices to determine whether amounts were being properly classified. Some of the invoices were missing. Brown listed the missing invoice numbers in the working papers with a note indicating that there should be a follow-up on the next engagement. Brown also discovered that the available records included the fixed asset values at estimated current replacement costs. Based on the records available, Brown prepared a balance sheet, income statement and statement of stockholder's equity. In addition, Brown drafted the footnotes but decided that any mention of the replacement costs would only mislead the readers. Brown suggested to Calhoun that readers of the financial statements would be better informed if they received a separate letter from Calhoun explaining the meaning and effect of the estimated replacement costs of the fixed assets. Brown mailed the financial statements and footnotes to Calhoun with the following note included on each page:

> "The accompanying financial statements are submitted to you without complete audit verification."

Required:

Identify the inappropriate actions of Brown and indicate what Brown should have done to avoid each inappropriate action.
    Organize your answer sheet as follows:

Inappropriate Action	*What Brown Should Have Done To Avoid Inappropriate Action*

(AICPA adapted)

3-31   Savage, CPA, has been requested by an audit client to perform a non-recurring engagement involving the implementation of an EDP information and control system. The client requests that in setting up the new system and during the period prior to conversion to the new system, that Savage:

- Counsel on potential expansion of business activity plans.
- Search for and interview new personnel.
- Hire new personnel.
- Train personnel.

In addition, the client requests that during the three months subsequent to the conversion, that Savage:

- Supervise the operation of the new system.
- Monitor client-prepared source documents and make changes in basic EDP generated data as Savage may deem necessary without concurrence of the client.
- Savage responds that he may perform some of the services requested, but not all of them.

Required:

a.   Which of these services may Savage perform and which of these services may Savage not perform?

b.   Before undertaking this engagement, Savage should inform the client of all significant matters related to the engagement. What are these significant matters?

c.   If Savage adds to his staff an individual who specializes in developing computer systems, what degree of knowledge must Savage possess in order to supervise the specialist's activities?

(AICPA adapted)

3-32   Ray, the owner of a small company, asked Holmes, CPA, to conduct an audit of the company's records. Ray told Holmes that an audit is to be completed in time to submit audited financial statements to a bank, as part of a loan application. Holmes immediately accepted the engagement and agreed to provide an auditor's report within three weeks. Ray agreed to pay Holmes a fixed fee plus a bonus if the loan was granted.

Holmes hired two accounting students to conduct the audit and spent several hours telling them exactly what to do. Holmes told the students not to spend time reviewing the controls, but instead to concentrate on proving the mathematical accuracy of the ledger accounts, and summarizing the data in the accounting records that support Ray's financial statements. The students followed Holmes' instructions and after two weeks gave Holmes the financial statements which did not include footnotes. Holmes reviewed the statements and prepared an unqualified auditor's report. The report, however, did not refer to generally accepted accounting principles nor to the year-to-year application of such principles.

Required:

Briefly describe each of the generally accepted auditing standards and indicate how the action(s) of Holmes resulted in a failure to comply with each standard.
    Organize your answer as follows:

Brief Description of Generally Accepted Auditing Standards	Holmes' Actions Resulting in Failure to Comply With Generally Accepted Auditing Standards

(AICPA adapted)

OBJECTIVE QUESTIONS*

3-33   A CPA examines the financial statements of a local bank. According to the AICPA Code of Professional Ethics, the appearance of independence ordinarily would *not* be impaired if the CPA

A.   Serves on the bank's committee that approves loans.
B.   Owns several shares of the bank's common stock.
C.   Obtains a short-term loan from the bank.
D.   Uses the bank's time-sharing computer service to solve client-related problems.

3-34   The AICPA Code of Professional Ethics recognizes that the reliance of the public, the government and the business community on sound financial reporting imposes particular obligations on CPAs. The code derives it authority from

A.   Public laws enacted over the years.
B.   General acceptance of the code by the business community.
C.   Requirements of governmental regulatory agencies such as the Securities and Exchange Commission.

Note: Questions marked with an asterisk are not AICPA adapted questions; otherwise, questions in this section have been taken from prior CPA examinations.

D. Bylaws of the American Institute of Certified Public Accountants.

3-35 Richard, CPA, performs accounting services for Norton Corporation. Norton wishes to offer its shares to the public and asks Richard to audit the financial statements prepared for registration purposes. Richard refers Norton to Cruz, CPA, who is more competent in the area of registration statements. Cruz performs the audit of Norton's financial statements and subsequently thanks Richard for the referral by giving Richard a portion of the audit fee collected. Richard accepts the fee. Who, if anyone, has violated professional ethics?

A. Only Richard.
B. Both Richard and Cruz.
C. Only Cruz.
D. Neither Richard nor Cruz.

3-36 To emphasize auditor independence from management, many corporations follow the practice of

A. Appointing a partner of the CPA firm conducting the examination to the corporation's audit committee.
B. Establishing a policy of discouraging social contact between employees of the corporation and the staff of the independent auditor.
C. Requesting that a representative of the independent auditor be on hand at the annual stockholders' meeting.
D. Having the independent auditor report to an audit committee of outside members of the board of directors.

3-37 In which of the following circumstances would a CPA be bound by ethics to refrain from disclosing any confidential information obtained during the course of a professional engagement?

A. The CPA is issued a summons enforceable by a court order which orders the CPA to present confidential information.
B. A major stockholder of a client company seeks accounting information from the CPA after management declined to disclose the requested information.
C. Confidential client information is made available as part of a quality review of the CPA's practice by a review team authorized by the AICPA.
D. An inquiry by a disciplinary body of a state CPA society requests confidential client information.

3-38   The AICPA's Code of Professional Ethics would be violated if a CPA accepted a fee for services and the fee was

A.   Fixed by a public authority.
B.   Based on a price quotation submitted in competitive bidding.
C.   Determined, based on the results of judicial proceedings.
D.   Payable after a specified finding was obtained.

3-39   The AICPA's Code of Professional Ethics states, in part, that a CPA should maintain integrity and objectivity. Objectivity in the code refers to a CPA's ability

A.   To maintain an impartial attitude on all matters which come under the CPA's review.
B.   To independently distinguish between accounting practices that are acceptable and those that are not.
C.   To be unyielding in all matters dealing with auditing procedures.
D.   To independently choose between alternate accounting principles and auditing standards.

3-40   Which of the following statements *best* describes why the profession of certified public accountants has deemed it essential to promulgate a code of ethics and to establish a mechanism for enforcing observance of the code?

A.   A distinguishing mark of a profession is its acceptance of responsibility to the public.
B.   A prerequisite to success is the establishment of an ethical code that stresses primarily the professional's responsibility to clients and colleagues.
C.   A requirement of most state laws calls for the profession to establish a code of ethics.
D.   An essential means of self-protection for the profession is the establishment of flexible ethical standards by the profession.

3-41   Jones and Barrow, CPAs, are partners in a public accounting firm that has a large tax practice. Jones is a member of the AICPA. Which of the following is the *best* firm name?

A.   Jones & Barrow, members AICPA.
B.   Jones & Barrow, Tax Accountants.
C.   Jones & Barrow, P.C. (Professional Corporation).
D.   Jones & Barrow, Certified Public Accountants.

3-42   With respect to records in a CPA's possession, rules of conduct provide that

    A.   Copies of client records incorporated into audit workpapers must be returned to the client upon request.

    B.   Worksheets in lieu of a general ledger belong to the auditor and need not be furnished to the client upon request.

    C.   An extensive analysis of inventory prepared by the client at the auditor's request are workpapers which belong to the auditor and need not be furnished to the client upon request.

    D.   The auditor who returns copies of client records must return the original records upon request.

3-43   The AICPA's Code of Professional Ethics requires compliance with accounting principles promulgated by the body designated by the AICPA Council to establish such principles. The pronouncements comprehended by the code include all of the following *except*

    A.   Opinions issued by the Accounting Principles Board.

    B.   AICPA Accounting Research Studies.

    C.   Interpretations issued by the Financial Accounting Standards Board.

    D.   AICPA Accounting Research Bulletins.

3-44   A CPA's retention of client records as a means of enforcing payment of an overdue audit fee is an action that is

    A.   Considered acceptable by the AICPA's Code of Professional Ethics.

    B.   Ill advised since it would impair the CPA's independence with respect to the client.

    C.   Considered discreditable to the profession.

    D.   A violation of generally accepted auditing standards.

3-45   Below are the names of four CPA firms and pertinent facts relating to each firm. Unless otherwise indicated, the individuals named are CPAs and partners, and there are *no* other partners. Which firm name and related facts indicates a violation of the AICPA's Code of Professional Ethics?

    A.   Arthur, Barry, and Clark, CPAs (Clark died about five years ago; Arthur and Barry are continuing the firm).

    B.   Dave and Edwards, CPAs (the name of Fredricks, CPA, a third active partner, is omitted from the firm name).

C. Jones & Co., CPAs, P.C. (the firm is a professional corporation and has ten other stockholders who are all CPAs).

D. George and Howard, CPAs (Howard died three years ago; George is continuing the firm as a sole proprietorship).

3-46   When a CPA prepares a federal income tax return for an audit client, one would expect

A. The CPA to take a position of client advocacy.

B. The CPA to take a position of independent neutrality.

C. The taxable net income in the audited financial statements to agree with taxable net income in the federal income tax return.

D. The expenses in the audited financial statements to agree with the deductions in the federal income tax return.

3-47   Which of the following is not a Management Advisory Service Practice Standard?

A. In performing management advisory service, a practitioner must act with integrity and objectivity and be independent in mental attitude.

B. The management advisory services engagement is to be performed by a person or persons having adequate technical training as a management consultant.

C. Management advisory service engagements are to be performed by practitioners having competence in the analytical approach and process, and in the technical subject matter under consideration.

D. Before undertaking a management advisory service engagement, a practitioner is to notify the client of any reservations regarding anticipated benefits.

3-48   According to the AICPA's Rules of Conduct, contingent fees are permitted by CPAs engaged in tax practice because

A. This practice establishes fees which are commensurate with the value of the services.

B. Attorneys in tax practice customarily set contingent fees.

C. Determinations by taxing authorities are a matter of judicial proceedings which do not involve third parties.

D. The consequences are based upon findings of judicial proceedings or the findings of tax authorities.

3-49   Auditing interpretations, which are issued by the staff of the AICPA's Auditing Standards Division in order to provide timely guidance on the application of pronouncements of the Auditing Standards Board, are

    A.   Less authoritative than a pronouncement of the Auditing Standards Board.

    B.   Equally authoritative as a pronouncement of the Auditing Standards Board.

    C.   More authoritative than a pronouncement of the Auditing Standards Board.

    D.   Nonauthoritative opinions which are issued without consulting members of the Auditing Standards Board.

3-50   It would not be appropriate for the auditor to initiate discussion with the audit committee concerning

    A.   The extent to which the work of internal auditors will influence the scope of the examination.

    B.   Details of the procedures which the auditor intends to apply.

    C.   The extent to which change in the company's organization will influence the scope of the examination.

    D.   Details of potential problems which the auditor believes might cause a qualified opinion.

3-51   The concept of materiality would be least important to an auditor in determining the

    A.   Transactions that should be reviewed.

    B.   Need for disclosure of a particular fact or transactions.

    C.   Scope of the CPA's audit program relating to various accounts.

    D.   Effects of direct financial interests in the client upon the CPA's independence.

3-52   The SEC has strengthened auditor independence by requiring that management

    A.   Engage auditors to report in accordance with the Foreign Corrupt Practices Act.

    B.   Report the nature of disagreements with former auditors.

    C.   Select auditors through audit committees.

    D.   Acknowledge their responsibility for the fairness of the financial statements.

3-53   In accordance with the AICPA's Statements On Responsibilities In Tax Practice, where a question on a federal income tax return has not been answered, the CPA should sign the preparer's declaration only if

A.   The CPA can provide reasonable support for this omission upon examination by IRS.

B.   The information requested is not available.

C.   The question is not applicable to the taxpayer.

D.   An explanation of the reason for the omission is provided.

3-54   A CPA while performing tax services for a client may learn of a material error in a previously filed tax return. In such an instance the CPA should

A.   Prepare an affidavit with respect to the error.

B.   Recommend compensating for the prior year's error in the current year's tax return where such action will mitigate the client's cost and inconvenience.

C.   Advise the client to file a corrected return regardless of whether or not the error resulted in an overstatement or understatement of tax.

D.   Inform the IRS of the error.

3-55   A CPA, who is a member of the American Institute of Certified Public Accountants, wrote an article for publication in a professional journal. The AICPA's Code of Professional Ethics would be violated if the CPA allowed the article to state that the CPA was

A.   A member of the American Institute of Certified Public Accountants.

B.   A professor at a school of professional accountancy.

C.   A partner in a national CPA firm.

D.   A practitioner specialized in providing tax services.

3-56   A CPA accepts an engagement for a professional service without violating the AICPA's Code of Professional Ethics if the service involves

A.   The preparation of cost projections for submission to a governmental agency as an application for a rate increase, and the fee will be paid if there is a rate increase.

B.   Tax preparation and the fee will be based on whether the CPA signs the tax return prepared.

C.   A litigatory matter, and the fee is not known but is to be determined by a district court.

D.   Tax return preparation, and the fee is to be based on the amount of taxes saved, if any.

3-57   The AICPA's Code of Professional Ethics states that a CPA shall not disclose any confidential information obtained in the course of a professional engagement except with the consent of the client. This rule should be understood to preclude a CPA from responding to an inquiry made by

A.   The trial board of the AICPA.
B.   An investigative body of a state CPA society.
C.   A CPA-shareholder of the client corporation.
D.   An AICPA voluntary quality review body.

3-58   Inclusion of which of the following in a promotional brochure published by a CPA firm would be most likely to result in a violation of the AICPA rules of conduct?

A.   Names and addresses, telephone numbers, number of partners, office hours, foreign language competence, and date the firm was established.
B.   Services offered and fees for such services, including hourly rates and fixed fees.
C.   Educational and professional attainments, including date and place of certification, schools attended, dates of graduation, degrees received, and memberships in professional associations.
D.   Names, addresses and telephone numbers of the firm's clients, including the number of years served.

3-59   The AICPA's Code of Professional Ethics provides, where a CPA is required to express an opinion on combined or consolidated financial statements which include a subsidiary, branch, or other component audited by another independent public accountant, that the CPA may

A.   Insist on auditing any such component which the CPA judges necessary to warrant the expression of an opinion.
B.   Insist only on performing a review of any such component.
C.   Not insist on auditing any such component but may request copies of all worksheets relevant to the other independent public accountant's examinations.
D.   Not insist on auditing any such component or reviewing worksheets belonging to the other independent public accountant.

3-60   When a CPA is associated with the preparation of forecasts, all of the following should be disclosed except the

A.   Sources of information.
B.   Character of the work performed by the CPA.
C.   Major assumptions in the preparation of the forecasts.
D.   Probability of achieving estimates.

3-61   Inclusion of which of the following statements in a CPA's advertisement is not acceptable pursuant to the AICPA's Code of Professional Ethics?

A.   Paul Fall
     Certified Public Accountant
     Fluency in Spanish and French
B.   Paul Fall
     Certified Public Accountant
     J.D., Evans Law School 1964
C.   Paul Fall
     Certified Public Accountant
     Free Consultation
D.   Paul Fall
     Certified Public Accountant
     Endorsed by AICPA

3-62   In which one of the following situations would a CPA be in violation of the AICPA's Code of Professional Ethics in determining his fee?

A.   A fee based on whether the CPA's report on the client's financial statements results in the approval of a bank loan.
B.   A fee based on the outcome of a bankruptcy proceeding.
C.   A fee based on the nature of the service rendered and the CPA's particular expertise instead of the actual time spent on the engagement.
D.   A fee based on the fee charged by the prior auditor.

3-63   Reed, a partner in a local CPA firm, performs free accounting services for a private club of which Reed is treasurer. Which of the following would be the most preferable manner for Reed to issue the financial statements of the club?

A.   On the firm's letterhead with a disclaimer for lack of independence.

B. On the firm's letterhead with a disclaimer for unaudited financial statements.

C. On plain paper with no reference to Reed so that Reed will not be associated with the statements.

D. On the club's letterhead with Reed signing as treasurer.

3-64 A CPA, while performing an audit, strives to achieve independence in appearance in order to

A. Reduce risk and liability.
B. Maintain public confidence in the profession.
C. Become independent in fact.
D. Comply with the generally accepted standards of field work.

3-65 Which of the following is required for a firm to designate itself "Member of the American Institute of Certified Public Accountants" on its letterhead?

A. At least one of the partners must be a member.
B. The partners whose names appear in the firm name must be members.
C. All partners must be members.
D. The firm must be a dues paying member.

3-66 Which of the following actions should be avoided by a CPA?

A. A CPA, who is in public practice, agrees to be the committee chairperson for a local fund-raising activity.
B. A CPA, who is an officer of a local bank, arranges a loan for another CPA, who is in private practice.
C. A CPA, who is in public practice, prepares a tax return for a friend without a fee and does *not* sign the return.
D. A CPA, who is retired from public practice, accepts a finder's fee from a public relations company for introducing a former client to that firm.

3-67 Which of the following *most* completely describes how independence has been defined by the CPA profession?

A. Performing an audit from the viewpoint of the public.
B. Avoiding the appearance of significant interests in the affairs of an audit client.
C. Possessing the ability to act with integrity and objectivity.
D. Accepting responsibility to act professionally and in accordance with a professional code of ethics.

3-68   In accordance with the AICPA's Statements On Responsibilities In Tax Practice, if after having provided tax advice to a client there are legislative changes which affect the advice provided, the CPA

A.   Is obligated to notify the client of the change and the effect thereof.

B.   Is obligated to notify the client of the change and the effect thereof if the client was not advised that the advice was based on existing laws which are subject to change.

C.   *Cannot* be expected to notify the client of the change unless the obligation is specifically undertaken by agreement.

D.   *Cannot* be expected to have knowledge of the change.

3-69   The AICPA's Committee on Management Services has stated its belief that a CPA should *not* undertake a management advisory service engagement for implementation of the CPA's recommendations unless

A.   The client has made a firm decision to proceed with implementation based on a complete undertaking and consideration of alternatives.

B.   The client does *not* understand the nature and implications of the recommended course of action.

C.   The client does *not* have sufficient expertise within its organization to comprehend the significance of the changes being made.

D.   The CPA withdraws as independent auditor for the client.

3-70   Cortney has moved to a distant city but desires to continue to retain Blake, CPA, to prepare his personal federal tax return. Blake telephones Cortney after receiving his written list of information to be used in the preparation of the tax return because it appears to contain an understatement of interest expense. Based upon the conversation, Blake learns that the interest expense should be double the amount indicated on the written list. Blake, who asked Cortney to send a photocopy of the support evidence indicating the correct amount of the interest expense, has not received the correspondence and the filing deadline is five days away. Under the circumstances, Blake should

A.   Prepare the return based upon the written information received and *not* sign the preparer's declaration.

B.   Prepare the return based upon the written information received, clearly indicating that an amended return will follow.

C. Prepare the return based upon the written and oral information received.

D. Send Cortney a telegram indicating that no tax return will be prepared until all requested data are received.

☐ BEGINNING THE AUDIT ENGAGEMENT

FAIR PRESENTATION ETHICAL CONDUCT INDEPENDENCE EVIDENCE DUE CARE FAIR PRESENTATION ETHICAL CONDUCT INDEPENDENCE EVIDENCE DUE CARE FAIR PRESENTATION
CARE FAIR PRESENTATION ETHICAL CONDUCT INDEPENDENCE EVIDENCE DUE CARE FAIR PRESENTATION ETHICAL CONDUCT INDEPENDENCE EVIDENCE DUE CARE FAIR PRESENTATI
UE CARE FAIR PRESENTATION ETHICAL CONDUCT INDEPENDENCE EVIDENCE DUE CARE FAIR PRESENTATION ETHICAL CONDUCT INDEPENDENCE EVIDENCE DUE CARE FAIR PRESEN
CE DUE CARE FAIR PRESENTATION ETHICAL CONDUCT INDEPENDENCE EVIDENCE DUE CARE FAIR PRESENTATION ETHICAL CONDUCT INDEPENDENCE EVIDENCE DUE CARE FAIR PRE
DENCE DUE CARE FAIR PRESENTATION ETHICAL CONDUCT INDEPENDENCE EVIDENCE DUE CARE FAIR PRESENTATION ETHICAL CONDUCT INDEPENDENCE EVIDENCE DUE CARE FAIR
EVIDENCE DUE CARE FAIR PRESENTATION ETHICAL CONDUCT INDEPENDENCE EVIDENCE DUE CARE FAIR PRESENTATION ETHICAL CONDUCT INDEPENDENCE EVIDENCE DUE CARE
CE EVIDENCE DUE CARE FAIR PRESENTATION ETHICAL CONDUCT INDEPENDENCE EVIDENCE DUE CARE FAIR PRESENTATION ETHICAL CONDUCT INDEPENDENCE EVIDENCE DUE CA
DENCE EVIDENCE DUE CARE FAIR PRESENTATION ETHICAL CONDUCT INDEPENDENCE EVIDENCE DUE CARE FAIR PRESENTATION ETHICAL CONDUCT INDEPENDENCE EVIDENCE DU

LEARNING OBJECTIVES

After studying this chapter, students should understand

1. The nature of the overall audit process.
2. Mechanisms for soliciting clients.
3. Procedures for investigating new and existing clients, including the required communication between successor and predecessor auditors.
4. The nature of analytic review procedures.
5. The nature of an overall audit plan, including the nature of an overall audit strategy, scheduling the audit work, using the work of a specialist, using the work of internal auditors, and audit programs and their purpose.
6. The nature of audit working papers.

DENCE EVIDENCE DUE CARE FAIR PRESENTATION ETHICAL CONDUCT INDEPENDENCE EVIDENCE DUE CARE FAIR PRESENTATION ETHICAL CONDUCT INDEPENDENCE EVIDENCE D
PENDENCE EVIDENCE DUE CARE FAIR PRESENTATION ETHICAL CONDUCT INDEPENDENCE EVIDENCE DUE CARE FAIR PRESENTATION ETHICAL CONDUCT INDEPENDENCE EVIDENC
NDEPENDENCE EVIDENCE DUE CARE FAIR PRESENTATION ETHICAL CONDUCT INDEPENDENCE EVIDENCE DUE CARE FAIR PRESENTATION ETHICAL CONDUCT INDEPENDENCE EVI
T INDEPENDENCE EVIDENCE DUE CARE FAIR PRESENTATION ETHICAL CONDUCT INDEPENDENCE EVIDENCE DUE CARE FAIR PRESENTATION ETHICAL CONDUCT INDEPENDENCE
DUCT INDEPENDENCE EVIDENCE DUE CARE FAIR PRESENTATION ETHICAL CONDUCT INDEPENDENCE EVIDENCE DUE CARE FAIR PRESENTATION ETHICAL CONDUCT INDEPENDEN
CONDUCT INDEPENDENCE EVIDENCE DUE CARE FAIR PRESENTATION ETHICAL CONDUCT INDEPENDENCE EVIDENCE DUE CARE FAIR PRESENTATION ETHICAL CONDUCT INDEPEN
ICAL CONDUCT INDEPENDENCE EVIDENCE DUE CARE FAIR PRESENTATION ETHICAL CONDUCT INDEPENDENCE EVIDENCE DUE CARE FAIR PRESENTATION ETHICAL CONDUCT IND
ETHICAL CONDUCT INDEPENDENCE EVIDENCE DUE CARE FAIR PRESENTATION ETHICAL CONDUCT INDEPENDENCE EVIDENCE DUE CARE FAIR PRESENTATION ETHICAL CONDUCT
ON ETHICAL CONDUCT INDEPENDENCE EVIDENCE DUE CARE FAIR PRESENTATION ETHICAL CONDUCT INDEPENDENCE EVIDENCE DUE CARE FAIR PRESENTATION ETHICAL COND
TATION ETHICAL CONDUCT INDEPENDENCE EVIDENCE DUE CARE FAIR PRESENTATION ETHICAL CONDUCT INDEPENDENCE EVIDENCE DUE CARE FAIR PRESENTATION ETHICAL C
SENTATION ETHICAL CONDUCT INDEPENDENCE EVIDENCE DUE CARE FAIR PRESENTATION ETHICAL CONDUCT INDEPENDENCE EVIDENCE DUE CARE FAIR PRESENTATION ETHIC
PRESENTATION ETHICAL CONDUCT INDEPENDENCE EVIDENCE DUE CARE FAIR PRESENTATION ETHICAL CONDUCT INDEPENDENCE EVIDENCE DUE CARE FAIR PRESENTATION ET
FAIR PRESENTATION ETHICAL CONDUCT INDEPENDENCE EVIDENCE DUE CARE FAIR PRESENTATION ETHICAL CONDUCT INDEPENDENCE EVIDENCE DUE CARE FAIR PRESENTATIO
RE FAIR PRESENTATION ETHICAL CONDUCT INDEPENDENCE EVIDENCE DUE CARE FAIR PRESENTATION ETHICAL CONDUCT INDEPENDENCE EVIDENCE DUE CARE FAIR PRESENTA
E CARE FAIR PRESENTATION ETHICAL CONDUCT INDEPENDENCE EVIDENCE DUE CARE FAIR PRESENTATION ETHICAL CONDUCT INDEPENDENCE EVIDENCE DUE CARE FAIR PRES
DUE CARE FAIR PRESENTATION ETHICAL CONDUCT INDEPENDENCE EVIDENCE DUE CARE FAIR PRESENTATION ETHICAL CONDUCT INDEPENDENCE EVIDENCE DUE CARE FAIR P
NCE DUE CARE FAIR PRESENTATION ETHICAL CONDUCT INDEPENDENCE EVIDENCE DUE CARE FAIR PRESENTATION ETHICAL CONDUCT INDEPENDENCE EVIDENCE DUE CARE FA
VIDENCE DUE CARE FAIR PRESENTATION ETHICAL CONDUCT INDEPENDENCE EVIDENCE DUE CARE FAIR PRESENTATION ETHICAL CONDUCT INDEPENDENCE EVIDENCE DUE CARE
E EVIDENCE DUE CARE FAIR PRESENTATION ETHICAL CONDUCT INDEPENDENCE EVIDENCE DUE CARE FAIR PRESENTATION ETHICAL CONDUCT INDEPENDENCE EVIDENCE DUE
NCE EVIDENCE DUE CARE FAIR PRESENTATION ETHICAL CONDUCT INDEPENDENCE EVIDENCE DUE CARE FAIR PRESENTATION ETHICAL CONDUCT INDEPENDENCE EVIDENCE C

Chapter 4

Planning the Audit Engagement

This chapter was written by
Thomas E. McKee, Ph.D., C.P.A.,
Professor of Accounting,
East Tennessee State University

INTRODUCTION

This chapter discusses the activities involved in obtaining clients and planning the resulting audit engagements. Detailed audit tests receive the greatest coverage in this text and in the audit literature generally. However, procedures for obtaining clients and planning the audit are equally, and perhaps more, important, because many audit failures result from poor judgment in obtaining (or continuing) clients and planning the audit.

Most people recognize the auditor's responsibility to conform with appropriate professional standards in providing auditing services. The auditor should plan and perform every part of the audit, from performing audit tests to issuing audit reports, with an awareness of the specific and the general professional standards that govern such actions. What many people do not recognize, however, is that some of the professional standards actually apply *prior* to the point when an audit begins and include auditor activities in soliciting prospective clients and accepting new ones. This chapter explains how auditors obtain and plan audit engagements and highlights the professional standards applicable to this process.

THE AUDIT PROCESS

It is necessary to have a general understanding of the overall sequence of audit activities before discussing the process of obtaining and planning audit engagements. This general understanding is helpful for the following reasons:

- Many audit activities depend on other activities that are normally performed at an earlier time.

- Many audit activities that are individually discussed in this chapter are actually performed simultaneously with other activities.

- It is generally easier to understand the individual activities if they can be related to the overall audit process.

The following diagram and explanations provide an overview of the audit process. Of course, a diagram oversimplifies many activities and events and does not illustrate those activities that may be performed simultaneously or concurrently.

In the diagram, the numbers at the bottom and top of each page indicate how the various pages of the diagram fit together. For example, the 1 at the bottom of the first page and the 1 at the top of the second page indicate that the flow of the diagram proceeds from the bottom of the first page to the top of the second page.

Summary Diagram of the
Overall Audit Process

Activity	*Description*

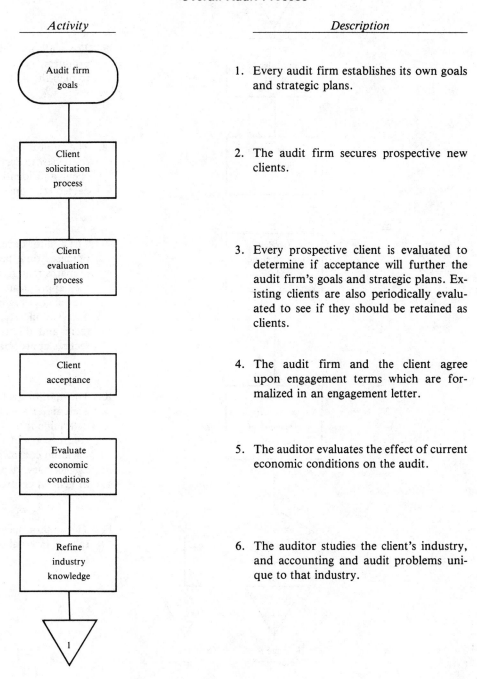

1. Every audit firm establishes its own goals and strategic plans.

2. The audit firm secures prospective new clients.

3. Every prospective client is evaluated to determine if acceptance will further the audit firm's goals and strategic plans. Existing clients are also periodically evaluated to see if they should be retained as clients.

4. The audit firm and the client agree upon engagement terms which are formalized in an engagement letter.

5. The auditor evaluates the effect of current economic conditions on the audit.

6. The auditor studies the client's industry, and accounting and audit problems unique to that industry.

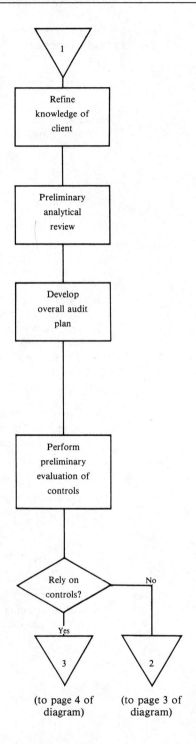

7. The auditor studies the client's business, products, goals, accounting system, etc. to plan the audit.

8. The auditor performs preliminary analytical review to further understanding of the client and identify any unusual or unexpected relationships.

9. The auditor develops an initial audit plan, prepares time budgets for various areas, prepares tentative audit programs, schedules appropriate personnel, confers with the client regarding dates (inventory observation, etc.), meets with the audit team and discusses the audit plan, and secures appropriate specialists, if needed.

10. The auditor evaluates internal controls in each major area of the client's business to determine if they appear reliable. General controls would be reviewed first and application controls would then be reviewed as necessary, dependent on the evaluation of general controls.

11. The auditor decides whether he or she can rely on internal controls.

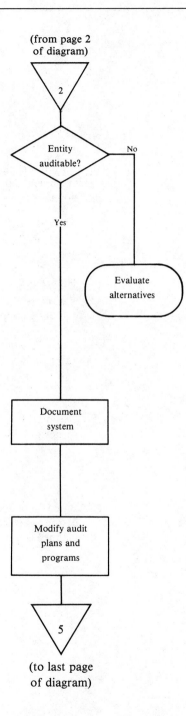

(from page 2
of diagram)

12. If controls may not be relied upon, the auditor must decide whether the entity may be audited using primarily substantive testing.

13. If entity is deemed to not be auditable, the auditor must consider alternatives such as issuing a disclaimer of opinion or withdrawing from the engagement.

14. The auditor will document the accounting system to the extent necessary to aid in designing an audit program which concentrates on substantive testing.

15. The auditor will design appropriate substantive tests, considering apparent control weaknesses.

(to last page
of diagram)

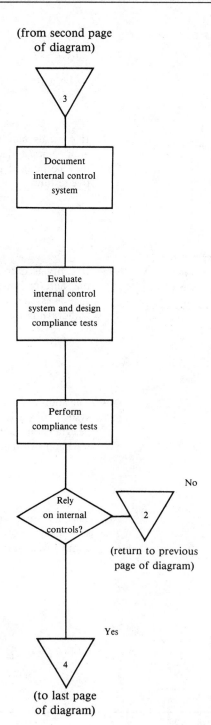

(from second page
of diagram)

16. The internal control system will be documented in detail by flowcharts, questionnaires, and narrative descriptions.

17. The auditor will evaluate strengths and weaknesses in the internal control system and design appropriate compliance tests.

18. The auditor will test the controls he or she wishes to rely on.

19. Based on previous testing, the auditor will decide whether controls he or she had planned to rely on are indeed reliable.

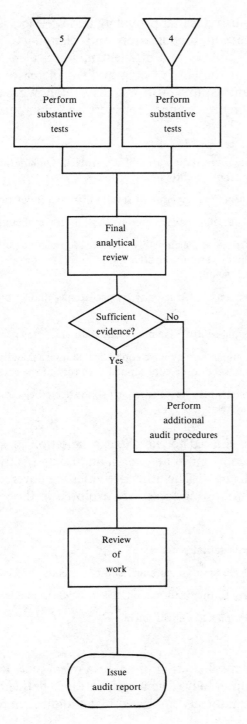

20. The auditor will perform substantive tests such as inventory observation, confirmation of cash, receivables, etc. The amount, type, and timing of substantive tests will vary depending on whether or not the auditor was able to place reliance on the internal control system.

21. The auditor will analyze financial statement amounts to identify unexpected or unusual relationships requiring further work. These analyses are a type of substantive testing procedure.

22. The auditor must evaluate whether sufficient evidence has been generated to support an opinion.

23. The auditor will perform additional audit procedures, if warranted. If the auditor cannot generate sufficient evidence, a qualified opinion or disclaimer of opinion may be warranted.

24. The accountant in charge and other appropriate parties, such as audit supervisors and partners, will review work performed to determine adequacy.

25. The auditor will issue the appropriate audit report. This would normally be an unqualified, qualified, adverse, or disclaimer opinion. Normally the auditor will issue a management letter commenting on areas where the client may improve its accounting system or operations.

The diagram illustrates that providing audit services is a complex process requiring careful organization and planning if it is to be accomplished in an orderly and efficient manner. Generally, as the size and complexity of the entity being audited increases, the amount of audit planning and control also increases. Following are some of the factors contributing to the need for increased planning and control for larger clients:

- Generally more audit staff will be involved. On large audits as many as 100 or more auditors may be necessary.

- Large clients may operate in several different industries.

- Large clients may have numerous subsidiaries or operating locations.

- Other offices of the audit firm may be requested to perform parts of the audit at various subsidiaries or branches located in their geographical vicinity.

- Other accounting firms may be performing audit work on various subsidiaries.

- The internal control system of large companies may be very complex.

- Large companies may have sophisticated internal audit staffs whose work may need to be coordinated with that of the external auditor.

- Large clients may have extremely sophisticated electronic data processing systems.

This chapter is limited to the client solicitation process (Activity 2) through the development of an overall audit plan (Activity 9), as shown in the previous diagram. The other activities are covered at other points in this text. The following topics are explored in the remainder of this chapter:

- Client solicitation process
- Client evaluation, acceptance, and continuance procedures
- Obtaining further information about the client and industry
- Planning the audit engagement

CLIENT SOLICITATION PROCESS

The term "client solicitation" may be a misnomer. It is used here for lack of better terminology. Client solicitation is defined as all activities, whether direct or indirect, employed by an audit firm to provide information to current and prospective clients about the firm's name, services, and activities.

Public accounting is a competitive profession. There are numerous accounting firms competing to obtain important new clients. A firm may obtain new clients in large groups when it acquires the practice of another firm, or through merger with another firm. More commonly, however, a firm acquires new clients individually as companies grow to the point where they require auditing services, or as companies become dissatisfied with their current auditors. Changes in audit firms may usually be attributed to one of the following reasons:

- The client has adopted the policy of regular auditor rotation (3 to 5 year rotation is typical).

- The client bases auditor choice on competitive bidding (discussed in more detail later).

- The client and the auditor disagree on the treatment of accounting or auditing matters.

- The client desires an improved image by association with a better-known auditing firm.

- The client desires an auditor who can provide services its former auditor could not (e.g., expertise in SEC work or a broader range of management advisory services).

However, regardless of the reasons for changing auditors, the competitive nature of the public accounting profession makes it imperative that CPA firms continually strive to develop new business. Four mechanisms for soliciting clients are:

- Community visibility
- Referrals
- Prospective clients soliciting bids for audit services
- Advertising

These methods are discussed in the subsequent paragraphs.

Community Visibility

One traditional way to obtain new clients is for the auditing firm to maintain a high degree of visibility in the communities it wishes to serve. This visibility may be accomplished by service in charitable organizations such as the United Fund, participation in community organizations such as the Lion's Club or Kiwanis, or service in religious organizations such as local churches. It may also be accomplished by membership in various organizations that are primarily social, such as the local country club. Accountants wishing to expand their practice typically seek organizations where they will be in contact with people who may at some time need accounting or auditing services. The contacts are usually individuals who are business executives or professional persons.

Many fruitful personal and business relationships have originated from friendships formed in organizations such as those mentioned above. This advantage does not imply, however, that accountants do not have a legitimate interest and concern for the purposes and activities of the organizations they are participating in. Such an interest and concern must be present in order for the accountant to participate effectively in the organization.

Referrals

Another traditional mechanism for obtaining new clients is by referral. Referral of prospective clients may be done by individuals who have dealt with the audit firm in the past and were impressed with the individuals in the audit firm and the quality of the firm's work. The principal source of such referrals is usually satisfied clients who tend to contribute greatly to the reputation of a firm. Other individuals in a position of influence to recommend accounting services are bankers, attorneys, and investment advisors.

Prospective Clients Soliciting Bids for Audit Services

Certain types of clients are often obtained by submitting a competitive bid for audit work. This type of work is typically for entities that are organizational units of the federal, state, or local governments. They normally advertise for bids before awarding the audit. A bid of this type results in a fixed price for the audit.

The AICPA formerly had an ethics rule prohibiting competitive bidding. The primary purpose of the rule was to prevent price competition that may have resulted in substandard work due to efforts to meet a low bid price. As indicated in Chapter 3, the ethical prohibition of competitive bidding was dropped by the AICPA in 1973 under threat of anti-trust prosecution by the U.S. Justice Department. Some state boards of accountancy still have ethical prohibitions against competitive bidding although these prohibitions may not stand up if tested in court.

Advertising

The newest mechanism for obtaining clients is formal advertising. It is new because the AICPA formerly had an ethics rule prohibiting advertising which was lifted in 1978. As indicated in Chapter 3, the AICPA's *Code of Professional Ethics* now permits advertising that is *not false, misleading,* or *deceptive.* Several state boards of accountancy still have ethical prohibitions against advertising in general. In view of a recent Supreme Court decision concerning the legal profession, it is believed that state ethics rules would *not* be upheld by the courts. The Supreme Court decision indicated that general advertising prohibitions are unwarranted restrictions on the right to free speech.

Since advertising is relatively new and is still used by only a small portion of the accounting profession, it is extremely difficult to determine the effectiveness of it in the client solicitation process. Most advertising that has been done has been the type that simply publicized the accounting firm's name, business locations, and general types of services offered. Exhibit 4-1 contains an example of a recent advertisement.

CLIENT EVALUATION, ACCEPTANCE AND CONTINUANCE PROCEDURES

Although auditors go to a great deal of time and expense to obtain prospective new clients, they do not automatically agree to provide audit services to any firm or individual who appears to be able to pay the audit fee. Both prudence and GAAS require that prospective clients be evaluated to determine whether they should be accepted.

Statement on Quality Control Standards 1, System of Quality Control for a CPA Firm, makes the following statement:

> **Acceptance and Continuance of Clients.** Policies and procedures should be established for deciding whether to accept or continue a client in order to minimize the likelihood of association with a client whose management lacks integrity. Suggesting that there should be procedures for this purpose does not imply that a firm vouches for the integrity or reliability of a client, nor does it imply that a firm has a duty to anyone but itself with respect to the acceptance, rejection, or retention of clients. However, prudence suggests that a firm be selective in determining its professional relationships.

Evaluation of Prospective Clients

The amount of investigation that is done on prospective new clients varies with how familiar the CPA firm is with the company. Large, well-known public companies ordinarily would not be investigated to the extent that smaller, privately-held companies would be. Frequently, some or all of this investigation may be done in conjunction with the client solicitation process.

Evaluation procedures might include the following:

- Requesting credit information about the prospective client from credit agencies. Such investigative procedures are subject to the Fair Credit Reporting Act of 1971.

Figure 4-1

Example of Advertising by National Accounting Firm

We have exan... the relatio... for the years the... ...78 and 1977 and the ...financial position and the ...anges in financial position for the years then auditing ...generally accepted auditing standards a...ch tests of the accounting records and such other auditing ...considered necessary in the circumstances present fairly the financial and generally accepted the Company at December 31, 1978 and 1977 and the results of its operations generally changes in its financial position for the years then ended, in conformity with generally accepted accounting principles applied on a consistent basis.

In our opinion, such financial statements present fairly the financial position of the Company at December 31, 1978 and 1977 and the results of its operations and the changes in its financial position for the years then ended, in conformity with generally accepted accounting principles applied on a consistent basis.

Deloitte Haskins & Sells

February 10, 1979

Your accountants should look beyond your bottom line. Your accountants should look at your business.

An accounting firm has to be conscientious about examining your financial statements, obviously.

But your accountants ought to be conscientious about reviewing your business, too — and helping you improve it.

At Deloitte Haskins & Sells, we think this often takes a specialized knowledge of your industry. Its accounting practices. Its regulatory environment. Its financial pressures.

So, we've organized teams to focus on the unique needs of specific industries.

The results? Well, look at some examples.

From our hospital experience, we just came up with ways to simplify SHUR—the system of uniform hospital reporting proposed by the Department of Health, Education and Welfare. Our approach would deliver essentially the data HEW wants, but at far less cost.

Or take municipal government. We showed some cities the best way to apply for Federal mass transit funds (and helped them get their fair share).

And from our knowledge of life insurance companies, we developed a computer program that lets them quickly run through their tax alternatives, to choose the one that hurts the least.

No two industries are exactly alike—any more than accounting firms are.

We think that when you treat a client's needs as something special, the results can be pretty special, too.

Deloitte Haskins+Sells
Beyond the bottom line

- Reviewing previous financial statements of the prospective client for unusual or controversial items.

- Inquiring about the prospective client's previous auditors. This is mandatory and is discussed in more detail in subsequent paragraphs.

- Asking third parties—such as the prospective client's banks, legal counsel, investment bankers, and others in the financial and business community—about the prospective client's reputation.

- Evaluating the financial stability of the prospective client. Clients threatened with insolvency or bankruptcy may have a higher propensity to intentionally misrepresent the financial statements.

- Evaluating the audit firm's ability to provide industry expertise and manpower sufficient to staff the engagement properly.

- Evaluating the timing of the engagement. Late appointment may prevent the auditor from performing procedures necessary to render an unqualified opinion.

Some national firms have a policy of accepting a few marginal clients because they feel that it is the responsibility of the public accounting profession to serve all business entities that need accounting or audit services provided by CPA firms.

Exhibit 4-2 is an example of a report that might be prepared to document information about a new client.

Communication With Predecessor Auditor

Guidance on communications when a change in auditors has taken place or is in process is found in *SAS No. 7, Communication Between Predecessor and Successor Auditors*. This statement requires that a successor auditor contact, either orally or in writing, the predecessor auditor for information that will help the successor auditor in deciding whether to accept the engagement. A "successor" auditor is one who has been invited to make a proposal for an engagement or who has tentatively accepted an engagement. Because of the ethical rule on disclosing confidential information, the predecessor auditor must obtain the client's permission before releasing any data, and all information exchanged must be held in confidence by both the successor and predecessor auditors.

If a client refuses to allow contact between predecessor and successor auditors, a successor will usually decline the engagement, unless the client has a good reason for the refusal, such as pending litigation. If a client does not have a good reason, the presumption is that the client is trying to conceal significant matters.

Exhibit 4-2
New Client Report[1]

Office _____
Date _____

Client's name _____ Fiscal year _____
Address _____
Phone _____ Major contact at client _____ Title _____
Nature of business _____ S.I.C. code number* _____
Latest year _____ Sales _____ Profits _____
Form of Organization: ☐ Individual ☐ Partnership ☐ Corporation ☐ Other-indicate _____
Publicly held: ☐ no ☐ yes-indicate: ☐ O.T.C.; ☐ N.Y.S.E.; ☐ A.S.E.; ☐ Other _____
a. Source of client: ☐ Personal acquaintance of partner or staff member; ☐ Client; ☐ Attorney;
     ☐ Bank; ☐ Another office, new client; ☐ Another office, existing client; ☐ Other _____
b. Name of source _____
c. Name of partner or staff member responsible for source contact _____
d. Acknowledgment to source by _____
Partner in charge _____ Client code number _____
Nature of assignment and assignment code number:
       ☐ Audit _____   ☐ Tax returns _____   ☐ MAS _____
       ☐ Compilation of Financial   ☐ Special tax _____   ☐ Monthly service _____
          Statements _____
       ☐ Review of Financial
          Statement _____
Estimated fees: a) Annual _____ b) Nonrecurring or special _____
Previous auditors _____
Reason for change (if known) _____
Attorney and law firm _____
                                          State unemployment   Sales tax
Federal identification no. _____   insurance no. _____   registration no. _____
Comments re assignment, fees, audit, etc. _____
Related clients, parent, or affiliates _____
_____

Approved _____   By _____
         Managing Partner   Account Administrator

INSTRUCTIONS

1. This report should be prepared on all new clients.
2. This report should also be prepared when an existing client is transferred from one office of the firm to another.
3. Multiple copies of this report should be prepared and distributed as indicated at the top of each copy.
4. Estimated fees must be recorded.
5. The report must be approved by the managing partner.

* Standard industrial classification code number.

---

[1]*Audit and Accounting Manual*, AU 3400.05, copyright 1979, American Institute of Certified Public Accountants, Inc.

SAS No. 7 requires that certain information be solicited by successor auditors, and it also suggests that obtaining other information may be helpful. Required successor-predecessor communication should include inquiries concerning:

- The integrity of management.

- Predecessor-client disagreements about accounting principles, auditing procedures, or similarly significant matters.

- The predecessor's understanding of the reasons for the change of auditors.

Suggested information inquiries may include:

- Review of a predecessor's working papers. This review would normally be limited to the single successor auditor actually accepting the engagement.

- Specific inquiries of matters the successor auditor believes may affect the conduct of his or her examination such as audit areas requiring inordinate amounts of time or problems stemming from the condition of the client's accounting system and records.

The purpose of *SAS No. 7* is to ensure that auditors considering new clients have the benefit of the previous auditor's knowledge concerning management and significant accounting and auditing problems that may exist. This information will prevent auditors from accepting "problem" clients without a reasonable knowledge of what they are becoming involved in.

If during the course of the engagement a successor auditor obtains information suggesting that previous financial statements may require revision, the successor should try to arrange a meeting with the client and the predecessor auditor to resolve the matter. The predecessor auditor may be required to take action (under *SAS No. 1*, Section 561) to correct previously issued financial statements that he or she was associated with. If the situation is not satisfactorily resolved in this manner, the successor auditor should consult an attorney to determine what further action to take.[2]

Engagement Letters

Once an audit firm and client have agreed on the nature and terms of the engagement, a recommended, but not required, procedure is to docu-

---

[2] *Statement on Standards for Accounting and Review Services No. 4, Communication Between Successor and Predecessor Accountants*, provides similar communication standards regarding compilation and review services for nonpublic clients. However, for these clients the communication is encouraged but not required.

ment this understanding in writing with an engagement letter. As explained in Chapter 1, the engagement letter spells out in detail the responsibilities of both parties and, when signed by both parties, becomes a contract between them. Although auditing or accounting and review services standards do not require engagement letters, the following list contains some good reasons why CPA firms should require engagement letters for all parts of their practice:

- **Reduced Chance of a Misunderstanding With the Client.** The engagement letter puts into writing the oral agreement between the auditor and the client. If an oral miscommunication has occurred, the client has an opportunity to correct it before signing the engagement letter.

- **Better Communication With Audit Staff.** The audit staff may not have been party to the negotiations and agreement with the client. A copy of the engagement letter gives them an authoritative source to supplement their oral instructions.

- **Reduced Legal Liability.** Since the engagement letter clearly spells out the services the accountant will perform, it should prevent a subsequent assertion regarding those contractual duties that were agreed upon.

- **Better Practice Management.** A written agreement helps the executive partner determine that the engagement will contribute to firm objectives with respect to types of services, fee structure, etc. It also helps in the drafting of extensions or amendments in later periods, particularly by accountants who may not have participated in the original agreement.

Engagement letters should be tailored to fit the needs of specific engagements. No single letter is suitable for all circumstances. An illustrative engagement letter was presented in Chapter 1.

Client Continuance

Auditors must not only decide whether to accept new clients; they also should periodically review their list of current clients and remove those clients the firm no longer wants to be associated with. Reasons for discontinuing clients might include:

- Evidence indicating a client's management may lack integrity.

- Continued non-payment of audit fees.

- Difficulty in working with client personnel.

- Inability to negotiate an acceptable increase in the audit fee.

- Client need for specialized services the current audit firm is unable or unwilling to provide.

UNDERSTANDING THE CLIENT AND INDUSTRY

As the diagram of the audit process shows, the next steps in the audit process after obtaining a signed engagement letter (Step 4) are to evaluate current economic conditions (Step 5), refine the auditor's knowledge of the client's industry (Step 6), refine the auditor's knowledge of the client (Step 7), and perform preliminary analytical review procedures (Step 8). These steps are essentially information-gathering processes which help the auditor comply with the first standard of field work: "The work is to be adequately planned and assistants, if any, are to be properly supervised." By gathering this information, the auditor will be able to recognize the client's unique aspects and potential problem areas. Such recognition is essential for proper planning.

This data-gathering process surprises some observers because many companies, particularly in the same industry, appear to be very similar. However, every company, and therefore every audit, is unique in some respects,—for example, management style, method of financing, or operating locations. The audit engagement should be tailored around the unique characteristics of the individual client. For example, a client with significant inventory saleability problems would require more audit work on inventory valuation.

SAS No. 22, Planning and Supervision, defines audit planning and lists some planning factors the auditor should consider. Audit planning involves developing an overall strategy for the expected conduct and scope of the examination. The nature, extent, and timing of planning vary with the size and complexity of the entity's business. In planning the examination, the auditor should consider the following:

- Matters relating to the entity's business and the industry in which it operates.
- The entity's accounting policies and procedures.
- Anticipated reliance on internal accounting control.
- Preliminary estimates of materiality levels for audit purposes.
- Financial statement items likely to require adjustment.
- Conditions that may require extension or modification of audit tests, such as the possibility of material errors or irregularities or the existence of related party transactions.
- The nature of reports expected to be rendered.

EVALUATING CURRENT ECONOMIC CONDITIONS

Since every company is affected to some extent by the overall economy it operates in, the auditor must know enough about current economic conditions to evaluate events that may have a significant impact on the financial statements. The auditor can learn much about the economy from reading regular business publications such as *The Wall Street Journal* or *Business Week*. This knowledge base is essential if the auditor is to evaluate the client's transactions. For example, an auditor who knows that the national prime loan rate is approximately 15 percent might question why a client obtained a loan at a 20 percent rate. Such an investigation might reveal that the client did not qualify for the prime rate, or it could possibly reveal a related-party transaction.

The auditor must be able to do more than check the mechanics of transactions. He or she must have the business judgment necessary to determine if significant transactions make business sense.

OBTAIN KNOWLEDGE OF CLIENT'S INDUSTRY

The auditor must obtain knowledge of the client's industry for the same reason he or she obtains knowledge of current economic conditions: to see if transactions and activities make sense and conform to normal industry practice. If a client uses an accounting method different from the normal method employed in the industry, the CPA must be aware of the industry accounting method to determine if the client's method is appropriate.

Many potential sources of information provide the CPA with knowledge about industries. Almost every industry has one or more trade magazines which contain helpful information. Government agencies typically publish statistics on many industries. Also, many industries have trade associations which publish data on members. The AICPA publishes accounting and audit guides for various industries. Another source is financial statements of key competitors in the same industry. Finally, data is published by many regular business periodicals. Industry statistics may be obtained from sources such as Dun and Bradstreets' *Key Business Ratios* or Robert Morris Associates' *Annual Statement Studies*. An example of statistics developed by the latter source is contained in Exhibit 4-3.

REFINE KNOWLEDGE OF CLIENT

SAS No. 22, Planning and Supervision, requires that the auditor be familiar with the client's business, its organization, and its operating characteristics so that he or she will have sufficient information to plan

Exhibit 4-3
Robert Morris Associates Statistics[3]

MANUFACTURERS · ELECTRONIC COMPUTING EQUIPMENT
SIC# 3573

	Current Data						Comparative Historical Data		
	67(6/30-9/30/78)		67(10/1/78-3/31/79)				6/30/76 3/31/77	6/30/77 3/31/78	6/30/78 3/31/79
0-250M	250M-1MM	1-10MM	10-50MM	ALL		ASSET SIZE	ALL	ALL	ALL
3	25	58	48	134		NUMBER OF STATEMENTS	128	110	134
%	%	%	%	%		**ASSETS**	%	%	%
	9.9	7.7	7.0	8.1		Cash & Equivalents	8.6	6.1	8.1
	29.6	29.6	31.7	30.4		Accts. & Notes Rec.- Trade(net)	30.6	32.3	30.4
	27.6	30.0	31.7	30.0		Inventory	30.8	32.3	30.0
	2.0	2.9	3.0	2.7		All Other Current	2.5	3.0	2.7
	69.0	70.2	73.5	71.3		Total Current	72.4	73.7	71.3
	23.3	21.0	19.5	20.9		Fixed Assets (net)	18.9	17.9	20.9
	.7	1.0	1.4	1.1		Intangibles (net)	1.4	1.4	1.1
	6.9	7.8	5.7	6.8		All Other Non-Current	7.2	7.0	6.8
	100.0	100.0	100.0	100.0		Total	100.0	100.0	100.0
						LIABILITIES			
	12.2	8.6	7.0	8.7		Notes Payable-Short Term	11.9	9.6	8.7
	7.5	3.2	2.1	3.7		Cur. Mat.-L/T/D	3.8	3.9	3.7
	15.2	15.2	13.1	14.3		Accts. & Notes Payable - Trade	14.4	16.0	14.3
	8.5	8.4	9.4	8.7		Accrued Expenses	7.9	9.5	8.7
	5.8	6.0	3.5	5.0		All Other Current	4.5	7.4	5.0
	49.2	41.5	35.0	40.4		Total Current	42.5	46.4	40.4
	15.5	17.5	17.7	17.2		Long Term Debt	17.8	15.7	17.2
	3.6	3.2	2.1	2.8		All Other Non-Current	2.8	3.2	2.8
	31.8	37.8	45.2	39.6		Net Worth	36.8	34.8	39.6
	100.0	100.0	100.0	100.0		Total Liabilities & Net Worth	100.0	100.0	100.0
						INCOME DATA			
	100.0	100.0	100.0	100.0		Net Sales	100.0	100.0	100.0
	58.2	60.0	62.0	60.4		Cost Of Sales	64.6	60.8	60.4
	41.8	40.0	38.0	39.6		Gross Profit	35.4	39.2	39.6
	36.8	30.9	26.8	30.5		Operating Expenses	33.2	29.9	30.5
	5.0	9.1	11.2	9.2		Operating Profit	2.2	9.2	9.2
	4.4	.8	1.3	0		All Other Expenses (net)	1.8	1.8	0
	9.4	8.3	9.8	9.2		Profit Before Taxes	.4	7.5	9.2
						RATIOS			
	2.0	2.3	2.9	2.6			3.0	2.7	2.6
	1.5	1.7	2.4	1.9		Current	2.1	1.9	1.9
	1.0	1.3	1.9	1.4			1.4	1.3	1.4
	1.2	1.4	1.7	1.5			1.7	1.5	1.5
	.8	.9	1.2	1.0		Quick	1.0	1.0	1.0
	.5	.7	.9	.7			.7	.7	.7
39	9.3	51 7.1	58 6.3	52 7.0			56 6.5	53 6.9	52 7.0
53	6.9	64 5.7	73 5.0	63 5.8		Sales/Receivables	68 5.4	66 5.5	63 5.8
72	5.1	78 4.7	104 3.5	83 4.4			89 4.1	94 3.9	83 4.4
31	11.6	87 4.2	94 3.9	76 4.8			78 4.7	76 4.8	76 4.8
53	6.9	122 3.0	126 2.9	118 3.1		Cost of Sales/Inventory	118 3.1	126 2.9	118 3.1
159	2.3	166 2.2	174 2.1	174 2.1			166 2.2	166 2.2	174 2.1
	5.4	3.5	2.9	3.2			3.0	3.3	3.2
	9.9	5.6	3.7	5.2		Sales/Working Capital	4.4	4.8	5.2
	-INF	10.5	5.4	10.3			8.2	8.9	10.3
	10.2	10.6	16.0	11.9			14.1	17.9	11.9
(21)	5.8	(48) 4.1	(39) 7.3 (111)	5.9		EBIT/Interest	(102) 4.0	(92) 6.2 (111)	5.9
	1.9	1.9	4.6	2.6			1.1	2.7	2.6
	8.3	25.6	20.7	20.3			9.7	19.5	20.3
(14)	3.3	(40) 7.1	(25) 5.8 (81)	5.8		Cash Flow/Cur. Mat. L/T/D	(79) 2.5	(60) 5.2 (81)	5.8
	.2	1.2	2.6	1.7			.7	1.9	1.7
	.2	.3	.2	.2			.2	.3	.2
	.6	.6	.4	.5		Fixed/Worth	.4	.4	.5
	1.0	1.0	.7	.9			.9	.8	.9
	1.5	.9	.7	.8			.7	.8	.8
	2.0	1.7	1.2	1.6		Debt/Worth	1.4	1.6	1.6
	3.8	3.0	2.6	3.0			3.4	3.2	3.0
	62.6	57.0	45.9	53.7		% Profit Before Taxes/Tangible	43.0	59.3	53.7
(23)	35.2	(57) 34.3	(46) 32.3 (129)	34.3		Net Worth	(119) 24.8 (104)	32.6 (129)	34.3
	17.3	16.8	20.1	18.7			3.4	17.9	18.7
	21.4	24.6	24.4	23.3		% Profit Before Taxes/Total	20.8	23.4	23.3
	15.5	13.4	15.6	14.9		Assets	10.0	14.7	14.9
	7.8	5.3	7.0	6.6			.6	5.6	6.6
	24.7	15.3	14.2	15.8			19.0	18.0	15.8
	10.9	8.2	7.9	8.6		Sales/Net Fixed Assets	9.2	10.7	8.6
	4.3	4.6	5.0	4.8			5.7	6.6	4.8
	2.7	2.0	1.7	2.0			2.0	2.1	2.0
	2.1	1.5	1.4	1.6		Sales/Total Assets	1.5	1.6	1.6
	1.4	1.3	1.2	1.3			1.2	1.3	1.3
	1.1	1.1	1.5	1.2			1.5	1.3	1.2
(22)	2.2	(52) 2.0	(38) 2.3 (115)	2.0		% Depr. Dep. Amort./Sales	(116) 2.6	(93) 2.0 (115)	2.0
	4.8	2.9	3.8	3.7			4.4	3.2	3.7
	1.4	1.0	.9	1.0			1.3	1.0	1.0
(12)	2.3	(30) 1.4	(15) 1.5 (60)	1.5		% Lease & Rental Exp/Sales	(67) 1.9	(51) 1.6 (60)	1.5
	3.4	1.9	2.2	2.6			3.2	1.9	2.6
				3.4			2.4	3.0	3.4
			(17)	4.8		% Officers' Comp/Sales	(12) 4.0	(15) 5.1 (17)	4.8
				6.4			11.7	8.9	6.4
999M	27165M	384589M	1523024M	1935777M		Net Sales ($)	1619061M	1452444M	1935777M
414M	12949M	241570M	1061246M	1316179M		Total Assets ($)	1218700M	947556M	1316179M

© Robert Morris Associates 1979

M = $thousand   MM = $million
See Pages 1 through 10 for Explanation of Ratios and Data

[3] Robert Morris Associates *Annual Statement Studies: 1979*, p. 100.

and perform the examination. A knowledge of economic conditions and the industry environment, as previously discussed, are part of this knowledge. In addition, the auditor also needs specific information about the client. According to *SAS No. 22*, decisions in the following areas are clarified by the auditor's knowledge of the client:

- Identifying areas that may need special consideration.
- Assessing conditions under which accounting data are produced, processed, reviewed, and accumulated within the organization.
- Evaluating the reasonableness of estimates, such as valuation of inventories, depreciation, allowances for doubtful accounts, and percentage of completion of long-term contracts.
- Evaluating the reasonableness of management representations.
- Making judgments about the appropriateness of the accounting principles applied and the adequacy of disclosures.

Obviously an auditor obtains some knowledge of the client in the engagement acceptance process. However, further detailed knowledge is usually necessary prior to planning specific audit procedures. The auditor will perform procedures such as the following to acquire additional information about the client:

- Reviewing the prior year's audit working papers, and annual and interim financial statements.
- Discussing items that may affect the audit with accounting firm personnel who provide non-audit services to the entity—for example, tax department personnel.
- Reading the current year's interim financial statements.
- Considering the potential effects of accounting and auditing pronouncements on the client.
- Reviewing previous SEC filings of the client.
- Identifying related parties by inquiry of management, review of SEC filings, and examination of stockholder listings.
- Touring client operating facilities and offices.
- Reading the minutes of recent meetings of directors and stockholders.
- Determining important government regulations which apply to the client.
- Reviewing internal audit reports.
- Reviewing important continuing contracts.
- Performing analytical review procedures (discussed on the next page).

ANALYTICAL REVIEW PROCEDURES

In refining his or her knowledge of the client the auditor also uses analytic review procedures. Analytical review is the study of an entity's accounting data to determine the entity's essential characteristics and the relationships among accounting data, such as the relationship among account balances. If an auditor understands the nature of an entity and the relationships among accounting data, then the auditor can identify unusual relationships or items and initiate an investigation or other appropriate action.

One basic assumption underlying analytical review is the existence of meaningful relationships among accounting data such as relationships among account balances, and the continued existence of such relationships in the absence of changed conditions. Understanding the relationships in the accounting data brings one closer to understanding the real economic events that have happened or may happen.

Although not required by auditing standards, analytical review procedures are normally performed in the planning phase of an audit and later during the procedural phase of the audit as substantive tests of financial information. According to *SAS No. 23, Analytical Review Procedures*, analytical review procedures may be employed "in the initial planning stage to assist in determining the nature, extent, and timing of other auditing procedures by identifying, among other things, significant matters that require consideration during the examination." Similarly, Section 320 of *SAS No. 1, Codification of Auditing Standards and Procedures*, describes analytical review procedures as one of the two classes of audit procedures in substantive testing, as follows:

> The evidential matter required by the third standard is obtained through two general classes of auditing procedures: (a) tests of details of transactions and balances and (b) analytical review procedures applied to financial information . . .

Benefits to be obtained from employing analytical review procedures include:

- **Better Understanding of the Audit Client.** By performing analytical review procedures such as ratio analysis, the auditor gains a better understanding of the client. This puts the auditor in a better position to ask meaningful questions of the client, plan the audit engagement, and deal with any problems that may arise.

- **Early Indication of Possible Problems.** Application of analytical review procedures such as discriminant analysis in planning the audit may indicate the client has a high probability of financial failure. By becoming aware of the problem at an early date, the auditor will be in a better position to counsel the client and modify audit plans appropriately.

- **Reduction of Other Audit Tests.**   Since analytical review is one of two types of substantive audit evidence, satisfactory completion of these tests will reduce the need for other audit tests.

- **Indication of Errors.**   Analytical review procedures may indicate that an error has occurred. For example, an auditor's calculation of interest expense based on long-term debt outstanding and the stated interest rate on such debt, may indicate interest expense is understated. Investigation may reveal that some interest payments were improperly debited to an asset account.

- **Recommendations to Client.**   Analytical review procedures may produce data the client was unaware of. For example, an analysis of gross profit by product line may indicate the company is concentrating promotional efforts on products that are relatively unprofitable.

There are really no significant differences in the analytical review procedures themselves when applied for planning purposes or for substantive tests. What is different is the data they are applied to and the significance of any problem area uncovered. In the planning stages of an audit, analytical review procedures typically involve previous year data and/or current period interim data. Problems or unusual relationships discovered at this time are considered in formulating the auditing plan. By uncovering potential problems early in the audit, the auditor will hopefully have done all the work necessary by year-end to have gathered enough competent evidence to support an appropriate opinion. When analytical review procedures are applied as substantive tests, they provide evidence about the reasonableness of amounts or balances in the year-end financial statements. Results of the substantive analytical review procedures contribute evidence as to whether the auditor should continue or modify the investigation of financial statements under audit.

If year-end analytical review procedures indicate a potential problem, the auditor will first ask management to explain the problem. The auditor will then evaluate management's response, considering such factors as the nature of the item, business conditions, the evaluation of internal control, and the results of other auditing procedures. If the auditor decides management's explanation is reasonable, then the auditor may accept management's response to the auditor's question.

No further work or attempts to corroborate management's response by employing other audit procedures would be required unless the matter were very significant.

If management's explanation is unacceptable, then the auditor should perform additional audit procedures to investigate the problem further. Failure to undertake the appropriate follow-up on any material difference or inconsistency revealed by analytical review procedures would be regarded as a failure to fulfill the requirement of due audit care.

Common analytical review procedures, as stated in *SAS No. 23*, include:

- Comparison of current-period data with comparable prior-period data.

- Comparison of current-period data with anticipated results, such as budgets or forecasts.

- Study of the relationships of elements of financial information that would be expected to conform to a predictable pattern based on the entity's experience. For example, if a company had consistently had a 40 percent gross profit margin for the past five years, the auditor would expect the current-year gross profit ratio to be 40 percent in the absence of information to the contrary.

- Comparison of company data with industry data.

- Study of the relationships of the financial information with relevant nonfinancial information. For example, administrative overhead may be related to the square feet of administrative office space the company uses.

Professional judgment is necessary in formulating specific tests. The general types of analytical review procedures may be implemented using dollars, physical quantities, ratios, or percentages.

The following paragraphs briefly discuss some techniques of analytical review.

Ratio Analysis.   Ratio analysis is one of the oldest analytical review procedures. It compares two or more variables in order to describe their relationship in a simpler, more comprehensible manner. An example would be the current ratio, which is the relationship of current assets to current liabilities. This relationship may be expressed as an absolute amount (3 to 1) or as a percentage (300%). Ratios generally relate one of four major economic aspects of a firm's operations:

- Short-term solvency (liquidity)

- Efficiency or activity (turnover)
- Long-term solvency (leverage)
- Profitability

Two basic approaches to using these ratios are time-series analysis, looking at historic behavior over time, or cross-sectional analysis, comparing client data with exogenous norms or standards such as industry norms.

In recent years auditors have used more advanced statistical techniques: these techniques offer several advantages. They are covered in college and university programs; they can be applied with the low cost electronic data processing now available, and they provide more effective and efficient audits without increased fees.

Financial Models.   This technique is actually a combination of other techniques. It is composed of a number of specific techniques used to forecast various elements of the overall financial statements. It is mentioned as a separate technique in order to emphasize its usefulness in analytical review.

Many accounting firms have developed computer-based financial modeling packages that are used primarily to advise and assist clients in a non-audit service context, such as budgeting. These models are useful for auditors because they can create a forecast to compare to actual financial amounts for clients who do not formally prepare their own forecasts. Also, they are useful in validating forecasts of clients who do prepare their own forecasts or budgets.

Time Series Analysis or Trend Analysis.   This category actually encompasses a number of statistical techniques that transform past experience into forecasts of future events. They range from relatively simple techniques such as exponential smoothing, to more sophisticated techniques, such as Box-Jenkins methodology. These techniques may be very helpful in verifying some significant financial statement amounts, such as sales and cost of goods sold.

Regression and Correlation Analysis.   These statistical techniques investigate and formally state the degree of association between variables. By using the formal statistical statement, the auditor can then use one variable to make inferences about the other. For example, the auditor may be able to predict sales based on sales' relationship to such variables as the advertising budget, the bank prime rate, and rate of growth in the consumer price index.

Discriminate Analysis.   This statistical method distinguishes between two or more groups. An equation is developed based on established group relationships for a sample. This equation can then be used to predict whether new observations will fall into one group or another.

Discriminate analysis is most commonly used in auditing to distinguish between going concerns and non-going concerns. Predictions about firm status can be made prior to the audit so auditors can decide whether to accept the client; the predictions can then be used to set the scope of the audit. The auditor can also use these predictions at the conclusion of the audit to decide whether to include a going-concern qualification in the auditor's report.

DEVELOPMENT OF OVERALL AUDIT PLAN

The next step in the audit process is development of an overall audit plan (Step 9 in the diagram). Developing the overall audit plan will usually involve the following specific activities.

- Developing an overall audit strategy.
- Requesting and scheduling appropriate staff personnel.
- Obtaining and coordinating specialists, if needed.
- Considering and coordinating the work with internal auditors.
- Preparing the tentative audit programs.
- Developing appropriate working paper files.

Developing an Overall Audit Strategy

After gathering appropriate information about the client, the industry and the economy, the auditor can develop a *preliminary* audit strategy. It should be emphasized that this strategy is *preliminary* and subject to modification and change if warranted by information developed during the course of the audit.

Audit strategy should include a formal plan to deal with any problem areas identified from information gathered up to that point in the audit. This strategy should also encompass the unique aspects of the client's operations. Many audit firms discuss these items and how they are to be handled in an audit planning memo. For example, if background data on the client indicates a possible excess inventory problem, the audit planning memo should mention this problem and describe how it will be dealt with. It may be necessary to assign an experienced staff accountant to the inventory work in response to the problem.

A unique aspect of the client's operations may be that it has converted to a computer system during the year under audit. This change will undoubtedly increase the time necessary to review and evaluate internal control since part of the year would involve manual controls and part of the year would involve EDP controls.

Developing a proper audit strategy involves considering the following types of questions:

- How much reliance is to be placed on internal control?

- How much work should be performed at interim dates?

- Are EDP audit techniques, such as a generalized audit software package, appropriate?

- Will significant statistical sampling be used?

- How large should the audit team be? How much and what type experience should they have had prior to the audit?

- What are the preliminary estimates of materiality levels?

- What conditions exist that may require the extension of audit procedures?

Scheduling the Audit Work

An audit is similar to many other complex activities in that proper management aids in the orderly and efficient completion of the work. The auditor will consider each area of the audit and will budget a specific amount of time to complete the work in that area.

The time budget is usually organized according to the firm's conceptual approach to the audit. Some firms use a traditional audit approach, commonly called the "related account concept." With this approach audit procedures are performed concurrently on related balance sheet and income statement accounts (e.g., long-term debt and interest expense), using a time budget similar to the one in Exhibit 4-4. Other firms use a version of the contemporary-cycle concept, in which the audit procedures are performed concurrently for accounts in a related processing cycle (e.g., the financing cycle, which includes the receipt of capital funds from investors and creditors, and temporary investment of capital funds). Firms using the contemporary-cycle concept might use a time budget organized around each cycle.

Once the auditor completes the time budget, he or she can use it to supervise the completion of the work and to review completed work. Assuming the time budget is realistic, a completed audit that is significantly over or under budget in any area may indicate a potential problem requiring investigation by the audit reviewer.

When the time budget is completed, the auditor can request the appropriate personnel for the engagement. Since there may be a large

Exhibit 4-4
Audit Time Budget Form[4]

	Date	*Budget*	*Actual*												
Total hours / *Accountant's initials color-coded*	Total														
	Supervisor/manager														
	Senior														
	Assistant														
General	Audit program														
	Prior period reports, workpapers, etc.														
	Trial balance and adjusting entries														
	Permanent file														
	Financial Statement Comparison														
	Transactions since balance sheet date														
	Preparation of reports														
	Internal control questionnaire and management letter														
	Time summary														
	Supervision														
	Correspondence and conferences														
Review in-house computer programs															
Audit of/with computer															
General ledger and journal entries															
Cash	In banks and on hand														
	Receipts and disbursements														
Notes/accounts receivable and allowance for losses															
Inventories	Observation														
	Comparison of Quantities														
	Valuation														
	Clerical accuracy and														
	Analytical review														
Prepaid expenses															
Other current assets															
Fixed assets and depreciation															
Investments and other assets															
Notes payable and long-term debt															
Accounts payable															
Other current liabilities															
Other long-term liabilities and deferred income															
Stockholders' equity															
Contingent liabilities															
Sales and revenue															
Payrolls															
Other expenses and income tests and analysis															
Preparation of tax returns															

[4] *AICPA Audit and Accounting Manual*, AAM 3600.08.

number of sometimes conflicting personnel requests, many firms formalize this process through a scheduling request form similar to the one in Exhibit 4-5. These forms are processed by a designated individual who matches personnel demand with availability.

**Using the
Work of a
Specialist**

In certain engagements an auditor may need skill or knowledge in fields other than accounting or auditing. For example, valuation of real estate may require a real estate appraiser. An auditor is not expected to

---

Exhibit 4-5
Staff Scheduling Request[5]

Client _____ Engagement No. _____ Year-End _____

Partner _____ Manager _____ Tax Ptr/Mgr _____

Personnel requested	Experience level	Interim			Year-End			Total
		From	Thru	Hours	From	Thru	Hours	Hours
_____	_____	_____	_____	_____	_____	_____	_____	_____
_____	_____	_____	_____	_____	_____	_____	_____	_____
_____	_____	_____	_____	_____	_____	_____	_____	_____
_____	_____	_____	_____	_____	_____	_____	_____	_____
_____	_____	_____	_____	_____	_____	_____	_____	_____

Audited?   Yes ____   No ____   Estimated total hours:

SEC?   Yes ____   No ____   Partner _____

Industry _____   Manager _____

                                        Staff _____

                                        Total _____

Can dates be adjusted?   Yes ____   No ____   Explain _____

Can personnel be changed? Yes ____   No ____   Explain _____

Comments _____

Requested by_____ Date _____ Scheduled _____ Date _____
                                          Assignment Manager

---

[5] Wayne G. Bremser, *Quality Control Systems in Accounting* (Maryland, Aspen Systems Corporation, 1979), p. 209.

have expertise in professions other than accounting or auditing. Thus an auditor will hire specialists for the audit, if appropriate.

Matters for which specialists are commonly used include:

- Valuation questions (e.g., real estate, art works, and gems).

- Quantity or condition determinations (e.g., oil reserves below ground, quantity of mined coal in above ground stockpile).

- Determination of amounts developed by other specialists (e.g., actuarial determinations).

- Legal or technical issues (e.g., legal title to land, legal significance of contract requirements).

If a specialist is necessary, the auditor must make sure, through inquiries or other appropriate procedures, that the specialist's professional qualifications and reputation are adequate. The auditor should consider matters such as:

- Whether the specialist has indicated competence by receiving a professional certification or license.

- Whether the reputation of the specialist among those knowledgeable about his or her performance is adequate.

- Whether the specialist has any relationship with the client that might impair or appear to impair the objectivity of his or her work. If possible, an auditor should attempt to obtain a specialist that is independent of the client.

In order to prevent any misunderstanding between the auditor, the client, and the specialist regarding the specialist's work, all parties should fully discuss the nature, extent, timing, and anticipated results of the specialist's work. This understanding would normally be documented by an engagement letter or contract. Although the specialist has primary responsibility for his or her work, the auditor must obtain a general understanding of the methods or assumptions used by the specialist to determine if the findings appear to be reasonable and support the financial statements. Additionally, the auditor is responsible for appropriately testing any accounting data supplied by the client to the specialist. The auditor would ordinarily rely on the work of the specialist unless the auditor's procedures lead him or her to believe the specialist's findings are unreasonable.

If the specialist's findings support the financial statement elements, then the auditor may conclude he or she has obtained sufficient competent evidential matter regarding the item(s) attested to by the specialist. In the event the specialist's findings do not support the financial statements or if the auditor believes they are unreasonable, the auditor should apply additional procedures sufficient to resolve the matter. If the matter is not resolved, the auditor would ordinarily qualify the opinion due to the inability to obtain sufficient competent evidential matter.

In order to avoid misleading readers of the audit report as to either the scope or responsibility for the audit work, an auditor should not refer to the work of the specialist when expressing an unqualified opinion. If some other type of opinion is issued, reference to the specialist may be made if the auditor believes such reference will assist report readers in understanding the reasons for the opinion.

Considering and Coordinating Work With Internal Auditors

The internal audit function is part of a company's internal control system. One objective of the internal audit function may be to study and evaluate other internal controls. It may also review various operations for economy, efficiency, and effectiveness (operational audits). Since much of the external auditor's work may also include evaluating internal control, the external auditor needs to determine the degree of reliance that can be placed on the work of the internal auditor. As noted in *SAS No. 9, The Effect of an Internal Audit Function on the Scope of the Independent Auditor's Examination*, the work of internal auditors cannot be substituted for the work of independent auditors. The internal audit function may, however, provide significant evidence regarding areas or controls examined by the internal auditors and may reduce the extent of testing done by the external auditor.

As used in this section, the term "internal auditor" refers to the modern definition of the term, which is an independent audit function that is not a direct part of the accounting system. For example, an individual who routinely verifies the mathematical accuracy of all invoices would not be considered an "internal auditor" since such clerical checking is an integral part of the accounting system and internal controls, rather than an independent review of the system and controls. The external independent auditor must obtain a sufficient understanding of the function and activities of the internal auditor to determine whether that function may be a factor affecting the external audit work.

If the external auditor wishes to place reliance on the internal auditor's work, the internal audit function must be evaluated as to competence of staff, the degree of independence within the client organization, and quality of work performed. In order to evaluate competence, the external auditor will consider factors such as the client's hiring practices, training of the internal auditors, and supervision of the internal audit staff. Their degree of independence typically involves a question as to whether the internal audit staff reports to a high enough level within their organization to act in an objective, unbiased manner. The quality of their work may be determined by reviewing the scope of the internal auditor's work, adequacy of audit programs used, appropriateness of the working papers prepared, and appropriateness of conclusions reached. The external auditor will also determine whether any reports prepared by the internal auditors appropriately reflect the results of work performed. The external auditor will also normally perform tests of the internal auditors' work to determine if the work was properly performed.

If the external auditor is satisfied regarding the internal auditors' competence, independence, and quality of work, he or she may place significant reliance on internal audit work. This will typically result in the external auditor reducing or eliminating completely work in the same area.

While planning his or her examination, the external auditor must consider work planned and completed by the internal auditors in order to avoid unnecessary duplication. For large companies, the audit committee of the board of directors frequently coordinates, to a degree, work between the internal and external auditors

In some instances, such as inventory observation, the internal auditors may provide direct assistance to the external auditors. In such circumstances the external auditors must evaluate the competence and objectivity of the internal auditors and supervise their work to the extent appropriate in the circumstances.

The external auditor bears final responsibility for all audit judgments, such as the effectiveness of internal accounting control, sufficiency of tests performed, materiality of transactions, and other matters affecting his or her report on the financial statement. He or she may not avoid this responsibility by using, directly or indirectly, the work of internal auditors.

Audit Programs

Development of audit programs may be viewed as consisting of three basic steps:

- *Identify the various assertions* the client makes in its financial statements. For example, one assertion normally implicit in the caption "Finished Goods Inventory" is existence of the inventories.

- From these identified assertions, *develop specific audit objectives* which, when tested, will result in an examination made in accordance with GAAS. For example, with respect to the above assertion, the related audit objective is "Inventories included in the balance sheet physically exist."

- *Design audit procedures* to achieve the specific audit objectives developed from the assertions. Continuing the previous example, two related audit procedures might be (a) observing physical inventory counts and (b) obtaining confirmation of inventories at locations outside the entity.

An audit program lists specific audit procedures for an audit engagement. This program should be tailored to accomplish the audit strategy and meet the unique needs of each individual audit engagement. Many audit firms use standard audit programs (audit checklists) appropriate for a particular industry and client size and add or delete program steps as necessary to tailor the program to the needs of an individual client. *SAS No. 22, Planning and Supervision*, specifically requires that audit programs be written but does not specify their form or content.

Audit programs are usually divided into logical units that correspond with either the "related account concept" based on financial statement classifications or with transaction cycles, depending on the CPA firm's audit methodology. For example, under the statement classification approach there may be separate audit programs for the areas of cash, accounts receivable, inventories, etc. By subdividing the overall audit procedures into appropriate subgroups, it is easier to assign staff to audit various audit sub-areas. Work with each audit area may be further subdivided by performance dates such as planning work, interim work, work at balance sheet date, and work associated with wrapping-up the engagement.

A portion of an audit program is illustrated in Exhibit 4-6. It should be noted that there is a column for the auditor to initial and date specific steps as the work is completed. This facilitates supervision and helps fix responsibility for the completed work.

**Audit
Working Papers**

Audit working papers are the written records of the audit process kept by the auditor. They should include all information necessary to document that the auditor conducted a proper examination in accordance with GAAS, applying all audit tests and procedures considered necessary in the circumstances of the particular engagement.

Working papers have a number of practical uses in addition to the

Exhibit 4-6
Illustrative Audit Program

Year-End Audit Program for Cash in Bank

Program Steps	Working Paper Reference	Done By
1. Confirm all bank accounts at year-end using standard bank confirmation form.		
2. Request cut-off bank statements from banks approximately two weeks after year-end.		
3. Obtain or prepare year-end reconciliations for all bank accounts.		
a. Foot reconciliations.		
b. Trace book balance to trial balance and general ledger.		
c. Trace bank balance to bank statement, cut-off bank statement, and bank confirmation.		
d. Agree outstanding checks to checks clearing with cut-off bank statement, noting appropriate time lags.		
e. Trace deposits in transit to cut-off bank statement and cash receipts journal, noting appropriate time lags.		
f. Appropriately test all other significant reconciling items.		
4. Prepare (using standard form) a schedule of interbank transfers for a period five days before and after year-end.		
5. Review all debit and credit memos clearing with cut-off bank statement for applicability to audit period.		
6. Obtain information concerning report disclosures such as cash withdrawal restrictions or bank overdrafts at year-end.		

obvious one of the auditor not having to rely too extensively on his or her memory:

- They provide a starting point for planning subsequent audits.
- They provide a written record that can be admitted as legal evidence that the auditor conducted a proper examination.
- They are the basis for review by managers and partners of the engagement performance.
- They are the basis for review of the CPA firm's quality control by firm peer reviewers.
- They are the source of information for preparing tax returns, SEC filings, or other reports.
- They are the source of information for issuing a management letter to the client.

Almost any type of document may be kept in working papers. On larger audits these documents may number in the thousands. To facilitate retrieval, they are usually organized in some logical manner. The various audit firms utilize different classification categories and indexing for working papers. One common classification scheme includes the following major categories.

- Working paper contents index.
- Planning and administrative data (engagement letter, planning memo, time budget, etc.).
- Financial statements, audit report, and footnotes.
- Permanent type data (minutes, contracts, articles of incorporation, etc.).
- Review of subsequent events, contingencies.
- Working trial balance.
- Adjusting journal entries.
- Internal control review and compliance testing (arranged by either related account or cycle concept).
- Non-analytical review substantive test working papers (arranged by either related account or cycle concept).
- Analytical review tests.

The major categories may include many different types of working papers. For example:

- Client-prepared documents (information prepared from basic accounting records by client personnel for audit testing).

- Reproductions of original documents (xerox copies of minutes, invoices, contracts, etc.).

- Audit checklists (planning checklists, review checklists, etc.).

- Audit programs (cash, receivables, inventory, etc.).

- Internal control questionnaires.

- Account or other data analyses.

- Trial balances or lists of account information.

- Account reconciliations.

- Information schedules (location of client personnel, audit time budget, etc.).

- Summary memos (auditors may write memos summarizing conclusions about the adequacy of work in each major area of audit).

Working papers are frequently indexed so that they may be better controlled and easily accessed. A common indexing scheme is presented in Exhibit 4-7.

As shown in Exhibit 4-7, each category of working papers has a unique numbering system which is used to number the working papers within that category. For example, the first working paper in the permanent file is numbered PF^1, the second working paper is number PF^2, etc. Likewise, the first working paper in the sales and revenue area is numbered PL^1, the second working paper is numbered PL^2, etc. Using an indexing scheme, such as the one depicted in Exhibit 4-7, facilitates arranging working papers in sequence so they may be easily reviewed or retrieved at a later date. Exhibit 4-8 contains an illustrative audit working paper.

Financial amounts in working papers are usually carried forward from detailed schedules to summary schedules or totals. In some firms, to reference a number forward, the auditor places the reference below or to the right of the number. On the other hand, to show that a number comes from another schedule, he or she places the reference above or to the left of the number being referenced (sometimes this reference is circled for emphasis). This referencing style is illustrated in Exhibit 4-8 and immediately following Exhibit 4-8.

Audit Symbols (Tick Marks)

Auditors commonly use audit symbols (tick marks) to explain work performed on a particular item of data. These symbols conserve time

Exhibit 4-7

	Category of Working Paper	Index Numbers Used
Summary Schedules	Permanent File	PF
	Working Trial Balance - Assets	B/S - A
	Working Trial Balance - Liabilities	B/S - L
	Working Trial Balance - Income and Expense	P/L
	Adjusting Journal Entries	AJ
Detail Schedules	Cash Area	A
	Receivables Area	B
	Inventory Area	C
	Property, Plant and Equipment area	D
	Investments Area	E
	Current Portion of Long-Term Debt Area	AA
	Accounts Payable Area	BB
	Accrued Liabilities Area	CC
	Sales or Revenue Area	PL^1-PL^9
	Cost of Goods Sold Area	PL^{10}-PL^{19}
	Selling Expenses Area	PL^{20}-PL^{29}

Exhibit 4-8
Illustrative Audit Working Paper

Schedule reference
Preparer and date
Reviewer and date

| Client name—work paper name Work paper date | ABC COMPANY - INVESTMENTS 12-31-x3 | | Work Paper No. | Accountant | TPM | Date 1-15-x4 |
| | | | | Reviewed by | DGH | 2-12-x4 |

1 DESCRIPTION	2	3 DATE	4 BALANCE 12-31-x2	5 ADDITIONS <DISPOSALS>	6 BALANCE 12-31-x3
XYZ WIDGETS, COMMON					
1,000 SHARES @ $25.50		6-17-X0	25500 ✓		25500 ∅ ✗
WHEELING IRON HORSE, COMMON					
500 SHARES @ $52		9-18-X1	26000 ✓		
500 SHARES @ $69		7-15-X3		< 26000 > 4 ✗	—0— ✗
GOLD GLITTER INC., COMMON					
1,000 SHARES @ $79		11-15-X3		79000 4	79000 ✗ ⊗
TOTALS			51500 ✓	53000	104500 Cx
			⌒	⌒	B/S-A

Audit Tick marks—
Explanation and
initials of pre-
parer of work paper

Total referenced
forward to
summary schedule

⌒ FOOTED / TPM
Cx CROSS COSTED / TPM
✓ AGREED TO PRIOR YEAR WORKING PAPERS / TPM
✗ AGREED ALL DETAILS TO BROKERS ADVICES / TPM
∅ 12-31-X3 MARKET PRICE $32 PER WALL STREET JOURNAL / TPM
⊗ 12-31-X3 MARKET PRICE $83 PER WALL STREET JOURNAL / TPM
4 GAIN CORRECTLY RECORDED IN INCOME ACCOUNT / TPM
✗ NO DIVIDENDS PAID PER STANDARD/POOR ANNUAL
   DIVIDEND RECORD / TPM

Working Paper Referencing

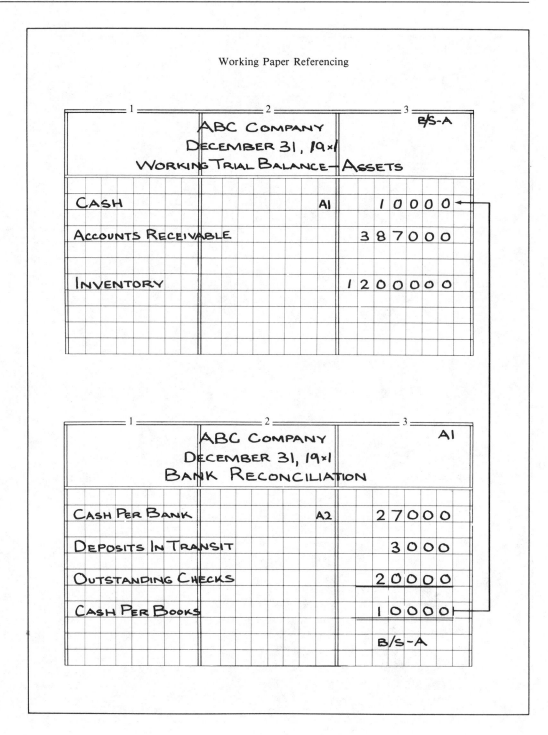

and space, particularly when the same procedure is being performed on a whole series of numbers. It is important that these symbols be kept simple, clear, and unique so they may be quickly written and reviewed. It is equally important that the explanation attached to the audit symbol (tick mark) be clear and precise so that a working paper reviewer other than the working paper preparer will know *exactly* what work was performed. Audit symbols (tick marks) are illustrated in Exhibit 4-8.

SUMMARY

This chapter has discussed the aspects of obtaining audit clients as well as planning, performing, and documenting the audit work. A summary diagram was presented depicting the overall audit process, which includes:

- Audit firm goals and client solicitation.
- Client evaluation and documentation of the engagement arrangement.
- Evaluating the client's business and industry and planning the audit procedures.
- Performing analytical review procedures.
- Documenting the audit in working papers.

The chapter discussed mechanisms for soliciting clients, such as community visibility, referrals, prospective clients soliciting bids for audit services, and advertising. Advertising has not been employed extensively in the accounting profession.

The importance of developing and continuing a good clientele was discussed, including the communication procedure that occurs between successor and predecessor auditors regarding acceptance of new clients. All CPAs, of course, seek to obtain quality clients that are financially sound and will permit the auditor to apply all the auditing procedures considered necessary in forming an opinion on the financial statements. It is often clients in financial difficulty that create problems regarding the application of accounting principles and attempt to place restrictions on the auditor's ability to gather evidence.

The development of an overall audit plan, including development of audit strategy, scheduling audit work, using the work of a specialist, and considering and coordinating the work of internal auditors were discussed.

REVIEW QUESTIONS

4-1   At what point in an audit do professional standards need to be considered?

4-2   Why is it difficult to place many audit activities in a proper time frame with respect to other audit activities?

4-3   List several factors that generally point toward a need for more planning and control in an audit.

4-4   What does the term "client solicitation" mean as it was employed in this chapter?

4-5   Discuss four mechanisms for soliciting prospective audit clients.

4-6   The AICPA previously banned all types of formal advertising. Now it permits certain types of advertising. What are the current limitations on advertising?

4-7   Why do auditors spend a great deal of time collecting and evaluating data about prospective clients before deciding whether to accept them as clients? Don't all audit firms want new clients to increase revenues?

4-8   What are the factors an auditor should consider prior to accepting an audit engagement?

4-9   Is contact with a predecessor auditor optional or mandatory?

4-10   What is the purpose of an engagement letter?

4-11   What subjects should be included in an engagement letter?

4-12   It is customary for the auditor to obtain background information on the client and industry. How may such information be useful?

4-13   What are some common information sources for an auditor to obtain knowledge about a client?

4-14   What are common analytical review procedures?

4-15   What are some specific techniques or tools for performing analytical review procedures?

4-16   At what point in an audit should analytical review procedures be performed? Why?

4-17   Why is it necessary for the auditor to formulate an audit strategy and document this in an audit planning memo?

4-18   Since the preliminary audit plan or approach is frequently revised based on information uncovered during the course of the audit, why is a detailed audit time budget prepared?

4-19   What are some common types of specialists that may be employed by a CPA during the course of an audit?

4-20   What are the general responsibilities an independent accountant may have for a specialist employed during an audit.

4-21   The work of the internal auditors may not be substituted for the work of the independent auditor. Why is this true and of what benefit to the external auditor is the work of the internal auditor?

4-22   What is an audit program? Give an example of an item that might be included in an audit program.

4-23   Of what benefit are *written* audit working papers as opposed to the auditor's memory?

4-24   What are major categories or files of working papers?

4-25   What are some different types of working papers?

DISCUSSION QUESTIONS AND PROBLEMS

4-26   Jones, CPA, is approached by a prospective client who desires to engage Jones to perform an audit which in prior years was performed by another CPA.

Required:

Identify the procedures which Jones should follow in accepting the engagement.

(AICPA adapted)

4-27   In late spring of 1984 you are advised of a new assignment as in-charge accountant of your CPA firm's recurring annual audit of a major client, the Lancer Company. You are given the engagement letter for the audit covering the calendar year December 31, 1984, and a list of personnel assigned to this engagement. It is your responsibility to plan and supervise the field work for the engagement.

Required:

Discuss the *necessary* preparation and planning for the Lancer Company annual audit prior to beginning field work at the client's office. In your discussion include the sources you should consult, the type of information you should seek, the preliminary plans and preparation you should make for the field work, and any actions you should take relative to the staff assigned to the engagement. Do not write an audit program.

(AICPA adapted)

4-28   In a properly planned examination of financial statements, the auditor coordinates his or her reviews of specific balance-sheet and income-statement accounts.

Required:

Why should the auditor coordinate his or her examination of balance-sheet accounts and income-statement accounts? Discuss and illustrate by examples.

(AICPA adapted)

4-29   The major written understandings between a CPA and his or her client, in connection with an examination of financial statements, are the engagement (arrangements) letter and the client's representation letters.

Required:

a.   What are the objectives of the engagement (arrangements) letter?
b.   Who should prepare and sign the engagement letter?
c.   When should the engagement letter be sent?
d.   Why should the engagement letter be renewed periodically?

(AICPA adapted)

4-30   The first generally accepted auditing standard of field work requires, in part, that "the work is to be adequately planned." An effective tool that aids the auditor in adequately planning the work is an audit program.

Required:

What is an audit program, and what purposes does it serve?

(AICPA adapted)

4-31 During the course of an audit engagement an independent auditor gives serious consideration to the concepts of materiality. This concept of materiality is inherent in the work of the independent auditor and is important for planning, preparing, and modifying audit programs. The concept of materiality underlies the application of all the generally accepted auditing standards, particularly the standards of field work and reporting.

Required:

a. Briefly describe what is meant by the independent auditor's concept of materiality.
b. What are some common relationships and other considerations used by the auditor in judging materiality?
c. Identify how the planning and execution of an audit program might be affected by the independent auditor's concept of materiality.

(AICPA adapted)

4-32 G. Johnson, a local real estate broker, is a member of the board of directors of Pennset Corporation. At a recent board meeting, called to discuss financial plans, Mr. Johnson discovered two planned expenditures for auditing. In the Controller's Department budget, he found an estimate for internal audit activity and in the Treasurer's budget he found an estimate for the annual audit by a CPA firm.

Mr. Johnson could not understand the need for two different expenditures for auditing. Since the CPA fee for the annual audit was less than the cost of the internal audit activity, he proposed eliminating the internal audit function.

Required:

a. Explain to Mr. Johnson the different purposes served by the two audit activities.
b. What benefits does the CPA firm performing an audit derive from the existence of an internal audit function?

(CMA adapted)

OBJECTIVE QUESTIONS*

4-33 The permanent section of the auditor's working papers generally should include

    A. Time and expense reports.
    B. Names and addresses of all audit staff personnel on the engagement.
    C. A copy of key customer confirmations.
    D. A copy of the engagement letter.

4-34 The first standard of field work recognizes that early appointment of the independent auditor has many advantages to the auditor and to the client. Which of the following advantages is least likely to occur as a result of early appointment of the auditor?

    A. The auditor will be able to plan the audit work so that it may be done expeditiously.
    B. The auditor will be able to complete the audit work in less time.
    C. The auditor will be able to better plan for the observation of the physical inventories.
    D. The auditor will be able to perform the examination more efficiently and will be finished at an early date after the year-end.

4-35 A CPA should comply with applicable generally accepted auditing standards on every engagement

    A. Without exception.
    B. Except in examinations that result in a qualified report.
    C. Except in engagements where the CPA is associated with unaudited financial statements.
    D. Except in examinations of interim financial statements.

4-36 A CPA establishes quality control policies and procedures for deciding whether to accept or continue a client. The primary purpose for establishing such policies and procedures is

    A. To enable the auditor to attest to the integrity or reliability of a client.
    B. To comply with the quality control standards established by regulatory bodies.

Note: Questions marked with an asterisk are not AICPA adapted questions; otherwise, questions in this section have been taken from prior CPA examinations.

C. To lessen the exposure to litigation resulting from failure to detect irregularities in client financial statements.

D. To minimize the likelihood of association with clients whose managements lack integrity.

4-37 A CPA may reduce the audit work on a first-time audit by reviewing the working papers of the predecessor auditor. The predecessor should permit the successor to review working papers relating to matters of continuing accounting significance such as those that relate to

A. Extent of reliance on the work of specialists.
B. Fee arrangements and summaries of payments.
C. Analysis of contingencies.
D. Staff hours required to complete the engagement.

4-38 Which of the following is a basic tool used by the auditor to control the audit work and review the progress of the audit?

A. Time and expense summary.
B. Engagement letter.
C. Progress flowchart.
D. Audit program.

4-39 Which of the following is generally included or shown in the auditor's working papers?

A. The procedures used by the auditor to verify the personal financial status of members of the client's managment team.
B. Analyses that are designed to be a part of, or a substitute for, the client's accounting records.
C. Excerpts from authoritative pronouncements that support the underlying generally accepted accounting principles used in preparing the financial statements.
D. The manner in which exceptions and unusual matters disclosed by the auditor's procedures were resolved or treated.

4-40 If the independent auditor decides that the work performed by internal auditors may have a bearing on the independent auditor's own procedures, the independent auditor should consider the objectivity of the internal auditors. One method of judging objectivity is to

A. Review the recommendations made in the reports of internal auditors.

B. Examine, on a test basis, documentary evidence of the work performed by internal auditors.

C. Inquire of management about the qualifications of the internal audit staff.

D. Consider the client's practices for hiring.

4-41   The independent auditor should acquire an understanding of the internal audit function as it relates to the independent auditor's study and evaluation of internal accounting control because

A. The audit programs, working papers, and reports of internal auditors can often be used as a substitute for the work of the independent auditor's staff.

B. The procedures performed by the internal audit staff may eliminate the independent auditor's need for an extensive study and evaluation of internal control.

C. The work performed by internal auditors may be a factor in determining the nature, timing, and extent of the independent auditor's procedures.

D. The understanding of the internal audit function is an important substantive test to be performed by the independent auditor.

4-42   During the course of an audit engagement an auditor prepares and accumulates audit working papers. The primary purpose of the audit working papers is to

A. Aid the auditor in adequately planning his work.

B. Provide a point of reference for future audit engagement.

C. Support the underlying concepts included in the preparation of the basic financial statements.

D. Support the auditor's opinion.

4-43   With respect to errors and irregularities, which of the following should be part of an auditor's planning of the audit engagement?

A. Plan to search for errors or irregularities that would have a material or immaterial effect on the financial statements.

B. Plan to discover errors or irregularities that are either material or immaterial.

C. Plan to discover errors or irregularities that are material.

D. Plan to search for errors or irregularities that would have a material effect on the financial statement.

4-44   Which of the following best describes the most important steps of an auditor's statistical analysis of significant ratios and trends?

A. Computation of significant ratios and trends.
B. Interpretation of significant variations and unusual relationships.
C. Reconciliation of statistical data to the client's accounting records.
D. Comparison of statistical data to prior-year statistics and to similar data published by governmental and private sources.

4-45   During the course of an audit, an auditor required additional research and consultation with others. This additional research and consultation is considered to be

A. An appropriate part of the professional conduct of the engagement.
B. A responsibility of the management, not the auditor.
C. A failure on the part of the CPA to comply with generally accepted auditing standards because of a lack of competence.
D. An unusual practice which indicates that the CPA should not have accepted the engagement.

4-46   Preliminary arrangements agreed to by the auditor and the client should be reduced to writing by the auditor. The best place to set forth these arrangements is in

A. A memorandum to be placed in the permanent section of the auditing working papers.
B. An engagement letter.
C. A client representation letter.
D. A confirmation letter attached to the constructive services letter.

4-47   Which of the following actions should be taken by a CPA who has been asked to examine the financial statements of a company whose fiscal year has ended?

A. Discuss with the client the possibility of an adverse opinion because of the late engagement date.
B. Ascertain whether circumstances are likely to permit an adequate examination and expression of an unqualified opinion.
C. Inform the client of the need to issue a qualified opinion if the physical inventory has already been taken.
D. Ascertain whether a proper study and evaluation of internal control can be conducted after completion of the field work.

4-48   Which of the following is an aspect of scheduling and controlling the audit engagement?

A. Include in the audit program a column for estimated and actual time.

B. Perform audit work only after the client's books of account have been closed for the period under examination.

C. Write a conclusion on individual working papers indicating how the results thereon will affect the auditor's report.

D. Include in the engagement letter an estimate of the minimum and maximum audit fee.

4-49 Those procedures specifically outlined in an audit program are primarily designed to

A. Prevent litigations.

B. Detect errors or irregularities.

C. Test internal systems.

D. Gather evidence.

4-50 Although the quantity, type, and content of working papers will vary with the circumstances, the working papers generally would include the

A. Copies of those client records examined by the auditor during the course of the engagement.

B. Evaluation of the efficiency and competence of the audit staff assistants by the partner responsible for the audit.

C. Auditor's comments concerning the efficiency and competence of client management and personnel.

D. Auditing procedures followed, and the testing performed in obtaining evidential matter.

4-51 Which of the following is not a factor that affects the independent auditor's judgment as to the quantity, type, and content of working papers?

A. The timing and the number of personnel to be assigned to the engagement.

B. The nature of the financial statements, schedules, or other information upon which the auditor is reporting.

C. The need for supervision of the engagement.

D. The nature of the auditor's report.

4-52 An auditor is planning an audit engagement for a new client in a business that is unfamiliar to the auditor. Which of the following would be the most useful source of information for the auditor during the preliminary planning stage, when the auditor is trying to obtain a general understanding of audit problems that might be encountered?

A. Client manuals of accounts and charts of accounts.
B. AICPA Industry Audit Guides.
C. Prior-year working papers of the predecessor auditor.
D. Latest annual and interim financial statements issued by the client.

4-53   Audit programs are modified to suit the circumstances on particular engagements. A complete audit program for an engagement generally should be developed

A. Prior to beginning the actual audit work.
B. After the auditor has completed an evaluation of the existing internal accounting control.
C. After reviewing the client's accounting records and procedures.
D. When the audit engagement letter is prepared.

4-54   Which of the following is an effective audit planning and control procedure that helps prevent misunderstandings and inefficient use of audit personnel?

A. Arrange to make copies, for inclusion in the working papers, of those client-supporting documents examined by the auditor.
B. Arrange to provide the client with copies of the audit programs to be used during the audit.
C. Arrange a preliminary conference with the client to discuss audit objectives, fees, timing, and other information.
D. Arrange to have the auditor prepare and post any necessary adjusting or reclassification entries prior to final closing.

4-55   Which of the following is not a factor affecting the independent auditor's judgment as to the quantity, type, and content of audit working papers?

A. The needs in the particular circumstances for supervision and review of the work performed by any assistants.
B. The nature and condition of the client's records and internal controls.
C. The expertise of client personnel and their expected audit participation.

D. The type of the financial statements, schedules, or other information upon which the auditor is reporting.

4-56 When a CPA is approached to perform an audit for the first time, the CPA should make inquiries of the predecessor auditor. This is a necessary procedure because the predecessor may be able to provide the successor with information that will assist the successor in determining

A. Whether the predecessor's work should be utilized.
B. Whether the company follows the policy of rotating its auditors.
C. Whether in the predecessor's opinion internal control of the company has been satisfactory.
D. Whether the engagement should be accepted.

4-57 An audit program provides proof that

A. Sufficient competent evidential matter was obtained.
B. The work was adequately planned.
C. There was compliance with generally accepted standards of reporting.
D. There was a proper study and evaluation of internal control.

4-58 Which of the following is the most likely *first* step an auditor would perform at the beginning of an initial audit engagement?

A. Prepare a rough draft of the financial statements and of the auditor's report.
B. Study and evaluate the system of internal administrative control.
C. Tour the client's facilities and review the general records.
D. Consult with and review the work of the predecessor auditor prior to discussing the engagement with the client management.

4-59 During an audit engagement pertinent data are compiled and included in the audit workpapers. The workpapers primarily are considered to be

A. A client-owned record of conclusions reached by the auditors who performed the engagement.
B. Evidence supporting financial statements.
C. Support for the auditor's representations as to compliance with generally accepted auditing standards.
D. A record to be used as a basis for the following year's engagement.

4-60   One reason why the independent auditor makes an analytic review of the client's operations is to identify

    A.   Weaknesses of a material nature in the system of internal control.

    B.   Non-compliance with prescribed control procedures.

    C.   Improper separation of accounting and other financial duties.

    D.   Unusual transactions.

4-61   In connection with an audit of financial statements by an independent CPA, the client suggests that members of the internal audit staff be utilized to minimize external audit costs. It would be *inappropriate* for the CPA to delegate which of the following tasks to the internal audit staff?

    A.   Selection of accounts receivable for confirmation based upon decision rules established by the independent CPA and with appropriate supervision by the CPA.

    B.   Investigation of negative accounts receivable responses for later review by the independent CPA.

    C.   Preparation of an accounts receivable aging schedule.

    D.   Determination of the adequacy of the allowance for uncollectible accounts.

4-62   For what minimum period should audit working papers be retained by the independent CPA?

    A.   For the period during which the entity remains a client of the independent CPA.

    B.   For the period during which an auditor-client relationship exists but not more than six years.

    C.   For the statutory period within which legal action may be brought against the independent CPA.

    D.   For as long as the CPA is in public practice.

4-63   When an independent auditor decides that the work performed by internal auditors may have a bearing on the nature, timing, and extent of the independent auditor's procedures, the independent auditor should evaluate the competence and objectivity of the internal auditors. Relative to objectivity, the independent auditor should

    A.   Consider the organizational level to which internal auditors report the results of their work.

    B.   Review the training program in effect for the internal audit staff.

C.   Examine the quality of the internal audit reports.
D.   Consider the qualifications of the internal audit staff.

4-64   The independent auditor should acquire an understanding of a client's internal audit function to determine whether the work of internal auditors will be a factor in determining the nature, timing, and extent of the independent auditor's procedures. The work performed by internal auditors might be such a factor when the internal auditor's work includes

A.   Verification of the mathematical accuracy of invoices.
B.   Review of administrative practices to improve efficiency and achieve management objectives.
C.   Study and evaluation of internal accounting control.
D.   Preparation of internal financial reports for management purposes.

RE FAIR PRESENTATION ETHICAL CONDUCT INDEPENDENCE EVIDENCE DUE CARE FAIR PRESENTATION ETHICAL CONDUCT INDEPENDENCE EVIDENCE DUE CARE FAIR PRESENTATION
CARE FAIR PRESENTATION ETHICAL CONDUCT INDEPENDENCE EVIDENCE DUE CARE FAIR PRESENTATION ETHICAL CONDUCT INDEPENDENCE EVIDENCE DUE CARE FAIR PRESENTA
DUE CARE FAIR PRESENTATION ETHICAL CONDUCT INDEPENDENCE EVIDENCE DUE CARE FAIR PRESENTATION ETHICAL CONDUCT INDEPENDENCE EVIDENCE DUE CARE FAIR PRESE
NCE DUE CARE FAIR PRESENTATION ETHICAL CONDUCT INDEPENDENCE EVIDENCE DUE CARE FAIR PRESENTATION ETHICAL CONDUCT INDEPENDENCE EVIDENCE DUE CARE FAIR P
IDENCE DUE CARE FAIR PRESENTATION ETHICAL CONDUCT INDEPENDENCE EVIDENCE DUE CARE FAIR PRESENTATION ETHICAL CONDUCT INDEPENDENCE EVIDENCE DUE CARE FA
E EVIDENCE DUE CARE FAIR PRESENTATION ETHICAL CONDUCT INDEPENDENCE EVIDENCE DUE CARE FAIR PRESENTATION ETHICAL CONDUCT INDEPENDENCE EVIDENCE DUE CARE
NCE EVIDENCE DUE CARE FAIR PRESENTATION ETHICAL CONDUCT INDEPENDENCE EVIDENCE DUE CARE FAIR PRESENTATION ETHICAL CONDUCT INDEPENDENCE EVIDENCE DUE
ENDENCE EVIDENCE DUE CARE FAIR PRESENTATION ETHICAL CONDUCT INDEPENDENCE EVIDENCE DUE CARE FAIR PRESENTATION ETHICAL CONDUCT INDEPENDENCE EVIDENCE D

LEARNING OBJECTIVES

After studying this chapter, students should understand

1. The basic internal controls which should be present in simple system of internal control.
2. The difference between accounting control and administrative control.
3. The nature of compensating controls.
4. The ten basic concepts of internal accounting control.
5. The nature of the Foreign Corrupt Practices Act.

E DUE CARE FAIR PRESENTATION ETHICAL CONDUCT INDEPENDENCE EVIDENCE DUE CARE FAIR PRESENTATION ETHICAL CONDUCT INDEPENDENCE EVIDENCE DUE CARE FAIR F
ENCE DUE CARE FAIR PRESENTATION ETHICAL CONDUCT INDEPENDENCE EVIDENCE DUE CARE FAIR PRESENTATION ETHICAL CONDUCT INDEPENDENCE EVIDENCE DUE CARE FA
EVIDENCE DUE CARE FAIR PRESENTATION ETHICAL CONDUCT INDEPENDENCE EVIDENCE DUE CARE FAIR PRESENTATION ETHICAL CONDUCT INDEPENDENCE EVIDENCE DUE CAR
CE EVIDENCE DUE CARE FAIR PRESENTATION ETHICAL CONDUCT INDEPENDENCE EVIDENCE DUE CARE FAIR PRESENTATION ETHICAL CONDUCT INDEPENDENCE EVIDENCE DUE
IDENCE EVIDENCE DUE CARE FAIR PRESENTATION ETHICAL CONDUCT INDEPENDENCE EVIDENCE DUE CARE FAIR PRESENTATION ETHICAL CONDUCT INDEPENDENCE EVIDENCE
EPENDENCE EVIDENCE DUE CARE FAIR PRESENTATION ETHICAL CONDUCT INDEPENDENCE EVIDENCE DUE CARE FAIR PRESENTATION ETHICAL CONDUCT INDEPENDENCE EVIDEN
INDEPENDENCE EVIDENCE DUE CARE FAIR PRESENTATION ETHICAL CONDUCT INDEPENDENCE EVIDENCE DUE CARE FAIR PRESENTATION ETHICAL CONDUCT INDEPENDENCE EV
CT INDEPENDENCE EVIDENCE DUE CARE FAIR PRESENTATION ETHICAL CONDUCT INDEPENDENCE EVIDENCE DUE CARE FAIR PRESENTATION ETHICAL CONDUCT INDEPENDENCE
NDUCT INDEPENDENCE EVIDENCE DUE CARE FAIR PRESENTATION ETHICAL CONDUCT INDEPENDENCE EVIDENCE DUE CARE FAIR PRESENTATION ETHICAL CONDUCT INDEPENDE
L CONDUCT INDEPENDENCE EVIDENCE DUE CARE FAIR PRESENTATION ETHICAL CONDUCT INDEPENDENCE EVIDENCE DUE CARE FAIR PRESENTATION ETHICAL CONDUCT INDEPE
ICAL CONDUCT INDEPENDENCE EVIDENCE DUE CARE FAIR PRESENTATION ETHICAL CONDUCT INDEPENDENCE EVIDENCE DUE CARE FAIR PRESENTATION ETHICAL CONDUCT IN
ETHICAL CONDUCT INDEPENDENCE EVIDENCE DUE CARE FAIR PRESENTATION ETHICAL CONDUCT INDEPENDENCE EVIDENCE DUE CARE FAIR PRESENTATION ETHICAL CONDUCT
ION ETHICAL CONDUCT INDEPENDENCE EVIDENCE DUE CARE FAIR PRESENTATION ETHICAL CONDUCT INDEPENDENCE EVIDENCE DUE CARE FAIR PRESENTATION ETHICAL COND
ITATION ETHICAL CONDUCT INDEPENDENCE EVIDENCE DUE CARE FAIR PRESENTATION ETHICAL CONDUCT INDEPENDENCE EVIDENCE DUE CARE FAIR PRESENTATION ETHICAL C
ESENTATION ETHICAL CONDUCT INDEPENDENCE EVIDENCE DUE CARE FAIR PRESENTATION ETHICAL CONDUCT INDEPENDENCE EVIDENCE DUE CARE FAIR PRESENTATION ETHIC
R PRESENTATION ETHICAL CONDUCT INDEPENDENCE EVIDENCE DUE CARE FAIR PRESENTATION ETHICAL CONDUCT INDEPENDENCE EVIDENCE DUE CARE FAIR PRESENTATION E
FAIR PRESENTATION ETHICAL CONDUCT INDEPENDENCE EVIDENCE DUE CARE FAIR PRESENTATION ETHICAL CONDUCT INDEPENDENCE EVIDENCE DUE CARE FAIR PRESENTATIO
ARE FAIR PRESENTATION ETHICAL CONDUCT INDEPENDENCE EVIDENCE DUE CARE FAIR PRESENTATION ETHICAL CONDUCT INDEPENDENCE EVIDENCE DUE CARE FAIR PRESENT
E CARE FAIR PRESENTATION ETHICAL CONDUCT INDEPENDENCE EVIDENCE DUE CARE FAIR PRESENTATION ETHICAL CONDUCT INDEPENDENCE EVIDENCE DUE CARE FAIR PRES
DUE CARE FAIR PRESENTATION ETHICAL CONDUCT INDEPENDENCE EVIDENCE DUE CARE FAIR PRESENTATION ETHICAL CONDUCT INDEPENDENCE EVIDENCE DUE CARE FAIR F
NCE DUE CARE FAIR PRESENTATION ETHICAL CONDUCT INDEPENDENCE EVIDENCE DUE CARE FAIR PRESENTATION ETHICAL CONDUCT INDEPENDENCE EVIDENCE DUE CARE F
VIDENCE DUE CARE FAIR PRESENTATION ETHICAL CONDUCT INDEPENDENCE EVIDENCE DUE CARE FAIR PRESENTATION ETHICAL CONDUCT INDEPENDENCE EVIDENCE DUE CAR
E EVIDENCE DUE CARE FAIR PRESENTATION ETHICAL CONDUCT INDEPENDENCE EVIDENCE DUE CARE FAIR PRESENTATION ETHICAL CONDUCT INDEPENDENCE EVIDENCE DUE
ENCE EVIDENCE DUE CARE FAIR PRESENTATION ETHICAL CONDUCT INDEPENDENCE EVIDENCE DUE CARE FAIR PRESENTATION ETHICAL CONDUCT INDEPENDENCE EVIDENCE

Chapter 5

Internal Control Principles and Standards

This chapter was written by
Johnny R. Johnson, Ph.D., C.P.A.,
Associate Professor of Accounting,
University of Georgia

INTRODUCTION

A system of internal control can be broadly defined as the set of techniques or procedures which an entity uses to (1) safeguard its assets, (2) provide reliable accounting information, (3) encourage adherence to management's policies, and (4) ensure operating efficiency.

Most individuals encounter internal control systems in their everyday life, but unless they are trained in auditing, they probably do not fully appreciate the significant role that such systems play in today's society. For example, when you eat in a restaurant, the waitress will likely write your order on a prenumbered check, which is then delivered to the kitchen where the food is prepared. After your meal, you deliver the check and cash to the cashier. The cashier retains the check.

Although the process which, from your viewpoint, begins with your order and ends with your payment probably seems of little significance, there are a number of internal control features in the process which are necessary for the operation of the restaurant.

This chapter continues the restaurant example to illustrate how a simple system of internal control might work. The chapter then discusses the nature of internal control, basic internal control concepts, and internal control and the Foreign Corrupt Practices Act.

**A SIMPLE
SYSTEM OF
INTERNAL
CONTROL**

This section describes how a system of internal control might work over the cash receipts in a restaurant.[1] This general discussion is designed to provide a framework for the discussion in the remainder of this chapter.

Most people that eat in restaurants probably do not appreciate the internal control techniques and procedures that they are indirectly exposed to. They notice that their order is written on a check which contains some sort of number, and of course, they realize that the check is presented to the cashier when they pay their bill. However, the procedures that the customer is exposed to represent only a small part of an underlying system designed to (1) safeguard the restaurant's assets, (2) provide reliable accounting information, (3) encourage adherence to management's policies, and (4) promote operational efficiency.

---

[1] Today many customers pay with a credit card. However, the credit card slips retained by the restaurant are similar to cash because they, like a customer's personal check, can be redeemed for cash at the bank which issued the card. In the remainder of this discussion, the term *cash* refers to currency, credit card slips, or personal checks which the customer uses to pay for the meal.

For example, in a restaurant with a good system of internal control the following procedures and techniques may be in effect:

- When a customer enters the restaurant, he or she is seated by a hostess who stamps the time on a prenumbered check, writes the waitress's name on the check and places the check on the table for the waitress. The significance of the time, the prenumbered check, and the waitress's name are discussed later.

- When the customer's order is taken, the waitress writes the customer's location in the restaurant on the check. In a large restaurant, this facilitates the prompt delivery of the food to the right person, and thus decreases customer dissatisfaction from having the order delivered to the wrong person.

- The specific food that the customer orders is written on the check so the chef will not misunderstand what the customer wanted. Also, since the check is written and is returned with the food, the waitress can compare the check with the food to determine that the customer is receiving what was ordered. This comparison decreases the chance of customer dissatisfaction or the chance that collusion between the customer and the chef could result in the customer receiving a steak and paying for a hamburger.

- When the customer pays the check, the cashier checks the price of the order to ensure that the customer pays the correct amount and verifies that any credit card used is not out of date. Also, the cash register is located near the exit to minimize the chance that the customer will leave without paying the bill.

- Before the restaurant opens for the day, the manager assigns prenumbered checks to each hostess. At the end of the day, the manager obtains the used checks from the cashier and accounts for the numerical sequence of the checks assigned to each hostess. This comparison should identify any checks which were used by the waitress, but not retained by the cashier. Any missing checks indicate some departure from the normal operation of the system. For example, if a customer takes the check and leaves without paying, the check for this customer will be missing.

- The cash register automatically prints the time on the check when the check is paid and keeps a cumulative balance of the cash which should be in the register at any time. Before the cashier leaves, the manager reconciles this balance with the actual cash on hand. This procedure helps to identify cash shortages or overages with the specific cashier on duty when the discrepancy occurs.

- When the numerical sequence of checks issued to the hostesses is accounted for, the manager reprices each order and prepares an adding machine tape of the check amounts. The tape total is then reconciled to the total cash on hand at the end of the day. This procedure helps to identify any pricing errors made by the waitresses and any discrepancy between the amount of cash which should have been collected and the amount actually collected.

- The manager deposits the cash collections at least on a daily basis. At various intervals during the day he or she may remove most of the cash from the cash register (leaving only enough cash for making change) and lock the cash in the restaurant's safe. Then at the end of the day, or the next morning, the manager deposits the cash from the safe in the bank. All of the procedures described above minimize the possible loss through robbery and the loss which could occur if, for example, the cashier stole the cash or unintentionally lost some of it by misplacing it or giving incorrect change.

- The bookkeeper uses the tape of the day's cash sales to post to the general ledger. This makes it unnecessary for the bookkeeper to have access to cash in posting the ledger. If the bookkeeper has access to cash, he or she could easily take the cash and cover up the theft by making a fictitious credit to cash with an offsetting debit to some other account.

- The person that reconciles the bank statement obtains the daily tapes of cash sales, the daily print-outs of the total cash receipts produced by the cash register, and the daily checks.[2] The bank statement reconciler first accounts for the numerical sequence of the daily checks and verifies the accuracy of the daily tapes. Then the totals from the tapes of the daily checks are compared with: (1) the daily print-out of the total cash receipts produced by the cash register, (2) the deposit shown on the bank statement, and (3) the daily debit to cash and credit to sales which are entered in the restaurant's books. The bank statement reconciler also determines that the deposit is made on a timely basis.

  The reconciler's comparisons and computations should reveal any discrepancy between actual sales for the day and (1) the cash deposited in the bank or (2) the entries to cash and sales in the restaurant's books.

  If these control procedures are not in effect, the manager of the restaurant could misappropriate cash, destroy the related customer

---

[2] The checks referred to here are the checks presented to the customers after their meals, not checks written by the restaurant in payment of various expenses.

checks, and perhaps not be detected. Also, posting errors by the bookkeeper would be more difficult to detect if this control were not in effect.

THE NATURE OF INTERNAL CONTROL

The restaurant illustrates a simple example of an internal control system. This section discusses further the nature of internal control, the difference between accounting and administrative control, compensating controls, and internal control and the size of the firm.

Accounting Versus Administrative Control

SAS No. 1 distinguishes between accounting and administrative controls.[3] Section 320 of *SAS No. 1* establishes the objectives of accounting control by providing the following definition:

> Accounting control comprises the plan of organization and the procedures and records that are concerned with the safeguarding of assets and the reliability of financial records, and consequently are designed to provide reasonable assurance that:
>
> a. Transactions are executed in accordance with management's general or specific authorization.
> b. Transactions are recorded as necessary (1) to permit preparation of financial statements in conformity with generally accepted accounting principles or any other criteria applicable to such statements and (2) to maintain accountability for assets.
> c. Access to assets is permitted only in accordance with management's authorization.
> d. The recorded accountability for assets is compared with the existing assets at reasonable intervals and appropriate action is then taken with respect to any differences.

The same section of *SAS No. 1* defines administrative control:

> Administrative control includes but is not limited to the plan of organization and the procedures and records that are concerned with the decision processes leading to management's authorization of transactions. Such authorization is a management function directly associated with the responsibility for achieving the objectives of the organization and is the starting point for establishing accounting control of transactions.

---

[3]*SAS No. 1, Codification of Auditing Standards and Procedures, Auditor's Study of Internal Control*, AU 320.

The key distinction between accounting control and administrative control is whether the control aids in safeguarding the assets and increasing the reliability of the financial records. If so, the control is classified as an accounting control. If not, the control is an administrative control.

The internal control system of the restaurant described previously uses both types of controls. Exhibit 5-1 summarizes the restaurant's controls over cash receipts. The exhibit explains the purpose of each control, indicates whether it is an accounting or administrative control, or both, and explains the control classification. In studying the classification of the restaurant's controls, remember that accounting controls safeguard assets and increase the reliability of financial records; all other controls are administrative controls.

As indicated in Exhibit 5-1, accounting controls and administrative controls are not mutually exclusive. For example, the first control, writing the waitress's name on the check, serves two purposes. First, a review of the checks can identify waitresses that make pricing errors. Thus, from this viewpoint the control is an accounting control. Second, the names help identify waitresses that give poor service. This identification is an important control for the restaurant, but the control does not safeguard assets or improve the reliability of the financial records. In short, the first control has two aspects: one is accounting and the other is administrative.

Some students may reason that poor service will eventually result in fewer customers and less profit; thus, in effect poor service may lead to the loss of assets (potential cash inflows). However, the Auditing Standards Board makes it clear in *SAS No. 1* that "the safeguarding of assets" refers to safeguards from intentional and unintentional errors in processing the transactions and handling the related assets. Thus, the definition of accounting control comprehends only the existing assets—not potential assets.

As a final point, some students may wonder why a distinction between accounting control and administrative control is necessary. The reason is that external auditors are concerned primarily with accounting control. This point is discussed further in Chapter 8.

Compensating Controls

A compensating control takes the place of another control. For example, a restaurant may not have a cash register that prints the time that a check is paid. Therefore, the manager cannot examine the checks to determine the time which elapses while the customer is in the

Exhibit 5-1
Analysis of Internal Control in the Restaurant

Internal Control	Purpose of Control	Accounting	Admin- istrative	Both	Explanation for Control Classification
1. The waitress's name is written on the check.	Waitresses who commit errors, such as incorrect pricing or poor service, can be identified.			X	Pricing errors involve the safeguarding of assets and reliable accounting information; service involves adherence to managerial policies *not* involving these accounting safeguards.
2. The time is written on the check when the customer arrives; the cash register prints the time on the check when the check is paid.	The manager can compare the time written on the check with time printed by cash register to identify possible poor service.		X		Service involves adherence to managerial policies, but it does not involve safeguarding assets and reliable accounting information.
3. All checks are prenumbered.	All checks can be accounted for to discover irregularities such as a customer leaving without paying. Also, the checks can be added up to verify the total cash which should have been received and deposited for each day. The total of the checks can also be used to verify total sales which should have been recorded for each day.	X			Safeguarding cash and providing reliable accounting information (cash and sales account amounts) are accounting controls.
4. The customer's location in the restaurant is written on the check.	It is easier for the waitress to deliver the right food to the right person and thus give better service.		X		Service involves adherence to managerial policies, but it does not involve safeguarding assets and providing reliable accounting information.
5. The waitress writes the customer's order on the check and then compares the food delivered with the original order.	A comparison of the food delivered with the food ordered serves two purposes: (1) it helps to ensure that the customer gets good service, i.e., the customer gets what was ordered, and (2) it helps to ensure that the chef and the customer do not defraud the restaurant.			X	Service is part of administrative control; preventing fraud involves safeguarding assets and providing reliable accounting information.

Exhibit 5-1 (continued):

Internal Control	Purpose of Control	Accounting	Administrative	Both	Explanation for Control Classification
6. The cashier checks the price of the order. If a credit card is used, the date that the card expires is examined.	There is less chance that the customer will pay the incorrect amount, and less chance that the sales will be recorded at an incorrect amount.			X	Ensuring that the customer pays the correct amount is an element of service. More importantly, ensuring that the customer pays the correct amount safeguards assets and provides reliable accounting information. If the incorrect amount of a sale is recorded, the balance in the sales account is misstated.
7. The cash register and the cashier are located near the exit.	It is more difficult for a customer to leave without paying.	X			Preventing customers from leaving without paying helps to safeguard assets and provide reliable accounting information.
8. The manager controls the prenumbered checks, assigns the checks to the hostesses, and accounts for the prenumbered checks.	If the manager does not maintain control over the prenumbered checks, internal controls 1, 2, and 3 are defeated. For example, if the prenumbered checks are issued at random, there is no way to account for the numerical sequence of the checks.			X	Since this control is an integral part of controls 1, 2, and 3, it encompasses the accounting and administrative aspects of control 1, the administrative aspects of control 2, and the accounting aspects of control 3.
9. The cash register accumulates the balance of cash which should be in the register, and the manager reconciles the two amounts before a cashier leaves for the day.	If this comparison is not made, any cash overages or shortages cannot be identified with a specific cashier and the cashier cannot be held accountable.	X			The primary purpose of this control is to safeguard assets and provide reliable accounting information.
10. The manager reprices each check, prepares an adding machine tape of the total cash which should have been collected, and reconciles the total on the tape with total cash collected for the day.	The purpose of this control is to detect pricing errors and cash overages or shortages.	X			Pricing errors and cash overages or shortages involve both safeguarding assets and providing reliable accounting information.

Exhibit 5-1 (continued):

Internal Control	Purpose of Control	Accounting	Administrative	Both	Explanation for Control Classification
11. Periodically during the day cash is removed from the cash register and locked in the safe.	If the cash in the register is minimized, there is less chance of loss through robbery, theft by the cashier, or misplacement of cash.	X			This control helps to safeguard assets and provide reliable accounting information.
12. Cash receipts are deposited daily.	If the cash on the premises (in the cash register or safe) is minimized, there is less chance of loss through robbery, etc. Also, if the cash receipts are deposited daily, the restaurant's cash management is improved.			X	The primary purpose of this control is to safeguard cash and provide reliable accounting information. However, the control also adheres to managerial policy of sound cash management.
13. The bookkeeper has no access to cash.	If the bookkeeper has access to cash, the bookkeeper could easily misappropriate it and cover up the theft with a fictitious entry.	X			The purpose of this control is to help safeguard assets and provide reliable accounting information.
14. The bank statement reconciler accounts for the numerical sequence of meal checks, verifies the accuracy of the daily tapes, and compares the total from the daily tapes to: the print-out of total cash receipts produced by the cash register, the deposit which is shown on the bank statement, and the debit to cash and credit to sales for the day.	If these control procedures are not in effect, the manager could misappropriate cash, destroy the related checks and perhaps not be detected. Also, posting errors by the bookkeeper would be more difficult to detect if this control were not in effect.	X			This control involves both the safeguarding of assets and the provision of reliable accounting information.

restaurant. However, the manager may compensate for this lack of formal control by simply observing the various waitresses and asking customers about the quality of service.

However, in many cases a given control may only partially compensate for the absence of another control. For example, the sixth control in Exhibit 5-1 requires the cashier to check the price of each order. Now the question is whether there is another control which would compensate if control number six were not present. Some may argue that control number ten, which requires the manager to reprice each order, would compensate for the absence of repricing by the cashier. However, the manager's price check is after the fact; the customer has left the premises. Therefore, the manager's price check would not totally compensate for the lack of a price check by the cashier.

Internal Control and Firm Size

A final point concerns the size of an entity and its internal control system. Many companies are not large enough to have a control system as sophisticated as that illustrated for the restaurant. In these companies, however, control is achieved by active involvement by the owners in all phases of the firm's operations. For example, in some small restaurants the owner operates the cash register and carefully supervises all aspects of the restaurant's operations.

BASIC CONCEPTS OF INTERNAL ACCOUNTING CONTROL

Now that the nature of internal control has been discussed, the discussion turns to the ten basic concepts of internal accounting control:

- Management Responsibility

- Reasonable Assurance

- Methods of Data Processing

- Limitations

- Personnel

- Segregation of Functions

- Execution of Transactions

- Recording of Transactions

- Access to Assets

- Comparison of Recorded Accountability With Assets

The first four concepts are implied in the definition of internal accounting control presented earlier. The last six concepts are referred to as the essential characteristics of internal accounting control. Each of the ten concepts is discussed in this section.

Management Responsibility

Management is responsible for implementing and maintaining the system of internal accounting control. In fact, as indicated in the last section of this chapter, the Foreign Corrupt Practices Act requires companies under the jurisdiction of the Securities and Exchange Commission to implement and maintain a reasonable system of internal accounting control.

Reasonable Assurance

The concept of reasonable assurance recognizes that the cost of internal control should not exceed the expected benefits which will accrue from having the control. For example, management may decide that service in a restaurant can be evaluated without incurring the cost of a cash register that prints the time on the check when the check is presented for payment.

The cost/benefit concept is often difficult to apply in practice because precise measurements of costs and especially benefits cannot usually be made. A considerable amount of judgment is required to apply cost/benefit analysis.

Methods of Data Processing

The definition and concepts of internal accounting control are stated in terms of objectives. These objectives, and thus the definitions and concepts, are not influenced by the method of data processing used. For example, all internal control systems designed in conjunction with manual, electromechanical, or electronic data processing methods should strive to attain the control objectives defined above.

Limitations

A number of limitations are inherent in a system of internal accounting control. Four are discussed and illustrated in this section.

Errors by personnel. The effectiveness of many accounting controls depends upon the quality of the work performed by the people involved. For example, the control which requires the cashier to verify the price charged the customer is only as effective as the cashier. Although the cashier may be competent, the control will be ineffective if he or she causes errors due to mistakes in judgment, misunderstanding instructions, or becomes careless due to boredom or fatigue.

Collusion. The effectiveness of many control steps depends on a proper segregation of duties, and these controls can be circumvented by collusion. In the restaurant exhibit, the bank statement reconciler re-computes the day's sales and compares this amount to the related bank deposit to check that the manager deposited the correct amount. However, if the two people get together and agree to steal, the bank statement reconciler would ignore the discrepancies or not perform the computations on certain days.

Management override.   In some cases, the management of the company may have so much power over the people assigned control functions that management can override the control. In the restaurant exhibit, the manager might have so much influence over the bank statement reconciler that the reconciler could be persuaded not to perform the required computations on certain days. Management override has been a major factor in many of the major frauds and misstatements of financial statements which have actually occurred.

The present is not the future.   One major limitation of a system of internal accounting control is that present conditions are not guaranteed in the future. The system of internal accounting control may work fine today, but this is no guarantee that the system will be effective tomorrow or next year.

Personnel

Another concept and important characteristic of internal accounting control is the integrity and quality of personnel in the organization. As indicated earlier, many control procedures depend upon the personnel who are assigned various duties. If these people are not honest and competent, the control functions which they are assigned will not be effective.

Segregation of Functions

Segregation of incompatible functions is an important concept and characteristic of internal accounting control. For internal control purposes, any two functions are incompatible if the same person can both perpetuate and conceal errors (unintentional mistakes) or irregularities (defalcations or intentional distortions of financial statements) in the normal course of that person's duties. In the restaurant exhibit, the bookkeeper has no access to cash. However, if the bookkeeper did have access to cash, he or she could take some cash and cover up the theft by making a credit to cash and a debit to some other account. In this case, the bookkeeper would be responsible for incompatible functions.

Execution of Transactions

Another concept and characteristic of internal accounting control deals with the execution of transactions. This concept requires an independent party within the organization to review transactions to determine that they were executed as authorized and that they were authorized by people with the appropriate authority. This independent party is usually the internal auditor. For example, in reviewing the property, plant, and equipment accounts, the internal auditor will determine that all major additions or disposals were properly authorized.

In a corporation, the stockholders have the ultimate authority, and they will generally approve major decisions such as the sale of stocks or bonds. However, much of their authority is delegated to the board of directors, which in turn delegates the less important decisions to various individuals in the organization. Authorization for various transactions may be general or specific and is usually provided for in the corporation's by-laws and procedures manual. For example, general authorization is normally delegated to sales representatives to make sales to all parties who maintain a certain credit standing. Specific authorization may be delegated by the board of directors to the treasurer of the corporation to buy a certain amount of marketable securities to be held for six months. For a partnership, the authorization of various transactions is usually specified in the partnership agreement and procedures manual. The auditor should keep a copy of the documents which indicate authority and review these documents carefully.

Recording of Transactions

Another important internal accounting control concept and characteristic requires that transactions be recorded at the proper amount and in the appropriate accounting period. Although this concept sounds simple, the practical application is much more complex. In the restaurant exhibit, each of the accounting controls is designed to ensure that the debit to cash and the credit to sales are made for the proper amount and in the proper accounting period.

Access to Assets

Yet another internal accounting control concept and characteristic is that access to assets should be limited to authorized personnel. In practice, a company's policy on access to assets is determined by the risk of the asset being lost by theft or otherwise. For example, obviously all employees of an electric utility have access to the building in which they work, but only a very few employees have access to cash or the utility's nuclear reactor.

One important point about access to assets is that employees may in fact have access without physically touching the asset. For example, a bank employee has access to cash if he or she is able to use a computer terminal to transfer amounts between various customers' account balances.

Comparison of Recorded Accountability With Assets

A final concept and characteristic of internal accounting control involves the comparison of recorded accountability with assets. This means that the assets should be examined by an independent party and compared with the amounts recorded in the accounting records. The way in which the comparison is made and the frequency of the comparison depends on the nature of the asset. For example, once an internal auditor verifies the cost of the bank's buildings, there is obviously no need to reverify the cost recorded in the accounting records until an event such as an addition occurs. On the other hand, cash held in the teller's drawers should be counted frequently, and the amount from each count should be compared to the amount recorded in the accounting records.

Two important points about the comparison process should be noted. First, if the amount determined by the physical count does not agree with the amount shown in the accounting records, there is an error or errors in either the count or the accounting records. On the other hand, if the two amounts agree, the agreement does not prove that there is a lack of error in either place. For example, the internal auditor might remove some cash from the teller's drawers and falsify the count to cover up the shortage.

FOREIGN CORRUPT PRACTICES ACT

As indicated earlier, some companies are required by law to maintain a system of internal control. Specifically, the Foreign Corrupt Practices Act of 1977 amended the Securities Exchange Act of 1934 to require all companies which are registered with the SEC to maintain a satisfactory system of internal control.

Although the Foreign Corrupt Practices Act (FCPA) adopts the same broad objectives for an internal accounting control system as defined by *SAS No. 1*, practicing accountants and business people have a problem in defining a satisfactory system of internal control. Since neither the FCPA of 1977 nor the Securities Exchange Act of 1934 defines a satisfactory system of internal control, business people and accountants are concerned about what they need to do to be in compliance with the law.

In addition to the points discussed in the two previous paragraphs, the FCPA of 1977 also makes it illegal for any business entity to pay a bribe to a foreign official, foreign political party, or candidate for political office for the purpose of influencing his acts or decisions about the business interests of the company.

SUMMARY

Nature of internal control.   Accounting controls are concerned with the safeguarding of assets and the reliability of financial records. Other controls are classified as administrative controls. A compensating control takes the place of another control. Small companies can best achieve internal control by having the owner actively involved in all aspects of the business.

Basic concepts of internal accounting control.   There are ten basic concepts of internal accounting control: (1) management responsibility, (2) reasonable assurance, (3) methods of data processing, (4) limitations, (5) personnel, (6) segregation of functions, (7) execution of transactions, (8) recording of transactions, (9) access to assets and (10) comparison of recorded accountability with assets. The first four concepts are implied in the definition of internal accounting control. The last six concepts are referred to as the *essential characteristics* of internal accounting control.

Foreign Corrupt Practices Act.   The Foreign Corrupt Practices Act of 1977 amended the Securities Exchange Act of 1934 to require companies under the SEC's jurisdiction to maintain a satisfactory system of internal control. However, since a satisfactory system of internal control is not defined by law, many business people are concerned about what they need to do to be in compliance with the law. The Foreign Corrupt Practices Act also makes it illegal for any business entity to pay a bribe to a foreign official, foreign political party, or candidate for political office for the purpose of influencing his acts or decisions about the business interests of the company.

REVIEW QUESTIONS

5-1   Broadly define a system of internal control.

5-2   Explain how the prenumbering of checks in a restaurant enhances internal control.

5-3   Discuss the differences between accounting and administrative control.

5-4   Are accounting and administrative control classifications mutually exclusive? Explain.

5-5   Does the "safeguarding of assets," as comprehended by *SAS No. 1*, include existing and potential assets? Discuss.

5-6   What is a compensating control?

5-7   How do small companies achieve good internal control when the entity is not large enough to support a sophisticated system?

5-8   List the ten basic concepts of internal accounting control. Identify the six concepts considered as essential characteristics of internal accounting control.

5-9   Who is responsible for implementing and maintaining an adequate system of internal accounting control?

5-10   Discuss the concept of reasonable assurance. Who is responsible for determining the level of reasonable assurance?

5-11   List and briefly discuss four limitations inherent in a system of internal control.

5-12   Explain the concept of collusion. How does this affect internal control systems? Give a brief example of how collusion could occur in a restaurant.

5-13   What is the most important characteristic of an internal accounting control system? Explain.

5-14   Distinguish between errors and irregularities.

5-15   Discuss the concepts of internal accounting control that deal with the execution and recording of transactions.

5-16   Must employees have physical possession to have access to assets? Explain.

5-17   Discuss the requirements of the Foreign Corrupt Practices Act of 1977 concerning internal accounting control systems.

DISCUSSION QUESTIONS AND PROBLEMS

5-18   Now that you are studying auditing, you have started to become curious about various procedures that are done in order to strengthen internal control. After eating in a cafeteria recently, you decided to get a cup of coffee. The waitress took your bill which was printed on an adding machine tape and stapled the bill for the coffee to it. Payment is made to the cashier at the exit.

Explain the purpose of the procedures described above and list those concepts of internal control that are involved.

5-19   During the past summer you were employed as a bookkeeper for a small company in your home town. Assume that there are two employees and yourself. How should the following duties be distributed among the three employees in order to achieve the most optimal internal control system?

1.   Maintain accounts payable ledger
2.   Maintain general ledger
3.   Maintain accounts receivable ledger
4.   Maintain disbursements journal
5.   Issue credits on returned merchandise
6.   Prepare checks for signature
7.   Reconcile bank statement
8.   Deposit cash receipts

(AICPA adapted)

5-20   The town of Commuter Park operates a private parking lot near the railroad station for the benefit of town residents. The guard on duty issues annual prenumbered parking stickers to residents who submit an application form and show evidence of residency. The sticker is affixed to the auto and allows the resident to park anywhere in the lot for twelve (12) hours if four quarters are placed in the parking meter. Applications are maintained in the guard office at the lot. The guard checks to see that only residents are using the lot and that no resident has parked without paying the required fee.

Once a week the guard on duty, who has a master key for all meters, takes the coins from the meters and places them in a locked steel box. The guard delivers the box to the town storage building where it is opened, and the coins are manually counted by a storage department clerk who records the total cash counted on a "Weekly Cash Report." This report is sent to the town accounting department. The storage department clerk puts the cash in a safe, and on the following day the cash is picked up by the town's treasurer, who manually recounts the cash, prepares the bank deposit slip, and delivers the deposit to the bank. The deposit slip, authenticated by the bank teller, is sent to the accounting department, where it is filed with the "Weekly Cash Report."

Required:

Describe weaknesses in the existing system and recommend one or more improvements for each of the weaknesses to strengthen the internal control over the parking lot cash receipts.

Organize your answer sheet as follows:

Weakness	*Recommended Improvement(s)*

(AICPA adapted)

5-21   You have been engaged by the management of Alden, Inc., to review its internal control over the purchase, receipt, storage, and issue of raw materials. You have prepared the following comments which describe Alden's procedures.

- Raw materials, which consist mainly of high-cost electronic components, are kept in a locked storeroom. Storeroom personnel include a supervisor and four clerks. All are well trained, competent, and adequately bonded. Raw materials are removed from the storeroom only upon written or oral authorization of one of the production foremen.

- There are no perpetual-inventory records; hence, the storeroom clerks do not keep records of goods received or issued. To compensate for the lack of perpetual records, a physical-inventory count is taken monthly by the storeroom clerks who are well supervised. Appropriate procedures are followed in making the inventory count.

- After the physical count, the storeroom supervisor matches quantities counted against a predetermined reorder level. If the count for a given part is below the reorder level, the supervisor enters the part number on a materials-requisition list and sends this list to the accounts-payable clerk. The accounts-payable clerk prepares a purchase order for a predetermined reorder quantity for each part and mails the purchase order to the vendor from whom the part was last purchased.

- When ordered materials arrive at Alden, they are received by the storeroom clerks. The clerks count the merchandise and agree the counts to the shipper's bill of lading. All vendor's bills of lading are initialed, dated, and filed in the storeroom to serve as receiving reports.

Required:

Describe the weaknesses in internal control and recommend improvements of Alden's procedures for internal control over raw materials.

(AICPA adapted)

OBJECTIVE QUESTIONS*

Select the best answer to the following multiple choice questions.

5-22   The primary distinction between accounting controls and administrative controls is that accounting controls are designed primarily to

    A.   Safeguard assets.
    B.   Encourage adherence to management's policies.
    C.   Ensure that accounting information is reliable.
    D.   Both A and C.

5-23   Which of the following is not an essential characteristic of internal accounting control?

    A.   Reasonable assurance.
    B.   Access to assets.
    C.   Personnel.
    D.   Segregation of functions.

5-24   The concept which recognizes that the cost of an internal control procedure should not exceed the benefits is known as

    A.   Materiality.
    B.   Reasonable assurance.
    C.   Relative risk.
    D.   The exposure principle.

5-25   A CPA has been engaged to examine the financial statements of the Foreign Corporation. In this case, the primary responsibility for the system of internal control rests with

---

*Note: Questions marked with an asterisk are not AICPA adapted questions; otherwise, questions in this section have been taken from prior CPA examinations.

A. The senior on the engagement.
B. The partner on the engagement.
C. All people assigned to the engagement.
D. The client.

5-26   The method of data processing used has an impact on

A. The objectives of internal control.
B. The concepts of internal control.
C. The way in which a specific objective is achieved.
D. None of the above.

5-27   Which of the following functions are most compatible within a company with a good system of internal control?

A. Bookkeeper and petty cash custodian.
B. Computer programmer and computer operator.
C. Bookkeeper and cashier.
D. Bookkeeper and manager.

5-28   Defalcations, embezzlements, or intentional distortions of financial statements are described in auditing as

A. Errors.
B. Fraud.
C. Errors and irregularities.
D. Irregularities.

5-29   A company's policy on access to assets should be determined by

A. The extent to which the company uses a computerized system.
B. The type of asset.
C. The risk of the asset being lost.
D. The extent to which duties are segregated.

5-30   Internal control can generally be subdivided into administrative controls and accounting controls. The scope of study and evaluation of internal control contemplated by generally accepted auditing standards requires the consideration of

A. Both administrative controls and accounting controls.
B. Administrative controls.

C. Accounting controls.

D. Accounting controls in an audit engagement and administrative controls in a management advisory service engagement.

5-31   As an in-charge auditor you are reviewing a write-up of internal-control weaknesses in cash receipt and disbursement procedures. Which one of the following weaknesses, standing alone, should cause you the *least* concern?

A. Checks are signed by only one person.

B. Signed checks are distributed by the controller to approved payees.

C. The treasurer fails to establish whether names and addresses of check payees are bona fide.

D. Cash disbursements are made directly out of cash receipts.

5-32   The primary purpose of internal control relating to heavy equipment is

A. To ascertain that the equipment is properly maintained.

B. To prevent theft of the equipment.

C. To determine when to replace the equipment.

D. To promote operational efficiency of the dollars invested in the equipment.

5-33   Which of the following is an invalid concept of internal control?

A. In cases where a person is responsible for all phases of a transaction there should be a clear designation of that person's responsibility.

B. The recorded accountability for assets should be compared with the existing assets at reasonable intervals and appropriate action should be taken if there are differences.

C. Accounting control procedures may appropriately be applied on a test basis in some circumstances.

D. Procedures designed to detect errors and irregularities should be performed by persons other than those who are in a position to perpetrate them.

5-34   A secondary objective of the auditor's study and evaluation of internal control is that the study and evaluation provide

A. A basis for constructive suggestions concerning improvements in internal control.

B. A basis for reliance on the system of internal accounting control.

C. An assurance that the records and documents have been maintained in accordance with existing company policies and procedures.

D. A basis for the determination of the resultant extent of the tests to which auditing procedures are to be restricted.

5-35   Internal accounting control comprises the plan of organization and the procedures and records that are concerned with the safeguarding of assets and the

A. Decision processes of management.
B. Reliability of financial records.
C. Authorization of transactions.
D. Achievement of administrative objectives.

5-36   The basic concept of internal accounting control which recognizes that the cost of internal control should *not* exceed the benefits expected to be derived is known as

A. Reasonable assurance.
B. Management responsibility.
C. Limited liability.
D. Management by exception.

5-37   Which of the following is the *least* likely reason for the auditor's study and evaluation of internal control?

A. To determine the extent of audit testing.
B. To serve as a basis for reliance on the controls.
C. To determine the nature of transactions.
D. To serve as a basis for constructive service suggestions.

5-38*   Internal control, in the broad sense, includes controls which may be characterized as

A. Administrative controls.
B. Accounting controls.
C. Auditing controls.
D. B and C.
E. A and B.

5-39*   Administrative controls ordinarily

A. Are concerned with operational efficiency.
B. Are *more* important in the audit of a warehouseman than industrial audits.

C. Relate only *indirectly* to the financial records, and, therefore, would not require evaluation by the auditor.

D. A and C.

E. A, B, and C.

5-40   When evaluating internal control, the auditor's primary concern is to determine

A. The possibility of fraud occurring.

B. Compliance with policies, plans, and procedures.

C. The reliability of accounting information.

D. The type of an opinion he or she will issue.

5-41   The auditor recognizes that a "system" of internal control extends beyond those matters which relate directly to the functions of the accounting and financial departments. Which one of the following would the auditor generally consider *least* likely to be a part of a manufacturing company's "system" of internal control?

A. Time and motion studies which are of an engineering nature.

B. Quarterly audits by an insurance company to determine the premium for workmen's compensation insurance.

C. A budgetary system installed by a consulting firm other than a CPA firm.

D. A training program designed to aid personnel in meeting their job responsibilities.

5-42   Which of the following activities would be *least* likely to strengthen a company's internal control?

A. Separating accounting from other financial operations.

B. Maintaining insurance for fire and theft.

C. Fixing responsibility for the performance of employee duties.

D. Carefully selecting and training employees.

5-43   Hickory Company, whose financial statements are unaudited, has engaged a CPA to make a special review and report on Hickory's internal accounting control. In general, to which of the following will this report be *least* useful?

A. Hickory's management.

B. Present and prospective customers.

C. A regulatory agency having jurisdiction over Hickory.

D. The independent auditor of Hickory's parent company.

5-44   A well-designed system of internal control that is functioning effectively is more likely to detect an irregularity arising from

A.   The fraudulent action of several employees.
B.   The fraudulent action of an individual employee.
C.   Informal deviations from the official organization chart.
D.   Management fraud.

5-45   For good internal control, the person who should sign the checks is the

A.   Person preparing the checks.
B.   Purchasing agent.
C.   Accounts-payable clerk.
D.   Treasurer.

5-46   To strengthen the system of internal accounting control over the purchase of merchandise, a company's receiving department should

A.   Accept merchandise only if a purchase order or approval granted by the purchasing department is on hand.
B.   Accept and count all merchandise received from the usual company vendors.
C.   Rely on shipping documents for the preparation of receiving reports.
D.   Be responsible for the physical handling of merchandise but *not* the preparation of receiving reports.

5-47   Which of the following is a standard internal accounting control for cash disbursements?

A.   Checks should be signed by the controller and at least one other employee of the company.
B.   Checks should be sequentially numbered and the numerical sequence should be accounted for by the person preparing bank reconciliations.
C.   Checks and supporting documents should be marked "Paid" immediately after the check is returned with the bank statement.
D.   Checks should be sent directly to the payee by the employee who prepares documents that authorize check preparation.

5-48   Which of the following is the *best* reason why an auditor should consider observing a client's distribution of regular payroll checks?

A.   Separation of payroll duties is less than adequate for effective internal control.

B. Total payroll costs are a significant part of total operating costs.

C. The auditor did *not* observe the distribution of the entire regular payroll during the audit in the prior year.

D. Employee turnover is excessive.

5-49   A factory foreman at Steblecki Corporation discharged an hourly worker but did *not* notify the payroll department. The foreman then forged the worker's signature on time cards and work tickets and, when giving out the checks, diverted the payroll checks drawn for the discharged worker to his own use. The most effective procedure for preventing this activity is to

A. Require written authorization for all employees added to or removed from the payroll.

B. Have a paymaster who has *no* other payroll responsibility distribute the payroll checks.

C. Have someone other than persons who prepare or distribute the payroll obtain custody of unclaimed payroll checks.

D. From time to time, rotate persons distributing the payroll.

5-50   Internal control over cash receipts is weakened when an employee who receives customer mail receipts also

A. Prepares initial cash receipts records.

B. Records credits to individual accounts receivable.

C. Prepares bank deposit slips for all mail receipts.

D. Maintains a petty cash fund.

5-51   When considering internal control, an auditor must be aware of the concept of reasonable assurance which recognizes that

A. The employment of competent personnel provides assurance that the objectives of internal control will be achieved.

B. The establishment and maintenance of a system of internal control is an important responsibility of the management and *not* of the auditor.

C. The cost of internal control should *not* exceed the benefits expected to be derived from internal control.

D. The segregation of incompatible functions is necessary to obtain assurance that the internal control is effective.

5-52   A system of internal accounting control normally would include procedures that are designed to provide reasonable assurance that

A. Employees act with integrity when performing their assigned tasks.

B. Transactions are executed in accordance with management's general or specific authorization.

C. Decision processes leading to management's authorization of transactions are sound.

D. Collusive activities would be detected by segregation of employee duties.

5-53   When considering the effectiveness of a system of internal accounting control, the auditor should recognize that inherent limitations do exist. Which of the following is an example of an inherent limitation in a system of internal accounting control?

A. The effectiveness of procedures depends on the segregation of employee duties.

B. Procedures are designed to assure the execution and recording of transactions in accordance with management's authorization.

C. In the performance of most control procedures, there are possibilities of errors arising from mistakes in judgment.

D. Procedures for handling large numbers of transactions are started on electronic data processing equipment.

5-54   Internal administrative control includes the overall plan of organization and the procedures that are concerned with

A. Safeguarding the assets and providing reliable financial records.

B. The decision process leading to management's authorization of transactions.

C. The execution of transactions in accordance with special or general authorization.

D. Providing reasonable assurance that access to assets is permitted only in accordance with management authorization.

5-55   Effective internal control in a small company that has an insufficient number of employees to permit proper division of responsibilities can *best* be enhanced by

A. Employment of temporary personnel to aid in the separation of duties.

B. Direct participation by the owner of the business in the record-keeping activities of the business.

C. Engaging a CPA to perform monthly "write-up" work.

D. Delegation of full, clear-cut responsibility to each employee for the functions assigned to each.

5-56   Which of the following *best* describes proper internal control over payroll?

A.   The preparation of the payroll must be under the control of the personnel department.
B.   The confidentiality of employee payroll data should be carefully protected to prevent fraud.
C.   The duties of hiring, payroll computation, and payment to employees should be segregated.
D.   The payment of cash to employees should be replaced with payment by checks.

5-57   For good internal control, the monthly bank statements should be reconciled by someone under the direction of the

A.   Credit Manager.
B.   Controller.
C.   Cashier.
D.   Treasurer.

5-58   Which of the following is a responsibility that should *not* be assigned to only one employee?

A.   Access to securities in the company's safe deposit box.
B.   Custodianship of the cash working fund.
C.   Reconciliation of bank statements.
D.   Custodianship of tools and small equipment.

5-59   Which of the following *best* describes the inherent limitations that should be recognized by an auditor when considering the potential effectiveness of a system of internal accounting control?

A.   Procedures whose effectiveness depends on segregation of duties can be circumvented by collusion.
B.   The competence and integrity of client personnel provides an environment conducive to accounting control and provides assurance that effective control will be achieved.
C.   Procedures designed to assure the execution and recording of transactions in accordance with proper authorizations are effective against irregularities perpetrated by management.
D.   The benefits expected to be derived from effective internal accounting control usually do *not* exceed the costs of such control.

5-60 Sanbor Corporation has an inventory of parts consisting of thousands of different items of small value individually, but significant in total. Sanbor could establish effective internal accounting control over the parts by requiring

A. Approval of requisitions for inventory parts by a company officer.

B Maintenance of inventory records for all parts included in the inventory.

C. Physical counts of the parts on a cycle basis rather than at year-end.

D. Separation of the store-keeping function from the production and inventory record-keeping functions.

5-61 Which of the following, if material, would be an irregularity as defined in Statements on Auditing Standards?

A. Errors in the application of accounting principles.

B. Clerical errors in the accounting data underlying the financial statements.

C. Misinterpretation of facts that existed when the financial statements were prepared.

D. Misappropriation of an asset or groups of assets.

5-62 Internal control is a function of management, and effective control is based upon the concept of charge and discharge of responsibility and duty. Which of the following is one of the overriding principles of internal control?

A. Responsibility for accounting and financial duties should be assigned to one responsible officer.

B. Responsibility for the performance of each duty must be fixed.

C. Responsibility for the accounting duties must be borne by the auditing committee of the company.

D. Responsibility for accounting activities and duties must be assigned only to employees who are bonded.

5-63 Effective internal control requires organizational independence of departments. Organizational independence would be impaired in which of the following situations?

A. The internal auditors report to the audit committee of the board of directors.

B. The controller reports to the vice president of production.

C. The payroll accounting department reports to the chief accountant.

D. The cashier reports to the treasurer.

5-64   In connection with the study and evaluation of internal control during an examination of financial statements, the independent auditor

A. Gives equal weight to internal accounting and administrative control.

B. Emphasizes internal administrative control.

C. Emphasizes the separation of duties of client personnel.

D. Emphasizes internal accounting control.

After studying this chapter, students should understand

1. The five categories of assertions about financial statements.
2. The five minimum substantive audit procedures which are applied to income statement account balances.
3. The five minimum substantive audit procedures which are applied to balance sheet account balances, including the differences in the ways the procedures are applied to the two types of balance sheet account balances.
4. The relationship between minimum substantive audit procedures for balance sheet and income statement accounts.
5. The nature of evidential matter, including factors which influence the auditor's judgment about the competency and sufficiency of evidential matter.
6. The nature of quality control for a CPA firm, and the elements of quality control for a CPA firm.

Chapter 6

Nature of Evidential Matter and Audit Tests

This chapter was written by
Johnny R. Johnson, Ph.D., C.P.A.,
Associate Professor of Accounting,
University of Georgia

INTRODUCTION

The third standard of field work requires the auditor to obtain sufficient competent evidential matter to afford a reasonable basis for an opinion regarding the financial statements under examination. The auditor obtains the evidence by using auditing procedures such as inspection, observation, inquiries, and confirmations. In fact, much of the auditor's work involves obtaining and evaluating evidence about the assertions which the client's management is making in their financial statements. In evaluating evidence, however, auditors must recognize that evidence differs in competence, and thus in the impact which the evidence should have on the auditor's decision process, which ultimately leads to an opinion on the client's financial statements. For example, factors such as pertinence, objectivity, timeliness, and the existence of other related evidential matter all influence the competence of evidence. Once the auditor has made a decision about the competence of the evidence, the auditor must then make a decision about the quantity of evidence, i.e., given the competence of the evidence, how much evidence is necessary to support the client's assertions which are reflected in the financial statements? The first part of this chapter discusses evidential matter.

In addition to evaluating evidential matter about financial statement assertions, an auditor must also gather evidential matter to indicate how he or she has complied with the statements of quality control for CPA firms, which have been issued by the profession. These statements on quality control are discussed in the second part of this chapter.

EVIDENTIAL MATTER

As indicated earlier, an auditor gathers evidential matter to evaluate the assertions which the client makes in the financial statements. This section begins with a discussion of the nature of financial statement assertions which management makes in its financial statements. This discussion is followed by discussions on the use of assertions in developing audit objectives and designing substantive tests, the nature of evidential matter, the competency of evidential matter, the sufficiency of evidential matter, and the evaluation of evidential matter.

NATURE OF ASSERTIONS

As indicated in Chapter 1, auditing is defined by the American Accounting Association as

. . . a systematic process of objectively obtaining and evaluating evidence regarding assertions about economic actions and events to ascertain the degree of correspondence between those assertions and established criteria and communicating the results to interested users.

According to *SAS No. 31, Evidential Matter*, management's assertions can be either explicit or implicit and can be classified in one or more of the following five categories:

- Existence or occurrence
- Completeness
- Rights and obligations
- Valuation or allocation
- Presentation or disclosure

Assertions about existence or occurrence deal with whether assets and liabilities which are shown in the client's financial statements exist at the date of the financial statements and whether the transactions which are reflected in the financial statement balances actually occurred. For example, when the client prepares financial statements, the client is asserting that the assets and liabilities which are shown in the financial statements exist. In addition, the client is asserting that the balances in the financial statements, such as revenues, expenses, gains, and losses, resulted from transactions which actually occurred.

In addition to assertions about existence or occurrence, management also makes assertions about the completeness of the financial statements. For example, when management presents a balance sheet for the company, management is asserting that the balance sheet contains all of the assets, liabilities, and equity amounts, including revenues, expenses, gains, and losses, which should be reported for the company in accordance with GAAP.

Assertions about rights and obligations deal with whether assets reported are the rights of the company and whether the liabilities reported are the obligations of the company. These assertions about assets and liabilities follow directly from the definitions of assets and liabilities which are presented by the FASB in *Statement of Financial Accounting Concepts No. 3*, "Elements of Financial Statements of Business Enterprises." In this document, the FASB defined assets in terms of probable future economic benefits which are obtained or controlled by the entity, i.e., assets are defined in terms of future economic benefits which the company has a right to receive. Likewise, liabilities are defined in terms of probable future economic sacrifices which the company has an obligation to make.

Assertions about valuation or allocation deal with whether the elements of the financial statements are recorded in accordance with generally accepted accounting principles. For example, when management reports a balance for equipment and related accumulated depreciation, management is asserting that the equipment is recorded at historical cost, that such cost is being allocated to the accounting periods which benefit from that cost, and that the allocation is being performed in a systematic and rational manner.

Finally, assertions about presentation or disclosure deal with whether particular components of the financial statements are properly classified, described, and disclosed in accordance with GAAP. For example, when management presents earnings per share data, management is asserting that the computations, presentations, and disclosures with respect to earnings per share are presented in accordance with GAAP.

USE OF ASSERTIONS IN DEVELOPING AUDIT OBJECTIVES AND DESIGNING SUBSTANTIVE TESTS

Over time auditors have developed a set of minimum audit procedures which they use to substantiate or validate the assertions which management makes about the income statement and balance sheet accounts which appear in the financial statements of the client. In developing these minimum audit procedures, auditors, of course, considered the five basic assertions which were discussed in the previous section and used experience and judgment in arriving at the minimum audit procedures which could best be used to substantiate or validate the assertions. These minimum audit procedures are applied to income statement and balance sheet accounts on every audit engagement, but the extent to which they are applied depends on the client's system of internal control. For example, if internal control is good, the minimum audit procedures may be applied to only the most material account balances, and some of the accounts with smaller balances, especially small income statement balances, may not be substantiated or validated at all. Likewise, the extent to which the minimum audit procedures are applied to a specific balance sheet or income statement balance also depends on the client's system of internal control. For example, if internal control over cash is good, the minimum audit procedures for balance sheet accounts may be applied to the largest bank account balances to substantiate the cash balance which appears on the balance sheet. On the other hand, if internal control over cash is poor, the minimum audit procedures for balance sheet accounts may be applied to every bank account balance and to petty cash. Also, if internal control is poor, the auditor may apply other procedures, in addition to the minimum audit procedures, to substantiate or validate an account balance which appears in the financial statements.

The relationship between substantive tests and internal control is considered in detail in Chapter 8. In this chapter, the concept of minimum audit procedures to substantiate an account balance is introduced. Students may find that it is helpful to refer to these minimum audit procedures, starting with Chapter 11, when they study audit programs for substantiating specific account balances because the audit programs to substantiate a specific account balance are based on the minimum audit procedures which are discussed in this section. Also, when students take professional examinations, they are likely to find that it is very helpful to have a general approach for writing audit programs to substantiate account balances because there is no guarantee that they will be asked to write an audit program to substantiate familiar account balances.

Before considering the minimum audit procedures for income statement balances, students should recognize three other important points. First, when applying any of the minimum audit procedures to either income statement or balance sheet accounts, the auditor is testing all of the assertions that management is making about the account balances. Thus, while the emphasis of a particular minimum audit procedure may be on one or two assertions, the auditor cannot ignore information about other assertions which is discovered when a particular minimum audit procedure is applied.

Second, the auditor's assessment of internal control and the extent to which minimum substantive audit procedures should be applied is a preliminary assessment which may change as the auditor applies the minimum substantive audit procedures. Accordingly, when the auditor applies the minimum substantive audit procedures, the auditor may change his or her assessment of internal control and the extent to which the minimum audit procedures should be applied.

Third, while the minimum substantive audit procedures for income statement and balance sheet accounts are discussed separately, the substantive procedures for all accounts are closely related. This point is discussed in more detail later in this chapter.

MINIMUM SUBSTANTIVE AUDIT PROCEDURES FOR INCOME STATEMENT BALANCES

In income statement balances the client accumulates financial information about transactions which have an impact on a specific accounting period, and these transactions are posted to the general ledger either monthly or daily. Over time, auditors have identified five minimum substantive audit procedures which are applied to income statement balances.

1. *Examine a sample of transactions for the period to determine that the transactions are properly recorded.* In applying this minimum audit procedure, auditors are trying to substantiate the client's assertions about the existence or occurrence of the transactions and the completeness of the transactions. To substantiate the existence or occurrence of transactions the auditor typically takes a sample of the transactions which have been posted to the account and verifies that the posted transactions did occur during the period and are recorded in accordance with GAAP. For example, if the auditor is auditing miscellaneous expense, the auditor will examine a sample of the transactions which have been posted to miscellaneous expense to determine that the transactions did occur and are recorded in accordance with GAAP. This verification can involve many detail procedures. For example, the auditor will first scan the journal entries which have been made to the account for the period to identify those transactions, especially any unusual transactions, which he or she believes should be substantiated. Then the auditor will substantiate that the transactions did occur and are recorded in accordance with GAAP by using audit procedures such as

   - Confirmation of the transaction with parties outside the client's organization. For example, auditors confirm sales to customers with the customer.

   - Examination of supporting documents such as cancelled checks, invoices, receiving reports, shipping reports, contracts, minutes of meetings, and leases. For example, an auditor might verify rent expense by comparing the rent expense with the client's lease and the cancelled check indicating the lease payment was made.

   - Making inquiries about the transaction to responsible people both within and outside the client's organization. For example, in substantiating the entries for depreciation expense, the auditor will have to make inquiries to responsible people about the useful life, salvage value, and depreciation method used for the asset. Of course, the auditor will also need to substantiate the cost of the asset, but the cost of the asset is usually substantiated by examining supporting documentation.

- Reading a description of and evaluating the appropriateness of a client's procedures and policies. For example, all large clients will have a chart of accounts which lists each account balance maintained by the client and the appropriate debits and credits which should be made to that account. Therefore, the auditor must examine the chart of accounts to determine that the chart of accounts, if followed, will result in the accumulation of financial information in accordance with GAAP. Also, the auditor will have to refer to the chart of accounts to determine that a particular entry is recorded in the proper account as indicated by the chart of accounts.

- Recalculation of the amounts of revenues or expenses. In addition to examining documents to support an entry for a revenue or expense, the auditor should also recalculate the amount of the entry. For example, in evaluating an entry to record depreciation expense, the auditor will recalculate the depreciation expense recorded by the client.

In addition to determining that recorded amounts are based on actual transactions which were properly recorded in accordance with GAAP, the auditor also substantiates that the amounts recorded are complete, i.e., the auditor verifies that the client has recorded all the transactions that it should have recorded in the particular income statement account. This verification is also accomplished by procedures such as recalculation, inquiries, examination of supporting documents, etc. However, the emphasis now is on examining a sample of transactions which should have been recorded and determining that the transactions were recorded in accordance with GAAP. In deciding on the transactions to examine, the auditor should exercise judgment and recognize the relationships between various accounts. For example, the auditor should exercise his or her experience and judgment in identifying any transaction, such as the accrual for the audit fee or a contingency, or depreciation on new equipment, that the client may either inadvertently or intentionally fail to record. Likewise, the auditor should also recognize the relationship between balance sheet and income statement accounts in identifying a sample of transactions which the client should have recorded. For example, any depreciable asset should have a related depreciation expense and vice versa. Likewise, any note receivable or payable should have a related interest accrual and vice versa.

2. *Once the auditor determines that his or her sample of transactions is properly recorded, the auditor must next verify the mathematical accuracy of the account balances.* Thus, the auditor must not only verify the existence and completeness of the individual entries, but the auditor must determine that the individual entries to the account are properly summarized to arrive at the account balance. In cases where the individual transactions are posted directly to the account balance, the auditor verifies the mathematical accuracy of the account balance by adding up the individual debits and credits to the account and making sure the debits and credits sum to the balance which is in the account. In cases where transactions are first posted to a special journal, the auditor first verifies the mathematical accuracy of the special journal, and then he or she verifies that the special journals were properly posted to the general ledger and that the postings to the general ledger accumulate to the balance which is shown in the account.

3. *The third minimum audit procedure which is applied to substantiate income statement balances is a procedure to verify the accuracy of the cutoff.* Since income statement balances accumulate amounts for a single accounting period, it is important that the balances only reflect transactions that relate to the accounting period being audited. Thus, an income statement balance should not reflect transactions that should have been reported in the previous accounting period or next accounting period.

   To verify the accuracy of the cutoff, the auditor takes a sample of transactions which occurred or should have occurred around the end of the accounting period. Then the auditor applies detailed audit procedures, such as confirmation, inquiries, and inspection of documents to verify the cutoff. For example, for the sales cutoff, the auditor will prepare a schedule of the last sales which were recorded in the current accounting period and the first sales which were recorded in the next accounting period. Then the auditor will examine shipping documents to verify the cutoff. In verifying the cutoff the auditor is concerned with both the existence of the transactions which were recorded and the completeness of the transactions which should have been recorded.

   As explained in the previous paragraph, when the auditor verifies the cutoff at the end of one accounting period, he or she also verifies the cutoff for the beginning of the next accounting period. However, when the auditor obtains a new client, the auditor must perform two cutoff tests: one for the beginning of the current period and the end of the previous period and one for the end of the current period and the beginning of the next period.

4. *After the auditor substantiates the existence and completeness of income statement balances, including the cutoff, the auditor next verifies that the account balance and any necessary disclosures related to that balance are fairly presented in accordance with GAAP.*   In applying this procedure, the auditor frequently makes use of checklists of disclosure and presentation principles which are required by GAAP. These disclosure and presentation checklists, which have been prepared by CPA firms, provide the auditor with a useful reminder list of disclosures and presentation principles which are required by GAAP so that the auditor does not have to review the details of each official pronouncement. However, the auditor should not rely too heavily on these checklists since any material information, whether disclosure is presently required by GAAP or not, should be disclosed if the information is important to the users of the financial statements.

    In addition, when the auditor performs this fourth minimum audit procedure to verify income statement balances, the auditor should also verify that the account balances, as well as detail relating to these account balances, are the same in every place that they appear in the working papers. Normally an account balance will appear in at least three places in the working papers: (1) on the financial statements, (2) on the working trial balance, and (3) on the specific working papers which the auditor uses to show the audit procedures which were followed in substantiating the assertions which the client is making about the balance. As indicated in Chapter 4, the auditor uses tick marks to cross reference the balances and to indicate that a given balance, or details relating to a balance, is reported at the same amount every time that it appears in the working papers.

5. *The fifth minimum audit procedure which is applied to income statement balances is analytical review.*   As discussed in more detail in Chapters 7 and 8, analytical review procedures include any technique which the auditor uses to review the reasonableness

of account balances and the reasonableness of the relationship between balances. For example, one analytical review procedure is to review the reasonableness of the relationship between interest expense and interest bearing debt and vice versa.

Analytical review procedures are applied continuously throughout the audit. For example, the auditor applies analytical review procedures at the beginning of the audit to identify account balances which appear to be out of line with the auditor's expectations. Then the results of this preliminary analytical review are combined with the auditor's preliminary assessment of internal control to determine the extent to which the minimum audit procedures will be applied. Also, analytical review procedures are used during the audit as the auditor obtains more detailed information about account balances and thus the reasonableness of the balances and the reasonableness of the relationships between account balances. Likewise, as indicated earlier, the auditor uses analytical review procedures when deciding on a sample of transactions to use to substantiate the completeness of account balances, e.g. every depreciable asset should be accompanied by depreciation expense and vice versa. Finally, the auditor uses analytical review procedures at the completion of the audit before the financial statements are released as a final check on the reasonableness of the account balances which are reported in the client's financial statements.

Exhibit 6-1 contains a sample audit working paper with tick marks to explain how the auditor applied the five minimum audit procedures, which apply to any income statement balance, to substantiate miscellaneous expense.

In reviewing this working paper, students may wonder why the auditors were not more explicit in describing the procedures which they performed to verify the completeness of the account, the cutoff, and to indicate the analytical review procedures which were performed. The answer is that this work was done, but the work was documented elsewhere in the working papers. Thus, firms frequently document analytical review procedures and cutoff work for all accounts together in one section of the working papers. However, the work is physically done separately as each account is substantiated.

Exhibit 6-1
Sample Substantive Audit Working Paper
for Miscellaneous Expense

Date: 1-23-84

Preparer: J.J.

Reviewer: P.T.

Bowler Lumber Company
Analysis of Miscellaneous Expense
12/31/83

Date	Description	Amount
3/14/83	Dinner for overtime workers...............	$ 60.00
5/16/83	Refreshments for board of director's meeting....................... ✗	200.00
9/22/83	Green fees for accounting systems consultants................... ✗	100.00
9/22/83	Dinner for accounting systems consultants............................ ✗	200.00
10/16/83	Political contribution to Joe Watt........... ✗	1,000.00
	Total of entries for less than $30 each........ φ	600.00
	Balance per general ledger..................	2,160.00
	Adjusting entry #6 to reclassify political contribution..................	(1,000.00)
		$1,160.00
		T/B ✓

✗   Examine cancelled check.

✓   Footed.

T/B   Agrees with trial balance and financial statements.

φ   Scanned general ledger for reasonableness of explanation and amount. No exception noted.

Working Paper #15

MINIMUM SUBSTANTIVE AUDIT PROCEDURES FOR BALANCE SHEET BALANCES

Balance sheet balances differ from income statement balances in that balance sheet account balances provide a cumulative history of financial information instead of financial information for one accounting period. Furthermore, there are two distinct types of balance sheet account balances: (1) balances, such as fixed assets and accumulated depreciation, which typically have only a few entries made to the account during the accounting period and (2) balances, such as inventory and accounts receivable, which typically have a large number of entries made to the account during the accounting period. The entries to both types of balances are typically posted daily or monthly, if special journals for cash receipts and cash disbursements are used. However, the amounts of the entries are quite different. Entries to the accounts which have only a few entries are typically for large amounts whereas the entries to the accounts which have a large number of entries are for relatively small amounts. In addition, for the balance sheet accounts which have a large number of entries, the details of the account balance at the end of the accounting period are typically totally different than they were at the beginning of the accounting period. For example, for accounts receivable or accounts payable, the subsidiary ledger accounts and balances at the end of the period are usually quite different, especially for the amount of the balances. On the other hand, accounts which require only a few entries during the period are by definition very similar, except in some cases for the amount of the balances.

Over time auditors have developed minimum substantive audit procedures for both types of balance sheet account balances, and these procedures include the same five basic procedures which are applied to income statement balances. However, the procedures are applied differently for balance sheet accounts because of basic differences in the nature of balance sheet and income statement balances. Also, the procedures are applied differently for the two types of balance sheet account balances because of the differences in the nature of the balances. This section repeats the five minimum substantive audit procedures with emphasis on how the procedures are applied for the two different types of balance sheet account balances.

1. *Examine a sample of transactions for the period to determine that the transactions are properly recorded.* As indicated earlier, when the auditor applies this minimum substantive audit procedure for income statement balances, he or she is testing client assertions about existence or occurrence, completeness, rights and

obligations, valuation or allocation and presentation or disclosure. These same assertions are also tested when the auditor carries out this first substantive procedure for balance sheet balances. However, the way in which the procedure is applied differs for the two types of balance sheet accounts.

When this first general substantive audit procedure is applied to balance sheet balances which have only a few entries for the period and for which, by definition, the ending balance is closely related to the beginning balance, the auditor, usually begins by having the client prepare a schedule which shows (1) the balance of the account at the beginning of the period, (2) the debits or credits to the account during the period, and (3) the ending balance in the account. Then the auditor compares the beginning balance on the schedule with the ending balance which is shown on the auditor's prior period's working papers. Next, the auditor substantiates the ending balance in the account by verifying the debits and credits which are, and should have been, posted to the account. In verifying these debits and credits, the auditor uses the same types of detailed audit procedures as he or she used in carrying out the first minimum substantive audit procedure for income statement balances. Thus, the auditor uses detailed audit procedures such as scanning, confirmation, examination of supporting documents, inquiries, reading and evaluating documents, and recalculation in auditing both income statement and balance sheet accounts.

When the auditor carries out the first minimum substantive audit procedure for balance sheet accounts which require many entries during the period and for which the beginning and ending balance are not closely related, usually the auditor first has the client prepare a schedule which shows the composition of the ending balance. For example, for receivables or payables the auditor has the client prepare a listing of the subsidiary ledger accounts and balances which make up the end of the period balance which is shown in the general ledger and financial statements. Likewise, the auditor has the client prepare a listing of the inventory items which add up to the balance which is shown in the financial statements. After the auditor receives these schedules which show the composition of the ending balances for these accounts, the auditor then uses detailed procedures such as scanning, confirmation, examination of supporting documents, etc. to evaluate whether the detail which is shown on the schedules and thus the balances which are shown in the financial statements are fairly stated in accordance with GAAP.

2. *Verify the mathematical accuracy of the general ledger account balance.*   This minimum substantive audit procedure for balance sheet accounts is carried out by verifying the mathematical accuracy of the client's schedules which show the composition of the general ledger balance. Thus, for balance sheet accounts with only a few entries for the period, the auditor verifies the mathematical accuracy of the general ledger when he or she verifies the footing (adding) of the client's schedule which shows the beginning balance, debits or credits for the period and ending balance. Also, the auditor indirectly verifies the mathematical accuracy of the ledger accounts which contain a large number of entries when he or she verifies the footing as well as individual balances from the schedules which show the composition of the ending balances in these accounts.

The other three minimum substantive audit procedures involve:

3. *Verifying the accuracy of the cutoff.*

4. *Verifying that the acccount balance and any necessary disclosures related to that balance are fairly presented in accordance with GAAP.*

5. *Applying analytical review procedures to the account balances.*

These three minimum substantive audit procedures are accomplished exactly the same way for both income statement and balance sheet accounts.

Exhibits 6-2 and 6-3 contain sample audit working papers with tick marks to explain how the auditor applied the five minimum audit procedures, which apply to any balance sheet balance, to substantiate retained earnings and accounts payable. Of course, retained earnings is an example of a balance sheet balance for which the beginning and ending balance are closely related whereas accounts payable is an example of a balance sheet balance for which the beginning and ending balances are not closely related. As indicated earlier, auditors usually document their tests for completeness, cutoff, and analytical review in separate sections of the working papers. However, this work is physically performed as each account is substantiated.

Exhibit 6-2
Sample Substantive Audit Working Paper
for Accounts Payable

Date: 2-15-84

Preparer: J.J.

Reviewer: P.J.

Bowler Lumber Company
Listing of Accounts Payable
12/31/83

Vendor	⋈ *Amount*
Johnson Electric Company.............................	$ 800.00
Gibson Lumber Company...............................	1,000.00
Vepco..	432.00
C&P Telphone..	318.00
Balance per general ledger............................	2,550.00
Adjusting entry #4 to accrue audit fee per Coopers and Lybrand WIP report dated 1/15/84.................	1,000.00
	T/B $3,550.00

⋈ Examined all cash disbursements and related invoices between 1/1/84 and 2/15/84 to verify that payables which should have been included on the list are in fact included and that bills which apply to 1984 are excluded from the list. No exceptions noted.

T/B Agrees with trial balance and financial statements.

✓ Footed.

Working Paper #19

Exhibit 6-3
Sample Substantive Audit Working Paper
for Retained Earnings

Date: 2-23-84
Preparer: J.J.
Reviewer: P.J.

Bowler Lumber Company
Schedule of Retained Earnings
12/31/83

Balance 12/31/82	$500,000	✓
Dividends		
6/30 10,000 shares at $10	(100,000)	⩗
1983 net income	400,000	T/B
	$800,000	T/B
	⩗	X

✓   Agrees with 1982 working paper #43.

⩗   Traced shares and amounts to 5/15/84 board of director's meeting. Verified extension. Examined all other minutes of board of directors, and no other dividends were declared.

T/B   Agrees with financial statements and working trial balance.

⩗   Footed.

X   The firm has reviewed the company's plans for expansion and concluded that the company does not have an accumulated earnings tax problem. See memo from Mike Ryan (WP #46).

Working Paper #70

RELATIONSHIP BETWEEN MINIMUM SUBSTANTIVE AUDIT PROCEDURES FOR BALANCE SHEET AND INCOME STATEMENT ACCOUNTS

Although the minimum substantive audit procedures for balance sheet and income statement accounts were discussed separately, students should realize, as indicated earlier, that there is a logical relationship between certain accounts, and that in practice related accounts are audited simultaneously. The following list which is not all inclusive contains some examples of accounts which are related and which are audited at the same time. Also, as indicated in Exhibit 6-4, one working paper is frequently used to document the work which was performed to substantiate several related account balances.

- Depreciable property, depreciation expense and accumulated depreciation.
- Prepaid insurance and insurance expense.
- Taxes payable and tax expense.
- Inventory and cost of goods sold.
- Sales and accounts receivable.

NATURE OF EVIDENTIAL MATTER

In the previous section, references were made to certain types of evidential matter such as invoices and cancelled checks. This section examines the nature of evidential matter.

According to *SAS No. 31*, evidential matter consists of all underlying accounting data and all corroborating information available to the auditor. The underlying accounting data includes the books of original entry, the general and subsidiary ledgers, related accounting manuals, such as a chart of accounts, and other informal records such as work sheets supporting cost allocations, computations, and reconciliations, such as a bank reconciliation. Students should recognize that the underlying accounting data is essential and without this data the auditor could probably not express an opinion on the financial statements. However, the auditor must also examine corroborating information which supports the underlying accounting information.

Corroborating information as indicated in *SAS No. 31* includes materials such as checks, invoices, contracts, and minutes of meetings. Corroborating information also includes confirmations and other written representations by knowledgeable people; information obtained by the auditor from inquiry, observation, inspection, and physical examination; and other information developed by, or available to, the auditor which permits the auditor to reach conclusions through valid reasoning.

Exhibit 6-4
Sample Substantive Audit Working Paper
for Prepaid Insurance and Insurance Expense

Date: 1-15-84

Preparer: J.J.

Reviewer: P.J.

Bowler Lumber Company
Analysis of Prepaid Insurance and Insurance Expense
12/31/83

① ∅ Description	① Period	Prepaid at 1/1/83	Premiums during 1983	Insurance expense	Prepaid at 12/31/83
Casualty Insurance on Buildings, Inventory, & Equipment ($1MM)	6/30/83 – 6/30/84	$12,000 ②	$24,000 ③	$24,000 ④	$12,000 ④ T/B

①   Examined policy—all details agree with policy.

②   Agrees with 1982 working paper #68.

③   Examined invoice.

④   Verified computation.

T/B   Agrees with financial statements and trial balance.

∅   The company has a policy of having its insurance coverage reviewed annually by Mike Dekel of State Farm. Examined Mike's report dated 6/18/83. He does not recommend any additional business coverage. However, he does recommend that the company purchase insurance on the lives of the officers. See WP #86 for analysis and management letter comment.

Working Paper #18

COMPETENCE OF EVIDENTIAL MATTER

When an auditor examines evidential matter, the auditor must evaluate both the competency and sufficiency of the evidence. The competency of evidential matter is considered in this section and the sufficiency of evidential matter is considered in the next section.

To be competent, evidential matter must be both valid and relevant. Of course, the relevancy of evidence is fairly easy to determine because a specific piece of evidence is generally either relevant or irrelevant to a specific assertion which is being examined.

The validity of evidential matter, however, is much more difficult to determine. The following presumptions about the validity of evidential matter are expressed in paragraph 18 of *SAS No. 31.*

- When evidential matter can be obtained from independent sources outside an entity, it provides greater assurance of reliability for purposes of an independent audit than that secured solely within the entity.

- When accounting data and financial statements are developed under satisfactory conditions of internal accounting control, there is more assurance about their reliability than when they are developed under unsatisfactory conditions of internal accounting control.

- The independent auditor's direct personal knowledge, obtained through physical examination, observation, computation, and inspection, is more persuasive than information obtained indirectly.

In addition to these presumptions which are discussed in *SAS No. 31*, the authors believe that there are two other useful presumptions about the validity of evidence.

- The validity of evidence which is determined from inquiries or confirmations depends to a large extent on the competence of the person responding to the inquiry or confirmation. Consequently, the auditors must consider the competence of the person who will provide the evidence before requesting oral or written evidence from that person.

- As a general rule, objective evidence is more valid than subjective evidence.

SUFFICIENCY OF EVIDENTIAL MATTER

As indicated in the introduction to this chapter, the independent auditor's purpose is to obtain sufficient competent evidential matter to provide a reasonable basis for an opinion on the financial statements. There are four important points with respect to the sufficiency of evidential matter.

First, the amount and kinds of evidence needed to support the auditor's opinion are largely a matter of professional judgment. However, statistical sampling techniques can give the auditor some objective ways of determining the quantity of evidence which is required. Techniques for determining sample sizes are discussed in Chapters 9 and 10.

Second, the fact that the auditor may be sued because of an opinion on financial statements which are subsequently found to be misleading, as a practical matter, cannot be ignored. Thus, as the risk of a lawsuit against the CPA increases, the amount of evidence which is required to support the auditor's opinion also must increase.

Third, more evidence is required to substantiate transactions with a related party than is required to substantiate transactions with an independent party. Related parties are defined in paragraph 2 of *SAS No. 6, Related Party Transactions*, as follows:

> The term related parties means the reporting entity; its affiliates, principal owners, management and members of their immediate families, entities for which investments are accounted for by the equity method; and any other party with which the reporting entity may deal when one party has the ability to significantly influence the management or operating policies of the other, to the extent that one of the transacting parties might be prevented from fully pursuing its own interest. Related parties also exist when one entity has the ability to significantly influence the management or operating policies of the transacting parties . . . .

Fourth, an auditor works within economic limits, and, if the auditor's opinion is to be useful, it must be formed within a reasonable length of time and at a reasonable cost. Thus, as a general rule there should be a relationship between the cost of obtaining evidence and the usefulness of the information obtained. However, the difficulty and expense involved in testing a particular item is not in itself a valid basis for omitting the test.

EVALUATION OF EVIDENTIAL MATTER

Most of the auditor's work in evaluating evidential matter takes place when he or she evaluates the competence and sufficiency of evidential matter. However, there are two general points about the evaluation of evidential matter which should be emphasized.

First, in designing audit procedures to obtain evidential matter, the auditor should recognize that the financial statements may not be fairly presented in accordance with GAAP.   Consequently, the auditor must be thorough in his or her search for edvidential matter and he or she must give consideration to relevant evidential matter regardless of whether it appears to corroborate or to contradict the assertions in the financial statements.

Second, if the auditor remains in doubt about any material assertion in the client's financial statements, the auditor must refrain from expressing an opinion on the financial statements until sufficient competent evidential matter is obtained to support the assertion.   Of course, if evidence cannot be obtained to support the opinion, the auditor must either qualify his or her opinion or disclaim an opinion because of the lack of sufficient competent evidential matter to express an opinion.

QUALITY CONTROL FOR CPA FIRMS

As indicated in the introduction to this chapter, auditors must not only obtain evidence about the assertions which the client is making in financial statements, but also, that they must accumulate evidence to indicate how they have complied with the quality control standards which have been established by the profession. This part of the chapter discusses quality control for CPA firms. It begins with a discussion on the nature of quality control for CPA firms followed by a discussion on the elements of quality control for a CPA firm.

NATURE OF QUALITY CONTROL FOR A CPA FIRM

Prior to September of 1977 a CPA firm could elect to have a voluntary quality control review by developing a quality control manual, which sets forth the firm's quality control practices and procedures, and having these practices and procedures reviewed by the firm's peers. Although this voluntary peer review is still in effect today, many firms, because of an action taken by the AICPA Council in September of 1977, are not participating in the old voluntary quality control review program. Instead, if they are participating in a quality control review program at all, they participate in the program which was started in 1977.

In September of 1977, the Council of the AICPA, under pressure from the United States Congress to formalize the profession's quality control review program, voted to establish two sections within the AICPA: (1) the Private Practices Section, and (2) the SEC Practices Section. Members of the AICPA do not have to join either section as of now, even if they have SEC clients. However, if a firm does join either section the firm has to develop a quality control manual and undergo peer review.

In a peer review, an independent peer review team evaluates the quality control practices and procedures of the CPA firm being reviewed. The peer review team is concerned with two basic questions about quality control: (1) Are the quality control policies and procedures which have been established by the firm adequate? and (2) Are the quality control practices and procedures which have been established being followed? The peer review team addresses these questions in its report on the peer review of the member firm, and these reports on peer reviews are in the public files of the SEC Section or Private Practices Section of the AICPA. Also, member firms may be sanctioned by their respective sections if they do not meet the quality control standards established by the section.

There are three sources of peer review teams. First, peer reviews may be conducted by teams which are appointed by the SEC Practices Section or the Private Practices Section of the AICPA. Second, a CPA firm may have its peer review performed by another CPA firm. This type of review is typically used by the larger national CPA firms. However, two firms cannot agree to exchange peer reviews. For example, Deloitte, Haskins, and Sells currently does the peer review for Arthur Andersen, and consequently Arthur Andersen cannot do the peer review for Deloitte, Haskins, and Sells. Finally, a CPA firm can have its peer review performed by a peer review team approved by an authorized entity such as a state society of CPAs or an association of CPA firms.

ELEMENTS OF QUALTIY CONTROL FOR A CPA FIRM

The Quality Control Standards Committee of the AICPA has identified nine elements of quality control for a CPA firm in *Statement on Quality Control Standards No. 1*. These elements of quality control are discussed in this section, with emphasis on the policies and procedures which a CPA firm might adopt to ensure that the firm achieves its quality control objectives.

Independence.   The first element of quality control is independence, and a CPA firm might adopt policies and procedures such as the following to ensure that the firm is independent in both fact and appearance.

- Establish an independence file in the library of each office of the firm. This file will typically include the independence requirements of the AICPA as well as the state board of accountancy, and a listing of the firm's clients for which independence is required.

- Designate one partner in each office as the partner in charge of independence, and require this partner to obtain a written representation from each person in the office which states that he or she has reviewed the firm's independence file and is independent in both fact and appearance with respect to each client for which independence is required.

- Emphasize the importance of independence in training programs and in the supervision and review of engagements.

- Require the partner in charge of independence matters to review any unpaid client bills to ensure that they do not in effect become loans to the client.

- Establish procedures for investigating the independence of correspondent firms, which the firm may use on some of its engagements.

Assigning personnel to engagements.   The second element of quality control deals with assigning personnel to engagements, and it requires a firm to establish policies and procedures to ensure that engagements are adequately staffed. A firm might comply with this element of quality control by adopting policies and procedures such as the following.

- Designate one person in each office of the firm as the person responsible for coordinating the assignment of personnel to engagements. This person will maintain an assignment schedule which shows the clients of that office and the various staff members which have been assigned to work on the engagements as well as the dates when the work will be done. Typically this information is entered on an assignment board, or displayed on a computer printout, and members of the staff can examine the board or printout and identify what they will be working on a month or so in advance. Also, the firm can identify peak periods in advance and plan for overtime or temporary help if needed.

- Require the partner on each engagement to request the staff for each engagement well in advance of the time the work will be done. The partner in charge of each engagement and the person in charge of assignments should consider factors such as the following in assigning personnel to engagements: (1) the special expertise which is required on the job, (2) previous personnel evaluations and the planned supervision of the staff member, (3) any potential conflict of interest between the staff member and the client, (4) the on-the-job training needs of the staff member, and (5) the need for both continuity and periodic rotation. With respect to this last point, the staff assigned to each engagement should not totally change from year to year, but at the same time the same staff should not be assigned to an engagement for too many years in a row because the staff may lose their objectivity. Consequently, some firms have a policy that one person cannot work on an engagement for more than a five year period.

- Establish policies and procedures for the use of detailed time budgets, with explanations for the difference between budgeted time and actual time on engagements. As indicated in Chapter 4, most firms use such budgets on all but the smallest engagements. However, even on these engagements a record should be maintained of the time which is spent on each engagement since the firm may have to justify the time spent on each aspect of the engagement either in court or to the client in cases where there might be a dispute over the fee.

Consultation. The third element of quality control is consultation and it requires firms to establish policies and procedures to ensure that members of the firm consult with a specialist in a given area when needed. To accomplish this goal, the firm typically identifies specialists, such as SEC specialists, both within the firm and within an office of the firm. These specialists are identified to each member of the firm, and members of the firm are encouraged, and in some cases required, to consult with the specialists as the need arises. For example, some firms have a policy that an EDP specialist spend at least a certain amount of time on all engagements which involve EDP applications.

Supervision. The fourth element of quality control is supervision, and it requires a firm to establish policies and procedures to ensure that each member of the firm is properly supervised. To accomplish this goal, a firm may establish policies and procedures such as the following.

- Require that work programs (audit programs for audits) be used on each engagement.

- Require that all work programs be approved by the partner in charge of the engagement.

- Establish standardized working papers for certain aspects of the audit.

- Identify the firm's policy on the review of working papers. Typically, all working papers are reviewed by the senior, manager, and partner on the engagement.

- Require that pre-engagement planning meetings be held on each engagement. In this meeting the partner in charge of the engagement discusses with the staff such factors as (1) background information for the client and how the partner used this information in planning the audit, (2) new tax, accounting, and auditing pronouncements which affect the client, (3) new developments for the client or its industry, and (4) the effect of current economic conditions on the client.

- Require that an engagement control checklist be prepared for each client. This checklist typically contains a listing of the key items which must be completed before the financial statements are released. A sample engagement control checklist is shown in Exhibit 6-5.

- Specify engagements for which a second partner review (horizontal review) is required and specify the duties and responsibilities of the second partner. Typically, firms specify that a second partner review

---

Exhibit 6-5
Sample Engagement Control Checklist

		Initials	Date
1.	Engagement letter prepared (Enter date of last letter _____)	_____	_____
2.	Work program approved by the partner in charge of the engagement................	_____	_____
3.	Work program steps completed and signed off.............................	_____	_____
*4.	Representation letter obtained from the client.............................	_____	_____
*5.	Legal letter obtained from client's counsel................................	_____	_____
6.	Material deficiencies in internal control communicated to the client in writing...	_____	_____
*7.	Second partner review completed (to be initialed only by the second partner).........	_____	_____
8.	Approval for continuance of client.............	_____	_____
9.	Other items, if applicable, list below...........	_____	_____

*Not required for unaudited financial statements or compilations.
Source: Johnny R. Johnson, "Quality Control in a Local Firm," *Journal of Accountancy*, February, 1979, p. 43.

be conducted for any engagement that involves an unusual degree of risk, and this assessment of risk differs among firms. For example, some of the large firms specify that a second partner review is required for all SEC clients whereas smaller firms specify that a second partner review is required for all audits. The second partner is usually responsible for reviewing and approving the audit program, the client's financial statements, and the firm's report on the financial statements.

- Specify the firm's policy with respect to indexing working papers.

- Identify the firm's rules on correspondence with clients and others outside the firm. Generally, all correspondence should be approved by a partner of the firm, and, in all cases, only a partner of the firm can sign the firm's report on financial statements.

- Communicate to the members of the firm that the firm's policy is to follow all official pronouncements of the AICPA, its committees, and the FASB and that members of the firm are responsible for keeping abreast of professional pronouncements.

- Specify policies for resolving differences in professional judgment among members of the firm.

Hiring.   The fifth element of quality control requires a CPA firm to establish policies and procedures over hiring personnel. Toward this goal, most CPA firms have formally established the qualifications which they expect in new employees and have developed procedures for communicating firm policies to job applicants as well as procedures for evaluating the qualifications of new personnel.

Professional development.   The sixth element of quality control is professional development, and it requires a CPA firm to establish policies and procedures to ensure that staff members receive adequate professional development. Professional development in CPA firms usually takes place both in centralized staff training schools which last one or two weeks and in staff training programs which take place in the local office and are typically for one or two days. In addition, professional pronouncements and the professional journals, such as the *Journal of Accountancy*, are made available to all staff members.

Advancement.   The seventh element of quality control is advancement, and it requires CPA firms to establish policies and procedures to ensure that staff members are capable of handling the duties which they are assigned. Toward this goal, CPA firms have established staff levels and have described what is expected of the staff at various levels. In addition, CPA firms carefully monitor personnel evaluations. A sample personnel evaluation form is shown in Exhibit 6-6.

Exhibit 6-6
Sample Personnel Evaluation Form

For each category, the staff member should be evaluated on a scale of 1 to 5, where a 5 represents superior performance and a 1 represents inadequate performance.

1. Technical competence........................... _____

2. Client relations............................... _____

3. Judgment .... _____

4. Written communication........................ _____

5. Oral communication........................... _____

6. Professional appearance....................... _____

7. Motivation .... _____

8. Supervision ability............................ _____
        Average score on 1 through 8................ _____

9. General evaluation of the staff
        member—please attach separate sheet

_____
Partner's signature

_____
Staff member's signature

_____
Date

Source: Johnny R. Johnson, "Quality Control in a Local Firm," *Journal of Accountancy*, February, 1979, p. 45.

Acceptance and continuance of clients.   The eighth element of quality control requires a CPA firm to establish policies and procedures to use in evaluating potential clients and existing clients. As indicated in Chapter 4, before a CPA firm accepts a client, the firm will consider such things as (1) the integrity of the client, (2) the ability of the firm to serve the client, (3) the required communication with the predecessor auditor, and (4) available financial information concerning the client. Many CPA firms have identified certain types of clients which they will not serve and certain other types of clients which present an unusual risk to the firm, and which require careful analysis before the firm accepts the client. For example, a CPA firm should not accept a client that lacks integrity or a client which the CPA firm does not have the expertise to serve. Also, for example, a CPA firm should consider a client to be a special risk if the client has a deteriorating financial position or has little or no internal control.

Inspection.   The ninth element of quality control requires a CPA firm to establish policies and procedures to ensure that the objectives of the firm's quality control program are being achieved. This inspection is accomplished by having internal and external peer reviews.

SUMMARY

The third standard of field work requires the auditor to obtain sufficient competent evidential matter to afford a reasonable basis for an opinion regarding the financial statements under examination. The auditor obtains the sufficient competent evidential matter by using auditing procedures such as inspection, observation, inquiries, confirmation, examination of supporting documents, and recalculations.

The assertions which management makes about its financial statements, and which the auditor tests, can be classified in one or more of the following five categories:

- Existence or occurrence
- Completeness
- Rights and obligations
- Valuation or allocation
- Presentation or disclosure

Over time auditors have developed a set of minimum audit procedures which they use to substantiate or validate the assertions which management makes about financial statement balances. These minimum audit procedures are applied to financial statement balances on every audit engagement, but the extent to which they are applied depends on the client's system of internal control. Also, there are slight differences in the ways the minimum audit procedures are applied to income statement balances and the two types of balance sheet balances. The five minimum substantive audit procedures are as follows:

1. Select a sample of transactions for the period to determine that the transactions are properly recorded.

2. Verify the mathematical accuracy of the account balance.

3. Verify the cutoff for the account balance.

4. Verify that the account balance and any necessary disclosures related to that balance are fairly presented in accordance with GAAP. In addition, verify that the account balances, as well as any detail relating to these account balances, are the same in every place that they appear in the working papers. Normally an account balance will appear in at least three places in the working papers: (1) on the financial statements, (2) on the working trial balance, and (3) on the specific working papers which the auditor uses to show the audit procedures which were followed in substantiating the assertions which the client is making about the balance.

5. Apply analytical review procedures to the account balance.

Evidential matter consists of all underlying accounting data and all corroborating information available to the auditor. When the auditor examines evidential matter, the auditor must evaluate both the competency and sufficiency of evidential matter.

There are five presumptions about the validity of evidential matter:

1. Evidential matter which is obtained from independent sources is generally more reliable than evidential matter secured solely within the entity.

2. Evidential matter which is developed under a satisfactory system of internal control is generally more reliable than evidential matter developed under an unsatisfactory system of internal control.

3. The independent auditor's direct personal knowledge is more persuasive than information obtained indirectly.

4. The validity of evidence which is determined from inquiries or confirmation depends to a large extent on the competence of the person, who responds to the inquiry or confirmation, to provide the evidence.

5. As a general rule, objective evidence is more valid than subjective evidence.

There are four important points with respect to the sufficiency of evidential matter.

1. The amount and kinds of evidence needed to support the auditor's opinion are largely a matter of professional judgment.

2. As the risk of a lawsuit against a CPA increases, the amount of evidence which is required to support the auditor's opinion also must increase.

3. More evidence is required to substantiate transactions with a related party than is required to substantiate transactions with an independent party.

4. As a general rule, there should be a relationship between the cost of obtaining evidence and the usefulness of the information obtained. However, the difficulty and expense involved in testing a particular item is not in itself a valid basis for omitting the test.

There are nine elements of quality control for a CPA firm:

- Independence
- Assigning personnel to engagements
- Consultation
- Supervision
- Hiring
- Professional development
- Advancement
- Acceptance and continuance of clients
- Inspection

REVIEW QUESTIONS

6-1   Why does an auditor gather evidential matter? List and explain two reasons in your answer.

6-2   Explain the differences between a client's assertions about existence and their assertions about completeness.

6-3   Explain how a client's assertions about rights and obligations relate to *Statement of Financial Accounting Concepts No. 3*.

6-4   When an auditor uses validation tests, what is the auditor trying to validate?

6-5   What determines the extent to which minimum audit procedures are applied?

6-6   Why might an auditor change his or her assessment of internal control as the auditor applies minimum audit procedures?

6-7   List and explain five minimum audit procedures which an auditor applies to substantiate management's assertions about income statement balances.

6-8   Give two examples of how an auditor might use judgment in testing the completeness of an account balance.

6-9   Give two examples of how an auditor might utilize the relationships between account balances in testing the completeness of account balances.

6-10   Explain how an auditor's verification of the mathematical accuracy of an account balance will differ depending on how frequently entries are posted to the account balance.

6-11   What do auditors mean by the term "cutoff"?

6-12   Why is it important for an auditor to verify the client's cutoff for account balances?

6-13   Explain how the auditor might verify the sales cutoff. The purchases cutoff.

6-14   When the auditor verifies the cutoff at the end of one accounting period, does he or she also verify the cutoff at the beginning of the next accounting period? Explain.

6-15   Explain how an auditor might use a checklist to substantiate that appropriate presentation and disclosure principles have been applied for a particular account.

6-16   State the general principle which governs disclosure in financial statements.

6-17   If a balance in an account is adjusted after the working trial balance is prepared, should the adjusting entry be shown in every place in the working papers where the account balance appears? Explain.

6-18   Define analytic review.

6-19   When does an auditor use analytic review procedures? Explain.

6-20   Should the auditor indicate on substantive audit working papers how the client's assertions about the completeness of an account balance was verified? Explain.

6-21   Is analytic review and cutoff work usually documented in a separate section of the working papers? Explain.

6-22   How do balance sheet balances differ from income statement balances?

6-23   List and describe two distinct types of balance sheet balances.

6-24   One minimum audit procedure is to examine a sample of transactions for the period to determine that the transactions are properly recorded in accordance with GAAP. Explain how this procedure is applied to both types of balance sheet balances.

6-25   Explain how an auditor verifies the mathematical accuracy of balance sheet balances. In your answer, indicate how this procedure differs for the two types of balance sheet balances.

6-26   Explain the relationship, if any, between minimum substantive audit procedures for balance sheet and income statement accounts.

6-27   What is evidential matter?

6-28   Explain the difference between underlying accounting data and corroborating information.

6-29 List and explain five presumptions about the validity of evidential matter.

6-30 List and explain four factors which have an impact on the sufficiency of evidential matter.

6-31 Are all CPA firms required to have a peer review? Explain.

6-32 What two basic questions does a peer review team try to answer about a CPA firm? Explain.

6-33 Identify three sources of peer review teams.

DISCUSSION QUESTIONS AND PROBLEMS

6-34 List and briefly explain the nine elements of quality control for a CPA firm. For each element of quality control, list and explain two policies and procedures which a firm might adopt to ensure that the firm achieves its quality control objective.

6-35 List and explain three auditing procedures which might be applied to substantiate each of the following assertions:

a. The existence of inventory.
b. The completeness of accounts payable.
c. The existence of petty cash.
d. The valuation of prepaid insurance.
e. The valuation of buildings.
f. The completeness of dividends.

6-36 During your audit of Jackson Candy, Inc., you obtain the following printout of the general ledger account for repairs and maintenance expense:

Date	Description	Amount	Balance
1- 1-84			0
2-15-84	Gas and oil	1,000.00	1,000.00
4-19-84	Rucker Repair Co.—repairs to forklift	2,000.00	3,000.00
6-15-84	Gas and oil	500.00	3,500.00
8-15-84	Peter Paint Co.—painting building	6,000.00	9,500.00
9-23-84	Gas and oil	2,000.00	11,500.00

Required:

1. Identify the specific assertions which the client is making about this account.
2. Write an audit program for your assistant to use in substantiating the assertions which you identified in part (1).

6-37 During your audit of the Tom Pushkin Company, you obtain the following printout of the general ledger account for Travel and Entertainment:

Date	Description	Amount	Balance
1- 1-85			0
3-28-85	Tom Pushkin—expenses for attending an EDP conference in New Orleans	1,000.00	1,000.00
8-15-85	Hotel Dal Cornoda-hotel room for Marty Hubbard-California Wine Convention	1,111.00	2,111.00
8-15-85	Hyatt Regency Atlanta-Ann Hubbard-hotel and meals-Southern Brewers Meeting	1,500.00	3,611.00

Required:

1. What assertion is the client making about this account balance?
2. Write an audit program for your assistant to use in substantiating the assertions which you identified in part (1).

6-38 During your audit of the Fred Company you obtain the following printout for the general ledger account for Due from officers:

Date	Description	Amount	Balance
1- 1-84	Loan to Rachel Fred, 8%, 180 days	10,000.00	10,000.00

Required:

1. What assertions is the client making about this account balance?
2. Given current economic conditions, do you see any problems with the presentation and disclosure for this account? Explain.
3. Write an audit program for your assistant to use in substantiating the assertions which you identified in part (1).

6-39 John Jones, CPA, has just completed a speech on Quality Control for CPA firms when a local television reporter posed the following question:

> "I don't see any quality in your quality control because quality control is not mandatory. It seems to me that this program was just a stopgap measure to get the government off of your backs. In addition, no CPA firm is going to report violations by another CPA firm."

Required:

Draft a response to the reporter's question.

6-40   After cocktails one night, a local CPA from Athens, Georgia makes the following comments to you.

> "I will have no part of peer review. This stuff is for the big firms in Atlanta and New York. I have been practicing for thirty years and I have never been sued. Can any of the big firms make this claim? You know that they can't. They need written policies and procedures because they are so big. My people have always done a good job, and they don't need a lot of paperwork to tell them what to do. Besides, I think peer review is simply a way for them to steal my clients. First, the New Yorkers eliminated encroachment, and now they want to come down here, review my clients, tell them what I am doing wrong, and take all my good clients away. No sir, I will have no part of peer review."

Required:

Draft a response to the CPA's comments.

6-41   The third generally accepted auditing standard of field work requires that the auditor obtain sufficient competent evidential matter to afford a reasonable basis for an opinion regarding the financial statements under examination. In considering what constitutes sufficient competent evidential matter, a distinction should be made between underlying accounting data and all corroborating information available to the auditor.

Required:

Discuss the nature of evidential matter to be considered by the auditor in terms of the underlying accounting data, all corroborating information available to the auditor, and the methods by which the auditor tests or gathers competent evidential matter.

(AICPA adapted)

6-42   In his examination of financial statements, an auditor must judge the validity of the audit evidence he obtains.

Required:

Assume that you have evaluated internal control and found it satisfactory.

a.   In the course of his examination, the auditor asks many questions of client officers and employees.

1. Describe the factors the auditor should consider in evaluating oral evidence provided by client officers and employees.
2. Discuss the validity and limitations of oral evidence.

b. An auditor's examination may include computation of various balance sheet and operating ratios for comparison with previous years and industry averages. Discuss the validity and limitations of ratio analysis.

c. In connection with his examination of the financial statements of a manufacturing company, an auditor is observing the physical inventory of finished goods, which consists of expensive, highly complex electronic equipment. Discuss the validity and limitations of the audit evidence provided by this procedure.

(AICPA adapted)

6-43 A CPA accumulates various kinds of evidence upon which he will base his auditor's opinion as to the fairness of financial statements he examines. Among this evidence are confirmations from third parties.

Required:

a. What is an audit confirmation?
b. What characteristics should an audit confirmation possess if a CPA is to consider it as valid evidence?

(AICPA adapted)

6-44 As auditor of the Star Manufacturing Company, you have obtained

A. A trial balance taken from the books of Star one month prior to year-end:

	Dr. (Cr.)
Cash in bank	$ 87,000
Trade accounts receivable	345,000
Notes receivable	125,000
Inventories	317,000
Land	66,000
Buildings, net	350,000
Furniture, fixtures, and equipment, net	325,000
Trade accounts payable	(235,000)
Mortgages payable	(400,000)
Capital stock	(300,000)
Retained earnings	(510,000)
Sales	(3,130,000)
Cost of sales	2,300,000
General and administrative expenses	622,000
Legal and professional fees	3,000
Interest expense	35,000

B.   There are no inventories consigned either in or out.

C.   All notes receivable are due from outsiders and held by Star.

Required:

Which accounts should be confirmed with outside sources? Briefly describe from whom they should be confirmed and the information that should be confirmed. Organize your answer in the following format:

Account Name	From Whom Confirmed	Information to Be Confirmed

(AICPA adapted)

OBJECTIVE QUESTIONS*

6-45   In the course of the examination of financial statements for the purpose of expressing an opinion thereon, the auditor will normally prepare a schedule of unadjusted differences for which the auditor did not propose adjustment when they were uncovered. What is the primary purpose served by this schedule?

A.   To point out to the responsible client officials the errors made by various company personnel.

B.   To summarize the adjustments that must be made before the company can prepare and submit its federal tax return.

C.   To identify the potential financial statement effects of errors or disputed items that were considered immaterial when discovered.

D.   To summarize the errors made by the company so that corrections can be made after the audited financial statements are released.

6-46   In planning an audit engagement, which of the following is a factor that affects the independent auditor's judgment as to the quantity, type, and content of working papers?

A.   The estimated occurrence rate of attributes.

B.   The preliminary evaluations based upon initial substantive testing.

---

*Note: Questions marked with an asterisk are not AICPA adapted questions; otherwise, questions in this section have been taken from prior CPA examinations.

C. The content of the client's representation letter.
D. The anticipated nature of the auditor's report.

6-47 Which of the following is the least persuasive documentation in support of an auditor's opinion?

A. Schedules of details of physical inventory counts conducted by the client.
B. Notation of inferences drawn from ratios and trends.
C. Notation of appraisers' conclusions documented in the auditor's working papers.
D. Lists of negative confirmation requests for which no response was received by the auditor.

6-48 In the context of an audit of financial statements, substantive tests are audit procedures that

A. May be eliminated under certain conditions.
B. Are designed to discover significant subsequent events.
C. May be either tests of transactions, direct tests of financial balances, or analytical tests.
D. Will increase proportionately with the auditor's reliance on internal control.

6-49 Which of the following procedures would ordinarily be expected to best reveal unrecorded sales at the balance sheet date?

A. Compare shipping documents with sales records.
B. Apply gross profit rates to inventory disposed of during the period.
C. Trace payments received subsequent to the balance sheet date.
D. Send accounts receivable confirmation requests.

6-50 Which of the following is not a primary purpose of audit working papers?

A. To coordinate the examination.
B. To assist in preparation of the audit report.
C. To support the financial statements.
D. To provide evidence of the audit work performed.

6-51 In verifying the amount of goodwill recorded by a client, the most convincing evidence which an auditor can obtain is by comparing the recorded value of assets acquired with the

A.   Assessed value as evidenced by tax bills.
B.   Seller's book value as evidenced by financial statements.
C.   Insured value as evidenced by insurance policies.
D.   Appraised value as evidenced by independent appraisals.

6-52   Which of the following elements ultimately determines the specific auditing procedures that are necessary in the circumstances to afford a reasonable basis for an opinion?

a.   Auditor judgment.
b.   Materiality.
c.   Relative risk.
d.   Reasonable assurance.

6-53   Which of the following is not a primary objective of the auditor in the examination of accounts receivable?

a.   Determine the approximate realizable value.
b.   Determine the adequacy of internal controls.
c.   Establish validity of the receivables.
d.   Determine the approximate time of collectibility of the receivables.

6-54   A sales cutoff test of billings complements the verification of

a.   Sales return.
b.   Cash.
c.   Accounts receivable.
d.   Sales allowances.

6-55   An audit program for the examination of the retained earnings account should include a step that requires verification of the

a.   Market value used to charge retained earnings to account for a two-for-one stock split.
b.   Approval of the adjustments to the beginning balance as a result of a write-down of an account receivable.
c.   Authorization for both cash and stock dividends.
d.   Gain or loss resulting from disposition of treasury shares.

6-56   The accuracy of perpetual inventory records may be established, in part, by comparing perpetual inventory records with

a.   Purchase requisitions.
b.   Receiving reports.
c.   Purchase orders.
d.   Vendor payments.

6-57   Which of the audit procedures listed below would be least likely to disclose the existence of related party transactions of a client during the period under audit?

A.   Reading "conflict-of-interest" statements obtained by the client from its management.
B.   Scanning accounting records for large transactions at or just prior to the end of the period under audit.
C.   Inspecting invoices from law firms.
D.   Confirming large purchase and sales transactions with the vendors and/or customers involved.

6-58   An example of a transaction which may be indicative of the existence of related parties is

A.   Borrowing or lending at a rate of interest which equals the current market rate.
B.   Selling real estate at a price that is comparable to its appraised value.
C.   Making large loans with specified terms as to when or how the funds will be repaid.
D.   Exchanging property for similar property in a nonmonetary transaction.

6-59   A common audit procedure in the audit of payroll transactions involves tracing selected items from the payroll journal to employee time cards that have been approved by supervisory personnel. This procedure is designed to provide evidence in support of the audit proposition that

A.   Only bona fide employees worked and their pay was properly computed.
B.   Jobs on which employees worked were charged with the approriate labor cost.
C.   Internal controls relating to payroll disbursements are operating effectively.
D.   All employees worked the number of hours for which their pay was computed.

6-60   Analytical review procedures may be classified as being primarily

A.   Compliance tests.
B.   Substantive tests.
C.   Tests of ratios.
D.   Detailed tests of balances.

6-61 The auditor's program for the examination of long-term debt should include steps that require the

A. Verification of the existence of the bondholders.
B. Examination of any bond trust indenture.
C. Inspection of the accounts payable subsidiary ledger.
D. Investigation of credits to the bond interest income account.

6-62 Which of the following explanations might satisfy an auditor who discovers significant debits to an accumulated depreciation account?

A. Extraordinary repairs have lengthened the life of an asset.
B. Prior years' depreciation charges were erroneously understated.
C. A reserve for possible loss on retirement has been recorded.
D. An asset has been recorded at its fair value.

6-63 To conceal defalcations involving receivables, the auditor would expect an experienced bookkeeper to charge which of the following accounts?

A. Miscellaneous income.
B. Petty cash.
C. Miscellaneous expense.
D. Sales returns.

6-64 To establish illegal "slush funds," corporations may divert cash received in normal business operations. An auditor would encounter the greatest difficulty in detecting the diversion of proceeds from

A. Scrap sales.
B. Dividends.
C. Purchase returns.
D. C.O.D. sales.

6-65 Which of the following is not a typical analytical review procedure?

A. Study of relationships of the financial information with relevant nonfinancial information.
B. Comparison of the financial information with similar information regarding the industry in which the entity operates.
C. Comparison of recorded amounts of major disbursements with appropriate invoices.
D. Comparison of the financial information with budgeted amounts.

6-66 In order to efficiently establish the correctness of the accounts payable cutoff, an auditor will be most likely to

A. Coordinate cutoff tests with physical inventory observation.
B. Compare cutoff reports with purchase orders.
C. Compare vendors' invoices with vendors' statements.
D. Coordinate mailing of confirmations with cutoff tests.

6-67 The auditor is most likely to verify accrued commissions payable in conjunction with the

A. Sales cutoff review.
B. Verification of contingent liabilities.
C. Review of post balance sheet date disbursements.
D. Examination of trade accounts payable.

6-68 Which of the following analytical review procedures should be applied to the income statement?

A. Select sales and expense items and trace amounts to related supporting documents.
B. Ascertain that the net income amount in the statement of changes in financial position agrees with the net income amount in the income statement.
C. Obtain from the proper client representatives, the beginning and ending inventory amounts that were used to determine costs of sales.
D. Compare the actual revenues and expenses with the corresponding figures of the previous year and investigate significant differences.

6-69 When examining a client's statement of changes in financial position, for audit evidence, an auditor will rely primarily upon

A. Determination of the amount of working capital at year-end.
B. Cross-referencing to balances and transactions reviewed in connection with the examination of the other financial statements.
C. Analysis of significant ratios of prior years as compared to the current year.
D. The guidance provided by the APB Opinion on the statement of changes in financial position.

6-70 When title to merchandise in transit has passed to the audit client, the auditor engaged in the performance of a purchase cutoff will encounter the greatest difficulty in gaining assurance with respect to the

A. Quantity.
B. Quality.
C. Price.
D. Terms.

6-71 To be competent, evidence must be both

A. Timely and substantial.
B. Reliable and documented.
C. Valid and relevant.
D. Useful and objective.

6-72 Most of the independent auditor's work in formulating an opinion on financial statements consists of

A. Studying and evaluating internal control.
B. Obtaining and examining evidential matter.
C. Examining cash transactions.
D. Comparing recorded accountability with assets.

6-73 In the audit of a medium-sized manufacturing concern, which one of the following areas would be expected to require the least amount of audit time?

A. Owners' equity.
B. Revenue.
C. Assets.
D. Liabilities.

6-74 Those procedures specifically outlined in an audit program are primarily designed to

A. Gather evidence.
B. Detect errors or irregularities.
C. Test internal systems.
D. Protect the auditor in the event of litigation.

6-75 An auditor will usually trace the details of the test counts made during the observation of the physical inventory taking to a final inventory schedule. This audit procedure is undertaken to provide evidence that items physically present and observed by the auditor at the time of the physical inventory count are

A. Owned by the client.
B. Not obsolete.

C. Physically present at the time of the preparation of the final inventory schedule.
D. Included in the final inventory schedule.

6-76 How does the extent of substantive tests required to constitute sufficient evidential matter vary with the auditor's reliance on internal control?

A. Randomly.
B. Disproportionately.
C. Directly.
D. Inversely.

6-77 One reason why the independent auditor makes an analytical review of the client's operations is to identify probable

A. Weaknesses of a material nature in the system of internal control.
B. Unusual transactions.
C. Non-compliance with prescribed control procedures.
D. Improper separation of accounting and other financial duties.

6-78 To test for unsupported entries in the ledger, the direction of audit testing should be from the

A. Ledger entries.
B. Journal entries.
C. Externally generated documents.
D. Original source documents.

6-79 Which of the following statements relating to the competence of evidential matter is always true?

A. Evidential matter gathered by an auditor from outside an enterprise is reliable.
B. Accounting data developed under satisfactory conditions of internal control are more relevant than data developed under unsatisfactory internal control conditions.
C. Oral representations made by management are not valid evidence.
D. Evidence gathered by auditors must be both valid and relevant to be considered competent.

6-80   The third standard of field work states that sufficient competent evidential matter may, in part, be obtained through inspection, observation, inquiries, and confirmations to afford a reasonable basis for an opinion regarding the financial statements under examination. The evidential matter required by this standard may, in part, be obtained through

A.   Auditor working papers.
B.   Proper planning of the audit engagement.
C.   Analytical review procedures.
D.   Review of the system of internal control.

6-81   Which of the following accounts should be reviewed by the auditor to gain reasonable assurance that additions to property, plant, and equipment are not understated?

A.   Depreciation.
B.   Accounts payable.
C.   Cash.
D.   Repairs.

6-82   An examination of the balance in the accounts payable account is ordinarily not designed to

A.   Detect accounts payable which are substantially past due.
B.   Verify that accounts payable were properly authorized.
C.   Ascertain the reasonableness of recorded liabilities.
D.   Determine that all existing liabilities at the balance sheet date have been recorded.

ETHICAL CONDUCT INDEPENDENCE EVIDENCE DUE CARE FAIR PRESENTATION ETHICAL CONDUCT INDEPENDENCE EVIDENCE DUE CARE FAIR PRESENTATION ETHICAL CONDUCT INDEPENDENCE EVIDENCE DUE CARE FAIR PRESENTATION ETHICAL CONDUCT INDEPENDENCE EVIDENCE DUE CARE FAIR PRESENTATION ETHICAL CONDUCT INDEPENDENCE EVIDENCE DUE CARE FAIR PRESENTATION ETHICAL CONDUCT INDEPENDENCE EVIDENCE DUE CARE FAIR PRESENTATION ETHICAL CONDUCT INDEPENDENCE EVIDENCE DUE CARE FAIR PRESENTATION

☐ FIELD WORK — COMPLIANCE TESTS

E FAIR PRESENTATION ETHICAL CONDUCT INDEPENDENCE EVIDENCE DUE CARE FAIR PRESENTATION ETHICAL CONDUCT INDEPENDENCE EVIDENCE DUE CARE FAIR PRESENTATION
CARE FAIR PRESENTATION ETHICAL CONDUCT INDEPENDENCE EVIDENCE DUE CARE FAIR PRESENTATION ETHICAL CONDUCT INDEPENDENCE EVIDENCE DUE CARE FAIR PRESENTA
DUE CARE FAIR PRESENTATION ETHICAL CONDUCT INDEPENDENCE EVIDENCE DUE CARE FAIR PRESENTATION ETHICAL CONDUCT INDEPENDENCE EVIDENCE DUE CARE FAIR PRESE
CE DUE CARE FAIR PRESENTATION ETHICAL CONDUCT INDEPENDENCE EVIDENCE DUE CARE FAIR PRESENTATION ETHICAL CONDUCT INDEPENDENCE EVIDENCE DUE CARE FAIR PR
DENCE DUE CARE FAIR PRESENTATION ETHICAL CONDUCT INDEPENDENCE EVIDENCE DUE CARE FAIR PRESENTATION ETHICAL CONDUCT INDEPENDENCE EVIDENCE DUE CARE FA
E EVIDENCE DUE CARE FAIR PRESENTATION ETHICAL CONDUCT INDEPENDENCE EVIDENCE DUE CARE FAIR PRESENTATION ETHICAL CONDUCT INDEPENDENCE EVIDENCE DUE CAR
NCE EVIDENCE DUE CARE FAIR PRESENTATION ETHICAL CONDUCT INDEPENDENCE EVIDENCE DUE CARE FAIR PRESENTATION ETHICAL CONDUCT INDEPENDENCE EVIDENCE DUE
NDENCE EVIDENCE DUE CARE FAIR PRESENTATION ETHICAL CONDUCT INDEPENDENCE EVIDENCE DUE CARE FAIR PRESENTATION ETHICAL CONDUCT INDEPENDENCE EVIDENCE C

LEARNING OBJECTIVES

DUCT INDEPENDENCE EVIDENCE DUE CARE FAIR PRESENTATION ETHICAL CONDUCT INDEPENDENCE EVIDENCE DUE CARE FAIR PRESENTATION ETHICAL CONDUCT INDEPENDENCE
CONDUCT INDEPENDENCE EVIDENCE DUE CARE FAIR PRESENTATION ETHICAL CONDUCT INDEPENDENCE EVIDENCE DUE CARE FAIR PRESENTATION ETHICAL CONDUCT INDEPENDE
AL CONDUCT INDEPENDENCE EVIDENCE DUE CARE FAIR PRESENTATION ETHICAL CONDUCT INDEPENDENCE EVIDENCE DUE CARE FAIR PRESENTATION ETHICAL CONDUCT INDEPE
THICAL CONDUCT INDEPENDENCE EVIDENCE DUE CARE FAIR PRESENTATION ETHICAL CONDUCT INDEPENDENCE EVIDENCE DUE CARE FAIR PRESENTATION ETHICAL CONDUCT IN

After studying this chapter, students should understand

1. The two phases of the study of an internal accounting control system.
2. The definition of a material weakness in internal accounting control, and the auditor's reporting responsibility with respect to these weaknesses.
3. The general nature of the relationship between compliance tests and substantive tests.
4. Techniques used in learning about a system of internal accounting control.
5. Techniques used in documenting a system of internal accounting control, including the advantages and disadvantages of each technique.
6. General and application controls in EDP systems.
7. Auditing techniques for EDP systems.
8. The ways in which EDP equipment may be used to facilitate substantive audit testing.

INDEPENDENCE EVIDENCE DUE CARE FAIR PRESENTATION ETHICAL CONDUCT INDEPENDENCE EVIDENCE DUE CARE FAIR PRESENTATION ETHICAL CONDUCT INDEPENDENCE EV
CT INDEPENDENCE EVIDENCE DUE CARE FAIR PRESENTATION ETHICAL CONDUCT INDEPENDENCE EVIDENCE DUE CARE FAIR PRESENTATION ETHICAL CONDUCT INDEPENDENCE
NDUCT INDEPENDENCE EVIDENCE DUE CARE FAIR PRESENTATION ETHICAL CONDUCT INDEPENDENCE EVIDENCE DUE CARE FAIR PRESENTATION ETHICAL CONDUCT INDEPENDI
L CONDUCT INDEPENDENCE EVIDENCE DUE CARE FAIR PRESENTATION ETHICAL CONDUCT INDEPENDENCE EVIDENCE DUE CARE FAIR PRESENTATION ETHICAL CONDUCT INDEPE
HICAL CONDUCT INDEPENDENCE EVIDENCE DUE CARE FAIR PRESENTATION ETHICAL CONDUCT INDEPENDENCE EVIDENCE DUE CARE FAIR PRESENTATION ETHICAL CONDUCT IN
ETHICAL CONDUCT INDEPENDENCE EVIDENCE DUE CARE FAIR PRESENTATION ETHICAL CONDUCT INDEPENDENCE EVIDENCE DUE CARE FAIR PRESENTATION ETHICAL CONDUCT
TION ETHICAL CONDUCT INDEPENDENCE EVIDENCE DUE CARE FAIR PRESENTATION ETHICAL CONDUCT INDEPENDENCE EVIDENCE DUE CARE FAIR PRESENTATION ETHICAL CON
NTATION ETHICAL CONDUCT INDEPENDENCE EVIDENCE DUE CARE FAIR PRESENTATION ETHICAL CONDUCT INDEPENDENCE EVIDENCE DUE CARE FAIR PRESENTATION ETHICAL
ESENTATION ETHICAL CONDUCT INDEPENDENCE EVIDENCE DUE CARE FAIR PRESENTATION ETHICAL CONDUCT INDEPENDENCE EVIDENCE DUE CARE FAIR PRESENTATION ETHI
R PRESENTATION ETHICAL CONDUCT INDEPENDENCE EVIDENCE DUE CARE FAIR PRESENTATION ETHICAL CONDUCT INDEPENDENCE EVIDENCE DUE CARE FAIR PRESENTATION E
FAIR PRESENTATION ETHICAL CONDUCT INDEPENDENCE EVIDENCE DUE CARE FAIR PRESENTATION ETHICAL CONDUCT INDEPENDENCE EVIDENCE DUE CARE FAIR PRESENTATI
ARE FAIR PRESENTATION ETHICAL CONDUCT INDEPENDENCE EVIDENCE DUE CARE FAIR PRESENTATION ETHICAL CONDUCT INDEPENDENCE EVIDENCE DUE CARE FAIR PRESENT
JE CARE FAIR PRESENTATION ETHICAL CONDUCT INDEPENDENCE EVIDENCE DUE CARE FAIR PRESENTATION ETHICAL CONDUCT INDEPENDENCE EVIDENCE DUE CARE FAIR PRE
E DUE CARE FAIR PRESENTATION ETHICAL CONDUCT INDEPENDENCE EVIDENCE DUE CARE FAIR PRESENTATION ETHICAL CONDUCT INDEPENDENCE EVIDENCE DUE CARE FAIR
ENCE DUE CARE FAIR PRESENTATION ETHICAL CONDUCT INDEPENDENCE EVIDENCE DUE CARE FAIR PRESENTATION ETHICAL CONDUCT INDEPENDENCE EVIDENCE DUE CARE F
EVIDENCE DUE CARE FAIR PRESENTATION ETHICAL CONDUCT INDEPENDENCE EVIDENCE DUE CARE FAIR PRESENTATION ETHICAL CONDUCT INDEPENDENCE EVIDENCE DUE CA
CE EVIDENCE DUE CARE FAIR PRESENTATION ETHICAL CONDUCT INDEPENDENCE EVIDENCE DUE CARE FAIR PRESENTATION ETHICAL CONDUCT INDEPENDENCE EVIDENCE DUE
DENCE EVIDENCE DUE CARE FAIR PRESENTATION ETHICAL CONDUCT INDEPENDENCE EVIDENCE DUE CARE FAIR PRESENTATION ETHICAL CONDUCT INDEPENDENCE EVIDENCE

Chapter 7

Internal Control Review — Manual and EDP Systems

This chapter was written by
Thomas E. McKee, Ph.D., C.P.A.,
Professor of Accounting,
East Tennessee State University

INTRODUCTION

This chapter provides an overview of the independent auditor's responsibilities for reviewing internal control as well as methods and procedures for conducting such a review. The general discussion in this chapter is supplemented by the material in Chapter 8, which uses an actual example, to reinforce the general concepts of internal control review which are illustrated in this chapter. This chapter also reviews EDP audit techniques. Since there is such a great diversity in the types and complexity of accounting systems, especially in relatively more sophisticated EDP systems, the coverage in this chapter has been designed to cover basic concepts and techniques that apply to all systems generally. Such a coverage will provide a central framework that is applicable to all systems.

REVIEW RESPONSIBILITY

The second standard of field work states:

> There is to be a proper study and evaluation of the existing internal control as a basis for reliance thereon and for the determination of the resultant extent of the tests to which auditing procedures are to be restricted.

This standard is applicable either to the internal control system as a whole or to major subsystems or cycles of an internal accounting control system. It requires the auditor to study and evaluate internal accounting control if he or she wishes to place any reliance on the system or major subsystem and thereby reduce or restrict substantive audit procedures. For example, if an auditor desires to restrict or reduce substantive audit procedures in the sales area, he or she must have reasonable assurance that the client has prescribed an appropriate internal control system for sales and that the system is operating as prescribed.

The study of the internal accounting control system normally encompasses two phases:

1. **Review of system** — The review phase is primarily a process of obtaining and documenting information about the procedures and methods of internal control prescribed for the entity by management. It is discussed in more detail later in this chapter.

2. **Tests of compliance** — The test-of-compliance phase consists of the auditor determining, with a reasonable degree of assurance, that controls prescribed by management which were documented during the review phase are in effect and operating as planned.

The auditor obtains assurance about the system by testing the controls. This type of testing is called compliance testing and is discussed in more detail in Chapter 8.

The study of the internal control system should be of the client's system in effect for the period under audit, that is, the system from which data for the audited financial statements were developed. Systems for prior or future periods are not relevant since the accounting data for the audit period was not generated from such systems. The study is also normally restricted to accounting controls rather than administrative controls, since accounting controls more directly impact financial statement preparation. As indicated in Chapter 5, administrative controls are those controls concerned with the decision processes leading to management's authorization of transactions. Accounting controls come into effect once a transaction has been authorized and are concerned with the safeguarding of assets and the reliability of the resulting financial records. Some controls are designed, of course, for both management control and accounting control. These controls are also included in the auditor's review and evaluation of the system.

REPORTING MATERIAL CONTROL WEAKNESSES

External auditors traditionally report to management all *significant* weaknesses in internal accounting control discovered during the course of the audit. Such reports are a byproduct of the audit and are made as a service to the client. They are usually reported in a written letter called a management letter. The management letter is formally issued after the conclusion of the audit although many of the comments may have been previously communicated orally to management during the course of the audit engagement. In addition to internal control recommendations, management letters usually include some comments or recommendations about how management may correct internal control weaknesses and improve business operations. For example, a management letter might contain a recommendation that a company consider automating its inventory record-keeping in order to improve operating efficiency in the inventory area and thereby reduce the level of inventory. External auditors are usually well qualified to make such recommendations because of their independent perspective and broad knowledge derived from working with many different companies.

The importance of businesses maintaining an adequate system of internal control was reinforced by the Foreign Corrupt Practices Act of

1977. As indicated in Chapter 5, the act contains the following two major provisions:

1. **Antibribery Provisions.** The essence of this portion of the act is that bribery or attempted bribery of any significant foreign official by any U.S. business or citizen for the purpose of obtaining or influencing business is illegal.

2. **Accounting Provisions.** This portion of the act makes it illegal for SEC registrants to fail to maintain a satisfactory system of internal accounting control.

Management and directors not complying with the act are subject to fines and/or imprisonment. Corporations found to be in noncompliance may be fined up to $1,000,000.

To assist management in carrying out their legal responsibility to maintain an adequate system of internal accounting control, *SAS No. 20, Required Communication of Material Weaknesses in Internal Accounting Control*, was issued in December, 1977. This pronouncement requires that the external auditor communicate to senior management and the board of directors all *material* weaknesses in internal accounting control that the auditor becomes aware of during the course of the audit. *SAS No. 20* left the form of communication optional. However, *SAS No. 30, Reporting on Internal Accounting Control*, issued in July, 1980, suggests a report form when management is presented with a written report on internal control weaknesses. The format of the report is discussed in Chapter 8.

It is important to recognize that *SAS No. 20* only requires the communication of *material* weaknesses in internal *accounting* (not administrative) control. A material weakness in internal accounting control is defined in *SAS No. 30* as:

> . . . a condition in which specific control procedures or the degree of compliance with them do not reduce to a relatively low level the risk that errors or irregularities in amounts that would be material in relation to the financial statements being audited may occur and not be detected within a timely period by employees in the normal course of performing their assigned functions.

Internal accounting control weaknesses not deemed material and other recommendations concerning the efficiency and effectiveness of operations will undoubtedly continue to be reported in the traditional management letter at the conclusion of the audit.

INTERNAL CONTROL REVIEW AND DOCUMENTATION PROCEDURES

Internal control review and documentation are normally performed simultaneously. That is, the auditor documents his or her findings during the review process. However, in order to more readily explain the procedures and concepts, the following discussion will first address the review process. A discussion and illustration of documentation methods will then follow.

Review of the System

The first step in the review process is to determine how the internal control review is to be organized. Two basic approaches are to review *major cycles* (for example, sales, billings, receivables, and collections may be one cycle) or to review *major functions* (for example, accounts receivable billing may be one function and cash disbursements may be another function). Since accounting firms use alternative approaches, firm policy will dictate which method will be used. Regardless of the review approach adopted, the auditor must consider how the entity being audited should be subdivided (subsidiary, division, branch, etc.) for purposes of organizing the internal control review. If accounting is centralized at one location (parent company), then segregation of the work may be unnecessary since essentially one system is being reviewed and the system will likely be reviewed by an audit team from one office of the CPA firm. On the other hand, if each division has its own accounting system, then the review will likely have to be divided to cover major subsidiaries.

During the review phase the auditor is trying to find answers to four general questions about specific internal control cycles or functions.

First, what internal controls have been prescribed by management? Management has the basic responsibility to specify the internal control system the company is to employ. Management's specification may be either general or specific. A general specification is a policy that employees follow whenever events fit the policy. For example, purchasing may be authorized to reorder inventory items any time the level falls below a four-week supply. Management may also specify controls for individual transactions. For example, all acquisitions of capital assets in excess of $10,000 may have to be approved in writing by an officer of the company.

Second, how has management communicated prescribed controls to employees? Specification of internal controls is not adequate if employees are not properly informed of them. In a good system of internal control, all employees will be properly informed of all control functions expected of them. Communication may be in oral instruction or written devices of various types, such as:

- Organization charts.
- Chart of accounts.
- Accounting policies and procedures manuals.
- Documents and forms, such as sales invoices, time cards, etc.
- Job descriptions.
- Accounting records, such as journals and ledgers.

Third, are incompatible functions adequately segregated? In a well designed accounting system, duties are appropriately segregated so that employees do not perform incompatible functions. Duties normally segregated include:

- **Operational responsibility and financial record-keeping responsibility.** Due to possible bias, organizational units should not prepare financial reports on their own operations.

- **Custody of assets and accounting for those assets.** Individuals should not be assigned responsibility for both assets and the related accounting records since they would be in a position to conceal a defalcation, and errors could go undetected.

- **Custody of assets and authorization of transactions related to those assets.** Individuals should not be assigned responsibility for assets and be allowed to initiate transactions for those same assets since this might permit a defalcation or erroneous transaction.

- **Separation of accounting tasks or duties.** Duties are normally divided so that one employee's work serves as a check on other employees.

Fourth, how is compliance with the authorized system maintained? If management does not have an effective system of monitoring compliance, then employees may intentionally or unintentionally use internal control procedures and methods different from those authorized. An effective system of compliance might include continuous review by an internal audit department, a reporting system which identifies departures from the prescribed system, and effective supervision at all levels in the company.

Data Gathering Techniques

The auditor must gain an understanding of the internal control system before he or she can document the system. Following is a discussion of major sources of data that auditors normally use in obtaining information about a client's system.

Interviews with employees. Interviewing responsible employees is probably the most common and productive way to obtain information regarding a client's internal control system. To be effective, the auditor must recognize that many employees perceive such interviews as "threat" situations. The auditor should try to minimize employee anxiety as much as reasonably possible. An interview will normally begin with an identification of functions performed by the employee. Each function will then be explored. Employees are normally asked to start at the beginning of each function performed by them and describe their performance of that function in a step-by-step manner.

Review of company documentation of the system. Many companies have some type of written description or documentation of their internal control system. The auditor may review items such as accounting policy and procedure manuals, narrative descriptions of the system, flowcharts of system procedures, charts of accounts, and EDP documentation to obtain an understanding of the procedures that have been formally established and approved for the internal control system.

Review of internal auditor files, reports, and recommendations. In many instances the internal audit department may have recently reviewed and tested areas of interest to the external auditor. The external auditor may review data generated by the internal auditors and extract relevant information.

System walk-through and observation. When the auditor believes that he or she has a reasonable understanding of the system from the data gathering techniques discussed, the auditor usually performs a transaction walk-through to confirm that understanding. The understanding may be erroneous because the previous data was incorrect or because the system is malfunctioning. A system or transaction walk-through is performed by selecting one or two transactions of each significant type and following those transactions step-by-step through the system. The auditor can determine whether the system description he or she obtained conforms to the actual operation of the system. Discrepancies must be resolved by amending the system description or by noting, for consideration in the evaluation of the internal accounting controls, an instance of system breakdown.

Documentation

The evaluation of the internal control system must be documented in the auditor's working papers. This documentation should include:

- **System inputs.**   The volume, types, authorization, and organization of transactions entering the system.

- **Processing activity.**   The persons, machines, and records involved in processing transactions.

- **System outputs.**   The records and reports generated by the system.

- **Significant controls.**   Significant controls either present (potential strengths of the system) or absent (potential weaknesses of the system) should be identified.

Three common documentation procedures are questionnaires, flowcharts, and narrative descriptions. These methods may be used individually or jointly in the case of flowcharts and narrative descriptions. Explanations and illustrations of these techniques follow.

Internal Control Questionnaires.   An internal control questionnaire is a preprinted list of questions about the system of internal accounting control. The staff accountant completes the questions during discussions with appropriate client personnel and the review of related transactions and supporting documentation. A "yes" answer indicates that the auditor believes a control to be in effect and operating. A "no" answer, on the other hand, indicates a control that is not in effect. "No" answers do not necessarily indicate weaknesses in the system. The auditor must consider the *overall system* to determine if a weakness exists. Remember, a material weakness in internal accounting control was previously defined as a condition which could permit a material error or irregularity to occur and not be detected within a timely period. The questionnaire might indicate the absence of a control which would prevent an error or irregularity from occurring and not being detected, such as the lack of numeric control of blank payroll checks. This could be a potential material weakness if the company does not have some type of alternative control, such as a monthly reconciliation of an imprest payroll account that would detect irregularities in a timely manner before they become material.

Internal control questionnaires are probably the most widely used method of documenting a system of internal control because of several significant advantages they offer, namely:

- **Comprehensiveness.** Experienced personnel spend considerable time designing them thus they are quite comprehensive and afford very little possibility of omitting an element of internal control from the review.

- **Level of training required.** Since each item on the questionnaire focuses on a single aspect of the internal control system, a high degree of expertise is not required to complete them.

- **Speed.** An internal control questionnaire may be completed relatively quickly since all that is involved is checking "yes" or "no" to a series of questions and perhaps adding some narrative explanations for "no" answers.

- **Potential weaknesses are highlighted.** Each "no" answer indicates a potential internal control weakness for the auditor to consider.

Despite their many advantages, internal control questionnaires do have some disadvantages:

- **Too comprehensive.** They may be too comprehensive for some companies, particularly smaller ones. A significant number of "no" answers may require a great deal of audit time in evaluating whether a system weakness exists.

- **Piecemeal approach.** Since they are completed question by question, they do not force the auditor to think about and visualize the overall system. This may result in insufficient integration of the overall system in the auditor's mind, thereby possibly causing the auditor to overlook some important relationship.

Exhibit 7-1 contains an example of the first question from a typical internal control questionnaire. Note that the auditor is asked to provide the basis for his or her understanding of the control. Frequently, copies of documents will be included in the audit working papers to supplement and illustrate points on the internal control questionnaire. For example, a question concerning whether sales personnel check credit limits before accepting sales orders may be accompanied by a copy of a sales invoice which has a blank space where credit approvals may be indicated.

Exhibit 7-1
Internal Control Questionnaire
General Controls Questionnaire

Questionnaire
Prepared by: _____

Questionnaire
Reviewed by: _____

Date: _____

Date: _____

Name of Company _____

Location of EDP Facility _____

Organization Controls:

1. Does the company's organizational structure and its division of duties appear to provide for adequate supervision and segregation of functions within the EDP department and between EDP and user departments?

Yes _____   No _____

In assessing organization controls the auditor should consider the following:	Contributes to Possible Reliance		Source of Information	Comments and/or Reference
	Yes	*No*		
Separation of programming, systems analysis, and operations functions.				
Application of management techniques to planning and reviewing the department's work.				
Data control function separate from user and operations functions.				
Regular rotation of duties.				
Independence of EDP department.				
Internal audit involvement in EDP.				

Source: *The Auditor's Preliminary Review of EDP Accounting Controls*, California CPA Foundation for Education and Research, 1976.

Flowcharts.   Flowcharting is an attempt to create a model of a system through the use of standardized symbols to represent various system components. Auditors need to understand flowcharting because it is a valuable way for them to document the functioning of a system. Also, since many companies flowchart their information systems as a means of documenting them, auditors need to be able to read flowcharts to comprehend such client-prepared system documentation.

There are three types of flowcharts the auditor needs to be familiar with:

Systems flowcharts. These flowcharts describe the flow of data through a system without regard to the exact details of how the data may be processed at various points in the system. This type of flowchart is very good at depicting the overall flows and functioning of the system. They are typically prepared by systems designers to document the nature and purpose of systems.

Program flowcharts. Program flowcharts describe how data is processed in a particular computer program. Program flowcharts are usually prepared by systems analysts to guide programmers in writing program code. Program flowcharts usually complement system flowcharts by describing in detail a particular program that may only be represented by a single symbol in a systems flowchart.

Auditor flowcharts. Auditor flowcharts are a special type of system flowcharts. They are an attempt to document significant data and document flows and to highlight the related internal accounting controls. An example of an auditor flowchart may be seen in Exhibit 7-2. Key features in an auditor flowchart usually include:

- An emphasis on the activities performed by employees, functions, or departments so as to highlight incompatible duties being performed.

- Clear indication of the origin and ultimate disposition of *all* copies of documents so as to clearly show who has access to such data.

- Supplemental narrative description of control points or processing activities that are not clearly shown on the flowchart.

- A clear indication of where and how documents in the system are filed.

Flowcharts have several advantages over other methods of documentation:

- **Easily understood.** Since flowcharts provide a visual description supplemented by a written narrative, they may be more easily understood than a straight narrative description or a questionnaire.

- **Better overall picture of complex system.** A complex system may be reduced to a one or two-page flowchart. The same system might require a 15-page internal control questionnaire or a 10-page narrative memo to describe its features.

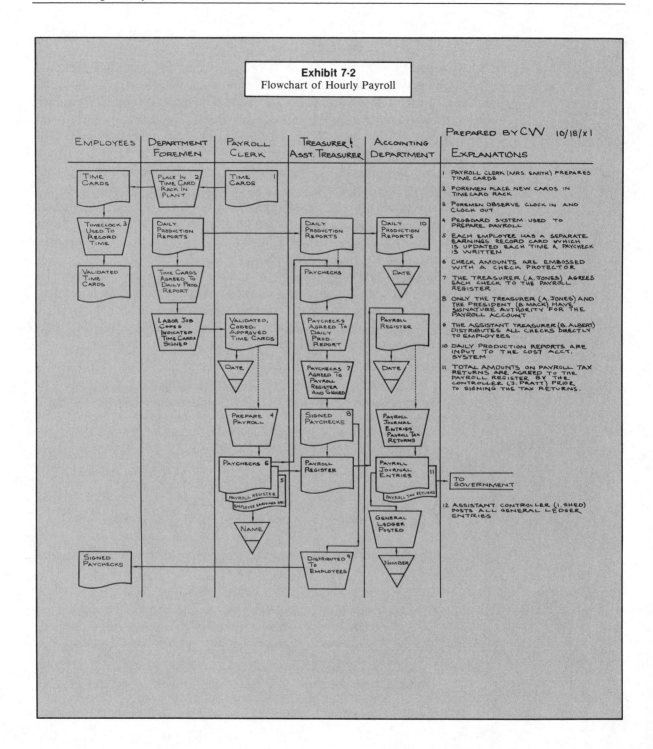

Exhibit 7-2
Flowchart of Hourly Payroll

PREPARED BY CW 10/18/X1

Explanations:

1. PAYROLL CLERK (MRS. SMITH) PREPARES TIME CARDS

2. FOREMEN PLACE NEW CARDS IN TIMECARD RACK

3. FOREMEN OBSERVE CLOCK IN AND CLOCK OUT

4. PEGBOARD SYSTEM USED TO PREPARE PAYROLL

5. EACH EMPLOYEE HAS A SEPARATE EARNINGS RECORD CARD WHICH IS UPDATED EACH TIME A PAYCHECK IS WRITTEN

6. CHECK AMOUNTS ARE EMBOSSED WITH A CHECK PROTECTOR

7. THE TREASURER (A. JONES) AGREES EACH CHECK TO THE PAYROLL REGISTER

8. ONLY THE TREASURER (A. JONES) AND THE PRESIDENT (B. MACK) HAVE SIGNATURE AUTHORITY FOR THE PAYROLL ACCOUNT

9. THE ASSISTANT TREASURER (B. ALBERT) DISTRIBUTES ALL CHECKS DIRECTLY TO EMPLOYEES

10. DAILY PRODUCTION REPORTS ARE INPUT TO THE COST ACCT. SYSTEM

11. TOTAL AMOUNTS ON PAYROLL TAX RETURNS ARE AGREED TO THE PAYROLL REGISTER BY THE CONTROLLER (J. PRATT) PRIOR TO SIGNING THE TAX RETURNS.

12. ASSISTANT CONTROLLER (I. SHED) POSTS ALL GENERAL LEDGER ENTRIES

- **Parallels EDP documentation.** EDP systems are commonly documented with flowcharts. Consequently, EDP personnel may be more able to relate to and advise the auditor of omissions or errors in a flowchart of a system.

- **Ease of update.** Flowcharts prepared in one audit may be easily updated in subsequent audits to reflect minor system changes. This means the auditor will not have to spend as much time documenting a relatively unchanged system in subsequent audits.

Flowcharts have three major disadvantages relative to other methods of documentation. First, to prepare a good flowchart of a complex system requires a higher level of knowledge and training than using an internal control questionnaire or a narrative memo. Second, flowcharts take more time to prepare than an internal control questionnaire. This increased time, however, should be weighed against less time on subsequent audits if there are minor system changes. Third, analysis of flowcharts, once prepared, to spot internal control weaknesses is more difficult and requires more knowledge than does the analysis of a completed internal control questionnaire where a "no" answer indicates a potential weakness.

Narrative Memos.   Narrative memos are a technique whereby the auditor writes a description of the system in narrative form. Narrative memos are probably used less than either questionnaires or flowcharts because they require a good deal of organization and composition ability for them to be clear and understandable. Narrative memos are used as the principal means of internal control documentation in smaller audits where the system may be more readily described in a few paragraphs than with a questionnaire or flowchart. Narrative memos are also frequently used in conjunction with questionnaires or flowcharts to further explain features which may not be adequately conveyed by the questionnaire or flowchart. An example of a narrative memo is contained in Exhibit 7-3.

EDP SYSTEMS AND CONTROLS

Whether an accounting system employs electronic data processing (EDP) or processes all data manually does not change the basic concepts of internal control. Internal control concepts are independent of the method of data processing. Procedures to accomplish the internal control objectives will be different in an EDP system, however, since different processing techniques are used. Therefore, the level of knowledge required of the auditor to comply with the first general

---

Exhibit 7-3
Narrative Memo

Prepared by and date _____
Reviewed by and date _____

ABC Manufacturing Co., Inc.
12/31/x1
Summary of Hourly Payroll Procedures

The company has approximately sixty hourly employees. All employees punch in and out of work via timecards through the time clock located in the west end (parking lot side) of the plant. The production foremen alternate in observing employees during this period to ensure that no employee handles more than one card. The payweek runs Friday to Thursday. At the conclusion of work on Thursday, each foreman removes the timecards for his department. The foremen agree the daily hours on the timecards to their daily production reports which list employees and daily assignments. The foremen fill in the jobs to be charged and indicate approval by signing the timecards. The foremen then turn in their timecards to Ms. Smith, the payroll clerk, who issues them new cards for the following week. The foremen place the new cards in the time clock rack so that employees will be able to punch in the following morning.

Ms. Smith then uses the timecards and employee withholding data to manually prepare the paychecks and payroll register on a pegboard payroll system. She updates each employee earnings record also.

The completed payroll register and paychecks are transported by Ms. Smith to Mr. A. Jones, Treasurer. Mr. Jones agrees each check to the payroll register and agrees the total hours on the payroll register to a summary of hours worked prepared from the daily production reports submitted by the foremen. Mr. A. Jones then manually signs each check. Employees are paid at the conclusion of work on Mondays and Mr. B. Albert, Assistant Treasurer, distributes the checks directly to the employees.

Payroll tax returns are prepared by the accounting department based upon the payroll registers maintained by Ms. Smith, the payroll clerk. Total amounts reported to the government are agreed to payroll register totals. The accounting department also uses the payroll registers as input for journal entries to record the weekly payroll.

---

auditing standard, requiring adequate technical training and proficiency, must necessarily be different in a situation where EDP processing is employed. The level of knowledge required is generally greater for EDP systems than for manual systems and increases as EDP systems increase in complexity.

Accounting firms have developed different approaches in coping with increased knowledge requirements for EDP systems. In some firms, EDP audit specialists are employed to evaluate internal control over EDP functions and to carry out audit procedures involving EDP processing. Other firms have taken the approach of educating the audit staff in basic EDP auditing so that a single audit team has responsibility for performing the overall audit. In the latter situation, EDP audit specialists are sometimes employed for engagements having particularly complex EDP operations. Both approaches have proven satisfactory in the past. It is apparent that in the future the average auditor will have to know more about EDP systems and EDP auditing since more and more businesses of all sizes are using EDP systems.

The use of EDP in an accounting system typically results in both greater concentration of processing ability (the EDP function may process data formerly processed by several independent departments) and greater concentration of data (the EDP function may have the responsibility for maintaining all data files). The concentration of both maintaining and processing data creates greater risk to the organization due to the decreased segregation of duties. In order to maintain an acceptable level of overall control, an EDP system may have to incorporate controls not present in its manual system counterpart. Many possible schemes for classifying EDP internal controls have been proposed in an attempt to logically organize such controls. A logical method for organizing EDP controls for audit purposes consists of classifying them into two groups: (1) general or environmental controls and (2) applications or systems controls.

General or environmental controls consist of those controls which apply to the overall environment in which specific EDP applications or systems are run. Applications or systems controls consist of those controls which apply solely to individual applications or systems. For example, all controls which are unique to a payroll system would be considered payroll application or system controls. The following sections describe the major elements of both general or environmental controls and applications or systems controls. An appreciation of these elements is needed in order to fully understand the EDP control review process.

GENERAL CONTROLS

According to *SAS No. 3, The Effects of EDP on the Auditor's Study and Evaluation of Internal Control*, general or environmental controls may be broken into five groups:

1. Organization and operation of the EDP department

2. Procedures for documenting, reviewing, testing, and authorizing applications or systems.

3.   EDP hardware controls.

4.   Controls over access to EDP equipment or data.

5.   Data or procedural controls affecting overall EDP operations.

**Organization
and Operation
of EDP
Department**

Since EDP activities are usually concentrated in a single department, control of the EDP department is very important. One aspect of control is the location of the EDP department in the organization structure. Although many organizations have achieved satisfactory control with different organizational patterns, the trend in larger companies is to place the head of the EDP department at an organizational level reporting to a vice-president of administration. This frees the EDP department, to a certain extent, from the pressures of particular functional areas, such as accounting or production and allows EDP to schedule current operations and systems development to the best advantage of the overall organization. If the EDP department reports to the head of some functional area such as production, then there is a tendency to favor that area at the expense of other areas in the organization.

Another aspect of control is separation of the various functions within the EDP department. Functions that are normally separated include:

- **Systems analysis and programming.**   This function involves system design and system maintenance. It also involves creation and maintenance of system documentation. Separation of this function from other functions, such as computer operations, is critical because personnel in the systems analysis and programming area possess sufficient knowledge of the system to perpetrate and conceal fraud.

- **Computer operations.**   This function involves physical operation of the computer and related equipment. Personnel operating the computer should not have knowledge of the system and related controls sufficient to circumvent them.

- **Data library.**   This function is charged with maintaining physical control of programs and files to insure that unauthorized persons do not access such data. Programs and files should be physically secured in a separate room with a check-in, check-out procedure in accordance with the daily operating schedule or as otherwise authorized.

- **Data control unit.**   Personnel in this function are charged with controlling data processed by the EDP department. They perform activities such as maintaining input batch totals (discussed later) and reconciling input and output totals with appropriate follow-up items not processed due to exception conditions or errors. They also have the responsibility for seeing that only authorized parties receive output.

An organization chart for these major functions might appear as shown in Exhibit 7-4.

Applications or Systems Approval and Documentation

In order to ensure that new and existing systems are appropriately designed and maintained, it is a common practice to have an EDP steering committee. Such a committee is composed of executives and personnel from various user areas within the overall organization. They meet periodically to monitor and approve requests for changes in the current system or the development of new system applications. Their purpose is to see that EDP resources, hardware, software, and personnel are employed in the best interests of the overall organization. The steering committee, to accomplish its purpose, would normally set priorities for systems development and attempt to resolve conflicts that might arise from various user departments' requests for what are usually limited EDP resources.

Since a great deal of time and money is spent in developing EDP systems and applications, it is important that they be appropriately documented. This is necessary to protect the investment made in developing the system and to provide a basis for making system changes and for management review and control. Documentation standards should be set and enforced for each EDP department. Normal documentation might include:

- Purpose and objectives of application or system.
- Complete set of flowcharts.
- Program source code listing.
- Compiled program listing.
- Computer operating instructions for computer operations group.
- Program testing documentation.
- Samples and layouts of all program inputs and outputs.
- Approvals for initial applications or systems and approvals for any subsequent changes.

EDP Hardware Controls

EDP hardware controls are those controls designed within the equipment by computer manufacturers to detect equipment failures. Although modern EDP equipment is very reliable, equipment failures do occur. Five of the more common hardware controls are discussed starting on page 281:

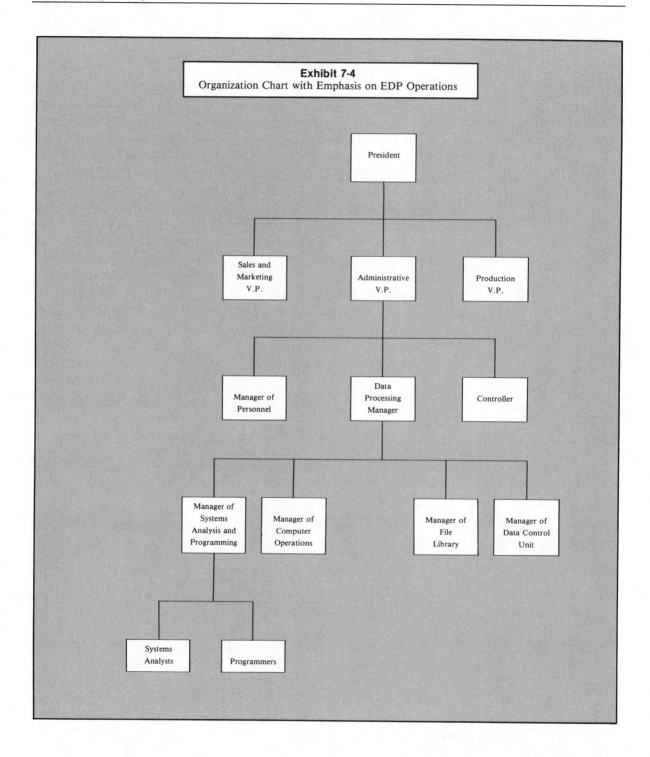

Exhibit 7-4
Organization Chart with Emphasis on EDP Operations

1. **Parity Check.** Data is represented within the computer in bits (*bi*nary dig*its*), and when that data is moved within a computer system, an extra bit is added to some data items so that all data items will either have an odd (odd parity system) or an even (even parity system) number of bits. Thus, after data has been transferred within the computer, the number of bits is counted. If a data item has an even number of bits in an odd parity system or vice-versa, this would indicate that the data was not properly transferred within the system. For example, in an even parity system, the number 9 (which has three bits in a binary form) would be represented by four bits, three for the number and one for parity. Every time the number 9 was moved from one location to another, it would be checked to see if it had four bits, and any discrepancies would indicate an error in data transfer.

2. **Echo Check.** When data is input to or output from a computer, there is a chance that the input or output will not be carried out properly. An echo check is a signal from the input or output device to the central processing unit (CPU) informing the CPU that the requested operation (e.g., printing an output) has been carried out properly. For example, if a computer was sending output in the form of punched cards, the CPU would send a message to the card punch, and the card punch would send a message back to the CPU indicating that the proper holes had been punched.

3. **Validity Check.** In any computer system, data items are converted (coded) into machine language, and there is a possibility that those data items will not be coded correctly. A validity check compares the bit structure of a data item with a list of all possible valid bit structures. If a match is not found, this indicates that the data item that was input was not properly coded. For example, punched paper tape is one method to input data into the computer. A validity check would compare the holes punched in that paper tape with a list of all valid sets of hole punches, and a discrepancy would indicate that an invalid character was being input.

4. **File Protection Rings.** To prevent accidental writing on a reel of magnetic tape, file protection rings are used. These rings attach to the reel, and the tape can be written on only when these rings are in

place. Thus, if a tape is not supposed to be written on, the file protection ring is removed. Then, if someone accidentally tries to write on the tape, the computer will not allow it.

5. **Dual Read Check.** To prevent data items from being read incorrectly, a dual read check reads data in twice and compares the results of both reads. If they differ, it indicates that data was not read in properly. For example, a card reader reads the same deck of cards twice, and if the two reads were the same, that would indicate that the data was read in properly.

While these are just some of the many hardware controls that exist, the auditor's primary concern with hardware controls is that the organization properly handle errors identified by the computer system. That is, the auditor is primarily concerned with the accuracy of the EDP generated information. Hardware failures themselves are normally corrected by the computer vendor, assuming a service contract exists. The auditor is more concerned with the client's procedures for identifying and correcting data processed by the faulty hardware.

Access Controls

Access controls are controls designed to restrict entry to all EDP facilities, records, and files. One aspect of access controls, use of a data library, was previously mentioned. This prevents unauthorized persons from obtaining physical access to copies of data or programs.

Physical access to EDP hardware is another aspect of access controls. Common procedures include physically restricting access to the central processing unit and related computer equipment by measures such as door locks and/or uniformed guards. Systems that may be accessed from remote locations through terminals pose unique access problems. Accessing a system through a terminal may provide many of the same opportunities for error or fraud as would exist if one were able to physically access the central processing unit and related computer equipment. Controls over systems subject to remote terminal access may include measures such as physical locks on terminals, passwords, and file protection codes.

Data or Procedural Controls

Many organizations have integrated computers into their operations to such an extent that their day to day operations are dependent on the computer system. Due to this dependency, physical protection of the EDP system and data is critical.

One aspect of physical protection concerns physical security of the computer hardware. This would include an installation that was reasonably protected against water damage, fire, or vandalism. To achieve this, many companies adopt such measures as locating the computer center in a building or floor level within a building where flooding is a minor risk. Fire prevention and detection procedures are mandatory requirements. In the event these procedures fail, the organization should maintain adequate insurance coverage to protect the company from loss.

Another aspect of data controls is the ability of the organization to recover from loss of programs or data either purposefully by vandalism or by accident. Protection in this area usually involves procedures for off-premises data storage, back-up facilities, and file or system reconstruction. Off-premises data storage involves the practice of regularly storing copies of all programs and data at remote locations so that copies will exist if the original versions are destroyed. This involves establishing a schedule of regularly copying programs or data on tape or disk and transporting them to the storage site. Also, in the event the computer hardware should be destroyed or rendered inoperable, the company should have an agreement with an organization with similar hardware for use of their facilities.

File reconstruction involves the ability to recreate individual files from back-up copies of the files. In a batch system this may involve a grandfather-father-son procedure, which works as follows. By definition, a batch system works by periodically (rather than continuously, as in an online system) updating a file by adding current transactions to it. The new (updated) file is called the son. The original file from which the son was made is called the father. The file the father was made from is called the grandfather. The father and the grandfather are backup copies which should be stored in a safe location either on or off premises. Then, if the son was destroyed, it could be reconstructed by reprocessing the father and the transaction record.

In a data base system this may involve processing transaction files against an old version of the data base in order to bring it up to date. System reconstruction involves the ability to actually use back-up facilities. This should normally involve a periodic "dry run" on the back-up facilities to make sure that all necessary programs and data are being maintained and that the company personnel can get the system operating in a reasonable time period.

APPLICATION CONTROLS

The focus in evaluating environmental or general controls is whether an overall environment is provided in which individual applications or systems may be run without material errors occurring, assuming adequate controls exist in each application or system. Since different applications or systems have different objectives and different potential errors, controls are evaluated based on the specific objectives and potential for error that exist in each application or system.

Application or system controls are usually categorized into three categories: input, processing, and output. There are usually several possible controls that could accomplish specific control objectives for each category. Therefore, the presence or absence of a specific control does not necessarily indicate a weakness. The auditor would have to consider all controls existing in that application or system to determine if an internal control weakness exists.

Input Controls

The general objectives of input controls are to ensure that (1) all data processed is properly authorized, (2) all data is properly converted into machine sensible form, (3) no data is lost, added, or altered during transmission for processing, and (4) rejected data is properly controlled and resubmitted. Several examples of input controls for each of these objectives follows:

1. **Authorization**

   - *Source documents* — acceptance of input only from properly filled out and appropriately signed source documents.

   - *Passwords* — online systems programmed to allow access only for authorized personnel.

2. **Conversion**

   - *Keypunch verification* — verifying selected fields on keypunched data by repunching by a second keypuncher on a machine which rejects transactions if the card does not agree with what is punched by second keypuncher.

   - *Turn-around documents* — the use of input documents on which most of the data has been generated by the computer in machine readable form thus eliminating much data conversion.

   - *Reasonableness or limit checks* — these are designed to check if the data that is input is reasonable. For example, in a payroll application, the computer can be programmed to not allow more than forty regular hours of work or more than seven days of work per week.

3.   **Transmission**

- *Transmittal forms* — when machine readable data are physically transmitted in batches, use of prenumbered transmittal forms with counts or record sequence will help ensure that no data is lost or added.

- *Control totals* — before and after a batch is processed, some meaningful total, such as total purchases for a group of purchase invoices, is computed. If the two totals differ, data has been lost in processing.

- *Hash totals* — these work in the same way as control totals, except the totals are themselves meaningless. For example, a total may be taken of all the social security numbers in a batch of payroll records.

- *Record counts* — by having the computer count the number of records it processed, the operator can make sure that this total agrees with the total number of records submitted to be processed.

4.   **Rejected Data**

- *Error control logs* — written record of all amounts rejected due to errors during normal processing.

- *Error correction* — only authorized personnel should be allowed access to data containing errors. Responsibility should be fixed for error correction and timely resubmission.

Processing Controls

The objectives of processing controls are to ensure that (1) all data submitted were correctly processed as authorized and (2) no data were added or omitted. Examples for each of these objectives follow:

1.   **Correct Processing**

- *Completeness check* — all input should be tested to determine that all required data is present. The payroll program might check inputs to determine that all employees had an approved employee number prior to processing their weekly payroll check.

- *File identification procedures* — applications should be programmed to accept and operate only with correct files. For example, a payroll program should be programmed to check, prior to processing, the header labels on tapes mounted for processing to determine that they are the correct tapes.

2.   **Data Integrity**

- *Machine-generated transactions* — applications should be programmed to perform appropriate checks over machine generated transactions such as automatic inventory reordering.

- *Programmed run-to-run control total and balancing* — this ensures that all data processed by one program in a system is also processed and/or balanced to data run in subsequent related programs.

Output Controls

The principal objectives of output controls are (1) to ensure the accuracy of processing results and (2) to restrict output to authorized personnel. Two examples of each of these include:

1.   **Accuracy**

- *Output totals* — output totals, such as total payroll hours processed, should be agreed back to input totals.

- *Review of reports* — authorized personnel should review reports generated for reasonableness and completeness prior to use.

2.   **Restricted Output**

- *Report distribution list* — a written list should exist of personnel authorized to receive each report generated.

- *Report log* — a written distribution log should be maintained to record when and to whom output was distributed.

REVIEW AND REPORTING RESPONSIBILITIES FOR EDP SYSTEMS

In a system with significant EDP applications, the auditor's review and reporting responsibilities are the same as it is for manual systems. First, the auditor reviews and evaluates the system. Then, if the auditor wishes to rely on the established controls, he or she must perform tests of compliance. Any material weaknesses found in either the design or operation of the EDP system should be reported in the auditor's management letter to the client or in a written report on internal control directed to the client's board of directors and to senior management.

Review and documentation procedures are also essentially the same for either manual or EDP systems. The major difference is the significance of the general controls relative to the application controls. If the auditor concludes, either by review or testing, that there are material weaknesses in the general controls, then there is no reason to review and test the controls over the individual applications. This is because of the significance of the general controls relative to the application controls. For example, if an organization had a general control weakness that allowed essentially anyone in the organization to access the payroll files, then it would not matter how good the controls were over the individual payroll application since they could be circumvented due to the general control weakness. Because of the importance of general controls, auditors normally review and evaluate general controls before reviewing controls over individual applications.

AUDITING TECHNIQUES FOR EDP SYSTEMS

As with audits of manual systems, there are two basic types of audit tests that may be applied to EDP systems: compliance tests and substantive tests. Based on the auditor's review and evaluation of the internal control system, both the manual and EDP portions, he or she will decide what combination of compliance and substantive tests is possible and appropriate. The auditor may decide not to rely on the internal controls due to apparent weaknesses in the controls or because testing such controls may not be justified on a cost/benefit basis. If the auditor decides not to rely on internal controls, for either reason, then he or she must perform sufficient substantive tests to obtain reasonable assurance regarding the fairness of the financial statements.

It is theoretically possible for the auditor to obtain all assurances strictly from substantive tests. This occurs very frequently in small companies where controls are weak or relatively nonexistent. As companies grow larger, it is much more difficult to obtain sufficient audit assurance from strictly substantive testing due to the volume of assets and transactions involved in a typical accounting period. For example, it would be virtually impossible to perform an audit based strictly on substantive tests in a reasonable time/cost framework for a company the size of General Motors or IBM.

In addition to considering company size in determining the audit approach for companies employing EDP, the auditor must also consider the degree of audit trail existence. As one moves from simple to complex systems, there tends to be a reduction in the human-readable audit trail. That is, the ability to follow transactions from origination through to final recording is diminished due to reduction or elimination of source documents and human-readable records. Many records may be maintained only in machine readable form on magnetic tapes, discs, or bubbles (a new form of electromagnetic storage), and the auditor must use the computer to access these records. Another factor to consider in more complex systems is the simultaneous updating of accounting records at the time the transaction takes place. For example, many cash registers are "point-of-sale" computer terminals which interface with a main CPU for updating inventory, sales, and accounts receivable records at the time the sale takes place. In these cases, the only way to determine the validity of such transactions is by auditing the system generating the transactions.

The following sections will review some common EDP audit techniques. Several of the techniques may be used for either compliance or substantive testing.

Audit Compliance Testing Without Utilizing the Computer

This technique involves a manual approach of auditing *around the computer*. The auditor will select a sample of source documents, manually determine processing results, and compare the results of the manual processing with computer printouts. Based on the degree of conformity between the auditor's manual processing results and the computer printouts, the auditor forms a conclusion about the computer processing even though the processing software is not examined directly. This approach is inappropriate if employed solely because the auditor lacks sufficient EDP expertise to use other techniques. It is appropriate when justified on a cost/benefit basis as compared to other available techniques. The manual approach would be primarily a compliance test but would also have some aspects of substantive tests since the transactions the auditor tests would be included in the financial statements. This approach is illustrated in the flowchart shown in Exhibit 7-5.

Techniques for Computer Audit Compliance Testing

In EDP systems where very little hard copy is produced and a human-readable audit trail is nonexistent, auditing around the computer or manual processing is very difficult and is usually not justified on a cost/benefit basis. In these situations, audit compliance testing using the computer to test hardware and software controls is necessary to obtain sufficient evidence that controls are functioning according to design. These techniques may involve the use of test data, parallel simulation, program code checking, integrated test facility, and transaction tagging.

Test Data.   A widely used technique to test computer controls is the test data approach. Using this approach, the auditor prepares test data which simulates both valid and erroneous transactions. Then the test data is processed by the client's computer system. The auditor then

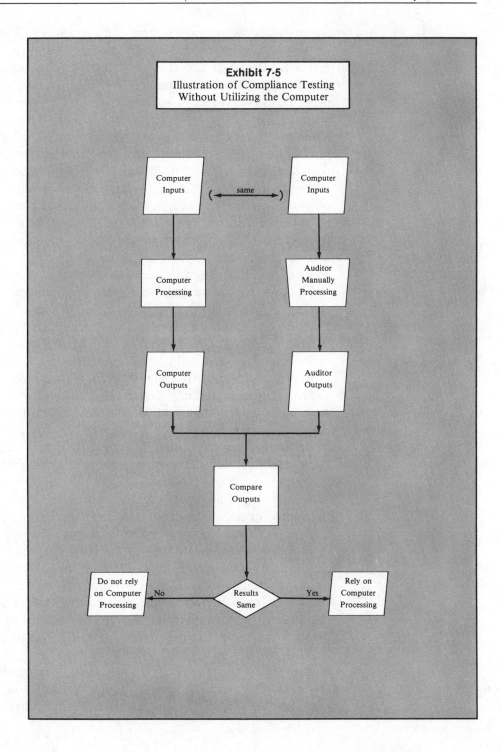

Exhibit 7-5
Illustration of Compliance Testing
Without Utilizing the Computer

compares the computer system output and reported exception conditions to the output expected based on the auditor's knowledge of the test data. Based on this comparison the auditor has a basis for forming a conclusion about the reliability of the client's system. The auditor must be very careful to ensure that such processing is done with the regular programs employed by the client. To achieve this, auditors sometimes request program copies on a surprise basis. Or, the auditor may obtain a copy of the client's program early in the current year and then later compare the retained copy with a new copy obtained from the client on a surprise basis. This procedure, however, is costly and time consuming. Furthermore, in most situations the auditor should examine the general controls over access to, and modification of, application programs. If these controls are good, the auditor will have more assurance that the application program given him or her by the client will be the same program used in day-to-day processing runs.

The tests should be designed to test data-editing routines written into the client's application programs. That is, the client's program should be written with built-in controls to accept only valid complete transactional data. Examples of editing routines for application programs include limit tests and field or numeric checks. A limit test for a payroll application could be that the program would not accept an employee's payroll data if such data reflected that the employee worked more than 40 regular hours. The auditor should include in the test data an erroneous transaction where hours worked for an employee reflected more than 40 regular hours. Then, the auditor would follow through to see if the program actually rejected the erroneous data and how the system reported the error.

A field check in an application program is a type of completeness test because it checks to see that data is recorded in all fields. If there are any blank fields, the program should reject that particular transaction. A numeric check in an application program tests fields to determine that only numeric data is recorded therein. In addition to the three edit routines discussed above, there are many different types of controls that can be designed into application programs. Before developing test data, the auditor should determine the controls built into the client's application programs so that he or she may design appropriate test data.

Also, all processing of the test data must be under the auditor's control to ensure that the client does not alter the results of processing the test data. The test data approach may be illustrated by reference to the previous flowchart for the around-the-computer manual approach.

There are two significant differences in the test data approach. The auditor determines the test data for input to the computer, and he or she also controls the processing of the test data. When using around-the-computer manual approach, the auditor simply uses actual transactions and the related processing is performed by the client.

Parallel Simulation.   This technique involves the auditor creating a set of computer programs that simulate or duplicate the major processing activities of the client's programs. Actual or test data may be processed by the auditor's computer programs and by the client's programs. The auditor then compares his or her program outputs with the client's program outputs and forms a conclusion about the reliability of the controls present in the client's program. This technique is essentially an automated version of the around-the-computer manual approach. The previous flowchart for the around-the-computer manual approach would depict parallel simulation by simply substituting "auditor computer processing" in the block for "auditor manually processing." The major advantage of this technique is that since the auditor is using the computer to do the processing, he or she may process much larger amounts of data than under the manual technique. This allows the auditor to achieve stronger assurances about the system since a larger sample is used.

Program Code Checking.   This technique requires the auditor to manually read program code and/or use automatic computer generated flowcharts to determine that programs perform as documented and as authorized. It requires detailed programming knowledge and can be very time consuming for complex applications. It may, however, be the only effective way to identify existing program controls in some systems.

Integrated Test Facility (ITF).   The ITF technique is used primarily with on-line, real-time (OLRT) systems. This technique involves the auditor submitting test data along with actual data into the client's actual processing system. If processed properly, such data should end up in a file established by the auditor to represent a dummy division or subsidiary. The major advantage is that the auditor is testing the client's system directly. The major disadvantage is the possible "contamination" of the client's actual data files with the test data.

Transaction Tagging.   Transaction tagging is used only with OLRT systems and involves the auditor marking or tagging selected actual client input data. The "mark" or "tag" is usually an indicator in a field that normally does not have major processing significance, such as an

"X" punch in card column eighty. "Tagged" data would then have special reports displayed or printed indicating all files affected by that transaction and the effect of the transaction on those files. In order to obtain such displays or reports, the tagging capability must be programmed into the client's system at the time it is designed.

Substantive Audit Testing Techniques Using the Computer

In performing substantive audit tests, the auditor usually employs many of the traditional manual techniques to test the results of computer processing. It may be desirable, however, to automate some of these tasks. Since the results of computer processing usually reside in data files or data bases, automation involves using the computer to perform certain audit tasks on such data. A discussion of three ways auditors have automated substantive testing of client-processed data follows.

Custom-Designed Audit Software.   Perhaps the earliest technique permitting auditors to retrieve and analyze data stored in machine readable files was customer-designed computer programs. Such programs were usually written to perform specific tasks in the system of one client. These tasks might include totaling a field in a file or printing all or portions of a file. This technique is very useful, but there are high development costs for the audit software.

Generalized Audit Software (GAS).   In order to reduce the high costs associated with using custom-designed audit software for a single client, auditors developed generalized audit software packages. Such packages usually have the capability of performing a wide variety of useful audit tasks and are designed to run on a variety of hardware. These packages have typically been sequential file manipulation tools. In essence they represent very high level programming languages that the average auditor can learn to use in two days to a week. The following is representative of tasks commonly performed by such software packages:

- Basic mathematical operations such as addition, subtraction, multiplication, or division for designated fields.

- Data output operations such as printing designated fields or writing a new file containing data created from or extracted from client files. A common use of such packages is to extract data and print confirmations.

- Statistical sampling including random sample selection and evaluation of results.

- Comparison of fields in different files.

- Advanced mathematical techniques such as correlation or multiple regression analysis.

Data Base Management Systems.   Most generalized audit software has been designed to operate on sequential files. The need to integrate separate data files into one data base has lead to the widespread use of data base management systems. This development has posed many problems for auditors. No consensus currently exists as to the best way to audit data stored in a data base. Certainly custom-designed audit software is an approach that may be useful even though expensive. Fortunately, many auditors will be able to avoid this method since a number of data base management systems have had basic audit functions and/or audit capabilities built into them in the form of utility programs. Also, data bases are sometimes output in a sequential-file format so that auditors can use generalized audit software to test such data.

SUMMARY

This chapter discussed the independent auditor's responsibility for reviewing and evaluating internal control in an audit engagement. Methods of internal control review and documentation were discussed encompassing both manual and EDP processing systems. Under the second standard of field work, the auditor reviews and evaluates internal accounting control to determine the extent of substantive testing appropriate or required in the particular audit circumstances. If the auditor intends to rely on accounting controls to restrict the amount of substantive testing, he or she must compliance test those controls. Material weaknesses discovered in reviewing and evaluating internal accounting control must be reported to senior-level management and to the board of directors. This information is usually communicated in the form of a management letter at the conclusion of the audit.

Three approaches are available to the auditor in documenting the review and evaluation of internal accounting control—the questionnaire, narrative description, and flowchart. Also, some combination of these three approaches may be used, such as development of a flowchart with narrative descriptions included to provide greater understanding.

Three types of flowcharts were discussed and explained—systems flowcharts, program flowcharts, and auditor flowcharts. Although flowcharting requires greater skill than the questionnaire approach to internal control review, flowcharts have the advantages of being easily understood and of providing a better overall understanding of a complex system. Furthermore, flowcharts parallel EDP documentation, and they may be readily updated in future engagements.

General controls and application controls for EDP systems were discussed. General controls relate to the overall EDP environment and form the foundation supporting application controls. Application controls relate to the input, processing, and output operations of a single task such as processing the payroll. In addition, auditing techniques for EDP systems were discussed. These included techniques for compliance testing with and without the computer and techniques for substantive audit testing using the computer.

REVIEW QUESTIONS

7-1   Under what circumstances is an auditor required to review and evaluate internal control?

7-2   If internal control is weak or non-existent in one area of a company's operations, does this preclude the auditor from placing reliance on the internal control system?

7-3   What are the two major phases in the study and evaluation of internal control?

7-4   Distinguish between internal accounting and administrative controls. Give an example of each.

7-5   What is a management letter?

7-6   What responsibility does the independent auditor have for material weaknesses in internal accounting control discovered during the course of an audit?

7-7   How does an auditor determine if an internal accounting control weakness is material?

7-8   Two basic approaches to organizing the review of internal control are to review major cycles or to review functions. Explain each of these approaches.

7-9   Discuss the four basic questions the auditor attempts to answer during the review phase of each control cycle or function.

7-10 What methods may the auditor use to gain an understanding of the client's internal control system?

7-11   Identify four components that should be included in the auditor's documentation of the internal control system.

7-12   List some advantages and disadvantages of internal control questionnaires, flowcharts and narrative memos.

7-13   How does the presence of a computer system alter an auditor's approach to the review and evaluation of an internal control system?

7-14   Distinguish between EDP general controls and application controls.

7-15   List five general controls.

7-16   Identify the functional areas within the EDP department that should be separated from one another.

7-17   List several different methods acceptable for documenting an EDP system.

7-18   Identify three access controls over remote-entry terminals.

7-19   Why is off-premises data storage important?

7-20   List the three categories of application controls.

7-21   What are the general objectives of input controls? Of processing controls? Of output controls?

7-22   Are review and reporting responsibilities different for EDP systems than for manual systems? Explain.

7-23   Under what circumstances might an auditor not be able to obtain sufficient assurances strictly from substantive testing, assuming that proper data exists and that there are no audit scope restrictions?

7-24   Under what circumstances might an auditor not be able to use an around-the-computer manual approach?

7-25   What are some major concerns of the auditor when using the test data approach?

7-26   List the major advantage of each of the following EDP audit techniques:

a. Parallel simulation
b. Program code checking
c. Integrated test facility
d. Transaction tagging

7-27 Why has the popularity of custom-designed audit software declined? Is there a current need for custom-designed audit software?

7-28 What are some significant advantages of generalized audit software packages?

7-29 What are two approaches the auditor may employ in accessing data stored in data base management systems?

DISCUSSION QUESTIONS AND PROBLEMS

7-30 Internal control comprises the plan of organization and all of the coordinate methods and measures adopted within a business to safeguard its assets, check the accuracy and reliability of its accounting data, promote operational efficiency, and encourage adherence to prescribed managerial policies.

Required:

a. What is the purpose of the auditor's study and evaluation of internal control?
b. What are the objectives of a preliminary evaluation of internal control?
c. How is the auditor's understanding of the system of internal control documented?
d. What is the purpose of tests of compliance?

(AICPA adapted)

7-31 You are reviewing audit work papers containing a narrative description of the Tenney Corporation's factory payroll system. A portion of that narrative is as follows:

Factory employees punch time clock cards each day when entering or leaving the shop. At the end of each week, the timekeeping department collects the time cards and prepares duplicate batch-control slips by department showing total hours and number of employees. The timecards and original batch-control slips are sent to the payroll accounting section. The second copy of the batch-control slips is filed by date.

In the payroll accounting section, payroll transaction cards are keypunched from the information on the timecards, and a batch-total card for each batch is keypunched from the batch-control slip. The timecards and batch-control slips are then filed by batch for possible reference. The payroll transaction cards and batch-total card are sent to data processing where they are sorted by employee number within batch. Each batch is edited by a computer program which checks the validity of the employee number against a master employee tape file and the total hours and number of employees against the batch total card. A detailed printout by batch and employee number is produced which indicates batches that do not balance and invalid employee numbers. This printout is returned to payroll accounting to resolve all differences.

In searching for documentation you found a flowchart of the payroll system which included all appropriate symbols (American National Standards Institute, Inc.) but was only partially labeled. The portion of this flowchart described by the above narrative follows:

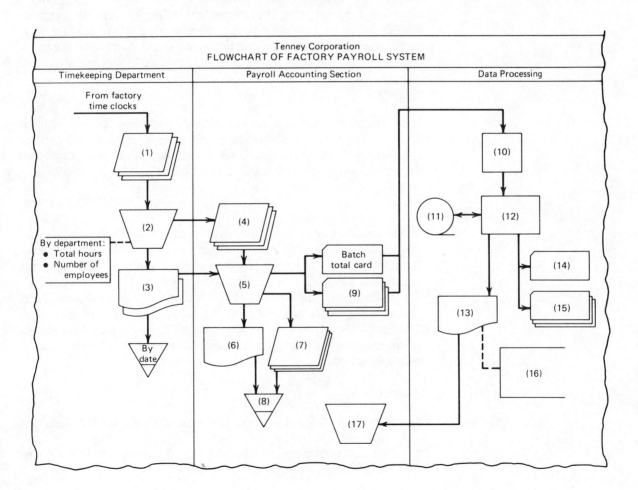

Required:

a. Number your answer 1 through 17. Next to the corresponding number of your answer, supply the appropriate labeling (document name, process description, or file order) applicable to each numbered symbol on the flowchart.

b. Flowcharts are one of the aids an auditor may use to determine and evaluate a client's internal control system. List advantages of using flowcharts in this context.

(AICPA adapted)

7-32   Anthony, CPA, prepared the flowchart on the following page which portrays the raw materials purchasing function of one of Anthony's clients, a medium-sized manufacturing company, from the preparation of initial documents through the vouching of invoices for payment in accounts payable. The flowchart was a portion of the work performed on the audit engagement to evaluate internal control.

Required:

Identify and explain the systems and control weaknesses evident from the flowchart on the following page. Include the internal control weaknesses resulting from activities performed or not performed. All documents are prenumbered.

(AICPA adapted)

7-33   When auditing an electronic data processing (EDP) accounting system, the independent auditor should have a general familiarity with the effects of the use of EDP on the various characteristics of accounting control and on the auditor's study and evaluation of such control. The independent auditor must be aware of those control procedures that are commonly referred to as "general" controls and those that are commonly referred to as "application" controls. General controls relate to all EDP activities, and application controls relate to specific accounting tasks.

Required:

a. What are the general controls that should exist in EDP-based accounting systems?

b. What are the purposes of each of the following categories of application controls?

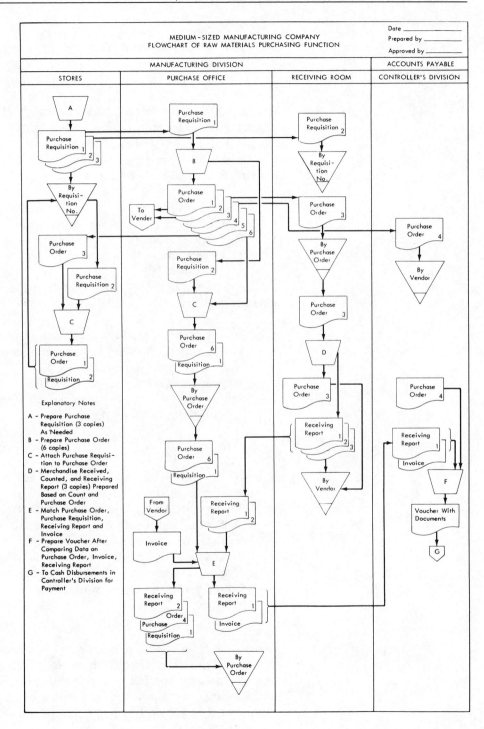

MEDIUM–SIZED MANUFACTURING COMPANY
FLOWCHART OF RAW MATERIALS PURCHASING FUNCTION

Date _____
Prepared by _____
Approved by _____

Explanatory Notes

A – Prepare Purchase Requisition (3 copies) As Needed
B – Prepare Purchase Order (6 copies)
C – Attach Purchase Requisition to Purchase Order
D – Merchandise Received, Counted, and Receiving Report (3 copies) Prepared Based on Count and Purchase Order
E – Match Purchase Order, Purchase Requisition, Receiving Report and Invoice
F – Prepare Voucher After Comparing Data on Purchase Order, Invoice, Receiving Report
G – To Cash Disbursements in Controller's Division for Payment

1. Input controls
2. Processing controls
3. Output controls

(AICPA adapted)

7-34 Savage, CPA, has been requested by an audit client to perform a non-recurring engagement involving the implementation of an EDP information and control system. The client requests that in setting up the new system and during the period prior to conversion to the new system, that Savage:

- Counsel on potential expansion of business activity plans.
- Search for and interview new personnel.
- Hire new personnel.
- Train personnel.

In addition, the client requests that during the three months subsequent to the conversion, that Savage:

- Supervise the operation of the new system.
- Monitor client-prepared source documents and make changes in basic EDP generated data as Savage may deem necessary without concurrence of the client.
- Savage responds that he may perform some of the services requested, but not all of them.

Required:

a. Which of these services may Savage perform and which of these services may Savage not perform?
b. Before undertaking this engagement, Savage should inform the client of all significant matters related to the engagement. What are these significant matters?
c. If Savage adds to his staff an individual who specializes in developing computer systems, what degree of knowledge must Savage possess in order to supervise the specialist's activities?

(AICPA adapted)

7-35 George Beemster, CPA, is examining the financial statements of the Louisville Sales Corporation, which recently installed an off-line electronic computer. The following comments have been extracted from Mr. Beemster's notes on computer operations and the processing and control of shipping notices and customer invoices:

To minimize inconvenience, Louisville converted without change its existing data processing system, which used tabulating equipment. The computer company supervised the conversion and has provided training to all computer department employees (except keypunch operators) in systems design, operations and programming.

Each computer run is assigned to a specific employee, who is responsible for making program changes, running the program, and answering questions. This procedure has the advantage of eliminating the need for records of computer operations because each employee is responsible for his or her own computer runs.

At least one computer department employee remains in the computer room during office hours, and only computer department employees have keys to the computer room.

System documentation consists of those materials furnished by the computer company — a set of record formats and program listings. These and the tape library are kept in a corner of the computer department.

The company considered the desirability of programmed controls but decided to retain the manual controls from its existing system.

Company products are shipped directly from public warehouses which forward shipping notices to general accounting. There a billing clerk enters the price of the item and accounts for the numerical sequence of shipping notices from each warehouse. The billing clerk also prepares daily adding machine tapes ("control tapes") of the units shipped and the unit prices.

Shipping notices and control tapes are forwarded to the computer department for keypunching and processing. Extensions are made on the computer. Output consists of invoices (in six copies) and a daily sales register. The daily sales register shows the aggregate totals of units shipped and unit prices which the computer operator compares to the control tapes.

All copies of the invoice are returned to the billing clerk. The clerk mails three copies to the customer, forwards one copy to the warehouse, maintains one copy in a numerical file, and retains one copy in an open invoice file that serves as a detailed accounts-receivable record.

Required:

Describe weaknesses in internal control over information and data flows and the procedures for processing shipping notices and customer invoices and recommend improvements in these controls and processing procedures. Organize your answer sheets as follows:

Weaknesses	Recommended Improvements

(AICPA adapted)

OBJECTIVE QUESTIONS*

7-36 The auditor's review of the client's system of internal control is documented in order to substantiate

A. Conformity of the accounting records with generally accepted accounting principles.
B. Representation as to adherence to requirements of management.
C. Representation as to compliance with generally accepted auditing standards.
D. The fairness of the financial statement presentation.

7-37 Which of the following is essential to determine whether the necessary internal control procedures were prescribed and are being followed?

A. Developing questionnaires and checklists.
B. Studying and evaluating administrative control policies.
C. Reviewing the system and testing compliance.
D. Observing employee functions and making inquiries.

7-38 In general, a material internal control weakness may be defined as a condition in which material errors or irregularities would ordinarily not be detected within a timely period by

A. An auditor during the normal study and evaluation of the system of internal control.
B. A controller when reconciling accounts in the general ledger.
C. Employees in the normal course of performing their assigned functions.
D. The chief financial officer when reviewing interim financial statements.

7-39 One reason why an auditor uses a flowchart is to aid in the

A. Evaluation of a series of sequential processes.
B. Study of the system of responsibility accounting.
C. Performance of important, required dual-purpose tests.
D. Understanding of a client's organization structure.

7-40 A secondary objective of the auditor's study and evaluation of internal control is that the study and evaluation provide

---

Note: All questions in this section are AICPA adapted questions.

A. A basis for constructive suggestions concerning improvements in internal control.

B. A basis for reliance on the system of internal accounting control.

C. An assurance that the records and documents have been maintained in accordance with existing company policies and procedures.

D. A basis for the determination of the resultant extent of the tests to which auditing procedures are to be restricted.

7-41   A client's materials-purchasing cycle begins with requisitions from user departments and ends with the receipt of materials and the recognition of a liability. An auditor's primary objective in reviewing this cycle is to

A. Evaluate the reliability of information generated as a result of the purchasing process.

B. Investigate the physical handling and recording of unusual acquisitions of materials.

C. Consider the need to be on hand for the annual physical count if this system is not functioning properly.

D. Ascertain that materials said to be ordered, received, and paid for are on hand.

7-42   One important reason why a CPA, during the course of an audit engagement, prepares systems flowcharts is to

A. Reduce the need for inquiries of client personnel concerning the operations of the system of internal accounting control.

B. Depict the organizational structure and document flow in a single chart for review and reference purposes.

C. Assemble the internal control findings into a comprehensible format suitable for analysis.

D. Prepare documentation that would be useful in the event of a future consulting engagement.

7-43   The basic concept of internal accounting control which recognizes that the cost of internal control should not exceed the benefits expected to be derived is known as

A. Management by exception.

B. Management responsibility.

C. Limited liability.

D. Reasonable assurance.

7-44   Which of the following is not a medium that can normally be used by an auditor to record information concerning a client's system of internal accounting control?

A.   Narrative memorandum.
B.   Procedures manual.
C.   Flowchart.
D.   Decision table.

7-45   Which of the following is an advantage of generalized computer audit packages?

A.   They are all written in one identical computer language.
B.   They can be used for audits of clients that use differing EDP equipment and file formats.
C.   They have reduced the need for the auditor to study input controls for EDP-related procedures.
D.   Their use can be substituted for a relatively large part of the required compliance testing.

7-46   After a preliminary phase of the review of a client's EDP controls, an auditor may decide not to perform compliance tests related to the control procedures within the EDP portion of the client's internal control system. Which of the following would not be a valid reason for choosing to omit compliance tests?

A.   The controls appear adequate.
B.   The controls duplicate operative controls existing elsewhere in the system.
C.   There appear to be major weaknesses that would preclude reliance on the stated procedure.
D.   The time and dollar costs of testing exceed the time and dollar savings in substantive testing if the compliance tests show the controls to be operative.

7-47   Accounting control procedures within the EDP activity may leave no visible evidence indicating that the procedures were performed. In such instances, the auditor should test these accounting controls by

A.   Making corroborative inquiries.
B.   Observing the separation of duties of personnel.
C.   Reviewing transactions submitted for processing and comparing them to related output.
D.   Reviewing the run manual.

7-48   Program controls are used as substitutes for human controls in a manual system. Which of the following is an example of a program control?

    A.   Dual read.
    B.   Echo check.
    C.   Validity check.
    D.   Limit and reasonableness test.

7-49   Auditors often make use of computer programs that perform routine processing functions such as sorting and merging. These programs are made available by electronic data processing companies and others and are specifically referred to as

    A.   User programs.
    B.   Compiler programs.
    C.   Supervisory programs.
    D.   Utility programs.

7-50   Where computers are used, the effectiveness of internal accounting control depends, in part, upon whether the organizational structure includes any incompatible combinations. Such a combination would exist when there is no separation of the duties between

    A.   Documentation librarian and manager of programming.
    B.   Programmer and console operator.
    C.   Systems analyst and programmer.
    D.   Processing control clerk and keypunch supervisor.

7-51   The primary purpose of a generalized computer audit program is to allow the auditor to

    A.   Use the client's employees to perform routine audit checks of the electronic data processing records that otherwise would be done by the auditor's staff accountants.
    B.   Test the logic of computer programs used in the client's electronic data processing systems.
    C.   Select larger samples from the client's electronic data processing records than would otherwise be selected without the generalized program.
    D.   Independently process client electronic data processing records.

7-52 An auditor evaluates the existing system of internal control in order to

A. Determine the extent of substantive tests which must be performed.
B. Determine the extent of compliance tests which must be perfomed.
C. Ascertain whether irregularities are probable.
D. Ascertain whether any employees have incompatible functions.

7-53 An independent auditor has concluded that the client's records, procedures, and representations can be relied upon based on tests made during the year, when internal control was found to be effective. The auditor should test the records, procedures, and representations again at year-end if

A. Inquiries and observations lead the auditor to believe that conditions have changed significantly.
B. Comparisons of year-end balances with like balances at prior dates revealed significant fluctuations.
C. Unusual transactions occurred subsequent to the completion of the interim audit work.
D. Client records are in a condition that facilitate effective and efficient testing.

7-54 The auditor's study and evaluation of internal control is done for each of the following reasons *except*

A. To provide a basis for constructive service suggestions.
B. To aid in the determination of the nature, timing, and extent of audit tests.
C. To establish a basis for reliance thereon.
D. To provide training and development for staff accountants.

7-55 Which of the following is an example of application controls in electronic data processing systems?

A. Input controls.
B. Hardware controls.
C. Documentation procedures.
D. Controls over access to equipment and data files.

7-56 In evaluating internal control, the first step is to prepare an internal-control questionnaire or a flowchart of the system. The second step should be to

A. Determine the extent of audit work necessary to form an opinion.

B. Gather enough evidence to determine if the internal-control system is functioning as described.

C. Write a letter to management describing the weaknesses in the internal-control system.

D. Form a final judgment on the effectiveness of the internal-control system.

7-57 Which of the following activities would be *least* likely to strengthen a company's internal control?

A. Separating accounting from other financial operations.

B. Maintaining insurance for fire and theft.

C. Fixing responsibility for the performance of employee duties.

D. Carefully selecting and training employees.

7-58 A well-designed system of internal control that is functioning effectively is most likely to detect an irregularity arising from

A. The fraudulent action of several employees.

B. The fraudulent action of an individual employee.

C. Informal deviations from the official organization chart.

D. Management fraud.

7-59 Which of the following best describes the principal advantage of the use of flowcharts in reviewing internal control?

A. Standard flowcharts are available and can be effectively used for describing most company internal operations.

B. Flowcharts aid in the understanding of the sequence and relationships of activities and documents.

C. Working papers are not complete unless they include flowcharts as well as memoranda on internal control.

D. Flowcharting is the most efficient means available for summarizing internal control.

7-60 The normal sequence of documents and operations on a well-prepared systems flowchart is

A. Top to bottom and left to right.

B. Bottom to top and left to right.

C. Top to bottom and right to left.

D. Bottom to top and right to left.

7-61   Effective internal control in a small company that has an insufficient number of employees to permit proper division of responsibilities can *best* be enhanced by

A.   Employment of temporary personnel to aid in the separation of duties.
B.   Direct participation by the owner of the business in the record-keeping activities of the business.
C.   Engaging a CPA to perform monthly "write-up" work.
D.   Delegation of full, clear-cut responsibility to each employee for the functions assigned to each.

7-62   Which of the following *best* describes the inherent limitations that should be recognized by an auditor when considering the potential effectiveness of a system of internal accounting control?

A.   Procedures whose effectiveness depends on segregation of duties can be circumvented by collusion.
B.   The competence and integrity of client personnel provides an environment conducive to accounting control and provides assurance that effective control will be achieved.
C.   Procedures designed to assure the execution and recording of transactions in accordance with prior authorizations are effective against irregularities perpetrated by management.
D.   The benefits expected to be derived from effective internal accounting control usually do *not* exceed the costs of such control.

7-63   Which of the following *best* describes how an auditor, when evaluating internal accounting control, considers the types of errors and irregularities that could occur and determines those control procedures that should prevent or detect such errors or irregularities?

A.   Discussions with management with respect to the system of internal accounting control and how management determines that the system is functioning properly.
B.   Review of questionnaires, flowcharts, checklists, instructions, or similar generalized materials used by the auditor.
C.   Exercise of professional judgment in evaluating the reliability of supporting documentation.
D.   Use of attribute sampling techniques to gather information for tests of compliance.

7-64   During which phase of an audit examination is the preparation of flowcharts *most* appropriate?

A. Review of the system of internal accounting control.

B. Tests of compliance with internal accounting control procedures.

C. Evaluation of the system of internal administrative control.

D. Analytic review of operations.

7-65 When preparing a record of a client's system of internal accounting control, the independent auditor sometimes uses a systems flowchart, which can *best* be described as a

A. Pictorial presentation of the flow of instructions in a client's internal computer system.

B. Diagram which clearly indicates an organization's internal reporting structure.

C. Graphic illustration of the flow of operations which is used to replace the auditor's internal control questionnaire.

D. Symbolic representation of a system or series of sequential processes.

7-66 Proper segregation of functional responsibilities calls for separation of the

A. Authorization, approval, and execution functions.

B. Authorization, execution, and payment functions.

C. Receiving, shipping, and custodial functions.

D. Authorization, recording, and custodial functions.

7-67 It is important for the CPA to consider the competence of the audit client's employees because their competence bears directly and importantly upon the

A. Cost/benefit relationship of the system of internal control.

B. Achievement of the objectives of the system of internal control.

C. Comparison of recorded accountability with assets.

D. Timing of the tests to be performed.

7-68 An auditor's flowchart of a client's internal control system is a diagrammatic representation which depicts the auditor's

A. Understanding of the system.

B. Program for compliance tests.

C. Documentation of the study and evaluation of the system.

D. Understanding of the types of irregularities which are probable, given the present system.

LEARNING OBJECTIVES

After studying this chapter, students should understand

1. The nature of substantive tests, including the five basic minimum audit procedures for substantive tests.
2. The relationship between substantive tests and internal control.
3. The techniques which auditors use to discover the existing system of internal control.
4. The techniques which an auditor uses to document a system of internal control.
5. The decision process which an auditor follows in deciding which controls to rely on.
6. The techniques which an auditor uses to compliance test a system of internal control.
7. The nature of reports on internal control.

Chapter 8

Internal Control Tests of Compliance and Evaluation

This chapter was written by
Johnny R. Johnson, Ph.D., C.P.A.,
Associate Professor of Accounting,
University of Georgia

INTRODUCTION

Chapter 5 discussed the nature of internal control, basic internal control concepts, and internal control and the Foreign Corrupt Practices Act. Also, Chapter 7 provided an overview of the independent auditor's responsibilities for reviewing internal control as well as methods and procedures for conducting such a review. This chapter explains in more detail how the auditor uses the system of internal control. The chapter begins with a discussion of the nature of substantive tests, followed by sections on the relationship between substantive tests and internal control and evaluating internal control. Special emphasis is placed on compliance testing of internal control.

NATURE AND ILLUSTRATION OF SUBSTANTIVE TEST

In Section 320 of *SAS No. 1, Auditor's Study of Internal Control,* substantive tests (sometimes referred to as validation tests) are defined as audit tests designed to "obtain evidence as to the validity and propriety of the accounting treatment of transactions and balances . . . ." In other words, substantive tests determine if a transaction or a series of transactions (an account balance) is properly recorded in accordance with generally accepted accounting principles.

There are two basic types of substantive tests. One type examines the details of a single transaction or an account balance to determine if the transaction or balance is recorded in accordance with generally accepted accounting principles. The second type of substantive tests, referred to as analytical review procedures, evaluates the overall reasonableness of account balances.

As indicated in Chapter 6, over the years auditors have developed a set of minimum audit proccedures which are used to substantiate the balances in the various financial statement accounts. These minimum audit procedures are usually considered each time a specific account is audited, but the extent of these procedures, as discussed in detail later, is determined by the reliance on internal control.

Illustration of Substantive Test for Sales

As indicated in Chapter 6, substantive tests for income statement balances employ five basic types of procedures. This section discusses these procedures as they would be used in auditing a sales account. The restaurant example which was discussed in Chapter 5, is continued for this illustration. The way in which the procedures are applied to other types of accounts is illustrated throughout the remainder of this text.

One type of audit procedure used in substantive tests for income statement balances verifies a sample of the individual entries which are posted to a specific account. For example, with sales the auditor usually computes the sales which should have been recorded for a sample of days, weeks, or months. Then the records are examined to determine that the entries which should have been recorded were in fact recorded.

To illustrate this verification procedure, consider the audit program in Exhibit 8-1. For a restaurant's sales account, as in this example, the entries for a sample of days can be verified by (1) obtaining the checks for each day in the sample, (2) recomputing the sales which should have been recorded for each day, and (3) verifying that each day's sales was properly recorded. In Exhibit 8-1, the verification procedures just described are accomplished by carrying out the first five audit program steps.

A second type of substantive audit procedure for income statement balances verifies the mathematical accuracy of the account balance. That is, the debits and credits which were posted to the account are summed to verify that the total balance in the account is mathematically correct. For the restaurant example, the mathematical accuracy is verified in audit program step number eight.

A third type of substantive audit procedure for income statement balances verifies the accuracy of the cutoff. Specifically, the entries around the end of the period are examined to determine that they were recorded in the proper accounting period. The cutoff in the restaurant example is verified by performing audit program steps six and seven.

A fourth type of substantive audit procedure for income statement balances verifies that the account is presented in accordance with GAAP and compares the balance in the account with the balance shown in the audit working papers. The balance in an account will normally appear in at least three places in the audit working papers: (1) in the financial statements, (2) in the working trial balance, and (3) in the specific working papers used to document the validation work done on that account. Audit program step nine illustrates this type of substantive procedure.

A fifth type of substantive test for income statement balances applies analytic review procedures to determine that the account balance is reasonable. Some examples of analytic review procedures for sales are given in audit program steps ten, eleven, and twelve of Exhibit 8-1. Analytic review procedures were discussed in detail in Chapter 4.

In summary, substantive audit procedures for income statement balances evaluate sample entries in the account and verify (1) that detail entries are properly recorded, (2) that the detail entries are accumulated

Exhibit 8-1
Audit Program Steps for the Substantive
Test of Sales in the Restaurant Example

Audit Program Steps	Initials	Date

1. Select a sample of days during the year and obtain the prenumbered checks for each day selected.

2. Account for the numerical sequence of checks for each day selected.

3. Obtain the menus for the selected days and reprice each order.

4. Prepare an adding machine tape of the checks for each day.

5. Compare the adding machine tape with the debit to cash and the credit to sales for that day. Also, determine that the debit to cash for each day agrees with the deposit which is shown on the next business day's bank statement.

6. Obtain the adding machine tapes which were prepared by the restaurant's manager for the last three business days of the accounting period under audit and for the first three days of the next accounting period.

7. Compare the totals on the tapes obtained in step six with the debit to cash and credit to sales for each day and note that there was a proper cutoff of sales.

8. Verify the mathematical accuracy of the addition in the general ledger sales account, i.e., add up the individual postings to determine that the total balance is mathematically correct.

9. Determine that the total balance in the sales account is presented in accordance with GAAP and agrees with the amounts shown in the working trial balance and in the earnings statement.

10. Have the client prepare a daily comparison of sales in the current year with sales in the previous year.

11. Trace a sample of the items from the client's schedule (from step 10) to the postings in the general ledger sales account. Also, compare the totals from the client's analysis with the respective totals in the general ledger sales account.

12. Review the daily sales analysis (from step 10) for any unusual fluctuations in daily sales. Clearly document the reasons for material daily fluctuations.

13. Review the cutoff bank statement for any credit card items or customer's personal checks not honored by the bank. Also, propose any necessary adjusting entry for items not honored by the bank.

to a correct total, (3) that there was a proper cutoff, (4) that the account balance is presented in accordance with GAAP and agrees with the balances in the working papers, and (5) that the balance appears reasonable.

THE RELATIONSHIP BETWEEN SUBSTANTIVE TESTS AND INTERNAL CONTROL

The relationship between substantive tests and internal control is explained in paragraph .08 of *SAS No. 39* as follows:

> .08 For purposes of this section, the uncertainty inherent in applying auditing procedures will be referred to as *ultimate risk*. Ultimate risk is a combination of the risk that material errors will occur in the accounting process used to develop the financial statements and the risk that any material errors that occur will not be detected by the auditor. The risk of these adverse events occurring jointly can be viewed as the product of the respective individual risks. The auditor may rely on internal accounting control to reduce the first risk and on substantive tests (tests of details of transactions and balances and analytical review procedures) to reduce the second risk.

The discussion in this paragraph can be summarized in two basic statements:

- If internal control is good, there is less chance that errors will occur, and therefore the auditor has less reason to substantiate the account balance.
- If internal control is poor, there is a greater chance for errors to occur, and therefore, the auditor must be very careful to thoroughly substantiate the account balance.

Although the two previous statements describe the relationship between substantive tests and internal control, auditors face a practical problem in deciding how much substantive testing must be performed when the system of internal control is somewhere between very good and very poor.

To illustrate the relationship between substantive tests and internal control, reconsider the controls given for the restaurant example which are summarized in Exhibit 8-2.

Most auditors would consider the system of control given in Exhibit 8-2 to be very good. The auditor would probably think that there is little chance of errors occurring, so the substantive tests could be restricted. Specifically, if the auditor used a judgment sample, he or she might verify a sample of only 20 to 25 days of sales. Alternatively, if statistical sampling were used to estimate total sales for the year, the auditor

Exhibit 8-2
Analysis of Internal Control in the Restaurant

Internal Control	Purpose of Control	Accounting	Administrative	Both	Explanation for Control Classification
1. The waitress's name is written on the check.	Waitresses who commit errors, such as incorrect pricing or poor service, can be identified.			X	Pricing errors involve the safeguarding of assets and reliable accounting information; service involves adherence to managerial policies *not* involving these accounting safeguards.
2. The time is written on the check when the customer arrives; the cash register prints the time on the check when the check is paid.	The manager can compare time written on the check with time printed by cash register to identify possible poor service.		X		Service involves adherence to managerial policies, but it does not involve safeguarding assets and reliable accounting information.
3. All checks are prenumbered.	All checks can be accounted for to discover irregularities such as a customer leaving without paying. Also, the checks can be added up to verify the total cash which should have been received and deposited for each day. The total of the checks can also be used to verify total sales which should have been recorded for each day.	X			Safeguarding cash and providing reliable accounting information (cash and sales account amounts) are accounting controls.
4. The customer's location in the restaurant is written on the check.	It is easier for the waitress to deliver the right food to the right person and thus give better service.		X		Service involves adherence to managerial policies, but it does not involve safeguarding assets and providing reliable accounting information.
5. The waitress writes the customer's order on the check and then compares the food delivered with the original order.	A comparison of the food delivered with the food ordered serves two purposes: (1) it helps to ensure that the customer gets good service, i.e., the customer gets what was ordered, and (2) it helps to ensure that the chef and the customer do not defraud the restaurant.			X	Service is part of administrative control; preventing fraud involves safeguarding assets and providing reliable accounting information.

Exhibit 8-2 (continued):

Internal Control	Purpose of Control	Accounting	Admin-istrative	Both	Explanation for Control Classification
6. The cashier checks the price of the order. If a credit card is used, the date that the card expires is examined.	There is less chance that the customer will pay the incorrect amount and less chance that the sales will be recorded at an incorrect amount.			X	Ensuring that the customer pays the correct amount is an element of service. More importantly, ensuring that the customer pays the correct amount safeguards assets and provides reliable accounting information. If the incorrect amount of a sale is recorded, the balance in the sales account is misstated.
7. The cash register and the cashier are located near the exit.	It is more difficult for a customer to leave without paying.			X	Preventing customers from leaving without paying helps to safeguard assets and provide reliable accounting information.
8. The manager controls the prenumbered checks, assigns the checks to the hostesses, and accounts for the prenumbered checks.	If the manager does not maintain control over the prenumbered checks, internal controls 1, 2, and 3 are defeated. For example, if the prenumbered checks are issued at random, there is no way to account for the numerical sequence of the checks.			X	Since this control is an integral part of controls 1, 2, and 3, it encompasses the accounting and administrative aspects of control 1, the administrative aspects of control 2, and the accounting aspects of control 3.
9. The cash register accumulates the balance of cash which should be in the register, and the manager reconciles the two amounts before a cashier leaves for the day.	If this comparison is not made, any cash overages or shortages cannot be identified with a specific cashier and the cashier cannot be held accountable.	X			The primary purpose of this control is to safeguard assets and provide reliable accounting information.
10. The manager reprices each check, prepares an adding machine tape of the total cash which should have been collected, and reconciles the total on the tape with total cash collected for the day.	The purpose of this control is to detect pricing errors and cash overages or shortages.	X			Pricing errors and cash overages or shortages involve both safeguarding assets and providing reliable accounting information.

Exhibit 8-2 (continued):

Internal Control	Purpose of Control	Accounting	Administrative	Both	Explanation for Control Classification
11. Periodically during the day cash is removed from the cash register and locked in the safe.	If the cash in the register is minimized, there is less chance of loss through robbery, theft by the cashier, or misplacement of cash.	X			This control helps to safeguard assets and provide reliable accounting information.
12. Cash receipts are deposited daily.	If the cash on the premises (in the cash register or safe) is minimized, there is less chance of loss through robbery, etc. Also, if the cash receipts are deposited daily, the restaurant's cash management is improved.			X	The primary purpose of this control is to safeguard cash and provide reliable accounting information. However, the control also adheres to managerial policy of sound cash management.
13. The bookkeeper has no access to cash.	If the bookkeeper has access to cash, the bookkeeper could easily misappropriate it and cover up the theft with a fictitious entry.	X			The purpose of this control is to help safeguard assets and provide reliable accounting information.
14. The bank statement reconciler accounts for the numerical sequence of meal checks, verifies the accuracy of the daily tapes, and compares the total from the daily tapes to: the print-out of total cash receipts produced by the cash register, the deposit which is shown on the bank statement, and the debit to cash and credit to sales for the day.	If these control procedures are not in effect, the manager could misappropriate cash, destroy the related checks and perhaps not be detected. Also, posting errors by the bookkeeper would be more difficult to detect if this control were not in effect.	X			This control involves both the safeguarding of assets and providing reliable accounting information.

might use a low confidence level, say 68%, and be willing to accept a confidence interval that estimates sales within a fairly wide range, say within plus or minus 20 percent.[1]

---

[1]As indicated in detail in Chapter 9, a confidence interval is a range within which the auditor is a certain percent confident (the confidence level) that the true amount of an item, such as an account balance, lies.

On the other hand, if internal control is poor, substantive tests must be extensive. For example, if the restaurant's manager also serves as the bookkeeper and bank reconciler, there is a very good chance that errors could occur. Therefore, the auditor that uses judgment sampling might select 75 to 100 days to verify. Likewise, the auditor that uses statistical sampling might now want to use 95% confidence and require a confidence interval that estimates sales within a range of plus or minus five percent.

Deciding on the amount of substantive testing necessary is fairly easy when internal control is either very good or very poor as in the above paragraphs. However, when the system of internal control is somewhere between very good and very poor, the decision on the amount of substantive testing is much more difficult.

To illustrate this point, consider the first control listed in Exhibit 8-2, which requires the waitress's name to be written on the check so that waitresses that make pricing errors (accounting control) or give poor service (administrative control) can be identified. It is clear that if this control is not in effect, accounting control over sales is weakened. However, if this is the only control missing from the system, what impact does this omission have on the extent of the substantive tests?

Questions such as this one are very difficult to answer; they will require much more audit research before definitive answers can be provided. For example, consider the following statement from page 33 of Peat, Marwick, Mitchell and Company's *Research Opportunities in Auditing*:

> The profession presently has no formal way of measuring the overall reliability of a related set of internal controls. Although present procedures are useful in identifying specific strengths and weaknesses in a system, such as payroll, they do not provide an objective measure of the likelihood that the payroll system will generate a materially misleading figure for total payroll expense. Thus, a more rigorous framework is needed for combining various findings related to an integrated set of internal controls and for relating these findings both to representations in the financial statements and to selected audit program procedures.

REVIEWING THE SYSTEM OF INTERNAL CONTROL

The previous section described the relationship between internal control and substantive testing. Therefore, before the auditor plans his or her substantive test, the system of internal control must be reviewed.

The auditor must make five broad decisions in reviewing a system of internal control:

- How can he or she find out about the existing system of internal control?

- How can the system be documented?

- Which controls in the system should the auditor rely on?

- How can the system be tested for compliance?

- How can the auditor report on the system?

The first four decisions are discussed in this section. The final section of this chapter discusses reports on internal control.

Discovering the Existing Control System

Once the auditor is assigned the task of reviewing a given part of a company's internal control system, such as the controls over sales, the first step is to find out how the system is supposed to work. As indicated in Chapter 6, this is done primarily by interviewing the people who are involved in the area under review. The auditor will ask these people questions about (1) how transactions originate, and (2) how transactions are processed from the time they originate to the time the accounting records are posted and verified. In performing these interviews, the auditor must recognize where errors are likely to occur and ask questions about the internal control techniques which the business has developed to prevent or detect the errors. The interviews must be thorough enough for the auditor to determine that if an error occurs the client's system is designed to detect and correct the error on a timely basis. In other words, the auditor must identify areas of weaknesses in the design of the client's system of internal accounting control.

To illustrate the interview process, reconsider the internal controls for the restaurant example which are summarized in Exhibit 8-2. In this exhibit, individual transactions originate when the customer enters the restaurant. The transactions for a given day are completed and verified once the bank reconciler verifies the sales for the day and compares the amount of sales which should have been recorded with the debit to cash and the credit to sales. In this example the auditor would find out about the system of internal controls by interviewing the people that are involved with sales transactions (the hostess, the waitresses, the chef, the cashier, the restaurant manager, the bookkeeper, and the bank reconciler). The auditor would ask questions about how a transaction is processed from the time the customer enters the door until the final verification of the transaction by the bank reconciler. Furthermore, at each stage in processing the auditor should be alert for possible errors that could occur and the method for detecting and correcting the error.

In this example it is fairly easy to find out about the existing system of internal control because common sense dictates how transactions originate and how they are processed from the time they originate to the time that the accounting records are posted and verified.

However, in practice the auditor frequently finds it helpful to use prior working papers and an internal control questionnaire in this part of the review of internal control. Prior working papers are useful in determining how the system operated in the previous year, which is frequently not different from the current year. In addition, an internal control questionnaire is useful in deciding what controls should be in effect in the existing system. As indicated in Chapter 7, the internal control questionnaire contains a list of questions which, if a good system exists, can be answered with "yes" answers. For example, the questionnaire for a restaurant might contain questions such as the following:

- Are all checks prenumbered?
- Is the bookkeeper prohibited from having access to cash?
- Does the cashier check to see that all credit cards which are used have a valid date?

The example could be continued, but the point is that the questionnaire should emphasize the controls which should be in effect in a given area. Over time, external and internal auditors have developed detailed internal control questionnaires for each audit area within specific industries, and these questionnaires are used by the auditor to get a basic understanding of the possible controls in a given area.

Documenting the Existing System of Internal Control

Once the auditor finds out about the existing system of internal control, he or she must document the system. The system can be documented either through a flowchart, a questionnaire or through a narrative description. An example of a narrative description of internal control was in Chapter 5; another variation of the narrative description is given in Exhibit 8-2. Flowcharting, questionnaires and narrative descriptions for a system of internal control were discussed in Chapter 7.

Deciding Which Controls to Rely On

Once the auditor decides on how to document the system of internal control, he or she must decide which of the controls will be tested and relied on. This decision involves the same principles used to show the relationship between internal control and substantive tests.

As indicated earlier, the basic relationship between internal control and substantive tests can be expressed in two statements:

- If internal control is good, there is less chance that errors will occur, and therefore, the auditor has less reason to substantiate the account balance.

- If internal control is poor, there is a greater chance for errors to occur, and therefore, the auditor must be very careful to thoroughly substantiate the account balance.

When deciding what controls to test and rely on, the auditor wants to get the most assurance about the fairness of an account balance for the least amount of audit work. Furthermore, as a practical matter certain controls are more important than other controls in ensuring the fairness of an account balance. These key controls are usually tested and relied on. However, the less important controls may not be tested because more efficient substantive procedures can be used to test the reasonableness of an account balance.

Consider the control in the restaurant example which requires that all checks be prenumbered and accounted for. As indicated earlier, this is a key control, and the substantive audit procedures must be increased significantly if this control is not in effect. Consequently, if this control is prescribed, the auditor will likely test the control (determine that the control is really working) and rely on it, rather than undertake the additional substantive procedures that would be necessary if number control is not in effect.

An example of a control the auditor might choose not to test and rely on is the requirement that the cashier examine each credit card to determine that the card is not out of date. There are two purposes of this control: (1) it safeguards assets by reducing the chance that bad credit cards will be accepted, and (2) it helps to ensure the reliability of the accounting records by reducing the chance that the debit to cash and the credit to sales will include invalid sales—sales for which no cash is subsequently received.

As indicated in the next section, controls of this type are very difficult to test. Furthermore, it may be a fairly simple matter to substantiate that errors resulting from the breakdown of this control do not exist. This conclusion can be reached by examining the bank statements and determining that the proper adjustments have been made (i.e., a debit to sales and a credit to cash) for any bad credit cards which were accepted. Therefore, it may very well be easier to do substantive tests for possible errors than to test and rely on the control.

In connection with this last point, it should be noted that different emphasis is placed by external and internal auditors on the system on internal control. As indicated earlier, the external auditor is concerned with two basic issues: (1) the chance that errors will occur, and (2) the chance that the errors will not be detected. However, the internal auditor is generally more concerned with preventing errors in the first place. Therefore, the internal auditor generally evaluates more controls than does the external auditor.

Deciding on How to Test the Internal Control System for Compliance

Once the system of internal control has been documented and the auditor has decided what controls to rely on, the next step in the review and evaluation of internal control is compliance testing the controls which will be relied on. Compliance testing includes any audit procedures performed to determine whether a given control is operating as designed. Exhibit 8-3 lists the controls for the restaurant example along with some possible techniques which could be used to test each control for compliance.

There are several important points which should be made about compliance tests for internal controls. First, the specific procedures performed are largely a function of the auditor's imagination; any audit procedure which provides evidence about whether the control is working as prescribed can be used. However, the auditor should not choose procedures which cost more than the value of the evidence obtained.

Second, there are few controls which can be directly tested for compliance after the control technique has been applied. For example, almost all of the techniques listed in Exhibit 8-3 for testing the controls, except those that involve observing the control in operation, are applied after the control has functioned. Therefore, it is possible that the control never worked. For example, the manager and the bank reconciler may assign to the cashier their tasks of (1) accounting for the prenumbered checks, (2) preparing an adding machine tape of the cash which should have been collected, and (3) comparing this total to the printout produced by the cash register. If the tasks are performed by the cashier, the controls which are supposed to be provided by the manager and the bank reconciler are certainly not in effect. Furthermore, as long as the cashier does not make errors or engage in fraud, none of the other compliance testing procedures would reveal the absence of the

---

Exhibit 8-3
Ways of Compliance Testing the Internal
Controls in the Restaurant Example

Control	*Ways of Compliance Testing the Control*
1. The waitress's name and the time is written on the check.	• Observe the waitress's name and the time being written on the check.
	• Obtain a sample of checks and see that the waitress's name and the time is written on each check.
	• Ask the hostess if she writes the waitress's name and the time of the customer's arrival on each check.
2. The cash register prints the time on the check when the check is paid.	• Examine the manufacturer's specifications for the cash register to see that it is designed to print the time on the checks when the checks are paid.
	• Ask the cashier if the cash register accurately prints the time on each check.
	• Obtain a sample of checks and see if the time is printed on the check.
3. All checks are prenumbered.	• Examine the file of order forms (purchase orders) which were used to order the checks throughout the period to see that prenumbered checks are being ordered.
	• Examine the supply of blank checks to see that they are prenumbered.
	• Ask the manager if only prenumbered checks are ordered.
	• Ask the hostesses if they receive only prenumbered checks and if they have to account for the numerical sequence to the manager.
	• Ask the bank reconciler if the checks are prenumbered.
	• Take a sample of days and account for the numerical sequence of checks used on each day.
4. The customer's location in the restaurant is written on the check.	• Observe the waitresses writing the customer's location on the check.
	• Obtain a sample of checks and see that the customer's location is written on each check.

Exhibit 8-3 (Continued):

Control	_Ways of Compliance Testing the Control_
	• Ask the cashier and chef if the customer's location is consistently written on the checks.
5. The customer's order is written on the check, and the waitress compares the food delivered with the original order.	• Observe the waitress writing the customer's order on the check and comparing the food delivered with the original order.
	• Ask the waitresses if they write the order on the check and compare the food delivered with the original order.
	• Ask the manager if he or she observes the waitresses writing the order on the check and comparing the food delivered with the original order.
6. The cashier checks the price of each order. If a credit card is used, the date that the card expires is examined.	• Ask each cashier how he or she performs the procedures required by this control.
	• Observe the cashier checking the price of each order and the date on any credit card used.
	• Examine a sample of checks and recheck the prices.
	• Examine the bank statements for credit card slips which were returned because the card was out of date.
7. The cash register and the cashier are located near the exit.	• Observe the location of the cash register and the cashier.
8. The manager controls the prenumbered checks, assigns the checks to the hostesses, and accounts for the prenumbered checks.	• Ask the manager how he or she achieves control over the prenumbered checks.
	• Observe the manager assigning the prenumbered checks and accounting for the numerical sequence of the checks.
	• Ask the hostesses about the way in which the manager assigns the checks and follows up to ensure that all checks are returned.
	• Obtain a sample of checks and account for the numerical sequence.
9. The cash register accumulates the balance	• Ask the manager how he or she reconciles the cash which should be on hand with the actual

Exhibit 8-3 (Continued):

Control	*Ways of Compliance Testing the Control*
of cash which should be in the register, and the manager reconciles the two amounts before a cashier leaves for the day.	cash on hand when each cashier leaves for the day.
	• Ask each cashier how the cash is reconciled before the cashier leaves for the day.
	• Examine the manufacturer's specifications to see that the cash register is designed so that the amount of cash which should be on hand at any point in time can be determined.
	• Examine any documentation which is signed by the manager and cashier to indicate that the reconciliation was performed.
	• Observe the manager performing the reconciliation.
	• Obtain a sample of the printouts produced by the cash register and reconcile the total cash which should have been received with the daily deposits shown on the bank statement.
10. The manager reprices each check, prepares an adding machine tape of the total cash which should have been collected, and reconciles the total on the tape with total cash collected for the day.	• Examine any documentation which indicates the duties were performed.
	• Ask the manager how he or she performs the required duties.
	• Obtain the adding machine tapes; reprice the checks and compare the checks with the entries on the adding machine tapes; compare the totals on the tapes with the debit to cash, the credit to sales, and the deposit shown on the bank statement.
11. Periodically during the day cash is removed from the cash register and locked in the safe.	• Ask the manager and the cashiers how the procedure is performed and how often it is performed.
	• Observe the manager removing the cash from the cash register and placing it in the safe.
12. Cash receipts are deposited daily.	• Ask the manager how the procedure is performed, e.g., how is the cash tranported to the bank, at what time, etc.
	• Observe the manager making the deposit.
13. The bookkeeper has no access to cash.	• Ask the bookkeeper, cashier, and manager if the bookkeeper ever has access to the cash register.

Exhibit 8-3 (Continued):

Control	Ways of Compliance Testing the Control
	• Ask the bookkeeper and manager if the bookkeeper has the combination to the safe.
	• Observe the bookkeeper to see that he or she does not serve as a cashier or open the safe.
14. The bank statement reconciler accounts for the numerical sequence of meal checks, verifies the accuracy of the daily tapes, and compares the totals from the daily tapes to: the print-out of total cash receipts produced by the cash register, the deposit which is shown on the bank statement and the debit to cash and credit to sales for the day.	• Ask the bank statement reconciler about his or her duties.
	• Examine any documentation signed by the bank reconciler indicating that the duties were performed.
	• Observe the bank reconciler performing his or her assigned duties.
	• Select a sample of days and obtain the meal checks used for the days, account for the numerical sequence of checks, compare the checks for each day to the daily tapes, compare the totals from the daily tapes to: the print-out of total cash receipts produced by the cash register, the deposit which is shown on the bank statement and the debit to cash and the credit to sales for the day.

control procedures which are supposed to be performed by the manager and the bank reconciler. In summary, as long as (1) errors or irregularities do not occur, and (2) the required documentation, such as the adding machine tapes, is prepared, many indirect tests of compliance may not indicate whether a required control procedure is being applied as it should be.

The fact that observation is the primary means of directly testing a control also causes a problem because common sense indicates that when an auditor is observing employees, the employees are likely to be more careful performing their duties than they would be otherwise.

Auditors use two basic approaches to overcome the problems associated with (1) indirect tests of compliance and (2) using observation as the primary direct test of compliance. One approach to overcome these problems is to thoroughly understand the procedure which is supposed to be performed and to ask in-depth questions about the procedure of the person charged with performing it. For example, if the auditor thoroughly understands what the manager is supposed to do and asks the manager in-depth questions about his or her duties, the auditor can likely tell whether the manager is really performing the procedures. Certainly, if the manager does not understand the basic forms and computations that he or she is expected to use and make, the manager is either not performing the procedures or at best is not performing them very well.

The second approach to overcome the problems associated with indirect tests of compliance and using observation as the primary direct test is to (1) test a control in several different ways and (2) redo any computations or comparisons made by the client whenever possible.

To illustrate this point, consider the third control in Exhibit 8-3, which requires all checks to be prenumbered. As indicated in the illustration, there are a number of different ways that the control can be tested. Furthermore, the auditor can actually perform the check of numerical sequence which is supposed to be done by the manager and the bank reconciler.

Another important point about tests of compliance is that the same procedure can be used to test several controls. For example, in Exhibit 8-3 the auditor is required to take a sample of days and account for the numerical sequence of checks used in those days as one way of testing controls 3, 8, and 14. In practice, the auditor would take the sample of days and test all three controls at the same time.

The same procedures can also be used in both substantive tests and compliance tests. For example, a comparison of the audit program for substantive tests in Exhibit 8-1 with the compliance tests given in Exhibit 8-3 indicates that some of the procedures are identical. These procedures for performing both types of tests are known as dual-purpose audit tests. The name arises because one test is performed which both tests the internal control system and validates the account balance.

Another consideration about compliance tests is the timing of these tests. Conceptually, since the auditor is relying on the controls for the entire period under audit, he or she should select items for testing from the entire period. However, in many cases compliance tests are performed at an interim period. *SAS No. 1*, Section 320, states that when compliance testing is done at an interim date, it may be necessary to test more extensively for the months which are available for testing. Whether the auditor will continue compliance testing at year-end will depend on the significance of the control being tested and whether any major changes have taken place in the internal accounting control system.

Once compliance tests are complete, the auditor then determines the extent to which substantive tests should be restricted or modified, given the control system which is actually in effect. The auditor must also revise the documentation of the internal control system so that the documentation reflects the actual system in effect.

REPORT ON INTERNAL CONTROL

Auditors may be requested to issue reports on internal control in several ways. For example, according to *SAS No. 30*, the auditor may be engaged to:

- Express an opinion on the entity's system of internal accounting control in effect as of a specified date. (An accountant may also be engaged to express an opinion on the entity's system of internal accounting control in effect during a specified period of time.)

- Report on the entity's system for the restricted use of management, specified regulatory agencies, or other specified third parties, based solely on an evaluation of internal accounting control made as part of an audit of the entity's financial statements.

- Report on all or part of an entity's system of internal accounting control for the restricted use of management or specified regulatory agencies, based on the regulatory agencies' pre-established criteria.

- Issue other special-purpose reports on all or part of an entity's internal accounting control system for the restricted use of management, specified regulatory agencies, or other specified third parties.

Currently, the most common type of report on internal accounting control is based solely on a study made as a part of an audit of the entity's financial statements (the second type of report listed). Consequently, this type of report is the only one discussed in this section. Other types of reports on internal control are discussed in Chapter 16.

When reporting on internal accounting control as a result of an audit of the entity's financial statements, there are three basic issues to consider: (1) the definition of material weaknesses in internal accounting control, (2) the reason for reporting on material weaknesses, and (3) the format of the report. These issues are discussed in this section.

Material Weaknesses in Internal Control

A material weakness in internal accounting control is defined in the Appendix to *SAS No. 30*, *Reporting on Internal Control*, as follows:

A material weakness in internal accounting control is a condition in which the specific control procedures or the degree of compliance with them do not reduce to a relatively low level the risk that errors or irregularities in amounts that would be material in relation to the financial statements being audited may occur and not be detected within a timely period by employees in the normal course of performing their assigned functions.

In evaluating weaknesses in internal accounting control, the auditor should recognize four basic points. First, the amount of errors or irregularities that can occur and remain undetected ranges from zero to the amount of assets or transactions exposed to the weakness.[2] For example, if the bookkeeper has access to cash, the bookkeeper may not steal any cash, or he or she may steal all of it.

Second, the probability that an error or irregularity may occur and not be detected depends on its amount. For example, it may be very likely that the bookkeeper could take a few dollars and not be detected, but it is very unlikely that he or she could take all of the cash and not be detected.[3]

Third, when evaluating the risk of *errors* (as opposed to irregularities), auditors are likely to find that historical information is useful. For example, if a given control weakness existed in the past, the auditor probably can get a good idea about the errors which have occurred in the past and thus predict the errors which are likely to occur in the future if the control weakness is not corrected.

On the other hand, past data is not likely to be very useful in predicting the risk of *irregularities* which may occur because of a control weakness. This difference in the usefulness of historical data arises because errors are unintentional and thus likely to be more predictable than intentional irregularities.

This difference between errors and irregularities, plus the accounting convention of conservatism, means that the auditor must assume a high probability of irregularities if a person can both perpetuate and conceal irregularities in the normal course of that person's duties.

---

[2] The thoughts which are expressed in this sentence are expressed in *SAS No. 30*. However, recent empirical work on errors in accounts receivable and inventory audits has indicated that this statement may not be true for errors. For example, see: Johnny R. Johnson, Robert A. Leitch, and John Neter, "Characteristics of Errors in Accounts Receivable and Inventory Audits," *The Accounting Review*, April, 1981.

[3] *Ibid.*

The fourth important point which must be considered in evaluating material weaknesses in internal accounting control is the probability that several immaterial weaknesses combined will create a material weakness.

Reasons for Reporting on Material Weaknesses in Internal Accounting Control

Historically, auditors have reported material weaknesses in internal accounting control to the client for two basic reasons. First, the report is likely to protect the auditor in the event of litigation by the client against the auditor; the auditor will be on record as saying that material weaknesses in internal control existed. Second, most clients want to know about material weaknesses in internal control so that corrective action can be taken. Clients want to avoid losses; if the client perceives that the auditor's internal control recommendations help avoid losses, the value of the audit to the client is increased.

Today, as indicated in Chapter 7, there is an additional reason for reporting to the client material weaknesses in internal control: the report is required by *SAS No. 20*. The next section explains the format of this report of internal control.

Format of Reports on Internal Control

SAS No. 20 requires the auditor to communicate material weaknesses in internal accounting control to senior management and the board of directors or its audit committee. According to *SAS No. 20*, the report may be oral or in writing, but most practicing auditors agree that the report should be in writing. When a written report is used, it should take the form of the report shown in Exhibit 8-4.

There are five important points concerning the report shown in Exhibit 8-4. First, when the report is prepared for management, it should be addressed to the board of directors, which, of course, includes senior management and the audit committee of the board. Also, the auditor should make it clear in the transmittal letter that accompanies the report that the report is exclusively for the use of the board of directors.

Second, in some cases a specified third party, such as a regulatory agency, may request the auditor's report on internal control. If so, the format should be the same as that shown in Exhibit 8-4. In these cases, the report should be addressed to the specified third party, and the transmittal letter should make it clear that the report was prepared for use exclusively by management and the specified third party.

Third, in the case where material weaknesses have been found, *SAS No. 30* requires the last sentence of the fourth paragraph to be modified as follows:

Exhibit 8-4
Report on Internal Control

To the Board of Directors of XYZ Company:

We have examined the financial statements of XYZ Company for the year ended December 31, 19x1, and have issued our report thereon dated February 23, 19x2. As part of our examination, we made a study and evaluation of the Company's system of internal accounting control to the extent we considered necessary to evaluate the system as required by generally accepted auditing standards. The purpose of our study and evaluation was to determine the nature, timing, and extent of the auditing procedures necessary for expressing an opinion on the company's financial statements. Our study and evaluation was more limited than would be necessary to express an opinion on the system of internal accounting control taken as a whole.

The management of XYZ Company is responsible for establishing and maintaining a system of internal accounting control. In fulfilling this responsibility, estimates and judgments by management are required to assess the expected benefits and related costs of control procedures. The objectives of a system are to provide management with reasonable, but not absolute, assurance that assets are safeguarded against loss from unauthorized use or disposition, and that transactions are executed in accordance with management's authorization and recorded properly to permit the preparation of financial statements in accordance with generally accepted accounting principles.

Because of inherent limitations in any system of internal accounting control, errors or irregularities may nevertheless occur and not be detected. Also, projection of any evaluation of the system to future periods is subject to the risk that procedures may become inadequate because of changes in conditions or that the degree of compliance with the procedures may deteriorate.

Our study and evaluation made for the limited purpose described in the first paragraph would not necessarily disclose all material weaknesses in the system. Accordingly, we do not express an opinion on the system of internal accounting control of XYZ Company taken as a whole. However, our study and evaluation disclosed no condition that we believed to be a material weakness.

This report is intended solely for the use of management (or specified regulatory agency or other specified third party) and should not be used for any other purpose.

However, our study and evaluation disclosed the following conditions that we believe result in more than a relatively low risk that errors or irregularities in amounts that would be material in relation to the financial statements of XYZ Company may occur and not be detected within a timely period. (A description of the material weaknesses that have come to the auditor's attention would follow.)

These conditions were considered in determining the nature, timing, and extent of the audit tests to be applied in our examination of the 19x1 financial statements, and this report does not affect our report on these financial statements dated (date of report).

Fourth, the auditor may want to report some weaknesses in internal accounting control which are not considered material. This is acceptable provided there is a clear distinction made in the report between the material and immaterial weaknesses.

Fifth, the auditor may want to report some immaterial weaknesses to one party and not to another. For example, the auditor may want to report some immaterial weaknesses to management, but he or she may not want to report these weaknesses to a regulatory agency that requests a copy of the auditor's report on internal control. This is acceptable provided (1) the auditor can justify his or her decision and (2) the more comprehensive report identifies the weaknesses not reported to the other party.

SUMMARY

Nature of substantive tests.   Substantive tests (sometimes referred to as validation tests) are defined as audit tests designed to determine if a transaction or a series of transactions (an account balance) is properly recorded in accordance with generally accepted accounting principles. There are two basic types of substantive tests. One type examines the details of a single transaction or an account balance to determine if the transaction or balance is recorded in accordance with generally accepted accounting principles. The second type of substantive tests, referred to as analytic review procedures, evaluates the overall reasonableness of account balances.

Substantive tests employ five basic types of procedures. One type of audit procedure used in substantive tests verifies a sample of the individual entries which are posted to a specific account. A second type of substantive audit procedure verifies the mathematical accuracy of the account balance. A third type of substantive audit procedure verifies the accuracy of the cutoff. Another type of substantive audit procedure verifies that the balance is presented in accordance with GAAP and compares the balance in the account with the balance shown in the audit working papers. A fifth type of substantive test applies analytic review procedures to determine that the account balance is reasonable.

Relationship between substantive tests and internal control.   If internal control is good, there is less chance that errors will occur, and therefore, less reason for the auditor to substantiate the account balance. Alternatively, if internal control is poor, there is a greater chance for errors to occur, and therefore, the auditor must be very careful to thoroughly substantiate the account balance. Deciding on the amount of substantive testing necessary in a given situation is fairly easy when internal control is either very good or very poor. However, when the system of internal control is somewhere between very good and very poor, the decision on the amount of substantive testing is much more difficult.

Reviewing the system of internal control.   The auditor must make five broad decisions in reviewing a system of internal control. The first decision is how can he or she find out about the existing system of internal control? This is done primarily by interviewing people who are involved in the area being reviewed. The auditor will ask these people questions about (1) how transactions originate, and (2) how transactions are processed from the time the transactions originate until the accounting records are posted and verified. In performing these interviews, the auditor must use judgment to recognize where errors are likely to occur and ask questions about the internal control techniques which the business has developed to provide reasonable assurance that errors will be detected and corrected. Internal control questionnaires and working papers from prior years are helpful in deciding what questions to ask.

Once the auditor finds out about the existing system of internal control, he or she must decide how the system is to be documented. The system can be documented either through a flowchart, a narrative description, or a questionnaire.

Once the auditor decides on how to document the system of internal control, he or she must decide which of the controls will be tested and relied on. When deciding what controls to test and rely on, the auditor wants to get the most assurance about the fairness of an account balance for the least amount of audit work. The key controls are usually tested and relied on. However, the less important controls may not be tested. Instead, substantive tests are designed to determine if an account is materially misstated.

After the system of internal control has been documented and the auditor has decided what controls to rely on, the auditor must decide how to test the controls for compliance. Compliance testing includes any audit procedure performed to determine whether a given control is working as the control was designed to work. One major problem in performing compliance testing is that there are very few controls which can be directly tested for compliance after the control technique has been applied. The fact that observation is the primary means of directly testing a control also causes a problem because common sense indicates that when an auditor is observing employees, the employees are likely to be more careful in performing their duties than they would be otherwise. Auditors try to overcome the problems associated with indirect tests of compliance and using observation as the primary direct test of compliance by (1) asking in-depth questions about control procedures of the persons charged with performing the procedures, (2) testing a given control in several different ways, and (3) redoing any computations or comparisons made by the client whenever possible.

Reports on internal control. Auditors may be requested to issue reports on internal control in several ways. However, the most common type of report on internal accounting control is based solely on a study made as a part of an audit of the entity's financial statements. In this report, material weaknesses in internal accounting control must be reported to senior management and the board of directors or its audit committee.

REVIEW QUESTIONS

8-1   Briefly define substantive tests and describe their purpose.

8-2   Describe the two basic kinds of substantive tests.

8-3   There are five basic types of procedures which are employed in substantive tests. Discuss each of these five procedures.

8-4   Describe the relationship between substantive testing and internal control.

8-5   Give an example of how a strong or poor system of internal control will affect substantive testing.

8-6   List the five broad decisions which the auditor must make in reviewing a system of internal control.

8-7   Describe how an auditor finds out about the existing system of internal control.

8-8   Briefly discuss how an auditor attempts to document a system of internal control.

8-9   Discuss how an auditor decides which controls to rely on.

8-10   What is the purpose of compliance testing?

8-11   What are the inherent limitations of indirect tests of compliance? Of observation as a direct compliance test?

8-12   Discuss techniques available to the auditor to overcome the limitations of indirect tests of compliance and of observation as a direct compliance test.

8-13   Define dual-purpose audit tests.

DISCUSSION QUESTIONS AND PROBLEMS

8-14   *Part a.*   The first generally accepted auditing standard of field work requires, in part, that "the work is to be adequately planned." An effective tool that aids the auditor in adequately planning the work is an audit program.

Required:

What is an audit program, and what purposes does it serve?

Part b.   Auditors frequently refer to the terms "Standards" and "Procedures." Standards deal with measures of the quality of the auditor's performance. Standards specifically refer to the ten generally accepted auditing standards. Procedures relate to those acts that are performed by the auditor while trying to gather evidence. Procedures specifically refer to the methods or techniques used by the auditor in the conduct of the examination.

Required:

List at least eight different types of procedures that an auditor would use during an examination of financial statements. For example, a type of procedure that an auditor would frequently use is the observation of activities and conditions. *Do not discuss specific accounts.*

(AICPA adapted)

8-15   As part of your annual audit of Call Camper Company, you have the responsibility for preparing a report on internal-control for management. Your workpapers include a completed internal-control questionnaire and documentation of other tests of the internal-control system which you have reviewed. This review identified a number of material weaknesses; for some of these, corrective action by management is not practicable in the circumstances.

Required:

Discuss the form and content of the report on internal control for management based on your annual audit and the reasons or purposes for such a report. *Do not write a report.*

(AICPA adapted)

8-16   The financial statements of the Tiber Company have never been audited by an independent CPA. Recently, Tiber's management asked Anthony Burns, CPA, to conduct a special study of Tiber's internal control; this study will not include an examination of Tiber's financial statements. Following completion of his special study, Mr. Burns plans to prepare a report that is consistent with the requirements of *Statement on Auditing Standards No. 30*, "Reports on Internal Control."

Required:

a.   Describe the inherent limitations that should be recognized in considering the potential effectiveness of any system of internal control.

b.   Explain and contrast the review of internal control that Mr. Burns might make as part of an examination of financial statements with his special study of Tiber's internal control, covering each of the following:

1.   Objectives of review or study.
2.   Scope of review or study.
3.   Nature and content of reports.

Organize your answer for Part b as follows:

Examination of Financial Statements	*Special Study*
1. Objective	1. Objective
2. Scope	2. Scope
3. Report	3. Report

(AICPA adapted)

8-17 You have been engaged by the management of Alden, Inc. to review its internal control over the purchase, receipt, storage, and issue of raw materials. You have prepared the following comments which describe Alden's procedures.

- Raw materials, which consist mainly of high-cost electronic components, are kept in a locked storeroom. Storeroom personnel include a supervisor and four clerks. All are well trained, competent, and adequately bonded. Raw materials are removed from the storeroom only upon written or oral authorization of one of the production foremen.

- There are no perpetual-inventory records; hence, the storeroom clerks do not keep records of goods received or issued. To compensate for the lack of perpetual records, a physical-inventory count is taken monthly by the storeroom clerks who are well supervised. Appropriate procedures are followed in making the inventory count.

- After the physical count, the storeroom superisor matches quantities counted against a predetermined reorder level. If the count for a given part is below the reorder level, the supervisor enters the part number on a materials-requisition list and sends this list to the accounts-payable clerk. The accounts-payable clerk prepares a purchase order for a predetermined reorder quantity for each part and mails the purchase order to the vendor from whom the part was last purchased.

- When ordered materials arrive at Alden, they are received by the storeroom clerks. The clerks count the merchandise and agree the counts to the shipper's bill of lading. All vendors' bills of lading are initialed, dated, and filed in the storeroom to serve as receiving reports.

Required:

Describe the weaknesses in internal control and recommend improvements of Alden's procedures for the purchase, receipt, storage, and issue of raw materials.

Organize your answer sheet as follows:

Weaknesses	*Recommended Improvements*

(AICPA adapted)

8-18   In connection with his examination of the financial statements of the Olympia Manufacturing Company, a CPA is reviewing procedures for accumulating direct labor hours. He learns that all production is by job order and that all employees are paid hourly wages, with time-and-one-half for overtime hours.

Olympia's direct labor hour input process for payroll and job-cost determination is summarized in the following flowchart:

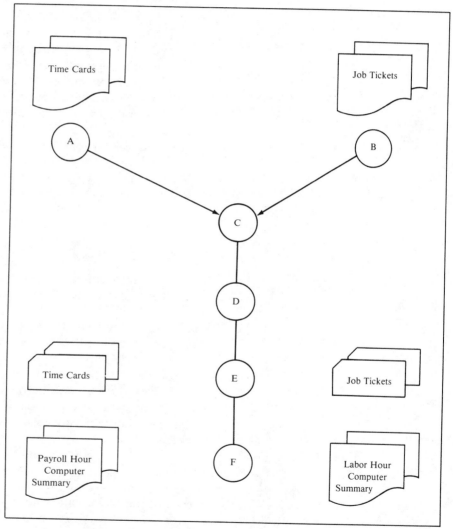

Steps A and C are performed in timekeeping, step B in the factory operating departments, step D in payroll audit and control, step E in data preparation (keypunch), and step F in computer operations.

Required:

For each input processing step A through F:

a. List the possible errors or discrepancies that may occur.
b. Cite the corresponding control procedure that should be in effect for each error or discrepancy.

> *Note:* Your discussion of Olympia's procedures should be limited to the input process for direct labor hours, as shown in steps A through F in the flowchart. **Do not discuss** personnel procedures for hiring, promotion, termination, and pay rate authorization. **In step F do not discuss** equipment, computer program, and general computer operational controls.

Organize your answer for each input-processing step as follows:

Step	Possible Errors or Discrepancies	Control Procedures

(AICPA adapted)

8-19 The following two statements are representative of attitudes and opinions sometimes encountered by CPAs in their professional practices:

1. Today's audit consists of test checking. This is dangerous because test checking depends upon the auditor's judgment, which may be defective. An audit can be relied upon only if every transaction is verified.
2. An audit by a CPA is essentially negative and contributes to neither the gross national product nor the general well-being of society. The auditor does not create; he merely checks what someone else has done.

Required:

Evaluate each of the above statements and indicate:

a. Areas of agreement with the statement, if any.
b. Areas of misconception, incompleteness or fallacious reasoning included in the statement, if any.

Complete your discussion of each statement (*both parts a and b*) before going on to the next statement.

(AICPA adapted)

8-20   Evidential matter supporting the financial statements consists of the underlying accounting data and all corroborating information available to the auditor. In the course of an independent audit of financial statements, the auditor will perform detail tests of samples of transactions from various large-volume populations. The auditor may also audit various types of transactions by tracing a single transaction of each type through all stages of the accounting system.

Required:

a.   What are the various audit objectives associated with a sample of transactions from a large-volume population?

b.   What evidential matter would the auditor expect to gain from auditing various types of transactions by tracing a single transaction of each type through all stages of the accounting system?

(AICPA adapted)

8-21   Dunbar Camera Manufacturing, Inc., is a manufacturer of high-priced precision motion picture cameras in which the specifications of components parts are vital to the manufacturing process. Dunbar buys valuable camera lenses and large quantities of sheetmetal and screws. Screws and lenses are ordered by Dunbar and are billed by the vendors on a unit basis. Sheetmetal is ordered by Dunbar and is billed by the vendors on the basis of weight. The receiving clerk is responsible for documenting the quality and quantity of merchandise received.

A preliminary review of the system of internal control indicates that the following procedures are being followed:

Receiving Report

1.   Properly approved purchase orders, which are prenumbered, are filed numerically. The copy sent to the receiving clerk is an exact duplicate of the copy sent to the vendor. Receipts of merchandise are recorded on the duplicate copy by the receiving clerk.

Sheetmetal

2.   The company receives sheetmetal by railroad. The railroad independently weighs the sheetmetal and reports the weight and

date of receipt on a bill of lading (waybill), which accompanies all deliveries. The receiving clerk only checks the weight on the waybill to the purchase order.

Screws

3. The receiving clerk opens cartons containing screws, then inspects and weighs the contents. The weight is converted to number of units by means of conversion charts. The receiving clerk than checks the computed quantity to the purchase order.

Camera lenses

4. Each camera lens is delivered in a separate corrugated carton. Cartons are counted as they are received by the receiving clerk and the number of cartons are checked to purchase orders.

Required:

a. Explain why the internal control procedures as they apply individually to receiving reports and the receipt of sheetmetal, screws, and camera lenses are adequate or inadequate. *Do not discuss recommendations for improvements.*

b. What financial statement distortions may arise because of the inadequacies in Dunbar's system of internal control and how may they occur?

(AICPA adapted)

OBJECTIVE QUESTIONS*

8-22 The actual operation of an internal control system may be most objectively evaluated by

A. Completing a questionnaire and flowchart related to the accounting system in the year under audit.
B. Review of the previous year's audit workpapers to update the report of internal control evaluation.
C. Selection of items processed by the system and determination of the presence or absence of errors and compliance deviations.
D. Substantive tests of account balances based on the auditor's assessment of internal-control strength.

8-23 If the auditor's reliance upon internal control and other factors increases and if the combined reliability level desired increases, the reliability level for substantive tests should

---

Note: All questions in this section are AICPA adapted questions.

A. Increase.
B. Decrease.
C. Remain the same.
D. Not enough information to determine.

8-24   Normally, the auditor does not rely upon his study and testing of the client's system of internal control to

A. Evaluate the reliability of the system.
B. Uncover embezzlements of the client's assets.
C. Help determine the scope of other auditing procedures to be followed.
D. Gain support for his opinion as to the accuracy and fairness of the financial statements.

8-25   Which of the following *best* describes how an auditor, when evaluating internal accounting control, considers the types of errors and irregularities that could occur and determines those control procedures that should prevent or detect such errors or irregularities?

A. Discussions with management with respect to the system of internal accounting control and how management determines that the system is functioning properly.
B. Review of the questionnaires, flowcharts, checklists, instructions or similar generalized materials used by the auditor.
C. Exercise of professional judgment in evaluating the reliability of supporting documentation.
D. Use of attribute sampling techniques to gather information for tests of compliance.

8-26   That segment of an auditor's internal control work which focuses directly on the purpose of preventing or detecting material errors or irregularities in financial statements is known as

A. Compliance with the existing system of internal control.
B. Review of the existing system of internal control.
C. Evaluation of the existing system of internal control.
D. Study of the existing system of internal control.

8-27   If, during the course of an annual audit of a publicly held manufacturing company, an independent auditor becomes aware of a material weakness in the company's internal accounting control, the auditor is required to communicate the material weakness to

A. The senior management and the board of directors of the company.

B. The senior management of the company.

C. The board of directors of the company.

D. The audit committee of the board of directors.

8-28 At interim dates an auditor evaluates a client's internal accounting control procedures and finds them to be effective. The auditor then performs a substantial part of the audit engagement on a continuous basis throughout the year. At a minimum, the auditor's year-end procedures must include

A. Determination that the client's internal accounting control procedures are still effective at year-end.

B. Confirmation of those year-end accounts that were examined at interim dates.

C. Tests of compliance with internal control in the same manner as those tests made at the interim dates.

D. Comparison of the responses to the auditor's internal control questionnaire with a detailed flowchart at year-end.

8-29 The two phases of the auditor's study of internal accounting control are referred to as "review of the system" and "tests of compliance." In the tests of compliance phase the auditor attempts to

A. Obtain a reasonable degree of assurance that the client's system of controls is in use and is operating as planned.

B. Obtain sufficient, competent evidential matter to afford a reasonable basis for the auditor's opinion.

C. Obtain assurances that informative disclosures in the financial statements are reasonably adequate.

D. Obtain knowledge and understanding of the client's prescribed procedures and methods.

8-30 The primary purpose of tests of compliance is to provide reasonable assurance that

A. The accounting and administrative control procedures are adequately designed to assure employee compliance therewith.

B. The accounting and administrative control procedures are being applied as prescribed.

C. The administrative control procedures are being applied as prescribed.

D. The accounting control procedures are being applied as prescribed.

8-31   Reliability levels for tests of compliance will

    A.   Vary more between audits than reliability levels for substantive tests.

    B.   Vary less between audits than reliability levels for substantive tests.

    C.   Be independent of the auditor's evaluation of internal controls.

    D.   Not influence the reliability levels for substantive tests.

8-32   Which of the following statements relating to compliance tests is most accurate?

    A.   Auditing procedures cannot concurrently provide both evidence of compliance with accounting control procedures and evidence required for substantive tests.

    B.   Compliance tests include physical observations of the proper segregation of duties which ordinarily may be limited to the normal audit period.

    C.   Compliance tests should be based upon proper application of an appropriate statistical sampling plan.

    D.   Compliance tests ordinarily should be performed as of the balance sheet date or during the period subsequent to that date.

8-33   Before relying on the system of internal control, the auditor obtains a reasonable degree of assurance that the internal control procedures are in use and operating as planned. The auditor obtains this assurance by performing.

    A.   Substantive tests.

    B.   Transaction tests.

    C.   Compliance tests.

    D.   Tests of trends and ratios.

8-34   An auditor may issue a report on internal control at the request of

    A.   The SEC (if the client has a listed security).

    B.   A major creditor.

    C.   The stockholders.

    D.   A and B.

    E.   A, B, and C.

8-35   Tests which are designed to validate an account balance are known as

    A.   Compliance tests.

    B.   Substantive tests.

C.   Dual purpose tests.

D.   Analytic review tests.

8-36   Tests which are designed to determine if a control is functioning as prescribed are known as

A.   Substantive tests.

B.   Dual purpose tests.

C.   Compliance tests.

D.   Analytic review tests.

8-37   The primary purpose of performing compliance tests is to provide reasonable assurance that

A.   Accounting control procedures are being applied as prescribed.

B.   The flow of transactions through the accounting system is understood.

C.   Transactions are recorded at the amounts executed.

D.   All accounting control procedures leave visible evidence.

8-38   Which of the following groups does *not* have the responsibility to decide whether reports on an auditor's evaluation of internal accounting control would be useful to the general public?

A.   Regulatory agencies.

B.   Directors.

C.   Officers.

D.   Stockholders.

8-39   Under which of the following conditions would the inclusion of the internal-control report in a document to stockholders be prohibited?

A.   If the document contains only the internal-control report and unaudited interim financial statements.

B.   If only a select class of stockholders receives the document.

C.   If a stockholder has requested the internal-control report because of a ruling by a regulatory agency.

D.   If the internal-control report indicates management negligence.

8-40   If the report on internal control is distributed to the general public, it must contain specific language describing several matters. Which of the following must be included in the specific language?

A. The distinction between internal administrative controls and internal accounting controls.

B. The various tests and procedures used by the auditor during his review of internal control.

C. The objective of internal accounting controls.

D. The reason(s) the company's management requested a report on internal control.

8-41 The opening paragraph of the internal-control report based solely on a study and evaluation made as part of an audit of the financial statement should indicate its timeliness by including which of the following pair of dates?

A. The date on which your review of internal control was completed and the date on which you agreed to prepare the internal-control report.

B. The date of the audit report issued on the client's financial statements and the date on which you agreed to prepare the internal-control report.

C. The date of the client's financial statements and the date on which your review of internal control was completed.

D. The date of the client's financial statements and the date of the audit report issued on those financial statements.

8-42 How should the report on internal control deal with the possibility that some stockholders might use the internal-control report for speculation about future adequacy of a client's internal-control system?

A. The report should contain an opinion as to whether the present internal-control system can be relied upon for the next accounting period.

B. The report should make no mention of the possibility of making such projections.

C. The report should disclose management's opinion about the number of future accounting periods during which the present internal-control system can be relied upon.

D. The report should discuss the risk involved in making such projections.

8-43 Dey, Knight, & Co., CPAs, has issued a qualified opinion on the financial statements of Adams, Inc., because of a scope limitation. Adams, Inc., requested a report on internal control which it intends to give to one of its major creditors. What effect, if any, would the qualified opinion have on the internal control report that Dey, Knight, & Co. intends to prepare based on its audit engagement?

A. The audit scope limitation should be indicated in the report on internal control.

B. A report on internal control cannot be issued based on a qualified opinion.

C. The audit scope limitation has no effect, but Dey, Knight, & Co. should not issue the report if it will be given to a creditor.

D. The audit scope limitation has no effect on a report on internal control.

8-44 Which of the following would be *least* likely to be included in an auditor's tests of compliance?

A. Inspection.
B. Observation.
C. Inquiry.
D. Confirmation.

8-45 Tests of compliance are concerned primarily with each of the following questions *except*

A. How were the procedures performed?
B. Why were the procedures performed?
C. Were the necessary procedures performed?
D. By whom were the procedures performed?

8-46 The sequence of steps in gathering evidence as the basis of the auditor's opinion is:

A. Substantive tests, internal control review and compliance tests.
B. Internal control review, substantive tests and compliance tests.
C. Internal control review, compliance tests and substantive tests.
D. Compliance tests, internal control review and substantive tests.

8-47 The purpose of tests of compliance is to provide reasonable assurance that the

A. Accounting treatment of transactions and balances is valid and proper.
B. Accounting control procedures are functioning as intended.

C.   The entity has complied with disclosure requirements of generally accepted accounting principles.

D.   The entity has complied with requirements of quality control.

8-48   In the audit of which of the following types of profit-oriented enterprises would the auditor be most likely to place special emphasis on testing the internal controls over proper classification of payroll transactions.

A.   A manufacturing organization.

B.   A retailing organization.

C.   A wholesaling organization.

D.   A service organization.

8-49   When evaluating inventory controls with respect to segregation of duties, a CPA would be *least* likely to

A.   Inspect documents.

B.   Make inquiries.

C.   Observe procedures.

D.   Consider policy and procedure manuals.

IR PRESENTATION ETHICAL CONDUCT INDEPENDENCE EVIDENCE DUE CARE FAIR PRESENTATION ETHICAL CONDUCT INDEPENDENCE EVIDENCE DUE CARE FAIR PRESENTATION
E FAIR PRESENTATION ETHICAL CONDUCT INDEPENDENCE EVIDENCE DUE CARE FAIR PRESENTATION ETHICAL CONDUCT INDEPENDENCE EVIDENCE DUE CARE FAIR PRESENTA
CARE FAIR PRESENTATION ETHICAL CONDUCT INDEPENDENCE EVIDENCE DUE CARE FAIR PRESENTATION ETHICAL CONDUCT INDEPENDENCE EVIDENCE DUE CARE FAIR PRESE
UE CARE FAIR PRESENTATION ETHICAL CONDUCT INDEPENDENCE EVIDENCE DUE CARE FAIR PRESENTATION ETHICAL CONDUCT INDEPENDENCE EVIDENCE DUE CARE FAIR P
CE DUE CARE FAIR PRESENTATION ETHICAL CONDUCT INDEPENDENCE EVIDENCE DUE CARE FAIR PRESENTATION ETHICAL CONDUCT INDEPENDENCE EVIDENCE DUE CARE FA
ENCE DUE CARE FAIR PRESENTATION ETHICAL CONDUCT INDEPENDENCE EVIDENCE DUE CARE FAIR PRESENTATION ETHICAL CONDUCT INDEPENDENCE EVIDENCE DUE CARE
EVIDENCE DUE CARE FAIR PRESENTATION ETHICAL CONDUCT INDEPENDENCE EVIDENCE DUE CARE FAIR PRESENTATION ETHICAL CONDUCT INDEPENDENCE EVIDENCE DUE
NCE EVIDENCE DUE CARE FAIR PRESENTATION ETHICAL CONDUCT INDEPENDENCE EVIDENCE DUE CARE FAIR PRESENTATION ETHICAL CONDUCT INDEPENDENCE EVIDENCE D

LEARNING OBJECTIVES

INDEPENDENCE EVIDENCE DUE CARE FAIR PRESENTATION ETHICAL CONDUCT INDEPENDENCE EVIDENCE DUE CARE FAIR PRESENTATION ETHICAL CONDUCT INDEPENDENCE
NCT INDEPENDENCE EVIDENCE DUE CARE FAIR PRESENTATION ETHICAL CONDUCT INDEPENDENCE EVIDENCE DUE CARE FAIR PRESENTATION ETHICAL CONDUCT INDEPENDE
ONDUCT INDEPENDENCE EVIDENCE DUE CARE FAIR PRESENTATION ETHICAL CONDUCT INDEPENDENCE EVIDENCE DUE CARE FAIR PRESENTATION ETHICAL CONDUCT INDEPE
L CONDUCT INDEPENDENCE EVIDENCE DUE CARE FAIR PRESENTATION ETHICAL CONDUCT INDEPENDENCE EVIDENCE DUE CARE FAIR PRESENTATION ETHICAL CONDUCT IND
HICAL CONDUCT INDEPENDENCE EVIDENCE DUE C

After studying this chapter, students should understand

1. How to define control attributes in relation to audit objectives.
2. Why auditors use sampling.
3. The nature of sampling risks and the nature of nonsampling risk.
4. The advantages and disadvantages of statistical sampling versus nonstatistical sampling.
5. Procedures for computing confidence intervals for attribute sampling plans.
6. The nature of alpha and beta risks.
7. The way in which various factors influence sample size.
8. The quantitative and qualitative techniques which are used to evaluate sample results.
9. The techniques used to select samples.
10. The nature of discovery sampling.

ENDENCE EVIDENCE DUE CARE FAIR PRESENTATION ETHICAL CONDUCT INDEPENDENCE EVIDENCE DUE CARE FAIR PRESENTATION ETHICAL CONDUCT INDEPENDENCE EVI
DEPENDENCE EVIDENCE DUE CARE FAIR PRESENTATION ETHICAL CONDUCT INDEPENDENCE EVIDENCE DUE CARE FAIR PRESENTATION ETHICAL CONDUCT INDEPENDENCE
T INDEPENDENCE EVIDENCE DUE CARE FAIR PRESENTATION ETHICAL CONDUCT INDEPENDENCE EVIDENCE DUE CARE FAIR PRESENTATION ETHICAL CONDUCT INDEPENDEN
DUCT INDEPENDENCE EVIDENCE DUE CARE FAIR PRESENTATION ETHICAL CONDUCT INDEPENDENCE EVIDENCE DUE CARE FAIR PRESENTATION ETHICAL CONDUCT INDEPE
ONDUCT INDEPENDENCE EVIDENCE DUE CARE FAIR PRESENTATION ETHICAL CONDUCT INDEPENDENCE EVIDENCE DUE CARE FAIR PRESENTATION ETHICAL CONDUCT IND
CAL CONDUCT INDEPENDENCE EVIDENCE DUE CARE FAIR PRESENTATION ETHICAL CONDUCT INDEPENDENCE EVIDENCE DUE CARE FAIR PRESENTATION ETHICAL CONDUCT
THICAL CONDUCT INDEPENDENCE EVIDENCE DUE CARE FAIR PRESENTATION ETHICAL CONDUCT INDEPENDENCE EVIDENCE DUE CARE FAIR PRESENTATION ETHICAL COND
IN ETHICAL CONDUCT INDEPENDENCE EVIDENCE DUE CARE FAIR PRESENTATION ETHICAL CONDUCT INDEPENDENCE EVIDENCE DUE CARE FAIR PRESENTATION ETHICAL C
TATION ETHICAL CONDUCT INDEPENDENCE EVIDENCE DUE CARE FAIR PRESENTATION ETHICAL CONDUCT INDEPENDENCE EVIDENCE DUE CARE FAIR PRESENTATION ETHICA
SENTATION ETHICAL CONDUCT INDEPENDENCE EVIDENCE DUE CARE FAIR PRESENTATION ETHICAL CONDUCT INDEPENDENCE EVIDENCE DUE CARE FAIR PRESENTATION ET
PRESENTATION ETHICAL CONDUCT INDEPENDENCE EVIDENCE DUE CARE FAIR PRESENTATION ETHICAL CONDUCT INDEPENDENCE EVIDENCE DUE CARE FAIR PRESENTATION
AIR PRESENTATION ETHICAL CONDUCT INDEPENDENCE EVIDENCE DUE CARE FAIR PRESENTATION ETHICAL CONDUCT INDEPENDENCE EVIDENCE DUE CARE FAIR PRESENTA
E FAIR PRESENTATION ETHICAL CONDUCT INDEPENDENCE EVIDENCE DUE CARE FAIR PRESENTATION ETHICAL CONDUCT INDEPENDENCE EVIDENCE DUE CARE FAIR PRESE
CARE FAIR PRESENTATION ETHICAL CONDUCT INDEPENDENCE EVIDENCE DUE CARE FAIR PRESENTATION ETHICAL CONDUCT INDEPENDENCE EVIDENCE DUE CARE FAIR PF
DUE CARE FAIR PRESENTATION ETHICAL CONDUCT INDEPENDENCE EVIDENCE DUE CARE FAIR PRESENTATION ETHICAL CONDUCT INDEPENDENCE EVIDENCE DUE CARE FAI
CE DUE CARE FAIR PRESENTATION ETHICAL CONDUCT INDEPENDENCE EVIDENCE DUE CARE FAIR PRESENTATION ETHICAL CONDUCT INDEPENDENCE EVIDENCE DUE CARE
DENCE DUE CARE FAIR PRESENTATION ETHICAL CONDUCT INDEPENDENCE EVIDENCE DUE CARE FAIR PRESENTATION ETHICAL CONDUCT INDEPENDENCE EVIDENCE DUE C
EVIDENCE DUE CARE FAIR PRESENTATION ETHICAL CONDUCT INDEPENDENCE EVIDENCE DUE CARE FAIR PRESENTATION ETHICAL CONDUCT INDEPENDENCE EVIDENCE D

Chapter 9

Internal Control and Attribute Sampling

This chapter was written by
Ann B. Pushkin, Ph.D., C.P.A.,
Assistant Professor of Accounting,
West Virginia University

INTRODUCTION

The previous chapter discussed techniques for compliance testing internal controls. This chapter explains how attribute sampling can be used to quantify conclusions about compliance testing. For example, attribute sampling can be used to determine the number of items for compliance testing and to make probability statements about the results of compliance tests. However, before using attribute sampling, the auditor must understand how to define control attributes in relation to audit objectives.

DEFINING CONTROL ATTRIBUTES IN RELATION TO AUDIT OBJECTIVES

In compliance testing the auditor wants to determine if prescribed internal accounting controls are operating as designed and the auditor looks at the characteristics, or attributes, of various controls to see that they are working properly. For example, the auditor may examine sales orders to see if they are stamped by the credit manager indicating credit approval for the customer. In this case, the characteristic or attribute is the credit manager's approval of the sales order. Each sales order examined is a sampling unit which can be put into one, and only one, of two possible categories. That is, each sales order will either show approval or it will not show approval. All attributes must be defined so that each sampling unit can be classified either as having the characteristic or as not having it. The proportion of sales orders lacking the stamp to the total number of sales orders examined in the sample is referred to as the sample rate of occurrence for the attribute tested.

The following credit approval/shipping subsystem is presented to illustrate further the definition of attributes in relation to audit objectives. Assume the procedure for shipment of goods, as shown in Exhibit 9-1, requires sales orders to be stamped by the credit manager indicating credit approval before goods are shipped to customers. After stamping the sales order, the credit manager sends two copies of the sales order to the finished goods storeroom as authorization to release the goods to shipping. The storeroom supervisor has the shipping department supervisor sign the first copy of the sales order to signify that the shipping department has control over the goods. The storeroom supervisor sends the stamped, signed sales order to billing while the shipping department uses the second copy to prepare a prenumbered bill of lading in triplicate with the corresponding sales order number typed on it. The shipping department has the carrier sign the bill of lading thus indicating receipt of the goods by the carrier. One copy of the bill of

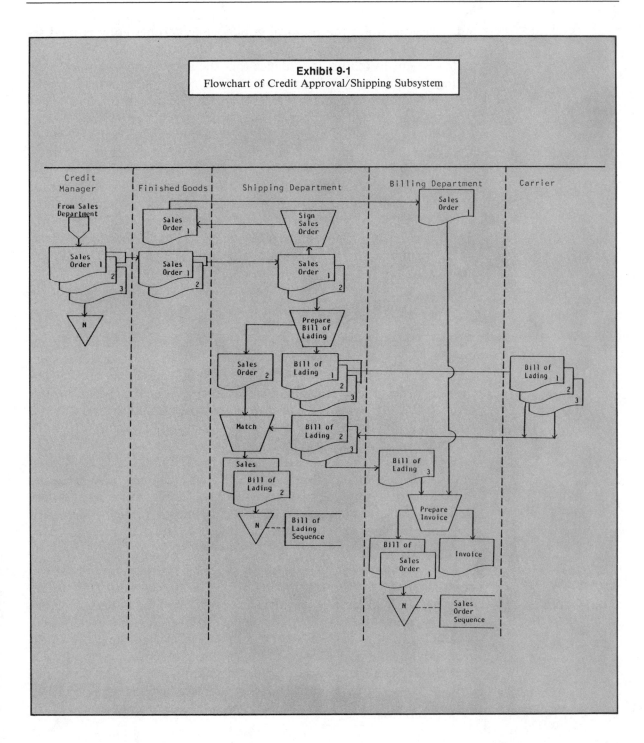

Exhibit 9-1
Flowchart of Credit Approval/Shipping Subsystem

lading accompanies the physical goods while another copy is filed sequentially in the shipping department. A third copy of the signed bill of lading is sent to billing as evidence that the goods where shipped. The billing department matches the bill of lading with the stamped, signed sales order before preparing a sales invoice. The sales order and bill of lading are then filed together in sales order number sequence.

If the specific audit objective is to determine that *all shipments of goods* are made to approved customers, i.e. to test the control that all shipments are properly approved, the auditor should take a sample from the file of duplicate bills of lading maintained in the shipping department, after testing the completeness of this file by examining the bill of lading numbers. After the auditor takes the sample, the auditor then traces each bill of lading in the sample to the billing department, which maintains the file of stamped, signed sales orders. The auditor then examines the sales order corresponding to the sampled bill of lading for the proper credit approval as indicated by the credit manager's stamp.

The auditor should not sample from the file of sales orders in the billing department because the evidence gathered would not satisfy the specific control objective that sales are properly authorized before shipment of goods. Sampling from this file only indicates credit approval of the sales orders filed in the billing department. When the audit objective is to test the approval of sales before shipment, the auditor should sample from a population representing *all* shipments. The sales order file may not represent such a population.

This example demonstrates the necessity of defining specific audit objectives of a compliance test before defining attributes of interest and identifying files (populations) from which to sample. Defining audit objectives is the key to developing a valid sampling plan which will provide relevant reliable data to support an audit conclusion.

DEFINING AUDIT OBJECTIVES

As the previous section stated, auditors must identify audit objectives before they can prepare a sampling plan. The auditor must first specify a general audit objective. For instance, one *general* audit objective may be to determine the effectiveness of controls over the sales cycle. Then, specific audit objectives should be defined within the framework of the general objective. Specific accounting control objectives may be divided into three categories: authorization, accounting, and asset safeguarding. That is, the auditor verifies that transactions have proper authorization, that the transactions are properly recorded in the accounting records, and that an entity's internal control system is adequate to safeguard its assets.

In some cases, one sample may be used to test several controls, and, in these cases, the sampling plan is said to be efficient. However, the auditor must be careful when he or she uses one common sample to investigate more than one attribute because one attribute may require a larger sample size than the second attribute. Procedures for determining sample size are discussed in subsequent sections of the chapter.

SAMPLING RISKS, METHODOLOGIES, AND PLANS

The auditor uses sampling to make inferences about auditing populations. When using a sampling plan, sampling risks—as well as non-sampling risks—are encountered. Moreover, the auditor must consider these risks regardless of the sampling methodology employed. After explaining why auditors use sampling, the next two sections discuss sampling and non-sampling risks and are followed by a discussion of the two basic sampling methodologies: statistical and nonstatistical. The last section identifies two statistical sampling plans for attributes.

Why Auditors Use Sampling

Rather than investigate each unit in the population, which is usually cost prohibitive, auditors use sampling to more efficiently gather evidence about auditing populations. Sampling is considered a necessary and acceptable practice for gathering sufficient evidential matter as required by the third standard of field work.[1] Evidence obtained by examining samples is used in conjuction with other types of audit evidence as the basis for expressing an opinion on a company's financial statements.

The auditor could not verify each item in a population and keep the cost of the audit at an amount acceptable to the client. In making a decision to use sampling, the auditor must, however, consider cost, time, and the potential consequences of an erroneous conclusion due to investigating only a portion of a population. There must be a balance between gathering enough relevant, reliable evidence to form an opinion on the financial statements and keeping the audit fee at a reasonable level. It is important that the auditor not oversample, which creates excessive auditing fees, but it is more important that the auditor not undersample because this could result in projecting erroneous

---

[1] *SAS No. 39, Audit Sampling*, American Institute of Certified Public Accountants, New York, 1981.

conclusions about an audit population. Consequently, the extent of sampling is an extremely important audit variable. The auditor's professional judgment and willingness to sustain a given level of sampling risk determine the extent of sampling in any audit situation.

Sampling Risks

In compliance testing, the auditor faces two types of sampling risks: the *risk of underreliance* and the *risk of overreliance*,[2] and *both risks are inherent in statistical and nonstatistical sampling.* To understand these sampling risks, it is necessary to understand that, regardless of the methodology used in compliance testing, the auditor judgmentally determines the proportion of times a control can break down and still be considered effective. For example, an auditor could specify that a control could break down 5 percent of the time (a noncompliance rate of 5 percent) and still be considered effective.

On each compliance test, the auditor is subjected to the *risk of overreliance.* This risk is the risk that sample results, because of sampling error, will indicate control effectiveness when in fact the control is not operating as it should. In other words, the true noncompliance rate is greater than the noncompliance rate which the auditor estimates from a sample. Yet the auditor will rely on the control as planned even though the control is operating ineffectively. In statistical terms, this sampling risk has been defined as the beta risk. The beta risk is discussed in more detail in the section on statistical sampling.

As stated above, the auditor is also subjected to the *risk of underreliance* on each compliance test. The risk of underreliance is the risk that sample results will indicate control ineffectiveness, again because of sample error, when in fact the *true* noncompliance rate is acceptable. In this situation, although the control is really operating effectively, the auditor will not rely on the control as planned. Since the internal accounting control under investigation is not relied on, the auditor must determine to what extent remaining auditing procedures should be modified. In statistical sampling plans, the risk of underreliance is defined as the alpha risk. The alpha risk is discussed again in the section on statistical sampling.

Nonsampling Risks

Nonsampling risks are of two basic types. One type consists of the auditor's inability to recognize a control breakdown. For example, when

---

[2] *SAS No. 39, Audit Sampling*, paragraph 12.

the auditor uses observation as a compliance testing technique, the auditor's observation may lead him or her to believe that a control is working as prescribed when such is not really the case.

The second type of nonsampling risk involves the inability of the auditor to design audit procedures compatible with audit objectives. If audit procedures do not provide evidence that is compatible with audit objectives, the competency and sufficiency of evidence are irrelevant, and audit conclusions may be invalid. For example, as indicated earlier, the auditor cannot test control over credit approval before shipment unless he or she samples from a file which indicates the shipments which were actually made.

Nonsampling risks are inherent in any audit engagement, even when sampling is not employed. That is, if the auditor investigates every item in an auditing population, nonsampling risks are still present. Control of nonsampling risks, however, may be reduced to a negligible level.[3] Nonsampling risks are controlled by auditor competence, proper planning and supervision, and the CPA's adherence to appropriate quality control standards. The higher the degree of auditor competency, of proper planning and supervision, and of adherence to high quality control standards, the lower the nonsampling risk. The competency of the auditor was discussed in both Chapters 1 and 2 in relation to the first general auditing standard. Proper planning and supervision was covered in Chapters 2 and 4 in relation to the first standard of field work. The necessity of developing quality control standards in a CPA firm was discussed in Chapter 3.

Sampling Methodologies

As mentioned above, there are two different approaches to sampling populations: nonstatistical (judgmental), and statistical. Both approaches are acceptable alternatives in practice and both are compatible with generally accepted auditing standards. Judgmental and statistical sampling are alike in defining general and specific audit objectives and in identifying populations and attributes. The two approaches differ, however, in the methods of determining sample size and selecting sample items from the populations.

Nonstatistical Sampling

When using nonstatiscal sampling, the auditor subjectively determines sample size and the items to be included in the sample. One

---

[3] *SAS No. 39, Audit Sampling*, paragraph 11.

nonstatistical method of determining sample size and of selecting sample items is *block sampling*. For example, the auditor may define an audit population as all cash disbursements during the fiscal year, and may specify that the sample consist of all cash disbursements in the last week of each quarter. Or a sample could be the first 100 cash disbursements in May and in September. The variety and pattern of blocks sampled should ensure that the sample is representative of the population characteristic being examined. For instance, if the auditor wants to estimate an average annual error rate for a class of transactions, and if there has been a high employee turnover throughout the fiscal year, smaller blocks of sample items from several months will more likely produce a representative sample than will larger blocks of items from a few months.

Another nonstatistical sampling method involves *judgment selection*. In this case, the auditor may select from an account or class of transactions all items in excess of a specified dollar amount or items of a particular type which represents a small portion of the total population. The idea is that the auditor selects the items based on his or her judgment. For example, the auditor may decide to examine supporting documentation for only the largest entries to an account or test credit approval for sales which exceed a certain dollar amount. Although the sample may not be representative of the population, it is justified on the basis that the sample serves the unique purpose identified by the auditor (e.g, to examine documentation or approval for the largest dollar amounts). However, when the auditor uses judgmental sampling, the auditor must be careful not to draw conclusions about the entire population based on a specialized sample.

Advantages of nonstatistical sampling.   Some auditors think that one advantage of nonstatistical sampling is the ability to concentrate on high-risk audit areas within a given audit population. In other words, the auditor may believe that certain types of errors or irregularities exist in a certain portion of the population. Thus, the auditor will want to test more heavily in those areas of the population which appear to have a high audit risk. However, the auditor must be careful not to extend conclusions formed about this high-risk area to the entire population.

Other auditors think that the ability to concentrate on high-risk areas within an audit population is not an advantage peculiar to nonstatistical sampling. The population could be stratified (as discussed later, stratification involves dividing the population into homogenous subgroups) so that those areas with potentially higher error rates or potential irregularities would form one stratum, and the remaining un-suspicious portion of the population would form another stratum. The stratum with a potentially higher audit risk could then be sampled more heavily than the other stratum with statistical or nonstatistical methods.

One advantage of nonstatistical sampling that auditors generally agree on is that it is less complex, and perhaps less costly, than statistical sampling. On occasion nonstatistical sampling may be the preferred approach in terms of cost and benefit. Consequently, nonstatistical sampling is an effective audit tool in many situations.

Disadvantages of nonstatistical sampling. Nonstatistical sampling can produce samples that are biased by the auditor's background or personal preferences. The number of blocks, the number of items in each block, and the location of each block will vary between auditors. In other words, it is difficult for the auditor to objectively determine a sample size and to objectively identify the items that should be selected from the population.

Also, after selecting the sample items and evaluating the sample, the auditor typically wants to make inferences about the population based on sample results. Nonstatistical sampling does not provide an objective framework for such inferences. The auditor cannot state the confidence with which a sampling conclusion is being made nor can nonstatistical sampling provide the quantification of sampling risks inherent in any sampling plan.

Statistical Sampling

When using statistical sampling, the auditor will mathematically determine the sample size by using either a formula, a graph, or a table, and will randomly select the sample items. When sample items are randomly selected, the sample should be representative of the population.

Advantages of statistical sampling. Statistical sampling uses mathematical methods to determine a sample size and to objectively justify its adequacy. Consequently, sample results are objective and defensible. Furthermore, the auditor has a tenable basis for expanding his or her audit procedures if the results of a statistical test indicate that such expansion is necessary in the circumstances. Another advantage of statistical sampling is that its use quantifies and controls the risk of underreliance or overreliance. Quantification and control of these sampling risks are discussed later in this chapter.

Disadvantages of statistical sampling. A disadvantage of statistical sampling is that it involves some complex sampling plans that are difficult to handle without the use of a computer. In other cases, the technical details of relating population items to the criteria for random sample item selection may be impractical without a computer facility. In such cases, the auditor must consider the cost/benefit factors before using statistical sampling techniques rather than nonstatistical sampling. However, many CPA firms have audit software packages that make statistical sampling efficient and less costly.

The following section discusses two basic types of statistical sampling plans—estimation sampling and discovery sampling.

Estimation Sampling Plans

There are two types of estimation sampling plans. One type is used to estimate "how much" while the other estimates "how often." "How much" refers to continuous measurements such as dollar values, and it can be used to estimate the dollar reasonableness of an account balance or the dollar error in a population. This type of estimation plan is called *variables sampling*; it is generally associated with substantive testing and is discussed in Chapter 10.

This chapter focuses on *attribute sampling*, the type of estimation plan which answers the question "How often?" In other words, attribute sampling establishes the frequency of some event such as an error or a missing document in a given population. Hence, this type of plan is used to estimate the frequency of deviations from prescribed internal accounting control procedures.

Discovery Sampling

Another type of sampling plan used to detect departures from prescribed control procedures is called discovery sampling. Discovery sampling is an extension of attribute sampling, but rather than estimate the frequency of procedural deviations from a control, discovery sampling attempts to discover at least one control breakdown when the population rate of breakdowns is equal to or greater than a critical noncompliance rate specified by the auditor. Discovery sampling techniques are discussed in the last section of this chapter.

STATISTICAL TERMINOLOGY

When using statistical sampling, the auditor examines sample items, calculates sample statistics, and uses these statistics to make inferences about the rate of deviation from prescribed internal control procedures which exists in the population. The rate of deviation may be defined as the rate of occurrence. The purpose of this section is to explain the following statistical terms in relation to attribute sampling: sampling risks, confidence level, and precision.

The auditor generally does not carry out many of the mathematical calculations demonstrated in this section because tables or graphs have been developed for practical use. Statistical calculations are presented, however, so that the student may learn the concepts. An understanding of statistical concepts is necessary to determine sample size and to properly evaluate and use sample results.

Sample Rate of Occurrence

After a sample size has been calculated and the sample items randomly selected from the population, the auditor must examine each item in the sample to determine how many of the sample units lack the control attribute under investigation. Then the auditor may calculate the sample rate of occurrence in the following manner. The formula is

$$p = \frac{q}{n}$$

where

p = the sample rate of occurrence,
q = number of sample items lacking the control attribute, and
n = sample size.

To illustrate, suppose the sample size equals 200 and the number of units in the sample lacking the control attribute equals 12. Then,

$$p = \frac{12}{200} = .06$$

The sample rate of occurrence (p) equals .06, meaning that the control under investigation broke down 6 percent of the time as determined from the sample.

The sample rate of occurrence is referred to as a point estimate. However, a conclusion that the population rate of occurrence is equal to the point estimate, p, is unreliable. The point estimate based on one sample is unreliable because the rate of occurrence of a second sample of the same size will probably differ from the rate of occurrence in the first sample. The third, fourth, and fifth sample rates of occurrences also will likely differ from one another. Theoretically, for large sample sizes, if all possible samples of the same size were randomly selected from the population, the sample rates of occurrence would be normally distributed around the population rate of occurrence. Consequently, any sample drawn from the population must come from this normal distribution of point estimates. How much any given point estimate will differ from the population rate of occurrence can be estimated by the standard error of the sample rate of occurrence.

Standard Error of the Sample Rate of Occurrence

The standard error of the sample rate of occurrence is a measure of the extent to which a sample rate of occurrence can be expected to deviate from the population rate of occurrence. The standard error of the sample rate of occurrence can be calculated using the following formula:

$$\hat{\sigma}_p = \sqrt{\frac{p\,(1 - p)}{n - 1}}$$

where

$\hat{\sigma}_p$ = standard error of the sample rate of occurrence.
The remaining notations were defined previously.

To follow through on the example given above, the standard error of the sample rate of occurrence would be calculated as follows:

$$\hat{\sigma}_p = \sqrt{\frac{.06\,(1 - .06)}{199}} = 0.0168$$

The standard error for the sample rate of occurrence is 0.0168. According to statistical theory, 99 percent of all samples of a given size, randomly selected from a population, will have a rate of occurrence which falls within plus or minus 2.58 standard errors of the population occurrence rate, and 95 percent of all samples will have a rate of occurrence which falls within plus or minus 1.96 standard errors of the population rate of occurrence. The number of standard errors for each probability can be determined from a standard normal table. The number of standard errors for each probability is generally symbolized with Z_α, where α (alpha) represents the complement of the probability factor. That is, if the probability equals 95 percent, then α equals 5 percent $(1 - .95)$. Alpha is a sampling risk which is discussed in more detail in a subsequent section of the chapter. Two of the more frequently used Z_α factors, in addition to the ones given above, are given in the following table:

Probability	*Z*
98	± 2.326
90	± 1.645

The fact that the true rate of occurrence for the population falls within a certain range of the sample rate of occurrence for any sample drawn from the population has been used to devise tests which determine the probability that the population rate of occurrence will fall between the computed upper and lower precision limits for any given sample.

Precision Limits and Confidence Level

After calculating the sample rate of occurrence and the standard error of the sample rate of occurrence, the auditor can determine the computed precision limits for a given probability. To find the computed upper precision limit for a given probability, the sample standard error is multiplied by the Z_α factor, and the product is added to the point estimate. The lower limit is found by subtracting this product from the point estimate. Symbolically, the computed upper and lower precision limits may be represented as follows:

$$CUPL = p + Z_\alpha (\hat{\sigma}_p)$$

$$CLPL = p - Z_\alpha (\hat{\sigma}_p)$$

where

CUPL = computed upper precision limit, and
CLPL = computed lower precision limit.
Remaining notations are defined above.

Continuing with the example, the computed precision limits for a 95 percent probability, which corresponds to a Z_α of 1.96, are calculated as follows:

$$CUPL = .06 + 1.96 (.0168) = .0929 = 9\%$$

$$CLPL = .06 - 1.96 (.0168) = .0271 = 3\%$$

The interval from the 6 percent point estimate to the upper precision limit of 9 percent is referred to as the *precision interval*. In this case the precision interval equals 3 percent (9 − 6 percent).

The confidence level is the *probability* that the true population occurrence rate will fall between the computed upper and lower precision limits for any given test. The confidence level (also referred to as the reliability level) and precision limits are directly related so that reference to one cannot be given without referring to the other. For the case given above, the auditor could state with 95 percent confidence that the population rate of occurrence is between 3 and 9 percent.

Since rates of occurrence generally concern rates for errors or control deviations, the auditor is primarily interested in the upper precision limit. Consequently, the remaining discussion on statistical sampling emphasizes the upper precision limit. The following discussion shows how the statistical procedures and conclusion given above will change when considering only the upper precision limit.

Computation of the sample rate of occurrence and the standard error of the sample rate of occurrence will not change. The Z_α factors will change, however, since the auditor will be considering only the upper precision limit. A few of the frequently used Z_α factors for *one-sided tests* (upper precision tests) are provided below:

Confidence Level	Z
99	+2.326
95	+1.645
90	+1.282
80	+ .842
75	+ .674

The computed upper precision limit for a one-sided 95 percent confidence level is calculated as follows:

$$CUPL = p + Z_\alpha (\hat{\sigma}_p)$$

$$CUPL = .06 + 1.645 (.0168) = .0876 = 9\%$$

In this case the auditor could state with 95 percent confidence that the population rate of occurrence is 9 percent or less.

The CUPL may be manipulated by changing the confidence level. Notice that Z_α factors get larger with higher levels of reliability. Consequently, the precision interval will be wider with a higher confidence level than with a lower confidence level for a particular sample. To illustrate, if the confidence level in the illustration discussed above were changed from 95 percent to 99 percent, the upper precision limit would be 10 percent rather than 9 percent. The computation of the CUPL for the 99 percent confidence level is as follows:

$$CUPL = .06 + 2.326 \ (.0168) = 10\%$$

For objectivity of sampling results, the auditor should specify a level of confidence before any sampling takes place. That is, it is not logical for the auditor to decide on a particular level of confidence which is required and then to change that level of confidence if the sample results do not support the level of confidence which the auditor believed was required in the first place.

Alpha Risk

As indicated earlier, the alpha risk is a sampling risk which may be defined as the risk of underreliance. It is the risk that an effective control will be considered ineffective. The alpha risk is the probability of a type one error. A type one error occurs when an effective control is deemed to be ineffective.

The alpha risk level (probability of a type one error) is quantified as the complement of the confidence level. Symbolically, the alpha risk is expressed as follows:

$$\alpha = 1 - CL$$

where

$$\alpha = \text{level of alpha risk, and}$$
$$CL = \text{confidence level.}$$

The formula clearly reflects the interrelationship between the confidence level and the level of alpha risk. This relationship is an important statistical concept. As confidence levels get larger, alpha risk levels get smaller. In other words, changing the confidence level from 90 percent to 95 percent decreases the probability from 10 percent to 5 percent that an effective control will erroneously be considered ineffective. The reverse relationship is also true: as confidence levels decrease, alpha risk levels increase. Consequently, auditors may control the alpha risk by specifying the confidence level.

When a compliance test indicates that a control is ineffective, the auditor must take steps to determine either that a type one error occurred or intensify subsequent substantive procedures. In either case, the auditor extends auditing tests as described below. Consequently, sampling procedures that indicate a control as ineffective affects the efficiency of the audit but not the effectiveness of the audit. Therefore, auditors are not as concerned with the risk of underreliance as they are with the risk of overreliance.

Beta Risk

The beta risk (risk of overreliance) is the risk that an ineffective control will be considered effective. This risk is also referred to as the probability of a type two error. A type two error occurs when a statistical test indicates that an ineffective control is effective.

If sampling procedures indicate that a control is effective, the auditor will rely on the control as planned even though a type two error may exist. In other words, the auditor will not know at this point in time whether a type two error is present or not. If a type two error does exist, the auditor may later discover through substantive tests that reliance on the control was unwarranted because a type two error occurred in the compliance test. That is, when substantive tests indicate that an account balance is materially misstated, the auditor may conclude that related controls must either be non-existent or operating ineffectively and that any reliance thereon would have been unwarranted.

However, when an auditor restricts substantive tests as a result of relying on accounting controls, the probability of discovering a materially misstated account balance is less than when substantive tests are not restricted. Consequently, the commission of a type two error affects the effectiveness of an audit. For this reason, auditors are more concerned with the risk of overreliance than with the risk of underreliance.

**SAMPLE SIZE
DETERMINATION**

The sample size is a critical factor statistically as well as an important audit variable. A small sample size will help keep the cost of an audit down. On the other hand, the sample size must be large enough to yield sufficient evidence whether the auditor is using statistical or nonstatistical sampling. The sampling conclusion is then used in conjunction with other audit evidence to formulate an audit decision either supporting or not supporting the degree of planned reliance on the control. Consequently, the sample size should be as small as possible to keep audit fees at a minimum and at the same time large enough to provide the necessary evidence for decision making.

Procedures to determine sample size for nonstatistical samples differ from procedures for statistical sample sizes although both types of plans have common factors which influence sample size. Statistical sample size determination will be presented first and will be followed by a discussion of nonstatistical sample sizes.

Statistical Sample Sizes

When an auditor determines a sample size for statistical sampling, statistical variables which influence sample size must be quantified. A discussion of the sample size variables follows the presentation on the sample size formula.

Sample Size Formula

A sample size formula is presented here although the auditor will probably not use the formula in practice. For practical purposes, tables for sample size determination have been developed. The following formula is given to explain sample size determinants and their interrelationships:[4]

$$n = \frac{Z_\alpha^2 \, p(1 - p)}{(TRO - ERO)^2}$$

where

$$
\begin{aligned}
n &= \text{sample size,} \\
Z_\alpha &= \text{factor from the standard normal distribution} \\
&\quad \text{necessary for the desired level of confidence,} \\
p &= \text{sample rate of occurrence,} \\
TRO &= \text{tolerable rate of occurrence,} \\
ERO &= \text{expected rate of occurrence in the population.}
\end{aligned}
$$

These sample size variables are defined and explained below. After discussing these variables, an example is given on computing sample size.

---

[4] The sample size formula is reliable only when p approximates 50 percent. The smaller the p, the more unreliable the formula in calculating an appropriate sample size. This undesirable characteristic is not present in the sample size tables presented in the appendix of this chapter. The formulas used for the tables are not presented here since (1) they are complex, and (2) they add little to the student's understanding of the concepts which are involved in determining sample sizes.

Sample Size Variables

The auditor must judgmentally specify the following sample size variables: the confidence level, the tolerable rate of occurrence (TRO), and the expected rate of occurrence in the population (ERO). Another variable that has a minor influence on sample size is the population size, which is discussed later.

Confidence level. When considering only an upper precision interval, the confidence level is the probability that the true population rate of occurrence is equal to or less than the computed upper precision limit. The level of confidence plays a dominant role in determining sample size. The higher the confidence level, the larger the sample size.

Traditionally, the risk of underreliance is used to determine sample size. However, *SAS No. 39* recommends that the risk of overreliance be used as a sample size determinant since this risk is of greater concern to the auditor. Consequently, the remaining discussions will use the *risk of overreliance to define reliability*. *SAS No. 39* also indicates that a low level, say 5 or 10 percent, be specified for the risk of overreliance because compliance testing provides the primary source of evidence for control effectiveness.

Tolerable rate of occurrence. The tolerable rate of occurrence (TRO) represents the maximum rate of noncompliance that could exist and still have the control considered effective. Statistically, the TRO is a *desired* upper precision limit. The TRO level specified by the auditor has a significant impact on sample size. For any practical audit application the higher the TRO for any given ERO, the smaller the sample size, and vice versa.[5]

In specifying the TRO, the auditor should consider the potential impact of control noncompliance on financial data in relation to the degree of planned reliance on the internal control system. When a high degree of reliance is planned for a control whose breakdown would have a significant impact upon financial data, the auditor should specify a low TRO. In other words, if the breakdown of a particular control could significantly affect the financial data and if the auditor intends to rely very heavily on that control, the auditor may set the TRO at a very low level, such as 1 or 2 percent. On the other hand, if a low degree of reliance is planned for controls whose potential impact upon

---

[5] As a practical matter, TRO will exceed ERO because it is not logical for the auditor to specify a tolerable rate of occurrence (TRO) which is less than the expected rate of occurrence (ERO). Therefore, as a practical matter, the larger the TRO the greater the distance between TRO and ERO and thus the smaller the sample size.

financial data is not significant, the auditor may specify a high TRO, such as 8 percent or higher.

Expected rate of occurrence.   The expected rate of occurrence (ERO) in the population must be estimated to determine sample size. The auditor may use the prior year's rate of occurrence adjusted for current changes in the internal accounting control system to estimate the ERO. Or, a preliminary sample of 30 (if the preliminary sample is less than 30, then the distributions of sample rates of occurrences is not expected to be normally distributed, but instead, is expected to follow a t distribution) items may be randomly selected and evaluated to estimate the ERO. If a preliminary sample is used to estimate the ERO, the preliminary sample would become part of the final sample.

The ERO has a significant impact on sample size. However, it is very difficult to generalize about the impact of ERO on sample size because, as the formula indicates, the key factor which influences sample size is the difference between ERO and TRO, and the larger this difference the smaller the sample size, and vice versa. As a practical matter, however, TRO will exceed ERO and TRO (see footnote 5) will be held to some minimum because it is not logical for the auditor to tolerate a rate of noncompliance which is greater than say 10 percent. Consequently, given that TRO will be held to a minimum level, increasing ERO will increase sample size, and vice versa.

Effect of changing sample size variables.   The effect on sample size when increasing one variable while holding all other sample size determinants constant is summarized below.

Variable Increased	Effect on Sample Size
Confidence Level	Larger
TRO	Smaller
ERO	Larger
Distance between TRO and ERO	Smaller

Effect of population size on sample size.   In attribute sampling the size of the population has a minor effect on sample size. Sampling may be carried out with replacement or without replacement. Sampling with replacement involves selecting a sample unit from the population and then placing the item back in the population so that it may be selected again. Sampling with replacement obviously permits duplication of sample units. The auditor is encouraged to use sampling without replacement because a sampling unit should be investigated and counted as evidence only once. Therefore, if sampling procedures select a particular item twice, the auditor should not use that item a second time, but he or she should select another population item for the sample.

The sample size tables discussed in the next section are constructed for sampling with replacement, but they may be used for sampling without replacement provided the calculated sample size is less than approximately 10 percent of the population size.[6] If the calculated sample size is larger than 10 percent of the population size, the sample sizes which are given by the tables will be slightly larger than necessary. However, the auditor may reduce the sample size by applying a finite population correction factor. The reduced sample size using a finite population correction factor may be calculated as follows:

$$n' = \frac{n}{1 + \dfrac{n}{N}}$$

where

n' = revised sample size,
n = sample size before considering the finite population correction factor, and
N = population size.

To illustrate use of the finite population correction factor, assume there are 1,250 bills of lading in the population and a sample of 150 units before considering the size of the population. Since $n/N = 12\%$, the finite population correction factor should be applied. The reduced sample size is calculated as follows:

$$n' = \frac{150}{1 + \dfrac{150}{1,250}} = 134$$

Calculating Sample Sizes From Tables

After the auditor has specified a confidence level, the TRO, and the ERO appropriate for the circumstances, a sample size may be determined. As indicated earlier, auditors seldom use the formula to determine

---

[6] The ten percent rule is arbitrary, but, as long as the sample size is less than ten percent of the population size, n' is approximately equal to n for sample sizes that auditors will use in practice. Of course, there is nothing wrong with applying the finite population correction factor whenever the auditor samples without replacement.

sample size because the tables developed for this purpose are easier to use. There is a different table for each confidence level. To illustrate sample size determination using a table, assume a confidence level of 95 percent, a TRO of 8 percent, and an ERO of 3 percent. In the chapter appendix find Table 3 which represents a 95 percent confidence level. The top row of the table lists the TROs while the left column provides the EROs. The matrix cells indicate sample sizes.

For example, locate the 8 percent TRO in the top row. Extend an imaginary perpendicular line downward from the 8 percent. Then, locate the ERO of 3 percent in the left column and extend a second imaginary line horizontally to the right. At the intersection of these two imaginary lines, the cell matrix indicates a required sample size of 100 units.

Stratification

Although sample size calculation for a stratified sampling plan used in conjunction with compliance testing is beyond the scope of this text, an introduction to stratification will indicate when a stratified attribute sampling plan may be advantageous.

Stratification means a population is divided into subgroups such that each population item belongs to one and only one of the subgroups. A subgroup is called a stratum. Each stratum should be as different as possible from other strata while the items in each stratum should be as homogeneous as possible. Such a structure generally requires a smaller sample size to produce the same precision as a non-stratified plan of the same type. When a smaller sample produces the same valid results as a larger sample, sampling efficiency is attained. Therefore, whenever the auditor believes that the population can be divided into homogeneous subgroups, i.e., subgroups which are similar in terms of the *attribute which is being measured*, the auditor should consider stratified sampling. For example, a population of transactions might be divided into subgroups based on the personnel who accounted for the transactions, if the auditor believes that the error rate differs between the various personnel. Likewise, a population of transactions might be divided into subgroups based on whether the transactions were processed manually or by EDP, if the two types of processing were used during the period and if the auditor believes that the attribute which is being measured, such as the error rate, differs between processing methods.

Nonstatistical Sample Sizes

As indicated previously, nonstatistical sampling plans have many factors in common with statistical sampling plans. Common factors which influence sample size are the tolerable rate of occurrence (TRO) and the expected population rate of occurrence (ERO). *SAS No. 39, Audit Sampling*, implies that the auditor should quantify these variables even for nonstatistical sampling plans.[7] Although the variables may be quantified, they are not used in a mathematical structure to compute a sample size. Instead the auditor will *subjectively* use the variables to determine a nonstatistical sample size. When specifying the TRO and ERO for judgmental samples, the auditor should take into consideration the same factors as discussed for statistical sampling plans. For example, a low TRO should be specified by the auditor when he or she intends to place heavy reliance on the internal control system. This type of situation calls for a larger sample size than when the auditor specifies a high TRO and plans to place very little reliance on the internal controls. How large, or how small, will depend on the professional judgment of the auditor.

Another factor that should be used in determining a nonstatistical sample size is the risk of overreliance. This is the risk that sample results support planned reliance when in fact the true compliance rate does not justify such reliance. *SAS No. 39* indicates that the auditor should specify a low level for the risk of overreliance because compliance testing provides the primary evidence for evaluating compliance with prescribed procedures.[8] The lower the risk level for overreliance that the auditor wants to obtain, the larger the sample size necessary to attain the desired level of risk.

Considering the factors discussed above for nonstatistical sample size determination, the auditor must subjectively combine these factors in order to identify the sampling units necessary for a representative sample of the population.

In nonstatistical sampling plans, sample items may be randomly selected or they may be chosen by any other selection method. However, if the auditor wants to make inferences about the population, the sample must be representative of the population under investigation.

SAMPLE ITEM SELECTION FOR STATISTICAL SAMPLES

After the auditor has determined the sample size for the statistical sampling plan, he or she must select the sample items from the population. It is necessary that sample items be randomly selected in order for the statistical conclusion to be unbiased and valid. Random selection is

---

[7] *SAS No. 39, Audit Sampling*, paragraphs 31-33.
[8] *SAS No. 39, Audit Sampling*, paragraph 36.

defined as a technique which allows every unit in the population an equal chance of being selected.

Under one method for random selection, the auditor must assemble random numbers and associate them with items in the population. The population must be in some numerical sequence for such an association. For illustration, assume a file of bills of lading for a given period is arranged in prenumbered sequence. Assume the first bill of lading for the current period under audit is number 23546, and the last numbered document is 73545. In other words, the population size is 50,000 bills of lading. Assuming a sample size of 50 units, the auditor should collect 50 random numbers of 5 digits each that correspond to the bill of lading numbers for the current period. There are two different ways to obtain random numbers. One method is to use a random number table and the other method uses computer generated random numbers.

Random Number Tables

An illustration of a random number table is provided in Table 1 of the appendix to this chapter. The table is divided into sets of 5 rows and 5 columns. After selecting a starting point at random from the table, the auditor may proceed in any systematic direction because the numbers are random in any direction. That is, the direction may be up or down, to the left or to the right. Once the direction is started, however, it should not be changed.

For example, assume that a random start results in the number 66801 being selected (row 21, column 21), which corresponds with the bill of lading number 66801 in the above illustration. Therefore, this bill of lading should be selected for the sample. Moving down the table, the second random number, 76813, cannot be associated with a bill of lading because the largest document number in the population is 73545. Therefore, this random number must be discarded and the next number tried. The next random number is 34868 which is usable because it corresponds with the number on a bill of lading. The auditor should continue in this manner until 50 random numbers are selected between 23456 and 73455. Once identified, the 50 random numbers can quickly be arranged in numerical sequence and the bills of lading pulled for investigation.

Computer-Generated Random Numbers

Most computer installations provide a utility program that generates random numbers. These programs typically require the following inputs: a seed number (*randomly* selected by the auditor as the first number in the random series), the number of desired random numbers, i.e., the sample size, and the first and last identification numbers, e.g. bill of lading numbers, of the population. As output, the auditor would receive a computer-printed list of random numbers. The auditor must associate these random numbers with the document numbers in the population in the manner described above.

If the auditor is working with a computerized system where the population file is stored on the system, a computer program or an audit software package may be used to randomly select the necessary records for investigation. The auditor will receive a computer printout for each randomly selected record. The auditor, however, must still investigate each record selected by the program.

If the above random sampling techniques are not economical or feasible, systematic sampling may simulate random selection in certain situations.

Systematic Sampling

Systematic sampling may be used to simulate random sampling when the population is already in random order. However, if the population items occur in any type of pattern, systematic sampling is not a valid statistical sampling procedure and should not be used. For example, an employee list would not be in random order if every 20th employee on the list represents a supervisor.

To use systematic sampling, an auditor must know the population size as well as the sample size. A quotient k is formed by dividing the population size by the sample size to obtain a selection interval. If the population size is 50,000 items and the sample size 200 units, the quotient k equals 250 items (50,000/200). After obtaining a random start, the auditor should select every 250th item in the population. A random starting number may be obtained from a random number table in the manner described previously.

For example, if an auditor is investigating the bill of lading file described perviously, he or she may use any random number between 23546 and 73545 for a starting point. If the beginning random number is 66801, the starting point in the bill of lading file is the document numbered 66801. The second sample item will be the document numbered 67051 (66801 + 250). The third sample item will be 67301; the fourth sample item will be 67551, etc. When the end of the file is reached, the auditor must loop back to the beginning of the file, still maintaining a 250 interval between sample item selections. In the case just described, the highest numbered document selected from the file will be 73301. Since only 244 more documents remain in the file, the next document to be selected should be 23552 (23546 + 6). The next document should be 23802 (23552 + 250). The auditor would continue pulling every 250th document for examination until the entire population file has been covered.

An alternative starting point could be randomly selected between 23546 and 23796. That is, the random starting point could be within the first 250 population items. The auditor would still select every 250th item from the random starting point to the end of the file. Regardless of the starting point, the sample will consist of 200 items as planned.

The randomness of systematic sampling may be improved by increasing the number of random starts. When an auditor uses more than one random start, the quotient k must be adjusted so that the interval is lengthened and the systematic selection yields the predetermined sample size. Specifically, the quotient k must be multiplied by the number of desired random starts to obtain the new interval to be used with the multiple starts.

Continuing the case illustrated above, if the auditor desires two random starts, the selection interval becomes every 500th (250 × 2) item in the population. The auditor may select a random number between 23546 and 24046 (23546 + 500) for one random starting point and select every 500th item until the entire file is covered. The auditor should then select a second random number between 23546 and 24046 for the second random start and again select every 500th item to the end of the file. Since the population size is 50,000 units, the selection procedures with 2 random starts and a 500 selection interval will yield a sample of 200 items as planned, of course, the auditor can also combine several random starts with the loop back procedure described earlier for systematic sampling.

SAMPLE EVALUATION

All types of attribute sampling plans and methodologies require two types of sample analyses: quantitative and qualitative. Quantitative analysis is used to make projections about the overall effectiveness of a particular control based on the number of occurrences found in the sample. Qualitative analysis attempts to determine the probable cause and effect of a control breakdown. Both statistical and nonstatistical sampling require similar qualitative analysis, but the two types of plans differ with respect to quantitative analysis.

Quantitative Analysis

For both types of sampling methodologies, the auditor must examine and classify each sample item as either having the attribute or as not having it. If the auditor cannot examine a sampling unit for some reason, the sample item should generally be considered as lacking the attribute of interest. The number of sample items lacking the attribute equals the number of occurrences. After the auditor has determined the number of occurrences in the sample, a sample rate of occurrence may be calculated. At this point, the remaining quantitative analysis procedures for the two sampling methodologies differ.

Statistical Samples

Based on sample results, statistical sampling provides for objective inferences about the population rate of occurrence. As pointed out in an earlier section of the chapter, the point estimate (sample rate of occurrence) is not a reliable indicator of the population rate of occurrence. An upper precision limit must be determined so that the auditor can state for a given confidence level that the population occurrence rate is no greater than the computed upper precision limit.

The auditor does not have to manipulate formulas or carry out mathematical calculations for sample evaluation because tables have been developed to determine the upper precision limit. Tables 5, 6, and 7 in the chapter appendix provide for "Evaluation of Results" at the 90, 95, and 99 percent confidence levels, respectively. Figures in the top row of the tables represent the computed upper precision limit while the left column indicates the sample size used in the statistical procedure. Cells in the matrix represent the *number* of occurrences found in the sample.

To illustrate the use of an evaluation table, assume a reliability level of 90 percent and a sample of 140 units with 6 sample items lacking the attribute of interest. In Table 5 find the sample size of 140 in the left column. Move horizontally in a straight line to the right until the number of occurrences, 6, is found. Then move vertically up the column to the top row of figures. In this case the figure 8 represents the computed upper precision limit of 8 percent. Consequently, the auditor is 90 percent confident that the population rate of occurrence is 8 percent or less.

The auditor should compare the computed upper precision limit (CUPL) with the tolerable rate of occurrence (TRO) to make a statistical decision as to control effectiveness. The decision would be based on the following criteria.

If	*Statistical Decision*
CUPL ≤ TRO	Control is effective
CUPL > TRO	Control is ineffective

In the example, if the TRO had been set at 7 percent or lower, the auditor would conclude statistically that the control is ineffective. If the TRO had been specified at 8 percent or above, statistically, the control would be considered effective.

If the statistical results indicate the control as ineffective, the auditor will probably not restrict related substantive testing. However, at this point the auditor will not know if a type one error occurred or whether the control is indeed ineffective as the statistical test indicates. To check for the possibility of a type one error, the auditor would have to expand the current attribute sampling by randomly selecting additional items. If the evaluation of the larger sample supports the previous statistical conclusion of an ineffective control, there is a high probability that a type one error did not occur and that substantive testing should not be restricted as planned. On the other hand, if the results of the larger sample indicate that the control is effective, the auditor may conclude that a type one error did occur with the smaller sample. The auditor can thus restrict substantive tests as planned.

The decision to expand the sample should be made on the basis of sampling costs for compliance testing and for substantive testing and the probability of a type one error. That is, if the auditor originally set the alpha risk level at a high level, say 20 or 30 percent, the auditor may want to lower the alpha risk level which will create a larger sample. Furthermore, the additional cost of increased compliance testing must be compared with the additional cost of increased substantive testing. The auditor must also consider that the expanded attribute sample may still support the results of the smaller sample indicating that a type one error did not occur and that substantive testing should not be restricted. If this situation occurs, no auditing efficiency is gained through further compliance testing. That is, if compliance testing is increased in these cases, there will be a high cost for compliance testing and a high cost for substantive testing.

A statistical decision based on the above criteria is quantitative in nature and by itself does not yield an audit decision. The auditor must also consider the results of the qualitative analysis in the decision to expand attribute sampling or to increase substantive testing. The results of the statistical decision should always be combined with the qualitative analysis to determine the impact upon remaining audit procedures.

Nonstatistical Samples

Nonstatistical sampling does not provide for objective inferences about the population rate of occurrence based on the sample rate of occurrence. Techniques used to evaluate statistical samples cannot be used with nonstatistical sampling because sample sizes are not statistically determined and the sample items may not have been randomly selected. The auditor must use professional judgment, based on a specified TRO and the sample rate of occurrence to decide whether the control is operating effectively or ineffectively. If the sample rate of occurrence is less than but very close to the TRO, the auditor may decide that there is an unacceptably high sampling risk that the true rate of occurrence is greater than the TRO. On the other hand, if the sample rate of occurrence is somewhat smaller than the TRO, the auditor may conclude that there is very little risk that the population rate of occurrence exceeds the TRO. For example, if one occurrence is found in a sample of 80 units (a sample rate of occurrence of 1¼ percent), the auditor may conclude that there is very little risk that the population rate of occurrence exceeds a TRO of 6 percent. Consequently, the auditor would accept the control as effective. However, if 4 occurrences are found in a sample of 80 units (a sample rate of occurrence of 5 percent), the auditor may decide that there is an unacceptably high sampling risk that the population occurrence rate is greater than a TRO of 6 percent. Therefore, the auditor would conclude that the control probably does not operate effectively.

If the control is considered effective, the auditor may rely on the control as planned. If the control is deemed ineffective, the auditor cannot rely on the control as planned and the extent of substantive testing will have to be increased over what was planned.

The type of decision referred to in the previous paragraph is quantitatively oriented and should be combined with the results of the qualitative analysis to form an audit decision. The final audit decision, which is based on both quantitative and qualitative analysis, will then modify, or not modify, the substantive audit procedures.

Qualitative Analysis

Qualitative analysis investigates the nature and cause of control breakdowns (occurrences in the sample) and their probable effect on financial data and statements. The auditor must be skeptical in attempting to determine whether control breakdowns result from intentional or unintentional behavior and whether the occurrences form a systematic pattern.

Unintentional behavior could indicate careless inattention to control duties, fatigue, or misunderstanding of instructions by employees. Intentional behavior could indicate fraud for personal gain or for company enhancement. Whether intentional or unintentional, the auditor should attempt to determine whether the control breakdown is an isolated incident or if there is evidence of a systematic pattern.

In addition to determining the nature and cause of control breakdowns, the auditor should identify the potential effects on financial data. For instance, he or she should consider the materiality of an isolated event. The auditor should also recognize that a systematic pattern of errors or irregularities, or a series of many small errors, may have a different effect, either larger or smaller, on the financial data than a series of a few large errors. Furthermore, the nature of the control also has a bearing on the potential effect. The failure of a credit manager to approve a sales order before shipment does not necessarily mean that the sale will be improperly recorded or that the account receivable will be uncollectible. However, a fraudulant act will have a direct impact on the financial statements.

Combining the results of the qualitative analysis with the quantitative conclusions, the auditor must determine the impact of controls upon remaining audit procedures. If the overall results of compliance testing indicate that internal controls are operating as designed, the auditor may place the degree of planned reliance on the controls and may restrict substantive tests as planned. If the overall compliance results show that controls are ineffective, the auditor may not place the planned reliance on the controls, and substantive tests must be extended. In addition, as indicated in Chapter 8, material weaknesses in internal accounting control must be communicated to senior management and the board of director or its audit committee.

If the qualitative investigation indicates control breakdowns due to intentional behavior, the auditor may extend the attribute sampling procedures just carried out, and/or modify remaining audit procedures. An extension or modification of audit procedures must be done in consideration of legal implications when it appears that control breakdowns are the result of intentional behavior. Legal implications and the auditor's responsibility for detecting fraud are discussed in Chapter 17.

Discovery sampling may be a useful technique in cases where the auditor suspects intentional control breakdown, and discovery sampling is discussed in the last section of this chapter.

DOCUMENTATION OF SAMPLING PROCEDURES AND EVALUATION

Audit working papers are an extremely important part of any audit. These papers document all steps and thought processes from the planning stages through the final drafting of the auditor's report. The area of attribute sampling is no exception. Whether a statistical or nonstatistical plan is used, the auditor must define all variables and document all factors considered in setting levels for the variables. Furthermore, the working papers must describe any problems encountered, statistical or otherwise, and indicate their resolution. In addition to complete documentation of the attribute sampling area, the auditor must cross-reference conclusions made in conjunction with compliance testing to those audit areas affected. In other words, the auditor should leave an "auditor's trail" in the audit working papers.

DISCOVERY SAMPLING

In some instances, an auditor may be working with sensitive areas such as unauthorized payroll disbursements. In these cases the auditor may want to determine a sample size necessary to reveal at least one occurrence in the sample *if* the population occurrence rate is equal to or greater than a specified critical rate of occurrence. Such a statistical sampling plan is called discovery sampling.

Discovery sampling is an extension of sampling for attributes where the expected rate of occurrence (ERO) in most cases is zero, and the tolerable rate of occurrence (TRO) is critical and thus small. The audit objective of discovery sampling, then, is to ensure that the auditor will find at least one incidence of an event if the population occurrence rate equals or exceeds the critical (TRO) rate. Discovery sampling tables have been developed to ascertain the necessary sample size to satisfy the audit objective. To use discovery sampling tables, the auditor must know the population size and specify the desired confidence level and the critical rate of occurrence. The confidence level is the probability of finding at least one occurrence in the sample.

To illustrate a discovery sampling plan, assume an auditor wants to be 90 percent confident of finding at least one example of an unauthorized payroll disbursement if the critical rate of occurrence is one percent or more. If 20,000 paychecks were prepared during the period, how many checks and related supporting documents will have to be examined to satisfy the audit objective? A discovery sampling table for populations in excess of 10,000 items is provided in Table 8 of the appendix. Critical rates of occurrence are reflected across the top of the table while the cells of the matrix reflect confidence levels. After locating the one percent critical rate of occurrence in the top row of the table, move vertically down the column until the desired confidence level is reached. When the desired confidence level falls between two cells, the higher confidence level should be selected for the statistical procedures. In this case a 91 percent confidence level should be used. Move horizontally to the left in a straight line to the column specifying the sample size. The sample size necessary to satisfy the audit objective is 240 items.

If *no* occurrence of an unauthorized payroll disbursement is found in the random sample of 240 items, the auditor may conclude at the desired reliability level that the population rate of occurrence does not exceed one percent. On the other hand, if one incidence of an unauthorized disbursement is discovered, the discovery sampling table *cannot* be used to formulate statistical conclusions. The discovery of one or more occurrences in the sample necessitates the use of attribute evaluation tables in the same manner discussed previously in this chapter. For example, suppose there is one unauthorized disbursement in the sample of 240 items. Using Table 5 for a 90 percent confidence level, the CUPL is determined to be two percent. Since the TRO is one percent, then TRO < CUPL. Consequently, the statistical test indicates an upper precision limit unacceptable to the auditor because the population rate of occurrence is greater than the critical rate of occurrence. The auditor must also make a thorough qualitative analysis of the exception to determine the effect on subsequent audit procedures.

In attribute sampling, auditors may use the discovery sampling table to make inferences about a population even though they do not use discovery sampling to determine sample size. For instance, if no occurrences are found in a sample of 120 units, the auditor may use the discovery sampling table (Table 8) to conclude with 91 percent confidence that the population rate of occurrence does not exceed two percent. To use the table for this purpose, find the sample size of 120 units in column one and then move horizontally to the right to the cell matrix representing a 91 percent confidence level. Continue moving vertically up this column to the top row reflecting two percent.

In addition to the statistical conclusion that the population rate of occurrence does not exceed two percent at the 91 percent reliability level, other statistical statements may be made by using other confidence levels in the row representing a 120 sample size. The auditor may also conclude with 70 percent confidence that the population occurrence rate does not exceed one percent. Or, with 45 percent confidence, the auditor may conclude that the rate does not exceed one-half percent.

Although the discovery sampling table may be used in this manner, students should remember that the audit objective of discovery sampling is to detect at least one occurrence of a specified event if the population occurrence rate is equal to or greater than a specified critical rate of occurrence.

SUMMARY

Attribute sampling consists of sampling plans to estimate the rate of noncompliance with prescribed internal accounting controls. Attributes are characteristics of control procedures upon which the auditor would like to rely. Before identifying attributes of interest, however, the auditor must define general and specific audit objectives. General audit objectives dictate the basic type of sampling plan necessary to attain specific audit objectives. Specific audit objectives help define appropriate attributes of control, and they also help identify populations from which evidence must be gathered for the basis of an audit conclusion.

Sampling must provide enough evidence upon which to base an opinion concerning an audit population. In other words, sampling relates to the sufficiency of evidence and not to the competency of evidential matter. The competency of individual items in the sample is not affected by the sampling methodology, plan, or sample size.

Regardless of the type of attribute sampling plan, auditors face two sampling risks: the risk of overreliance and the risk of underreliance. The risk of underreliance pertains to the efficiency of the sampling plan because the auditor must extend either compliance or substantive procedures if the statistical test indicates an ineffective control. If *extended compliance* procedures show that the control actually operates as designed, a type one error occurred with the smaller sample, and since the control is actually effective, substantive testing may be restricted as originally planned. If the *extended compliance* test supports the results of the smaller sample that the control is ineffective, substantive testing may not be restricted as planned. In this case there would be a high cost for compliance testing and for substantive testing.

A type two error is related to the risk of overreliance. The risk of overreliance pertains to the effectiveness of the sampling plan because the auditor will not know if a type two error occurs when statistical results indicate that a control is effective. If a type two error exists, reliance on the control under investigation is unwarranted.

Sampling risks, type one errors and type two errors, are inherent in statistical and nonstatistical sampling plans. In nonstatistical sampling plans, however, the risks and errors cannot be quantified. Both types of sampling plans are valuable auditing tools. Nonstatistical sampling is generally less complex and in some cases less costly than statistical sampling. Many benefits, however, are associated with statistical techniques. Under both methods it is necessary to define audit objectives and to identify populations and attributes of interest. The two methods differ in determining sample size. Nonstatistical sample sizes are subjectively determined, while statistical sampling provides for objectively determined sample sizes with randomly selected sample items.

All samples, whether statistical or nonstatistical, must be representative of the population being examined unless the sample is to serve a unique purpose. If samples are not representative, erroneous inferences could be made about the control under investigation. Although auditors should consider cost/benefit factors when deciding whether to use nonstatistical or statistical sampling, they should use statistical sampling for compliance testing where possible because of (1) the control that statistical techniques give over the risk of underreliance and overreliance, and (2) the objectivity of sample results.

When using statistical sampling, the auditor will judgmentally set levels for the confidence level, tolerable rate of occurrence (TRO), and the expected rate of occurrence (ERO). The confidence level is the probability that the true rate of ocurrence is equal to or smaller than the upper precision limit. Consequently, the confidence level and the precision limit are dependent on one another, and each must be defined in terms of the other. That is, the auditor may state with a given level of reliability that the population rate of occurrence is equal to or smaller than the upper precision limit. The specified confidence level also defines the alpha risk level since this sampling risk is the complement of the reliability level. When specifying the confidence level, the auditor should consider the degree of reliance to be placed on the internal control being examined. High reliance dictates a high confidence level. A high confidence level also yields a large sample size. The reverse situation is also true.

The TRO is the maximum rate of control noncompliance that could exist and still have the control considered effective. When setting the level for the TRO, the auditor should consider the potential impact of control breakdowns on financial data in relation to the degree of reliance planned for the control, and the likelihood that subsequent auditing procedures will detect a material misstatement of related financial data. The larger the potential impact of control breakdowns upon financial data and the less likely a subsequent auditing procedure would detect a material misstatement, the lower the TRO should be set. A low

TRO creates a large sample size, and vice versa.

The ERO is a necessary input for sample size determination. To estimate the ERO, the auditor may use the prior year's rate of occurrence adjusted for current changes in the internal control system, or the auditor may take a preliminary sample. In estimating the ERO, the auditor should consider that the larger the ERO, the larger the sample size.

Although statistical sample size determination is objective, the auditor must judgmentally set levels for sample size variables. However, setting levels for statistical variables is not arbitrary because the auditor must evaluate and consider factors which influence the sample size variables.

The auditor should also set specific levels for sample size variables when using a nonstatistical sampling plan. In this case, however, the variables do not fit into a mathematical framework which requires manipulation to arrive at a sample size. Nonstatistical sampling requires the auditor to assess factors that have a bearing on sample size and to combine these factors intuitively to identify sampling units to be selected from the population for investigation.

In nonstatistical sampling plans, sample items may be randomly selected or they may be chosen by any other selection method so long as the sample is representative of the population. On the other hand, it is important that sample items be randomly selected from a population for statistical sampling plans so that statistical conclusions have validity. Random numbers may be obtained from a random number table or from a random number generator in a computer program. The random numbers must correspond to document numbers on the sampling units in the population because each random number represents the number of a document to be included in the sample.

An alternative to random sampling, if the population is in random order, is systematic selection. In this approach, every k^{th} item is selected from the population. The interval k is found by dividing the population size by the sample size. Increases in the number of random starts improve the randomness of this approach. In the case of multiple random starts, the interval k must be multiplied by the number of random starts to provide the selection interval.

After selecting the sample items and investigating each unit, the sample must be evaluated quantitatively and qualitatively. For statistical sampling plans, the quantitative evaluation involves the comparison of the computed upper precision limit (CUPL) with the TRO. If the CUPL is less than or equal to the TRO, the auditor may statistically conclude that the control is effective. If the CUPL is greater than the TRO, the auditor should consider the control ineffective or expand compliance tests.

For nonstatistical samples, the quantitative evaluation involves the comparison of the sample rate of occurrence with the TRO. If the sample rate of occurrence is smaller but very close to the TRO, the auditor may decide that there is an unacceptably high sampling risk that the true population rate of occurrence is greater than the TRO. In this case, the auditor may conclude that the control is not operating as designed. On the other hand, if the sample rate of occurrence is much lower than the TRO, the auditor may decide that there is little risk that the true rate of occurrences exceeds the TRO, and therefore the control is operating effectively.

Qualitative evaluation of the sample is the same for statistical and nonstatistical sampling. Qualitative analysis investigates the nature and cause of control breakdowns and their probable effect on financial data. Using the qualitative evaluation in conjunction with the quantitative analysis, the auditor must determine the impact of controls upon remaining audit procedures. Substantive tests may be restricted as planned if the overall results of compliance testing indicate that controls are operating as designed. If the overall compliance results show that controls are ineffective, substantive tests may not be restricted as planned. In this case, substantive tests must be extended to gather sufficient competent evidence for a basis to form an opinion on the financial statements under audit.

CHAPTER APPENDIX

Table 1
Table of Random Digits

08149	14776	83594	25074	00184	83366	52998	42104	81540	11126
69393	16793	26625	03626	93300	21854	71725	18831	52906	60561
07127	28219	15917	42137	10713	95124	57960	05683	43756	05025
67448	61562	40266	23938	90957	52162	01177	90182	08454	96561
86214	53821	81970	23142	42933	93478	30378	18495	48373	97689
21568	19342	07821	29941	84094	38074	22429	67170	41001	57467
80376	95821	97763	91328	25063	02004	71503	82970	61669	28335
04265	23100	73964	45774	15753	31831	59817	20633	92268	82581
52382	67432	94394	67879	11303	41356	96669	46031	80327	98777
41948	99708	55353	81160	43200	48243	37044	46103	65464	21671
09201	35481	83003	23514	02844	78075	65420	67535	32447	34575
12379	36696	08556	03309	21587	07065	87588	07954	46624	39729
96328	82959	31874	87005	08728	91636	18986	98453	18663	10773
33004	64495	76596	87233	49788	45582	95749	84642	89299	92760
56796	12936	76308	03529	33361	43442	11350	59165	70198	88570
20887	43157	74092	19950	81312	82117	80948	49051	78442	26003
58773	50675	68623	36991	65293	52509	22069	33326	33164	24959
17542	12554	64286	76034	90353	04714	13614	11349	92165	99212
95002	30153	31722	66744	63397	41530	81338	67986	51478	98720
57807	77433	65367	64861	36395	45595	17574	48568	73159	36830
78394	97930	72476	81628	66801	06838	53938	02116	31290	35484
36010	00874	61554	03930	76813	04110	80237	56992	58885	82395
35736	49271	60789	09339	34868	09009	72530	18735	64332	03697
25323	56652	55557	19128	99012	68240	74399	63812	57213	17417
85278	21251	40588	02478	56420	99299	28412	83989	89082	83173
86114	58859	90474	81029	52698	06727	13753	62728	72986	64711
67430	57097	39476	53242	22233	20613	25136	09443	83084	22925
06964	90193	70344	46617	88997	39555	76652	34255	82586	04720
89983	59718	33004	19795	83779	90326	90185	18240	11673	70968
60718	30714	47309	25051	18095	28725	08346	98810	02209	58208
74024	90794	99100	24031	69005	12944	67732	22424	29221	79654
37033	17764	59482	12790	95015	27273	65531	20187	60790	57358
49246	59630	43635	02931	95923	14749	02529	02694	79631	97723
52978	20248	07296	53257	55027	21790	75655	87355	23715	05433
31425	39865	60729	70449	43054	85834	73832	52815	37998	25696
04402	26377	19057	86671	58288	31367	95663	70948	82881	42306
45389	43993	28279	14144	61256	47718	19017	24024	51852	85436
74187	62120	63159	75454	29647	59915	74184	47261	46941	61024
65624	31299	53494	35822	54612	25054	27475	89887	07347	55895
58428	17582	18339	13867	98191	21556	34049	42139	29373	33628
50626	40047	41078	65809	93332	05759	36533	76154	53981	96183
35706	97649	32802	26107	01466	83932	75217	07618	63642	74751
87633	10424	93235	65113	11385	23673	48544	98040	54496	92004
83126	63377	81018	51621	98097	95515	36879	15966	06685	40393
70090	05750	43225	63728	66615	68807	22251	60175	22681	73598
17382	39493	85125	52023	41381	72824	76163	52644	55398	81201
22214	57511	99807	64671	50244	12345	99347	21606	31123	72781
51139	50509	66346	75458	80228	47405	37597	T2683	74525	71035
18864	71938	84707	81152	27322	80417	10993	52930	68340	51329
40108	66030	03600	77583	27036	94382	10674	09531	11786	90382

Source: The Rand Corporation. *A Million Random Digits with 100,000 Normal Deviates* (Glencoe: The Free Press, 1955), p. 391.

Table 2
Determination of Sample Size
Reliability = 90%

UPPER PRECISION LIMIT: PERCENT RATE OF OCCURRENCE

EXPECTED PERCENT RATE OF OCCURRENCE	1	2	3	4	5	6	7	8	9	10	12	14	16	18	20	25	30	35	40	45	50
0.25	400	200	140	100	80	70	60	50	50	40	40	30	30	20	20	20	20	10	10	10	10
0.50	800	200	140	100	80	70	60	50	50	40	40	30	30	30	20	20	20	10	10	10	10
1.0		400	180	100	80	70	60	50	50	40	40	30	30	30	20	20	20	10	10	10	10
1.5			320	180	120	90	60	50	50	40	40	30	30	30	20	20	20	10	10	10	10
2.0		*	600	200	140	90	80	50	50	40	40	30	30	30	20	20	20	10	10	10	10
2.5			*	360	160	120	80	70	60	40	40	30	30	30	20	20	20	10	10	10	10
3.0				800	260	160	100	90	60	60	50	30	30	30	20	20	20	10	10	10	10
3.5				*	400	200	140	100	80	70	50	40	40	30	20	20	20	10	10	10	10
4.0					900	300	200	100	90	70	50	40	40	30	20	20	20	10	10	10	10
4.5					*	550	220	160	120	80	60	40	40	30	20	20	20	10	10	10	10
5.0						*	320	160	120	80	60	40	40	30	20	20	20	10	10	10	10
5.5						*	600	280	160	120	70	50	40	30	30	20	20	10	10	10	10
6.0							*	380	200	160	80	50	40	30	30	20	20	10	10	10	10
6.5							*	600	260	180	90	60	40	30	30	20	20	10	10	10	10
7.0								*	400	200	100	70	40	40	40	20	20	10	10	10	10
7.5								*	800	280	120	80	40	40	40	20	20	10	10	10	10
8.0									*	460	160	100	50	50	40	20	20	10	10	10	10
8.5									*	800	200	100	70	50	40	20	20	10	10	10	10
9.0										*	260	100	80	50	40	20	20	10	10	10	10
9.5										*	380	160	80	50	40	20	20	10	10	10	10
10.0											500	160	80	50	40	20	20	10	10	10	10
11.0											*	280	140	70	60	30	30	20	20	10	10
12.0												550	180	90	70	30	30	20	20	10	10
13.0												*	300	160	90	30	30	20	20	10	10
14.0													600	200	100	40	30	20	20	10	10
15.0													*	300	140	40	30	20	20	10	10
16.0														650	200	50	30	30	20	10	10
17.0														*	340	70	40	30	20	20	10
18.0															700	100	50	30	20	10	10
19.0															*	100	50	30	20	10	10
20.0																160	50	30	20	10	10
22.0																400	80	40	30	20	20
24.0																*	120	50	30	20	20
26.0																	260	80	30	30	20
28.0																	1000	100	50	30	20
30.0																		180	50	30	20
33.0																		1000	100	50	30
36.0																			280	80	40
39.0																			*	160	60
42.0																				500	90
46.0																					300

NOTE: * = more than 1000

Source: Ernst & Whinney, *Audit Sampling*, 1979.

Table 3
Determination of Sample Size
Reliability = 95%

UPPER PRECISION LIMIT: PERCENT RATE OF OCCURRENCE

EXPECTED PERCENT RATE OF OCCURRENCE	1	2	3	4	5	6	7	8	9	10	12	14	16	18	20	25	30	35	40	45	50
0.25	650	240	160	120	100	80	70	60	60	50	40	40	30	30	30	20	20	20	10	10	10
0.50	*	320	160	120	100	80	70	60	60	50	40	40	30	30	30	20	20	20	10	10	10
1.0		600	260	160	100	80	70	60	60	50	40	40	30	30	30	20	20	20	10	10	10
1.5		*	400	200	160	120	90	60	60	50	40	40	30	30	30	20	20	20	10	10	10
2.0			900	300	200	140	90	80	70	50	40	40	40	30	30	20	20	20	10	10	10
2.5			*	550	240	160	120	90	70	70	40	40	30	30	30	20	20	20	10	10	10
3.0				*	400	200	160	100	90	90	60	50	30	30	30	20	20	20	10	10	10
3.5				*	650	280	200	140	100	80	70	50	40	40	30	20	20	20	10	10	10
4.0					*	500	240	180	100	90	70	50	40	40	30	20	20	20	10	10	10
4.5					*	800	360	200	160	120	80	50	40	40	30	20	20	20	10	10	10
5.0						*	500	240	150	120	90	60	40	40	30	20	20	20	10	10	10
5.5						*	900	360	200	160	90	70	50	50	30	30	20	20	10	10	10
6.0							*	550	280	180	100	80	50	50	30	30	20	20	10	10	10
6.5							*	1000	400	240	120	90	60	50	30	30	20	20	10	10	10
7.0								*	600	300	140	100	70	50	40	30	20	20	10	10	10
7.5								*	*	460	160	100	80	50	40	30	20	20	10	10	10
8.0									*	650	200	100	80	50	50	30	20	20	10	10	10
8.5									*	*	280	140	80	70	50	30	20	20	10	10	10
9.0										*	400	180	100	70	50	30	20	20	10	10	10
9.5										*	550	200	120	70	50	30	20	20	10	10	10
10.0											800	220	120	70	50	30	20	20	10	10	10
11.0											*	400	180	100	70	40	30	20	20	20	20
12.0												900	280	140	90	40	30	20	20	20	20
13.0												*	460	200	100	50	30	20	20	20	20
14.0													1000	300	160	50	40	20	20	20	20
15.0													*	500	200	60	40	20	20	20	20
16.0														*	300	80	50	30	30	20	20
17.0														*	550	100	50	40	30	20	20
18.0															*	140	50	40	30	20	20
19.0															*	180	70	40	30	20	20
20.0																220	70	40	30	20	20
22.0																600	100	50	30	30	20
24.0																*	200	70	40	30	20
25.0																	400	100	50	30	30
28.0																	*	160	60	40	30
30.0																		280	80	40	30
33.0																		*	160	60	30
36.0																			460	100	50
39.0																			*	220	80
42.0																				800	140
46.0																					550

NOTE: * = more than 1000

Source: Ernst & Whinney, *Audit Sampling*, 1979.

Table 4
Determination of Sample Size
Reliability = 99%

UPPER PRECISION LIMIT: PERCENT RATE OF OCCURRENCE

EXPECTED PERCENT RATE OF OCCURRENCE	1	2	3	4	5	6	7	8	9	10	12	14	16	18	20	25	30	35	40	45	50
0.25	*	340	240	180	140	120	100	90	80	70	60	50	40	40	40	30	20	20	20	20	20
0.50	*	500	280	180	140	120	100	90	80	70	60	50	40	40	40	30	20	20	20	20	20
1.0		*	400	260	180	140	100	90	80	70	60	50	40	40	40	30	20	20	20	20	20
1.5		*	800	360	200	180	120	120	100	90	60	50	40	40	40	30	20	20	20	20	20
2.0			*	500	300	200	140	140	100	90	70	50	40	40	40	30	20	20	20	20	20
2.5			*	1000	400	240	200	160	120	100	70	60	40	40	40	30	20	20	20	20	20
3.0				*	700	360	260	160	160	100	90	60	50	50	40	30	20	20	20	20	20
3.5				*	*	550	340	200	160	140	100	70	50	50	40	40	20	20	20	20	20
4.0					*	800	400	280	200	160	100	70	50	50	40	40	20	20	20	20	20
4.5					*	*	600	380	220	200	120	80	60	60	40	40	20	20	20	20	20
5.0						*	900	460	280	200	120	80	60	60	40	40	20	20	20	20	20
5.5						*	*	650	380	280	160	90	70	70	50	40	30	30	20	20	20
6.0						*	1000	500	300	180	100	80	70	50	40	30	30	20	20	20	20
6.5							*	*	800	400	240	120	90	70	60	40	30	30	20	20	20
7.0							*	*	600	240	140	100	70	70	40	30	30	20	20	20	20
7.5									*	800	280	160	120	80	70	40	30	30	20	20	20
8.0									*	*	400	200	140	100	70	50	30	30	20	20	20
8.5									*	*	500	240	140	100	70	50	30	30	20	20	20
9.0										*	700	300	180	100	90	50	30	30	20	20	20
9.5										*	1000	360	200	140	90	50	30	30	20	20	20
10.0											*	420	220	140	90	50	30	30	20	20	20
11.0											*	800	300	180	140	60	40	30	30	20	20
12.0												*	500	240	160	70	40	30	30	20	20
13.0												*	600	360	200	90	50	30	30	20	20
14.0													*	500	280	100	50	40	30	20	20
15.0													*	900	360	120	60	40	30	20	20
16.0														*	550	160	80	40	30	30	20
17.0														*	1000	180	80	40	40	30	20
18.0															*	240	100	50	40	30	20
19.0															*	300	100	60	40	30	20
20.0																420	120	60	40	30	20
22.0																*	200	90	50	40	30
24.0																*	340	120	70	40	30
26.0																	800	180	80	50	30
28.0																	*	280	100	60	40
30.0																		550	140	70	40
33.0																		*	300	100	60
36.0																			900	180	80
39.0																			*	400	140
42.0																				*	240
46.0																					900

NOTE: * = more than 1000

Source: Ernst & Whinney, *Audit Sampling*, 1979.

Table 5
Evaluation of Results
Reliability = 90%
Number of Observed Occurrences

UPPER PRECISION LIMIT: PERCENT RATE OF OCCURRENCE

SAMPLE SIZE	1	2	3	4	5	6	7	8	9	10	12	14	16	18	20	25	30	35	40	45	50
10																0		1		2	
20											0				1	2		3	4	5	6
30								0				1			2	4	6		8	9	10
40						0				1	2	3			4	6	7	9	11	13	15
50					0				1		2	3	4	5		8	10	12	15	17	19
60								0	1	2	3	4	5	6	7	10	13	15	18	21	24
70							0	1	2	3	4	5	6	8	9	12	15	18	22	25	29
80						0	1	2	3	4	5	6	8	9	10	14	18	22	25	29	33
90					0	1	2	3	4	5	6	7	9	11	12	16	20	25	29	33	38
100				0	1	2	3	4	5	6	7	9	10	12	14	19	23	28	33	38	43
120			0	1	2	3	4	5	6	7	9	11	13	15	17	23	29	34	40	46	52
140		0	1	2	3	4	5	6	7	9	11	13	16	18	21	27	34	41	48	54	61
160		0	1	2	4	5	6	8	9	10	13	16	19	22	25	32	40	47	55	63	71
180		0	2	3	4	6	7	9	10	12	15	18	22	25	28	37	45	54	63	71	80
200		1	2	4	5	7	8	10	12	14	17	21	24	28	32	41	51	60	70	80	90
220		1	2	4	6	8	10	12	13	15	19	23	27	31	35	46	56	67	78	89	99
240	0	1	3	5	7	9	11	13	15	17	21	26	30	35	39	50	62	74	85	97	109
260	0	1	3	5	8	10	12	14	17	19	24	28	33	38	43	55	68	80	93	106	119
280	0	2	4	6	8	11	13	16	18	21	26	31	36	41	46	60	73	87	101	114	128
300	0	2	4	7	9	12	14	17	20	22	28	33	39	45	50	64	79	93	108	123	138
320	0	2	5	7	10	13	16	18	21	24	30	36	42	48	54	69	85	100	116	132	148
340	0	3	5	8	11	14	17	20	23	26	32	38	45	51	58	74	90	107	123	140	157
360	0	3	6	9	12	15	18	21	25	28	34	41	48	55	61	79	96	113	131	149	167
380	0	3	6	9	13	16	19	23	26	30	37	44	51	58	65	83	102	120	139	158	177
400	1	4	7	10	14	17	21	24	28	31	39	46	54	61	69	88	107	127	146	166	186
420	1	4	7	11	14	18	22	26	29	33	41	49	57	65	73	93	113	134	154	175	196
460	1	4	8	12	16	20	24	28	33	37	45	54	63	71	80	102	124	147	170	192	215
500	1	5	9	13	18	22	27	31	36	40	50	59	69	78	88	112	136	160	185	210	235
550	2	6	10	15	20	25	30	35	40	45	55	66	76	87	97	124	150	177	204	232	259
600	2	7	12	17	22	28	33	39	44	50	61	72	84	95	107	135	165	194	224	253	283
650	2	8	13	19	24	30	36	42	48	54	66	79	91	104	116	147	179	211	243	275	308
700	3	8	14	20	27	33	39	46	52	59	72	85	99	112	126	159	194	228	262	297	332
800	4	10	17	24	31	38	46	53	61	68	83	99	114	129	145	183	222	262	301	341	381
900	4	12	20	28	36	44	52	61	69	78	95	112	129	146	164	207	251	296	340	385	430
1000	5	13	22	31	40	49	59	68	77	87	106	125	144	164	183	232	280	330	379	429	479

Source: Ernst & Whinney, *Audit Sampling*, 1979.

Table 6
Evaluation of Results
Reliability = 95%
Number of Observed Occurrences

SAMPLE SIZE	UPPER PRECISION LIMIT: PERCENT RATE OF OCCURRENCE

SAMPLE SIZE	1	2	3	4	5	6	7	8	9	10	12	14	16	18	20	25	30	35	40	45	50
10																0		1			
20												0				1	2	3		4	5
30									0				1			2	3	4	5	8	10
40							0				1		2		3	5	6	8	10	12	14
50					0					1		2	3	4	5	7	9	11	13	16	18
60				0					1		2	3	4	5	6	9	11	14	17	20	23
70				0			1		2		3	4	5	7	8	11	14	17	20	24	27
80			0		1			2		3	4	5	7	8	9	13	16	20	24	28	32
90			0		1	2			3	4	5	6	8	9	11	15	19	23	27	32	36
100		0		1			2	3	4		6	8	9	11	13	17	22	26	31	36	41
120			0	1	2	3	4	5	6		8	10	12	14	16	21	27	33	38	44	50
140			0	1	2	3	4	5	6	7	10	12	14	17	19	26	32	39	46	52	59
160		0	1	2	3	4	5	6	8	9	12	14	17	20	23	30	38	45	53	61	69
180		0	1	2	3	5	6	8	9	11	14	17	20	23	26	35	43	52	60	69	78
200		0	1	3	4	6	7	9	11	12	16	19	23	26	30	39	48	58	68	77	87
220		0	2	3	5	7	8	10	12	14	18	22	25	29	33	44	54	64	75	86	97
240		1	2	4	6	8	10	12	14	16	20	24	28	33	37	48	59	71	83	94	106
260		1	3	4	7	9	11	13	15	17	22	26	31	36	41	53	65	77	90	103	116
280		1	3	5	7	10	12	14	17	19	24	29	34	39	44	57	71	84	98	111	125
300	0	1	3	6	8	11	13	16	18	21	26	31	37	42	48	62	76	91	105	120	135
320	0	2	4	6	9	11	14	17	20	22	28	34	40	45	51	66	82	97	113	128	144
340	0	2	4	7	10	12	15	18	21	24	30	36	42	49	55	71	87	104	120	137	154
360	0	2	5	8	10	13	17	20	23	26	32	39	45	52	59	76	93	110	128	146	163
380	0	2	5	8	11	14	18	21	24	28	34	41	48	55	62	80	98	117	135	154	173
400	0	3	6	9	12	15	19	22	26	29	37	44	51	59	66	85	104	123	143	163	183
420	0	3	6	9	13	16	20	24	27	31	39	46	54	62	70	90	110	130	151	171	192
460	0	4	7	11	15	18	22	26	31	35	43	51	60	68	77	99	121	143	166	188	211
500	1	4	8	12	16	21	25	29	34	38	47	56	66	75	84	108	132	157	181	197	221
550	1	5	9	14	18	23	28	33	38	43	53	63	73	83	94	120	146	173	200	227	255
600	1	6	10	15	20	26	31	36	42	47	58	69	80	92	103	132	161	190	219	249	279
650	2	6	12	17	23	28	34	40	46	52	64	76	88	100	112	143	175	207	239	271	303
700	2	7	13	19	25	31	37	43	50	56	69	82	95	108	122	155	189	223	258	292	327
800	3	9	15	22	29	36	43	51	58	65	80	95	110	125	141	179	218	257	296	336	376
900	4	10	18	26	34	42	50	58	66	74	91	108	125	142	159	203	247	291	335	379	424
1000	4	12	20	29	38	47	56	65	74	84	102	121	140	159	178	227	275	324	374	423	473

Source: Ernst & Whinney, *Audit Sampling*, 1979.

Table 7
Evaluation of Results
Reliability = 99%
Number of Observed Occurrences

SAMPLE SIZE	UPPER PRECISION LIMIT: PERCENT RATE OF OCCURRENCES																				
	1	2	3	4	5	6	7	8	9	10	12	14	16	18	20	25	30	35	40	45	50
10																			0		
20																0	1		2	3	4
30													0			1	3	4	5	6	8
40											0		1		2	3	5	7	8	10	12
50									0			1	2		3	5	7	9	11	13	16
60											0	1	2	3	4	7	9	12	14	17	20
70									0	1	2	3	4	5	6	9	11	14	18	21	24
80									0	1	2	4	5	6	7	10	14	17	21	25	29
90								0	1	2	3	5	6	7	9	12	16	20	24	29	33
100							0	1	2	3	4	6	7	9	10	14	19	23	28	33	37
120						0	1	2	3	4	6	8	9	11	13	18	24	29	35	40	46
140					0	1	2	3	4	5	7	10	12	14	16	22	29	35	42	48	55
160				0	1	2	3	5	6	7	9	12	14	17	20	27	34	41	49	56	64
180			0	1	2	3	4	6	7	8	11	14	17	20	23	31	39	47	56	65	73
200			0	1	3	4	5	7	8	10	13	16	19	23	26	35	44	54	63	73	83
220			0	2	3	5	6	8	10	11	15	18	22	26	30	39	50	60	70	81	92
240		0	1	2	4	6	7	9	11	13	17	21	25	29	33	44	55	66	78	89	101
260		0	1	3	5	6	8	10	12	14	19	23	27	32	36	48	60	72	85	97	110
280		0	2	3	4	7	9	12	14	16	21	25	30	35	40	53	65	79	92	106	120
300		0	2	4	6	8	10	13	15	18	23	28	33	38	43	57	71	85	99	114	129
320		0	2	4	7	9	11	14	17	19	24	30	35	41	47	61	76	91	107	122	138
340		1	3	5	7	10	13	15	18	21	26	32	38	44	50	66	82	98	114	131	148
360		1	3	6	8	11	14	16	19	22	28	35	41	47	54	70	87	104	122	139	157
380		1	3	6	9	12	15	18	21	24	30	37	44	50	57	75	93	111	129	148	166
400		1	4	7	10	13	16	19	22	26	32	39	46	54	61	79	98	117	136	156	176
420		2	4	7	10	14	17	20	24	27	35	42	49	57	64	84	103	124	144	164	185
460	0	2	5	8	12	15	19	23	27	31	39	47	55	63	72	93	114	136	159	181	204
500	0	3	6	10	13	17	21	26	30	34	43	52	60	70	79	102	125	149	174	198	223
550	0	3	7	11	15	20	24	29	34	38	48	58	68	78	88	113	139	166	192	219	247
600	0	4	8	13	17	22	27	32	37	43	53	64	78	86	97	125	153	182	211	241	271
650	0	4	9	14	19	25	30	36	41	47	58	70	82	94	106	136	167	198	230	262	294
700	1	5	10	16	21	27	33	39	45	51	64	76	89	102	115	148	181	215	249	283	318
800	1	7	13	19	25	32	39	46	53	60	74	89	103	118	133	171	209	248	287	326	366
900	2	8	15	22	29	37	45	53	61	69	85	101	118	135	152	194	237	281	325	369	414
1000	2	9	17	25	34	42	51	60	69	78	96	114	133	151	170	218	266	314	363	412	462

Source: Ernst & Whinney, *Audit Sampling*, 1979.

Table 8
Discovery Sampling Table
(Probability in Percent of Including at
Least One Occurrence in a Sample)
For Populations Over 10,000

Upper Precision Limit: Critical Rate of Occurrence

Sample Size	.01%	.05%	.1%	.2%	.3%	.5%	1%	2%
50		2%	5%	9%	14%	22%	39%	64%
60	1%	3	6	11	16	26	45	70
70	1	3	7	13	19	30	51	76
80	1	4	8	15	21	33	55	80
90	1	4	9	16	24	36	60	84
100	1	5	10	18	26	39	63	87
120	1	6	11	21	30	45	70	91
140	1	7	13	24	34	50	76	94
160	2	8	15	27	38	55	80	96
200	2	10	18	33	45	63	87	98
240	2	11	21	38	51	70	91	99
300	3	14	26	45	59	78	95	99+
340	3	16	29	49	64	82	97	99+
400	4	18	33	55	70	87	98	99+
460	5	21	37	60	75	90	99	99+
500	5	22	39	63	78	92	99	99+
600	6	26	45	70	84	95	99+	99+
700	7	30	50	75	88	97	99+	99+
800	8	33	55	80	91	98	99+	99+
900	9	36	59	83	93	99	99+	99+
1,000	10	39	63	86	95	99	99+	99+
1,500	14	53	78	95	99	99+	99+	99+
2,000	18	63	86	98	99+	99+	99+	99+
2,500	22	71	92	99	99+	99+	99+	99+
3,000	26	78	95	99+	99+	99+	99+	99+

Source: Ernst & Whinney, *Audit Sampling*, 1979.

REVIEW QUESTIONS

9-1   What is the purpose of attribute sampling?

9-2   Discuss the importance of defining audit objectives before identifying attributes of interest and the related audit population.

9-3   Explain the relationship between sampling and the third standard of field work. Does sampling provide sufficient competent evidence upon which an audit decision may be based?

9-4   The sampling risks of overreliance and underreliance are inherent in any sampling plan or methodology. What is the risk of overreliance? The risk of underreliance?

9-5   Explain the two basic types of nonsampling risks. How are nonsampling risks controlled?

9-6   Why should all samples be representative of the audit population? What is meant by a representative sample?

9-7   Discuss the advantages and disadvantages of block sampling when using the nonstatistical methodology.

9-8   Discuss the advantages and disadvantages of statistical sampling.

9-9   Discuss the relationship between a sample rate of occurrence and its standard error.

9-10   Discuss the relationship between the confidence level and the upper precision limit when considering a one-sided statistical test.

9-11   Explain the relationship between the confidence level and the alpha risk level.

9-12   Discuss how the degree of planned reliance on internal control affects the level of confidence specified by the auditor.

9-13   Define the tolerable rate of occurrence (TRO).

9-14   What factors must be considered by the auditor when specifying the TRO?

9-15   State the effect on sample size when each of the following sample size determinant is *increased* and all other variables are held constant.

a. Confidence level.
b. Tolerable rate of occurrence (TRO).
c. Expected rate of occurrence (ERO).
d. Distance between TRO and ERO.

9-16 Why should auditors use sampling without replacement?

9-17 Random selection of sampling units from an audit population is an important concept in statistical sampling. What is meant by random selection?

9-18 Describe systematic sampling.

9-19 Under what condition does systematic sampling approximate random selection? When this condition exists, how may randomness be improved?

9-20 Distinguish between quantitative and qualitative analyses of samples and state the importance of each.

9-21 Distinguish between the tolerable rate of occurrence and the upper precision limit.

9-22 Discuss the alternative procedures the auditor could pursue if the quantitative analysis of a sample indicates that a control is ineffective. How does the cost of sampling influence the auditor's decision as to which course of action should be taken?

9-23 Assume that quantitative and qualitative analyses do not support the degree of planned reliance on an internal control under investigation. How will the results of these analyses affect the substantive tests associated with the control?

9-24 What is the objective of discovery sampling? Under what circumstances would the auditor want to use discovery sampling?

DISCUSSION QUESTIONS AND PROBLEMS

9-25 Sam Smart, a recent accounting graduate from Illinois Tech, wanted to impress his new boss, Patsy Perfect, CPA, with his newly acquired statistical skills. While on his new assignment to compliance test transaction details, Sam decided to select a random sample of shipping documents. The shipping documents were to be investigated for proper credit approval of the customer before shipment was made. He thought that in the circumstances a tolerable rate of occurrence of 9 percent and a confidence level of 95 percent would be appropriate. Patsy told Sam that last year's working paper showed that 5 percent of the shipping documents examined lacked proper credit approval. Sam determined that a sample of 280 shipping documents would provide sufficient evidence for a statistical decision on control effectiveness. After randomly selecting 280 items, Sam proceeded to investigate the documents for proper credit approval.

Required:

a.   Compute a statistical sample size for Sam's sampling plan.
b.   What are three probable explanations for the error in Sam's sample size? Be specific indicating values that Sam might have used for statistical variables in determining the 280 sample size.
c.   Discuss the adequacy of Sam's sample size in relation to your computed sample size. Will Sam's larger sample size have an effect on (1) the statistical results, or (2) on auditing fees?

9-26   Based on the information in question 9-25, it is quite evident to Patsy Perfect, CPA, that Sam Smart, new staff auditor, needed help in determining sample sizes. She decided to have an in-house training session on statistical sampling techniques for entry-level personnel. Patsy was very thorough in her explanation of sample size determinants for statistical samples. Sam memorized that higher confidence levels, larger EROs, and larger populations called for larger sample sizes while higher TROs created smaller samples. When Patsy gave a quiz on sample size determination, Sam could not properly relate what he had memorized to quiz questions. Sam missed 83% of the questions on the quiz. Patsy has asked you to go over the quiz with Sam indicating the correct answers and explaining in detail why your answers are correct. Sam's answers are underlined in the quiz.

Quiz

Case	Population 1 Relative to Population 2		Specified Statistical Variables for Population 1 Relative to Population 2		Sample Size for Population 1 Relative to
	Size	**ERO**	**TRO**	**Confidence Level**	**Population 2**
1	Equal	Smaller	Equal	Equal	*Larger*
2	Equal	Equal	Smaller	Equal	*Smaller*
3	Equal	Equal	Equal	Lower	*Smaller*
4	Larger	Smaller	Equal	Higher	*Larger*
5	Equal	Equal	Larger	Higher	*Larger*
6	Equal	Larger	Smaller	Higher	*Indeterminable*

Required:

Correct Sam's answers in each case, if necessary, for the relative sample size of population 1 compared to population 2. Answers should indicate whether the sample size for population 1 should be larger than, equal to, or smaller than the sample size for population 2, or if the answer is indeterminable.

9-27   Sam Smart, the recent graduate in accounting from Illinois Tech, continues to bungle audit jobs. His employer, Patsy Perfect, CPA, has agreed to give him a last chance to prove himself capable of carrying out an attribute sampling plan. Patsy assigned Sam the job of investigating controls over the authorization of cash disbursements. Sam decided he would randomly sample the disbursement vouchers and investigate the rate of occurrence for disbursements that were not properly supported by purchase orders and receiving reports.

In looking over last year's working papers, Sam noticed that 3% of the vouchers did not have proper supporting documents. Given favorable changes in systems personnel, Sam thought a TRO equal to 7% would be appropriate while specifying a 90 percent confidence level. Sam computed the sample size and randomly selected the vouchers for examination. Since 5 vouchers were found without supporting documentation, Sam concluded that the control requiring supporting documentation for each cash disbursement was effective.

Required:

a.   How many vouchers should Sam examine to satisfy the sampling plan?
b.   Was Sam's statistical conclusion satisfactory? If not, state the statistical conclusion that Sam should have documented in the working papers.
c.   If sample results indicate an ineffective control, describe the alternative courses of action that Sam should consider in light of the statistical conclusion.

9-28   In a nonstratified sampling plan, 80 bills of lading are to be selected from a population of 3,200 documents. The documents are in random order although the bills of lading are numbered consecutively from 5420 to 8619. The bills of lading have been stored in 80 binders of 40 documents each.

Required:

a.   Using the random number table in the chapter appendix and starting with row 32, column 22, and moving down the column, select the first 5 random numbers which correspond to the bills of lading that would be used in the sample of 80 units.

b.   Assuming that one bill of lading would be randomly selected from each binder, describe how the first 3 random bills of lading would be selected for the sample of 80 units.

c.   Using the systematic selection technique to simulate random sampling, describe the process of using 2 random starts within the first selection interval.

9-29   There are 9 different situations given below. The first 3 situations illustrate the effect of changing the confidence level on the computed upper precision limit (CUPL) while holding the sample size and tolerable rate of occurrence (TRO) constant. The next 3 situations point out the effect of changing the sample size on the CUPL while holding the other given factors constant. The last 3 situations illustrate the effect of changing the TRO upon the CUPL while holding the confidence level and sample size constant.

a.   Compute the CUPL for each situation given below. Then, discuss the effect of changing the confidence level upon the CUPL. What are the implications of this effect on the statistical decision concerning the effectiveness of the control under investigation?

	(1)	(2)	(3)
Confidence level..........	90%	95%	99%
TRO....................	7%	7%	7%
Sample size..............	200	200	200
Rate of sample exceptions...	3.5%	3.5%	3.5%
CUPL	_____	_____	_____

b.   Compute the CUPL for each situation given below. Discuss the effect on the CUPL of increasing the sample size. What are the implications of this effect on the statistical decision to rely on the internal control as planned?

	(4)	(5)	(6)
Confidence level..........	95%	95%	95%
TRO....................	10%	10%	10%
Sample size..............	100	200	400
Rate of sample exceptions...	6%	6%	6%
CUPL	_____	_____	_____

c.   Compute the CUPL for the following situations. Then discuss the effect on the CUPL of increasing the TRO and the difference in the statistical decision for each situation given.

	(7)	(8)	(9)
Confidence level	95%	95%	95%
TRO	3%	6%	9%
Sample size	160	160	160
Rate of sample exceptions	2.5%	2.5%	2.5%
CUPL	___	___	___

9-30   The following is an exercise in using the discovery sampling table.

a.   Assume populations in excess of 10,000 units for each situation given. Fill in the missing data.

Situation	Critical Rate of Occurrence	Desired Confidence Level	Sample Size
(1)	.1%	95%	—
(2)	.5%	95%	—
(3)	1.0%	95%	—
(4)	.5%	—	800
(5)	1.0%	—	460
(6)	2.0%	—	160
(7)	—	91%	120
(8)	—	98%	400
(9)	—	97%	700

b.   Based on situations 1, 2, and 3 above, what is the impact upon sample size when the critical rate of occurrence is increased and the desired confidence level is held constant?

9-31   Patsy Perfect, CPA, sent Sam Smart on a sensitive assignment. Patsy did not think Sam would bungle this job because she documented every audit and statistical procedure in detail on the audit program.

The client, Neatless Bookkeeping Forms, Inc., appeared to have potential problems in the area of cash disbursements. Mr. Wise, Chairman of the Audit Committee, had told Patsy that Mr. Katchem, Director of Internal Auditing, was suspicious of the newly hired cashier, Mr. Sly. Mr. Wise asked Patsy if her firm would handle a special assignment to investigate cash disbursements. Patsy accepted the assignment after Mr. Wise signed the engagement letter which she had prepared.

Patsy's audit program stated that one specific audit objective was to determine that cash disbursements had proper supporting documentation authorizing each disbursement. The program specified that the population should consist of all cancelled checks of Neatless from the beginning of Mr. Sly's employment as cashier five months ago to the end of the prior month. Patsy's program included a discovery sampling plan which specified a critical rate of .5 percent and a reliability level of 99 percent.

With the audit program locked in his briefcase, Sam Smart began the assignment with enthusiasm because this was his big chance to prove that he really was a competent auditor. Sam determined that Mr. Sly had written 10,500 checks over the past five months. After calculating the sample size and randomly selecting the cancelled checks, Sam discovered only two checks without proper supporting documentation. Since two occurrences were found, Sam concluded with 99 percent confidence that the population rate of occurrence does not exceed one-half of one percent and that he could rely on the control as effective.

Required:

a.   How many cancelled checks should Sam have investigated for proper supporting documentation to satisfy Patsy's discovery sampling plan?

b.   Assuming Sam calculated the correct sample size and properly sampled the cancelled checks, was Sam's statistical conclusion appropriate? If not, what should have been Sam's conclusion?

9-32   The use of statistical sampling techniques in an examination of financial statements does not eliminate judgmental decisions.

Required:

Identify and explain five areas where a CPA may use professional judgment to plan a statistical sampling test.

(AICPA adapted)

9-33   The Cowslip Milk Company's principal activity is buying milk from dairy farmers, processing the milk, and delivering it to retail customers. You are auditing the retail accounts receivable of the company and determine the following:

1.   The company has 50 retail routes; each route consists of 100 to 200 accounts, the number that can be serviced by a driver in a day.

2.   The driver enters cash collections from the day's deliveries to each customer directly on a statement form in record books maintained for each route. Mail remittances are posted in the route record books by office personnel. At the end of the month, the statements are priced, extended, and footed. Photocopies of

the statements are prepared and left in the customers' milk boxes with the next milk delivery.

3. The statements are reviewed by the office manager, who prepares for each route a list of accounts with 90-day balances or older. The list is used for intensive collection action.

4. The audit program used in prior audits for the selection of retail accounts receivable for confirmation stated: "Select two accounts from each route, one to be chosen by opening the route book at random and the other as the third item on each list of 90-day or older accounts."

Required:

Your review of the accounts receivable leads you to conclude that statistical sampling techniques may be used for their examination.

a. Since statistical sampling techniques do not relieve the CPA of responsibilities to exercise professional judgment, of what benefit are they to the CPA? Explain.

b. Give the reasons why the audit procedure previously used for selection of accounts receivable for confirmation (as given in item *4* above) would not produce a valid statistical sample.

c. What are the audit objectives or purposes in selecting 90-day accounts for confirmation? Can the application of statistical sampling techniques help in attaining these objectives or purposes? Discuss.

d. Assume that the company has 10,000 accounts receivable and that your statistical sampling disclosed 6 errors in a sample of 200 accounts. Is it reasonable to assume that 300 accounts in the entire population are in error? Explain.

(AICPA adapted)

9-34   Mavis Stores had two billing clerks during the year. Snow worked three months and White worked nine months. As the external auditor for Mavis Stores, Jones, CPA, uses attributes sampling to test clerical accuracy for the entire year. Due to the lack of internal verification, the system depends heavily upon the competence of the billing clerks. The quantity of bills per month is constant.

Required:

a. Jones decided to treat the billing by Snow and White as two separate populations. Discuss the advisability of this approach, considering the circumstances.

b. Jones decided to use the same confidence level, expected error rate, and desired upper precision limit for each population. Assuming he decided to select a sample of 200 items to test Snow's work, approximately how large a sample would be necessary to test White's?

(AICPA adapted)

9-35 You are now conducting your third annual audit of the financial statements of Elite Corporation. The current audit is for the year ended December 31, 1983. You decide to employ statistical sampling techniques, using unrestricted random numbers, to test the effectiveness of the company's internal control procedures relating to sales invoices. The sales invoices are serially numbered. In prior years, after selecting one representative two-week period during the year, you tested all invoices issued during that period and resolved to your satisfaction all errors that were found in the sample.

a. Explain the statistical procedures you would use to determine the sample size of the invoices to be examined.
b. Once the sample size has been determined, how would you select the individual invoices to be included in the sample? Explain.
c. Would statistical sampling procedures improve the examination of sales invoices as compared with the selection procedure used in prior years? Discuss.
d. Assume that the company issued 50,000 sales invoices during the year and that the auditor specified a confidence level of 95 percent with a precision range of plus or minus 2 percent.

1. Does this mean that the auditor would be willing to accept the reliability of the sales invoice data if errors are found on no more than 4 sales invoices out of every 95 invoices examined? Discuss.
2. If the auditor specified a precision range of ± 1 percent, would the confidence level be higher or lower than 95 percent assuming that the size of the sample remains constant? Why?

(AICPA adapted)

OBJECTIVE QUESTIONS*

9-36 Auditors who prefer statistical to judgmental sampling believe that the principal advantage of statistical sampling flows from its unique ability to

---

Note: Questions marked with an asterisk are not AICPA adapted questions; otherwise, questions in this section have been taken from prior CPA examinations.

A. Define the precision required to provide audit satisfaction.
B. Provide a mathematical measurement of uncertainty.
C. Establish conclusive audit evidence with decreased audit effort.
D. Promote a more legally defensible procedural approach.

9-37   Auditors often utilize sampling methods when performing tests of compliance. Which of the following methods is *most* useful when testing for compliance?

A. Attribute sampling.
B. Variables sampling.
C. Unrestricted random sampling with replacement.
D. Stratified random sampling.

9-38   Which of the following *best* describes the distinguishing feature of statistical sampling?

A. It requires the examination of a smaller number of supporting documents.
B. It provides a means for measuring mathematically the degree of uncertainty that results from examining only part of a population.
C. It reduces the problems associated with the auditor's judgment concerning materiality.
D. It is evaluated in terms of two parameters: statistical mean and random selection.

9-39   When using statistical sampling for tests of compliance, an auditor's evaluation of compliance would include a statistical conclusion concerning whether

A. Procedural deviations in the population were within an acceptable range.
B. Monetary precision is in excess of a certain predetermined amount.
C. The population total is not in error by more than a fixed amount.
D. Population characteristics occur at least once in the population.

9-40   Which of the following *best* describes the distinguishing feature of statistical sampling?

A. It provides for measuring mathematically the degree of uncertainty that results from examining only a part of the data.

B. It allows the auditor to have the same degree of confidence as with judgment sampling but with substantially less work.

C. It allows the auditor to substitute sampling techniques for audit judgment.

D. It provides for measuring the actual misstatements in financial statements in terms of reliability and precision.

9-41 Precision is a statistical measure of the maximum likely difference between the sample estimate and the true but unknown population total, and is directly related to

A. Reliability of evidence.
B. Relative risk.
C. Confidence level.
D. Cost benefit analysis.

9-42 Which of the following *best* describes what the auditor means by the rate of occurrence in an attribute sampling plan?

A. The number of errors that can reasonably be expected to be found in a population.
B. The frequency with which a certain characteristic occurs within a population.
C. The degree of confidence that the sample is representative of the population.
D. The dollar range within which the true population total can be expected to fall.

9-43 The "reliability" (confidence level) of an estimate made from sample data is a mathematically determined figure that expresses the expected proportion of possible samples of a specified size from a given population

A. That will yield an interval estimate that will encompass the true population value.
B. That will yield an interval estimate that will not encompass the true population value.
C. For which the sample value and the population value are identical.
D. For which the sample elements will not exceed the population elements by more than a stated amount.

9-44 When using a statistical sampling plan, the auditor would probably require a smaller sample if the

A. Population increases.
B. Desired precision interval narrows.
C. Desired reliability decreases.
D. Expected error occurrence rate increases.

9-45   If all other factors specified in a sampling plan remain constant, changing the specified reliability level from 90 percent to 95 percent would cause the required sample size to

A. Remain the same.
B. Decrease.
C. Increase.
D. Become indeterminate.

9-46*   When holding all other sample size variables constant, which of the following would *DECREASE* the size of the auditor's statistical sample in an attribute sampling plan?

A. Changing the confidence level from 90% to 95%.
B. Increasing the tolerable rate of occurrence from 5% to 8%.
C. Raising the estimated error rate from 1% to 3%.
D. Changing the confidence interval from ±2% to ±1%.

9-47   A CPA's client wishes to determine inventory shrinkage by weighing a sample of inventory items. If a stratified random sample is to be drawn, the strata should be identified in such a way that

A. The overall population is divided into subpopulations of equal size so that each subpopulation can be given equal weight when estimates are made.
B. Each stratum differs as much as possible with respect to expected shrinkage but the shrinkages expected for items within each stratum are as close as possible.
C. The sample mean and standard deviation of each individual stratum will be equal to the means and standard deviations of all other strata.
D. The items in each stratum will follow a normal distribution so that probability theory can be used in making inferences from the sample data.

9-48   The objective of attribute sampling is to satisfy the auditing standard, which states:

A. The work is to be adequately planned.

B. Sufficient competent evidential matter is to be obtained through inspection, observation, inquiries, and confirmation to afford a reasonable basis for an opinion.

C. The examination is to be performed by a person . . . having adequate technical training and proficiency as an auditor.

D. There is to be a proper study and evaluation of the existing internal control as a basis for reliance thereon, and for the determination of the resultant extent of the tests to which auditing procedures are to be restricted.

9-49* The following statements apply to unrestricted random sampling with replacement, a sampling technique which may be employed by an auditor under proper circumstances. Circle the T if the statement is true; if the statement is false, circle the F.

T   F   1. If the auditor wishes to use a table of random digits to select a random sample, he must first find a table conforming to the numbering employed by the items in the population he wishes to sample.

T   F   2. If a usable digit appears more than once in the table of random digits during the selection of the sample, the item should be included in the sample only once and another digit selected from the table.

T   F   3. A preliminary random sample of at least 30 items would have to be discarded if it produced one item disproportionately large in relation to the other items selected.

T   F   4. The effect of the inclusion by chance of a very large or very small item in a random sample can be lessened by increasing the size of the sample.

T   F   5. The reliability specified by the auditor for a sample estimate expresses the degree of confidence that the true value will be within the precision limits determined.

T   F   6. The standard deviation is a measure of variability of items in the universe.

T   F   7. Variability of items in the population is a factor which usually causes a sample mean and a population mean to be different.

T   F   8. It is necessary to determine the true standard deviation for a population in order to determine the size of the sample to be drawn from that population.

9-50 An important statistic to consider when using a statistical sampling audit plan is the population variability. The population variability is measured by the

    A   Sample mean.
    B.   Standard deviation.
    C.   Standard error of the sample mean.
    D.   Estimated population total minus the actual population total.

9-51 The statement, "A CPA tests disbursement vouchers to determine whether or not compliance deviations exceed 0.2 percent," omits which of the following necessary elements of a discovery sampling plan?

    A.   Characteristic being evaluated.
    B.   Definition of the population.
    C.   Maximum tolerable occurrence rate.
    D.   Specified reliability.

9-52 If a CPA selects a random sample for which he specified a confidence level of 99 percent and upper precision limit of 5 percent and subsequently changes the confidence level to 90 percent, the sample will produce an estimate which is

    A.   More reliable and more precise.
    B.   More reliable and less precise.
    C.   Less reliable and more precise.
    D.   Less reliable and less precise.

9-53 If an auditor, planning to use statistical sampling, is concerned with the number of a client's sales invoices that contain mathematical errors, the auditor would most likely utilize

    A.   Random sampling with replacement.
    B.   Sampling for attributes.
    C.   Sampling for variables.
    D.   Stratified random sampling.

9-54 From a random sample of items listed from a client's inventory count a CPA estimates with 90 percent confidence that the error occurrence rate is between 4 percent and 6 percent. The CPA's major concern is that there is one chance in twenty that the true error rate in the population is

A. More than 6 percent.
B. Less than 6 percent.
C. More than 4 percent.
D. Less than 4 percent.

9-55   Which of the following is an application of sampling for attributes?

A. Estimating the total dollar value of accounts receivable.
B. Estimating the reliability of a sample estimate.
C. Estimating the precision of a sample estimate.
D. Estimating the percentage of sales invoices with totals of less than $10.

9-56   In connection with his test of the accuracy of inventory counts, a CPA decides to use discovery sampling. Discovery sampling is concerned with the occurrence rate of a characteristic and therefore may be considered a special case of

A. Judgmental sampling.
B. Sampling for variables.
C. Stratified sampling.
D. Sampling for attributes.

9-57   Discovery sampling should be used to estimate whether a population contains

A. Errors of any kind.
B. Noncritical errors.
C. Critical errors.
D. No errors.

9-58   A CPA using discovery sampling is looking for a characteristic which, if discovered in his sample, might be indicative of more widespread irregularities or serious errors in the financial statements being examined. If a CPA discovers one such error while using a discovery sampling plan, the CPA

A. Is satisfied.
B. Must test more extensively.
C. Must expand his testing to 100 percent.
D. May not use any sampling plan.

9-59   What is the primary objective of using stratification as a sampling method in auditing?

A. To increase the confidence level at which a decision will be reached from the results of the sample selected.

B. To determine the occurrence rate for a given characteristic in the population being studied.

C. To decrease the effect of variance in the total population.

D. To determine the precision range of the sample selected.

9-60 The auditor's failure to recognize an error in an amount or an error in an internal-control data-processing procedure is described as a

A. Statistical error.

B. Sampling error.

C. Standard error of the mean.

D. Nonsampling error.

9-61 There are many kinds of statistical estimates that an auditor may find useful, but basically every accounting estimate is either of a quantity or of an error rate. The statistical terms that roughly correspond to "quantities" and "error rate," respectively, are

A. Attributes and variables.

B. Variables and attributes.

C. Constants and attributes.

D. Constants and variables.

9-62 How should an auditor determine the precision required in establishing a statistical sampling plan?

A. By the materiality of an allowable margin of error the auditor is willing to accept.

B. By the amount of reliance the auditor will place on the results of the sample.

C. By reliance on a table of random numbers.

D. By the amount of risk the auditor is willing to take that material errors will occur in the accounting process.

9-63 Which of the following is an advantage of systematic sampling over random number sampling?

A. It provides a stronger basis for statistical conclusions.

B. It enables the auditor to use the more efficient "sampling with replacement" tables.

C. There may be correlation between the location of items in the population, the feature of sampling interest, and the sampling interval.

D. It does not require establishment of correspondence between random numbers and items in the population.

9-64 An example of sampling for attributes would be estimating the

A. Quantity of specific inventory items.
B. Probability of losing a patent infringement case.
C. Percentage of overdue accounts receivable.
D. Dollar value of accounts receivable.

9-65 Statistical sampling generally may be applied to test compliance with internal accounting control when the client's internal accounting control procedures

A. Depend primarily on appropriate segregation of duties.
B. Are carefully reduced to writing and are included in client account manuals.
C. Leave an audit trail in the form of documentary evidence of compliance.
D. Enable the detection of material irregularities in the accounting records.

9-66 A CPA examining inventory may appropriately apply sampling for attributes in order to estimate the

A. Average price of inventory items.
B. Percentage of slow-moving inventory items.
C. Dollar value of inventory.
D. Physical quantity of inventory items.

9-67 Jones, CPA, believes the industry-wide occurrence rate of client billing errors is 3% and has established a maximum acceptable occurrence rate of 5%. In the review of client invoices Jones should use

A. Discovery sampling.
B. Attribute sampling.
C. Stratified sampling.
D. Variable sampling.

9-68 If certain forms are not consecutively numbered

A. Selection of a random sample probably is not possible.
B. Systematic sampling may be appropriate.

C. Stratified sampling should be used.
D. Random number tables cannot be used.

9-69 The objective of precision in sampling for compliance testing on an internal control system is to

A. Determine the probability of the auditor's conclusion based upon reliance factors.
B. Determine that financial statements taken as a whole are not materially in error.
C. Estimate the reliability of substantive tests.
D. Estimate the range of procedural deviations in the population.

CONDUCT INDEPENDENCE EVIDENCE DUE CARE FAIR PRESENTATION ETHICAL CONDUCT INDEPENDENCE EVIDENCE DUE CARE FAIR PRESENTATION ETHICAL CONDUCT INDEPE
AL CONDUCT INDEPENDENCE EVIDENCE DUE CARE FAIR PRESENTATION ETHICAL CONDUCT INDEPENDENCE EVIDENCE DUE CARE FAIR PRESENTATION ETHICAL CONDUCT IND
THICAL CONDUCT INDEPENDENCE EVIDENCE DUE CARE FAIR PRESENTATION ETHICAL CONDUCT INDEPENDENCE EVIDENCE DUE CARE FAIR PRESENTATION ETHICAL CONDUCT
N ETHICAL CONDUCT INDEPENDENCE EVIDENCE DUE CARE FAIR PRESENTATION ETHICAL CONDUCT INDEPENDENCE EVIDENCE DUE CARE FAIR PRESENTATION ETHICAL COND
ATION ETHICAL CONDUCT INDEPENDENCE EVIDENCE DUE CARE FAIR PRESENTATION ETHICAL CONDUCT INDEPENDENCE EVIDENCE DUE CARE FAIR PRESENTATION ETHICAL C
ENTATION ETHICAL CONDUCT INDEPENDENCE EVIDENCE DUE CARE FAIR PRESENTATION ETHICAL CONDUCT INDEPENDENCE EVIDENCE DUE CARE FAIR PRESENTATION ETHICA
RESENTATION ETHICAL CONDUCT INDEPENDENCE EVIDENCE DUE CARE FAIR PRESENTATION ETHICAL CONDUCT INDEPENDENCE EVIDENCE DUE CARE FAIR PRESENTATION ET
IR PRESENTATION ETHICAL CONDUCT INDEPENDENCE EVIDENCE DUE CARE FAIR PRESENTATION ETHICAL CONDUCT INDEPENDENCE EVIDENCE DUE CARE FAIR PRESENTATION

UE CARE FAIR PRESENTATION ETHICAL CONDUCT INDEPENDENCE EVIDENCE DUE CARE FAIR PRESENTATION ETHICAL CONDUCT INDEPENDENCE EVIDENCE DUE CARE FAIR PR
E DUE CARE FAIR PRESENTATION ETHICAL CONDUCT INDEPENDENCE EVIDENCE DUE CARE FAIR PRESENTATION ETHICAL CONDUCT INDEPENDENCE EVIDENCE DUE CARE FAI
IENCE DUE CARE FAIR PRESENTATION ETHICAL CONDUCT INDEPENDENCE EVIDENCE DUE CARE FAIR PRESENTATION ETHICAL CONDUCT INDEPENDENCE EVIDENCE DUE CARE
EVIDENCE DUE CARE FAIR PRESENTATION ETHICAL CONDUCT INDEPENDENCE EVIDENCE DUE CARE FAIR PRESENTATION ETHICAL CONDUCT INDEPENDENCE EVIDENCE DUE C
CE EVIDENCE DUE CARE FAIR PRESENTATION ETHICAL CONDUCT INDEPENDENCE EVIDENCE DUE CARE FAIR PRESENTATION ETHICAL CONDUCT INDEPENDENCE EVIDENCE DI
DENCE EVIDENCE DUE CARE FAIR PRESENTATION ETHICAL CONDUCT INDEPENDENCE EVIDENCE DUE CARE FAIR PRESENTATION ETHICAL CONDUCT INDEPENDENCE EVIDENCI
PENDENCE EVIDENCE DUE CARE FAIR PRESENTATION ETHICAL CONDUCT INDEPENDENCE EVIDENCE DUE CARE FAIR PRESENTATION ETHICAL CONDUCT INDEPENDENCE EVID
INDEPENDENCE EVIDENCE DUE CARE FAIR PRESENTATION ETHICAL CONDUCT INDEPENDENCE EVIDENCE DUE CARE FAIR PRESENTATION ETHICAL CONDUCT INDEPENDENCE E
CT INDEPENDENCE EVIDENCE DUE CARE FAIR PRESENTATION ETHICAL CONDUCT INDEPENDENCE EVIDENCE DUE CARE FAIR PRESENTATION ETHICAL CONDUCT INDEPENDENC
NDUCT INDEPENDENCE EVIDENCE DUE CARE FAIR PRESENTATION ETHICAL CONDUCT INDEPENDENCE EVIDENCE DUE CARE FAIR PRESENTATION ETHICAL CONDUCT INDEPEN
L CONDUCT INDEPENDENCE EVIDENCE DUE CARE FAIR PRESENTATION ETHICAL CONDUCT INDEPENDENCE EVIDENCE DUE CARE FAIR PRESENTATION ETHICAL CONDUCT INDE
IICAL CONDUCT INDEPENDENCE EVIDENCE DUE CARE FAIR PRESENTATION ETHICAL CONDUCT INDEPENDENCE EVIDENCE DUE CARE FAIR PRESENTATION ETHICAL CONDUCT I
ETHICAL CONDUCT INDEPENDENCE EVIDENCE DUE CARE FAIR PRESENTATION ETHICAL CONDUCT INDEPENDENCE EVIDENCE DUE CARE FAIR PRESENTATION ETHICAL CONDU
ION ETHICAL CONDUCT INDEPENDENCE EVIDENCE DUE CARE FAIR PRESENTATION ETHICAL CONDUCT INDEPENDENCE EVIDENCE DUE CARE FAIR PRESENTATION ETHICAL CON
ITATION ETHICAL CONDUCT INDEPENDENCE EVIDENCE DUE CARE FAIR PRESENTATION ETHICAL CONDUCT INDEPENDENCE EVIDENCE DUE CARE FAIR PRESENTATION ETHICAL
ESENTATION ETHICAL CONDUCT INDEPENDENCE EVIDENCE DUE CARE FAIR PRESENTATION ETHICAL CONDUCT INDEPENDENCE EVIDENCE DUE CARE FAIR PRESENTATION ETHI
I PRESENTATION ETHICAL CONDUCT INDEPENDENCE EVIDENCE DUE CARE FAIR PRESENTATION ETHICAL CONDUCT INDEPENDENCE EVIDENCE DUE CARE FAIR PRESENTATION I
FAIR PRESENTATION ETHICAL CONDUCT INDEPENDENCE EVIDENCE DUE CARE FAIR PRESENTATION ETHICAL CONDUCT INDEPENDENCE EVIDENCE DUE CARE FAIR PRESENTATI
IRE FAIR PRESENTATION ETHICAL CONDUCT INDEPENDENCE EVIDENCE DUE CARE FAIR PRESENTATION ETHICAL CONDUCT INDEPENDENCE EVIDENCE DUE CARE FAIR PRESENT
E CARE FAIR PRESENTATION ETHICAL CONDUCT INDEPENDENCE EVIDENCE DUE CARE FAIR PRESENTATION ETHICAL CONDUCT INDEPENDENCE EVIDENCE DUE CARE FAIR PRES
DUE CARE FAIR PRESENTATION ETHICAL CONDUCT INDEPENDENCE EVIDENCE DUE CARE FAIR PRESENTATION ETHICAL CONDUCT INDEPENDENCE EVIDENCE DUE CARE FAIR
NCE DUE CARE FAIR PRESENTATION ETHICAL CONDUCT INDEPENDENCE EVIDENCE DUE CARE FAIR PRESENTATION ETHICAL CONDUCT INDEPENDENCE EVIDENCE DUE CARE F
VIDENCE DUE CARE FAIR PRESENTATION ETHICAL CONDUCT INDEPENDENCE EVIDENCE DUE CARE FAIR PRESENTATION ETHICAL CONDUCT INDEPENDENCE EVIDENCE DUE CAR
E EVIDENCE DUE CARE FAIR PRESENTATION ETHICAL CONDUCT INDEPENDENCE EVIDENCE DUE CARE FAIR PRESENTATION ETHICAL CONDUCT INDEPENDENCE EVIDENCE DUE
ENCE EVIDENCE DUE CARE FAIR PRESENTATION ETHICAL CONDUCT INDEPENDENCE EVIDENCE DUE CARE FAIR PRESENTATION ETHICAL CONDUCT INDEPENDENCE EVIDENCE
PENDENCE EVIDENCE DUE CARE FAIR PRESENTATION ETHICAL CONDUCT INDEPENDENCE EVIDENCE DUE CARE FAIR PRESENTATION ETHICAL CONDUCT INDEPENDENCE EVIDEN
IDEPENDENCE EVIDENCE DUE CARE FAIR PRESENTATION ETHICAL CONDUCT INDEPENDENCE EVIDENCE DUE CARE FAIR PRESENTATION ETHICAL CONDUCT INDEPENDENCE EVI
T INDEPENDENCE EVIDENCE DUE CARE FAIR PRESENTATION ETHICAL CONDUCT INDEPENDENCE EVIDENCE DUE CARE FAIR PRESENTATION ETHICAL CONDUCT INDEPENDENCE
DUCT INDEPENDENCE EVIDENCE DUE CARE FAIR PRESENTATION ETHICAL CONDUCT INDEPENDENCE EVIDENCE DUE CARE FAIR PRESENTATION ETHICAL CONDUCT INDEPENDE
CONDUCT INDEPENDENCE EVIDENCE DUE CARE FAIR PRESENTATION ETHICAL CONDUCT INDEPENDENCE EVIDENCE DUE CARE FAIR PRESENTATION ETHICAL CONDUCT INDEPE
CAL CONDUCT INDEPENDENCE EVIDENCE DUE CARE FAIR PRESENTATION ETHICAL CONDUCT INDEPENDENCE EVIDENCE DUE CARE FAIR PRESENTATION ETHICAL CONDUCT INI
THICAL CONDUCT INDEPENDENCE EVIDENCE DUE CARE FAIR PRESENTATION ETHICAL CONDUCT INDEPENDENCE EVIDENCE DUE CARE FAIR PRESENTATION ETHICAL CONDUCT
N ETHICAL CONDUCT INDEPENDENCE EVIDENCE DUE CARE FAIR PRESENTATION ETHICAL CONDUCT INDEPENDENCE EVIDENCE DUE CARE FAIR PRESENTATION ETHICAL COND
ATION ETHICAL CONDUCT INDEPENDENCE EVIDENCE DUE CARE FAIR PRESENTATION ETHICAL CONDUCT INDEPENDENCE EVIDENCE DUE CARE FAIR PRESENTATION ETHICAL C
ENTATION ETHICAL CONDUCT INDEPENDENCE EVIDENCE DUE CARE FAIR PRESENTATION ETHICAL CONDUCT INDEPENDENCE EVIDENCE DUE CARE FAIR PRESENTATION ETHICA
RESENTATION ETHICAL CONDUCT INDEPENDENCE EVIDENCE DUE CARE FAIR PRESENTATION ETHICAL CONDUCT INDEPENDENCE EVIDENCE DUE CARE FAIR PRESENTATION ET

☐ FIELD WORK — SUBSTANTIVE TESTS

FAIR PRESENTATION ETHICAL CONDUCT INDEPENDENCE EVIDENCE DUE CARE FAIR PRESENTATION ETHICAL CONDUCT INDEPENDENCE EVIDENCE DUE CARE FAIR PRESENTA
CARE FAIR PRESENTATION ETHICAL CONDUCT INDEPENDENCE EVIDENCE DUE CARE FAIR PRESENTATION ETHICAL CONDUCT INDEPENDENCE EVIDENCE DUE CARE FAIR PRESE
UE CARE FAIR PRESENTATION ETHICAL CONDUCT INDEPENDENCE EVIDENCE DUE CARE FAIR PRESENTATION ETHICAL CONDUCT INDEPENDENCE EVIDENCE DUE CARE FAIR PR
CE DUE CARE FAIR PRESENTATION ETHICAL CONDUCT INDEPENDENCE EVIDENCE DUE CARE FAIR PRESENTATION ETHICAL CONDUCT INDEPENDENCE EVIDENCE DUE CARE FA
ENCE DUE CARE FAIR PRESENTATION ETHICAL CONDUCT INDEPENDENCE EVIDENCE DUE CARE FAIR PRESENTATION ETHICAL CONDUCT INDEPENDENCE EVIDENCE DUE CARE
EVIDENCE DUE CARE FAIR PRESENTATION ETHICAL CONDUCT INDEPENDENCE EVIDENCE DUE CARE FAIR PRESENTATION ETHICAL CONDUCT INDEPENDENCE EVIDENCE DUE C
NCE EVIDENCE DUE CARE FAIR PRESENTATION ETHICAL CONDUCT INDEPENDENCE EVIDENCE DUE CARE FAIR PRESENTATION ETHICAL CONDUCT INDEPENDENCE EVIDENCE D
DENCE EVIDENCE DUE CARE FAIR PRESENTATION ETHICAL CONDUCT INDEPENDENCE EVIDENCE DUE CARE FAIR PRESENTATION ETHICAL CONDUCT INDEPENDENCE EVIDENC

LEARNING OBJECTIVES

After studying this chapter, students should understand
1. The nature of substantive tests and the relationship between
substantive tests and compliance tests.
2. The risks associated with substantive testing.
3. The relationship between financial statement assertions and audit
objectives.
4. The nature of evidence-gathering procedures.
5. The factors which influence sample sizes for variables sampling.
6. Qualitative and quantitative analysis of sample results.
7. The nature of the various variable sampling plans.
8. Procedures for computing sample sizes, point estimater, standard
error of the mean, precision limits, and confidence levels for the
mean per unit and difference estimators. ATION ETHICAL CONDUCT INDEPENDENCE EVIDENCE

PENDENCE EVIDENCE DUE CARE FAIR PRESENTATION ETHICAL CONDUCT INDEPENDENCE EVIDENCE DUE CARE FAIR PRESENTATION ETHICAL CONDUCT INDEPENDENCE EVIDE
NDEPENDENCE EVIDENCE DUE CARE FAIR PRESENTATION ETHICAL CONDUCT INDEPENDENCE EVIDENCE DUE CARE FAIR PRESENTATION ETHICAL CONDUCT INDEPENDENCE EV
T INDEPENDENCE EVIDENCE DUE CARE FAIR PRESENTATION ETHICAL CONDUCT INDEPENDENCE EVIDENCE DUE CARE FAIR PRESENTATION ETHICAL CONDUCT INDEPENDENCE
DUCT INDEPENDENCE EVIDENCE DUE CARE FAIR PRESENTATION ETHICAL CONDUCT INDEPENDENCE EVIDENCE DUE CARE FAIR PRESENTATION ETHICAL CONDUCT INDEPENDE
CONDUCT INDEPENDENCE EVIDENCE DUE CARE FAIR PRESENTATION ETHICAL CONDUCT INDEPENDENCE EVIDENCE DUE CARE FAIR PRESENTATION ETHICAL CONDUCT INDEPE
CAL CONDUCT INDEPENDENCE EVIDENCE DUE CARE FAIR PRESENTATION ETHICAL CONDUCT INDEPENDENCE EVIDENCE DUE CARE FAIR PRESENTATION ETHICAL CONDUCT IN
ETHICAL CONDUCT INDEPENDENCE EVIDENCE DUE CARE FAIR PRESENTATION ETHICAL CONDUCT INDEPENDENCE EVIDENCE DUE CARE FAIR PRESENTATION ETHICAL CONDUCT
IN ETHICAL CONDUCT INDEPENDENCE EVIDENCE DUE CARE FAIR PRESENTATION ETHICAL CONDUCT INDEPENDENCE EVIDENCE DUE CARE FAIR PRESENTATION ETHICAL CON
TATION ETHICAL CONDUCT INDEPENDENCE EVIDENCE DUE CARE FAIR PRESENTATION ETHICAL CONDUCT INDEPENDENCE EVIDENCE DUE CARE FAIR PRESENTATION ETHICAL C
SENTATION ETHICAL CONDUCT INDEPENDENCE EVIDENCE DUE CARE FAIR PRESENTATION ETHICAL CONDUCT INDEPENDENCE EVIDENCE DUE CARE FAIR PRESENTATION ETHIC
PRESENTATION ETHICAL CONDUCT INDEPENDENCE EVIDENCE DUE CARE FAIR PRESENTATION ETHICAL CONDUCT INDEPENDENCE EVIDENCE DUE CARE FAIR PRESENTATION ET
AIR PRESENTATION ETHICAL CONDUCT INDEPENDENCE EVIDENCE DUE CARE FAIR PRESENTATION ETHICAL CONDUCT INDEPENDENCE EVIDENCE DUE CARE FAIR PRESENTATIO
E FAIR PRESENTATION ETHICAL CONDUCT INDEPENDENCE EVIDENCE DUE CARE FAIR PRESENTATION ETHICAL CONDUCT INDEPENDENCE EVIDENCE DUE CARE FAIR PRESENTA
CARE FAIR PRESENTATION ETHICAL CONDUCT INDEPENDENCE EVIDENCE DUE CARE FAIR PRESENTATION ETHICAL CONDUCT INDEPENDENCE EVIDENCE DUE CARE FAIR PRES
DUE CARE FAIR PRESENTATION ETHICAL CONDUCT INDEPENDENCE EVIDENCE DUE CARE FAIR PRESENTATION ETHICAL CONDUCT INDEPENDENCE EVIDENCE DUE CARE FAIR
ICE DUE CARE FAIR PRESENTATION ETHICAL CONDUCT INDEPENDENCE EVIDENCE DUE CARE FAIR PRESENTATION ETHICAL CONDUCT INDEPENDENCE EVIDENCE DUE CARE FA
IDENCE DUE CARE FAIR PRESENTATION ETHICAL CONDUCT INDEPENDENCE EVIDENCE DUE CARE FAIR PRESENTATION ETHICAL CONDUCT INDEPENDENCE EVIDENCE DUE CARE
EVIDENCE DUE CARE FAIR PRESENTATION ETHICAL CONDUCT INDEPENDENCE EVIDENCE DUE CARE FAIR PRESENTATION ETHICAL CONDUCT INDEPENDENCE EVIDENCE DUE C
NCE EVIDENCE DUE CARE FAIR PRESENTATION ETHICAL CONDUCT INDEPENDENCE EVIDENCE DUE CARE FAIR PRESENTATION ETHICAL CONDUCT INDEPENDENCE EVIDENCE D

INTRODUCTION

This chapter discusses sampling for variables within the framework of substantive testing. This framework will enable students to extend their knowledge of substantive testing and variables sampling to the remaining chapters of the text and to other situations, both academic and practical. The chapter is divided into four major sections. The first section discusses the nature, objectives, and risks associated with substantive testing and reviews the relationship of substantive testing to compliance testing. The second section reviews the importance of developing audit objectives in conjunction with substantive tests and it also reviews procedures for gathering evidence for substantive testing. The third section is devoted to a review of designing and evaluating different types of substantive tests. The final section demonstrates the applicability of statistical sampling techniques to substantive testing.

SUBSTANTIVE TESTS

The auditor's primary decision is to determine whether the client's recorded book values are reasonably stated or if they are materially misstated. Substantive tests provide evidence for such a decision. These tests may be used to estimate the dollar error in an account balance or in a class of related transactions, such as the dollar error in the accounts receivable balance or in the recorded total for sales. Substantive tests may also be used to determine the reasonableness of an account balance or class of recorded transactions.

The quantity and quality of substantive tests are directly associated with the field work standards. The first standard of field work requires that all substantive tests be adequately planned and properly supervised. The second standard of field work requires that the nature, extent, and timing of substantive testing be based on the degree of reliance on the existing internal control system. The third standard of field work requires that substantive tests contribute to the necessary sufficient competent evidence upon which to base an opinion regarding the financial statements under investigation. This chapter provides guidance in designing and carrying out an audit plan in compliance with the field work standards.

Relationship With Compliance Tests

As indicated in Chapter 8, substantive testing is used to estimate the reasonableness of a financial statement amount. On the other hand, compliance testing determines the degree of compliance with prescribed control procedures. If internal accounting controls are strong, the probability of a materially misstated financial amount is lower than when the internal accounting controls are weak or nonexistent. The second standard of field work is based on this inverse relationship between internal accounting control and the probability of a materially misstated account. If the results of compliance testing indicate effective internal accounting controls for a particular account or class of transactions, the extent of substantive testing in that account or class of transactions may be restricted. The auditor must be cautious, however, because strong controls in one audit area do not necessarily mean effective controls in other areas.

The extent of compliance testing and the extent of substantive testing are, of course, a matter of professional judgment as long as the latter is not eliminated. The second field work standard does not allow complete reliance on internal accounting control to the exclusion of substantive tests. The combination of compliance tests and substantive tests should provide the auditor with valid reliable evidence upon which to base an opinion regarding the financial statements under audit.

The auditor must also consider time/cost/benefits received from each type of testing when determining the level of compliance testing in relation to substantive testing. The extent of compliance testing should not be greater than the cost savings resulting from reduced substantive testing.

Risks Associated With Substantive Testing

As with compliance testing, substantive testing includes both sampling and nonsampling risks. With substantive testing, however, the combination of both risks is referred to as the *ultimate risk*. These risks, as they relate to substantive testing, are discussed below.

Sampling Risks

Since the auditor investigates only a portion of the auditing population, there is the risk that the conclusion based on a sample may be different from a conclusion based on an examination of every item in the population. This type of risk is referred to as sampling risk and it may be classified into two different types: (1) risk of incorrect acceptance and (2) risk of incorrect rejection.[1] These risks are encountered whether the auditor is using statistical or nonstatistical procedures.

---

[1] AICPA Auditing Standards Board, Statement on Auditing Standards 39, *Audit Sampling*, (New York: American Institute of Certified Public Accountants, Inc., June 1981), paragraph 12. Hereinafter referred to as SAS No. 39, *Audit Sampling*.

Risk of incorrect acceptance. The risk of incorrect acceptance is the risk that sample results will support the client's book amount as reasonably stated when the true unknown status of the amount is materially different from the recorded amount. In other words, it is the risk that the auditor will conclude that the financial statement amount is reasonably stated when the amount is actually materially misstated.

The auditor may control this risk through sample size. If the auditor uses nonstatistical sampling, the desired level of risk will be used subjectively to determine sample size. The higher the level of risk for incorrect acceptance the auditor is willing to sustain in the circumstances, the smaller the sample size necessary to attain the sampling objectives. Determination of statistical sample sizes in relation to an acceptable risk level is discussed in more detail in a subsequent section of the chapter.

For any given substantive test, an acceptable risk level for incorrect acceptance is a function of (1) the degree of reliance assigned to internal controls, (2) the probability that other substantive tests will detect a material misstatement of the account under investigation, and (3) in cases where internal control is weak or nonexistent because of management's lack of concern with controls, the risk which the auditor perceives because of this lack of concern. A high degree of risk for incorrect acceptance may be acceptable for a given substantive test when a high degree of reliance can be placed on internal controls or when there is a high probability that other substantive tests will detect a material misstatement of the account under consideration. On the other hand, when the auditor places relatively little reliance on internal controls and on other related substantive tests, the acceptance risk level for incorrect acceptance chould be specified at a low level. Concerning the risk because of management's disregard for internal controls, the acceptable risk level for incorrect acceptance should vary inversely with the auditor's subjective probability of the risks of errors or irregularities because of this lack of concern. In other words, if the subjective probability for errors or irregularities is high because of management's disregard of controls, the acceptable risk level for incorrect acceptance should be low.

Risk of incorrect rejection. The risk of incorrect rejection is the risk that sample results will not support a fairly presented financial statement amount. That is, it is the risk that the auditor will conclude that a reasonably stated financial statement amount is materially misstated.

If the sampling results indicate that the recorded amount is unreasonable, the auditor will likely apply additional substantive procedures to

(1) resolve whether a sampling error caused an erroneous rejection, or (2) determine that the account is actually materially misstated.

The risk of incorrect rejection also influences statistical and non-statistical sample sizes for substantive testing. The auditor subjectively uses the desired level of risk of incorrect rejection to determine a nonstatistical sample size: the higher the level of risk acceptable to the auditor for incorrect rejection, the smaller the sample size. The relationship between this risk level and statistical sample sizes varies in the same way and is discussed in a subsequent section.

Nonsampling Risks

As discussed in the previous chapter, nonsampling risks are inherent in every audit procedure. These risks exist whether the auditor applies auditing procedures to every item in the population or to just a portion of the population. Nonsampling risks consist of the inability of the auditor to (1) design audit procedures to satisfy the established audit objectives, or (2) to effectively carry out auditing procedures specified in a well-designed audit program. Nonsampling risks may be reduced to a negligible level, however, by (1) having proper planning and supervision of the audit, (2) by adherence to high quality control standards, and (3) by maintaining a high level of auditor competency.

Ultimate Risk

Ultimate risk is the combination of sampling and nonsampling risks. It is of the utmost importance that CPA firms keep nonsampling risks at a negligible level at all times. Assuming nonsampling risks are negligible, the ultimate risk becomes the joint probability that (1) the internal accounting control system will allow material errors to occur and to go undetected, and (2) that the auditor will not detect the materially misstated financial data. The auditor relies on the system of internal control to reduce the first risk and depends on substantive tests to reduce the second risk.[2]

Ultimate risk is inherent in any sampling plan whether the auditor uses statistical techniques or nonstatistical sampling. When using nonstatistical sampling, the auditor will use the concept of ultimate risk in a subjective manner. To control for this risk, the auditor will judgmentally determine the balance desired between compliance testing and substantive testing.

---

[2] An interesting discussion of this point is provided by William R. Kinney, Jr. in "A Note on Compounding Probabilities in Auditing," working paper, University of Iowa, September, 1982.

On the other hand, with statistical sampling techniques, the ultimate risk may be quantified and used to determine other sampling variables. This aspect of ultimate risk is discussed in a later section covering statistical sampling techniques.

AUDIT OBJECTIVES AND FINANCIAL STATEMENT ASSERTIONS

Chapter 9 discussed why auditors should define audit objectives before they carry out auditing procedures. Defining general and specific audit objectives is the key to developing valid sampling plans, whether the auditor uses statistical or nonstatistical techniques.

Defining Audit Objectives

If the general audit objective is to test the compliance of internal controls with prescribed procedures, an attribute sampling plan is appropriate. On the other hand, if the general audit objective is to determine the amount of dollar error in an account, the auditor should design a variables sampling plan for substantive testing.

After general objectives have been stated, specific objectives are developed to attain the general objectives. Specific audit objectives for compliance and substantive testing are developed simultaneously so that one sample from an audit population may be used for both types of testing. Sampling efficiency is attained when an auditor uses one sample concurrently for a compliance test and a substantive test. A "dual-purpose test" is carried out when one test satisfies both types of audit objectives.

For example, if a specific audit objective for compliance testing is to determine that adequate controls exist to ensure that all goods shipped *are* billed for the proper amount, the parallel audit objective for substantive testing may be to determine that all goods shipped *were* billed for the proper amount. Consequently, when tracing a bill of lading, which is filed in the shipping department, to the corresponding sales invoice filed in the billing department, the auditor should not only check the correspondence between the quantity on the bill of lading and the sales invoice, but he or she will also have to compare the unit sales price on the sales invoice to an approved price list. After carrying out these procedures, the auditor should also extend the quantity and unit price on the invoice to verify the mathematical accuracy of the amount billed. After performing these procedures, the auditor has performed both a compliance test and a substantive test with one sample.

The auditor must document the work performed by preparing a working paper showing the number of missing invoices in relation to bills of lading, the number of discrepancies between the billed unit price and authorized unit price, and the number of erroneous extensions. In addition to maintaining a record of the number of differences, the auditor should note the dollar differences between the billed unit price and the authorized unit price, and the dollar differences between invoice extensions and the recomputed extensions, if any. The auditor will use the number of discrepancies in compliance tests to determine rates of exceptions, while the dollar differences will be used in substantive tests to estimate the dollar overstatement or understatement of billings. If the rate of errors or dollar differences found in the sample is compatible with acceptable levels, the auditor will continue the examination as specified in the audit program. On the other hand, if the rate of exceptions or the dollar differences found are not acceptable to the auditor, remaining substantive tests must be modified as to their nature, timing, or extent.

The auditor may thus increase audit efficiency by developing specific audit objectives concurrently for compliance and substantive testing so that one sample may be used for both types of testing.

When performing substantive tests, the auditor must develop specific audit objectives in light of management assertions embodied in financial statements. The next section discusses the nature of these financial statement assertions.

Nature of Financial Statement Assertions

Since financial statements are the responsibility of management, assertions in financial statements are representations of management. As indicated in Chapter 6, management's assertions may be explicit or implicit.

SAS No. 31, *Evidential Matter*, provides the following classification of major financial statement assertions: (1) existence or occurrence, (2) completeness, (3) rights and obligations, (4) valuation or allocation, and (5) presentation and disclosure.[3]

> *Assertions about existence or occurrence* deal with whether assets or liabilities of the entity exist at a given date and whether recorded transactions have occurred during a given period. For example, management asserts that finished goods inventories in the balance sheet are available for sale. Similarly, management asserts that sales in the income statement represent the exchange of goods or services with customers for cash or other consideration.

---

[3] American Institute of Certified Public Accountants, SAS No. 31, *Evidential Matter*, (New York: American Institute of Certified Public Accountants, August 1980).

Assertions about completeness deal with whether all transactions and accounts that should be presented in the financial statements are so included. For example, management asserts that all purchases of goods and services are recorded and are included in the financial statements. Similarly, management asserts that notes payable in the balance sheet include all such obligations of the entity.

Assertions about rights and obligations deal with whether assets are the rights of the entity and liabilities are the obligations of the entity at a given date. For example, management asserts that amounts capitalized for leases in the balance sheet represent the cost of the entity's rights to leased property and that the corresponding lease liability represents an obligation of the entity.

Assertions about valuation or allocation deal with whether asset, liability, revenue, and expense components have been included in the financial statements at appropriate amounts. For example, management asserts that property is recorded at historical cost and that such cost is systematically allocated to appropriate accounting periods. Similarly, management asserts that trade accounts receivable included in the balance sheet are stated at net realizable value.

Assertions about presentation and disclosure deal with whether particular components of the financial statements are properly classified, described, and disclosed. For example, management asserts that obligations classified as long-term liabilities in the balance sheet will not mature within one year. Similarly, management asserts that amounts presented as extraordinary items in the income statement are properly classified and described.

In addition to these broad categories of financial statement assertions, the overall assertion of management that the financial statements are prepared in accordance with generally accepted accounting principles (GAAP) consistently applied is implicit in the statements if they purport to show financial position, results of operations, and changes in financial position. Consequently, in developing audit objectives the auditor must consider the broad categories of assertions discussed above as well as the overall assertion concerning GAAP. Of course, numerous substantive tests carried out to satisfy an objective based on a specific assertion will also confirm adherence to GAAP.

As previously stated, these categories of assertions enable the auditor to develop specific audit objectives for substantive testing. These assertions may also be related to the audit objectives of each audit cycle as presented in subsequent chapters.

Evidence-Gathering Procedures

The following discussion summarizes the different types of evidence-gathering procedures, some of which apply to both compliance and substantive testing. Common audit techniques include the following:

- Inquiry
- Observation
- Counting
- Scanning
- Recomputation or recalculation
- Confirmation
- Retracing
- Vouching

An *inquiry* made by the auditor may be oral or written. The auditor should insist, however, that many of the responses be confirmed in writing. For example, as discussed in more detail in Chapter 14, the auditor will make inquiries of the client's legal counsel about contingent liabilities of the client. The client's attorney should respond to the inquiry in writing. On the other hand, the auditor may ask a stock room clerk about slow-moving inventory items. The inquiry and the response are both oral. In this situation, however, evidence gathered by inquiry must be supported by corroborating evidence. The auditor will carry out independent procedures to verify and identify the slow-moving inventory items, if any. As a general rule, any inquiry obtained from the client, either oral or written, should be substantiated by corroborating evidence.

Observation by the auditor consists of two important tasks. The first aspect of observation requires visual inspection of tangible items. For example, the auditor may visually verify the existence and physical quality of an item such as a building, or the auditor may read and examine documents for certain types of information.

The second aspect of observation requires the auditor to witness the performance of duties by client personnel. Such observation provides evidence of the proper separation of conflicting duties. Or the auditor may observe the client's personnel counting physical inventory to determine that the physical inventory plan is being carried out according to written instructions.

Counting is directly related to the observation of tangible items because the auditor may be required to count what is being physically observed. For instance, the auditor may count some physical inventory items while he or she observes the quality of the goods. Or, the auditor may account for all prenumbered documents in a file under investigation.

Scanning does not produce corroborating evidence the auditor can rely on without further evidential matter, but the procedure does identify items that should be investigated in more detail. For example, the auditor may look very quickly at the entries in the repairs and maintenance expense accounts to detect unusual items which should be investigated more thoroughly.

Recomputation or recalculation involves duplicating mathematical procedures carried out by the client. For example, the auditor may recalculate the annual depreciation expense. This type of evidence is convincing and relevant if the underlying data has been verified. On the other hand, if the depreciable base and depreciation method have not been verified, the evidence gained from recomputing annual depreciation expense is not very persuasive.

Confirmation of financial data requires the auditor to interact directly with an independent third party. The third party may be a customer requested to confirm an account receivable, a vendor asked to confirm an accounts payable, a lessor asked to confirm a lease agreement, or a banker asked to confirm cash balances or outstanding loan balances. Evidence furnished by confirmation with independent third parties is quite reliable, assuming that the third party has the competence to provide the evidence, because the client does not come in contact with the evidence.

Retracing involves following a transaction through the accounting system in the direction of normal occurrence. For instance, the auditor may retrace a credit sales invoice to the sales journal and to the subsidiary accounts receivable ledger to determine that the sale is properly recorded in both places. This procedure helps determine that all transactions captured on source documents are properly recorded in journals and ledgers so that related financial statement accounts are not *understated*.

Vouching involves following a transaction through the accounting system in the opposite direction of normal occurrence. For example, the auditor might vouch an entry in the sales journal back to the sales invoice or vouch an entry in the accounts receivable subsidiary ledger back to the sales invoice. This procedure helps determine that all journal and ledger entries have proper supporting documentation and that related financial statement accounts are not *overstated*.

It is important that appropriate conclusions are drawn in conjunction with retracing and vouching procedures. The auditor must distinguish between *vouching* which provides evidence that recorded entries have proper supporting documentation and *retracing* which provides evidence that source documents are properly recorded.

DESIGNING AND EVALUATING SUBSTANTIVE TESTS

Types of Substantive Tests

The auditor must design substantive tests in light of specific audit objectives. To satisfy the specific objectives, the auditor can gather evidence from two general types of substantive tests: (1) analytical review techniques, and (2) tests of details. The second general type may be further subdivided into tests of details of transactions and direct tests of balances (a series of transactions). As indicated in Chapter 6, when an auditor applies substantive tests to an account balance, he or she not only validates the existence and completeness of the individual transactions, but also evaluates the account balance in terms of the mathematical accuracy, the cutoff and fair presentation in accordance with GAAP.

Analytical Review Techniques

Substantive tests involving analytical review techniques and procedures consist of studying and comparing relationships among data. Analytical review techniques and procedures were discussed in Chapter 4. Therefore, the current section is designed to review analytic review techniques and place this technique within the framework of statistical sampling.

Analytical review techniques include the study of financial ratios, percentages, dollar values reflected on the financial statements, or related physical quantities. For example, the auditor may compare the gross profit percentage of the current year with the percentage of previous years. Or, the auditor may compare the current year's ratio of net income to sales with the ratio of previous years. Auditors may apply analytical review techniques to the overall financial statements of a consolidated group of companies, to the financial information of an individual subsidiary of the consolidated group, or to the individual elements of the financial statements.[4]

Comparisons of data as suggested in Chapter 4 and in the previous paragraph may be made at the beginning of the audit, during the examination, or near the end of the audit. Regardless of when analytical review procedures are carried out, an unusual fluctuation, or lack of an anticipated fluctuation, will have to be investigated. The auditor may ask

---

[4] American Institute of Certified Public Accountants, *SAS No. 1*, Section 318.07, *Analytical Review Procedures,* (New York: American Institute of Certified Public Accountants, Inc., October 1978).

management to interpret the unusual fluctuation. Management's response is evaluated based on knowledge of the client's business and industry, the economy, and knowledge learned thus far from the application of audit procedures. Even though management's response to such an inquiry may be acceptable, the auditor generally will examine corroborating evidence related to the response. If management's response is unacceptable, the auditor will have to perform additional auditing procedures to investigate the unusual fluctuation. On the other hand, the auditor may be able to explain the analytical deviation by knowing that some specific event caused the unusual fluctuation. For example, an involuntary shutdown of operations due to an employee strike could cause a fluctuation in the level of sales for a particular period. Nevertheless, the auditor would want to document the event fully in the working papers.

If analytical review procedures are carried out at the beginning of the audit, the results may be used as a planning tool. In this case analytical information involves unaudited data and unusual fluctuations may indicate high risk audit areas requiring an intense investigation. Consequently, analytical results may be used to develop an effective and efficient audit plan which will provide sufficient competent evidence necessary for an audit opinion.

Analytical tests performed during the examination in conjunction with other audit procedures may, or may not, involve audited data. The results of the tests, in either event, may be used to modify remaining auditing procedures or to support conclusions based on the application of other auditing procedures. Analytical comparisons made near the end of an audit, after considering adjusting and reclassifying entries, provide an overall review of the financial information.[5]

As can be seen by the discussion above, analytical review techniques involve relationships of summarized data and generally do not require sampling plans. The remainder of the chapter is devoted to substantive tests of details and direct tests of balances and related sampling plans.

Tests of Details of Transactions or Balances

Substantive tests involving tests of details of transactions or balances may focus on the balance of a financial statement account or on a specific class of transactions. The auditor may vouch items from, or retrace items to, the financial statement account or class of transactions. The direction of testing depends on the specific audit objective. If

---

[5] *Ibid.*, Section 318.05

the objective concerns the assertion of existence or occurrence, the auditor should select items from a financial statement account and vouch those items back to supporting documentation. Stating the specific audit objective of evaluating existence or occurrence in a different way, the auditor may indicate that the objective is to search for unauthorized or ficticious transactions. That is, the auditor is concerned that the account may be overstated.

For example, if the specific audit objective is to verify the occurrence of sales in the period under audit, the auditor could vouch summarized sales figures from the general ledger to the sales journal, and vouch individual sales from the journal to appropriate sales invoices and to related shipping documents. This procedure establishes that recorded sales have proper supporting documentation which provides evidence of their occurrence. This procedure may also help satisfy the specific objective of proper valuation, since vouching in substantive tests compares recorded sales values to values on supporting documentation. Thus, the auditor, by vouching prices reflected on the sales invoices to approved price lists, provides evidence of proper valuation.

On the other hand, if the specific audit objective concerns the assertion of completeness, the auditor should select sample items from source documents and *retrace* those items to the appropriate journals and ledger accounts. This procedure verifies that the account is complete as to transactions captured on source documents, and is appropriate when the auditor is concerned that the account balance or class of transactions may be understated due to unrecorded transactions. For example, to satisfy the objective concerning completeness of the sales figure, the auditor could select a sample of sales orders and retrace those documents to related shipping documents, to appropriate sales invoices, and to the recording in the sales journal. Then the auditor should retrace summarized sales figures in the journal to the general ledger. This procedure provides evidence about unrecorded transactions that have been captured on source documents. It also provides evidence about whether transactions are properly recorded and valued. Therefore, retracing may also be used to support the audit objective concerning proper valuation of an account or class of transactions.

The direction of testing is extremely important in relation to specific audit objectives. If the direction of testing is not commensurate with the objective, audit conclusions will not be supported with appropriate evidence. Therefore, it is of the utmost importance that specific audit objectives be defined before any testing takes place so that audit procedures may be designed to provide appropriate evidence upon which to base an audit conclusion.

Sampling and Substantive Tests

Generally, in substantive tests a sample of items from the audit population is investigated rather than investigating every item in the population. In some cases, however, where sampling risks cannot be accepted, the auditor should examine every item in the population. For example, sampling cannot be justified when any item in the population represents a potential error that would cause the account to be materially misstated.[6] Otherwise, sampling may be justified on the basis of cost versus benefit. The justification of sampling presented in Chapter 9 concerning compliance testing is also applicable to substantive testing.

Identifying Audit Populations

As discussed previously, any sampling plan, whether statistical or nonstatistical, must provide appropriate evidence to satisfy general and specific audit objectives. Therefore, the sampling plan must identify the relevant audit population. If the auditor is concerned about overstatement of an account, the sampling plan should identify the population of recorded items from which to select sample items. The sample items may then be confirmed with third parties or vouched back to their source, thus verifying the existence or occurrence of the recorded items.

For example, if the specific audit objective is to determine that recorded sales do not include unauthorized transactions, the audit population from which to sample would be the sales journal. The sampling unit would be the individual lines in the journal where each line represents a sale.

Sampling units selected from the sales journal should be vouched back (1) to the related sales invoice providing evidence as to the equivalency of the recorded sales amount and the total billed the customer, (2) to shipping documents which indicate that the goods were actually shipped to the customer, thus establishing the right to recognize a sale and a receivable, and (3) to sales orders to provide evidence of credit approval of the customer before shipment of the goods.

Vouching sales transactions back through the system provides evidence that recorded sales are not overstated due to ficticious transactions.

---

[6] *SAS No. 39, Audit Sampling*, paragraph 21.

If the auditor's concern is that of account understatement, the sampling plan should identify the audit population as the file of source documents in which omitted items would be included. The auditor would trace the sample items forward through the system to determine that they were properly recorded. This procedure substantiates completeness of an account balance or class of transactions.

For example, if the specific audit objective is to determine that recorded sales are not understated and the company uses bills of lading for the shipment of all items sold, the audit population would consist of all bills of lading used for the period. All sales, whether recorded or unrecorded in the sales journal, should be represented in a complete file of bills of lading for the period under audit. The sampling unit would be the bills of lading. After selecting a sample, the auditor would trace the bills of lading information to sales orders, to sales invoices, and to the sales journal. Retracing the sales transactions through the system provides evidence that recorded sales are not understated due to unrecorded transactions. Of course, the auditor must also establish the correspondence between recorded sales in the journal and in the general ledger. In addition, the auditor must verify the equivalency of the sales total reflected on the income statement with the sales total in the general ledger.

Factors Influencing Sample Size

This section presents factors that influence sample size while the actual calculation of a statistical sample size is provided in a subsequent section on statistical sampling techniques. In determining statistical sample sizes, the auditor will quantify determinants of sample size and will use these determinants (variables) in a mathematical structure. The same sample size determinants should be used subjectively in specifying a nonstatistical sample size.

As previously stated, desired levels of sampling risks affect sample size. The lower the desired sampling risk for incorrect acceptance and for incorrect rejection, the larger the sample size necessary to satisfy audit objectives. The converse is also true. Factors influencing the desired sampling risk were discussed previously in the section on "Risks Associated with Substantive Testing."

In addition to sampling risk levels, the sample size depends on the maximum amount of monetary error that could exist in an account balance or in a class of transactions without causing the financial statements to be materially misstated. This maximum amount of monetary error that could exist without causing a material misstatement is referred to as the *tolerable error*.[7] Therefore, the dollar amount of tolerable error is equivalent to the amount considered material in the circumstances. The smaller the amount of tolerable error acceptable in the circumstances, the larger the sample size necessary to attain audit objectives. The reverse of this statement is also true: the larger the amount of tolerable error, the smaller the sample size.

Selecting Sample Items

After determining the sample size, the auditor must select sample items from the audit population. With a statistical plan or with non-statistical sampling, selection of sample items should, except for judgmental samples, be random so that results will be valid. Random selection techniques were presented in Chapter 9 and will not be repeated in this chapter. Sample selection for nonstatistical plans was also discussed in the prior chapter.

Regardless of the selection technique used, the sample must be representative of the population, or the unique part of the population which is of interest is judgmental sampling, so that valid inferences will be made concerning the audit population. If the sample is not representative of the population of interest, erroneous conclusions based on sample data may be made. Erroneous conclusions could lead to excessive audit work or to accepting a materially misstated financial statement account.

Evaluation of Sample Results

In substantive testing, sample results will reflect the magnitude and direction of dollar errors found in sample items. A dollar error is defined as the difference between an audited value and a client-recorded value. Dollar errors must be evaluated both quantitatively and qualitatively. Quantitative evaluation examines the amount and direction of errors found in sample items. Qualitative evaluation investigates the probable cause and nature of the errors.

Qualitative Analysis.   The qualitative analyses made in conjunction with substantive tests are comparable to qualitative analyses carried out for compliance testing. Qualitative evaluation of sample results will also be the same for statistical and nonstatistical sampling plans.

The cause of dollar errors could be employee fatigue, carelessness, inattentiveness, or misunderstanding of instructions. On the other hand, dollar errors may be intentional. Regardless of the nature of the dollar

---

[7] *Ibid.*, paragraph 18.

errors, intentional or unintentional, the auditor will have to investigate the errors thoroughly, and the results of the investigation will be used with the results of the quantitative evaluation to modify subsequent auditing procedures. If the dollar errors are intentional, however, subsequent auditing procedures must be made in light of *SAS No. 17, Illegal Acts by Clients*, and *SAS No. 16, The Independent Auditor's Responsibility for the Detection of Errors or Irregularities*. These topics are discussed further in Chapter 17.

Quantitative Analysis.   Quantitative evaluation of sample results for statistical sampling plans differs from the evaluation for nonstatistical sampling plans. Statistical sampling plans provide a mathematical framework for making inferences about financial statement accounts based on sample results. A statistical plan indicates the reasonableness of an account balance or the probable dollar difference between the audited value and the client-recorded value. The auditor must decide whether to consider the difference material. If the difference is material, the statistical conclusion indicates that the financial statement account is materially misstated, and the auditor may have to carry out additional auditing procedures.

Nonstatistical sampling plans do not provide a mathematical framework for making inferences about a financial statement account. The auditor must subjectively determine the impact of potential dollar errors upon financial statement accounts. If the impact appears to be material, the auditor may conclude that the account is materially misstated, even though the magnitude of the missstatement cannot be measured mathematically.

Using the quantitative and qualitative analyses, the auditor must make an audit decision either to accept the financial statement account as reasonably stated or to carry out additional auditing procedures.

The Audit Decision

If the quantitative evaluation for either a statistical or a nonstatistical sampling plan indicates an immaterial difference between the audited value and the client-recorded value, the auditor may accept the financial statement account as reasonably stated, provided the qualitative analysis reflects only unintentional errors. However, as indicated previously, if the qualitative analysis indicates the presence of intentional errors, the auditor will have to investigate the errors in more detail in light of *SAS No. 17, Illegal Acts by Clients*, and *SAS No. 16, The Independent Auditor's Responsibility for the Detection of Errors or Irregularities*.

If the quantitative investigation indicates a material misstatement of a financial statement account, the auditor must modify subsequent auditing procedures taking into consideration the qualitative analysis. The auditor may take one or a combination of the following alternative courses of action after weighing the benefits against costs. The materiality of the account in relation to the financial statements taken as a whole must also be considered. For example, the audit decision may be different for an immaterial current asset, such as prepaid insurance, as compared to a material current asset, such as accounts receivable. The potential courses of action are discussed below.

Increase sample size.   When the quantitative analysis indicates a materially misstated financial account balance and when the qualitative analysis indicates that dollar errors occur randomly and do not occur in a systematic pattern, the auditor may increase the sample size. Just how much the sample should be increased will depend on the materiality of the account in relation to the financial statements and on the original sample size. Generally, the more significant the account to the financial statements, the more evidence needed to establish a material misstatement and to recommend an adjustment of the account balance. If a statistical sampling plan has been used, the sample size may be increased by reducing the sampling risk levels. With an increased sample, the new achieved sample statistic may fall within acceptable limits. That is, sample results from the increased sample size may reverse the statistical conclusion of the smaller sample, thus indicating that the account is reasonably stated and that the smaller sample produced a sampling error.

There is also the possibility that the increased sample size will not change the original sampling results. If the new sampling results do not change the conclusion as to material misstatement of an account, the auditor will have substantial evidence to support a recommendation for an account adjustment.

Increasing sample size is expensive in terms of audit time and costs, and there may be instances where an increase in sample size is impossible or prohibitive in terms of cost and time. In those cases, the auditor will have to revert to alternative auditing procedures, such as a more in-depth analytic review or a more in-depth audit of the sample items, to gather evidence about the reasonableness of an account.

Extend auditing procedures in problem areas.   When the qualitative analysis indicates a pattern of errors or errors of a particular type, the auditor may restrict subsequent audit procedures to the problem area or areas. Of course this means that the new items sampled in the problem areas cannot be used to increase sample size because the new items are not randomly selected. Additional testing in the problem areas is a separate test and must be extensive enough to determine the full financial impact of the errors on the financial statement account. Furthermore, there must be sufficient evidence to support a recommendation of an account adjustment if the account is materially misstated.

Ask client to "rework" the account. If the qualitative analysis reveals unintentional errors due to a misunderstanding of instructions or a misapplication of an accepted accounting principle, to the extent that the related financial statement account is materially misstated, the auditor may ask the client to reconstruct the account using the proper applications or instructions. (For example, if additions to plant were recorded in the journal at appraised values, which differed from historical cost, plant would be overstated.) The auditor may ask the client to correct the journal entries using historical cost. Of course, when the client corrects the records, the modified records must be examined.

Request adjustment of the account. When the auditor requests the client to adjust the balance of a materially misstated account, the auditor should have sufficient evidence to convince the client of the necessity of making the account adjustment. The auditor can only recommend the account adjustment to the client. The client's reaction to the recommendation will dictate the type of opinion the auditor may render for the audit engagement.

Adopt an appropriate opinion. If the client makes the recommended adjustment, the auditor may render an unqualified opinion. If the client refuses to make the adjustment, the auditor must decide whether to render a qualified or adverse opinion on the financial statements.

VARIABLES SAMPLING PLANS

Variables sampling plans are statistical sampling plans designed to attain the objectives of substantive tests of details of transactions and of direct tests of balances. Variables sampling plans are estimation plans designed to estimate the dollar reasonableness of a financial statement account or the amount of material misstatement if the account is not reasonably stated.

There are several types of variables sampling plans. In practice, deciding which type of plan should be used for a particular case is a complex and difficult process because there is not one variables sampling plan that is appropriate in all circumstances. Differing population characteristics warrant different statistical estimators.[8]

This section considers some of the major estimators and when they may be appropriate. Two types of variables estimators, the mean-per-unit (MPU) estimator and the difference estimator, are illustrated.

Descriptions of Different Variables Sampling Plans

The following discussions briefly describe variables sampling plans and point out conditions under which each plan may be appropriate.

Mean-Per-Unit Estimator.   The mean-per-unit (MPU) estimator is the least complex of all the estimators and thus provides a basis for understanding other variables estimation techniques. The usefulness of the MPU estimator, however, is limited in practice.[9]

The MPU estimator uses only the audited value of a sample item. Consequently, this estimator can be used when there are no book values for the individual sample items, e.g., when the company uses a periodic inventory system. Furthermore, the MPU estimator does not require particular error patterns, or a particular frequency of errors in the sample, like most of the other estimators. The major limitation of the MPU estimator is the inefficiency of the technique compared to other variables estimators. The MPU estimator for accounting populations generally requires a larger sample size than that required by other estimators to achieve a given statistical objective. In many instances, however, the MPU estimator is the only estimator compatible with population characteristics. In these cases, the auditor may use a stratified MPU technique to reduce sample size. The MPU estimator is also used to explain the theory of controlling sampling risks, which is provided in the chapter appendix.

Difference Estimator.   Statistical computations for the difference estimator are similar to the computations for the MPU estimator except the difference estimator uses differences between the audited sample values and the respective book values rather than just the audited values. That is, the differences between the audited sample values and the client-recorded values are the sample items to be manipulated in the statistical test. Consequently, there is less variability between the sample items within a sample for the difference estimator than between sample items for the MPU estimator. For this reason, the difference estimator

---

[8] See for example John Neter and James K. Loebbecke, *Behavior of Major Statistical Estimators in Sampling Accounting Population—An Empirical Study*, (New York: American Institute of Certified Public Accountants, Inc. 1975).

[9] *Ibid.*

yields more precise estimates than the MPU estimator.

Ratio Estimator. The ratio estimator is very similar to the difference estimator. The sample items for the ratio estimator are the ratios of the audited values to the client-recorded values. This estimator also gives more precise estimates than the MPU estimator because the variability of the ratios in a sample is smaller than the variability within a sample of audited values. The ratio estimator is especially effective when there is a linear relationship through the origin between audit values and book values and when the variance of the audit values is proportional to the variance of the book values. This condition is present when a plot of audit values against book values reveals a pattern like the following:

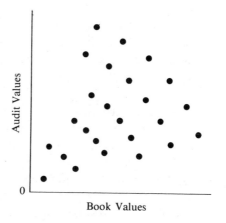

One problem with both the ratio and difference estimators occurs when there are no errors, or only a few errors, discovered in the sample. In these cases, the standard error of the point estimate is zero or very near zero, and this implies that the total book value is exactly correct or nearly exactly correct, which as a practical matter is not likely to be true. Therefore, many authors believe that the use of the ratio and difference estimators is inadvisable when the expected error rate in the population is low.[10] The ratio estimator, as well as the difference estimator, may be used in a stratified sampling plan. Stratified sampling is discussed in general terms below without referring to particular estimators, although stratification may be used with all of the estimators discussed above.

_____

[10] _Ibid._

Stratified Sampling Plans. Stratification consists of dividing an audit population into two or more relatively homogeneous subgroups. Auditors use an informal stratification procedure when they separate the population into two subgroups with one subgroup consisting of all high-valued items over a specified amount while the other subgroup consists of items under the specified amount.

A statistical stratified plan separates a population into nonoverlapping subgroups, called strata. Population items within each stratum should be as homogeneous as possible, but each stratum should be as different as possible from other strata. This type of structure increases the efficiency of most sampling plans by reducing the variability of items in each stratum. Consequently, stratification generally achieves sampling efficiency.

A statistical stratified sampling plan calculates a sample size and allocates a certain number of sample items for random selection from each stratum. Auditors select random items from each stratum in the same way that they select a random sample from an unstratified population.

Auditors investigate the sampled items from each stratum as they would for any sampling plan. Then, the results of each stratum are combined into one cohesive quantitative conclusion which should be used in conjunction with the qualitative analysis of the sample items to evaluate the reasonableness of a class of transactions or an account balance.

Dollar-Unit Sampling Plans. Dollar-unit sampling is relatively new in auditing compared to other sampling plans. Dollar-unit sampling defines a sampling unit as an individual dollar in the audit population. If the audit population is defined as all sales transactions of the period, as reflected in a sales journal totaling $100,000, the population consists of 100,000 potential sampling units without regard to the number of sales transactions. In other words, the audit population is composed of 100,000 units, each of which must have an equal opportunity of being selected for the sample. When a particular dollar is selected for the sample, the entire sales transaction which contains that dollar must be investigated. Consequently, sales transactions with greater dollar values are more likely to be selected.

To illustrate dollar-unit sampling, consider the following simple population which consists of four accounts:

Account	Book Amount	Cumulative Book Amount Range
A	$ 50	$ 1- 50
B	100	51-150
C	25	151-175
D	30	176-205

This population consists of 205 dollar units. To select a random sample of two dollar units, two random numbers are selected, and the cumulative dollar column is used to identify the accounts which contain the dollars. Then these accounts are selected for audit. For example, if the random numbers were 38 and 180, accounts A and D would be selected for audit.

Dollar-unit sampling appears to be a fruitful technique for audit use, and researchers continue to investigate the behavior of various statistical estimators which are based on the concept of dollar-unit sampling.

Advantages and Disadvantages of Variables Sampling

Advantages and disadvantages of statistical sampling discussed in the previous chapter are applicable to variables sampling except sampling risks associated with variables sampling are the risks of incorrect acceptance and incorrect rejection rather than risks of overreliance and underreliance. Variables sampling techniques, of course, can be used to control sampling risks.

Control of Sampling Risks in Statistical Plans

Auditors use sample size to control the sampling risks of incorrect acceptance and incorrect rejection by specifying the desired risk levels to be used in determining sample size. The following sections discuss (1) control of the risk incorrect rejection, (2) quantification of the ultimate risk, and (3) control of the risk of incorrect acceptance.

Controlling the Risk of Incorrect Rejection. In statistical sampling plans, the risk of incorrect rejection is called the alpha risk, which is the probability that statistical results will indicate that a reasonably stated account is materially misstated. Alpha risk is also known as the probability of a type one error. The alpha risk level is the complement of the desired confidence level. The confidence level is the probability that the true population value will fall between the computed upper and lower precision limits. Confidence levels and precision limits are explored further in a subsequent illustrative case.

Quantification of the Ultimate Risk. As stated previously, the ultimate risk is the joint probability that (1) material errors will occur and go undetected in the accounting process by which the financial statements are developed, and (2) that the auditor's investigation will not detect the materially misstated amount. The auditor relies on the system of internal control to reduce the first risk and depends on substantive tests to reduce the second risk. Consequently, the ultimate risk is a function of reliance on the internal accounting controls and on substantive tests. Symbolically, this function may be expressed as follows:

$$UR = (IC)(AR)(TD)$$

$$TD = \frac{UR}{IC \times AR}$$

where:

UR = ultimate risk,

IC = risk expressed as the probability that internal accounting controls will allow errors to occur which materially affect the financial statement account and that the system will not detect the errors,

AR = risk expressed as the probability that analytical review procedures will not detect a materially misstated financial account, and

TD = risk expressed as the probability that substantive tests of details and direct tests of balances will fail to detect a materially misstated financial account.

The auditor may subjectively specify the IC risk after evaluating and compliance testing internal accounting controls associated with the account under investigation. If the system is properly designed and compliance tests indicate that the controls are operating effectively, the auditor may assign a low probability, such as 5 percent, to the IC risk. If very little reliance is placed on internal accounting controls, the auditor may assign a 50 percent or higher probability to the IC risk.

The AR risk is very difficult to quantify. It is generally treated conservatively by assigning to it a very high probability, such as 80 percent. Some auditors assign a value of 1 to the AR risk because of the difficulty in determining the effectiveness of analytical review procedures to detect a materially misstated financial statement account.

The TD risk is equivalent to the risk of incorrect acceptance. An acceptable level for the risk of incorrect acceptance, as indicated earlier, is a function of (1) the degree of reliance assigned to internal controls, (2) the probability that other substantive tests will detect a material misstatement of the account under investigation, and (3) one minus the risk, if any, which the auditor perceives because of management's disregard for internal controls.

The formula (stated earlier) for the ultimate risk is generally not used to calculate the ultimate risk level; rather, the formula is used to determine the appropriate risk level for incorrect acceptance, TD. Consequently, the auditor judgmentally sets the ultimate risk level and then manipulates the formula to calculate the risk level for incorrect acceptance. Manipulation of the formula is presented in the following section. When the auditor *judgmentally* sets the ultimate risk level, he or she should take into consideration (1) the materiality and nature of the account under investigation in relation to the financial statements taken as a whole and (2) the adverse consequences of failing to detect a material misstatement of the financial statement account. For instance, the adverse consequences of failing to detect a materially misstated office supplies inventory account may not be as severe as not detecting a materially misstated finished goods inventory account. As the materiality of the account balance increases and as the impact of a material misstatement on the fairness of the financial statements increases, the ultimate risk level should decrease.

Controlling the Risk of Incorrect Acceptance. Traditionally in a statistical sampling plan, the risk of incorrect acceptance is referred to as the beta risk. The beta risk is the probability that statistical results will indicate an account as reasonably stated when it is materially misstated. Beta risk is also referred to as the probability of a type two error.

Quantification of the acceptable beta risk level is a function of the formula presented in the discussion on ultimate risk. The formula given for the ultimate risk may be manipulated as follows to yield the appropriate beta risk level.

$$R = (IC)(AR)(TD) \quad \text{(the formula as stated)}$$

sas 39

$$TD = \frac{\mathcal{U}R}{(IC)(AR)} \quad \begin{array}{l}\text{[the result from dividing both sides by}\\ (IC)(AR) \text{ and rearranging]}\end{array}$$

The notation should be interpreted as previously defined. The values of R, IC, AR are set by the auditor as described in previous discussions.

ILLUSTRATIVE CASE

The following example has two purposes. First, it will illustrate statistical concepts associated with variables sampling. Second, it will demonstrate the MPU and difference estimators. Included in this example are sample size calculations, point estimates, standard errors, precision intervals, confidence levels, and statistical sample evaluation.

Sample Size Determination

Sample size formulas for the MPU and difference estimators may be represented as follows:

$$\text{MPU} \qquad\qquad \text{Difference}$$

$$n = \left[\frac{S_y(Z_\alpha + Z_\beta)}{M/N} \right]^2 \qquad\qquad n = \left[\frac{S_d(Z_\alpha + Z_\beta)}{M/N} \right]^2$$

where:

n = sample size,

S_y = sample standard deviation for the MPU estimator,

S_d = sample standard deviation for the difference estimator,

Z_α = factor from the normal table for a two-sided alpha risk,

Z_β = factor from the normal table for a one-sided beta risk,

M = minimum amount considered material for the account under investigation, and

N = population size.

The sample size formulas for the MPU and difference estimators are identical except for the sample standard deviation. The sample standard deviation for the MPU estimator is based on audited values, while the sample standard deviation for the difference estimator is based on the differences between the audited values and the client-recorded book values.

In theory, the standard deviation in the sample size formula represents the population standard deviation and not that of the sample. Since it is impossible to know the population standard deviation, it must be estimated for sample size determination. The auditor may base this estimate on prior years' standard deviations or take a pilot sample of 30 items. (If the preliminary sample is less than 30, the distribution of sample means is not expected to be normally distributed.)[11] The auditor

---

[11] The distribution of sample means is expected to follow a t distribution if sample sizes are 30 or less. However, there is nothing wrong with the auditor's preliminary sample being substantially greater than 30 because empirical work has shown that sample sizes of 100 or even 200 are often not sufficient to meet the assumption of a normal distribution. For example, see the Neter reference in footnote number eight.

would audit the 30 sample items and calculate a sample standard deviation for use in the sample size formula. After the sample size is calculated, the original 30 sample items may be included in the final sample. Assume for purposes of illustrating the sample size formulas that S_y equals 31 and S_d equals 15.

Next, acceptable alpha and beta risk levels must be specified and translated into Z factors using a standard normal table. However, before discussing alpha and beta risk in detail, students must understand the nature of a normal distribution and the confidence intervals which are determined from a normal distribution.

The central limit theorem states that as sample size increases, the means from repeated samples from any population will form a normal distribution. For example, consider a population of accounts receivable, and assume that the auditor (1) takes all possible samples of a given size from this population, (2) computes the mean for each of these individual samples, and (3) examines the distribution of means. The central limit theorem states that the distribution of sample means will be normally distributed if the constant sample size used for each of the possible samples is large. How large the sample size needs to be, however, depends on the distribution of the individual account balances in the population. However, statisticians do know that if the constant sample size which is used for each of the possible samples is large enough, the resulting distribution of sample means will be a normal distribution. This statement about normality is true regardless of how the means are defined. For example, the sample means could be based on audited values, book values, differences between audited values and book values, the ratio of audited values to book values, or the proportion of accounts in each sample which have a certain attribute, e.g., the proportion of accounts which are over thirty days past due. Statisticians also know that the mean from the distribution of means, i.e., the average of all possible sample means, will equal the true mean for the population, and that the variation in the distribution of means is described by the standard error of the mean. Thus, if the auditor takes all possible samples of a given size from a population of accounts receivable, not only will the means from these samples tend to be normally distributed if the sample size is large enough, but also, (1) the mean of the sample means will equal the mean per account from the population, and (2) the variability of the distribution of sample means will be described by the standard error of the mean.

A table of areas under a normal curve is provided in Table 1 of Appendix A. Z factors are reflected in the left column of the table with the hundredth place of a Z factor shown in the top row of the table. Cells in the table show the proportion of the sample means, regardless of how the means are computed, which are expected to fall between the true mean for the population and this true mean, plus, minus, but not both, Z standard errors of this mean. For example, .4750 or 47.5 percent of the possible means from a population are expected to fall between the true mean for the population and this true mean plus 1.96 standard errors of the mean. (See the probability which appears at the intersection of the .06 column and the 1.9 row in Table 1.) Likewise, since the normal distribution is a symmetric distribution, 47.5 percent of all possible means from a population are expected to fall between the true mean for the population and the true mean minus 1.96 standard errors of the mean. Finally, 95 percent of all sample means from a population are expected to fall between the true mean for the population and this true mean plus or minus 1.96 standard errors of the mean. Similar statements may be made about any other combinations of Z and related probabilities which are listed in Table 1. For example, if one is interested in a Z of 1.18 (see the intersection of the .08 column and the 1.1 row) the following three statements can be made:

- 38.1 percent of all possible means for the population will fall between the true mean for the population and the true mean plus 1.18 standard errors of the mean.

- 38.1 percent of all possible means for the population will fall between the true mean for the population and the true mean less 1.18 standard errors of the mean.

- 76.2 (38.1 × 2) percent of all possible means for the population will fall between the true mean for the population and the true mean plus or minus 1.18 standard errors of the mean.

In practice, of course, the auditor never knows the true mean for the population, but he or she can compute a sample mean and the standard error of the mean based on the data in the sample. Then the auditor takes the sample mean plus, minus, or plus or minus the standard error of the mean to compute an appropriate confidence interval. The question is then, "What statements can the auditor make about the resulting interval?"

To understand the answer to this question, the student must understand that if the auditor took all possible samples of a given size from a population, the means from these samples will fall within a certain distance of the true mean for the population. For example, as indicated earlier, 95 percent of all sample means will fall within plus or minus 1.96 standard errors of the true mean for the population.

Given that the means of all possible samples will fall within a certain distance of the true population mean, the auditor can make the following statements about the confidence intervals which he or she computes by taking his or her sample mean plus, minus, or plus or minus Z standard errors of the mean:

- If the auditor computes the interval by taking the sample mean plus or minus Z standard errors of the mean, the auditor is a certain percent confident that the resulting interval contains the true mean for the population. The extent of the auditor's confidence can be computed from Table 1 by first obtaining the cell value for the Z which the auditor used, expressing this value as a percent and multiplying the percentage by two. For example, if the auditor uses a Z value of 1.96, the auditor is 95 percent confident that the resulting interval contains the true population mean. Another way of saying this is that, since the auditor knows that 95 percent of all means from the population will fall within plus or minus 1.96 standard errors of the true mean, there is a 95 percent chance that the mean from the auditor's sample will fall within plus or minus 1.96 standard errors of the true mean for the population. Consequently, for any possible mean from the population that the auditor obtains, he or she is 95 percent confident that the sample mean plus or minus 1.96 standard errors of the mean will include the true mean for the population.

- If the auditor computes the interval by taking the sample mean plus Z standard errors of the mean, the auditor is a certain percent confident that the true population mean is less than the upper end of the confidence interval. The extent of the auditor's confidence is obtained by obtaining the cell value for the Z which the auditor used, expressing this value as a percent, and adding 50 percent to the percentage computed from the table. For example, if the auditor uses a Z of 1.96, the auditor is 97.5 percent (47.5 + 50) confident that the true population mean is less than the upper end of the interval. Another way of saying this is that, since the auditor knows that only 2.5 percent of the possible means from the population will fall *below* the true mean minus 1.96 standard errors of the mean, there is a 97.5 percent chance that the mean from the auditor's sample will be greater than the true mean for the population less 1.96 standard errors of the mean. Of course, if any of these means, which the auditor expects to obtain 97.5 percent of the time, is obtained, the mean value plus 1.96 standard errors of the mean will be greater than the true mean for the population.

- If the auditor computes the interval by taking the sample mean minus Z standard errors of the mean, the auditor is a certain percent confident that the true population mean is more than the lower end of the interval. The extent of the auditor's confidence is obtained by obtaining the cell value for the Z that the auditor used, expressing this value as a percent, and adding 50 percent to the percentage computed from the table. For example, if the auditor uses a Z of 1.96, the auditor is 97.5 percent (47.5 + 50.0) confident that the true population mean is greater than the lower end of the auditor's confidence interval. Another way of saying this is that, since the auditor knows that only 2.5 percent of the possible means from the population will fall *above* the true mean plus 1.96 standard errors of the mean, there is a 97.5 percent chance that the mean from the auditor's sample will be less than the true mean for the population plus 1.96 standard errors of the mean. Of course, if any of these means, which the auditor expects to obtain 97.5 percent of the time, is obtained, the mean value less 1.96 standard errors of the mean will be less than the true mean.

In practice, the auditor sets the appropriate confidence interval, identifies an acceptance region, and either accepts or rejects the average balance per account which is implied by the client, i.e., the total book balance shown on the client's financial statements divided by the number of accounts, depending on whether the average balance per account which is implied by the client falls within the auditor's acceptance region or not.

The appropriate acceptance region can be established in one of three ways depending on the auditor's objectives. One way to set an acceptance region is to take the sample mean plus Z standard errors of the mean to obtain an upper precision limit. As indicated earlier, when the auditor sets the interval in this way, the auditor, depending on the Z factor used, e.g., 1.96 for 97.5 percent, is a certain percent confident that the true mean for the population is less than the upper precision limit. In these cases, the auditor accepts the client's balance as being correct if the balance which is implied by the client is less than or equal to the upper precision limit. That is, the acceptance region is any value which is less than or equal to the upper precision limit. The auditor should use this form of acceptance region when the auditor's primary concern is that the client's balance is *overstated*, and thus, the auditor is willing to accept the client's balance as being correct only if the balance which is implied by the client is less than or equal to some upper limit.

A second way to set an acceptance region is to take the sample mean less Z standard errors of the mean to obtain a lower precision limit. As indicated earlier, when the auditor sets the interval in this way, the auditor, depending on the Z factor used, is a certain percent confident that the true mean for the population is more than the lower precision limit. In these cases, the auditor accepts the client's balance as being correct if the balance which is implied by the client is greater than or equal to the lower precision limit. That is, the acceptance region is any value which is greater than or equal to the lower precision limit. The auditor should use this form of acceptance region when the auditor's primary concern is that the client's balance is *understated*, and thus, the auditor is willing to accept the client's balance as being correct only if the balance wich is implied by the client is greater than or equal to some lower limit.

A third way to set an acceptance region is to take the sample mean plus or minus Z standard errors of the mean to obtain a confidence interval which is between two points inclusive: an upper and lower precision limit. As indicated earlier, when the auditor sets the interval in this way, the auditor, depending on the Z factor used, is a certain percent confident that the true mean for the population is between the two precision limits inclusive. In these cases, the auditor accepts the client's balance as being correct if the balance which is implied by the client is between the upper and lower precision points inclusive, and the acceptance region is any value between the upper and lower precision points inclusive. The auditor should use this form of acceptance region when the auditor is concerned that the client's balance is either overstated or understated, and thus, the auditor is willing to accept the client's balance as being correct only if the balance which is implied by the client is between two points inclusive. Generally in substantive tests the auditor is concerned with either an overstatement or understatement, and therefore, the auditor should use the two-sided tests, or intervals, described in this paragraph as opposed to the one-sided tests, or intervals, which were described earlier.

When using either of the three types of tests, however, the auditor should remember that the true mean for the population is never known in practice. All that the auditor knows is that if all possible samples of a given size were taken from the population and the constant sample size for these samples is large enough, (1) the mean of the sample means will equal the true population mean, whatever the true mean is, and (2) the sample means will be normally distributed.

Since the auditor never knows the true mean of the population, the auditor, as indicated earlier, incurs sampling risk whenever the auditor uses a sample to make inferences about a population. These sampling risks, as indicated earlier, are the risk of rejecting a balance of the client's which is fairly stated, the risk of incorrect rejection, and the risk of accepting a client's balance which is not fairly stated, the risk of incorrect acceptance. The risk of incorrect rejection is also known as the alpha risk or the probability of a type one error, whereas the risk of incorrect acceptance is also known as the beta risk or the probability of a type two error.

Once the student understands these points about the normal distribution, the nature of alpha and beta risk as well as the nature of Z_α and Z_β are easier to understand. As indicated earlier, the alpha risk is always equal to one minus the auditor's confidence, where confidence is expressed as a decimal. Furthermore the Z_α factor which the auditor should use in the sample size formula is the same as the Z_α factor which the auditor uses in setting his or her confidence interval. Consequently, if the auditor wants to set a 95 percent two sided confidence interval (an alpha risk of .05), the appropriate Z_α is 1.96. Likewise, if the auditor wants to set a 97.5 percent one sided confidence interval (an alpha risk of .025) the appropriate Z_α is also 1.96. In the sample size computations which follow, an alpha risk of .05 is used for illustrative purposes.

Further insight into the computation of alpha risk can be obtained by recognizing that when an auditor sets a 95 percent two-sided confidence interval, he or she is 95 percent confident that the interval contains the true mean for the population because 95 percent of all sample means from the population will fall within 1.96 standard errors of the true mean. However, it is possible that the auditor's sample mean differs from the true mean by more than 1.96 standard errors of the mean, and thus the auditor's confidence interval will not contain the true mean. Thus, even if the balance which is implied by the client is correct, the auditor, based on his or her confidence interval, would erroneously conclude that the client's balance is incorrect if the auditor by chance obtained a sample mean which differed from the true mean by more than 1.96 standard errors of the mean. The probability of obtaining a sample mean which differs from the true mean by more than 1.96 standard errors is of course .05, if the auditor uses a two-sided 95 percent confidence interval. Similar reasoning for other types of confidence intervals can be used to understand that the alpha risk is always equal to one minus the confidence level, expressed as a decimal.

As indicated earlier, beta risk, or the probability of a type two error, is the risk of incorrect acceptance. An auditor incurs beta risk or makes a type two error if he or she accepts a client's reported balance which is either too small or too large in relation to the actual balance. However, as a practical matter the auditor has some feeling about the direction of beta risk. Consequently, the auditor computes the sample size to protect against beta risk in only one direction. For example, if the auditor computes the required sample size for a beta risk of .20, the sample size is large enough to have only a 20 percent chance of accepting a client's balance which is in fact overstated (understated) by a material amount. However, the sample size is not large enough for the auditor to have only a 20 percent chance of accepting a balance which is either overstated or understated by a material amount. The risk of accepting a balance which is either overstated or understated by a material amount is 40 percent (20 × 2). However, the auditor, as a practical matter, is not concerned with the risk of either a material overstatement or understatement because, at least after looking at the data, the auditor is fairly sure of the direction of a type two error, if any.

To obtain Z_β, the auditor finds .5 minus the beta risk which he or she is willing to accept in the appropriate cell of Table 1, and then reads the Z_β factor by referring to the row and column which intersect at the cell which contains .5 minus the beta risk that the auditor is willing to accept. In cases where the exact value for .5 minus the beta risk is not given in the body of Table 1, the auditor should select the next closest value which is given in the table. For example, Z_β for a 20 percent beta risk is approximately .84. A 20 percent beta risk and a Z_β of .84 is used in the example which immediately follows this discussion.

Further insight into the computation of beta risk can be obtained by recognizing that in practice the auditor never knows the true mean for the population. Instead, all that he or she knows is that if the constant sample size is large enough (1) the means of repeated samples from any population will be normally distributed and (2) the mean of all possible sample means from the population will equal the true mean for the population. Consequently, it is entirely possible that the auditor will obtain a sample mean which will cause the auditor's confidence interval to include the balance implied by the client when the client's balance is incorrect.

To illustrate this point, assume the following data:

True mean for the population	10
Auditor's sample mean	11
Balance implied by the client (total book value divided by the number of items)	12
Standard error of the mean computed from the sample	1
Minimum amount considered material	2

Given the auditor's sample mean and the standard error of the mean, the auditor's acceptance region for a two-sided 95 percent confidence interval would be 9.04 to 12.96 [11 ± 1.96(1)]. Consequently, the auditor would accept the balance implied by the client as being correct when in fact the balance, as the example indicates, is incorrect. In other words, given the assumed data, the auditor would make a type two error. What happened in this case, of course, was that the auditor was fooled into thinking that the distribution of sample means centered around 12 (as indicated earlier, the distribution of sample means for a population will center around the true mean for the population) when in fact the distribution centered around 10. Notice in this case that 95 percent of the possible means from the actual population will fall between the true mean for the population (10) plus or minus 1.96 standard errors of the mean (1). Thus, 95 percent of the means will fall between 8.04 and 11.96 inclusive [10 ± 1.96(1)]. Consequently, in this example it is not at all unreasonable to assume that the auditor obtained a sample mean of 11 and thus made a type two error.

In the previous illustration, the auditor made a type two error because the auditor believed that he or she was sampling from a distribution with a center of 12 when he or she was really sampling from a distribution with a center of 10. In fact, whenever an auditor makes a type two error, the auditor has been fooled into thinking that he or she is sampling from a distribution with a given center when in fact he or she is sampling from a distribution which has a center value above or below this value. Consequently, when an auditor specifies the probability of a type two error he or she is willing to accept, the auditor is actually specifying the chance that he or she is willing to accept that a sample mean will be obtained from a distribution which has a center which is close enough to the balance that is implied by the client that the auditor will be fooled, based on his or her confidence interval, into thinking that the client's balance is correct when in fact the balance is incorrect. Of course, the probability of a type two error is dependent on the amount of the error in the client's balance. For example, if the client implies that the average balance per account is $12 when it is really $12.01, there is a very good chance that the auidtor will make a type two error, but of course, the amount of the error in this case is clearly immaterial. On the other hand, if the client implies that the average balance per account is $12 when it is really $1,000, there is very little chance that the auditor will make a type two error because there is practically no chance that the auditor would obtain a sample mean from a distribution that actually centers around $1,000 that is close enough to $12 so that the auditor's confidence interval would include $12. This point as well as the derivation of the way in which alpha and beta risk influence sample size are discussed in more detail in Appendix B of this chapter.

The remaining quantification for sample size determination concerns materiality. Materiality was previously defined as the dollar amount of tolerable error that could exist in the population without causing a material misstatement. The auditor may subjectively determine a material amount by specifying a certain sum or a percent of an account balance. For instance, if an inventory book value is $70,000, the auditor may indicate that 3 percent of the book value ($2,100) is material. In the sample size formula provided above, materiality is converted to a per-unit basis by dividing the minimum amount considered material by the population size. In the present case, assume a population size of 1,000 units, and a materiality amount of $2,100.

Sample sizes for the MPU and difference estimators may be calculated as follows:

$$\underline{MPU} \qquad\qquad\qquad \underline{Difference}$$

$$n = \left[\frac{31(1.96 + .84)}{2,100/1,000}\right]^2 \qquad\qquad n = \left[\frac{15(1.96 + .84)}{2,100/1,000}\right]^2$$

$$n = 1,708 \qquad\qquad\qquad n = 400$$

This example demonstrates the efficiency of the difference estimator compared to the MPU estimator. Note also that the sample size formula for the MPU estimator yields a sample size larger than the population size. When this happens in practice, it simply means that the auditor needs to sample every item in the population to be able to achieve the results which he or she had planned. However, the auditor would not use these sample sizes without the adjustment factor explained below.

The formulas given above represent sampling with replacement. Of course, auditors should sample without replacement. To adjust the above sample size to reflect sampling without replacement, the auditor should use the following sample size adjustment formula.

$$n' = \frac{n}{1 + \dfrac{n}{N}}$$

where:

n′ = sample size without replacement,

n = sample size with replacement, and

N = population size.

To adjust the calculated sample sizes above:

	MPU		*Difference*

$$n' = \frac{1{,}000}{1 + \frac{1{,}000}{1{,}000}} \qquad\qquad n' = \frac{400}{1 + \frac{400}{1{,}000}}$$

$$n' = 500 \qquad\qquad\qquad n' = 286$$

When the sample size with replacement is approximately 10 percent or more of the population size, the auditor should adjust the sample size to reflect sampling without replacement. That is, when n/N is greater than 10 percent, make the adjustment. When n/N is less than 10 percent, the adjustment to sample size is optional since its effect on sample size will likely be immaterial.

Assumed Data for Illustrative Case

For the remaining portions of the case, substitute a sample size of 10 for the calculated sizes of 500 and 286. It is necessary to reduce the sample size to a manageable number so that unwieldy calculations will not detract from the presentation of concepts.

Assume the following additional data for the illustrative case.

Inventory book value	$70,000
Population size, N	1,000
Sample size, n	10
Confidence level = 80%	
Alpha risk level = 20%, Z_α	1.282
Beta risk level = 20%, Z_β	.842
Materiality factor (3% of book)	$ 2,100
Total *book* value of all items in the sample	$ 566
Total *audited* value of all items in the sample	$ 493

In this example, the auditor has randomly selected 10 sample items from an inventory population of 1,000 items and has prepared the following worksheet.

WORKSHEET

Sample Item (i)	Audited Value (y_i)	Book Value (x_i)	Difference (d_i)	$(d_i - D^*)^2$	$(y_i - Y\#)^2$
1	26	30.	− 4	10.89	542.89
2	72	69.	3.	106.09	515.29
3	53	63.	− 10.	7.29	13.69
4	46	46.	0	53.29	10.89
5	14	24.	− 10.	7.29	1,246.09
6	21	18	3.	106.09	800.89
7	86	96.	− 10.	7.29	1,346.89
8	110	120.	− 10.	7.29	3,684.49
9	38	83.	− 45.	1,421.29	127.69
10	27	17.	10.	299.29	497.29
	$\Sigma y_i = 493$	$\Sigma x_i = 566.$	$\Sigma d_i = -73.$	$\Sigma(d_i - D)^2 = 2,026.10$	$(\Sigma y_i - Y)^2 = 8,786.10$

*D = average difference in sample
#Y = average audited value in sample ⎤— See calculation of sample means in the following section.

Point Estimates

A point estimate is an estimate of the audited value of the account under investigation. The sample mean is used to calculate the point estimate. Sample means for the MPU and difference estimators may be calculated as shown below:

MPU	Difference
$Y = \Sigma y_i/n$	$D = \Sigma d_i/n$
$= 493/10$	$= -73/10$
$= \underline{49.30}$	$= \underline{-7.30}$

where:

Y = MPU sample mean (average audited value of sample),

D = Difference sample mean (average difference in sample),

y_i = audit value of the ith sample item,

d_i = difference between the audited value and the book value of the ith sample item, and

n = sample size.

When using the MPU estimator to obtain the point estimate for the population total, multiply the sample mean by the population size. For the difference estimator, multiplying the sample mean by population size yields the estimated population difference. The estimated population difference must be added to, or subtracted from, the book value of the financial statement account to arrive at the point estimate for the population total. Point estimates for the population totals are computed as follows:

	MPU		*Difference*

MPU   *Difference*

Point estimate = Y(N)   Estimated population difference = D(N)

Pt_y = 49.30(1,000)   = − 7.30(1,000)

      = 49,300.   = − 7,300.

Point estimate = Book Value + D(N)

Pt_d = 70,000 + (− 7,300.)

    = 62,700.

Point estimates are unreliable because sample means are unreliable. Sample means are unreliable because a second sample of the same size (assuming valid sample sizes) will probably yield a sample mean different from the first sample mean. And a third and fourth sample will probably produce means different from the first and second sample means. As indicated earlier, if all possible samples of the same size were randomly selected from a population and the constant sample size for each sample is large enough, the sample means would be normally distributed around the true population mean. Consequently, any sample drawn from the population must come from this normal distribution of sample means. How much any given sample mean will differ from the true population mean can be estimated by the standard error of the sample means.

Standard Error of Sample Means

The standard error of sample means is a measure of the extent to which a sample mean may be expected to deviate from the population mean. The standard error of sample means is found by dividing the standard deviation of the sample by the square root of the sample size. First, the standard deviation of the sample must be calculated. The standard deviation of the two different estimators may be computed as follows:

MPU   *Difference*

$$S_y = \sqrt{\frac{\sum\limits_{i=1}^{n}(y_i - Y)^2}{n-1}} \qquad\qquad S_d = \sqrt{\frac{\sum\limits_{i=1}^{n}(d_i - D)^2}{n-1}}$$

where:

S_y = sample standard deviation for the MPU estimator, and
S_d = sample standard deviation for the difference estimator.

The remaining notation is the same as previously defined. Sample standard deviations for the case may be computed as indicated below:

$$
\begin{array}{cc}
\textit{MPU} & \textit{Difference} \\[4pt]
S_y = \sqrt{\dfrac{8786.10}{10-1}} & S_d = \sqrt{\dfrac{2026.10}{10-1}} \\[10pt]
= \underline{\underline{31.2447}} & = \underline{\underline{15.0040}}
\end{array}
$$

The following formula shows the relationship of the standard deviation to the standard error and reflects the calculation of the standard error of sample means for the MPU and difference estimators:

$$
\begin{array}{cc}
\textit{MPU} & \textit{Difference} \\[4pt]
SE_y = S_y/\sqrt{n} & SE_d = S_d/\sqrt{n} \\[6pt]
= 31.2447/\sqrt{10} & = 15.0040/\sqrt{10} \\[6pt]
= \underline{\underline{9.8804}} & = \underline{\underline{4.7446}}
\end{array}
$$

where:

SE_y = standard error for the MPU estimator, and
SE_d = standard error for the difference estimator.

The standard error is used in calculating precision limits for a given confidence level.

Precision Limits and Confidence Levels

After calculating the point estimate and the standard error, the auditor can determine the precision limits for the given confidence level. Precision limits may be calculated for sample means (the point estimate of the amount per account) or for point estimates of the total. The illustrative case uses point estimates of the total as the basis for calculating achieved precision limits.[12]

First the precision interval for the average must be determined by using the following formula:

---

[12] As indicated earlier, the auditor can make a decision about the fairness of the client's balance by determining whether the balance per account which is implied by the client, i.e., the book value divided by the number of accounts, falls within the auditor's acceptance region. Alternatively, as this example illustrates, the auditor can convert the acceptance region to an acceptance region based on the total, and then determine if the client's total book amount falls within this acceptance region. Both procedures always give the same conclusion.

<table>
<tr><td colspan="2">MPU</td><td colspan="2">Difference</td></tr>
<tr><td>Precision interval
for the average =</td><td>$Z_\alpha SE_y$</td><td>Precision interval
for the average =</td><td>$Z_\alpha SE_d$</td></tr>
<tr><td>=</td><td>1.282(9.8804)</td><td>=</td><td>1.282(4.7446)</td></tr>
<tr><td>=</td><td>12.6667</td><td>=</td><td>6.0826</td></tr>
</table>

The precision interval for the average must be multiplied by the population size to convert it to the precision interval for the population. This mathematical procedure is demonstrated below:

<table>
<tr><td colspan="2">MPU</td><td colspan="2">Difference</td></tr>
<tr><td>Precision interval
for population =</td><td>$N \cdot z_\alpha \cdot SE_y$</td><td>Precision interval
for population =</td><td>$N \cdot Z_\alpha \cdot SE_d$</td></tr>
<tr><td>PI_y =</td><td>1,000(12.6667)</td><td>PI_d =</td><td>1,000(6.0826)</td></tr>
<tr><td>=</td><td>12,666.70</td><td>=</td><td>6,082.60</td></tr>
</table>

The precision interval for the population total is added to, and subtracted from, the point estimate to determine the upper and lower precision limits for the confidence level specified. This mathematical process is shown below:

<table>
<tr><td colspan="2">MPU</td><td colspan="2">Difference</td></tr>
<tr><td>UPL_y =</td><td>$Pt_y + PI_y$</td><td>UPL_d =</td><td>$Pt_d + PI_d$</td></tr>
<tr><td>=</td><td>49,300. + 12,666.70</td><td>=</td><td>62,700. + 6,082.60</td></tr>
<tr><td>=</td><td>61,966.70</td><td>=</td><td>68,782.60</td></tr>
<tr><td>LPL_y =</td><td>$Pt_y - PI_y$</td><td>LPL_d =</td><td>$Pt_d - PI_d$</td></tr>
<tr><td>=</td><td>49,300. − 12,666.70</td><td>=</td><td>62,700. − 6,082.60</td></tr>
<tr><td>=</td><td>36,633.30</td><td>=</td><td>56,617.40</td></tr>
</table>

where:

UPL_y = upper precision limit for the MPU estimator,
LPL_y = lower precision limit for the MPU estimator,
UPL_d = upper precision limit for the difference estimator, and
LPL_d = lower precision limit for the difference estimator.

The auditor can state with 80 percent confidence that the true population value falls between the upper and lower precision limits. For the MPU estimator, the auditor is 80 percent confident that the population value falls between $36,633.30 and $61,966.70. For the difference estimator, the auditor is 80 percent confident that the population value falls between $56,617.40 and $68,782.60. The auditor will use this information to form a statistical conclusion.

Some readers may wonder why the precision interval is so wide in the sample case. The answer is that the results are due to the small sample size, 10, used in the example. In practice, the auditor can make the precision interval as small as he or she wants by increasing the sample size.

Statistical Conclusion. For a statistical conclusion the upper and lower precision limits are compared to the client-recorded book value of the account under investigation. If the book value falls between the upper and lower precision limits, the auditor may statistically conclude at the confidence level stated in the plan that the recorded book value is reasonably stated. If the book value falls outside the decision interval, statistical results indicate that the account is not reasonably stated. The comparison for the current case is presented below:

MPU estimator:

$$LPL_y < \text{Book Value} < UPL_y$$
$$36{,}633.30 < 70{,}000 \not< 61{,}966.70$$

Difference estimator:

$$LPL_d < \text{Book Value} < UPL_d$$
$$56{,}617.40 < 70{,}000 \not< 68{,}782.60$$

Comparisons for both estimators reflect that the book value falls outside the acceptance region. Consequently, for both estimators the auditor could statistically conclude with 80 percent confidence that the client's book value is materially misstated.

However, the auditor must recognize that sample size determination was based on an estimate of the population standard deviation. If the estimate used in determining sample size does not approximate the sample standard deviation, the beta risk level will differ from the planned beta risk level. Therefore, when the standard deviation for the sample differs from the standard deviation used in determining sample size, the auditor may want to adjust the precision interval to be compatible with the desired beta risk level before reaching a final statistical decision. This point is illustrated later.

Impact of changing confidence level.   Changing the confidence level while holding the sample size constant influences the width of the precision interval. Remember that the precision interval is the product of the Z_α factor, standard error, and population size. Of course, when auditors evaluate a sample, they cannot alter the standard error and population size. The confidence level, however, can be changed in the evaluation. When the confidence level is increased from 80 percent to 90 percent, the Z_α factor increases from 1.282 to 1.645, causing a wider precision interval. Computation of the wider precision interval with a 90 percent confidence level is demonstrated below:

	MPU		*Difference*
$PI_y =$	$N \cdot Z_\alpha \cdot SE_y$	$PI_d =$	$N \cdot Z_\alpha \cdot SE_d$
$=$	$1,000(1.645)(9.8804)$	$=$	$1,000(1.645)(4.7446)$
$=$	$16,253.25$	$=$	$7,804.86$

Accordingly, precision limits are further apart with a 90 percent confidence level than with an 80 percent confidence level. Precision limits associated with the higher confidence level are reflected below:

	MPU		*Difference*
$UPL_y =$	$Pt_y + PI_y$	$UPL_d =$	$Pt_d + PI_d$
$=$	$49,300. + 16,253.25$	$=$	$62,700. + 7,804.86$
$=$	$65,553.25$	$=$	$70,504.86$
$LPL_y =$	$Pt_y - PI_y$	$LPL_d =$	$Pt_d - PI_d$
$=$	$49,300. - 16,253.25$	$=$	$62,700. - 7,804.86$
$=$	$33,046.75$	$=$	$54,895.14$

The auditor may compare these precision limits to the related book value as a basis for a statistical decision at the 90 percent confidence level. The comparison of the client's book value with the precision limits is provided below:

MPU estimator:

LPL_y < Book value < UPL_y
33,046.75 < 70,000. ≮ 65,553.25

Difference estimator:

LPL_d < Book value < UPL_d
54,895.14 < 70,000. < 70,504.86

For the MPU estimator, the statistical conclusion does not change with the higher confidence level. The auditor may still conclude that the book value is materially misstated, but the statistical decision in this case is at the 90 percent reliability level. The difference estimator indicates a change in the statistical decision at the 90 percent confidence level. With the wider acceptance region, the book value falls inside the acceptance region indicating a reasonably stated book value. The above situations illustrate the statistical phenomenon that the level of confidence and the preciseness of the acceptance region have an inverse relationship. That is, the auditor may have more confidence in a decision but the acceptance region will be less precise.

Furthermore, the auditor must also consider that with higher reliability levels there is a lower probability of committing a type one error of statistically concluding that a reasonably stated account is materially misstated. For the MPU case above, if the recorded book value is reasonably stated, the probability of committing a type one error changes from 20 percent to 10 percent.

For the difference estimator above, the probability of committing a type one error in the first situation, with an 80 percent confidence level, is 20 percent. The 90 percent confidence level, however, created a precision interval wide enough to allow a statistical decision of fair statement of the account. Consequently, a type one error cannot be committed; only a type two error may occur in this case, and a type two error can only occur if the client-recorded value is materially misstated. Adjusting the precision interval to control the beta risk level is the topic of the following section. However, before considering the control of beta risk, one other important point must be considered.

As this section indicates, the confidence level used has an important impact on the acceptance region and the probability of a type one error. However, the *auditor's confidence level must be established in advance, and the level must not be changed simply because a different statistical conclusion can be obtained by changing the confidence level.* For example, when the auditor decides to use an 80 percent confidence level for the difference estimator, he or she makes the decision in view of all of the information, such as his or her assessment of internal control available at that time. Consequently, the auditor must not change the confidence level to 90 percent simply because the auditor can accept the client's balance at a 90 percent confidence level but not at the 80 percent confidence level. In short, any decisions about confidence level must be based on valid audit judgment and not only on the impact that the confidence level has on the results of a statistical test.

Adjusting the precision interval and limits to control beta risk[13]. In certain situations the auditor may want to adjust the precision interval so that the computed and desired beta risk levels are equivalent. The computed beta risk level will not be equivalent to the desired level when the standard deviation differs from the estimated standard deviation used in sample size determination. When this difference occurs, the precision interval will be either too wide or too narrow for the desired beta risk level. If the standard deviation is less than the estimated standard deviation, the precision interval will be too small for the desired beta risk level; the beta risk will be smaller than the planned level.

To understand this point, recognize that the size of the standard deviation determines the size of the standard error of the mean; the smaller the standard deviation, the smaller the standard error of the mean. Furthermore, the smaller the standard error of the mean, the smaller the acceptance region which the auditor computes. Therefore, if the acceptance region is smaller than the auditor planned, there is less chance that the acceptance region will contain a balance which is in fact incorrect. Or, in other words, there is less beta risk than the auditor had planned on when he or she determined the sample size.

When statistical results indicate a reasonably stated account, the auditor will probably not object to the lower beta risk. On the other hand, if statistical results imply that the account is materially misstated, the auditor may increase the precision interval to reflect the desired beta risk level.

To illustrate adjusting precision intervals to reflect the desired beta risk level, assume the following data for the MPU estimator:

---

[13] Some students, who have not had previous experience in computing beta risk, may find that it is helpful to read Appendix B before studying this section.

Book value.............................. $100,000.
Point estimate........................... 98,000.
Computed precision interval............... 1,500.
Materiality (3%)......................... 3,000.
Planned beta risk........................ 20%
Planned alpha risk....................... 10%

Also assume that the sample standard deviation is less than the estimated standard deviation used in sample size determination. Notice that the assumed statistical results above indicate that the book value of $100,000 is materially misstated since the book value is larger than the upper precision limit of $99,500 ($98,000 + $1,500). In this case, the beta risk will be smaller than the planned 20 percent risk. To calculate an adjusted precision interval for a beta risk of 20 percent, the desired precision interval must first be calculated using the following formula:

$$DPI = \frac{M}{1 + \dfrac{Z_\beta}{Z_\alpha}}$$

where:

DPI = desired precision interval,
M = minimum amount considered material,
Z_β = factor from the normal table for a one-sided beta risk, and
Z_α = factor from the normal table for a two-sided alpha risk.

$$DPI = \frac{3{,}000}{1 + \dfrac{.842}{1.645}}$$

$$= \underline{1{,}984}$$

To calculate an adjusted precision interval for a beta risk equal to the planned beta, substitute the appropriate data in the following formula:

$$PI_y{'} = PI_y + M[1. - (PI_y/DPI)]$$
$$= 1{,}500. + 3{,}000.[1. - (1{,}500/1{,}984.)]$$
$$= \underline{2{,}232}$$

where:

$PI_y{'}$ = adjusted precision interval,
PI_y = original precision interval,
DPI = desired precision interval, and
M = minimum amount considered material.

Then, the adjusted precision interval is used to calculate adjusted precision limits. Adjusted precision limits are reflected below:

$$UPL_{y'} = Pt_y + PI_{y'} = 98,000. + 2,232. = 100,232.$$
$$LPL_{y'} = Pt_y - PI_{y'} = 98,000. - 2,232. = 95,768.$$

where:

$UPL_{y'}$ = adjusted upper precision limit, and

$LPL_{y'}$ = adjusted lower precision limit.

Remaining notation was defined previously.

Since the book value of $100,000 falls within the adjusted precision limits, the auditor may conclude that the book value is not materially misstated; however, the auditor does not know the level of confidence with which this statement is being made because the size of the confidence level has been expanded. However, since the auditor is now accepting the book value as reasonable, a type one error cannot occur; only a type two error is possible. Therefore, the auditor is not concerned so much with confidence and the related probability of a type one error. The probability of a type two error is 20 percent, the desired beta risk level.

Although it is not necessary to know the final alpha risk level, since the auditor will not be committing a type one error, the auditor may compute the alpha risk and confidence level as described below. The following formula can be used to calculate the $Z_{\alpha'}$ factor which is associated with the adjusted confidence level:

$$Z_{\alpha'} = Z_\alpha(PI_{y'}/PI_y)$$
$$= 1.645(2,232/1,500)$$
$$= \underline{\underline{2.44}}$$

where:

$Z_{\alpha'}$ = factor from the normal table for the adjusted confidence level.

Using Table 1 in Appendix A of the chapter, find 2.4 in the left column and .04 in the top row. Draw an imaginary horizontal line to the right of 2.4 and an imaginary vertical line down from .04. At the intersection of these two imaginary lines, find the factor .4927 which represents the probability for one-half the curve or one-half the reliability level. Doubling the Z_{α} factor of .4927 yields a confidence level of 98 percent.

The illustration above on adjusting precision limits will enable the auditor to accept the recorded book value as reasonably stated because it falls within the adjusted precision limits. On the other hand, if the book value did not fall within the adjusted precision limits, the auditor would have to evaluate and choose between alternative paths of action as described in the prior section, "The Audit Decision." The above illustration demonstrates how to adjust the precision interval when the beta risk level is smaller than the desired risk level.

The auditor may also want to adjust the precision interval when the beta risk is larger than the desired beta risk. This will occur when the standard deviation is greater than the estimated standard deviation used to determine sample size. When this situation occurs, the precision interval will be too large to keep the beta risk as small as desired. In this case, the auditor will make the adjustment only when statistical results indicate that the financial statement balance is reasonably stated. If the adjustment were not made, the auditor might be accepting the reasonableness of the account under unacceptable conditions. Therefore, when the standard deviation is greater than the estimated standard deviation and when statistical results indicate that the financial statement balance is reasonably stated, the auditor should adjust the precision interval so that the beta risk and desired beta risk levels are equivalent. The adjustment would be made by using the formulas given earlier.

To understand this point recognize that, when the standard deviation is larger that the estimated standard deviation, the standard error of the mean is larger than the auditor anticipated. Therefore, the auditor's acceptance region is larger than the auditor expected. Consequently, there is more chance than the auditor anticipated that the acceptance region will contain a balance which is in fact incorrect. Or, in other words, there is more beta risk than the auditor had planned on when he or she determined the sample size.

On the other hand, when the standard deviation is greater than the estimated standard deviation and when statistical results indicate that the account is materially misstated, the precision interval should not be adjusted because a type two error cannot occur. Only a type one error may be made. The auditor will have to evaluate additional auditing procedures in light of alternative paths of action as discussed in the prior section, "The Audit Decision."

In summary, the precision interval should be adjusted for a statistical decision when either of the following two situations occur: (1) when the standard deviation is smaller than the estimated standard deviation and when statistical results indicate a materially misstated account, and (2) when the standard deviation is greater than the estimated standard deviation and when statistical results imply that the account is reasonably stated.

An appendix to this chapter provides an auditing derivation of the sample size formula and a theoretical discussion of controlling the beta risk. Although the appendix may be omitted without jeopardizing the continuity of the following chapters, the student is strongly encouraged to read this appendix to gain a better understanding of statistical concepts in relation to variables sampling.

SUMMARY

The purpose of substantive testing is to estimate the amount of dollar error in a financial statement account or to determine the reasonableness of an account balance. The nature, extent, and timing of substantive testing are influenced by the degree of reliance which the auditor places on the relevant internal accounting controls. If the internal accounting control system over the account or class of transactions under investigation is strong, the auditor may restrict substantive tests. Complete reliance on internal accounting controls, however, is not permitted by the second standard of field work. There must be some substantive testing. The auditor judgmentally determines the balance between compliance testing and substantive testing. Evidence gained from these two types of testing must be sufficient and competent so that the auditor may form an opinion regarding the financial statements under audit.

Substantive testing includes both sampling and nonsampling risks. Nonsampling risks are controlled by proper planning and supervision of the audit, by firm adherence to high quality control standards, and by maintaining a high level of auditor competency.

The auditor may control the sampling risks of incorrect acceptance and of incorrect rejection through sample size. The lower the sampling risk levels, the larger the sample size necessary to attain the sampling objectives. In addition to sampling risks, sample size depends on the amount of tolerable error (materiality) considered acceptable in the circumstances. The smaller the amount of tolerable error, the larger the sample size necessary to attain the audit objectives.

If sampling results indicate a materially misstated account, the auditor must apply additional audit procedures to the account balance or to the class of transactions so that he or she can determine if the population was erroneously rejected or determine why the account is materially misstated.

An acceptable risk level for incorrect acceptance is a function of the degree of reliance assigned to internal controls, the probability that analytical review techniques will detect a material misstatement of the account under investigation, and the ultimate risk.

The ultimate risk is the joint probability that the internal accounting control system will allow a material error to occur and go undetected and that the auditor will not detect the material misstatement of financial data. The auditor relies on internal accounting controls to reduce the first risk and depends on substantive testing to reduce the second risk.

The risk of incorrect acceptance may be subjectively determined based on the factors specified above. Or, this risk level may be determined using an algebraic formula where the auditor must quantify the (1) ultimate risk level, (2) the risk that internal accounting controls will allow material errors to occur and remain undetected, and (3) the risk that analytical review techniques will fail to detect a materially misstated financial statement account.

Substantive testing includes analytical review procedures, tests of details of transactions, and direct tests of balances. Analytical review techniques use summarized data and generally do not involve sampling procedures. Tests of details and direct tests of balances use sampling procedures unless each item in the population should be investigated. Analytical review techniques provide corroborating evidence for a materially misstated account but the techniques generally are not used to measure the amount of misstatement. Statistical sampling plans, however, provide an objective method for determining the probable amount of misstatement. Statistical techniques employed in conjunction with tests of details and direct tests of balances have been defined as variables sampling plans.

The auditor should develop tests of details and direct tests of balances to satisfy specific audit objectives. Auditors should define specific audit objectives before developing a substantive sampling plan because the objectives determine the appropriate audit population from which to sample.

If the specific audit objective is to ascertain the existence or occurrence of an item or class of transactions reflected on the financial statement, the procedure is one of vouching from a population containing all recorded items in the account to their source in a search for unauthorized or ficticious transactions. If the specific audit objective is to determine completeness of a financial statement account, the procedure is one of retracing to search for unrecorded transactions captured on source documents. In substantive tests, either retracing or vouching may be used to ascertain proper valuation of a financial statement account or class of transactions.

Evaluation of sample results consists of quantitative and qualitative analyses. Qualitative analyses investigate the nature and cause of the dollar errors. The auditor uses the results of qualitative analysis in conjunction with the quantitative analysis to form an audit conclusion. Quantitative and qualitative evaluation of the sample may indicate that the financial statement account under investigation is reasonably stated, and the auditor may proceed as planned. If the evaluation indicates that the account is materially misstated, the auditor may follow one or a combination of alternative courses of action.

One potential course of action would be to increase the sample size, while another possibility would be to extend auditing procedures where patterns of errors are indicated. Either alternative should establish the degree of material misstatement or determine that the original sample had produced an incorrect rejection of a reasonably stated account. Another alternative is to ask the client to reconstruct the account if the account is materially misstated due to unintentional errors, such as misunderstanding instructions or misapplying an acceptable accounting principle. If the auditor has sufficient evidence that an account is materially misstated, he or she should recommend that the client adjust the account. If the client makes the adjustment, the auditor can give an unqualified opinion. If the client refuses to make the adjustment, the auditor must render either a qualified or an adverse opinion.

The mean-per-unit (MPU) and difference estimators were used to illustrate a variables sampling plan and statistical concepts. There are several other variables estimators, but there is not one estimator that is more reliable than all other estimators under all conditions. Several variables sampling plans were described indicating conditions under which each estimator would be reliable.

Variables sampling plans which estimate the reasonableness of an account, or the degree of misstatement, offer the advantages of controlling sampling risks and providing conclusive evidence to support a recommendation to adjust a materially misstated financial account.

Furthermore, variables sampling plans satisfy the field work standards. Valid variables sampling plans require advance planning before statistical techniques are carried out. Thus, with proper supervision of the testing, the first standard of field work is satisfied. Auditors judgmentally set levels for many statistical variables which influence the extent of sampling. Quantification of some of these statistical variables which influence the extent of testing is based on the degree of reliance that can be placed on the internal control system. Consequently, variables sampling techniques help attain the second field work standard.

Evidence gained through variables sampling provides sufficient competent evidence upon which to base an opinion regarding the financial statement under investigation. A variables sampling plan specifies the sufficiency of testing while the auditor professionally determines the competency of the evidence. Therefore, statistical sampling plans help attain the third standard of field work since the extent of sampling is objectively determined in such plans.

APPENDIX A

Table 1
Areas of the Normal Curve

Z Standard deviation units	.00	.01	.02	.03	.04	.05	.06	.07	.08	.09
0.0	.0000	.0040	.0080	.0120	.0160	.0199	.0239	.0279	.0319	.0359
0.1	.0398	.0438	.0478	.0517	.0557	.0596	.0636	.0675	.0714	.0753
0.2	.0793	.0832	.0871	.0910	.0948	.0987	.1026	.1064	.1103	.1141
0.3	.1179	.1217	.1255	.1293	.1331	.1368	.1406	.1443	.1480	.1517
0.4	.1554	.1591	.1628	.1664	.1700	.1736	.1772	.1808	.1844	.1879
0.5	.1915	.1950	.1985	.2019	.2054	.2088	.2123	.2157	.2190	.2224
0.6	.2257	.2291	.2324	.2357	.2389	.2422	.2454	.2486	.2517	.2549
0.7	.2580	.2611	.2642	.2673	.2704	.2734	.2764	.2794	.2823	.2852
0.8	.2881	.2910	.2939	.2967	.2995	.3023	.3051	.3078	.3106	.3133
0.9	.3159	.3186	.3212	.3238	.3264	.3289	.3315	.3340	.3365	.3389
1.0	.3413	.3438	.3461	.3485	.3508	.3531	.3554	.3577	.3599	.3621
1.1	.3643	.3665	.3686	.3708	.3729	.3749	.3770	.3790	.3810	.3830
1.2	.3849	.3869	.3888	.3907	.3925	.3944	.3962	.3980	.3997	.4015
1.3	.4032	.4049	.4066	.4082	.4099	.4115	.4131	.4147	.4162	.4177
1.4	.4192	.4207	.4222	.4236	.4251	.4265	.4279	.4292	.4306	.4319
1.5	.4332	.4345	.4357	.4370	.4382	.4394	.4406	.4418	.4429	.4441
1.6	.4452	.4463	.4474	.4484	.4495	.4505	.4515	.4525	.4535	.4545
1.7	.4554	.4564	.4573	.4582	.4591	.4599	.4608	.4616	.4625	.4633
1.8	.4641	.4649	.4656	.4664	.4671	.4678	.4686	.4693	.4699	.4706
1.9	.4713	.4719	.4726	.4732	.4738	.4744	.4750	.4756	.4761	.4767
2.0	.4772	.4778	.4783	.4788	.4793	.4798	.4803	.4808	.4812	.4817
2.1	.4821	.4826	.4830	.4834	.4838	.4842	.4846	.4850	.4854	.4857
2.2	.4861	.4864	.4868	.4871	.4875	.4878	.4881	.4884	.4887	.4890
2.3	.4893	.4896	.4898	.4901	.4904	.4906	.4909	.4911	.4913	.4916
2.4	.4918	.4920	.4922	.4925	.4927	.4929	.4931	.4932	.4934	.4936
2.5	.4938	.4940	.4941	.4943	.4945	.4946	.4948	.4949	.4951	.4952
2.6	.4953	.4955	.4956	.4957	.4959	.4960	.4961	.4962	.4963	.4964
2.7	.4965	.4966	.4967	.4968	.4969	.4970	.4971	.4972	.4973	.4974
2.8	.4974	.4975	.4976	.4977	.4977	.4978	.4979	.4979	.4980	.4981
2.9	.4981	.4982	.4982	.4983	.4984	.4984	.4985	.4985	.4986	.4986
3.0	.4987	.4987	.4987	.4988	.4988	.4989	.4989	.4989	.4990	.4990
3.1	.4990	.4991	.4991	.4991	.4992	.4992	.4992	.4992	.4993	.4993
3.2	.4993	.4993	.4994	.4994	.4994	.4994	.4994	.4995	.4995	.4995
3.3	.4995	.4995	.4995	.4996	.4996	.4996	.4996	.4996	.4996	.4997
3.4	.4997	.4997	.4997	.4997	.4997	.4997	.4997	.4997	.4997	.4998
3.5	.499767									
3.6	.499841									
3.7	.499892									
3.8	.499928									
3.9	.499952									
4.0	.499968									
4.1	.499979									
4.2	.499987									
4.3	.499991									
4.4	.499995									
4.5	.499997									
4.6	.499998									
4.7	.499999									
4.8	.499999									
4.9	.500000									

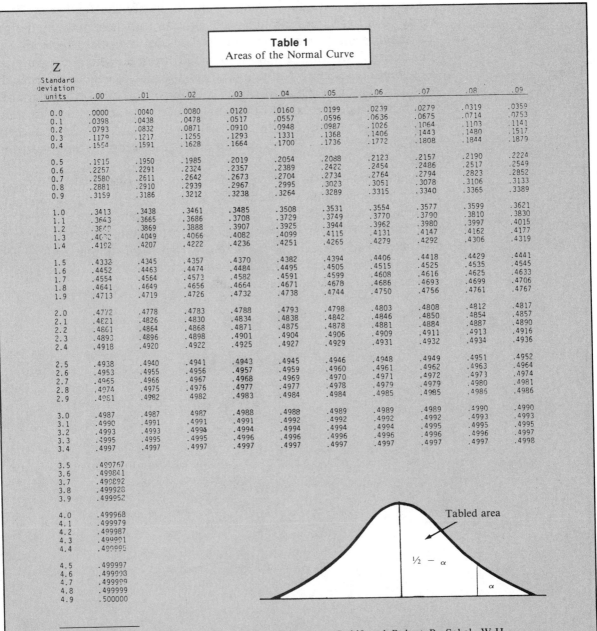

Tabled area

½ − α

α

From Statistical Tables, Second Edition, by F. James Rohlf and Robert R. Sokal. W.H. Freeman and Company, c. 1981.

APPENDIX B

DERIVATION OF SAMPLE SIZE FORMULA AND CONTROL OF THE BETA RISK

The purpose of this appendix is to provide an auditing derivation of the sample size formula and a theoretical discussion of controlling the beta risk. These concepts will be applied to the mean-per-unit (MPU) estimator because of its simplicity. The concepts and theory presented, however, are applicable to the other variables estimators. Theoretical concepts are based on sampling from a large population so that the finite correction factor does not have to be applied to the sample size.

Derivation of Sample Size Formula

The sample size formula for the MPU estimator is given below.

$$n = \left[\frac{S_y (Z_\alpha + Z_\beta)}{m} \right]^2$$

where:

n = sample size,

S_y = sample standard deviation,

Z_α = factor from the normal table for a two sided alpha risk.

Z_β = factor from the normal table for a one-sided beta risk.

m = minimum amount considered material per sample item which is equivalent to M/N as suggested in the chapter.

The auditor may use this formula to calculate the sample size for a substantive test used to determine the reasonableness of a client-recorded account balance. When the auditor wants to determine the reasonableness of an account balance, he or she must consider (1) the probability of rejecting the recorded book value when it is correct and (2) the probability of rejecting the book value when it is materially misstated. If the recorded book value is reasonably stated, the probability of rejecting it is equal to the alpha risk, α. If the recorded book value is materially misstated, the probability of rejecting the client's book value is $(1 - \beta)$, where β symbolizes the beta risk.

The same statements about rejecting the recorded book value could be made in terms of the average recorded book value and per unit materiality. Exhibit 1 illustrates the probabilities of rejecting the average recorded book value. The curves in Exhibit 1 represent sampling distributions of sample means. Referring to Exhibit 1, if the average book value is reasonable, the probability of rejecting it is equal

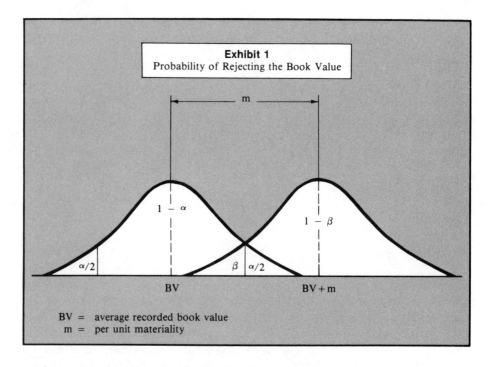

Exhibit 1
Probability of Rejecting the Book Value

BV = average recorded book value
m = per unit materiality

to the alpha risk. If the average recorded book value is materially understated so that the *true* average book value equals the average book value plus per unit materiality (BV + m), the probability of rejecting the average recorded book value as reasonable is (1 − β).

The minimum amount considered material on a per unit basis should be the amount by which the auditor would like to detect a misstatement of data. In other words, the auditor would like to detect a misstatement if the true average book value equals the average recorded book value plus per unit materiality. Since the auditor wants to detect a misstatement by this amount, the distance *m* in Exhibit 1 needs to be translated into statistical terms. Distance *m* in Exhibit 2 reflects the translation. The distance between BV and X can be represented by $Z_\alpha \sigma/\sqrt{n}$ which is the traditional plus and minus factor in computing precision intervals where σ represents the true standard deviation.

Assuming the true average book value to be Q, the distance between X and Q can be represented by $Z_\beta \sigma/\sqrt{n}$. Therefore, the distance *m*, materiality, can be expressed as follows:

$$m = Z_\alpha \sigma/\sqrt{n} + Z_\beta \sigma/\sqrt{n}$$

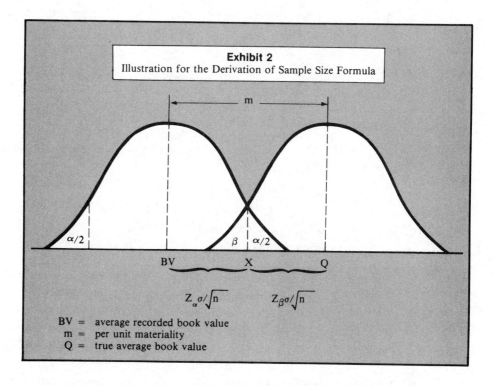

Exhibit 2
Illustration for the Derivation of Sample Size Formula

BV = average recorded book value
m = per unit materiality
Q = true average book value

Multiplying through by $\sqrt{n}$ and dividing by m the equation becomes:

$$\sqrt{n} = \frac{Z_\alpha \sigma + Z_\beta \sigma}{m}$$

Squaring both sides so that:

$$n = \frac{\sigma^2 (Z_\alpha + Z_\beta)^2}{m^2} = \left[\frac{\sigma(Z_\alpha + Z_\beta)}{m} \right]^2$$

Generally, the true standard deviation, σ, is unknown. Therefore, an estimate of σ must be used. The estimate of σ is given by S_y which is calculated from a sample taken from the population. When S_y is substituted for σ in the above formula, it is the form shown below:

$$n = \left[\frac{S_y(Z_\alpha + Z_\beta)}{m} \right]^2$$

As can be seen, this is the sample size formula for the MPU estimator. As indicated above, the distance between BV and X in Exhibit 2 may be symbolized by $Z_\alpha \sigma/\sqrt{n}$. Substituting the sample standard deviation for the unknown true standard deviation, σ, the distance may be represented by $Z_\alpha S_y/\sqrt{n}$. The symbols $S_y/\sqrt{n}$ may be referred to as the standard error which is discussed in the chapter. Therefore, the distance between BV and X in Exhibit 2 may also be represented by $Z_\alpha SE_y$ where SE_y refers to the standard error of sample means. In other words, the distance between BV and X depicts the desired precision interval for the average.

Control of the Beta Risk

The auditor may control the beta risk by varying the relationship between precision and materiality. In Exhibit 2, the smaller the distance between BV and X (representing the precision interval) in proportion to the distance m, the smaller the beta risk. The larger the precision interval in relation to materiality, the larger the beta risk. Consequently, when an auditor evaluates the sample, he or she can modify the degree of beta risk by varying one of the determinants of precision, given a constant amount of materiality.

The beta risk may be controlled when the auditor determines the sample size and when the sample is being evaluated. The beta risk is controlled at the time of sample size determination by specifying the level of beta risk acceptable in the circumstances. Holding materiality constant, the lower the level specified for both alpha and beta risks, the larger the sample size causing the sampling distribution of sample means to cluster more closely around the true population mean. Consequently, there will not be much overlap between the two sampling distributions as shown in Exhibit 2. The areas under the sampling distribution curves representing the β and α risks are reduced with larger samples. Accordingly, to reduce the beta risk, specify a low level for this variable in sample size determination.

If higher levels of sampling risks are specified, the sample size will be smaller and the sampling distributions will be more flat and spread out. In this case, there will be more overlap between the two sampling distributions and the areas under the curves representing the β and α risks will be much larger. Therefore, the smaller the sample size, the higher the beta risk.

Control of the beta risk at the time of sample evaluation is necessary when the sample standard deviation differs from the standard deviation used to determine sample size. When the standard deviation differs from the estimated standard deviation, the beta risk differs from the desired beta risk. In some instances, the auditor may want to adjust the precision interval so that the beta risk equals the desired risk level. These procedures were discussed in the chapter in conjunction with the illustrative case in the section, "Adjusting the Precision Interval and Limits."

REVIEW QUESTIONS

10-1   Discuss the relationship between compliance and substantive testing.

10-2   What is the basic difference between sampling and nonsampling risks?

10-3   Explain the risk of incorrect acceptance. How does this risk affect sample size?

10-4   An acceptable risk level for incorrect acceptance is a function of what factors?

10-5   Discuss the risk of incorrect rejection. How does this risk affect sample size?

10-6   What factors should be considered in specifying an acceptable risk level for incorrect rejection?

10-7   Discuss how nonsampling risks may be reduced to a negligible level.

10-8   Explain the ultimate risk.

10-9   Why is it important to define specific audit objectives simultaneously for compliance testing and substantive testing?

10-10   Management assertions embodied in financial statements provide a basis for developing specific audit objectives. Discuss each of the management assertions of existence or occurrence, completeness, rights or obligations, valuation or allocation, and presentation or disclosure.

10-11   What type of evidence is gathered by vouching procedures? By retracing procedures?

10-12   Identify two general types of substantive tests.

10-13   In substantive tests of details of transactions, what type of evidence-gathering procedure should be used to establish the existence or occurrence of a financial statement account or class of transactions? To establish completeness?

10-14   What are the primary audit procedures for direct tests of balances?

10-15   Explain the relationship between management assertions, audit objectives, and audit populations.

10-16   Define the tolerable error and point out how it affects sample size.

10-17   What are the basic differences between quantitative and qualitative analyses?

10-18   Under what conditions will the auditor pursue additional procedures when the quantitative analysis indicates a reasonably stated financial statement account?

10-19   When the quantitative analysis indicates a materially misstated financial account, under what conditions would the auditor increase sample size? Extend auditing procedures in problem areas? Ask the client to "rework" the account under investigation? Request an adjustment of the account balance?

10-20   Discuss the relationship between variables sampling and substantive testing.

10-21   Identify four variables sampling plans and briefly discuss the conditions under which each plan may be appropriate.

10-22   Discuss the relationship between the alpha risk level and the confidence level. What is the probability that the auditor will reject an account as reasonably stated when the client-recorded value is fairly stated.

10-23   Discuss the factors the auditor should consider in judgmentally setting the ultimate risk level.

10-24   Discuss the quantification of the beta risk level. Express the formula that may be used to determine the beta risk level.

DISCUSSION QUESTIONS AND PROBLEMS

10-25   Patsy Perfect, CPA, recently fired a new entry-level employee, Sam Smart, because of incompetence. Patsy was fortunate, however, to recruit an experienced CPA, Nancy Neat. Patsy assigned Nancy to a variables sampling job to determine the reasonableness of the finished goods inventory account balance. Patsy had previously observed the year-end count and was satisfied as to the count and the summarization of the count on the inventory summary sheets. Patsy wrote an audit program which indicated that Nancy should randomly select a sample of inventory items listed on the inventory summary sheets and should vouch those items to appropriate vendor invoices, comparing the unit prices on the inventory summary sheets with the unit prices on the vendor invoices. The difference estimator was to be used in evaluating the results of this sample. The audit program specified the risk levels for incorrect rejection and incorrect acceptance at 20 and 10 percent, respectively, and indicated that the tolerable amount of error in the account should be 5 percent of the finished goods inventory account balance. Based on the prior year's working paper, a $12.50 standard deviation of differences was to be used in calculating a sample size.

When Nancy Neat arrived at the client's place of business, she discovered that there were 2,250 inventory items and that the final inventory valuation was $126,000.

Required:

a. Using Table 1 in Appendix A, determine the appropriate Z factors for the risk levels of incorrect rejection and incorrect acceptance.

b. Using the sample size formula presented in the chapter, calculate a sample size for the difference estimator. Adjust the sample size using the finite population correction factor if the calculated sample size is greater than 10 percent of the population size.

10-26 Given the situation in Problem 10-25, assume a sample size of 6 items. Nancy Neat randomly selected 6 inventory items from the inventory summary sheets and vouched the items to appropriate vendor invoices. She started the following working papers.

Sample Item (i)	Audited Value (y_i)	Book Value (x_i)	Difference $(y_i - x_i = d_i)$	$(d_i - D)^2$
1	66.	61.		
2	36.	46.		
3	72.	72.		
4	38.	83.		
5	51.	59.		
6	20.	22.		

Required:

a. Find the average difference for the sample and complete the working paper.

b. Estimate the population difference and calculate the population point estimate.

c. Calculate the sample standard deviation and the standard error of the sample mean.

d. Determine the precision interval for the sample (for the average) and the precision interval for the population.

e. Calculate the upper and lower precision limits based on the point estimate for the population.

f. Indicate the statistical conclusion that Nancy Neat should make concerning the reasonableness of the finished goods inventory account.

g. Is the sample deviation equivalent to the standard deviation used in determining sample size? If there is a difference, what is the impact upon desired risk levels? Should Nancy Neat adjust precision interval? Why or why not?

h. In the event that Nancy Neat must statistically reject the reasonableness of the finished goods inventory account, discuss the alternative courses of action available to Nancy.

10-27 Nancy Neat has performed exceptionally well as an experienced auditor when assigned to variables sampling procedures. Her variables sampling skills appear to be superior. Patsy Perfect, CPA, has asked Nancy to prepare an in-house workshop on the techniques of variables sampling. Nancy feels that entry-level personnel needed additional skills in determining when the precision interval should be adjusted so that the beta risk level will approximate the desired beta risk. Nancy has prepared the following worksheet to be completed by participants in the workshop. She has also asked the participants to discuss the questions given on the second part of the worksheet.

Required:

a. Complete the worksheet given below.

b. Answer the questions on the lower part of the worksheet.

(a)

Sample Standard Deviation Relative to that Used in Sample Size Formula	Effect Upon Precision Interval Relative to Desired Interval	Effect Upon Beta Risk Relative to Desired Risk
1. Less than	?	?
2. Greater than	?	?

(b) 1. In situation 1 above, discuss when the precision interval should be adjusted so that the beta risk level will approximate the desired risk level. Include in your answer the rationale for the precision interval adjustment.

  2. In situation 2 above, discuss when the precision interval should be adjusted so that the beta risk will approximate the desired beta risk. Include in your answer the rationale for such an adjustment.

10-28 (a) Distinguish between the following statistical terms: point estimate, upper and lower precision limits, confidence level, precision interval, and acceptance region.

  (b) If an auditor states that the population value is $80,000 ± $2,400 with a reliability level of 95 percent, numerically identify or calculate each statistical term specified in part (a) above.

10-29 During the course of an audit engagement, a CPA attempts to obtain satisfaction that there are no material misstatements in the client's accounts receivable. Auditors often use statistical sampling to obtain representative evidence that an account is recorded accurately.

  On a particular engagement an auditor determined that the precision should be $35,000. To obtain satisfaction, the auditor had to be 95 percent confident that the population of accounts was not in error by more than $35,000. The auditor decided to use unrestricted random sampling with replacement and took a preliminary random sample of 100 items (n) from a population of 1,000 items (N). The sample produced the following data:

Arithmetic mean of sample items ($\bar{x}$)............... $4,000
Standard deviation of sample items (SD)........... 200

The auditor also has available the following information:

$$\text{Standard error of the mean (SE)} = \text{SD} \div \sqrt{n}$$

$$\text{Population precision (P)} = N \times R \times SE$$

Partial list of reliability coefficients

If Reliability Coefficient (R) is	Then Reliability is
1.70	91.086%
1.75	91.988
1.80	92.814
1.85	93.568
1.90	94.256
1.95	94.882
1.96	95.000
2.00	95.450
2.05	95.964
2.10	96.428
2.15	96.844

Required:

a. If all necessary audit work is performed on the preliminary sample items and no errors are detected,

    1. What can the auditor say about the total amount of accounts receivable at 95 percent reliability level?

    2. At what confidence level can the auditor say that the population is not in error by $35,000?

b. Assume that the preliminary sample was sufficient.

    1. Compute the auditor's estimate of the population total.

    2. Indicate how the auditor should relate this estimate to the client's recorded amount.

(AICPA adapted)

10-30   The workshop directed by Nancy Neat (Question 10-27) was a success and the participants felt that the time invested in studying variables sampling was beneficial. Consequently, Patsy Perfect, CPA, asked Nancy to prepare a workshop on sample sizes for a variables sampling plan using the difference estimator. The following sample size formula was included in study materials presented to workshop participants.

$$n = \left[\frac{S_d(Z_\alpha + Z_\beta)}{M/N} \right]^2$$

where:

n = sample size,

S_d = sample standard deviation for the difference estimator,

Z_α = factor from the normal table for a two-sided alpha risk,

Z_β = factor from the normal table for a one-sided beta risk,

M = minimum amount considered material for the account under investigation, and

N = population size.

Following a thorough discussion on the sample size formula, Nancy Neat administered the following quiz.

Quiz

	Population 1 Relative to Population 2				
	Minimum Considered Material	*Estimated Standard Deviation*	*Acceptable Level for*		*Sample Size*
			Alpha Risk	*Beta Risk*	
Case 1	Larger	Equal	Equal	Equal	_____
Case 2	Equal	Smaller	Equal	Equal	_____
Case 3	Smaller	Equal	Equal	Smaller	_____
Case 4	Equal	Larger	Smaller	Equal	_____
Case 5	Smaller	Smaller	Equal	Equal	_____
Case 6	Equal	Equal	Larger	Equal	_____

Required:

Complete the quiz Nancy Neat prepared for the in-house workshop. Your answers should be selected from the following potential responses: Larger, Smaller, or Indeterminable. These terms express the sample size for population 1 in relation to population 2.

10-31   You desire to evaluate the reasonableness of the inventory book value of your client, Draper, Inc. You satisfied yourself earlier as to inventory quantities. During the examination of the pricing and extension of the inventory, the following data were gathered using appropriate unrestricted random sampling with replacement procedures.

- Total items in the inventory (N).................... 12,700
- Total items in the sample (n)....................... 400
- Total audited value of items in the sample............ $38,400
- $\sum\limits_{j=1}^{400} (x_j - \bar{x})^2$............................. 312,816
- Formula for estimated population standard deviation

$$S_{x_j} = \sqrt{\frac{\sum\limits_{j=1}^{j=n} (x_j - \bar{x})^2}{n-1}}$$

- Confidence level coefficient of the standard error of the mean at a 95 percent confidence (reliability) level .... ±1.96

Required:

a. Based on the sample results, what is the estimate of the total value of the inventory? Show computations in good form where appropriate.

b. What statistical conclusion can you reach regarding the estimated total inventory value calculated in item *a* above at the confidence level of 95 percent? Present computations in good form where appropriate.

c. Independent of your answers to items *a* and *b*, assume that the book value of Draper's inventory is $1,700,000, and based on the sample results the estimated total value of the inventory is $1,690,000.

   The auditor desires a confidence (reliability) level of 95 percent. Discuss the audit and statistical considerations the auditor must evaluate before deciding whether the sampling results support acceptance of the book value as a fair presentation of Draper's inventory.

(AICPA adapted)

OBJECTIVE QUESTIONS*

10-32* Which of the following responses will not reduce nonsampling risks to a negligible level in a CPA firm?

    A.   Maintaining a policy on continuing professional education for all professional staff.

    B.   Having every audit properly planned and supervised.

    C.   Having every client sign an engagement letter.

    D.   Adherence to high quality control standards.

10-33* Assuming nonsampling risks are negligible, ultimate risk is the joint probability that (1) the internal accounting control system will allow material errors to occur and to go undetected, and (2) that the auditor will not detect the materially misstated financial data. To reduce the first risk, the auditor relies on

    A.   Management's representation letter stating that the company has maintained an adequate system of internal accounting control throughout the period under audit.

    B.   The design of the client's system of internal accounting control and the compliance of the controls to prescribed procedures.

    C.   Substantive tests of details disclosing material misstatements of financial statement accounts.

    D.   Analytical review procedures to indicate areas of noncompliance with prescribed control procedures.

10-34* Using the same situation described in Question 10-33 above, the auditor depends on which of the following responses to reduce the second risk?

    A.   Analytical review procedures to corroborate evidence gathered in substantive tests of details.

    B.   Evidence gathered in compliance tests.

    C.   Evidence gathered in attribute sampling plans.

    D.   All of the above.

10-35* The second standard of field work is based on the concept that when there is a high probability of a materially misstated account

    A.   Internal controls are weak.

    B.   Internal controls are strong.

    C.   The standard does not depend on such a probability.

    D.   Validation tests are insufficient.

Note: Questions in this section have been taken from prior CPA examinations except for those questions marked with an asterisk.

10-36* The sampling risk of incorrect acceptance involves

    A.   A large sample size when the auditor must sustain a small risk level.

    B.   Accepting a materially misstated financial account as unreasonable.

    C.   A high risk level when the auditor relies extensively on internal accounting controls.

    D.   All of the above.

    E.   None of the above.

10-37* An acceptable risk level for incorrect rejection is a function of

    A.   The probability that other substantive tests will detect a material misstatement of the account under investigation.

    B.   The subjective probability of management's disregard for internal controls.

    C.   The degree of reliance assigned to internal controls.

    D.   All of the above.

    E.   None of the above.

10-38* The sampling risk of incorrect rejection involves

    A.   A large sample when the costs to extend subsequent auditing procedures are high.

    B.   A small sample when the auditor is willing to sustain a small risk level.

    C.   Accepting a reasonably stated financial statement account when there is a material misstatement.

    D.   All of the above.

    E.   None of the above.

10-39* Management's assertions in the financial statements about existence or occurrence deal with whether

    A.   Inventories are properly valued at lower of cost or market.

    B.   Inventories are properly classified in the balance sheet.

    C.   Inventories reflected on the balance sheet physically exist.

    D.   All of the above.

    E.   None of the above.

10-40*   Management's assertions in the financial statements about completeness reflect

     A.   That all liabilities of the company have been recorded and included in the balance sheet.

     B.   That listings of inventories include goods owned by the company that are in transit.

     C.   That all probable contingencies which can be reasonably estimated have been recorded.

     D.   All of the above.

     E.   None of the above.

10-41*   The assertion embodied in financial statements concerning proper valuation and allocation implies that

     A.   Accounts receivable are shown gross of sales discounts.

     B.   The bases of inventory valuation are adequately disclosed in the management letter.

     C.   Depreciable assets are recorded at historical cost and that this cost is being systematically allocated to appropriate accounting periods.

     D.   All of the above.

     E.   None of the above.

10-42*   When evaluating the results of a variables sampling plan, if the auditor increases the reliability level from 90 percent to 95 percent, the precision interval will

     A.   Not change.

     B.   Increase.

     C.   Decrease.

     D.   Be indeterminable.

10-43*   The size of a statistical sample for a variables estimation plan is influenced by

     A.   The minimum amount considered material and the expected amount of error.

     B.   The minimum amount considered material, the population standard deviation, and the recorded book value.

     C.   The minimum amount considered material, the population standard deviation, and the level of sampling risks the auditor is willing to sustain in the circumstances.

     D.   None of the above.

10-44* In a variables sampling plan, the larger the estimated standard deviation of the population

A. The larger the sample size necessary to attain reliable statistical results.
B. The larger the confidence level should be in determining sample size.
C. The more likely the precision interval will include the true population value.
D. None of the above.

10-45* In gathering evidence, retracing a transaction involves

A. Following the transaction through the accounting system in the opposite direction of normal occurrence.
B. Following the transaction through the accounting system in the direction of normal occurrence.
C. Observing the clerk recording the transaction.
D. None of the above.

10-46 In estimation sampling for variables, which of the following must be known in order to estimate the appropriate sample size required to meet the auditor's needs in a given situation?

A. The total amount of the population.
B. The desired standard deviation.
C. The desired confidence level.
D. The estimated rate of error in the population.

10-47 Which of the following sampling plans would be designed to estimate a numerical measurement of a population, such as a dollar value?

A. Numerical sampling.
B. Discovery sampling.
C. Sampling for attributes.
D. Sampling for variables.

10-48 The ultimate risk against which the auditor requires reasonable protection is a combination of two separate risks. The first of these is that material errors will occur in the accounting process by which the financial statements are developed, and the second is that

A. A company's system of internal control is not adequate to detect errors and irregularities.

B.   Those errors that occur will not be detected in the auditor's examination.

C.   Management may possess an attitude that lacks integrity.

D.   Evidential matter is not competent enough for the auditor to form an opinion based on reasonable assurance.

10-49   An important statistic to consider when using a statistical sampling audit plan is the population variability. The population variability is measured by the

A.   Sample mean.
B.   Standard deviation.
C.   Standard error of the sample mean.
D.   Estimated population total minus the actual population total.

10-50   An auditor selects a preliminary sample of 100 items out of a population of 1,000 items. The sample statistics generate an arithmetic mean of $120, a standard deviation of $12 and a standard error of the mean of $1.20. If the sample was adequate for the auditor's purposes and the auditor's desired precision was plus or minus $2,000, the minimum acceptable dollar value of the population would be

A. $122,000.
B. $120,000.
C. $118,000.
D. $117,600.

10-51   Use of the ratio estimation sampling technique to estimated dollar amounts is *inappropriate* when

A.   The total book value is known and corresponds to the sum of all the individual book values.
B.   A book value for each sample item is unknown.
C.   There are some observed differences between audited values and book values.
D   The audited values are nearly proportional to the book value.

10-52   An auditor selects a preliminary sample of 100 items out of a population of 1,000 items. The sample statistics generate an arithmetic mean of $60, a standard deviation of $6 and a standard error of the mean of $.60. If the sample was adequate for the auditor's purposes and the auditor's desired precision was plus or minus $1,000, the *maximum* acceptable dollar value of the population would be

A. $61,000.
B. $60,000.
C. $59,000.
D. $58,800.

10-53   The major reason that the difference and ratio estimation methods would be expected to produce audit efficiency is that the

A. Number of members of the populations of differences or ratios is smaller than the number of members of the population of book values.
B. Beta risk may be completely ignored.
C. Calculations required in using difference or ratio estimation are less arduous and fewer than those required when using direct estimation.
D. Variability of the populations of differences or ratios is less than that of the populations of book values or audited values.

10-54   The frequency distribution of employee years of service for Henry Enterprises is right skewed (i.e., it is not symmetrical). If a CPA wishes to describe the years of service of the typical Henry employee in a special report, the measure of central tendency that he should use is the

A. Standard deviation.
B. Arithmetic mean.
C. Mode.
D. Median.

10-55   Mr. Murray does not know the standard deviation of the cost of the items in Rasmussen's inventory. He can assume that the standard deviation computed from his sample is an adequate estimate of the population standard deviation if the sample

A. Is randomly selected, regardless of the number of items in the sample.
B. Is randomly selected and contains at least 30 items.
C. Contains at least 30 items, even if not randomly selected.
D. Is either randomly selected or contains at least 30 items.

10-56 The greater the variability in the cost of the items being sampled (as measured by population standard deviation) the

A. Greater the usefulness of a table of random numbers in selecting a sample.
B. Larger the sample size required to make reliable statements with a given precision.
C. Greater should be the level of confidence required when establishing the estimate.
D. More likely that an interval estimate made from sample data will be correct.

10-57 A CPA specifies that a sample shall have a confidence level of 90 percent. The specified confidence level assures her of

A. The true estimate of the population characteristic being measured.
B. An estimate that is at least 90 percent correct.
C. A measured precision for her estimate.
D. How likely she can estimate the population characteristic being measured.

10-58 If all other factors specified in a sampling plan remain constant, changing the specified reliability from 90 percent to 95 percent would cause the required sample size to

A. Increase.
B. Remain the same.
C. Decrease.
D. Become indeterminate.

10-59 In connection with her examination of the financial statements of the Patricia Roberts Corporation, a CPA is making a rough estimate of the total value of an inventory of 2,000 items. Her estimate of the total, based upon the mean of the unrestricted random sample, will be within the desired precision limits of ± $18,000 provided that the difference between the sample mean and the true population mean is not more than

A. $36.
B. $18.
C. $ 9.
D. $ 4.50.

10-60   There are many kinds of statistical estimates that an auditor may find useful, but basically every accounting estimate is either of a quantity or of an error rate. The statistical terms that roughly correspond to "quantities" and "error rate," respectively, are

A.   Attributes and variables.
B.   Variables and attributes.
C.   Constants and attributes.
D.   Constants and variables.

10-61   What is the primary objective of using stratification as a sampling method in auditing?

A.   To increase the confidence level at which a decision will be reached from the results of the sample selected.
B.   To determine the occurrence rate for a given characteristic in the population being studied.
C.   To decrease the effect of variance in the total population.
D.   To determine the precision range of the sample selected.

10-62   Mr. Johnson decides to use stratified sampling. The basic reason for using stratified sampling rather than unrestricted random sampling is to

A.   Reduce as much as possible the degree of variability in the overall population.
B.   Give every element in the population an equal chance of being included in the sample.
C.   Allow the person selecting the sample to use his own judgment in deciding which elements should be included in the sample.
D.   Reduce the required sample size from a non-homogeneous population.

10-63   The auditor's failure to recognize an error in an amount or an error in an internal-control data-processing procedure is described as a

A.   Statisticial error.
B.   Sampling error.
C.   Standard error of the mean.
D.   Nonsampling error.

After studying this chapter, students should understand

1. The nature of the revenue cycle.
2. Audit objectives of the revenue cycle.
3. Procedures used in planning the audit of the revenue cycle, including analytic review.
4. The internal controls which are frequently encountered in the revenue cycle.
5. Procedures for compliance testing internal controls in the revenue cycle.
6. Dual-purpose audit procedures for the revenue cycle.
7. Substantive audit procedures for the revenue cycle, including the use of positive and negative confirmations and alternative auditing procedures.

Chapter 11

Audit of the Revenue Cycle

This chapter was written by
Wesley T. Andrews, Ph.D., C.P.A.,
Associate Professor of Accounting,
Florida Atlantic University

INTRODUCTION

The revenue cycle may be thought of as those segments of the information processing system that record, summarize and accumulate information about the company's sales, cash collection and sales return functions. As such, information generated about these activities is reflected in the cash accounts, the account and note receivable accounts, and the sales and sales returns accounts. Also, the allowance for doubtful accounts and the bad debt expense account may also be thought of as accumulating data generated through the revenue cycle.

This chapter begins with an overview of the three segments of the revenue cycle: sales, sales returns, and cash receipts. This first section is followed by sections on internal control and compliance testing for the revenue cycle. The chapter concludes with a discussion of substantive tests for accounts in the revenue cycle. However, since cash is affected by both the revenue cycle and the expense and production cycle, substantive tests for cash balances are deferred until Chapter 12.

OVERVIEW OF THE REVENUE CYCLE

The segment of the information processing system that records, summarizes, and accumulates information about sales is the sales segment. When a sale takes place, detailed information about the transaction is recorded on some document, which is called the initial document. For example, in a retail establishment, the initial document recording the occurrence of a sale may be a cash register tape. In a company that employs outside salesmen, the initial document may be a sales order prepared by the salesman when the sale is made.

Subsequently, data concerning sales may be either entered directly in a sales journal from the initial document (journalized), or the data may be summarized on some intermediate document, such as a weekly sales summary. In this latter case, the summarized information (for example, sales for the week and the total debit to accounts receivable) would be entered in the sales journal, while detailed information concerning each sale on account would be entered in the individual customer's account receivable in the accounts receivable subsidiary ledger. This detailed information may be journalized to the accounts receivable ledger from either the initial record or from the detail listing of sales on the intermediate document. In the case of an accounting system maintained on EDP equipment, it is fairly common for postings to individual customer accounts to be made directly from data contained on the initial document.

The next step in the sales segment is the posting of the data from the sales journal to the general ledger. After this step (and after data from the cash receipts and sales return cycles have also been posted to the accounts receivable control account in the general ledger), the balance in the accounts receivable control account can be computed. This balance can then be compared to the total of the balances in the individual customer accounts in the subsidiary accounts receivable ledger. Agreement of the general ledger control account balance with the total of the individual subsidiary ledger balances gives some assurance of the integrity of the summarized data after it has moved through the sales segment to the general and subsidiary ledgers.

The segment of the information processing system that records, summarizes and accumulates information about sales returns and allowances is the sales return segment. Sales returns and allowances occur when a customer returns the purchased goods or claims that credit should be given for defective merchandise or some other valid reason. If management agrees that the customer's claim is valid, the result will be either a journal entry to credit the customer's account receivable account or an authorization to issue a check to the customer for the amount claimed. Of course, one or the other of these events (but not both) should be authorized by management, depending upon whether the customer has paid the account balance prior to filing the claim for the sales return or allowance.

The responsibility for authorizing a credit to a customer's account receivable account (or for issuing a check, in the event the customer has previously remitted the amount claimed) is usually assigned to specific personnel, often personnel in a customer relations department. If goods are returned by the customer, a sales return should be documented with a receiving report. Further, the approval of a request for a sales allowance is usually documented by the issuance of a credit memorandum by the customer relations department. Thus, the initial document in the sales return segment of the revenue cycle may be viewed as being either the receiving report for the returned goods or the correspondence from the customer who makes the request for an allowance. In turn, documentation of the investigative activities of the customer relations department (to establish that the customer's claim is valid and, if so, to determine whether the credit memorandum should create a credit to accounts receivable or be the basis for issuance of a check) may be viewed as intermediate documents in the sales return segment of the revenue cycle.

Once the investigative activities to support the issuance of the credit memorandum have been completed and documented, the credit memorandum is issued and may also be thought of as an intermediate document, providing the documentary support for the journalizing of the sales returns and allowance entry. This entry, a debit to the sales returns and allowances account (or to a previously established allowance account), and a credit to accounts receivable may then be posted to both the general ledger account and to the subsidiary accounts receivable ledger.

The segment of the revenue cycle that records, summarizes, and accumulates information about cash receipts is the cash receipts segment. Data concerning cash received is introduced into the system whenever cash is received, an event that can occur under a variety of circumstances. In a retail establishment whose sales are primarily for cash, the receipt of cash occurs at the point of sale. In such cases, a cash register, containing an imprest currency fund for making change and equipped with an internal mechanism to record and sum cash receipts, is usually provided as the initial repository for the cash collected. In this circumstance, the cash register tape provides the initial record of cash received and is frequently the initial document in the cash receipts segment. However, as indicated in Chapters 5 and 8, there may be an initial document, such as the customer's check in a restaurant, which is prepared before the sale is recorded on the cash register.

In the case of a company with substantial sales on account, cash is received through the mail. In such cases, cash is usually received in the form of checks rather than currency, although currency may occasionally be remitted through the mail. If customers enclose remittance advices with their remittances (for example, the portion of a utility bill that says "Detach and return this portion with your payment"), then this remittance advice may be viewed as the initial document in the cash receipts segment. (In computerized information processing systems such as those of oil companies and most utilities, the remittance advices will be prepunched data processing cards with customer account information already punched in the card.)

Occasionally, cash may be collected by route salesmen or delivery personnel. In such cases, the usual practice is to furnish such personnel with an imprest cash fund for making change and to require that collections be reported to the cashier in a timely manner. In such cases, a copy of the customer receipt issued at time of collection is the typical initial document for the cash receipts segment.

Regardless of the nature of cash receipts, for control purposes certain personnel in the organization are authorized to receive cash and to prepare initial documentation. Further, this cash, along with a copy of the documentation, will be turned over to a person who performs the depository function. This person will usually prepare some form of intermediate document, perhaps a daily cash summary, and will prepare the cash for deposit. Preparation of the deposit involves counting total cash, endorsing checks (if they have not been previously endorsed by the person who collected the cash), and preparing the deposit slip. With respect to deposit slip preparation, a good practice for controlling cash is to prepare the deposit slip in duplicate and to require the bank to "authenticate" one copy at the time of deposit. These authenticated copies of the deposit slip provide excellent documentary evidence that the cash has been deposited.

As soon as the deposit has been prepared, some authorized person (either the cashier or some other authorized employee) will deliver the deposit to the bank. As an alternative to physically taking the deposit to the bank, some companies use mail deposit, a practice which is not recommended if large amounts of currency are involved. Another practice is called "lock box depositing." Under this alternative, some banks offer the service of receiving company mail directly from the post office and preparing the deposit entirely at the bank. In such cases, the report from the bank, usually received on a daily basis, provides the initial document for the cash receipts segment.

After the deposit has been made, the document which provides the record of cash received becomes the documentary support for the entry to record cash receipts in the cash receipts journal, and, of course, after the cash receipts entry has been journalized, information is then posted to the general ledger and to the subsidiary accounts receivable ledger.

The foregoing description can be generalized as a description of any accounting information processing system. Obviously, wide variations in the specific details of different systems exist, but in general, certain common characteristics exist. For example, the concept of information processing segments which collect, summarize, and direct data about specific transactions to the appropriate general and subsidiary ledgers is useful in visualizing how the system works. In addition, the notion that data about specific transactions is first recorded on some initial document, then transferred to a book of original entry (journal), and finally is posted, in summary form, to appropriate ledger accounts is also extremely useful in describing any accounting system.

There are certain other non-routine transactions which can affect the accounts which are normally impacted by the three segments of the revenue cycle. Since these transactions do not occur with the same regularity as cash receipts, sales, and sales returns, they are normally recorded through the general journal and hence do not involve a formal information processing segment. Entries concerning these transactions involve the write-off of a bad debt, periodic adjustment of the allowance for doubtful accounts, reclassification entries to segregate notes receivable from accounts receivable and employee receivables from trade receivables, the accrual of interest income on notes receivable, and other adjustments to accounts receivable.

The write-off of a bad debt should usually be initiated by someone in the collection department who has reached the conclusion that extensive efforts at collection are likely to be unsuccessful. For control purposes, this decision should be documented by the person who makes the decision and approved by someone who has authority to approve such transactions (usually the person who approves the decision should not be connected with either the sales department or the credit department). This document, properly approved, becomes the support for the general journal entry to debit the allowance for doubtful accounts and credit accounts receivable.

A fairly common practice is to use the services of a collection agency before completely admitting defeat in collecting an account. Such agencies will accept old accounts and make an effort at collection in exchange for a fee, which is customarily one-third of the amounts recovered. In such cases, the write-off of a bad account may involve two steps; recording the turnover of the account to the collection agency and subsequently writing off the account when collection agency efforts have failed, if in fact they do fail.

Periodically, management will want to review the adequacy of the allowance for doubtful accounts. At such times, it is appropriate to review the company's bad debt history, perhaps to prepare an aging of accounts receivable, and prepare a general journal entry to adjust the allowance for doubtful accounts and bad debt expense as needed. Of course, this review, as well as the conclusions thereof, should be documented and approved by personnel in authority, this documentation providing the support for the resulting general journal entry.

In some businesses, it is customary to hold notes receivables in addition to accounts receivable (this is particularly true if the client business is a financial institution, such as a bank). In such cases, it is usual to maintain two control accounts in the general ledger, one for accounts receivable and the other for notes receivable. In addition, it is also customary to maintain two subsidiary ledgers of individual debtor balances, one for trade accounts receivable and one for notes receivable. In some systems, the notes receivable subsidiary ledger takes the form of a notes receivable register which contains information about each note, such as a maker, amount, due date, interest rate and description of collateral, if any.

In most commercial and industrial enterprises, entries to the general and subsidiary ledgers for note receivable transactions occur infrequently and are normally journalized through general journal entries. Examples of such transactions are the receipt of a note in settlement of a trade account receivable, the periodic accrual of interest, the recording of the discounting of a note receivable, and the write-off of an uncollectible note receivable. Of course, the collection of interest and principal, when due, is normally recorded through the cash receipts segment.

Other non-routine adjustments to accounts affected by the revenue cycle would include such transactions as recording bank service charges, recording a customer's bad check as an account receivable, and recording the recovery of a bad debt previously written off. Such non-routine adjustments are normally made by general journal entry, supported by some form of appropriately approved documentation.

AUDIT OBJECTIVES AND THE REVENUE CYCLE

With respect to the audit of the system segments which make up the revenue cycle, as well as the audit of the balances in the accounts affected by those segments, the audit plan is developed in order to achieve two overall audit objectives:

1. To do the work necessary to furnish a reasonable basis for an opinion on the financial statements being audited; and

2. To plan and execute this work in accordance with the three field work standards and to properly document the results.

In order to achieve these overall objectives (which, incidentally, are appropriate objectives for the planning of any phase of the audit), the audit of the revenue cycle segments and related account balances should be designed to accomplish the specific objectives listed below:

1. To obtain and document a description of the existing procedures and controls involved in each of the three information processing segments which comprise the revenue cycle;

2. To review information relevant to the environment in which the client company operates and to review analytically interim data regarding the client company's operations to establish areas where audit test work should be concentrated;

3. If, after preliminary evaluation of the procedures and controls so described, it appears that the controls existing in any or all of the information processing segments of the revenue segment may be relied upon, to compliance test these controls in order to establish the reliability of the controls in existence;

4. To obtain sufficient substantive evidence to support an opinion that the integrity of the data which flowed through the particular segment is acceptable;

5. To obtain further substantive evidence as a result of analytical review of account balances that those account balances are reasonable in the light of what is already known about the client's operating environment; and

6. To conduct specific additional substantive tests of the balances in the accounts affected by the revenue cycle, if needed.

Notice several things about these specific objectives. First, the objectives provide a logical basis for attacking the audit programming problem, thereby providing a logical, integrated planning basis for developing the audit program. Thus, designing the audit program to satisfy these specific objectives will satisfy the first standard of field work which requires adequate planning of the progress of the work.

Second, notice that specific objectives 1, 2, and 3 are designed primarily to satisfy the second standard of field work (i.e., the required review, testing, and evaluation of the system of internal accounting control as a basis for reliance thereon), while specific objectives 3, 4, 5, and 6 are designed primarily to satisfy the third standard of field work (i.e., the requirement to gather sufficient, competent evidential matter to support an opinion on the financial statements being audited). Further, notice that the third specific objective (which requires compliance testing of those controls which, after preliminary evaluation, appear to be reliable) also involves the gathering of evidence which supports an opinion on the financial statements, so that this specific objective might also be thought of as satisfying the requirements of both the second and third field work standards.

Viewed another way, specific objectives 1, 2, and 3 may be thought of as accomplishing the objective of the second field work standard (to place audit reliance on those control features of the internal accounting control system which show themselves reliable, based upon appropriate compliance testing), while specific objectives 4, 5, and 6 are balance testing oriented.

PLANNING THE AUDIT OF THE REVENUE CYCLE

In order to plan the audit of the revenue cycle so as to accomplish the general and specific audit objectives listed above, an audit plan should be designed to accomplish the following:

1. To obtain a description of existing procedures and controls in each of the segments of the revenue cycle, as well as a description of existing procedures and controls over data entry and processing through the general journal;

2. To gather and document environmental data about the existing sales and credit situation in which the client is operating and to reach conclusions about the probable effect of the environmental circumstances noted on the accounting data being audited; and

3. Using the insights gained from steps 1 and 2 above, to gather and analytically review interim operating data for months (or quarters) during the year under review.

Once the results of the above three steps are available, the auditor should be able to make some preliminary judgments about areas within the revenue cycle where audit effort should be concentrated and about controls where reliance can be placed. At this stage, then, it is a good idea to discuss these preliminary findings with the client. Such a conference can accomplish three things. First, the client may offer insights about additional controls and explanations for unusual results of the analytical review process. Second, the client has an opportunity to correct any misimpressions the auditor may have about the system or the client's operating environment and results before substantial audit time is expended based upon such possible misimpressions. Finally, the client becomes apprised of the auditor's initial assessment of the magnitude of the audit task, so that the client may be better prepared for the size of the audit fee that may result.

Following this conference with the client, the audit plan can be further developed to accomplish the following:

4. Make a preliminary evaluation of the strengths and weaknesses in the controls purported to be in existence in each segment of the revenue cycle;

5. Based upon the results of this preliminary evaluation, plan and conduct compliance tests to determine if those controls upon which audit reliance is to be placed are actually operating as described in step 1 above;

6. Evaluate the results of the compliance tests performed in step 5 above to reach conclusions about the reliability of the controls actually in effect in each of the segments of the revenue cycle; and

7. Concurrent with the compliance tests performed in step 5 above, to perform limited substantive tests of the accuracy of the data flowing through the segments of the revenue cycle to the general ledger and to the subsidiary accounts receivable ledger.

Note that, if the audit program is efficiently planned, the compliance tests of the system conducted in step 5 and the substantive tests of accounting data conducted in step 7 may be conducted concurrently with one operation. Tests designed in this manner are often called dual-purpose tests.

Finally, the last step in the audit process of the revenue cycle can now be programmed and executed, namely:

8. To perform substantive tests of the year-end balances in the accounts affected by the revenue cycle (i.e., petty cash, cash in bank, accounts and notes receivable, allowance for doubtful accounts, sales, sales returns and allowances, and bad debts expense).

In planning this last step, the results of the testing and evaluation of the system segments described above, as well as the results of the analytical review of interim operating results will be determining factors in making decisions about the nature, extent, and timing of the substantive tests performed in step 8. Of course, the exact nature of the impact of these results on the nature, extent, and timing of substantive tests of balances is largely a matter of professional judgment which is developed through experience. In the remaining section of this chapter, considerations involved in the development of specific audit programs to accomplish the steps of the audit plan will be discussed.

DEVELOPING AUDIT PROGRAMS RELATED TO THE REVENUE CYCLE

The result of the above described planning activities should be a set of audit programs which outlines in detail the procedural steps and audit tests to be performed in order to audit the information processing segments of the revenue cycle and the balances in cash, accounts and notes receivable, and the related allowance for doubtful accounts, as well as the balance in sales, sales returns and allowances, and bad debt expense. In this section, detailed audit procedures will be discussed for each aspect of the audit of the revenue cycle, and the justification for each procedural step, in terms of the general and specific audit objectives mentioned earlier, will be discussed.

Audit Program for Preliminary Evaluation of Controls

As discussed above, the overall objective of the audit program for a preliminary evaluation of controls is two-fold: to obtain an overview of the environment in which the client conducts its revenue generating activities and to obtain a preliminary description of the controls that are supposed to exist in the sales, sales returns and allowances, and cash receipts segments of the information processing system relevant to the revenue cycle. Therefore, the following procedures are likely to be appropriate on most engagements:

1. Using the information obtained from industry and financial media, prepare a memorandum summarizing the market(s) in which the client operates. Note specifically:

   a. Client's share of market(s) and change in market share(s) as compared to previous periods.

   b. The entry or exit of competitors in the market(s) in which the client operates. Obtain, if possible, information about the quality of competing products and the likelihood of product obsolescence. Also note any market factors that might suggest increased or decreased demand for the company's product(s);

2. Discuss the above findings with knowledgeable company personnel. Include the client's observations about its various marketing environments in the memo describing the markets in which the client sells its product(s);

3. Discuss with knowledgeable company personnel any environmental factors which affect the granting of credit to customers and/or the collection of receivables. Support these findings by reference to appropriate trade literature, Dun & Bradstreet reports, and the financial media;

4. Based upon the findings in steps 1 through 3 above, prepare a memo which describes the probable impact of any environmental factors noted on the data for the current period;

5. Obtain from the client any available interim data regarding activity within the revenue cycle. In this regard, information such as the following will be useful:

    a.   Monthly (and quarterly) data of sales by product line, by division, and by geographic region, if available;

    b.   Monthly (and quarterly) data concerning sales returns by product line, by division, and by geographic region, if available;

    c.   Monthly (and quarterly) data concerning cost of goods sold and inventory levels, along with computed turnover rates for inventory, if available;

    d.   Copies of interim agings of accounts receivable and computed turnover rates for accounts receivable, along with monthly (and quarterly) summaries of write-offs of customer bad debts, if available; and

    e.   Copies of monthly cash forecasts, along with a summary of the month-end cash balances in all cash accounts, if available;

6.   Using comparable data for previous periods (and comparable industry data, if available), analytically review trends in sales, sales returns, bad debts, and cash and receivable balances. Prepare a memo for the working papers documenting the results of this review.

These six initial procedural steps are designed to obtain an overview of the environment in which the client conducts marketing activities. Steps 1 through 4 are designed to assist the auditor in "getting the feel" of the client's marketing environment, while steps 5 and 6 look for unusual fluctuations in accounting data.

Once the auditor has conducted the tests required by steps 1 through 6 above, the next step is to obtain a description of the controls which the client believes exist in each of the segments of the revenue cycle. This initial description of the client's control system for the revenue cycle is usually obtained by discussion with knowledgeable company personnel and documented as indicated in Chapter 7 by use of either a descriptive memo, a completed internal control questionnaire, or a flowchart (or, indeed, all these forms of documentation may be used). Hence, the following audit program step is appropriate:

7.   Based upon inquiry of knowledgeable company personnel, prepare an internal control questionnaire, a narrative description, or a flowchart for the following segments of the revenue cycle:

    a.   Sales,

     b.   Sales returns and allowances (i.e., credit memorandum processing), and

     c.   Cash receipts.

As indicated in Chapter 8, before the auditor documents the controls which are supposed to exist in any cycle, it is often helpful for the auditor to review an internal control questionnaire to become familiar with controls which are used in a particular cycle. Exhibit 11-1 shows some controls which are frequently encountered in the revenue cycle as well as an explanation for each control.

Also, as indicated earlier in this chapter, when an auditor compliance tests controls, he or she first identifies the controls to be relied on. Then, as indicated in Chapter 8, the auditor basically uses common sense to identify procedures which can be used to determine if the control is operating as prescribed. For example, procedures for compliance testing include techniques such as observing employees performing control functions, inspecting documents for evidence which indicates that control procedures were carried out, and redoing control procedures such as footing, whenever possible.

Exhibit 11-1
Controls Frequently Encountered in the Revenue
Cycle and Explanation of Controls

	Control	*Explanation*
1.	Are all sales commitments recorded on prenumbered documents, and are the documents periodically reviewed by a responsible person to determine possible losses?	Some companies make sales commitments at firm prices and, if the cost of the goods increases, the firm may incur losses. This control decreases the chance that these losses will fail to be recorded.
2.	Are sales invoices and shipping documents prenumbered, and does a responsible person periodically account for the numerical sequence of these documents?	If prenumbered documents are not used, it is nearly impossible to identify goods shipped and sales billed during a period.

Exhibit 11-1 Continued:

Control	Explanation
3. Is a copy of the shipping document filed with the sales invoice and sales order to indicate shipment, and does a responsible person review the file for items ordered but not shipped, items ordered but improperly shipped, or items shipped without a sales order?	If a company requires sales orders before shipment, there is less chance that goods will be shipped to a ficticious customer. Also, customer satisfaction is increased if customers receive what they order promptly. Furthermore, if customers are shipped what they ordered, there is less chance of sales returns.
4. Does a responsible person match the prenumbered shipping documents against sales invoices and sales orders?	If a responsible person matches shipping documents against sales orders and sales invoices, there is less chance that items will be shipped but not billed. Notice that this control also helps to ensure that the objectives of the third control are obtained. However, the direction of the review is different. In the third control, a responsible person matched what was billed i.e., the sales invoice, with what was ordered and shipped. However, with this control a responsible person is starting with what was shipped i.e., the prenumbered shipping document, and matching the information on the shipping document to what was ordered and billed.
5. Is credit approval made by a responsible person, and are shipping documents matched to sales orders by a responsible person to ensure that credit approval was noted on the sales order before the goods were shipped?	The risk of uncollectable accounts is decreased if credit is approved before the goods are shipped.
6. Is a price list, which has been approved by a responsible person, used to price all invoices, and does a responsible person examine sales invoices for pricing, extension, and discount terms?	There is less chance of billing errors if an approved price list is used to price invoices, and if prices, extensions and discount terms are reviewed by a responsible person.
7. Are cash sales recorded with a cash register, and does a responsible person reconcile the cash which should be on hand at the end of each day with the actual cash on hand?	As indicated in Chapter 8, a cash register which accumulates the cash which should be on hand at any point in time, is an effective technique for controling cash receipts.

Exhibit 11-1 Continued:

Control	*Explanation*
8. Are prenumbered documents used for cash sales, and does a responsible person reconcile the cash which should have been collected for the day with the cash actually collected for the day?	As indicated in Chapter 8, prenumbered documents, such as prenumbered checks in a restaurant, are frequently used to control over-the-counter receipts.
9. Are shipping documents used to make credit entries to perpetual inventory records, and does a responsible person compare the prenumbered shipping documents with the credits made in the perpetual inventory records and the debits made in the cost of goods sold account?	As indicated in controls two, three, and four, shipping documents are an important part of control in the revenue cycle. Since these documents are used to ensure that what was shipped was in fact billed, they should be used to post the credits to the perpetual inventory records and the debits to cost of goods sold, thus ensuring that entries to record cost of goods sold are based on goods actually sold.
10. Are prenumbered receiving reports used to record sales returns, and does a responsible person examine the merchandise and prepare a prenumbered credit memorandum for all goods returned?	Any merchandise which the company receives should be recorded on a prenumbered receiving report. Also, effective control over sales returns requires a responsible official to examine the merchandise, and thus approve the return, and prepare a prenumbered credit memorandum.
11. Does a responsible person examine the prenumbered credit memorandum for approval, compare the credit memorandums with the receiving reports, verify the prices and extensions of credit memorandums, and examine the debit to inventory and credit to accounts receivable or cash?	If a responsible person reviews credit memorandums, there is less chance that credit memorandums will be used to cover up errors in accounts receivable or other accounts. Also, if a responsible person reviews the sales return process, there is less chance that sales returns which are not justified will be made. Also, a careful review of the sales return process may indicate improvements in product quality which are needed.
12. Are the accounts (notes) receivable general ledger account and the subsidiary ledger accounts posted by different people, and is the control account periodically reconciled to the subsidiary ledger accounts by a responsible person?	All information which is posted to the general ledger account is also posted to the subsidiary ledger accounts, but the documents which are used for postings are different i.e., totals are posted to the general ledger account whereas

Exhibit 11-1 Continued:

Control	*Explanation*
	details are posted to the subsidiary ledger accounts. Consequently, if the postings are done by different people and, if the general ledger balance is reconciled to the balances in the subsidiary ledger, the accuracy of the posting process is improved. Also, if the accounts are posted by different people, it is more difficult for ficticious entries to be posted to accounts receivable, since any ficticious entry must be posted by two different people.
13. Are the totals for cash collected for the day and sales for each day reconciled by a responsible person with the debit to cash and the credit to accounts receivable and the debit to accounts receivable and the credit to sales?	As indicated in Chapter 8, control totals, such as the cash which should have been collected for the day, can be used effectively to verify the postings to accounts.
14. Are customer statements mailed at least monthly, and does a responsible person compare the amounts on the statements with the balances in the subsidiary ledger accounts?	Customer statements are obviously used to bill customers, but these statements are also an effective control device, since customers will usually complain if they are billed for the wrong amount, especially when they are billed too much.
15. Does a responsible person in the mailroom open all mail, stamp checks for deposit only, and prepare a listing of the total cash received for the day?	The mail should be opened by a responsible person who has no accounting responsibility. This person should stamp all checks for deposit only and prepare a listing of cash receipts which can be used in control thirteen to verify the debit to cash and the credit to accounts receivable.
16. Is cash deposited on a daily basis by a responsible person?	As indicated in Chapter 8, if cash is deposited on a daily basis, there is less chance of theft. Also, if cash is deposited promptly, it is easier for the business to optimize its cash management.
17. Have adequate physical safeguards been developed to maintain control over assets which may easily be misappropriated, such as cash on hand and inventory?	As indicated in Chapter 8, cash on hand should be minimized, and the cash should be stored in a safe. Likewise, fences and other safeguards should be established to

Exhibit 11-1 Continued:

Control	Explanation
	prevent unauthorized access to inventory.
18. Are physical inventories taken at least annually?	If physical inventories are not taken, perpetual inventory records are likely to contain substantial errors.
19. Are bank reconciliations prepared at least monthly by a responsible person who verifies that the credits to the client's account shown on the bank statement agree with the listing of cash which should have been received for each day (see control fifteen) and vice versa. Also, does the bank reconciler determine that all deposits were made promptly?	Bank reconciliations provide an important control because they reconcile the cash which should have been received with the cash deposited to the client's account.
20. Is the petty cash fund the responsibility of one person, and does the size of the fund appear optimum? Does a responsible person periodically count the fund, and examine the disbursements for propriety?	Petty cash funds are established to avoid writing numerous checks for small amounts. The fund should be large enough so that it does not have to be replenished too often, and thus defeat the purpose of the fund, but at the same time the fund should be small enough so that if the fund is misappropriated, the company does not suffer a material loss. When the fund is replenished, the various expenses made by the custodian should be reviewed by a responsible person. Also, the fund and the documentation for expenses incurred should be periodically counted on a surprize basis.
21. Does adequate documentation exist for all entries to the accounts in the revenue cycle, and are the entries and related documentation reviewed by a responsible person?	Most entries to the accounts in the revenue cycle result from sales, cash collections, and sales returns, and the way in which these entries are reviewed is discussed in connection with controls one, nine, eleven, thirteen, and nineteen. However, all entries to the accounts must be documented and reviewed by a responsible person. For example, when the control

Exhibit 11-1 Continued:

Control	Explanation
	procedures described in the previous sentence are carried out, other material entries to the accounts, such as a write-off of a bad debt, should be reviewed and appropriate documentation examined.
22 Are duties in the revenue cycle properly segregated?	As indicated in Chapter 5, incompatible duties should be performed by different people. The decision on what duties are incompatible is largely a matter of common sense. For example, the bookkeeper should clearly not have access to cash. Likewise, the person who reviews transactions should not be the same person who records the transactions.
23. Are remittance advices used to post the entries to the individual customer accounts?	If remittance advices are used to post to customer accounts, the number of people who have access to cash can be restricted easier.

The next section of the audit program is designed to compliance test controls which exist in each of the information processing segments of the revenue cycle and upon which the auditor wants to place reliance. Steps 8 through 20 below are directed at testing the sales segment of the revenue cycle. Note that while the primary purpose of this audit program is to test the controls which exist in the sales segment of the revenue cycle, some tests may also be directed at obtaining substantive evidence to support the validity of the information flowing through the sales cycle. Hence, some of the steps in this program may be both compliance test and substantive test oriented and the program may therefore be thought of as being a dual-purpose program.

Before reading the audit program steps, however, it is important that the student understand that the program is presented to illustrate the types of audit programs which are likely to be found in practice, and that it would be impossible to present an audit program which covered the testing of all controls which auditors may encounter in their professional practice without making the program excessively complex. Therefore, in reading the program the student should recognize that

(1) the program is presented for illustrative purposes only, and (2) in practice, auditors identify controls which they want to rely on for their specific clients and develop specific audit programs to gather evidence about whether those controls are working as prescribed. *The same word of caution is applicable for all audit programs presented in this text.*

8. Determine that the client uses prenumbered documents where appropriate, and use techniques, such as those indicated in Chapter 8, to compliance test the use of prenumbered documents.

9. Define the statistical population to be the set of all initial documents which record sales (such as sales orders, cash register tapes, etc.) for the period under review, and design a sampling plan to randomly select and evaluate a sample of initial sales documents for test purposes;

Although the audit procedures initially focus on the initial document, e.g., the sales order, the auditor will also need, as indicated in step 11, to obtain all related documents, such as the sales invoices and bills of lading which correspond to the sales orders which are sampled. Also, the auditor will select the sample by sampling from the bill of lading file because this file contains a record of all shipments made during the period. Thus, the auditor will sample from the bill of lading file and then obtain the sales orders and sales invoices which correspond to the bills of lading in the sample.

10. Review the sales documents selected in step 9 above noting any information required by client's policy, such as initials indicating checks made on extensions, prices, footings, and quantities, which is missing from the document. Note particularly the presence of initials of the person responsible for authorizing the sale transaction and for the presence of documentation for approval of granting credit to the customer. When possible, redo control procedures, such as footings, pricing, and extensions, which were applied to the documents;

11. For all sales selected in step 9 above, obtain and examine any available supporting documentation to provide evidence of shipment of inventory, such as shipping documents prepared in the shipping department and copies of bills of lading. Compare information according to shipping documents with information on the sales order and sales invoice, determining that merchandise descriptions and quantities shipped agree with the descriptions and quantities ordered and billed according to the sales order and sales invoice;

12. Trace all data from the initial sales documents selected in step 9 above to any sales summaries which serve as intermediate documents. If such sales summaries are aggregated with totals which are to be entered in the sales journal, foot the sales summaries. Also note the initials of the

employee who checks the mathematical accuracy of the sales summary (If the initial document, tested in 10 above, is the posting media for entry directly to the sales journal, this step should be marked as "not applicable.");

13. For all initial sales documents tested in step 10 above, or for all sales summaries tested in step 12 above, if applicable, trace sales data from initial document to the sales journal, or from the sales summary, if applicable, to the sales journal;

14. Test the footing of data in the sales journal and trace the posting of total sales to the general ledger account;

15. For those sales transactions selected for test in step 9 above, trace information concerning inventory description and quantity to perpetual inventory records, if such detailed perpetual records are part of the client's inventory system. Determine that the cost and inventory quantities have been removed from the inventory records;

16. For those sales transactions selected for testing in step 9 above, trace the posting of the debit to the customer's individual account receivable account in the subsidiary accounts receivable ledger. For those individual customer accounts so tested, foot the total debits and credits to the customer's account for the month in which the sale took place and prove the mathematical accuracy of the balance in the customer's account as of month end;

17. In the accounts receivable control account, test the footing of the total debits and credits as well as the footing of the total credits in the sales accounts to prove the mathematical accuracy of the balances in those accounts for the months tested;

18. Review the client's procedure for preparation of periodic reconciliations of the accounts receivable subsidiary ledger with the accounts receivable control account in the general ledger. Obtain a copy of an interim trial balance of the accounts receivable subsidiary ledger (or prepare one, if the client does not routinely do so), foot the trial balance and agree the total to the general ledger accounts receivable control balance. Select a sample of individual customer account balances from the trial balance and trace them to the accounts receivable subsidiary ledger, if the trial balance was prepared by the client. Also, select a sample of balances of individual customer accounts from the accounts receivable subsidiary ledger and trace the balances into the trial balance, if the trial balance was prepared by the client; and

19. List both compliance and substantive errors noted in steps 8 through 18 on a work paper and prepare a statistical evaluation of these errors. For this purpose, evaluate the results to determine if the sample is ac-

ceptable as defined in the sampling plan with respect to the maximum tolerable error rate for compliance errors and with respect to the maximum tolerable amount of dollar error which would be considered not material for substantive errors.

Evaluation of sample results and subsequent alternative courses of action that may be taken after sample evaluation for compliance and substantive testing were discussed in Chapters 9 and 10, respectively.

Notice several aspects of the foregoing steps. First, the test selects a sample of sales transactions from all sales transactions that took place during the period under audit.

Second, notice that the set of procedures calls for tracing data about the selected sales transaction through the various steps in the sales segment, testing the aggregation process and the controls over the aggregation process.

Third, notice the direction of the test from detailed transactions towards the general ledger. Thus, the procedure provides some assurance that proper effect has been given in the general and subsidiary ledgers for all sales for which a shipping document was prepared. The set of procedures does not provide any assurance that shipments were in fact made for all recorded sales; hence the set of procedures only tests sales for understatement.

In order to provide some assurance that sales are not overstated, the auditor may perform an additional test which provides additional assurance over and above the general sense of the propriety of recorded sales achieved from the analytic review procedures conducted in steps 5 and 6 previously. For example, the auditor may wish to reverse the direction of test, as follows:

20. Select a sample of debits posted to individual customer account receivable accounts and trace the record of these debits to the sales journal, then to the initial sales summaries, if applicable, and then to the initial sales document. Examine initial sales documents for transactions so selected, noting approval of credit by authorized client personnel, as well as documentary evidence of shipment of inventory, such as shipping documents, bills of lading, etc.

Finally, notice that as a part of the sales test, documentary evidence was gathered to support the fact that, for each sale tested, inventory was in fact shipped and the quantities and costs of the inventory shipped were properly removed from the perpetual inventory records. This portion of the sales test fulfills two functions. First, additional documentary evidence is examined to support the assertion that a sale did take place (this is one of the purposes of the sales test). And second, the test also provides evidence that, when a sale does take place, the quantities and costs of the inventory shipped are properly removed from the perpetual inventory records. Debits to inventory records will be tested in connection with the auditor's review of the expense and production cycle, which will be discussed in detail in Chapter 12.

So far, the audit program has been directed at achieving three goals: to learn about the marketing and revenue generating environment in which the client operates, to identify those areas of the revenue generating activities of the client about which unusual interim data has been produced, and to test the controls in and the data flowing through the sales segment of the revenue cycle. Now, attention is directed at that portion of the audit program that tests the controls in the sales returns and allowances segment of the revenue information processing cycle.

First, it is helpful to understand that the auditor's chief concern regarding recorded sales returns and allowances is that credit memorandums may be issued when, in fact, no return or allowance has taken place. If one is in a position to authorize and issue credit memorandums, one can credit accounts receivable when cash has not been collected, thereby removing from the books a receivable which is related to a previously intercepted and misappropriated cash receipt. Hence, the primary concern of the auditor is to be sure that recorded sales returns and allowances are not overstated. With respect to unrecorded sales returns and allowances, an irate customer provides a reasonable control to ensure that, when a credit memo should be issued, it will be issued. The auditor usually relies on substantive tests (primarily confirmations) to detect unrecorded sales returns and allowances. Confirmation of accounts receivable is discussed later in this chapter.

Since the objective of the auditor's test of recorded sales returns and allowances is to test for overstatement, it makes sense to begin the test at the general ledger and proceed through the sales returns and allowances segment in the reverse direction of the normal flow of processing. A generalized dual-purpose audit program for the audit of the sales returns and allowances segment follows:

1. Defining the population to be the set of all debits to sales returns and allowances in the general ledger, select a sample of recorded debits to sales returns and allowances;

2. For each debit selected in step 1 above, trace the amount of the debit to the book of original entry in which the entry was journalized. Scan

the entry for reasonableness. For example, the credit to the entry should be to accounts receivable or possibly to cash. In the latter case, the original entry should be in the cash disbursements journal and will be tested in connection with the cash disbursements segment of the expense and production cycle; hence, no further testing of sales returns requiring the payment of cash is required at this time;

3. For those debits involving a credit to accounts receivable which were selected for test, obtain supporting documentation that shows the detail of the individual credit memorandums that make up the total debit. In most cases, this supporting documentation will be an intermediate document such as a weekly summary of credit memorandums issued. In other cases, the supporting documentation may be copies of the individual credit memorandums themselves;

4. For each debit entry in step 3, foot the individual credit memorandum totals to prove the mathematical accuracy of the total debit to sales returns and allowances .(In the event that the debit is summarized on some form of intermediate document such as a weekly summary, foot this summary and obtain copies of the individual credit memorandums that make up the total, comparing the copies of the individual credit memorandums to the intermediate record.);

5. For all of the credit memorandums selected above (or for a reasonable subsample, if the number of credit memorandums is large), obtain and examine documentary support for the following:

    a. Evidence that the credit memorandum was properly approved by authorized company personnel (this will usually take the form of an authorizing signature on the memorandum itself);

    b. Evidence about the authenticity of the credit. This evidence is usually obtained by examining the customer correspondence files which contain letters and other correspondence with the customer indicating the history of the return or allowance;

    c. Evidence that the goods were actually returned. Documentary evidence, such as receiving reports and inspection reports, is useful here; and

    d. The effectiveness of numerical control over credit memorandums; and

6. List both compliance and substantive errors noted in steps 1 through 5. Evaluate these results in order to determine if reliance upon the controls existing in the sales return and allowance segment of the revenue cycle is justified, as well as to determine if the conclusion that the data flowing through the sales returns and allowances segment is substan-

tially free of material error. If the desired results are not achieved as a result of the foregoing tests, consider repeating steps 1 through 5 with an expanded sample.

The final segment of the revenue cycle to be tested in this phase of the audit is the cash receipts segment. Here, it is more difficult to develop a generalized audit program to compliance test controls, since there are a variety of ways in which cash may be received into a business. As discussed earlier, some businesses may receive the majority of their cash through the mail, representing collections on account. Indeed, other businesses, such as mail order houses, may receive the majority of their cash through the mail, but in this case cash receipts may not represent collections on account, but rather cash collected in advance of shipments made to customers. Other businesses, such as a large department store or a large supermarket, may receive the majority of their cash at the point of sale.

In each case, however, initial control over cash received should be established by the person within the client's organization who receives the cash. This control should be established by preparation of an initial record of cash received.

In the ideal internal control situation, this original document will be the basis for recording cash receipts in the books by persons who do not have access to cash. The cash itself, on the other hand, should be deposited immediately and intact by a person who does not have access either to the initial document, to any intermediate documentation of cash receipts, or to the books of the company.

The principal weakness in most systems will occur at the point of creation of the initial document, since the preparer of that document is the only person in the client's organization who (a) can affect the cash receipts entry on the books by alteration of the initial document and (b) has access to cash. For example, a checker in the local supermarket can fail to ring up a customer's purchase on the register and misappropriate the cash, or a mailroom clerk can intercept a cash receipt from a credit customer and not report the cash receipt on the initial record of cash receipts.

Often, in such situations, there are controls which compensate for the weakness. For example, at the checkout counter in the supermarket, the digital readout feature of the cash register is placed in full view of the customer, so that the customer will complain if the amount of the cash receipt exceeds the amount rung up on the register by the clerk. In addition, the store may assign management personnel to be constantly present in the checkout area, not only to provide timely customer service, if needed, but also to observe the checkout process. In the case of the mailroom clerk, management's policy may require two persons to be present when mail is opened and the initial record is prepared. An additional control in the case of collections on account is provided if the general ledger and the subsidiary accounts receivable ledger are in the custody of someone other than the person who initially receives cash and prepares the initial record thereof. If, for example, cash is intercepted and misappropriated in the mailroom by the person who initially receives and records cash receipts, a statement of the customer's account which does not reflect the receipt will be mailed to the customer at the end of the month, and the customer will complain, unless the perpetrator of the misappropriation and the accounts receivable bookkeeper act in collusion to prevent the mailing of the statement or alter the statement before it is mailed.

Finally, the direction of the test of cash receipts should be from the detailed records of cash receipts towards the general ledger, since the auditor's primary concern is with cash receipts that are not properly recorded as such. Hence, the following dual-purpose audit program steps are appropriate on many engagements:

1. Determine that the client uses prenumbered documents where appropriate, e.g., customer checks in a restaurant, and uses techniques, such as those indicated in Chapter 8, to compliance test the use of prenumbered documents;

2. Define the population to be all of the initial documents that record cash receipts (such as individual cash register tapes, in the case of a retail establishment, or remittance advices, in the case where collections are routinely received through the mail). Design a sampling plan, and from the population identified above, select a sample of individual initial cash receipt records for test purposes;

3. For each of the initial records selected in step 2 above, trace the total cash received to any intermediate summary record, if appropriate. Note specifically on the intermediate record the propriety of information concerning:

   a. The amount of the cash receipt,

   b. The identification of the source of the cash receipt,

c. The propriety of the account to be credited (sales, other income, interest income, etc.), and

d. The approval for the accounting distribution in step 3c above;

4. Prove the footing of any summarization of data that takes place on the intermediate record (such as footing of the cash received through each of several cash registers to produce a total of cash received for the day). Trace the totals from the intermediate record to the cash receipts journal. (Of course, if the client journalizes the individual details of cash receipt data directly from the initial record of cash receipt, steps 3 and 4 are not applicable.);

5. Prove the mathematical accuracy of any summarization of data that takes place in the cash receipts journal and trace postings from the cash receipts journal to the general ledger;

6. Obtain copies of authenticated duplicate deposit slips for deposits that contain cash receipts selected for test in step 2 above. Compare the total deposit, as well as the detail of any checks included in the deposit, with entries in the cash receipts journal (or intermediate document supporting aggregated entries to the cash receipts journal, if appropriate);

7. Trace deposits tested in step 6 above to the appropriate bank statement. Ascertain that deposits are made intact and on a timely basis;

8. From the detailed initial records of cash receipts selected for the test in step 2 above, trace the detailed cash received data to postings to the appropriate accounts in the accounts receivable subsidiary ledger; and

9. List both compliance and substantive errors noted in steps 1 through 8 and prepare a statistical evaluation thereof. For this purpose, evaluate the results to determine if the objectives of the sampling plan are attained. If the sampling objectives are not achieved with respect to both types of errors, consider repeating steps 1 through 8 with an expanded sample of cash receipts transactions.

Notice that in the above program, no attempt is made to review the reconciliation of the accounts receivable subsidiary ledger with its related control account, even though reliance on this mechanism is necessary to offset the control weakness associated with the initial receiver of cash having access both to cash and the original document which is used to record the cash receipt. It is not necessary to test this control here, however, since it has been tested in step 18 of the test of the sales segment, noted previously.

**Developing
Substantive Tests
of Balances
of the Accounts
Affected by
the Revenue Cycle**

The preceding section of this chapter illustrated specific audit programs (a) to familiarize the auditor with the client's revenue generating environment, (b) to identify those areas of the revenue cycle where unusual transactions and events have occurred during the year, (c) to review, test, and evaluate the controls in the sales segment, the sales returns and allowances segment, and the cash receipts segment of the revenue cycle, and (d) to gather some substantive evidence to support the propriety of the data being channelled to the general and subsidiary ledgers through the various segments of the revenue cycle. Normally, this work is performed prior to, but close to, year-end, so that the results of these tests may be used to make decisions regarding the nature, extent and timing of the substantive tests of balances that are to be undertaken subsequently. Hence, auditors normally refer to this first phase of work as "preliminary" work, while the subsequent substantive tests of balances (most of which are performed after year-end, when a trial balance of the ledger for the year is available) are normally referred to as "final" or "year-end" work.

This section of the chapter is devoted to a discussion of the audit programs related to specific balances associated with the revenue cycle. Specifically, programs for the review of balances in sales, sales returns and allowances, bad debt expense, accounts receivable, and allowance for doubtful accounts will be discussed here. (Although the cash receipts segment of the revenue cycle also affects the cash accounts, discussion of audit programs to substantively test balances in cash accounts will be deferred until Chapter 12, which will also discuss the cash disbursements segment of the expense and production cycle.)

At this point, the perceptive reader may have noticed that the preceding discussion of audit programs to compliance test the segments of the revenue information processing cycle failed to provide any testing of one source of data in revenue-related accounts — the general journal. Consequently, the following initial audit program step is appropriate in a substantive program to test balances:

> As soon as the general ledger is available for the year, scan those accounts effected by the revenue cycle, noting postings of unusual size or from unusual sources. Specifically, note entries from journals other than the sales journal, the sales returns and allowances journal, and the cash receipts journal. Obtain documentary evidence to support the propriety of any such entries noted.

Two observations are in order regarding this procedure. First, scanning is a valid audit procedure and provides a quick way to identify those unusual general journal entries that may be posted to the accounts. Also, while the primary purpose of the procedure is to provide substantive evidence of the propriety of entries recorded in the general journal, the procedure also allows the auditor, by examining the documentation supporting such general journal entries, to obtain evidence concerning the procedures in effect over preparation and recording of general journal entries. Second, while the above procedural step calls for the procedure to be performed after year-end, auditors usually review the general ledger at an interim date and then complete the review after year-end.

With respect to substantive tests of the balances in the sales and the sales returns and allowances accounts, most audit programs do not require extensive procedures after year-end to provide additional substantive evidence, since operating results for the year have been reviewed analytically, as indicated earlier, and data for the year has already been tested substantively in connection with the review of the sales and sales returns and allowances segments of the revenue cycle.

As noted in Chapter 6, five minimum substantive audit procedures are applied to substantiate accounts. These procedures are used to:

1. Verify a sample of the individual entries which are posted to the account for existence or occurrence, and verify the completeness of the account by examining a sample of entries which should have been recorded in the account to determine that the entries were recorded;

2. Verify the mathematical accuracy of the account balance;

3. Verify the accuracy of the cut-off;

4. Verify that the account is presented in accordance with GAAP, and compare the account balance with the balances which are shown in the audit working papers for the account. The balance in an account will normally appear in at least three places in the audit working papers: (1) in the financial statements, (2) in the working trial balance, and (3) in the specific working papers used to document the substantive work done on that account; and

5. Verify that the account balance is reasonable by applying analytic review procedures.

As indicated in Chapters 4 and 6, and as discussed again in Chapter 14, the fourth minimum substantive audit procedure is usually accomplished by using checklists to determine that the account balance is presented in accordance with GAAP and crossreferencing all balances for a given account every time the balance appears in the working papers. Although this minimum substantive audit procedure is not routine, and in fact requires a comprehensive knowledge of GAAP, the procedure does not differ much for any of the client's accounts. Consequently, this procedure is not emphasized in the following discussion. Also, since analytic review procedures were discussed in the first part of this chapter, these procedures are not repeated in the following discussion. Consequently, the audit program steps in the following discussion emphasize the first three minimum substantive audit procedures.

Sales, Sales Returns and Allowances, Accounts Receivable, and Notes Receivable

As indicated earlier, year-end audit procedures for sales and sales returns and allowances are usually not extensive because a substantial amount of substantive audit evidence is obtained about these balances when the dual-purpose audit procedures, and analytic review procedures which were discussed earlier, are applied. In addition, since the sales, sales returns and allowances, and accounts receivable accounts are closely related, some additional evidence about the fairness of the sales and sales returns and allowances balances is obtained when the accounts receivable balance is substantiated, as indicated in the following audit program.

Before discussing a sample audit program for accounts receivable, however, it is necessary to discuss confirmation, since confirmation is the primary *audit procedure* which is used to substantiate accounts receivable balances. A confirmation is a request from the client to its customers for the customer to provide information directly to the auditor about the amount of the customer's balance. Although a confirmation is a request from the client to its customers, the confirmation should be carefully controlled and mailed by the CPA because, if the requests were mailed by the client, the client might fail to mail confirmations to customers whose balances were incorrect. There are two basic types of confirmations: positive and negative. A positive confirmation always requires the customer to respond to the CPA, stating whether his or her balance is correct or incorrect. A negative confirmation, on the other hand, only requires the customer to respond to the CPA if the balance is incorrect. Examples of negative and positive confirmations are shown in Exhibit 11-2.

Exhibit 11-2
Example of Positive and Negative Confirmation Requests

(a) *Positive Confirmation*

Bowler Lumber Co.
Tretna, Virginia

January 4, 1984

Tibson Lumber Co.
P.O. Box 3211
Tretna, VA 24557

Gentlemen:

In connection with an examination of our financial statements, please confirm directly to our auditors the balance of your account with us as of December 31, 1983, as shown below.

This is not a request for payment; please do not send your remittance to our auditors.

Your prompt attention to this request will be appreciated. An enclosed addressed envelope is provided for your convenience.

David Bowler,
Controller

Cole and Armbrister
370 West Monroe Street
Wytheville, Virginia 26602

The balance receivable from us of *$15,102* as of December 31, 1983 is correct except as noted below:

_____

_____

_____

_____

Date _____   By _____

Exhibit 11-2 Continued:

(b) *Negative Confirmation*

Auditor's Account Confirmation

Please examine this statement carefully. If it does not agree with your records, please report any exceptions directly to our auditors

Cole and Armbrister
370 West Monroe Street
Wytheville, Virginia 26602

who are making an examination of our financial statements. An enclosed addressed envelope is provided for your convenience.

Do not send your remittance to our auditors.

Although there has been no conclusive evidence to indicate that positive confirmations are superior to negative confirmations[1], there is a presumption among most auditors that positive confirmations are superior to negative confirmations because positive confirmations require the customer to respond whether its balance is correct or not. For example, *SAS No. 1* states that the use of the positive form is preferable "when individual account balances are large or when there is reason to believe that there may be a substantial number of accounts in dispute or with inaccuracies or irregularities." On the other hand, "the negative form is useful particularly when internal control surrounding accounts receivable is considered to be effective, when a large number of small balances are involved, and when the auditor has no reason to believe the persons receiving the requests are unlikely to give them consideration." *SAS No. 1* goes on to state that as a practical matter, both negative and positive confirmations will be used on most engagements.

In addition to confirming account balances, auditors in some cases confirm several of the sales invoices which make up the account

---

[1] For example, see Carl S. Warren, "Confirmation Reliability - The Evidence," *Journal of Accountancy*, February, 1975, pp. 85-89.

balance. This technique is usually required when the customer uses a voucher system and pays each invoice separately, as the invoices are received, instead of paying the total account balance on a monthly basis. Frequently, many government agencies pay using a voucher system, and, if they receive a request to confirm a balance, they typically will respond by stating that their accounting system does not accumulate balances owed to a particular supplier. Instead, they can only confirm specific invoices from a particular supplier.

Although confirmations are a basic technique for substantiating accounts receivable, auditors frequently apply other audit procedures to accounts receivable, especially to large balances or balances which for some reason cannot be confirmed. These procedures include examining cash receipts on the account after the balance sheet date and/or reconstructing the balance which should be in the account. The balance which should be in the account, of course, can be reconstructed by taking the beginning balance plus the debits minus the creidts to arrive at the ending balance. Of course, when the auditor reconstructs an account, he or she must examine evidence to support the beginning balance and debits and credits. For example, the auditor might reconstruct the debits to an account by examining the sales order, sales invoice, bill of lading, and price listing, and then use this information to recompute the debit which should have been made to the account. Likewise, the auditor can examine remittance advices and cash receipts records to verify a sample of the credits to the account.

With respect to the timing of confirmation requests, it is important to recognize that an irregularity that is sometimes encountered in the audit of accounts receivable is lapping. Lapping involves misappropriating the receipts from customers and covering the shortages in these customers accounts with receipts from subsequent customers. Thus, the shortage is not eliminated but transferred to other accounts. For example, an employee may misappropriate $100 of the receipt from customer A. Then, when customer B pays, $100 of customer B's payment is credited to customer A's account. Then, when customer C pays, $100 of customer C's payment is credited to customer B's account, etc.

Although lapping is difficult to accomplish unless there is collusion between the bookkeeper and a person that has access to cash, auditors should recognize that lapping may occur. However, if the accounts for all customers are confirmed as of the same date, there is a greater chance that lapping will be discovered if it exists. Thus, while auditors, as indicated later, may confirm accounts receivable either at year-end or sometime during the year, the auditor generally should design his or her sampling plan so that account balances which are confirmed are confirmed as of the same date.

Finally, students should recognize that the confirmation of accounts receivable is a generally accepted auditing procedure. This means that the auditor must either confirm receivables if (1) the receivables are material, and (2) it is possible and practicable to confirm receivables, or disclaim or qualify his or her opinion because of the scope limitation. However, there is no scope limitation in cases where it is impossible or impracticable to confirm the receivables, e.g., the auditor is engaged after year-end, and the auditor uses alternative procedures, e.g., examing subsequent receipts or reconstructing the receivable balances, to evaluate the fair presentation of receivables.

Now that the basic procedures which are used to substantiate accounts receivable have been reviewed, a sample audit program for substantiating accounts receivable is presented followed by a sample audit program for substantiating notes receivable. In reviewing the audit programs, students should recognize that accounts receivable is a balance sheet account where the beginning and ending balances are not closely related whereas notes receivable is a balance sheet account where the beginning and ending balances are closely related, as these terms were defined in Chapter 6. Consequently, the audit program steps for accounts receivable parallel the minimum substantive procedures which were given in Chapter 6 for a balance sheet account for which the beginning and ending balances are not closely related, whereas the audit program steps for notes receivable parallel the audit program steps for an account balance where the beginning and ending balances are closely related.

1. As of the confirmation date, obtain a trial balance of the subsidiary accounts receivable ledger and trace the total of this trial balance to the balance in the accounts receivable control account in the general ledger;

2. If the trial balance obtained in step 1 was client-prepared, perform the following additional steps:

    a. Foot the trial balance;

    b. Select a sample of balances from the trial balance and trace amounts to individual customer accounts in the subsidiary ledger;

    c. Select a sample of balances from the subsidiary accounts receivable ledger and trace amounts to the trial balance;

3. Using an appropriate variables sampling plan, select a random sample of individual customer account balances from the trial balance (note in determining the size of the sample to be selected, desired confidence level and precision should be established after considering the results of compliance tests of the revenue cycle, conducted earlier);

4. As soon as possible after the confirmation date, mail, under control of the auditor, confirmation requests to customers represented in the sample;

5. If positive confirmation requests are used in step 4, mail second requests to nonrespondents 10 days after initial requests are mailed. Mail third requests, registered mail, 10 days following the mailing of second requests;

6. Prepare a schedule of exceptions returned by customers. In this schedule, indicate the customer name, account number, balance from the subsidiary accounts receivable ledger, balance as confirmed, and difference. Also include the reason for the difference, according to the confirmation exception. Furnish the client with a copy of this schedule and have the client determine if the exception is genuine;

7. With respect to the explanations of exception differences furnished by the client in step 6, document the client's explanations for all exceptions which do not represent substantive errors in the balance of accounts receivable as of the confirmation date. Summarize the remaining exceptions (those that do represent substantive errors in the balance of accounts receivable) and statistically evaluate these errors;

8. If, as a result of the evaluation in step 7, the auditor is unable to reach the conclusion that accounts are free of material error with the desired level of confidence, consider expanding the scope of the tests and repeating steps 1 through 7.

With respect to the timing of the above-described confirmation procedure, the confirmation date will normally be as of year-end. If the results of the preliminary review, test, and evaluation of the controls in existence in the revenue cycle indicated that reliance can be placed upon the system, the timing of the confirmation procedure can be moved ahead to some more convenient interim date, say one or two months in advance of year-end. In this event, the following audit step should be added to the confirmation procedure:

9. If the confirmation procedure is conducted as of an interim date, prepare a schedule that reconciles the balance in accounts receivable as of the confirmation date to the balance as of year-end. Also, reconcile

the balances in the allowance for doubtful accounts and in bad debt expense from the confirmation date to year-end. Trace all postings to these accounts from the general ledger to their respective books of original entry. Review these entries and balances analytically, noting and documenting explanations for any unusual entries to these accounts.

Next, steps should be included in the audit program to determine that any receivables which are evidenced by a note are reviewed. In the event that significant notes receivable exist, they should be included in the confirmation procedures called for in steps 1 through 9 above and the following steps relating to notes receivable only should also be performed.

10. At the same time that surprise counts of imprest currency funds and undeposited cash are scheduled (see Chapter 12), examine the notes themselves. For this purpose, arrange to examine notes in the presence of an authorized employee and prepare a worksheet showing date of each note, the principal amount, the date each note is due, the interest rate, the payee, the maker, and a description of any collateral. Obtain a receipt from the client's employee who was present during the examination, indicating that the notes were examined by the auditor in the employee's presence and returned to the employee intact;

11. Subsequent to the examination of notes, trace information from the schedule prepared in step 10 to the detail record of individual notes receivables on the books;

12. Trace details of information confirmed in step 4 previously to the detailed records of individual notes receivable on the books as of the confirmation date of receivables;

13. Reconcile the totals of principal and accrued interest receivable, computed from information contained on the schedule prepared in step 10 previously, to the books as of the date of examination of the notes receivable. Also prepare a reconciliation of these balances to the balances in notes receivable and accrued interest receivable as of year-end. (Note: Clearly, if the examination of notes receivable is conducted as of year-end, this step should be marked "not applicable.");

14. Prepare a schedule which analyzes the activity in the general ledger accounts for notes receivable, accrued interest receivable and interest income for the year. Trace information concerning beginning balances to prior year's work papers. (Note: In the event of an initial audit, this step should be modified, as indicated later, to provide other appropriate evidence of the propriety of the beginning of year information.) Calculate the proper amount of interest income for the year, trace collections of notes and interest collected during the year to cash receipts journal and reconcile accrued interest receivable from begin-

ning to end of year. Finally, trace year-end balances from the schedule to respective balances in notes receivable, accrued interest receivable and interest income accounts in the general ledger;

15. Determine that there was a proper cut-off for sales, notes receivable, and accounts receivable;

16. Prepare a memo which indicates suggested wording for any required footnote disclosure of the description of collateral and or guarantees of notes receivable. At the end of the audit, compare this memo to footnote disclosure in final draft of client's financial statements to ensure that the statements reflect all required disclosures.

With respect to the modified procedures required in step 14 in the case of an initial audit, several alternative procedures may be appropriate, depending on the circumstances. For example, if the previous year was audited by another auditor, beginning-of-year information can be traced to the predecessor auditor's working papers, providing that satisfactory arrangements have been made with the predecessor auditor. (For a discussion of the proper way to make arrangements with a predecessor auditor, see Chapter 4). In the event that this is the first year that the client's financial statements have been audited, an additional step designed to gather evidence to support the propriety of the beginning-of-year information should be included in the audit program. Typically, the auditor would have the client prepare a schedule of the notes receivable and accrued interest as of the beginning of the year. Then the auditor would (1) examine the notes, (2) confirm the details of the notes with the makers of the notes, and (3) verify the computation of accrued interest.

With respect to audit program step 15, the cut-off for notes receivable is easy to verify. For example, when the auditor examines the notes he or she will see the date of the note, and thus the auditor will verify that the note was recorded in the proper period. Likewise, when the auditor verifies the computation of interest receivable and interest revenue, the auditor automatically verifies the cut-off for these accounts.

The cut-off for sales, sales returns and accounts receivable is also very easy to accomplish. However, the auditor should exercise care in testing the cut-off because it is very easy for sales, accounts receivable or sales returns to be recorded in the wrong accounting period. To verify the cut-off for sales and accounts receivable, the auditor visits the client's shipping department on the last day of the accounting period and makes inquiries of the shipping department's personnel to determine that the title to all goods which were shipped before year-end passed to the buyer before the last day of the accounting period. The auditor also examines the last few bills of lading for the period to verify that title did in fact pass to the buyer before year-end for these shipments. Then the auditor writes down the last bill of lading number used for the period and examines the unused bills of lading to determine that they are prenumbered and in numerical order. Then when the auditor returns to begin the year-end work, he or she examines the last sales recorded in the sales journal for the period under audit and the first entries in the sales journal for the next accounting period, and, by reference to the bill of lading for each sale, determines that the sales are recorded in the proper accounting period. For example, if the last bill of lading used in 1984 was numbered 2,000, then 1984 sales should have bills of lading with a number of 2,000 or less, and 1985 sales should have bills of lading with a number greater than 2,000.

The cut-off for sales returns could be accomplished in a similar manner, except of course the auditor would use receiving reports for the numerical information. The problem with this type of analysis, however, is that some returns or allowances for the current accounting period will physically take place in the next accounting period. For example, returns from December sales will, in many cases, not take place until January. Therefore, the last return which should be recorded in any given accounting period is frequently not the last item which was physically returned in that accounting period.

Because of this problem, the auditor relies to a large extent on the information received from customers through confirmation about returns or allowances which have not been recorded but should be recorded in the current accounting period. For example, it is likely that customers will complain on a confirmation if they do not expect to pay the full amount of their balance, but instead expect to make or return or receive an allowance for goods. Of course, analytic review procedures also provides evidence about unrecorded sales returns.

Exhibits 11-3 and 11-4 show examples of the primary audit working papers which are used to document the substantive work performed on accounts receivable and notes receivable. Also, these exhibits show how the primary audit working papers should be crossreferenced to other audit working papers (not shown) where other aspects of the substantive audit work are performed.

+---+
| **Exhibit 11-3** |
| Example of Primary Substantive Audit Working Paper |
| for Accounts Receivable |
+---+

Prepared by: *J. J.*
Date: 1-14-84
Reviewed by: P. J.
Date: 2-1-84

Bowler Lumber Co.
Accounts Receivable
12/31/83

Customer Name	Balance	Age of Balance in Days			
		0-30	31-60	61-90	Over 90
B.B. Crane	$ 1,000 N, ✓	$ 1,000			
Virgil Crosby	5,000 N		$ 5,000		
Helen Dunn	10,000 P, ✓	5,000	5,000		
—	—	—	—	—	—
—	—	—	—	—	—
—	—	—	—	—	—
Herbert Warlick, Inc.	15,000 P				$15,000 1
	$396,000 ⟋ T/B 2,3	$300,000 ⟋ 3	$80,000 ⟋ 3	$1,000 ⟋ 3	$15,000 ⟋ 3 ⊘

⟋   Footed.

⊘   Crossfooted.

P,N   Positive confirmation (P), Negative confirmation (N) — mailed on 1/4/84. All confirmation exceptions resolved to our satisfaction—see working paper #43.

✓   Verified aging and traced amounts to subsidiary ledger.

T/B   Agrees with general ledger control account, trial balance, and financial statements. Discussed presentation of receivables with client. Based on their discussion and other audit work performed, all receivables are properly classified as current assets.

1   Customer sells Christmas items—purchases are made in September and balance is typically paid in January. Examined remittance advice and cash receipts journal. Payment received on January 21, 1984.

2   Upper and lower precision limits for 95% confidence interval are $400,000 and $390,000, respectively. See working paper #44.

3   Agrees with amounts used to compute the allowance for doubtful accounts. Note to students: The dashes in the schedule indicate lines which were omitted for presentation in text. Clearly, in practice, the auditor uses a complete schedule and no lines are omitted.

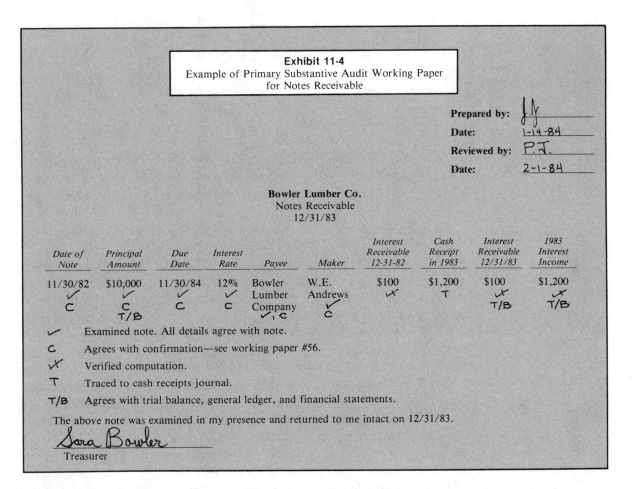

Exhibit 11-4
Example of Primary Substantive Audit Working Paper
for Notes Receivable

Prepared by: J.V.
Date: 1-14-84
Reviewed by: P.J.
Date: 2-1-84

Bowler Lumber Co.
Notes Receivable
12/31/83

Date of Note	Principal Amount	Due Date	Interest Rate	Payee	Maker	Interest Receivable 12-31-82	Cash Receipt in 1983	Interest Receivable 12/31/83	1983 Interest Income
11/30/82 ✓ C	$10,000 ✓ C T/B	11/30/84 ✓ C	12% ✓ C	Bowler Lumber Company ✓, C	W.E. Andrews ✓ C	$100 ✗	$1,200 T	$100 ✗ T/B	$1,200 ✗ T/B

✓ Examined note. All details agree with note.

C Agrees with confirmation—see working paper #56.

✗ Verified computation.

T Traced to cash receipts journal.

T/B Agrees with trial balance, general ledger, and financial statements.

The above note was examined in my presence and returned to me intact on 12/31/83.

Sara Bowler
Treasurer

Allowance for Doubtful Accounts and Bad Debts Expense

Next, audit program steps designed to provide the auditor with some assurance that the allowance for doubtful accounts is reasonable are added to the audit program. When reviewing these steps, the student should understand that the allowance for doubtful accounts is an example of a balance sheet account where the beginning and ending balance are closely related, and thus, the audit procedures parallel the minimum substantive audit procedures which were illustrated in Chapter 6 for balance sheet accounts for which the beginning and ending balance are closely related.

Thus, the audit of the allowance for doubtful accounts requires the auditor to examine some form of schedule which shows the beginning balance in the account, less the accounts written off, plus the bad debts expense for the period, to arrive at the ending balance in the account.

The two key amounts on this schedule are the accounts written off for the period and the bad debts expense for the period.

The auditor substantiates the accounts written off for the period by having the client prepare a listing of these accounts and by examining each writeoff for proper approval by a responsible official. Since there are usually not many writeoffs for the period, the auditor typically examines approval for all of the writeoffs, or at least a large percentage of them, instead of examining a sample.

The auditor substantiates the bad debts expense for the period in one of three ways, depending on the number of receivables that the client has and whether the client uses the balance sheet method or the income statement method of accounting for bad debts.

As indicated in most intermediate and introductory accounting texts, there are two methods of accounting for bad debts: the income statement method and the balance sheet method. Under the income statement method, the client estimates the proportion of credit sales which are expected to be uncollectible and then multiplies this proportion by credit sales for the year to arrive at an estimate of bad debts expense. Then this estimated amount is credited to the allowance for doubtful accounts and debited to bad debts expense. On the other hand, if the client uses the balance sheet method, the client estimates the dollar amount of accounts receivable which is expected to be uncollectible, and then the client debits bad debts expense and credits the allowance for doubtful accounts with an amount which will make the balance in the allowance for doubtful accounts equal the estimated amount of uncollectible accounts receivable. A refinement of the balance sheet method involves first aging the accounts and then determining the dollar amount of the uncollectible accounts by reference to the dollar amounts which are in each age category.

When the client uses either of these methods, the auditor evaluates the reasonableness of the client's addition to the allowance for doubtful accounts. To evaluate the reasonableness of the addition to the allowance for doubtful accounts, the auditor typically verifies the client's computation and determines that the appropriate percentage, i.e., percentage of credit sales or percentage of receivables, reflects the trends experienced in the past and is adjusted for current economic condition if they differ from past economic condition.

A third method which is used to compute the credit to the allowance for doubtful accounts is used by clients that do not have a sufficient number of receivables for the percentage methods to be reliable. These clients use a variation of the balance sheet method in which they determine the addition to the allowance for doubtful accounts by evaluating the collectibility of each specific receivable.

In such a case, the auditor usually confirms a high percentage of the accounts, or perhaps all of the accounts, and thus the auditor has a substantial amount of evidence about whether the accounts are in dispute. Also, since there is a small number of accounts, the auditor typically has past experience with the customer's payment history which would indicate whether delays in paying are typical for a particular customer or whether the delay represents an amount which likely would not be collected. The auditor uses this information along with information from credit agencies about each customer to evaluate the reasonableness of the client's assessment about the collectibility of each account.

Audit program steps 17 through 21 illustrate a sample audit program for substantiating the balance in the allowance for doubtful accounts. The program is written for a client that uses the balance sheet method, based on an aging schedule, to determine the required addition to the allowance for doubtful accounts. Also, Exhibit 11-5 illustrates a sample working paper which might be prepared for audit program step 20 for accounts receivable.

17. If the client prepares an aging of accounts and notes receivables as of year-end, obtain a copy of this aging for the working papers. Foot the aging schedule, trace totals of accounts and notes receivable from the aging schedule to the general ledger and test the detail of the individual customer account and note balances to the proper subsidiary ledger. (If the client does not routinely prepare such an aging schedule, one should be prepared by audit personnel from the subsidiary accounts and notes receivable ledgers.);

18. Test the propriety of the aging of specific accounts by examination of underlying supporting documentation, such as copies of invoices, shipping documents, etc.;

19. Compare the current aging schedule with those of prior years, noting particularly changes in relative column totals in the current year as compared with prior years. Reach a conclusion as to the reasonableness of the aging and the related percentage allowance for each aging classification;

20. Prepare a schedule which compares annual data as follows for the current year and for the preceding four years:

Exhibit 11-5
Example of Primary Substantive Audit Working Paper
for Bad Debts Expense and Allowance for Doubtful Accounts

Prepared by:	J.J.
Date:	1-15-84
Reviewed by:	P.J.
Date:	1-21-84

Bowler Lumber Company
Bad Debts Expense and Allowance for Doubtful Accounts
12/31/83

Year	1983	1982	1981	1980	1979
Accounts receivable balance	$ 150,000 T/B	$ 134,000 ✓	$ 98,000 ✓	$ 110,000 ✓	$ 100,000 ✓
Credit sales	1,500,000 T	1,340,000 ✓	980,000 ✓	1,100,000 ✓	1,000,000 ✓
Allowance for doubtful accounts activity:					
Beginning balance	6,000 ✓	6,200 ✓	6,000 ✓	5,500 ✓	5,000 ✓
Writeoffs	(500) E	(1,000) ✓	(800) ✓	(600) ✓	(500) ✓
Bad debt expense	(500) C, T/B	800 ✓	1,000 ✓	1,100 ✓	1,000 ✓
Ending balance	$ 6,000 ✓ T/B	$ 6,000 ✓	$ 6,200 ✓	$ 6,000 ✓	$ 5,500 ✓

✓ Agrees with 1982 working paper #56.

T Traced to schedule of credit sales for the year. See working paper #53.

E Traced to client's schedule of accounts written off. Examined each write off for proper approval. See working paper #60.

C Computation verified. Percentage of accounts in each age category which are expected to become bad debts appear reasonable. See working paper #61 for computation and our review of the reasonableness of the computation.

✓ Footed.

T/B Agrees with general ledger, trial balance, and financial statements.

a. End-of-year balance in accounts and notes receivable,

b. Credit sales for the year,

c. Allowance for doubtful accounts at the beginning and the end of the year,

d. Amount of accounts and notes actually written off during the year, and

e. Amount of bad debt expense for the year.

Compare current year's data to prior year's data for these items and determine if the current year's data appears reasonable. Investigate and explain unusual fluctuations. (Note: Information for this schedule is also needed for the corporation tax return.)

21. Review the results of steps 19 and 20 with responsible client personnel. Based upon the information gathered, reach a conclusion as to the propriety of the allowance for doubtful accounts as of year-end.

The final steps in the audit program for substantive tests of accounts receivable and related allowance accounts provide for a review of the classification considerations concerning accounts and notes receivable and the consistency of application of generally accepted accounting principles with respect to receivable accounting.

The following audit program steps complete the audit program for substantive testing of accounts and notes receivable and related allowance accounts as of year-end:

22. Review the composition of the individual account balances in accounts and notes receivable as of year-end. Separate amounts due from affiliates, officers and employees, subsidiaries, and amounts which are not properly classified as current assets. Determine that these amounts are properly classified in the final draft of the client's financial statements;

23. Discuss with the client the consistency of application of generally accepted accounting principles regarding accounts receivable and notes receivable, as compared with the previous year. Prepare a memorandum for the working papers describing any inconsistencies in application discussed. Document that all inconsistencies in application of principle have been identified and justified. If such inconsistencies in application of principle have occurred, determine that disclosure of the nature and effect of the changes is appropriate in the client's financial statements. Also, consider the impact of these changes, if any, on the opinion paragraph of the report to be issued;

24. Draft a paragraph to be included in the client's letter of representation, to be obtained from the client at the completion of the field work, which will include all representations desired.

SUMMARY

The revenue cycle accumulates information about a company's sales, cash collections, and sales returns. Information generated about these activities is reflected in the cash accounts, the accounts and notes receivable accounts, the sales and sales returns accounts, and the bad debt expense and allowance for doubtful accounts.

Compliance tests of the revenue cycle are usually accomplished by using dual-purpose audit programs. These programs require the auditor to select a sample of transactions and follow these transaction through the accounting system and related controls until the transactions are posted to the general ledger. These programs are dual-purpose programs because they allow the auditor not only to test the controls which are built into the system, but also to test the accuracy of the information which is accumulated in account balances. Controls which are frequently encountered in the revenue cycle and an explanation for these controls were summarized in Exhibit 11-1. One of the first steps in compliance testing in any cycle requires the auditor to determine that the client uses prenumbered documents where appropriate and to test the use of prenumbered documents. In many cases, the auditor will find that it is useful to evaluate the results of compliance tests by using attribute sampling procedures.

In the sales cycle, the auditor samples from the bill of lading file, which indicates the merchandise which was shipped, and then obtains the related sales order and sales invoice. Then the auditor tests the summarization and processing of these transactions until they are posted to the general ledger. To test sales for overstatement, the auditor also takes sample of recorded sales and obtains the related bill of lading, sales invoice, and sales order. Then the auditor tests the processing and summarization of these transactions until they are posted to the general ledger. In testing the summarization and processing of sales transaction, the auditor is concerned not only with the accuracy of the summarization and processing, but also with the controls over the process. Whenever possible, the auditor should redo required computations and examine other evidence to determine that the controls are functioning as prescribed.

In the sales return cycle, the auditor's primary concern for *recorded* sales returns and allowances is that credit memorandum may have been processed when in fact no return took place; the auditor relies primarily on confirmation to detect returns which should be recorded but which have not been recorded. Consequently, the auditor takes a sample of transactions from the debits to sales returns and allowances. Then the auditor tests the summarization and processing of sales returns and allowances from their inception to the posting to the general ledger. In testing the summarization and processing of sales returns and allowances, the auditor is concerned not only with the accuracy of the summarization and processing, but also with the controls over the process. Whenever possible, the auditor should redo required computation and examine other evidence to determine that the controls are functioning as prescribed.

In the cash receipts cycle, the auditor selects a sample of cash receipts by sampling from the initial documents, such as remittance advises, which are used to record cash receipts. Then the auditor tests the summarization and processing of these cash receipts until they are posted to the general ledger. As with any compliance test, the auditor is concerned not only with the accuracy of the summarization and processing, but also with the controls over the process. Consequently, whenever possible, the auditor should redo required computation and examine other evidence to determine that the controls are functioning as prescribed.

After compliance tests are complete, the auditor then determines the nature, timing, and extent of substantive tests. Usually, substantive tests in the revenue cycle are directed towards the balances in cash, accounts receivable, notes receivable, allowance for doubtful accounts, and bad debts expense. Very little substantive work is required for the balances in sales and sales returns and allowances for three reasons. First, these balances have already been analyzed by analytic review procedures. Second, a substantial amount of substantive evidence is obtained about these balances from performing the dual-purpose audit procedures which were used for compliance tests. And third, a substantial amount of substantive audit evidence about these balances is obtained when substantive procedures are applied to accounts receivable.

The primary substantive audit procedure for accounts receivable is confirmation. A confirmation is a request from the client to its customer for the customer to provide information directly to the auditor about the amount of the customer's balance. There are two types of confirmation: positive and negative, and usually a combination of the two is used in practice. Although a confirmation is a request from the client to its customers, the confirmation should be carefully controlled and mailed by the CPA. Other substantive audit procedures for accounts receivable include examining cash receipts on the account after the balance sheet date and/or reconstructing the balance which should be in the account.

Substantive audit procedures for notes receivable include confirmation and examination of notes receivable. In addition, the balances in interest receivable and interest income should be computed, based on the terms of the note, and any cash received should be traced to the cash receipts journal.

To substantiate the balances in bad debts expense and the allowance for doubtful accounts, the auditor reviews the reasonableness of the client's computation of these balances.

REVIEW QUESTIONS

11-1   Discuss journalization of a sale for manual and EDP systems.

11-2   After a sale is journalized, what is the next step in an accounting information system?

11-3   Other than a sale, what types of transactions affect the balance of the accounts receivable account?

11-4   Why is it necessary to balance the total of individual customer accounts in the subsidiary accounts receivable ledger with the control account in the general ledger?

11-5   How are sales returns and allowances documented?

11-6   What is the purpose of a credit memorandum?

11-7   What is the initial record for cash received in a cash sale transaction? For cash received through the mail? For cash collected by a route salesmen or delivery personnel?

11-8   Discuss procedures that may be used by a firm to provide evidence that cash received has been deposited in the bank.

11-9   Who should initiate the write-off of an account receivable as a bad debt? Who should approve the write-off?

11-10   Identify non-routine transactions and adjustments in the revenue cycle which are usually journalized in a general journal and then posted in the general ledger.

11-11   What are the two general audit objectives that an audit plan must achieve?

11-12   Discuss three specific audit objectives for the revenue cycle which satisfy the second standard of field work.

11-13   Discuss four specific audit objectives for the revenue cycle which relate to the third standard of field work.

11-14   What sources does the auditor use to make preliminary judgments concerning controls which may be relied upon in identifying high risk audit areas?

11-15   Briefly identify and discuss factors the auditor should consider when making decisions concerning the nature, extent, and timing of substantive tests performed at year-end.

11-16   What is the primary purpose of an audit program?

11-17   Discuss the nature of the first six procedural steps in an audit program for the revenue cycle as illustrated in the chapter.

11-18   List the primary media auditors use to document their findings concerning the client's information processing system.

11-19   List the tests that should be performed on the sample of initial sales documents.

11-20   If the auditor wants to test sales for understatement, should the direction of the test go from detailed transactions toward the general ledger? Explain.

11-21   What should be the direction of testing if the auditor wants to attain assurance that sales are not overstated?

11-22   When the client records a sale, how does the auditor determine that goods were actually shipped and that perpetual inventory records were properly adjusted?

11-23   What is the objective of the auditor's test when examining recorded sales returns and allowances?

11-24   Briefly discuss the incompatible custodial and record-keeping functions in a cash receipts system.

11-25   What is the primary concern of the auditor when testing cash receipts? Discuss the direction of testing in relation to the auditor's primary concern.

11-26   When are substantive tests of balances generally performed?

11-27   What is the purpose of scanning general ledger accounts after year-end?

11-28   Give a general description of procedures for sending accounts receivable confirmations.

11-29   Briefly describe the procedures the auditor should use in following up on responding and nonresponding positive accounts receivable confirmation requests.

11-30   Under what circumstances may confirmations of accounts receivable be moved from year-end to an interim date?

11-31   The auditor should apply the same procedures to notes receivable as to accounts receivable. However, additional procedures may be performed only for notes receivable. What is the objective(s) of these additional procedures for notes receivable?

11-32   What is the nature of the procedures that should be carried out to determine the reasonableness of the balance in the allowance for doubtful accounts?

11-33   What is the primary purpose for investigating (1) the classification of accounts and notes receivable and (2) the consistent application of generally accepted accounting principles concerning accounts and notes receivable?

DISCUSSION QUESTIONS AND PROBLEMS

11-34   Dodge, CPA, is examining the financial statements of a manufacturing company with a significant amount of trade accounts receivable. Dodge is satisfied that the accounts are properly summarized and classified and that allocations, reclassifications, and valuations are made in accordance with generally accepted accounting principles. Dodge is planning to use accounts receivable confirmation requests to satisfy the third standard of field work as to trade accounts receivable.

Required:

a.   Identify and describe the two forms of accounts receivable confirmation requests and indicate what factors Dodge will consider in determining when to use each.

b.   Assume Dodge has received a satisfactory response to the confirmation requests. Describe how Dodge could evaluate collectibility of the trade accounts receivable.

(AICPA adapted)

11-35 The Art Appreciation Society operates a museum for the benefit and enjoyment of the community. During hours when the museum is open to the public, two clerks who are positioned at the entrance collect a five dollar admission fee from each nonmember patron. Members of the Art Appreciation Society are permitted to enter free of charge upon presentation of their membership cards.

At the end of each day, one of the clerks delivers the proceeds to the treasurer. The treasurer counts the cash in the presence of the clerk and places it in a safe. Each Friday afternoon the treasurer and one of the clerks deliver all cash held in the safe to the bank and receive an authenticated deposit slip which provides the basis for the weekly entry in the cash receipts journal.

The board of directors of the Art Appreciation Society has identified a need to improve their system of internal control over cash admission fees. The board has determined that the cost of installing turnstiles, sales booths, or otherwise altering the physical layout of the museum will greatly exceed any benefits which may be derived. However, the board has agreed that the sale of admission tickets must be an integral part of its improvement efforts.

Smith has been asked by the board of directors of the Art Appreciation Society to review the internal control over cash admission fees and provide suggestions for improvement.

Required:

Indicate weaknesses in the existing system of internal control over cash admission fees which Smith should identify and recommend one improvement for each of the weaknesses identified. Organize the answer as indicated in the following illustrative example:

Weakness	*Recommendation*
1. There is no basis for establishing the documentation of the number of paying patrons.	1. Prenumbered admission tickets should be issued upon payment of the admission fee.

(AICPA adapted)

11-36 The customer billing and collection functions of the Robinson Company, a small paint manufacturer, are attended to by a receptionist, an accounts receivable clerk, and a cashier who also serves as a secretary. The company's paint products are sold to wholesalers and retail stores.

The following describes *all* the procedures performed by the employees of the Robinson Company pertaining to customer billings and collections:

a. The mail is opened by the receptionist, who gives the customers' purchase orders to the accounts receivable clerk. Fifteen to twenty orders are received each day. Under instructions to expedite the shipment of orders, the accounts receivable clerk at once prepares a five-copy sales invoice form which is distributed as follows:

  1. Copy 1 is the customer billing copy and is held by the accounts receivable clerk until notice of shipment is received.
  2. Copy 2 is the accounts receivable department copy and is held for ultimate posting of the accounts receivable records.
  3. Copies 3 and 4 are sent to the shipping department.
  4. Copy 5 is sent to the storeroom as authority for release of the goods to the shipping department.

b. After the paint order has been moved from the storeroom to the shipping department, the shipping department prepares the bills of lading and labels the cartons. Sales invoice copy 4 is inserted in a carton as a packing slip. After the trucker has picked up the shipment, the customer's copy of the bill of lading and copy 3, on which are noted any undershipments, are returned to the accounts receivable clerk. The company does not "back order" in the event of undershipments; customers are expected to reorder the merchandise. The Robinson Company's copy of the bill of lading is filed by the shipping department.

c. When copy 3 and the customer's copy of the bill of lading are received by the accounts receivable clerk, copies 1 and 2 are completed by numbering them and inserting quantities shipped, unit prices, extensions, discounts, and totals. The accounts receivable clerk then mails copy 1 and the copy of the bill of lading to the customer. Copies 2 and 3 are stapled together.

d. The individual accounts receivable ledger cards are posted by the accounts receivable clerk by a bookkeeping machine procedure whereby the sales register is prepared as a carbon copy of the postings. Postings are made from copy 2 which is then filed, along with staple-attached copy 3, in numerical order. Monthly the general ledger clerk summarizes the sales register for posting to the general ledger accounts.

e. Since the Robinson Company is short of cash, the deposit of receipts is also expedited. The receptionist turns over all mail receipts and related correspondence to the accounts receivable clerk who examines the checks and determines that the accompanying vouchers or correspondence contain enough detail to permit posting of the accounts. The accounts receivable clerk then endorses the checks and gives them to the cashier who prepares the daily deposit. No currency is received in the mail, and no paint is sold over the counter at the factory.

f. The accounts receivable clerk uses the vouchers or correspondence that accompanied the checks to post the accounts receivable ledger cards. The bookkeeping machine prepares a cash receipts register as a carbon copy of the postings. Monthly the general ledger clerk summarizes the cash receipts register for posting to the general ledger accounts. The accounts receivable clerk also corresponds with customers about unauthorized deductions for discounts, freight or advertising allowances, returns, etc., and prepares the appropriate credit memos. Disputed items of a large amount are turned over to the sales manager for settlement. Each month the accounts receivable clerk prepares a trial balance of the open accounts receivable and compares the resultant total with the general ledger control account for accounts receivable.

Required:

Identify weaknesses in Robinson's system of internal accounting control over customer billings and remittances and the accounting for these transactions. Make a recommendation to correct or improve each weakness.

Organize your answer as follows:

Weakness	Recommendations to Improve Weakness

(AICPA adapted)

11-37 Mountaineer Paper Company engaged you to review its internal control system. Mountaineer does not prelist cash receipts before they are recorded and has other weaknesses in processing collections of trade receivables, the company's largest asset. In discussing the matter with the controller, you find he is chiefly interested in economy when he assigns duties to the 15 office personnel. He feels the main considerations are that the work should be done by people who are most familiar with it, capable of doing it, and available when it has to be done.

The controller says he has excellent control over trade receivables because receivables are pledged as security for a continually renewable bank loan and the bank sends out positive confirmation requests occasionally, based on a list of pledged receivables furnished by the company each week.

Required:

a.   Explain how prelisting of cash receipts strengthens internal control over cash.

b.   Assume that an employee handles cash receipts from trade customers before they are recorded. List the duties which that employee should not do to withhold from him the opportunity to conceal embezzlement of the receipts.

(AICPA adapted)

11-38 Your examination of the financial statements of Hymar Department Store, Inc. disclosed the following:

1.   The store has 30,000 retail accounts which are billed monthly on a cycle basis. There are twenty billing cycle divisions of the subsidiary accounts receivable ledger, and accounts are apportioned alphabetically to the divisions.

2.   All charge sales tickets, which are prenumbered, are microfilmed in batches for each day's sales. These sales tickets are then sorted into their respective cycle divisions, and adding machine tapes are prepared to arrive at the total daily sales for each division. The daily totals for the divisions are then combined for comparison with the grand daily total charge sales determined from cash register readings. After the totals are balanced, the daily sales tickets are filed behind the related customer account cards in the respective cycle divisions.

3.   Cycle control accounts for each division are maintained by postings of the tapes of daily sales.

4. At the cycle billing date the customers' transactions (sales, remittances, returns, and other adjustments) are posted to the accounts in the individual cycle. The billing machine used automatically accumulates six separate totals: previous balances, purchases, payments, returns, new balances, and overdue balances. After posting, the documents and the customers' statements are microfilmed and then mailed to the customer.

5. Within each division a trial balance of the accounts in the cycle, obtained as a by-product of the posting operations, is compared with the cycle control account.

6. Credit terms for regular accounts require payment within 10 days of receipts of the statement. A credit limit of $300 is set for all accounts.

7. Before the statements are mailed they are reviewed to determine which are past due. Accounts are considered past due if the full balance of the prior month has not been paid. Past due accounts are noted for subsequent collection effort by the credit department.

8. Receipts on account and customer account adjustments are accumulated and posted in a similar manner.

Required:

Discuss audit procedures that should be applied to testing transactions for sales and charges to accounts receivable in one billing cycle division. Identify the billing cycle division that should be selected for testing.

(AICPA adapted)

11-39 *Part a.* In a properly planned examination of financial statements, the auditor coordinates his reviews of specific balance-sheet and income-statement accounts.

Required:

Why should the auditor coordinate his examination of balance-sheet accounts and income-statement accounts? Discuss and illustrate by examples.

Part b. A properly designed audit program enables the auditor to determine conditions or establish relationships in more than one way.

Required:

Cite various procedures that the auditor employs that might lead to detection of an inadequate allowance for doubtful accounts-receivable.

(AICPA adapted)

11-40   The Meyers Pharmaceutical Company, a drug manufacturer, has the following system for billing and recording accounts receivable:

1.   An incoming customer's purchase order is received in the order department by a clerk who prepares a prenumbered company sales order form in which is inserted the pertinent information, such as the customer's name and address, customer's account number, quantity and items ordered. After the sales order form has been prepared, the customer's purchase order is stapled to it.

2.   The sales order form is then passed to the credit department for credit approval. Rough approximations of the billing values of the orders are made in the credit department for those accounts on which credit limitations are imposed. After investigation, approval of credit is noted on the form.

3.   Next the sales order form is passed to the billing department where a clerk types the customer's invoice on a billing machine that cross-multiples the number of items and the unit price, then adds the automatically extended amounts for the total amount of the invoice. The billing clerk determines the unit prices for the items from a list of billing prices.

The billing machine has registers that automatically accumulate daily totals of customer account numbers and invoice amounts to provide "hash" totals and control amounts. These totals, which are inserted in a daily record book, serve as predetermined batch totals for verification of computer inputs.

The billing is done on prenumbered, continuous, carbon-inter-leaved forms having the following designations:

a.   "Customer's copy."
b.   "Sales department copy," for information purposes.
c.   "File copy."
d.   "Shipping department copy," which serves as a shipping order. Bills of lading are also prepared as carbon copy by-products of the invoicing procedure.

4. The shipping department copy of the invoice and the bills of lading are then sent to the shipping department. After the order has been shipped, copies of the bill of lading are returned to the billing department. The shipping department copy of the invoice is filed in the shipping department.

5. In the billing department, one copy of the bill of lading is attached to the customer's copy of the invoice and both are mailed to the customer. The other copy of the bill of lading, together with the sales order form, is then stapled to the invoice file copy and filed in invoice numerical order.

6. A keypunch machine is connected to the billing machine so that punched cards are created during the preparation of the invoices. The punched cards then become the means by which the sales data are transmitted to a computer.

    The punched cards are fed to the computer in batches. One day's accumulation of cards comprises a batch. After the punched cards have been processed by the computer, they are placed in files and held for about two years.

Required:

List the procedures that a CPA would employ in his examination of his selected audit samples of the company's (1) typed invoices, including the source documents, and (2) punched cards.

(AICPA adapted)

11-41 Several accounts receivable confirmations have been returned with the notation that "verification of vendors' statements is no longer possible because our data processing system does not accumulate each vendor's invoices."

Required:

What alternative auditing procedures could the auditor use to audit the accounts receivable?

(AICPA adapted)

11-42 The ABC Appliance Company, a manufacturer of minor electrical appliances, deals exclusively with 20 distributors situated at focal points throughout the country. At December 31, the balance sheet date, receivables from these distributors aggregated $875,000. Total current assets were $1,300,000.

With respect to receivables, the auditor followed the procedures outlined below in the course of the annual examination of financial statements:

1. Reviewed the system of internal accounting control. It was found to be exceptionally good.
2. Tied detail with control account at year-end.
3. Aged accounts. None were overdue.
4. Examined detail sales and collection transactions for the months of February, July, and November.
5. Received positive confirmations of year-end balances.

Required:

You are to criticize the completeness or incompleteness of the above program, giving reasons for your recommendations concerning the addition or omission of any procedures.

OBJECTIVE QUESTIONS*

11-43 The confirmation of the client's trade accounts receivable is a means of obtaining evidential matter and is specifically considered to be a generally accepted auditing

A. Principle.
B. Standard.
C. Procedure.
D. Practice.

11-44 The auditor obtains corroborating evidential matter for accounts receivable by using positive or negative confirmation requests. Under which of the following circumstances might the negative form of the accounts receivable confirmation be useful?

A. A substantial number of accounts are in dispute.
B. Internal control over accounts receivable is ineffective.
C. Client records include a large number of relatively small balances.
D. The auditor believes that recipients of the requests are likely to give them consideration.

Note: Questions marked with an asterisk are not AICPA adapted questions; otherwise, questions in this section have been taken from prior CPA examinations.

11-45   A sales clerk at Schackne Company correctly prepared a sales invoice for $5,200, but the invoice was entered as $2,500 in the sales journal and similarly posted to the general ledger and accounts-receivable ledger. The customer remitted only $2,500, the amount on his monthly statement. The most effective procedure for preventing this type of error is to

A.   Use predetermined totals to control posting routines.
B.   Have an independent check of sales-invoice serial numbers, prices, discounts, extensions, and footings.
C.   Have the bookkeeper prepare monthly statements which are verified and mailed by a responsible person other than the bookkeeper.
D.   Have a responsible person who is independent of the accounts-receivable department promptly investigate unauthorized remittance deductions made by customers or other matters in dispute.

Items 11-46 through 11-49 are based on the following information:

The following sales procedures were encountered during the regular annual audit of Marvel Wholesale Distributing Company.

Customer orders are received by the sales-order department. A clerk computes the dollar amount of the order and sends it to the credit department for approval. Credit approval is stamped on the order and returned to the sales-order department. An invoice is prepared in two copies and the order is filed in the "customer order" file.

The "customer copy" of the invoice is sent to the billing department and held in the "pending" file awaiting notification that the order was shipped.

The "shipping copy" of the invoice is routed through the warehouse and the shipping department as authority for the respective departments to release and ship the merchandise. Shipping-department personnel pack the order and prepare a three-copy bill of lading: the original copy is mailed to the customer, the second copy is sent with the shipment, and the other is filed in sequence in the "bill of lading" file. The invoice "shipping copy" is sent to the billing department.

The billing clerk matches the received "shipping copy" with the customer copy from the "pending" file. Both copies of the invoice are priced, extended, and footed. The customer copy is then mailed directly to the customer, and the "shipping copy" is sent to the accounts-receivable clerk.

The accounts-receivable clerk enters the invoice data in a sales-accounts-receivable journal, posts the customer's account in the "subsidiary customers' accounts ledger," and files the "shipping copy" in the "sales invoice" file. The invoices are numbered and filed in sequence.

11-46 In order to gather audit evidence concerning the proper credit approval of sales, the auditor would select a sample of transaction documents from the population represented by the

A. "Customer order" file.
B. "Bill of lading" file.
C. "Subsidiary customers' accounts ledger."
D. "Sales invoice" file.

11-47 In order to determine whether the system of internal control operated effectively to minimize errors of failure to post invoices to customer's accounts ledger, the auditor would select a sample of transactions from the population represented by the

A. "Customer order" file.
B. "Bill of lading" file.
C. "Subsidiary customers' accounts ledger."
D. "Sales invoice" file.

11-48 In order to determine whether the system of internal control operated effectively to minimize errors of failure to invoice a shipment, the auditor would select a sample of transactions from the population represented by the

A. "Customer order" file.
B. "Bill of lading" file.
C. "Subsidiary customers' accounts ledger."
D. "Sales invoice" file.

11-49 In order to gather audit evidence that uncollected items in customers' accounts represented valid trade receivables, the auditor would select a sample of items from the population represented by the

A. "Customer order" file.
B. "Bill of lading" file.
C. "Subsidiary customers' accounts ledger."
D. "Sales invoice" file.

11-50 A CPA examines a sample of copies of December and January sales invoices for the initials of the person who verified the quantitative data. This is an example of a

A. Compliance test.
B. Substantive test.
C. Cut-off test.
D. Statistical test.

11-51 An auditor is reviewing sales cut-off as of March 31, 1976. All sales are shipped F.O.B. destination, and the company records sales three days after shipment. The auditor notes the following items:

| | | (Amounts in thousands) | |
Date Shipped	Month Recorded	Selling Price	Cost
March 18	March	$192	$200
March 29	March	44	40
March 30	April	77	81
April 2	March	208	220
April 5	April	92	84

If the client records the required adjustment, the net effect on income in thousands of dollars for the period ended March 31, 1976 is

A. An increase of 12.
B. An increase of 8.
C. A decrease of 12.
D. A decrease of 8.

11-52 An auditor is reviewing changes in sales for two products. Sales volume (quantity) declined 10% for product A and 2% for product B. Sales prices were increased by 25% for both products. Prior year sales were $75,000 for A and $25,000 for B. The auditor would expect this year's total sales for the two products to be approximately

A. $112,500.
B. $115,000.
C. $117,000.
D. $120,000.

11-53 Which of the following audit procedures is most effective in testing credit sales for understatement?

A. Age accounts receivable.
B. Confirm accounts receivable.

C. Trace sample of initial sales slips through summaries to recorded general ledger sales.

D. Trace sample of recorded sales from general ledger to initial sales slip.

11-54 To determine that sales transactions have been recorded in the proper accounting period, the auditor performs a cut-off review. Which of the following *best* describes the overall approach used when performing a cut-off review?

A. Ascertain that management has included in the representation letter a statement that transactions have been accounted for in the proper accounting period.

B. Confirm year-end transactions with regular customers.

C. Examine cash receipts in the subsequent period.

D. Analyze transactions occurring within a few days before and after year-end.

11-55 A not-for-profit organization published a monthly magazine that had 15,000 subscribers on January 1, 1976. The number of subscribers increased steadily throughout the year and at December 31, 1976, there were 16,200 subscribers. The annual magazine subscription cost was $10 on January 1, 1976, and was increased to $12 for new members on April 1, 1976. An auditor would expect that the receipts from subscriptions for the year ended December 31, 1976, would be approximately

A. $179,400.
B. $171,600.
C. $164,400.
D. $163,800.

11-56 Which of the following would be the *best* protection for a company that wishes to prevent the "lapping" of trade accounts receivable?

A. Segregate duties so that the bookkeeper in charge of the general ledger has *no* access to incoming mail.

B. Segregate duties so that *no* employee has access to both checks from customers and currency from daily cash receipts.

C. Have customers send payments directly to the company's depository bank.

D. Request that customers' payment checks be made payable to the company and addressed to the treasurer.

11-57 Which of the following internal control procedures will *most* likely prevent the concealment of a cash shortage resulting from the improper write-off of a trade account receivable?

    A.   Write-offs must be approved by a responsible officer after review of credit department recommendations and supporting evidence.

    B.   Write-offs must be supported by an aging schedule showing that only receivables overdue several months have been written-off.

    C.   Write-offs must be approved by the cashier who is in a position to know if the receivables have, in fact, been collected.

    D.   Write-offs must be authorized by company field sales employees who are in a position to determine the financial standing of the customers.

11-58 Which of the following might be detected by an auditor's cut-off review and examination of sales journal entries for several days prior to and subsequent to the balance sheet date?

    A.   Lapping year-end accounts receivable.

    B.   Inflating sales for the year.

    C.   Kiting bank balances.

    D.   Misappropriating merchandise.

11-59 Which of the following analytical review procedures should be applied to the income statement?

    A.   Select sales and expense items and trace amounts to related supporting documents.

    B.   Ascertain that the net income amount in the statement of changes in financial position agrees with the net income amount in the income statement.

    C.   Obtain from the proper client representatives the beginning and ending inventory amounts that were used to determine costs of sales.

    D.   Compare the actual revenues and expenses with the corresponding figures of the previous year and investigate significant differences.

11-60 During the first part of the current fiscal year, the client company began dealing with certain customers on a consignment basis. Which of the following audit procedures is least likely to bring this new fact to the auditor's attention?

A. Tracing of shipping documents to the sales journal.
B. Test of cash receipts transactions.
C. Confirmation of accounts receivable.
D. Observation of physical inventory.

11-61 For the purpose of proper accounting control, post-dated checks remitted by customers should be

A. Restrictively endorsed.
B. Returned to customer.
C. Recorded as a cash sale.
D. Placed in the joint custody of two officers.

11-62 A company policy should clearly indicate that defective merchandise returned by customers is to be delivered to the

A. Sales clerk.
B. Receiving clerk.
C. Inventory control clerk.
D. Accounts receivable clerk.

11-63 A sales cut-off test of billings complements the verification of

A. Sales return.
B. Cash.
C. Accounts receivable.
D. Sales allowances.

11-64 The use of the positive (as opposed to the negative) form of receivables confirmation is indicated when

A. Internal control surrounding accounts receivable is considered to be effective.
B. There is reason to believe that a substantial number of accounts may be in dispute.
C. A large number of small balances is involved.
D. There is reason to believe a significant portion of the requests will be answered.

11-65 The primary difference between an audit of the balance sheet and an audit of the income statement lies in the fact that the audit of the income statement deals with the verification of

A. Transactions.
B. Authorizations.
C. Costs.
D. Cut-offs.

11-66 A CPA auditing an electric utility wishes to determine whether all customers are being billed. The CPA's best direction of test is from the

A. Meter department records to the billing (sales) register.
B. Billing (sales) register to the meter department records.
C. Accounts receivable ledger to the billing (sales) register.
D. Billing (sales) register to the accounts receivable ledger.

11-67 When scheduling the audit work to be performed on an engagement, the auditor should consider confirming accounts receivable balances at an interim date if

A. Subsequent collections are to be reviewed.
B. Internal control over receivables is good.
C. Negative confirmations are to be used.
D. There is a simultaneous examination of cash and accounts receivable.

11-68 To conceal defalcations involving receivables, the auditor would expect an experienced bookkeeper to charge which of the following accounts?

A. Miscellaneous income.
B. Petty cash.
C. Miscellaneous expense.
D. Sales returns.

11-69 In determining validity of accounts receivable, which of the following would the auditor consider *most* reliable?

A. Documentary evidence that supports the accounts receivable balance.
B. Credits to accounts receivable from the cash receipts book after the close of business at year-end.
C. Direct telephone communication between auditor and debtor.
D. Confirmation replies received directly from customers.

11-70 Which of the following is an effective internal accounting control over accounts receivable?

    A   Only persons who handle cash receipts should be responsible for the preparation of documents that reduce accounts receivable balances.

    B.   Responsibility for approval of the write-off of uncollectible accounts receivable should be assigned to the cashier.

    C.   Balances in the subsidiary accounts receivable ledger should be reconciled to the general ledger control account once a year, preferably at year-end.

    D.   The billing function should be assigned to persons other than those responsible for maintaining accounts receivable subsidiary records.

11-71 Once a CPA has determined that accounts receivable have increased due to slow collections in a "tight money" environment, the CPA would be likely to

    A.   Increase the balance in the allowance for bad debts account.

    B.   Review the going concern ramifications.

    C.   Review the credit and collection policy.

    D.   Expand tests of collectibility.

11-72 Confirmation of individual accounts receivable balances directly with debtors will, of itself, normally provide evidence concerning the

    A.   Collectibility of the balances confirmed.

    B.   Ownership of the balances confirmed.

    C.   Validity of the balances confirmed.

    D.   Internal control over balances confirmed.

11-73 The audit working papers often include a client-prepared aged trial balance of accounts receivable as of the balance sheet date. This aging is *best* used by the auditor to

    A.   Evaluate internal control over credit sales.

    B.   Test the accuracy of recorded charge sales.

    C.   Estimate credit losses.

    D.   Verify the validity of the recorded receivables.

11-74   In determining the adequacy of the allowance for uncollectible accounts, the *least* reliance should be placed upon which of the following?

    A.   The credit manager's opinion.
    B.   An aging schedule of past due accounts.
    C.   Collection experience of the client's collection agency.
    D.   Ratios calculated showing the past relationship of the valuation allowance to net credit sales.

11-75   Johnson is engaged in the audit of a utility which supplies power to a residential community. All accounts receivable balances are small and internal control is effective. Customers are billed bi-monthly. In order to determine the validity of the accounts receivable balances at the balance sheet date, Johnson would most likely

    A.   Examine evidence of subsequent cash receipts instead of sending confirmation requests.
    B.   Send positive confirmation requests.
    C.   Send negative confirmation requests.
    D.   Use statistical sampling instead of sending confirmation requests.

11-76   An auditor is testing sales transactions. One step is to trace a sample of debit entries from the accounts receivable subsidiary ledger back to the supporting sales invoices. What would the auditor intend to establish by this step?

    A.   All sales have been recorded.
    B.   Debit entries in the accounts receivable subsidiary ledger are properly supported by sales invoices.
    C.   All sales invoices have been properly posted to customer accounts.
    D.   Sales invoices represent bona fide sales.

11-77   Internal control over cash receipts is weakened when an employee who receives customer mail receipts also

    A.   Prepares initial cash receipts records.
    B.   Records credits to individual accounts receivable.
    C.   Prepares bank deposit slips for all mail receipts.
    D.   Maintains a petty cash fund.

11-78 Those procedures specifically outlined in an audit program are primarily designed to

A. Gather evidence.
B. Detect errors or irregularities.
C. Test internal systems.
D. Protect the auditor in the event of litigation.

11-79 Which of the following is *not* a principal objective of the auditor in the examination of revenues?

A. To verify cash deposited during the year.
B. To study and evaluate internal control, with particular emphasis on the use of accrual accounting to record revenue.
C. To verify that earned revenue has been recorded, and recorded revenue has been earned.
D. To identify and interpret significant trends and variations in the amounts of various categories of revenue.

11-80 In order to safeguard the assets through proper internal control, accounts receivable that are written off are transferred to a (an)

A. Separate ledger.
B. Attorney for evidence in collection proceedings.
C. Tax deductions file.
D. Credit manager since customers may seek to reestablish credit by paying.

11-81 Smith Manufacturing Company's accounts-receivable clerk has a friend who is also Smith's customer. The accounts-receivable clerk, on occasion, has issued fictitious credit memorandums to his friend for goods supposedly returned. The most effective procedure for preventing this activity is to

A. Prenumber and account for all credit memorandums.
B. Require receiving reports to support all credit memorandums before they are approved.
C. Have the sales department independent of the accounts-receivable department.
D. Mail monthly statements.

11-82   Which of the following is *not* a primary objective of the auditor in the examination of accounts receivable?

A.   Determine the approximate realizable value.
B.   Determine the adequacy of internal controls.
C.   Establish validity of the receivables.
D.   Determine the approximate time of collectibility of the receivables.

11-83   A corporation is holding securities as collateral for an outstanding account receivable. During the course of the audit engagement the CPA should

A.   Verify that title to the securities rests with the corporation.
B.   Ascertain that the amount recorded in the investment account is equal to the fair market value of the securities at the date of receipt.
C.   Examine the securities and ascertain their value.
D.   Refer to independent sources to determine that recorded dividend income is proper.

11-84   It is sometimes impracticable or impossible for an auditor to use normal accounts receivable confirmation procedures. In such situations the *best* alternative procedure the auditor might resort to would be

A.   Examining subsequent receipts of year-end accounts receivable.
B.   Reviewing accounts receivable aging schedules prepared at the balance sheet date and at a subsequent date.
C.   Requesting that management increase the allowance for uncollectible accounts by an amount equal to some percentage of the balance in those accounts that *cannot* be confirmed.
D.   Performing an overall analytic review of accounts receivable and sales on a year-to-year basis.

After studying this chapter, students should understand

1. The nature of the expense and production cycle.
2. Audit objectives of the expense and production cycle.
3. Procedures used in planning the audit of the expense and production cycle, including analytic review.
4. The internal controls which are frequently encountered in the expense and production cycle.
5. Procedures for compliance testing internal controls in the expense and production cycle.
6. Dual-purpose audit procedures for the expense and production cycle.
7. Substantive audit procedures for the expense and production cycle, including the use of alternative procedures for inventory.

CONDUCT INDEPENDENCE EVIDENCE DUE CARE FAIR PRESENTATION ETHICAL CONDUCT INDEPENDENCE EVIDENCE DUE CARE FAIR PRESENTATION ETHICAL CONDUCT INDEPEND
AL CONDUCT INDEPENDENCE EVIDENCE DUE CARE FAIR PRESENTATION ETHICAL CONDUCT INDEPENDENCE EVIDENCE DUE CARE FAIR PRESENTATION ETHICAL CONDUCT INDE
HICAL CONDUCT INDEPENDENCE EVIDENCE DUE CARE FAIR PRESENTATION ETHICAL CONDUCT INDEPENDENCE EVIDENCE DUE CARE FAIR PRESENTATION ETHICAL CONDUCT I
N ETHICAL CONDUCT INDEPENDENCE EVIDENCE DUE CARE FAIR PRESENTATION ETHICAL CONDUCT INDEPENDENCE EVIDENCE DUE CARE FAIR PRESENTATION ETHICAL CONDU
ATION ETHICAL CONDUCT INDEPENDENCE EVIDENCE DUE CARE FAIR PRESENTATION ETHICAL CON

Chapter 12

Audit of the Expense and Production Cycle

This chapter was written by
Wesley T. Andrews, Ph.D., C.P.A.,
Associate Professor of Accounting,
Florida Atlantic University

INTRODUCTION

The expense and production cycle is similar to the revenue cycle in that it is helpful to visualize the expense and production cycle as a group of information processing segments which channel information from the initial record of the transaction to the appropriate general ledger accounts. More specifically, the expense and production cycle may be thought of as being comprised of the voucher segment and the cash disbursements segment. The cash disbursements segment may be further subdivided into the general cash disbursements (by check) subsegment, the payroll subsegment, and the petty cash (or currency) disbursement subsegment. Likewise, the voucher segment may be subdivided into the general voucher subsegment and the payroll voucher subsegment.

This chapter begins with an overview of the various segments in the expense and production cycle followed by sections on internal control and substantive tests for the expense and production cycle. Although most asset and liability balances are influenced by activity in the expense and production cycle, this chapter only discusses substantive tests for cash and inventory balances. Substantive tests for other asset and liability balances are deferred until Chapter 13, where the financing and investing cycle is discussed.

Overview of General Voucher Segment

Activity in the general voucher segment of the expense and production cycle is initiated any time there is a need for the business to acquire goods or services from outside the entity. Some such needs arise regularly and routinely, such as the need to purchase inventory, supplies, acquire utility services, pay rent, and the like. Other needs may be non-routine in nature, such as the need to acquire a new plant or some other large capital item.

In any event, the initial document to record the need to acquire any goods or services is usually termed a purchase requisition. Purchase requisitions may be created either manually or automatically, as in the case of an automated EDP inventory control system. In this latter case, the controls inherent in the inventory control system should ensure that purchase requisitions are created only when inventory levels fall to designated reorder points, thus ensuring that purchase requisitions for the acquisition of inventory are properly authorized. Where purchase requisitions are issued manually, company policy should explicitly require that all purchase requisitions be issued only by authorized personnel and that requisitions also be approved by some authorized person other than the preparer of the requisition. In both cases, preparation of the purchase requisition should be independent of the purchasing department, and access to blank purchase requisition forms should be physically controlled and restricted to authorized personnel only. In addition, the use of prenumbered purchase requisition forms, along with the policy requirement that purchase requisitions be issued in numerical order, facilitates subsequent accounting to ensure that all purchase requisitions have been properly entered in the voucher segment of the information processing system.

In most cases, the preparation of multiple copies of the purchase requisition is normal. Usually, the preparer of the requisition (for example, a raw materials storeroom clerk) will retain one copy of the requisition, and send copies to the purchasing agent, the receiving department, and the accounts payable department.

Receipt of a properly authorized purchase requisition initiates purchasing activity on the part of the purchasing agent. The purchasing agent has the responsibility for maintaining contact with present and potential suppliers and for keeping abreast of price information, available discounts, shipping terms, and information about the quality of goods and services offered by various suppliers. Upon receipt of a properly authorized purchase requisition, the purchasing agent issues a purchase order to the best supplier of the goods or services requisitioned. One copy of the purchase order is normally forwarded to the supplier to constitute an order, another copy is sent to the originator of the purchase requisition (in order to indicate that action has been taken on the purchase requisition), and one copy is usually forwarded to the accounts (or vouchers) payable department. Another copy of the purchase order is usually filed in the purchasing agent's office, along with the purchasing agent's copy of the purchase requisition. This file constitutes the purchasing agent's documentation that all purchase orders issued are supported by a properly approved purchase requisition.

As was the case with purchase requisitions, good practice suggests that purchase orders should be prenumbered, and company policy should require that the purchasing agent issue purchase orders in numerical sequence. This will facilitate subsequent accounting for purchase orders to ensure that all purchase orders that have been issued have been entered on the books. In addition, company policy should require unissued purchase order forms to be controlled physically (that is, maintained in a locked fireproof place where access is restricted to authorized personnel). Finally, company policy should require that all purchase orders be properly approved by authoritative personnel before the purchase order is issued.

Receipt of goods is usually documented by the preparation of a receiving report by receiving department personnel. Again, multiple copies of the receiving report are usually prepared, with one copy being routed to the person who initiated the requisition (to indicate that the goods have been received) and one copy being forwarded to the accounts (or vouchers) payable department. A third copy of the receiving report is usually filed in the receiving department.

The use of prenumbered receiving report forms and the requirement that receiving department personnel issue receiving reports in numerical sequence, along with the requirement that copies of receiving reports be filed in numerical order, greatly facilitates the establishment of proper purchase cut-off (that is, the assurance that goods physically received in the receiving department prior to the end of an accounting period are recorded on the books during the period). A more detailed discussion of the effects of an improper purchase cut-off and auditing considerations related to the cut-off problem will be discussed later in this chapter.

One fairly common practice is to use copies of the purchase order to substitute for the receiving report. In such cases, three copies of the purchase order, rather than one, are forwarded to the receiving department by the purchasing agent when the purchase order is issued. These copies contain all information that appears on other copies of the purchase order, except that quantities ordered are not shown on receiving department copies. The omission of quantities, of course, forces the receiving department to accurately count what was received instead of reporting that the quantities received agree with the quantities ordered. When goods are received in the receiving department, quantities received are entered on the receiving department copies for subsequent comparison with quantities ordered. This comparison, usually made in the accounts (or vouchers) payable department, facilitates the maintenance of records regarding backorders and overshipments, allowing for follow-up of such matters at a later time.

At this point, the purchase requisition function has occurred, the goods have been ordered, and they have been received. Each of these activities is documented by either a purchase requisition, a purchase order or a receiving report. For a given purchase, a copy of each of these documents has been forwarded to the accounts (or vouchers) payable department, which files these documents, usually alphabetically by vendor. These files are usually referred to as the open requisition file, the open order file, and the open receiver file.

The remaining functions in the vouching process occur in the accounts (or vouchers) payable department. Preparation of the voucher involves the matching together of a purchase requisition, a purchase order, and a receiving report for each transaction. These documents provide a basis for checking the propriety of the details of the supplier's invoice, which should also be routed to the accounts (or vouchers) payable department when received from the supplier. Thus, the invoice, supported by a copy of the requisition, the purchase order, and the receiving report, constitutes the voucher itself.

Once these supporting documents have been matched and a voucher document attached, the voucher is assigned a number, such numbers being issued sequentially to facilitate later accounting for the recording of all vouchers. At this point, company procedures usually require clerical checking of all aspects of the data on the supplier's invoice. For example, a clerk will usually check to see that the description and quantity of the items ordered on the purchase order agrees with the description and quantity of the items requisitioned on the purchase requisition. Also, the clerk will compare this information with the description and quantity of the information on the receiving report in order to determine that the goods received are the goods actually ordered. Finally, this information is compared to the description and quantities of items on the supplier's invoice, to ensure that the supplier is billing the company for the correct items and quantities actually shipped.

In addition, clerical checking of the prices charged on the invoice is necessary to determine that they are proper, according to either prices indicated on the purchase order or to published price lists from the supplier. Also, the mathematical accuracy of the invoice (i.e., that the extension and footing of the invoice is proper) is checked by clerical personnel in the accounts (or vouchers) payable department. Finally, good practice suggests that the performance of each of these checks be documented. This is usually accomplished by having the clerk who performs the checks initial the voucher in a space provided to represent each check operation.

Once the voucher has been checked completely, the accounting distribution (the account to be debited) of the voucher should be entered on the voucher by some authorized person. The voucher is then approved for recording and entered in the appropriate book of original entry (usually referred to as the voucher register). The voucher itself is then usually filed in a tickler file (a file organized by date when payment is to be made in order to take advantage of any cash discounts). This file facilitates the payment of vouchers in timely fashion and may also be thought of as a subsidiary accounts (or vouchers) payable ledger, so that the total of the unpaid vouchers in the tickler file at any time may be totaled and agreed to the balance in the accounts payable account in the general ledger.

The voucher register lists the vouchers in numerical order, summarizes the total credit to be posted to accounts payable in the general ledger, accumulates the various debits that make up the distribution of the vouchers entered during the period, and is the basis for posting to the general ledger.

The foregoing describes the process of voucher preparation and recording for a normal acquisition of goods and services where payment is expected to be made by check. Indeed, a large number of businesses who use such a voucher system have policy requirements that all disbursements by check must be supported by a properly prepared and recorded voucher. (Of course, in the event that services are purchased, such as utility services or the services of an attorney or CPA, some of the supporting documents for the voucher will not be appropriate, e.g., a receiving report.)

Overview of General Cash Disbursements Segment

In the case of a voucher system, the cash disbursement function becomes relatively simple, since all disbursements have previously been recorded by a credit to accounts payable and debits to the appropriate accounts through the voucher register. The only entry required to record cash disbursements is a debit to accounts payable and a credit to cash in bank for the total dollar value of checks issued. Thus, the cash disbursements journal becomes a simple listing of the checks issued during the period, noting the check number, the payee, the number of vouchers being paid, the date of the check, and the amount of the check.

The process of issuing a check involves some procedures that are of interest to the auditor. This process is initiated by treating the vouchers in the tickler file, described above, as initial documents for the cash disbursements segment of the expense and production cycle. On any given day, the vouchers that have been previously filed by payment date for payment on that day are pulled from the tickler file and used as a basis for preparation of the checks to be issued.

The checks themselves are usually made of protective paper (that is, the paper is printed in such a manner that any attempt to alter what is originally written on the check will be prominently noticeable). The checks are usually prenumbered, and it is a good practice to require that checks be issued in numerical sequence in order to facilitate accounting in the cash disbursements journal for all checks issued.

It is not unusual for company policy to require two signatures on each check, thus ensuring that no single individual can issue a check without the knowledge of someone else in the organization (unless, of course, forgery is involved). Another common practice which accomplishes the same result is the use of a signature facsimile machine (where the signature is affixed to the check mechanically by a machine which contains a signature plate, somewhat similar to engraving). Usually, facsimile machines require one or more keys in order to operate the machine; where two keys are required, the keys can be issued to two different employees, thereby achieving the same control as the requirement for two check signers.

The check may be prepared in duplicate, in which case the copy of the check can serve as the cash disbursements journal [an adding machine tape of the total credit to cash for each batch of check copies provides the data for the entry of the credit to the cash account and the debit to the accounts (or vouchers) payable account]. When only one copy of the check is prepared (as in the case of the standard checkbook), the check stub should contain information about the payee, the date of check, the amount of the check, the check number, and the voucher number supporting the disbursement. An adding machine tape of the check amounts from the check stubs can provide the data necessary for the cash disbursements entry to the general ledger.

Once each check is prepared and approved by some responsible person, the voucher supporting the disbursement should be cancelled in such a manner as to prevent its resubmission to support issuance of another check. This is usually accomplished by stamping the face of the voucher "paid" in some prominent fashion; often this cancellation will involve mutilation of the voucher by perforation. Also, once the voucher is paid and cancelled, the fact that it has been paid should be noted in the voucher register, indicating the date of payment and the check number. If this is done promptly upon payment, the voucher register provides a current record of open (i.e., unpaid) vouchers, the total dollar value of which should agree with the balance in the accounts (or vouchers) payable account in the general ledger. In this manner, the voucher register can serve the same function as the accounts receivable subsidiary ledger, described in Chapter 11.

In those situations where a voucher system is not in operation, the cash disbursements segment has to perform the additional function of journalizing the accounting distribution of all debits and credits associated with a payment of cash, since the voucher segment is not performing this function. This means that, for example, when a purchase of inventory is made, the debit to the purchases account does not get journalized until the purchase is paid for, whereas it would be journalized through the voucher segment much earlier, if a voucher system were in operation. Hence, the cash disbursements journal, in the absence of a voucher register and previous recording of vouchers, must be expanded to summarize the account distribution of all cash disbursements.

The perceptive reader will also realize that in the absence of a formal voucher segment, the accounts payable account will be unaffected by day to day recording of transactions occurring in the expense and production cycle. Thus, the accounts payable account must be adjusted at the end of each accounting period to record the liability for accounts payable, after reversing the accrual of accounts payable as of the end of the previous period. In other words, in the absence of a formal voucher segment, transactions in the expense and production cycle are recorded on a cash basis during the period and must be adjusted to an accrual basis at year-end.

Overview of Petty Cash Disbursement Segment

One specialized subfunction of the cash disbursements segment is the imprest petty cash function. In most businesses, there is a need to make small disbursements in currency periodically, particularly when it is either inconvenient or inefficient to issue a check for small amounts. The use of imprest cash (currency) funds also occurs in retail establishments and financial institutions, where it is necessary to have cash on hand for making change.

Procedures for operating an imprest petty cash fund are based upon the fundamental principle of internal control that suggests that all assets of the enterprise should be in the custody of specifically designated employees, and access to assets should be restricted to such specifically designated employees. For example, one employee should be assigned primary responsibility for all raw materials stored at a particular location and that one employee should have the only key to the storage area. Only under such an arrangement can responsibility be established for any shortage of these assets. (For a review of this idea, the reader is encouraged to review Chapter 5 on internal control principles and standards.)

This idea is applied to control funds held in currency, either to make small disbursements or to provide change funds. When the fund is established, a check is drawn on the general bank account, payable to the newly appointed petty cash fund custodian, in the amount of the fund (say, $1,000).

The custodian of the fund now has $1,000 of company funds. The custodian should be instructed that he or she has sole responsibility for the funds and that the funds are to be physically kept in a locked drawer or box to which the custodian has the only key. The custodian should also be instructed not to allow access to the funds to anyone unless he or she (the custodian) is present. Thus, the custodian should understand that, in the event of a shortage in the fund, the custodian will be held responsible.

If the fund is to be used to make small disbursements (i.e., it is a "petty cash" fund), the custodian is instructed to disburse currency only upon receipt of a properly approved receipt, or "petty cash voucher." Such vouchers, which indicate the date of the disbursement, the amount of the disbursement, the accounting distribution of the transaction (i.e., the account to be debited), the person to whom payment was made, and the approval for the disbursement are to be placed in the fund by the custodian and viewed as the equivalent of currency. Therefore, at any point in time the custodian is accountable for the original amount and must have that amount in the fund, either in the form of vouchers or currency.

At some point in time, the custodian will have made total disbursements large enough to exhaust the currency in the fund. At that time, it is necessary to replenish the fund by issuing a check from the general cash account in the amount of the total of the vouchers in the fund. This check is issued to the custodian of the fund in exchange for the vouchers, thus restoring the amount of currency in the fund to the original amount. The recording of the issuance of the reimbursement check in the cash disbursements journal provides the first opportunity to record the expense distribution of the vouchers being reimbursed. Notice two things about the above-described procedure for the operation of an imprest petty cash fund. First, the petty cash account, an asset account, will have a balance equal to the original amount of the fund at all times. This balance will not change unless the amount of the fund is changed. (For example, management may decide to raise the amount of the fund from $1,000 to $1,500, in which case a check for the additional $500 would be issued to the custodian, and a debit to petty cash would be recorded in the cash disbursements journal). The issuance of a routine reimbursement check, however, does not affect the balance in the petty cash account in the general ledger.

Second, notice that disbursements made from petty cash which have not been reimbursed represent unrecorded disbursements. If a material amount of such unrecorded disbursements exists at year-end, the petty cash fund should be reimbursed on the last day of the year in order to record these items.

In the event that the purpose of the imprest fund is to make change, there is no need to provide for petty disbursements from the fund. In the typical retail situation, a change fund of, say, $100 will be issued for a particular cash register. Usually, company policy will require that only one employee be able to record sales on that register and, when a sale is recorded, the register will automatically accumulate total sales. At the end of the day, the amount of cash in the drawer should equal the imprest cash amount ($100) plus the total sales figure provided by the cash register. In a bank or savings and loan association, teller cash is controlled in a similar fashion; the custodian (teller) begins each day's work with a fixed imprest amount and at the end of the day must have an amount determined by adding all receipts to the fund during the day and subtracting all disbursements from the fund during the day.

Overview of Payroll Segment

A second specialized subfunction of the cash disbursements segment is the payroll function. Indeed, in most companies the payroll function accounts for a significant percentage of the total disbursements of the enterprise. Further, the payroll involves a specialized type of transaction, justifying a separate set of procedures and controls for processing information concerning these transactions.

In the case where the payroll is based upon hourly wages, the initial document for a payroll transaction is usually a time card, the card which the employee uses to "punch in" and "out" for each shift. At the end of the week, these cards are collected and each employee's immediate supervisor approves the hours worked by the employee.

Payroll cards are summarized as to hours worked, overtime premium hours, and accounting distribution. This work is usually done by the payroll department. However, in computerized applications this summarization is done by computer, after detailed information is entered from the time cards. Frequently a summary of hours worked by department, by employee, and by account debited is produced at this stage, to be used by production supervisory personnel to assist in the control of labor costs.

Next, payroll department personnel must identify the correct hourly rate for each employee. This requires that someone who has authority to establish hourly rates of pay (usually these rates are subject to several influences, such as company policy and union contract agreements) to maintain an up-to-date list of all employees and their authorized rates of pay. This list must be available to the payroll department in order to provide the basis for computation of gross pay. On the other hand, good internal control over payroll requires that authorizations for changes in rates of pay be the responsibility of someone other than payroll personnel.[1]

The computation of the net pay for each employee is usually summarized in the payroll register, which is a book of original entry in columnar form. The register lists for each employee the number of hours worked, the pay rate per hour, the overtime premium and shift premium hours, the gross pay (hours × rate), the details of the payroll deductions, and net pay (gross pay − total deductions). Typical deductions are for withholding of employee's share of FICA, withholding of federal and state income taxes, retirement contributions, and voluntary deductions, such as automatic savings plans, Christmas Club, and union dues.

In computing deductions, payroll department personnel must have other information which is usually found in the employee's personnel file. The computation of the amount of withholding of federal income tax is done by using a set of withholding tables furnished by the Internal Revenue Service. The computation also requires information about the filing status and number of dependents claimed by the employee. This information is usually obtained from the employee when the employee is hired, and the information is filed in the employee's personnel file.

Once the payroll has been computed and the net pay determined for each employee, the computations are usually reviewed by someone other than the person who made the original computations. Not only does this procedure require collusion between the preparer of the payroll and the reviewer in order to perpetrate an irregularity, but the review will also often detect unintentional errors in the computation.

Once the payroll register has been reviewed, footed, and balanced, the column totals for the payroll may then be posted to the general ledger, with the credit for the amount of the net payroll being posted to

---

[1] One warning is in order at this point. Needless to say, information concerning rates of pay is considered highly confidential in most companies, and the auditor working with such information should take particular care to maintain that confidentiality.

a cash-in-bank account (the procedure for issuance of payroll checks will be described below). In addition, the detail of each employee's pay computation is posted to individual employee earnings records, usually also maintained by the payroll department. These records reflect gross pay, deductions, and net pay for each employee for each pay period that the employee received a check, in addition to cumulative monthly, quarterly, and annual information for each employee. These records are the basis for preparation of the various payroll tax returns (federal and state income tax withheld, FICA tax withheld, and federal and state unemployment compensation tax, all of which are usually filed at least quarterly).

At this point, paychecks are prepared to complete the payroll process. Checks are prepared from information contained on the payroll register. In more automated systems, both the payroll register and the checks can be prepared by the computer after information concerning hours worked and master files containing the withholding information necessary to compute deductions have been input.

In any event, all of those control procedures that were recommended for general cash disbursements and discussed earlier are also recommended for the issuance of payroll checks. These controls would include (a) issuing prenumbered checks in numerical sequence, (b) using protective paper, and (c) using either dual manual signatures or facsimile signature with a dual access machine. In addition, once the paychecks are ready for signature and distribution, they should be reviewed and compared to the payroll register by someone other than the preparer of the payroll or the preparer of the checks themselves. At this point, the reviewer should approve the signing and issuance of paychecks.

Although the practice is not recommended, some businesses pay the payroll in currency. In this case, instead of issuing paychecks to each individual employee, only one check, in the amount of the total net pay, is drawn for each payroll. This check is cashed by the payroll clerk, who then places the amount of each employee's net pay in a pay envelope for that employee.

Once the paychecks have been signed (or, in the case where the payroll is to be paid in currency, the currency has been placed in the pay envelopes), the signed checks should be distributed immediately and directly by an employee independent of the employees being paid. The reason for this should be fairly obvious; signed checks (or currency) are highly liquid and therefore susceptible to misappropriation and should therefore be distributed as quickly as possible after completion of the payroll preparation function. Further, distribution of paychecks (or envelopes) directly to employees deters, for example, the unscrupulous supervisor who has discharged an employee but failed to notify the payroll department from intercepting the check or currency for that employee.

Some companies make available to their employees the service of direct deposit of paychecks. In such cases, the employee who wishes his or her paycheck deposited directly to his or her bank account can authorize the employer to do so each pay period. In this case, the payroll department will prepare a deposit slip for the employee and mail the deposit directly to the employee's bank. The bank in turn mails an authenticated copy of the deposit slip directly to the employee, indicating that credit has been given in the employee's bank account.

The procedures and controls involved in the preparation of salaried payrolls are essentially the same as the procedures and controls involved in the preparation and payment of hourly payrolls. The only essential difference is that the initial document is not a time card which records hours worked, since the employee is paid a fixed salary for each normal work week or month. The initial document, instead, may take the form of a payroll action form which initially places the employee on the payroll at a given salary, or the initial document may be a payroll action form that authorizes a salary change for a salaried employee.

The fact that an employee is on a fixed salary does not preclude the payment of overtime to that employee, if company policy so dictates. In such a case there will be some time-reporting document where the employee can report the total hours worked in a pay period, and overtime is computed at a rate implied by the employee's salary. Such time reporting is very common in CPA firms, not only to provide a basis for payment of overtime to staff but also to maintain a record of chargeable hours worked by professional staff.

AUDIT OBJECTIVES OF THE EXPENSE AND PRODUCTION CYCLE

Overall Objectives

As was the case with the revenue cycle, the overall audit objectives of the audit of the expense and production cycle are:

1. To do the work necessary to furnish a reasonable basis for an opinion on the financial statements being audited, and

2. To plan and execute this work in accordance with the three field work standards and to document the results in the work papers.

Specific Objectives of the Audit of the Expense and Production Cycle

To accomplish these overall audit objectives with respect to those elements of the information processing system and those accounts that are a part of the expense and production cycle, audit programs must be designed to accomplish certain specific audit objectives. These audit objectives are related to each of the segments of the expense and production cycle and to each of the account balances affected by that cycle. These specific objectives include:

1. To obtain and document descriptions of the procedures and controls that are part of the client's information processing system for each of the subsegments of the expense and production cycle discussed earlier;

2. To review analytically any relevant information concerning the environment in which the client conducts its expense and production activities. More specifically, this involves obtaining a general familiarity with the markets in which the client obtains resources, such as markets for raw materials, labor and overhead items, as well as markets for advertising and other selling and distribution expenses. In addition, interim monthly or quarterly data concerning the client's production activities should be reviewed analytically and compared with comparable data for prior periods;

3. To compliance test the controls that the auditor wants to rely on to establish their reliability;

4. To simultaneously with the testing of the procedures and controls for compliance described in objective 3 above, test substantively the data processed through the segments and subsegments of the expense and production cycle, gathering evidence that the integrity of that data is reasonably assured; and

5. Finally, to conduct tests of the balances in those accounts affected by the expense and production cycle to gather substantive evidence (in addition to the substantive evidence gathered through analytical review and the dual-purpose audit tests in objectives 2 and 3 above) to support the fairness of the balances in those accounts.

The discussion now turns to a detailed discussion of the specific procedures which should be included in the detailed audit programs related to the accounts affected by the expense and production cycle.

DEVELOPING AUDIT PROGRAMS RELATED TO THE EXPENSE AND PRODUCTION CYCLE

As was the case with the audit programs developed in Chapter 11 for the audit of the revenue cycle, the following audit programs represent logically organized sequences of audit testing procedures designed to accomplish the foregoing overall and specific audit objectives related to the expense and production cycle. The initial steps in the program are designed to obtain an overview of the market environment(s) in which the client obtains the resources to conduct business and to review analytically interim purchasing and inventory results.

1. Using the information obtained from industry and financial media, prepare a memorandum summarizing current conditions in the market(s) in which the client obtains resources. Note particularly:

   a. The presence or absence of major suppliers who may tend to exercise control over resource markets, and

   b. The entry or exit of competitors to or from these resource markets upon which the client depends. Obtain, if possible, information about the quality of available resources in these markets;

2. Discuss the above information with knowledgeable client personnel and include the client's observations in the memo prepared in step 1 above;

3. Based upon the findings in steps 1 and 2 above, prepare a memorandum which describes the probable impact of any environmental factors noted on the accounting data for the current period; and

4. Refer to steps 5 and 6 in the audit program for the revenue cycle (see Chapter 11, pages 499 and 500). Note that interim data regarding sales and inventory levels by product line, by division, and by geographical region was obtained and analytically reviewed. Based upon this work, prepare a memorandum discussing the probable impact of the findings of that analytical review on inventory levels and/or on other audit problem areas related to the expense and production cycle which might be suggested by the results.

After completion of the above four initial steps in the audit of the expense and production cycle, the auditor should have a reasonable understanding of the environmental factors which affect the client's operations in its resource markets. The next step is to obtain a description of the controls which are included in each of the segments of the expense and production cycle.

5. Based upon inquiry of knowledgeable company personnel, prepare an internal control questionnaire and/or a flowchart for each of the following segments of the expense and production cycle:

a. Voucher (purchases/accounts payable),

b. General cash disbursements, and

c. Payroll.

For a detailed description of the use of internal control questionnaires and flowcharting, see Chapter 7. Also, as indicted in Chapter 8, before the auditor documents the controls which are suppose to exist in any cycle, it is often helpful for the auditor to review an internal control questionnaire to become familiar with controls which are often used in a particular cycle. Exhibit 12-1 shows some controls which are frequently encountered in the expense and production cycle as well as an explanation for each control.

Exhibit 12-1
Controls Frequently Encountered in Expense and
Production Cycle and Explanation of Controls

Controls	*Explanation*
1. Are all purchase commitments recorded on prenumbered documents, and are the documents periodically reviewed by a responsible person to determine possible losses?	If these procedures are followed, there is less chance that losses on purchase commitments will fail to be recorded.
2. Are purchase orders prenumbered, and does a responsible person approve all purchase orders?	If purchase orders are not prenumbered, it is nearly impossible to identify the orders which have been placed by the company. If all purchase orders are approved by a responsible person, there is less chance that the company will order in less than optimum quantities and pay prices that are not the best prices available, consistent with quality. Also, there is less chance that the company will purchase inferior goods.

Exhibit 12-1 Continued:

Controls	Explanation
3. Are prenumbered receiving reports used, and does a responsible official account for the numerical sequence of receiving reports used?	If prenumbered receiving reports are not used, it is nearly impossible for a company to identify what has in fact been received. Also, if prenumbered receiving reports are not used, it is very difficult to establish a proper cutoff for receipts at year-end.
4. Does a responsible person inspect merchandise received for quality, and are quantities accurately determined and entered on the receiving report along with a description of the merchandise?	If merchandise is not inspected when received, there is a greater chance that the company will accept inferior goods. Also, if the receiving reports are not accurate with respect to quantities and description of what was received, there is a greater chance that the company will pay for goods not received.
5. Does a responsible person match the vendor's invoice with the purchase order and receiving report, and are prices, extensions, discount terms, and footings checked before invoices are approved for payment?	If these procedures are not performed, there is a greater chance that the company will pay for goods that were not received or pay incorrect amounts for goods which were received. Notice that if these procedures are performed, the following three documents would have to be forged before payments were made to a ficticious vendor: (1) the purchase order, (2) the receiving report, and (3) the vendor's invoice.
6. Are vendor's invoices used to post the debit to purchases, or the debit to inventory when a perpetual inventory system is used? Also, are the detailed inventory records posted from receiving reports?	Since vendor's invoices and receiving reports indicate what was received and what was paid for, the accuracy of inventory records is improved if receiving reports are used to post inventory records.
7. Are prenumbered documents used to record purchase returns, and are purchase return documents prepared by a responsible person who enters the description, quantities, and prices on the documents? Also, does a responsible person review the purchase return documents to ensure that the company receives cash or credit for purchase returns?	If these procedures are not followed, there is a greater chance that the client will not receive cash or appropriate credit for purchase returns.

Exhibit 12-1 Continued:

Controls	*Explanation*
8. Are the prenumbered purchase return documents used to post credits to purchase returns or inventory, including the detailed inventory quantity records when a perpetual system is used?	Since the purchase return documents establish what was returned, these documents should be used to post inventory records.
9. Are the accounts payable general ledger account and the subsidiary ledger accounts posted by different people and, is the control account periodically reconciled to the subsidiary ledger accounts by a responsible person? Are the general ledger inventory account and the detailed inventory records posted by different people, and is the general ledger account periodically reconciled to the detailed inventory records by a responsible person?	All information which is posted to the general ledger is also posted to the detailed records, but the documents which are used for postings are different, i.e., vendors invoices are used to post the general ledger whereas receiving reports are used to post the detailed inventory records. Consequently, if the postings are done by different people and if the general ledger balance is reconciled to the balances in the detailed records, the accuracy of the posting process is improved. Also, if the accounts are posted by different people, it is more difficult for ficticious entries to be posted, since any ficticious entry must be posted by two different people.
10. Are the accounts payable subsidiary records periodically reconciled to vendors monthly statements by a responsible person?	Many clients prepare a separate voucher for each invoice, but many vendors send monthly statements of the total amount which is due, which of course may include several invoices. If the individual vouchers are reconciled to the monthly statements, disputes between the client and vendors can be promptly reconciled. Also, if this procedure is followed, the chance of error in the client's and vendor's records is reduced.
11. Are prenumbered forms used to record hirings and dismissals as well as changes in pay rates? Are hirings and dismissals as well as changes in pay rates approved by a responsible person, and is this information communicated to the payroll department in writing?	It is convenient to design one prenumbered form which can be used to record hirings, firings, and changes in the rate of pay. Also, this form should be designed to reflect the initial rate of pay, in addition to changes in the rate of pay, and appropriate withholding

Exhibit 12-1 Continued:

Controls	*Explanation*
	information, such as the number of exemptions. Usually hirings, dismissals, initial pay rates, and changes in rates of pay are initiated in the production departments and approved by the personnel department. Then a copy of the prenumbered form is forwarded to the payroll department.
12. Does a responsible person account for the numerical sequence of the prenumbered forms discussed in control 11 and determine that (1) the payroll reflects only authorized employees, (2) these employees are being paid at the correct rate of pay, and (3) the payroll computation, including the accounting entries to journalize the payroll, are being made correctly.	Periodically the internal audit department should reconcile the prenumbered forms to the payroll register and verify that the payroll includes only authorized employees and that all payroll computations are being made correctly. Of course, if these procedures are followed, there is less chance of errors or irregularities in the accounting process.
13. Are production reports used to accumulate the hours worked during each pay period to determine manufacturing efficiency, and does a responsible person reconcile the hours paid on each payroll with the production reports?	Typically, production supervisors are held accountable for the hours their employees work, and variances are analyzed to identify those production supervisors who are inefficient. If these reports are reconciled to the hours paid from the payroll records, there is less chance of errors in the production reports or the payroll records. Also, since production supervisors are held accountable for the hours worked, they have an incentive to ensure that employees are efficient.
14. Does a responsible person compare payroll checks, as well as checks to discharge payroll withholding liabilities, e.g., taxes withheld, with the payroll register before the checks are signed and distributed?	Controls 12 and 13 are designed to ensure that the payroll register is error-free before checks are written. However, before the checks are signed and distributed, the check signer should have evidence that controls 12 and 13 have been applied. Then he or she should compare each payroll check, as well as checks to discharge payroll withholding liabilities, with the entries in the payroll register.

Exhibit 12-1 Continued:

Controls	Explanation
15. Are all checks prenumbered and controlled by someone other than the authorized check signer? Does a responsible person other than the authorized check signer complete the check for dates, amounts, and payee before the check and supporting documentation is submitted to the authorized check signer?	If checks are not prenumbered, it is nearly impossible to identify all disbursements which are made during a given period of time, and therefore it is nearly impossible for someone to review the disbursements for propriety. If the authorized check signer only receives checks to sign which are complete, and supported by adequate documentation, e.g., vouchers or the payroll register, there is less chance that improper checks will be written.
16. Does the check signer compare checks with supporting documentation before the checks are signed, and is supporting documentation effectively cancelled before the checks are signed?	Controls 5, 12, 13, and 15 are designed to ensure that checks and supporting documentation are correct before they are submitted to the authorized check signer. However, the authorized check signer must carefully review the check and supporting documentation before he or she signs the check and thus assumes final responsibility for the disbursement. Also, he or she must cancel the supporting documentation so that the same disbursement cannot be submitted twice.
17. Are checks distributed directly to vendors or employees by the authorized check signer or someone under his or her control, such as a paymaster, without being returned to other employees involved in the cash disbursements function?	If checks are distributed directly by the authorized check signer, there is less chance that the check could be altered or misplaced.
18. Are special bank accounts maintained for dividends, payrolls, and other disbursements where the total amount of the disbursement is fixed for a given period of time? For example, for payroll the net amount of the payroll can be transferred from the regular bank account to the payroll account, and then the payroll checks can be written on the payroll bank account.	When this procedure is followed, there is only enough money in the bank to cover the amount of the approved disbursement, and any unauthorized disbursements will cause the account to be overdrawn and therefore the improper disbursement will automatically come to the client's attention.

Exhibit 12-1 Continued:

Controls	*Explanation*
19. Are all bank accounts reconciled at least monthly by a responsible person who has no other responsibility for cash disbursements or cash receipts? Does this person compare the deposits which should have been made to the account with the deposits which were made to the account? Does this person account for the numerical sequence of cancelled checks and compare cancelled checks with the appropriate disbursements journal, i.e., the cash disbursements journal or the payroll register, for the date, the payee, and the amount? Does this person examine the signature on the check to determine that the signature is authorized? Finally, does this person examine endorsements, such as an endorsement which is different from the payee?	Bank reconciliations, if done properly, reconcile what should have been recorded with what was actually deposited or disbursed from the bank.
20. Have adequate physical safeguards been developed to maintain control over assets which may easily be misappropriated, such as cash on hand and inventory?	As indicated in Chapter 8, cash on hand should be minimized, and the cash should be stored in a safe. Likewise, fences and other safeguards should be established to prevent unauthorized access to the inventory.
21. Are physical inventories taken at least annually, and are the perpetual records adjusted for the physical count?	If physical inventories are not taken, perpetual inventory records are likely to contain substantial errors.
22. Is the petty cash fund the responsibility of one person, and does the size of the fund appear optimum? Does a responsible person periodically count the fund and exmine the disbursements for proprierty?	Petty cash funds are established to avoid writing numerous checks for small amounts. The fund should be large enough so that it does not have to be replenished too often, and thus defeat the purpose of the fund, but at the same time the fund should be small enough so that if the fund is misappropriated, the company does not suffer a material loss. When the fund is replenished, the various expenses made by the custodian should be reviewed by a responsible person.

Exhibit 12-1 Continued:

Controls	Explanation
	Also, the fund and the documentation for expenses should be periodically counted on a surprise basis.
23. Does adequate documentation exist for all entries to the accounts in the expense and production cycle, and are the entries and related documentation reviewed by a responsible person?	Most entries to the accounts in the expense and production cycle result from purchases, purchase returns, and payroll, and the ways these entries are reviewed are discussed in connection with the controls discussed previously. However, all entries to the accounts must be documented and reviewed by a responsible person. For example, when inventory is written down to market value, a responsible person must review the entry and supporting documentation.
24. Are duties in the expense and production cycle properly segregated?	As indicated in Chapter 5, incompatible duties should be performed by different people. For example, the bookkeeper should clearly not be authorized to sign checks. Likewise, the person who reviews transactions should not be the person who records the transactions.

The next four sections of the audit program relate to compliance testing the controls described in each of the segments. The tests are designed so that the auditor can also test the data flowing through each of these segments for substantive error, so they may be characterized as dual-purpose tests.

At this point, it is useful to recall the requirements of the second standard of field work regarding the review, testing, and evaluation of the system of internal accounting control. The purpose of this review process is to provide the auditor with a basis for determining answers to questions concerning the nature, extent, and timing of substantive audit tests to be performed. Step 5 above fulfills the requirements of the second field work standard with respect to the auditor's understanding of the system that is supposed to be in effect; it does not give the necessary assurance that the described controls are actually in place and functioning. In order to obtain this assurance, compliance testing is necessary. After performing these compliance testing procedures, the auditor then has some assurance about whether the controls described in step 5 above are in fact operating.

Further, these compliance tests need only be performed if the auditor wants to rely on the controls to justify the reduction or modification of the nature, extent, or timing of the substantive tests of balances to be performed subsequently. This means that, in the case where the control aspects of the expense and production cycle segments described in step 5 appear to be unreliable even if they do exist, the auditor is justified in not performing the compliance tests. In this case the auditor would proceed directly to substantive tests of balances which should accordingly be designed with the lack of underlying system controls in mind.

Before reading the audit program steps, however, it is important that the student understand that the program is presented to illustrate the types of audit programs which are likely to be found in practice. It would be impossible to present an audit program which covered the testing of all controls which auditors may encounter in their professional practice without making the program excessively complex. Therefore, in reading the program the student should recognize that (1) the program is presented for illustrative purposes only, and (2) in practice, auditors identify controls which they want to rely on for their specific clients and develop specific audit programs to gather evidence about whether the controls are working as prescribed. *The same word of caution is applicable for all audit programs presented in this text.*

The first segment to be discussed is the voucher segment. One objective of the set of procedures is to determine if all recorded vouchers are, in fact, proper liabilities of the company; that is, the audit program is designed to test vouchers payable (and accordingly the various asset and expense accounts that are debited through the voucher system) for overstatement. As will be discussed in Chapter 13, vouchers payable will be tested as of year-end for understatement by the search for unrecorded liabilities.

Since the voucher test is a test for overstatement, the direction of test is from the general ledger towards the detailed supporting documentation; hence, the conclusion to be drawn from the test is that recorded liabilities are proper, not that all liabilities have been recorded.

A generalized voucher test audit program follows:

6. Determine that the client uses prenumbered documents where appropriate, e.g., receiving reports and vouchers, and use techniques such as those indicated in Chapter 8 to compliance test the use of prenumbered documents;

7. Scan the credits to vouchers (or accounts) payable recorded in the general ledger. Investigate any credits posted to vouchers payable from any journal source other than the voucher register;

8. Trace a sample of credits from the general ledger account to the voucher register;

9. For the period being audited, test the voucher register for mathematical accuracy by refooting and crossfooting the register. (If the voucher register is voluminous, this may be done on a test basis, if the register has appropriate subtotals.) Test the posting of debits from the voucher register to the proper general ledger accounts by tracing all (or a sample) of such debits to the general ledger. If a perpetual inventory system is in use, also trace the detail of information concerning purchases of inventory to the perpetual inventory records;

10. Defining a population to be the set of all vouchers recorded in the voucher register during the period, select a sample of vouchers for examination of supporting documentation;

11. For those vouchers selected in step 10 above, examine the following supporting documentation:

    a. Purchase requisition,

    b. Purchase order,

    c. Receiving report, and

    d. Supplier's invoice.

    Note particularly that the purchase requisition was prepared by an authorized person and approved by someone other than the preparer of the requisition. Note further that the purchase order is properly approved by the purchasing agent and that the goods ordered are the same as the goods requisitioned (both in terms of description of ordered goods and quantities ordered). In addition, note that the goods received, according to the receiving reports, were the same as the goods ordered, according to the purchase order. Any goods not received are said to be "backordered"; note any such goods and determine (a) that these goods were not invoiced to the client, and (b) that the goods were subsequently received under a separate voucher. Finally, review the supplier's invoice, noting that the descriptions and quantities on the invoice agree with the purchase requisition, the purchase order, and the receiving report. In addition, check the pricing used on the invoice to approved suppliers' price lists and check the extensions and footing of the invoice. Examine evidence to indicate that the checking described in this paragraph was performed by client personnel.

With respect to the voucher itself, note that the voucher was entered in the voucher register properly and that the voucher is properly approved for recording by some authorized person. Further note that the voucher has been mutilated or otherwise stamped so that the same voucher cannot be reused to support additional disbursement;

12. Discuss the exceptions noted in step 11 with client personnel. Determine if each exception noted is, in fact, a proper exception; and

13. Evaluate the results of the test in terms of precision of the test. If, as a result of this evaluation, the precision of the test indicates that the error rate in the population is probably less than the maximum tolerable error rate, given the confidence level required for the test, the voucher test is complete. If, on the other hand, the precision of the test indicates that this conclusion cannot be supported by the test, consider whether to expand the test by selection of additional vouchers for examination or to conclude that internal controls in the voucher segment of the expense and production cycle are in fact weak and proceed to expand the scope of the subsequent substantive tests of balances accordingly.

In addition to the voucher test outlined above, it is proper to conduct a test of the general cash disbursements function as a part of the tests of the controls in the expense and production cycle. If, of course, a voucher system is in effect (requiring that all disbursements be based upon a properly recorded voucher), then the cash disbursements journal will be a relatively simple journal. That is, all checks for payments of vouchers will represent a debit to vouchers payable and a credit to cash in bank.

The following steps represent an audit program to test the controls in the cash disbursements segment of the expense and production cycle. Of course, if the client does not have a voucher system and expenses are recorded when the disbursement is made, the following program will have to be modified to examine supporting documentation for expense propriety, as was done in conjunction with the voucher test above.

14. Determine that the client uses prenumbered documents where appropriate, e.g., checks, and use techniques such as those indicated in Chapter 8 to compliance test the use of prenumbered documents;

15. Defining a population to be the set of all checks issued during the period under audit, select a sample of disbursements from the cash disbursements journal for test;

16. For the checks selected for test above, obtain cancelled checks from the bank statements which have been returned to the client by the bank. Compare these checks to the cash disbursements journal, noting:

    a.   Check number,

    b.   Date of check,

    c.   Payee,

    d.   Amount of check, and

    e.   Authorized signature.

    Further, examine the endorsement(s) on the checks, noting that the checks are in fact endorsed by the payee and that the checks do not bear second endorsements. If any checks bear second endorsements, note the names of second endorsers and determine that such second endorsers are not company employees. Examine evidence to indicate that the tests performed in this section were done by the client when the bank reconciliation was prepared;

17. For each of the checks selected in step 15, trace the checks to the voucher register to determine that the voucher supporting the disbursement has been properly removed from vouchers payable; and

18. List any exceptions noted in steps 14 through 17 above and discuss exceptions with client personnel. Once the client agrees that these are truly compliance exceptions to the cash disbursements segment controls, evaluate the exceptions in terms of the precision of the test. If this evaluation does not support the conclusion that the error rate in the population is less than the maximum tolerable error rate, consider expanding the sample used for testing or expanding the scope of the subsequent substantive tests of balances of those accounts which are affected by the cash disbursements segment of the expense and production cycle.

Next, a separate set of audit program steps will be included to test the controls and the data concerned with payrolls. For hourly payrolls, the following audit program steps are appropriate. In each case, it is important that the auditor not only make the computation or verification which is described but also obtain evidence that the computation or verification was done by the client. Of course, *this same statement is true for any compliance test because the client's computations and verifications represent the actual controls.*

19. Determine that the client uses prenumbered documents where appropriate, e.g., payroll checks, time cards, forms for hiring, dismissal, and pay rate changes, and use techniques such as those indicated in Chapter 8 to compliance test the use of prenumbered documents;

20. Obtain the payroll registers for the period under review and

   a. Test the footing and crossfooting of the registers, and

   b. Test the posting of the totals from the payroll register (gross pay, FICA tax withheld, federal and state income taxes withheld, other deductions, and net pay) to the appropriate general ledger accounts;

21. Defining a population to be the set of all payroll checks written during the period, select a sample of payroll line entries (i.e., paychecks listed in the payroll registers) for test. For each of the line items so selected, perform the following tests:

   a. Trace the employee's name and social security number to an approved list of employees obtained from the personnel department;

   b. Trace the total number of hours worked to a time clock card or some other appropriate form of documentation. Note that the clock card or other documentation bears the employee's supervisor's approval of the number of hours worked;

   c. Refer to the company's policy manual for hourly personnel (or the union contract, if appropriate) to determine the appropriate method of computation of overtime pay and/or shift differential pay;

   d. Obtain from the personnel department (or from some other authorized source within the client's organization) a list of authorized pay rates for each employee;

e. Using the information obtained in steps c and d above, recheck the computation of gross pay, including the computation of overtime pay and/or shift differential pay included therein;

f. Refer to payroll files for each employee and note documentation of authorization to withhold any discretionary payroll deductions, such as Christmas Club, union dues, and savings bond purchases. Also, note the employee's federal form W-4, and similar state tax form where appropriate, authorizing the number of dependents to be used in computing the employee's federal and state income tax withholding;

g. Referring to appropriate federal (and state, if appropriate) payroll withholding tables, verify the computation of federal (and state) income tax withheld. Also, verify the computation of FICA tax withheld; and

h. Verify the computation of net pay for each employee; and

22. For each of the payroll register line items (each representing a paycheck to an employee), obtain the payroll bank statements with cancelled payroll checks and examine the related cancelled paycheck, noting:

a. The date of the paycheck, the name of the employee, the amount of the check (i.e., the net pay), the gross pay and the amounts withheld. Trace these items to the payroll register and note that they agree with the payroll register;

b. Examine the signature on the check and determine that paychecks have been signed by an authorized checksigner;

With respect to this point, many companies use mechanical check signing equipment to sign checks. Such equipment usually uses an engraved signature plate which is removable from the equipment, so that it can be conveniently maintained by the checksigner. In addition, most check signing equipment requires two keys in order to activate the equipment. If these two keys are maintained by two separate employees, so that both employees must be present to operate the equipment, this control has the same effect as the requirement for dual signatures on the check, even though only one signature appears on the signature plate. If such mechanical check signing equipment is in use, attend the signing of a payroll, observing the procedures used by the client to take advantage of the control features, such as dual keying, of the equipment.

    c.   Examine the endorsement(s) on the reverse side of the paycheck, noting that the first endorser is in fact the payee. Note the names of second endorsers and subsequently determine that such endorsers are not employees of the company;

With respect to this point, the suspicion of the auditor should particularly be aroused if the second endorser is an employee of the company because there is always a chance that the check is to a ficticious employee and the check has been intercepted by a regular employee, such as a supervisor.

    d.   In the event the payroll is paid in currency, observe the preparation and distribution of a payroll, noting particularly that the physical security around the operation of handling a large amount of currency is appropriate. Further, this procedure gives the auditor assurance that an employee in fact exists for each employee on the payroll; and

23.   For the employees selected for test in step 21 above, trace detailed payroll information concerning gross pay, payroll deductions, and net pay to the employee's individual earnings record. For each employee so selected, test the footing and crossfooting of the earnings record to verify the mathematical accuracy of the quarterly and annual earnings data for that employee. Trace the quarterly totals of gross pay, deductions, and net pay to the appropriate quarterly payroll tax returns, such as Form 941. After the end of the client's calendar year, compare annual individual earnings information from the earnings records to the employer's copies of the federal Form W-2s for the selected employees.

The foregoing detailed audit programs are designed to test the various elements of the expense and production cycle which are of interest to the auditor. As such, the foregoing procedures are essentially designed to compliance test the controls that exist in the voucher segment, the cash disbursements segment, and the payroll segment of the expense and production information processing system. However, it is also true that, as a result of performing these procedures, the auditor gathers substantive evidence supporting the propriety of the actual data flowing through the system, so that the foregoing procedures have, in fact, a dual purpose.

With respect to the timing of the foregoing procedures, they may all be completed during the year, that is, prior to the client's year-end. It is also particularly important that they be completed well in advance of the time that a trial balance of the general ledger as of year-end becomes available, so that the results of the procedures may be analyzed as a basis for reaching conclusions regarding the reliability of the internal accounting controls involved in the expense and production cycle; these conclusions are necessary in turn to make necessary planning decisions regarding the nature, extent, and timing of substantive tests of balances which are to be conducted essentially with regard to year-end trial balance data.

The following audit programs are typical of the substantive year-end balance tests that would normally be performed with respect to those accounts affected by the information processing segments of the expense and production cycle.

Substantive Audit Programs

As indicated in Chapter 6, there are two types of balance sheet accounts, and the way in which substantive audit procedures are applied differs slightly for the two different types of accounts. Therefore, in reviewing the substantive audit programs which follow, students should recognize that cash and inventory accounts are balance sheet accounts where the beginning and ending balances are not closely related. Also, students should remember that while accounts payable, accrued salaries and wages, and payroll tax accruals may be technically part of the expense and production cycle, these accounts are also liabilities, and the discussion of substantive audit procedures for these accounts is deferred until Chapter 13.

Substantive Audit Program for Imprest Petty Cash Funds

1. Well in advance of year-end (say, 30 to 90 days before), review the general ledger to determine the existence of and amount of imprest petty cash funds. Determine the name of the custodian of each fund. If there are many such funds, select a sample of the funds for subsequent verification.

With respect to this point, it is not uncommon for larger clients to have several petty cash funds in operation, even though for small imprest amounts. Further, although the auditor may technically be justified in not conducting any verification procedures on imprest funds for immaterial amounts, clients usually want the auditor to make surprise counts of at least some of the funds, since they may view this procedure as being a significant part of the internal accounting control over the fund. Said another way, the client may be willing to incur the additional audit expense involved in making surprise counts in order to "keep the custodians of the funds on their toes."

2. For those funds selected for verification, plan a count of each imprest fund to be conducted on a surprise basis. Counts of funds should involve the following specific steps:

    a. Present identification to the custodian of the fund (or arrange for the client's supervisory personnel to make an introduction, so that the custodian understands that the auditor is authorized to count the fund);

    b. In the presence of the custodian, count the fund, noting (1) the amount of currency and coin in the fund, (2) a listing of any petty cash vouchers in the fund, including each voucher's amount, payee, account distribution, date, and authorization, (3) a listing of any checks included in the fund, including the date, amount, payee, maker, and endorsements for each check, and (4) any other items in the fund which are the equivalent of cash (such as postage stamps);

    c. Total the amount counted in b above and reconcile the total counted to the imprest amount of the fund; and

    d. Return the contents of the fund to the custodian, and obtain a receipt from the custodian indicating that the contents of the fund was counted and returned intact.

In the event that there are several such funds to be counted, it is important to schedule the counts of the funds to occur simultaneously, in order to minimize the risk that cash from one fund will be used to cover a shortage in another fund. Also, as discussed further in Chapter 13, if the client also has a material amount of marketable securities and/or notes receivable which require verification by physical examination, the counts of imprest cash funds should be conducted at the same time that the examination of marketable securities and notes receivable take place, since these liquid assets may be either sold, discounted, or pledged to obtain cash to replace shortages in imprest petty cash funds. This consideration is particularly important in audits of financial institutions such as banks, savings and loan associations, and brokerage firms because of the large percentage of such firms' assets held in liquid assets of this type.

Further, it is important to note that the entire count of the imprest fund should occur in the presence of the fund custodian; indeed, the auditor should not allow the custodian to leave the fund in the auditor's custody without the custodian present. A moment's reflection will suggest the reason why: in the event the fund is significantly short, it is convenient not to be in a position where one can be accused of causing the shortage.

In order to cover the contingency that the count may be interrupted and the element of surprise lost, the auditor should have in his possession a supply of gummed seals to seal the fund until the count can be resumed and completed. These seals usually bear the CPA's name and can be placed over the lock of a strongbox; removal (and consequent destruction) of the seal in order to gain access to the contents of the fund therefore cannot take place prior to resumption of the count without being detected by the auditor. A sample substantive audit working paper for the petty cash count is shown in Exhibit 12-2.

Substantive Audit Program for Cash in Bank—General Accounts

1. About ten days prior to year-end, arrange to have the client request, in writing, from each bank which holds funds on deposit, that a cut-off bank statement for the first ten days of the period immediately following year-end be mailed directly to the auditor. Include in this letter a request for a standard bank confirmation form, to be returned directly to the auditor from the bank;

Since the above step is customary in all audits, banks are used to receiving such requests from their customers and are usually very cooperative. An example of a standard bank confirmation form is included in Exhibit 12-3.

A cut-off bank statement is like a regular bank statement except that it covers a shorter period of time: from the client's year-end up to the date specified by the auditor. The auditor will use the cancelled checks and other documentation returned with the cut-off bank statement to substantiate the items, e.g., deposits in transit and outstanding checks, which appear on the client's year-end reconciliation. Consequently, in selecting the time period for the cut-off bank statement, the auditor should specify a long enough period of time so that most reconciling items on the client's year-end bank reconciliation have time to clear the bank during the period covered by the cut-off bank statement and usually ten business days is a sufficient period of time. When the auditor finishes with the cut-off bank statements, the statements should be returned to the client because the bank will not include copies of the items, e.g., cancelled checks, in the client's bank statement for the first month of the client's new accounting period.

2. Obtain a copy of the client's reconciliation, as of year-end, for each bank account. Foot the reconciliation and trace the balance per general ledger as listed on the reconciliation to the general ledger and to the working trial balance and financial statements;

Exhibit 12-2
Sample Working Paper for Petty Cash Count

Prepared by: _J.Y._
Date: _12-31-83_
Reviewed by: _P.J._
Date: _1-14-84_

Bowler Lumber Co.
Petty Cash Count
12/31/83

$10	× 2	$ 20
5	× 3	15
1	× 6	6
.50	× 2	1
Petty cash vouchers.............................		E 58
		$100
		⩗
		T/B

The above fund was counted in my presence and
returned to me intact.

David Bowler
Petty Cash Custodian
12/31/83

⩗   Footed.

T/B   Agrees with general ledger, trial balance, and financial
statements.

E   Examined petty cash vouchers. All expenses appear to be
proper. Examined check #1206, which was written after
the petty cash count, to replenish the account.

Exhibit 12-3

STANDARD BANK CONFIRMATION INQUIRY
Approved 1966 by
AMERICAN INSTITUTE OF CERTIFIED PUBLIC ACCOUNTANTS
and
BANK ADMINISTRATION INSTITUTE (FORMERLY NABAC)

O R I G I N A L
To be mailed to accountant

_____19_____

Your completion of the following report will be sincerely appreciated. **IF THE ANSWER TO ANY ITEM IS "NONE,"**
PLEASE SO STATE. Kindly mail it in the enclosed stamped, addressed envelope _direct_ to the accountant named below.

Report from   Yours truly, _____

_____
(ACCOUNT NAME PER BANK RECORDS)

(Bank) _____   By _____
                                                              Authorized Signature

_____   Bank customer should check here if confirma-
                                                    tion of bank balances only (item 1) is desired.

_____   ☐

                                                    NOTE—If the space provided is inadequate,
                                                    please enter totals hereon and attach a state-
                                                    ment giving full details as called for by the
                                                    columnar headings below.

Accountant

1. At the close of business on_____19_____our records showed the following balance(s) to the
credit of the above named customer. In the event that we could readily ascertain whether there were any balances
to the credit of the customer not designated in this request, the appropriate information is given below.

AMOUNT	ACCOUNT NAME	ACCOUNT NUMBER	Subject to With-drawal by Check?	Interest Bearing? Give Rate
$				

2. The customer was directly liable to us in respect of loans, acceptances, etc., at the close of business on that
date in the total amount of $_____, as follows:

AMOUNT	DATE OF LOAN OR DISCOUNT	DUE DATE	INTEREST Rate	INTEREST Paid to	DESCRIPTION OF LIABILITY, COLLATERAL, SECURITY INTERESTS, LIENS, ENDORSERS, ETC.
$					

3. The customer was contingently liable as endorser of notes discounted and/or as guarantor at the close of
business on that date in the total amount of $_____, as below:

AMOUNT	NAME OF MAKER	DATE OF NOTE	DUE DATE	REMARKS
$				

4. Other direct or contingent liabilities, open letters of credit, and relative collateral, were

_____

5. Security agreements under the Uniform Commercial Code or any other agreements providing for restrictions,
not noted above, were as follows (if officially recorded, indicate date and office in which filed):

_____

_____

Yours truly, (Bank) _____

Date_____19_____   By _____ _____
                                        Authorized Signature

The program given herein assumes that the auditor intends to verify all bank accounts as of year-end; which is normally the case. In the event that the client has multiple bank accounts (and particularly in the situation where some of the bank accounts are imprest at nominal balances), the auditor may decide not to verify all cash-in-bank accounts. In such cases, all bank accounts which have significant balances should be verified, along with a sample of the smaller balance accounts. Further, the auditor's assessment of the relative strength of the controls in the cash receipts and disbursements segments of the revenue cycle and the expense and production cycle, will be a determining factor in this decision.

3. Obtain from the client bank statements for each bank account for the month ending with the client's year-end. Trace the ending balance from the bank statement to the balance per bank statement listed on the year-end reconciliation.

4. Compare checks returned with the bank statement to the cash disbursements journal for the last month of the fiscal year. Trace

   a. All checks returned in the bank statement which were written prior to the beginning of the month to the previous month's outstanding check list, and

   b. All recorded disbursements for the month which did not clear during the month to the outstanding check list at the end of the month. (Note that all checks that were outstanding at the beginning of the month and did not clear during the month should also be outstanding at the end of the month); and

5. Foot the outstanding check list and agree total outstanding checks to the bank reconciliation as of year-end.

Note that after steps 3, 4 and 5 have been completed the auditor should have accounted for all checks outstanding at the end of the previous month as either having cleared the bank during the last month of the year or as being outstanding as of the end of the year. Also, all checks recorded as cash disbursements during the last month of the year are accounted for as either clearing the bank during the last month of the year or as being outstanding as of year-end.

6. Compare checks returned with the cut-off bank statement, obtained directly from the bank in step 1 above, to the outstanding check list at year-end. Examine checks carefully, noting that they are dated

during the year being audited, are properly signed and endorsed, and are for correct amounts. For the remaining checks returned with the cut-off bank statement, trace each check to the cash disbursements journal for the month immediately following year-end; and

7. With respect to deposits, trace all deposits from the bank statement for the last month of the year to the cash receipts journal for that month. Any deposits in transit at the beginning of the month should also be traced to the bank statement. Deposits from the cash receipts journal which did not reach the bank during the last month of the year should be traced to the year-end bank reconciliation as deposits in transit.

Once step 7 has been completed, the auditor, as was the case with cash disbursements in step 5 above, should have accounted for all deposits in transit as of the beginning of the month, tracing such deposits to the bank statement. In addition, all deposits from the cash receipts book for the last month of the year should be accounted for, either as being deposited in the bank during the month or properly handled as deposits in transit on the year-end bank reconciliation.

The auditor should pay particular attention to the delay time between recording of cash receipts in the cash receipts journal and the actual deposit according to the bank statement. Significant delays (say, more than one or two days) indicate, at best, a weakness in the internal control over cash receipts.

8. Trace deposits from the cut-off bank statement either to the cash receipts book for the first month of the subsequent year or to the bank reconciliation as of year-end. Note delays of more than one or two business days, obtaining an explanation for any deposits with significant delays;

9. Examine evidence to support the propriety of all other reconciling items in the year-end reconciliation; and

10. Compare the balance confirmed by the bank according to the confirmation obtained in step 1 above with the balance per bank statement used in the year-end reconciliation. Trace all other information contained on the confirmation form to the general ledger to determine that items, such as confirmed liabilities to the bank, have been properly reflected on the books.

An example of an audit working paper indicating the substantive audit procedures applied to a client's year-end bank reconciliation is shown in Exhibit 12-4.

Exhibit 12-4
Example of Audit Working Paper Indicating
Substantive Audit Procedures Applied to
Clients Year-End Bank Reconciliation

Prepared by: *J.K.Y.*
Date: 1-14-84
Reviewed by: *P.J.*
Date: 1-20-84

Bowler Lumber Co.
Cash—General Bank Account
12/31/83

Balance per bank		$2,000 Ⓐ
Outstanding checks:		
104	$100 ✓	
106	200 ✓	
107	50 ✓	
108	25 ✓	
109	25 ✓	⟨400⟩
Deposit in transit		5,000 T
Balance per books		$6,600

T/B, ⟋

Ⓐ   Agrees with 12/31/83 bank statement, 1/1/84 beginning balance on cut-off bank statement, and bank confirmation (see working paper #43).

⟋   Footed.

T/B   Agrees with general ledger, trial balance, and financial statements.

✓   Examined cancelled check clearing with cut-off bank statement. Reconstructed outstanding check list, and verified cut-off by applying audit program, steps 3-6.

T   Traced to cut off bank statement. Amount cleared on 1/2/84. Also, traced to 12/31/83 cash receipts journal. Applied audit program steps 7 and 8 to reconstruct the deposit in transit and verify cut-off.

While reviewing the client's cash receipts and disbursements, the auditor should carefully examine interbank transfers. These occur when a check is written on one bank and deposited in another bank. One problem which may occur when these transfers are not under effective control is called *kiting*.

Kiting involves drawing a check on one bank and depositing the check in another bank to cover a shortage in the latter bank. However, neither the receipt or the disbursement are recorded in the accounting records. Consequently, until the check clears the disbursing bank, it appears that the cash balance in the bank which was short has been increased with no change in the book balances for either account.

To illustrate kiting, assume that $50,000 has been misappropriated from Bank S, and thus a reconciliation of this account will show a $50,000 difference between the adjusted balance per bank and the adjusted balance per books, i.e., the adjusted balance per bank will be $50,000 less than the adjusted balance per books. An embezzler might try to cover this shortage by writing a $50,000 check on another one of the client's bank accounts, depositing the amount in Bank S, and not recording the receipt or disbursement in the client's records. Thus, until the check clears the disbursing bank, the balance per bank in Bank S will increase by $50,000 with no apparent change in balances per books or in the balance per bank for the disbursing bank. Thus, for a short period of time the fraud can be covered up.

Of course, the auditor should be able to detect kiting when he or she examines the cash receipts and disbursements as indicated in the previous audit program steps. However, in many cases the auditor will prepare a formal schedule of bank transfers which occurred around the client's year-end. The auditor will examine each transfer to determine (1) that the receipt and disbursement were recorded on the books in the same accounting period, and (2) that items which were recorded on the books, but which did not clear the bank until the next period, are properly shown as a reconciling item on the appropriate bank reconciliation. An example of a bank transfer schedule is shown in Exhibit 12-5.

Substantive Audit Program for Cash in Bank—Imprest Accounts

The procedures involved in auditing an imprest bank account are essentially the same as those for general cash-in-bank accounts, except that the balance per books should be a fixed, imprest amount. Therefore, only one additional step is needed to accommodate the imprest status of such accounts:

Exhibit 12-5
Example of a Bank Transfer Schedule

Prepared by: _J.J._
Date: _1-16-84_
Reviewed by: _P.J._
Date: _1-20-84_

Bowler Lumber Co.
Bank Transfer Schedule
12/31/83

Transfer		Receipt		Disbursement	
		Books	Bank	Books	Bank
First and Merchant to Chase.....T.		12/31	1/4	12/31	1/6
Bank of the South to Continental Illinois..........		1/4	1/8	1/4	1/10

Examined all cash receipts and cash disbursements for the period 12/20/83 to 1/10/84. The only transfers during this period were the two noted above, and, as this schedule indicates, these transfers were properly accounted for.

T   Traced to outstanding check list for F&M and deposit in transit list for Chase.

Determine that imprest amounts are properly authorized by the client. Review the amounts of imprest balances to determine if they are reasonable (unnecessarily large imprest balances represent an unproductive use of cash, while balances that are too small require frequent reimbursement and related expense).

Substantive Audit Program for Inventories

The following audit programs for validating inventory amounts are extremely generalized; this must be so because of the inherent complexity of inventory accounting. In other words, there is a wide variety of inventory problems in actual practice, so that no two firms are faced with exactly the same inventory accounting systems and/or problems. As a result, each inventory audit program requires considerable tailoring to fit the client's individual situation.

Nevertheless, the following generalized audit program is useful to demonstrate the basic considerations involved in programming the audit of inventories. Further, the following programs are designed to audit inventory in a merchandising or non-manufacturing company. Similar program steps are also appropriate for auditing raw material inventories and finished goods inventories in a manufacturing company.

The audit of inventories can be considered as taking place in two parts: verification of physical quantities of the inventory and verification of inventory valuations. In the following discussion, the audit of physical quantities is discussed first, followed by a discussion of the audit of inventory values.

Even if the client maintains extensive perpetual inventory records and the auditor's compliance tests of the controls inherent in the perpetual inventory recordkeeping process indicate that the perpetual records should be reliable, the client should take some form of physical inventory for comparison of quantities actually on hand with the perpetual records. Of course, the timing of the inventory taking may be modified somewhat if the controls over the perpetual recordkeeping process are evaluated as being good. For example, if the controls are judged to be reliable, the client may wish to take the physical inventory at some time other than at year-end and the auditor can agree with this conclusion. Indeed, with reliable controls, the client may physically verify less than 100% of the quantities in the inventory, basing the selection of items to be physically counted on some statistically reliable sampling plan.

Also, some clients may follow a practice of cycle counting the inventory — i.e., certain parts of the inventory may be counted at different points during the year, so that it is not necessary to take a complete physical inventory at any one time during the year. The auditor can modify his or her inventory quantity verification procedures to correspond to cycle consenting if the controls in the perpetual recordkeeping process have been reviewed and judged to be adequate.

Based upon the above considerations and after completing a review and evaluation of the internal accounting controls in the sales and voucher segments of the client's information processing system, the auditor may discuss and agree with the client as to an appropriate time for the client to take physical inventory. Unless the client is using some type of cycle counting approach, in which case all elements of the inventory will not be counted at the same time, it is highly advisable to secure the client's agreement to suspend operations entirely while the physical inventory is conducted. The reason for this is that it is very difficult to obtain an accurate count of inventory while goods are moving from one place to another in the inventory storage area. In manufacturing companies where the client is operating second and third shifts, the client may be somewhat reluctant to suspend operations and, indeed, in the case of some continuous process types of manufacturing, it may be technologically impossible to suspend operations. In these cases, particular attention should be given to the problem by incorporating controls into the inventory-taking procedure to account for inventory movement during the count to protect against double counting or omissions in the count.

Before discussing inventory observation in detail, however, students should recognize that the observation of inventory is a generally accepted auditing procedure. This means that the auditor must observe the inventory if (1) the inventory is material, and (2) it is possible and practicable to observe the inventory, or disclaim or qualify his or her opinion because of the scope limitation. However, there is no scope limitation in cases where it is impossible or impracticable to observe the inventory, and the auditor uses alternative procedures to evaluate the fair presentation of the inventory. For example, it would be impossible for the auditor to observe the ending inventory if he or she was engaged after the client's year-end. Also, in some of these cases, the auditor would be able to substantiate the year-end inventory by observing the inventory when he or she is engaged as auditor and reconstructing the year-end inventory by taking the inventory at the observation date *minus* purchases and *plus* sales since the year-end date. However, this alternative procedure would only help the auditor substantiate the year-end inventory and not the beginning inventory. Consequently, the auditor would still have to disclaim an opinion or qualify his or her opinion because of the failure to observe the beginning inventory unless the beginning inventory was examined by another CPA and the auditor, as discussed in Chapter 4, could rely on the work performed by the other CPA.

The following audit program steps are appropriate for audit of the taking of a physical inventory by the client:

1. Prior to the date scheduled for the taking of the physical inventory, meet with the client to discuss the inventory procedures and the instructions for inventory-taking that the client will issue to company employees involved in the counting process. Obtain a copy of the client's written inventory-taking procedures for the working papers.

The client's plans for taking inventory should include:

a. Plans to suspend operations before the actual count is to begin, in order to give client's personnel time to arrange the inventory in an orderly manner prior to the beginning of the actual count. The client should ensure that similar inventory items are located in the same area, that any inventory held on consignment is appropriately physically segregated, and that trash and other non-inventory items are removed from the storage area;

b. Procedures for control of the documents to be used to record the inventory count. Usually, counts are recorded on prenumbered documents issued by one employee responsible for document control. Employees making counts should be instructed to use the count documents in sequence and return unused documents to the document control employee, whereupon the document control employee can account for all count documents as either being used or returned;

c. Plans for assigning counting duties to employees (preferably to work in teams of two, one counting and one recording counts);

d. Plans for dual counts of inventory. Usually, dual counting is accomplished by requiring one count team to count an area of inventory; leaving copies of the count documents in the inventory storage area but with quantities deleted. A second count team then repeats the counts, recording the second counts on the copies. Then the copies of the count documents are removed from the inventory storage area and matched with the originals. Any count differences noted are recounted and reconciled; and

e. Plans that counts be compared to perpetual inventory records and that differences between physical count and quantities from the perpetual records be reconciled before the inventory is completed and movement of inventory is resumed.

At the time of the physical inventory, the auditor should plan to observe the count and perform the following audit program steps:

1. Tour the inventory storage area, noting whether or not the client's personnel have in fact complied with the inventory instructions regarding such items as the clean-up of the storage area. Prepare a memo for the working papers, commenting upon observed compliance with the inventory-taking instructions;

2. Review the client's implementation of the count document control procedures. If appropriate, prepare a worksheet showing the range of numbers assigned to count sheets in each inventory storage area. At the conclusion of the count, determine that all count documents are accounted for, either as being used in the count or as being returned to the document control employee unused. Working papers of the auditor should document the numbers of the count sheets used and the numbers not used; and

3. Select a sample of items for verification of counts. Locate items selected and make a count of the quantity in inventory. Record the following information on a worksheet for each item counted:

    a. Item description,

    b. Item location,

    c. Count document number,

    d. Quantity per auditor count,

    e. Quantity per inventory count,

    f. Difference (if any), and

    g. Explanation of difference (if any).

Selection of items for test counting may be either based upon some random statistical selection plan or upon a judgmental basis. If the basis for selection is judgmental, most auditors will attempt to select items of high dollar value or items which appear to be more susceptible to errors in counting.

In addition, the auditor should consider the "direction of test" implications of selecting items to be test-counted. If the client maintains a perpetual inventory system, some items may be selected from the perpetual inventory records to be located in the storage area and counted by the auditor. This procedure gives the auditor assurance of the physical existence of inventory that is supposed to exist. This procedure does not, however, give the auditor any assurance concerning understatement of the perpetual inventory record. That is, selecting items for count from the perpetual records can never identify inventory that is physically on hand but not recorded on the books. For this reason, the auditor also selects some items from the inventory storage area for count, later tracing these items to the perpetual inventory records.

In the event that substantial, numerous count errors are detected during the inventory, the auditor should discuss the errors with the client, considering whether or not to reach a conclusion that the entire count procedure is improper [such a decision would require that the inventory be recounted, after correction of the cause(s) of the bad counts]. In any event, if numerous count errors are noted during the count, the auditor should consider extending his or her audit tests to include more test counts than originally contemplated. Exhibit 12-6 shows an example of a test count working paper which might be prepared by the auditor.

In addition to making test counts of the inventory, several other audit tasks should be accomplished by the auditor while the count is in progress:

4. While touring the inventory storage area, note any inventory that does not appear to have moved recently (such inventory may be dusty and stored in a remote part of the storage area). Also, note any inventory which appears not to be in a salable condition. Prepare a listing of such questionable inventory for subsequent consideration of a write-down to market for obsolete or slow-moving items;

5. Inquire of client's personnel regarding the nature of any items in the storage area which are not included in the physical inventory. Such inventory may be held on consignment or may have been invoiced to customers on a "bill and hold" basis prior to the inventory count. Make a list of such items for subsequent verification of the propriety of treatment of these items;

6. Make a tour of the receiving area, noting any inventory that arrives during (or immediately before) the taking of the physical inventory.

Exhibit 12-6
Example of Test Count Working Paper

Prepared by: J.J.
Date: 12-31-83
Reviewed by: P.J.
Date: 1-14-83

Johnson Electric Co.
Test Counts of Inventory
12/31/83

Description	Location	Count Document Number	Auditor's Count Quantity
10-2 wire (2,000 feet)	Storage Area E-6	1502	2,000 feet Ⓐ
Six heat pumps—GE Model 23012	Storage Area E-12	2001	6 A
1,500 bags of insulation	Front of main warehouse	63	1,500 bags Ⓐ

Ⓐ   Agrees with final inventory listing as working paper #52. These items are not maintained on perpetual records.

A   Agrees with perpetual inventory records and final inventory listing (working paper #53).

Note to Student: In practice the auditor should make a representative number of test counts of all classes of inventory items. Only three counts are shown here to conserve space.

Prepare a working paper listing the last few (say, five or ten) receiving reports used for the accounting period. Determine that the goods entered on these receiving reports have been counted and included in the inventory. Also inspect a few of the blank receiving reports which will be issued after the inventory count to verify that the blank receiving reports are in numerical order; and

7.   Make a tour of the shipping area, noting any inventory which is in the shipping area for shipment immediately after the inventory count. Examine copies of the last few (say, five or ten) shipping documents for shipments made immediately before the inventory count and examine a few blank shipping documents which will be used for shipments to be made immediately after the inventory count to verify that the blank shipping reports are in numerical order.

The purpose of steps 6 and 7 is to establish that there is a good cut-off of both purchases and shipments as of the inventory date. As indicated in Chapter 11 and later in this chapter, information collected at this time can be traced to purchase and sales records after inventory has been completed to test the propriety of the cut-offs.

The remaining procedures concerning inventory verification are directed towards two goals: follow-up of items noted during the physical inventory and verification of the valuation of the physical inventory. These procedures can be undertaken after the physical inventory has been completed and the auditor has been furnished with a listing of the inventory quantities and prices as determined by the client. An example of a inventory listing is shown in Exhibit 12-7.

8.   As soon as the client has a copy of the final physical inventory listing available, obtain a copy of the listing for the working papers. Trace the items selected in step 3 previously (i.e., those items selected by the auditor for test-counting while the inventory count was in progress) to the inventory listing;

9.   Test the inventory listing obtained in step 8 above to determine that the listing is complete, i.e., that the listing contains all of the count documents that should be included in the listing but excludes count documents not used. To accomplish this step, the information gathered in step 2 previously should be related to the final inventory listing; and

10.   Review with the client the comparison of the quantities according to the physical inventory listing with the quantities according to the client's perpetual inventory records. Determine that the client has made proper adjustment of the accounting records to reflect the results of the physical inventory.

Exhibit 12-7
Example of Final Inventory Listing

Prepared by: _J.J._
Date: _1-8-84_
Reviewed by: _P.J._
Date: _1-14-84_

University of Georgia Bookstore
Final Inventory Listing
12/31/83

② Count Document	Description	Quantity	FIFO Cost/ Unit	Total Cost
1004	Edwards, Johnson, Roemmick — Intermediate Accounting	100 ✓	$21 V	$2,100 ⌾

1005	Hubbard, Johnson, Pushkin —
	    Auditing Concepts-Standards-
	    Procedures
		200 ✓	20 V	4,000 ⌾

1006	Johnson and Brown — Intermediate Software Diskettes	100 ✓	10 V	1,000 ⌾
		•	•	•
		•	•	•
		•	•	•
		•	•	•
				431,000 w, T/B

✓ Agrees with test counts.

V Verified computation of FIFO cost per unit.

⌾ Verified extension and traced to perpetual records.

w Footed.

T/B Agrees with general ledger, trial balance and financial statements.

② Count documents on the final inventory listing agree with count documents used for inventory taking on 12/31/83, as recorded by us. No unused count documents appear on listing.

Note to Students: Dots indicate lines were omitted to conserve space. In practice, the final inventory listing frequently contains thousands of lines, i.e., one line for each item of inventory.

The student should keep in mind that when an auditor performs this step, the proper action to correct a discrepancy between the client's perpetual inventory record and the physical count is to adjust the book figure to the actual physical count.

11. Conduct a test of the valuation of the year-end inventory listing by selecting a sample of items from the final inventory listing and verifying the value(s) used.

For example, if the client is using a FIFO assumption, the values used should represent the invoice cost of the most recent purchases. If, on the other hand, the client is using a LIFO assumption, the dollar values used should represent the oldest invoice costs.

In the case where the client is using dollar value LIFO, the retail method, or some other valuation estimation procedure, the auditor should obtain a copy of the client's computational worksheets for valuation of the inventory, review the propriety and accuracy of the computations, and test the valuations used by the client, as appropriate.

12. If, while performing step 4 discussed previously, any inventory was noted that appeared to be obsolete or slow-moving, examine perpetual inventory records for such inventory to determine the date of last shipment or usage of the inventory. In addition, scan inventory records, noting any material amounts of inventory that are slow-moving. Discuss the results of this test with the client, considering the possibility of a write-down of obsolete or slow-moving items, if appropriate;

13. Use the information gathered in steps 6 and 7 previously to test the propriety of the cut-off of purchases and sales transactions at year-end. With respect to purchases cut-off, trace the receiving reports noted in step 6 previously to the purchases journal, noting that the liability for the purchase was recorded prior to year-end and that the inventory was reflected in the perpetual inventory records prior to year-end. Further, note that invoices for inventory which was received after year-end are not included in accounts payable as of year-end and that the inventory represented by these invoices is debited to the perpetual inventory records in the subsequent year. With respect to sales cut-off, trace the sales invoices corresponding to the shipping documents which were used before year-end to the sales journal noting that the sale is properly recorded in the current year and that the perpetual inventory records are reduced prior to year-end. Also, note that the entries for sales subsequent to year-end are recorded in the next period;

14. Test the extensions and footing of the inventory listing and trace the total inventory value to the general ledger, trial balance, and financial statements; and

15. Review the client's procedures for determining that the inventory is valued at the lower of cost or market. Select a sample of items from the final inventory listing and determine

   a. Current replacement cost (by reference to recent vendors' invoices or price lists),

   b. Selling price (based upon prices currently in effect for the client's products), and

   c. Costs to complete and sell (by discussion with client's production personnel regarding the readiness of the inventory for sale and/or the cost to complete the inventory and render it in a salable state).

   Based upon this information, reach a conclusion about the need for a possible write-down of the inventory to market.

In connection with this latter step, the requirements of FASB Statement No. 33, *Financial Reporting and Changing Prices*, apply to any public enterprise that prepares its financial statements in U.S. dollars and in accordance with U.S. generally accepted accounting principles and, as of the beginning of its fiscal year, has either

   Inventories and property, plant and equipment with (before depreciation or amortization) a value of more than $125 million, or

   Total assets (after deducting depreciation and amortization allowances) of more than $1 billion.

In such cases, additional audit steps should be included in the audit program to review the appropriateness of the computations related to the supplemental disclosures required for such companies and to ensure that the client's financial statements and supplemental disclosures meet the requirements of FASB Statement No. 33.

Finally, in the event the client has material amounts of inventory in the custody of others as of the physical inventory date, e.g., inventories stored in public warehouses, the auditor should arrange in advance of the actual physical inventory to obtain confirmations of such inventory as of the inventory date. Also, the auditor should review the internal control over inventory exercised by the custodian, in addition to reliance upon confirmation. Furthermore, if these controls are not adequate, the auditor should consider physical observation of the inventory in the custody of others.

As discussed further in Chapter 14, the auditor will normally obtain a letter of representation from the client. It is customary, in this letter, for the client to make various representations concerning the inventory, such as:

- That all inventory is properly reflected upon the books as of year-end;

- That the inventory is valued on a basis that is in accordance with generally accepted accounting principles (that is, for example, lower of first-in, first-out cost or market, LIFO, or some other acceptable basis);

- That all slow-moving or obsolete inventory has been written down to market value or has been removed from the inventory total; and

- In the event the inventory is being constructed under a long-term construction contract, that the percent-complete estimates used to value the contract in progress are reasonable and in accordance with management's best estimate of the status of the contract(s).

SUMMARY

This chapter discussed the procedures involved in the audit of the expense and production cycle. The expense and production cycle includes the voucher segment and the cash disbursements segment. The cash disbursements segment is further subdivided into the cash (check) disbursements subsegment, the payroll subsegment, and the petty cash or currency subsegment. The voucher segment is subdivided into the general voucher subsegment and the payroll voucher subsegment. Activity in the general voucher segment is initiated by the acquisition of goods and services such as the purchase of inventory, supplies, utility services, payment of rent, and so forth. All expenditures must be properly supported by an authorized and approved voucher before the expenditure of funds can occur. Good internal control requires the initiation of a purchase requisition and the creation of a purchase order, a receiving report, and an approved voucher for payment by check. Control over disbursements by check requires procedures such as the use of prenumbered checks prepared on protective paper and dual-signed manually or by facsimile machine.

Small cash disbursements are made from an imprest fund. Such funds are used for minor daily expenditures and for change funds. Responsibility for imprest funds is fixed with one responsible individual. When the fund is established, a check is drawn on the general bank account, payable to the custodian, in the amount of the fund. The debit for the transaction is to an asset, Petty Cash, and the amount of this asset is not changed unless the fund is increased or decreased. Daily expenditures are supported by vouchers which are recorded on the books when the fund is replenished.

Controls which are frequently encountered in the expense and production cycle were summarized in Exhibit 12-1. To test the controls in the expense and production cycle, the auditor takes a sample of transaction and follows these transactions through the accounting system and related controls until the transactions are posted to the general ledger. The audit programs which are used for compliance testing are dual-purpose programs because they allow the auditor not only to test the controls which are built into the system, but also to test the accuracy of the information which is accumulated in the accounts. One of the first steps in compliance testing in any cycle requires the auditor to determine that the client uses prenumbered documents where appropriate and to test the use of prenumbered documents. In many cases, the auditor will find that it is useful to evaluate the results of compliance tests by using attribute sampling procedures. In testing the summarization and processing of transactions, the auditor is concerned not only with the accuracy of the summarization and processing, but also with the controls over the process. Whenever possible, the auditor should redo required computations and examine other evidence to determine that the controls are functioning as prescribed.

Substantive audit procedures for cash, petty cash, and inventories were also discussed. The principle substantive audit procedure for petty cash is the petty cash count. The principle audit procedure for cash involves the auditors review of the client's year-end bank reconciliation. The principle audit procedures for inventory involve the observation of the client's inventory counts and the verification of the client's inventory pricing.

REVIEW QUESTIONS

12-1   Explain why companies use prenumbered purchase requisition forms. Who should control blank purchase requisitions? Who should prepare and authorize purchase requisitions? Who should receive copies of purchase requisitions?

12-2   What is the purpose of prenumbering purchase orders? Who prepares purchase orders? Who should control blank purchase orders? Who should receive copies of purchase orders?

12-3   Explain why companies use prenumbered receiving reports. Who should receive copies of the receiving report?

12-4   Describe the documents that support a voucher payable package. Discuss the purpose of comparing the supporting documents of a voucher package with the vendor's invoice.

12-5   Describe a tickler file and discuss its function.

12-6   What is the purpose of a voucher register?

12-7   Describe a cash disbursements journal and explain its function.

12-8   Explain why a firm may require two signatures on a check.

12-9   Why should a voucher and supporting documents be cancelled at the time a check is prepared based on the voucher?

12-10   Describe the difference in recognizing and recording accounts payable when a voucher system is used and when such a system is not used.

12-11   Describe the operation of an imprest petty cash fund.

12-12   What is the initial document for hourly paid employees? The original book of entry?

12-13   What is the function of a payroll register?

12-14   Who should (or should not) distribute payroll checks or payroll currency?

12-15   List the different functions in a payroll system that should be independent of one another.

12-16   Does a perpetual inventory system preclude a company from taking a physical count of inventory? Why or why not?

12-17   Discuss the five specific audit objectives of the expense and production cycle.

12-18   What is the purpose of the initial four audit program steps discussed in the chapter for the audit of the expense and production cycle? Briefly discuss each of the four steps.

12-19   Under what circumstances would the auditor by-pass compliance testing of system controls and proceed directly to substantive tests of balances?

12-20   In a voucher test for overstatement, what is the direction of testing? What is the nature of the conclusion that can be drawn from such a test?

12-21   Under what circumstances could vouchers selected for a sample in a voucher test also be used as sample items in testing the cash disbursements segment? That is, when would the auditor examine the checks representing payment of the sample vouchers rather than select a different sample of checks issued during the period under audit?

12-22   What is the objective of each audit program step for hourly payrolls as discussed in the chapter?

12-23   When should compliance testing be carried out by the independent auditor? When should substantive testing of balances?

12-24   Why is it important that imprest cash funds, marketable securities and notes receivable be counted simultaneously by independent auditors? Why is it important that such a count be conducted in the presence of the fund custodian?

12-25   What is a cut-off bank statement?

12-26   List and briefly discuss the five different types of information provided for on a standard bank confirmation.

12-27   Why is it important that cancelled checks returned with the cut-off bank statement be compared to the outstanding check list as of year-end?

12-28   What are the purposes of auditing deposits in transit at the beginning and ending of the last month in the client's accounting period?

12-29   Identify the two basic phases in the audit of inventories.

12-30   Under what circumstances may the client take a physical count of inventory items other than at year-end?

12-31   Under what circumstances may the client physically verify less than 100 percent of the inventory items?

12-32   Identify the population from which the auditor should sample to test for understatement of perpetual inventory records. For overstatement of perpetual inventory records. Briefly discuss procedures that should be carried out on the sampling items.

12-33   Discuss the initial steps the auditor should take to determine that there are proper cut-offs of purchases and of shipments of inventory.

12-34   Briefly describe how the CPA would use the client's final inventory listing in auditing the physical count of inventory and the valuation of the inventory.

12-35   What are the basic inventory audit procedures that the auditor should consider if the client owns inventory which is in the custody of a third party?

12-36   What types of information concerning inventory should be provided in the client's representation letter to the auditor?

DISCUSSION QUESTIONS AND PROBLEMS

12-37   Often an important aspect of a CPA's examination of financial statements is his observation of the taking of the physical inventory.

Required:

a.   What are the general objectives or purposes of the CPA's observation of the taking of the physical inventory? (Do not discuss the procedures or techniques involved in making the observation.)

b.   For what purposes does the CPA make and record test counts of inventory quantities during his observation of the taking of the physical inventory? Discuss.

12-38   Ace Corporation does not conduct a complete annual physical count of purchased parts and supplies in its principal warehouse but uses statistical sampling instead to estimate the year-end inventory. Ace maintains a perpetual inventory record of parts and supplies and believes that statistical sampling is highly effective in determining inventory values and is sufficiently reliable to make a physical count of each item of inventory unnecessary.

Required:

a.   Identify the audit procedures that should be used by the independent auditor that change or are in addition to normal required audit procedures when a client utilizes statistical sampling to determine inventory value and does not conduct a 100 percent annual physical count of inventory items.

b.   List at least ten normal audit procedures that should be performed to verify physical quantities whenever a client conducts a periodic physical count of all or part of its inventory.

(AICPA adapted)

12-39   In connection with his examination of the financial statements of Knutson Products Co., an assembler of home appliances, for the year ended May 31, 19x0, Ray Abel, CPA, is reviewing with Knutson's controller the plans for a physical inventory at the Company warehouse on May 31. (*Note:* In answering the two parts of this question do not discuss procedures for the physical inventory of work-in-process, inventory pricing or other audit steps not directly related to the physical inventory taking.)

1.   Finished appliances, unassembled parts and supplies are stored in the warehouse, which is attached to Knutson's assembly plant. The plant will operate during the count. On May 30, 19x0, the warehouse will deliver to the plant the estimated quantities of unassembled parts and supplies required for May 31 production, but there may be emergency requisitions on May 31. During the count the warehouse will continue to receive parts and supplies and to ship finished appliances. However, appliances completed on May 31 will be held in the plant until after the physical inventory.

2.   Warehouse employees will join with accounting department employees in counting the inventory. The inventory-takers will use a tag system.

Required:

a.   What procedures should the company establish to ensure that the inventory count includes all items that should be included and that nothing is counted twice?

b.   What instructions should the company give to the inventory takers?

(AICPA adapted)

12-40   A processor of frozen foods carries an inventory of finished products consisting of fifty different types of items valued at approximately $2 million. About $750,000 of this value represents stock produced by the company and billed to customers prior to the audit date. This stock is being held for the customers at a monthly rental charge until they request shipment and is not separated from the company's inventory.

The company maintains separate perpetual ledgers at the plant office for both stock owned and stock being held for customers. The cost department also maintains a perpetual record of stock owned. The above perpetual records reflect quantities only.

The company does not take a complete physical inventory at any time during the year since the temperature in the cold storage facilities is too low to allow one to spend more than fifteen minutes inside at a time. It is not considered practical to move items outside or to defreeze the cold storage facilities for the purpose of taking a physical inventory. Due to these circumstances, it is impractical to test count quantities to the extent of completely verifying specific items. The company considers as its inventory valuation at year-end the aggregate of the quantities reflected by the perpetual record of stock owned, maintained at the plant office, priced at the lower or cost of market.

Required:

a.   What are the two principal problems facing the auditor in the audit of the inventory? Discuss briefly.

b.   Outline the audit steps that you would take to enable you to render an unqualified opinion with respect to the inventory. (You may omit consideration of a verification on unit prices and clerical accuracy.)

(AICPA adapted)

12-41   Your audit client, Household Appliances, Inc., operates a retail store in the center of town. Because of lack of storage space Household keeps inventory that is not on display in a public warehouse outside of town. The warehouseman receives inventory from suppliers and, on request from your client by a shipping advice or telephone call, delivers merchandise to customers or to the retail outlet.

The accounts are maintained at the retail store by a bookkeeper. Each month the warehouseman sends to the bookkeeper a quantity report indicating opening balance, receipts, deliveries, and ending balance. The bookkeeper compares book quantities on hand at month-end with the warehouseman's report and adjusts his books to agree with the report. No physical counts of the merchandise at the warehouse were made by your client during the year.

You are now preparing for your examination of the current year's financial statements in this recurring engagement. Last year, you rendered an unqualified opinion.

Required:

a.   Prepare an audit program for the observation of the physical inventory of Household Appliances, Inc. (1) at the retail outlet and (2) at the warehouse.

b.   As part of your examination, would you verify inventory quantities at the warehouse by means of

   1.   A warehouse confirmation? Why?
   2.   Test counts of inventory at the warehouse? Why?

c.   Since the bookkeeper adjusts books to quantities shown on the warehouseman's report each month, what significance would you attach to the year-end adjustments if they were substantial? Discuss.

(AICPA adapted)

12-42   An auditor is conducting an examination of the financial statements of a wholesale cosmetics distributor with an inventory consisting of thousands of individual items. The distributor keeps its inventory in its own distribution center and in two public warehouses. An inventory computer file is maintained on a computer disk and at the end of each day the file is updated. Each record of the inventory file contains the following data:

1. Item number.
2. Location of item.
3. Description of item.
4. Quantity on hand.
5. Cost per item.
6. Date of last purchase.
7. Date of last sale.
8. Quantity sold during year.

The auditor is planning to observe the distributor's physical count of inventories as of a given date. The auditor will have available a computer tape of the data on the inventory file on the date of the physical count and a general purpose computer software package.

Required:

The auditor is planning to perform basic inventory auditing procedures. Identify the basic inventory auditing procedures and describe how the use of the general purpose software package and the tape of the inventory file data might be helpful to the auditor in performing such auditing procedures. Organize your answer as follows:

Basic Inventory Auditing Procedure	*How General Purpose Computer Software Package and Tape of the Inventory File Data Might Be Helpful*
1. Observe the physical count, making and recording test counts where applicable.	Determining which items are to be test counted by selecting a random sample of a representative number of items from the inventory file as of the date of the physical count.

(AICPA adapted)

12-43   A CPA's audit working papers contain a narrative description of a segment of the Croyden Factory, Inc., payroll system and an accompanying flowchart as follows:

Narrative

The internal control system with respect to the personnel department is well-functioning and is not included in the accompanying flowchart.

At the beginning of each work week payroll clerk No. 1 reviews the payroll department files to determine the employment status of factory employees and then prepares time cards and distributes them as each individual arrives at work. This payroll clerk, who is also responsible for custody of the signature stamp machine, verifies the identity of each payee before delivering signed checks to the foreman.

At the end of each work week the foreman distributes payroll checks for the preceding work week. Concurrent with this activity, the foreman reviews the current week's employee time cards, notes the regular and overtime hours worked on a summary form, and initials the aforementioned time cards. The foreman then delivers all time cards and unclaimed payroll checks to payroll clerk No. 2.

Required:

a. Based upon the narrative and accompanying flowchart, what are the weaknesses in the system of internal control?

b. Based upon the narrative and accompanying flowchart, what inquiries should be made with respect to clarifying the existence of possible additional weaknesses in the system of internal control?

NOTE: Do not discuss the internal control system of the personnel department.

Flowchart appears on page 616.

(AICPA adapted)

12-44   James, who was engaged to examine the financial statements of Talbert Corporation, is about to audit payroll. Talbert uses a computer service center to process weekly payroll as follows.

Each Monday Talbert's payroll clerk inserts data in appropriate spaces on the preprinted service center prepared input form, and sends it to the service center via messenger. The service center extracts new permanent data from the input form and updates master files. The weekly payroll data are then processed. The weekly payroll register and payroll checks are printed and delivered by messenger to Talbert on Thursday.

12-43 (Continued):

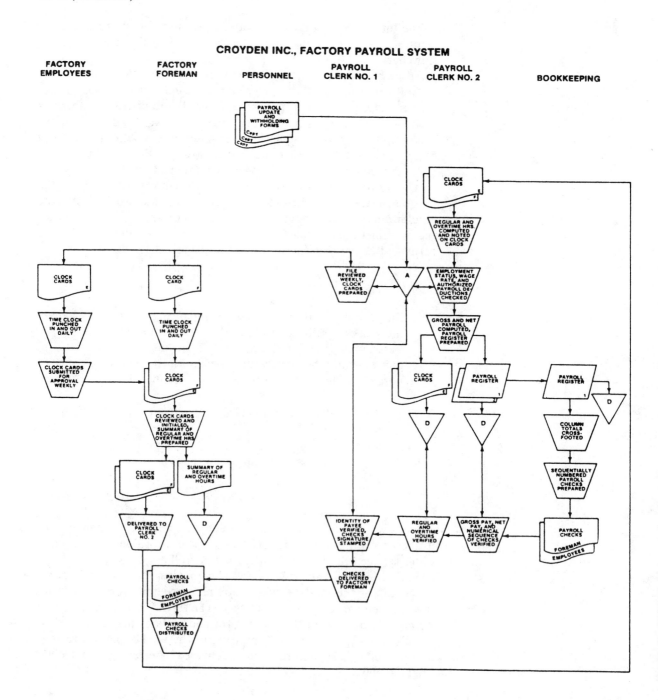

CROYDEN INC., FACTORY PAYROLL SYSTEM

Part of the sample selected for audit by James includes the following input form and payroll register:

See chart on page 618.

Required:

a. Describe how James should verify the information in the payroll input form shown on the following page.
b. Describe (but do not perform) the procedures that James should follow in the examination of the November 12, 1985, payroll register shown on the following page.

(AICPA adapted)

12-45 You are engaged in auditing the financial statements of Henry Brown, a large independent contractor. All employees are paid in cash because Brown believes this arrangement reduces clerical expenses and is preferred by his employees.

During the audit, you find in the petty cash fund approximately $200 of which $185 is stated to be unclaimed wages. Further investigation reveals that Brown has installed the procedure of putting any unclaimed wages in the petty cash fund so that the cash can be used for disbursements. When the claimant to the wages appears, he is paid from the petty cash fund. Brown contends that this procedure reduces the number of checks drawn to replenish the petty cash fund and centers the responsibility for all cash on hand in one person inasmuch as the petty cash custodian distributes the pay envelopes.

Required:

1. Does Brown's system provide proper internal control of unclaimed wages? Explain fully.
2. Because Brown insists on paying salaries in cash, what procedures would you recommend to provide better internal control over unclaimed wages?

(AICPA adapted)

12-46 Long, CPA, has been engaged to examine and report on the financial statements of Maylou Corporation. During the review phase of the study of Maylou's system of internal accounting control over pur-

12-44 (Continued):

Talbert Corporation Payroll Input — Week Ending Friday, Nov. 23, 1985

| | — Employee Data — Permanent File — | | | — Current Week's Payroll Data — | | | | |
Name	Social Security	W-4 Information	Hourly Rate	Reg	OT	Bonds	Union	Other
				Hours		Special Deductions		
A. Bell	999-99-9991	M-1	10.00	35	5	18.75		
B. Carr	999-99-9992	M-2	10.00	35	4			
C. Dawn	999-99-9993	S-1	10.00	35	6	18.75	4.00	
D. Ellis	999-99-9994	S-1	10.00	35	2		4.00	50.00
E. Frank	999-99-9995	M-4	10.00	35	1		4.00	
F. Gillis	999-99-9996	M-4	10.00	35			4.00	
G. Hugh	999-99-9997	M-1	7.00	35	2	18.75	4.00	
H. Jones	999-99-9998	M-2	7.00	35			4.00	25.00
J. King	999-99-9999	S-1	7.00	35	4		4.00	
New Employee								
J. Smith	999-99-9990	M-3	7.00	35				

Talbert Corporation Payroll Register — Nov. 23, 1985

Employee	Social Security	Hours		Payroll		Gross Payroll	Taxes Withheld			Other Withheld	Net Pay	Check No.
		Reg	OT	Reg	OT		FICA	Fed	State			
A. Bell	999-99-9991	35	5	350.00	75.00	425.00	26.05	76.00	27.40	18.75	276.80	1499
B. Carr	999-99-9992	35	4	350.00	60.00	410.00	25.13	65.00	23.60		296.27	1500
C. Dawn	999-99-9993	35	6	350.00	90.00	440.00	26.97	100.90	28.60	22.75	260.78	1501
D. Ellis	999-99-9994	35	2	350.00	30.00	380.00	23.29	80.50	21.70	54.00	200.51	1502
E. Frank	999-99-9995	35	1	350.00	15.00	365.00	22.37	43.50	15.90	4.00	279.23	1503
F. Gillis	999-99-9996	35		350.00		350.00	21.46	41.40	15.00	4.00	268.14	1504
G. Hugh	999-99-9997	35	2	245.00	21.00	266.00	16.31	34.80	10.90	22.75	181.24	1505
H. Jones	999-99-9998	35		245.00		245.00	15.02	26.40	8.70	29.00	165.88	1506
J. King	999-99-9999	35	4	245.00	42.00	287.00	17.59	49.40	12.20	4.00	203.81	1507
J. Smith	999-99-9990	35		245.00		245.00	15.02	23.00	7.80		199.18	1508
Totals		350	24	3,080.00	333.00	3,413.00	209.21	540.90	171.80	159.25	2,331.84	

chases, Long was given the document flowchart for purchases which appears on the following page.

Flowchart appears on page 620

Required:

a. Identify the procedures, relating to purchase requisitions and purchase orders, that Long would expect to find if Maylou's system of internal control over purchases is effective. For example, purchase orders are prepared only after giving proper consideration to the time to order and quantity to order. Do not comment on the effectiveness of the flow of documents as presented in the flowchart or on separation of duties.

b. What are the factors to consider in determining

   1. The time to order?
   2. The quantity to order?

(AICPA adapted)

12-47   Anthony, CPA, prepared the flowchart on the following page which portrays the raw materials purchasing function of one of Anthony's clients, a medium-sized manufacturing company, from the preparation of initial documents through the vouching of invoices for payment of accounts payable. The flowchart was a portion of the work performed on the audit engagement to evaluate internal control.

Required:

Identify and explain the systems and control weaknesses evident from the flowchart on the following page. Include the internal control weaknesses resulting from activities performed or not performed. All documents are prenumbered.

Flowchart appears on page 621.

(AICPA adapted)

12-48   William Green recently acquired the financial controlling interest of Importers and Wholesalers, Inc., importers and distributors of cutlery. In his review of the duties of employees, Mr. Green became aware of loose practices in the signing of checks and the operation of the petty cash fund.

   You have been engaged as the company's CPA, and Mr. Green's first request is that you suggest a system of sound practices for the

12-46 (Continued):

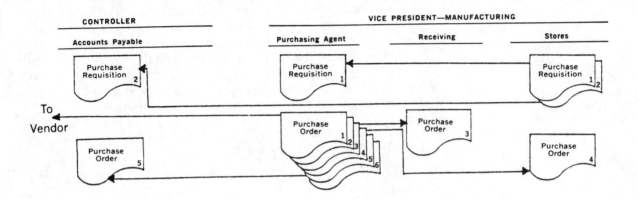

Maylou Corporation
DOCUMENT FLOWCHART FOR PURCHASES

12-47 (Continued):

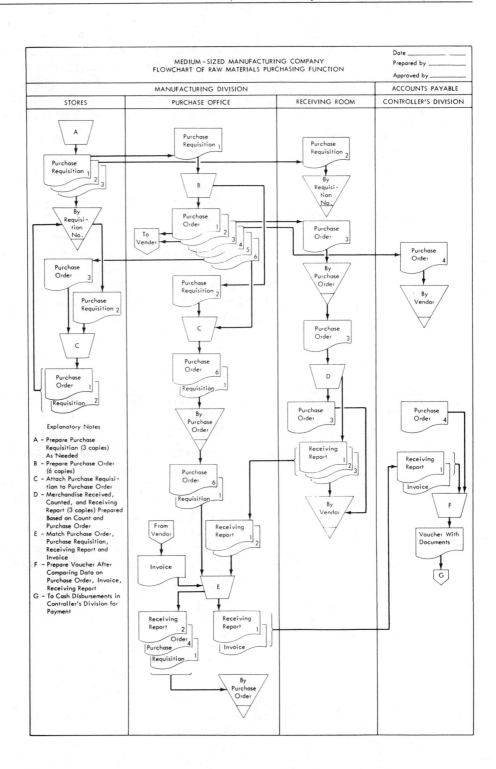

signing of checks and the operation of the petty cash fund. Mr. Green prefers not to acquire a check-signing machine.

In addition to Mr. Green, who is the company president, the company has twenty employees including four corporate officers. About 200 checks are drawn each month. The petty cash fund has a working balance of about $200 and about $500 is expended by the fund each month.

Required:

Prepare a letter to Mr. Green containing your recommendations for good internal control procedures for

a.   Signing checks. (Mr. Green is unwilling to be drawn into routine check signing duties. Assume that you decided to recommend two signatures on each check.)
b.   Operation of the petty cash fund. (Where the effect of the control procedure is not evident, give the reason for the procedure.)

(AICPA adapted)

OBJECTIVE QUESTIONS*

12-49   The primary objective of a CPA's observation of a client's physical inventory count is to

A.   Discover whether a client has counted a particular inventory item or group of items.
B.   Obtain direct knowledge that the inventory exists and has been properly counted.
C.   Provide an appraisal of the quality of the merchandise on hand on the day of the physical count.
D.   Allow the auditor to supervise the conduct of the count so as to obtain assurance that inventory quantities are reasonably accurate.

Note: Questions in this section have been taken from prior CPA examinations except for those questions marked with an asterisk.

12-50 Which of the following is a primary function of the purchasing department?

    A.   Authorizing the acquisition of goods.
    B.   Ensuring the acquisition of goods of a specified quality.
    C.   Verifying the propriety of goods acquired.
    D.   Reducing expenditures for goods acquired.

12-51 Jackson, the purchasing agent of Judd Hardware Wholesalers, has a relative who owns a retail hardware store. Jackson arranged for hardware to be delivered by manufacturers to the retail store on a C.O.D. basis thereby enabling his relative to buy at Judd's wholesale prices. Jackson was probably able to accomplish this because of Judd's poor internal control over

    A.   Purchase orders.
    B.   Purchase requisitions.
    C.   Cash receipts.
    D.   Perpetual inventory records.

12-52 Which of the following audit tests would be regarded as a test of compliance?

    A.   Tests of the specific items making up the balance in a given general ledger account.
    B.   Tests of the inventory pricing to vendors' invoices.
    C.   Tests of the signatures on cancelled checks to board of director's authorizations.
    D.   Tests of the additions to property, plant, and equipment by physical inspections.

12-53 Propex Corporation uses a voucher register and does not record invoices in a subsidiary ledger. Propex will probably benefit most from the additional cost of maintaining an accounts payable subsidiary ledger if

    A.   There are usually invoices in an unmatched invoice file.
    B.   Vendors' requests for confirmation of receivables often go unanswered for several months until paid invoices can be reviewed.
    C.   Partial payments to vendors are continuously made in the ordinary course of business.
    D.   It is difficult to reconcile vendors' monthly statements.

12-54   For internal control purposes, which of the following individuals should preferably be responsible for the distribution of payroll checks?

     A.   Bookkeeper.
     B.   Payroll clerk.
     C.   Cashier.
     D.   Receptionist.

12-55   Proper internal control over the cash payroll function would mandate which of the following?

     A.   The payroll clerk should fill the envelopes with cash and a computation of the net wages.
     B.   Unclaimed pay envelopes should be retained by the paymaster.
     C.   Each employee should be asked to sign a receipt.
     D.   A separate checking account for payroll be maintained.

12-56   A CPA reviews a client's payroll procedures. The CPA would consider internal control to be less than effective if a payroll department supervisor was assigned the responsibility for

     A.   Reviewing and approving time reports for subordinate employees.
     B.   Distributing payroll checks to employees.
     C.   Hiring subordinate employees.
     D.   Initiating requests for salary adjustments for subordinate employees.

12-57   Which of the following is an internal control weakness for a company whose inventory of supplies consists of a large number of individual items?

     A.   Supplies of relatively little value are expensed when purchased.
     B.   The cycle basis is used for physical counts.
     C.   The storekeeper is responsible for maintenance of perpetual inventory records.
     D.   Perpetual inventory records are maintained only for items of significant value.

12-58   Effective internal accounting control over the payroll function should include procedures that segregate the duties of making salary payments to employees and

     A.   Controlling unemployment insurance claims.
     B.   Maintaining employee personnel records.

    C.   Approving employee fringe benefits.

    D.   Hiring new employees.

12-59   Effective internal control over the payroll function would include which of the following?

    A.   Total time recorded on time-clock punch cards should be reconciled to job reports by employees responsible for those specific jobs.

    B.   Payroll department employees should be supervised by the management of the personnel department.

    C.   Payroll department employees should be responsible for maintaining employee personnel records.

    D.   Total time spent on jobs should be compared with total time indicated on time-clock punch cards.

12-60   Effective internal control over the purchasing of raw materials should usually include all of the following procedures except

    A.   Systematic reporting of product changes which will affect raw materials.

    B.   Determining the need for the raw materials prior to preparing the purchase order.

    C.   Obtaining third-party written quality and quantity reports prior to payment for the raw materials.

    D.   Obtaining financial approval prior to making a commitment.

12-61   Which of the following is an effective internal accounting control measure that encourages receiving department personnel to count and inspect all merchandise received?

    A.   Quantities ordered are excluded from the receiving department copy of the purchase order.

    B.   Vouchers are prepared by accounts payable department personnel only after they match item counts on the receiving report with the purchase order.

    C.   Receiving department personnel are expected to match and reconcile the receiving report with the purchase order.

    D.   Internal auditors periodically examine, on a surprise basis, the receiving department copies of receiving reports.

12-62   To strengthen the system of internal accounting control over the purchase of merchandise, a company's receiving department should

    A.   Accept merchandise only if a purchase order or approval granted by the purchasing department is on hand.

B. Accept and count all merchandise received from the usual company vendors.

C. Rely on shipping documents for the preparation of receiving reports.

D. Be responsible for the physical handling of merchandise but not the preparation of receiving reports.

12-63 A client's materials-purchasing cycle begins with requisitions from user departments and ends with the receipt of materials and the recognition of a liability. An auditor's primary objective in reviewing this cycle is to

A. Evaluate the reliability of information generated as a result of the purchasing process.

B. Investigate the physical handling and recording of unusual acquisitions of materials.

C. Consider the need to be on hand for the annual physical count if this system is not functioning properly.

D. Ascertain that materials said to be ordered, received, and paid for are on hand.

12-64 Effective internal accounting control over unclaimed payroll checks that are kept by the treasury department would include accounting department procedures that require

A. Effective cancellation and stop payment orders for checks representing unclaimed wages.

B. Preparation of a list of unclaimed wages on a periodic basis.

C. Accounting for all unclaimed wages in a current liability account.

D. Periodic accounting for the actual checks representing unclaimed wages.

12-65 With respect to a small company's system of purchasing supplies, an auditor's primary concern should be to obtain satisfaction that supplies ordered and paid for have been

A. Requested by and approved by authorized individuals who have no incompatible duties.

B. Received, counted, and checked to quantities and amounts on purchase orders and invoices.

C. Properly recorded as assets and systematically amortized over the estimated useful life of the supplies.

D. Used in the course of business and solely for business purposes during the year under audit.

12-66   In order to efficiently establish the correctness of the accounts payable cut-off, an auditor will be most likely to

A.   Coordinate cut-off tests with physical inventory observation.
B.   Compare cut-off reports with purchase orders.
C.   Compare vendors' invoices with vendors' statements.
D.   Coordinate mailing of confirmations with cut-off tests.

12-67   The auditor's count of the client's cash should be coordinated to coincide with the

A.   Study of the system of internal controls with respect to cash.
B.   Close of business on the balance sheet date.
C.   Count of marketable securities.
D.   Count of inventories.

12-68   An auditor would be most likely to learn of slow-moving inventory through

A.   Inquiry of sales personnel.
B.   Inquiry of stores personnel.
C.   Physical observation of inventory.
D.   Review of perpetual inventory records.

12-69   When title to merchandise in transit has passed to the audit client, the auditor engaged in the performance of a purchase cut-off will encounter the greatest difficulty in gaining assurance with respect to the

A.   Quantity.
B.   Quality.
C.   Price.
D.   Terms.

12-70   An auditor will usually trace the details of the test counts made during the observation of the physical inventory taking to a final inventory schedule. This audit procedure is undertaken to provide evidence that items physically present and observed by the auditor at the time of the physical inventory count are

A.   Owned by the client.
B.   Not obsolete.
C.   Physically present at the time of the preparation of the final inventory schedule.
D.   Included in the final inventory schedule.

12-71 The physical count of inventory of a retailer was higher than shown by the perpetual records. Which of the following could explain the difference?

    A.   Inventory items had been counted but the tags placed on the items had not been taken off the items and added to the inventory accumulation sheets.

    B.   Credit memos for several items returned by customers had not been prepared.

    C.   No journal entry had been made on the retailer's books for several items returned to its suppliers.

    D.   An item purchased "FOB shipping point" had not arrived at the date of the inventory count and had not been reflected in the perpetual records.

12-72 In verifying debits to perpetual inventory records of a non-manufacturing firm, the auditor would be most interested in examining the purchase

    A.   Journal.
    B.   Requisitions.
    C.   Orders.
    D.   Invoices.

12-73 The auditor tests the quantity of materials charged to work-in-process by tracing these quantities to

    A.   Cost ledgers.
    B.   Perpetual inventory records.
    C.   Receiving reports.
    D.   Material requisitions.

12-74 An inventory turnover analysis is useful to the auditor because it may detect

    A.   Inadequacies in inventory pricing.
    B.   Methods of avoiding cyclical holding costs.
    C.   The optimum automatic reorder points.
    D.   The existence of obsolete merchandise.

12-75 During 1984, a bookkeeper perpetrated a theft by preparing erroneous W-2 forms. The bookkeeper's FICA withheld from all other employees was understated. Which of the following is an audit procedure which would detect such a fraud?

A. Multiplication of the applicable rate by the individual gross taxable earnings.

B. Using form W-4 and withholding charts to determine whether deductions authorized per pay period agree with amounts deducted per pay period.

C. Footing and crossfooting of the payroll register followed by tracing postings to the general ledger.

D. Vouching cancelled checks to federal tax forms 941.

12-76   An audit program provides proof that

A. Sufficient competent evidential matter was obtained.

B. The work was adequately planned.

C. There was compliance with generally accepted standards of reporting.

D. There was a proper study and evaluation of internal control.

12-77   A client's procurement system ends with the assumption of a liability and the eventual payment of the liability. Which of the following best describes the auditor's primary concern with respect to liabilities resulting from the procurement system?

A. Accounts payable are not materially understated.

B. Authority to incur liabilities is restricted to one designated person.

C. Acquisition of materials is not made from one vendor or one group of vendors.

D. Commitments for all purchases are made only after established competitive bidding procedures are followed.

12-78   Which of the following is the best way for an auditor to determine that every name on a company's payroll is that of a bona fide employee presently on the job?

A. Examine personnel records for accuracy and completeness.

B. Examine employees' names listed on payroll tax returns for agreement with payroll accounting records.

C. Make a surprise observation of the company's regular distribution of paychecks.

D. Visit the working areas and confirm with employees their badge or identification numbers.

12-79   Which of the following would detect an understatement of a purchase discount?

A.   Verify footings and crossfootings of purchases and disbursement records.

B.   Compare purchase invoice terms with disbursement records and checks.

C.   Compare approved purchase orders to receiving reports.

D.   Verify the receipt of items ordered and invoiced.

12-80   The accuracy of perpetual inventory records may be established, in part, by comparing perpetual inventory records with

A.   Purchase requisitions.

B.   Receiving reports.

C.   Purchase orders.

D.   Vendor payments.

12-81   The auditor should ordinarily mail confirmation requests to all banks with which the client has conducted any business during the year, regardless of the year-end balance, since

A.   The confirmation form also seeks information about indebtedness to the bank.

B.   This procedure will detect kiting activities which would otherwise not be detected.

C.   The mailing confirmation forms to all such banks is required by generally accepted auditing standards.

D.   This procedure relieves the auditor of any responsibility with respect to nondetection of forged checks.

12-82   A common audit procedure in the audit of payroll transactions involves tracing selected items from the payroll journal to employee time cards that have been approved by supervisory personnel. This procedure is designed to provide evidence in support of the audit proposition that

A.   Only bona fide employees worked and their pay was properly computed.

B.   Jobs on which employees worked were charged with the appropriate labor cost.

C.   Internal controls relating to payroll disbursements are operating effectively.

D.   All employees worked the number of hours for which their pay was computed.

12-83   As an in-charge auditor you are reviewing a write-up of internal-control weaknesses in cash receipt and disbursement procedures. Which one of the following weaknesses, standing alone, should cause you the least concern?

A.   Checks are signed by only one person.
B.   Signed checks are distributed by the controller to approved payees.
C.   Treasurer fails to establish *bona fides* of names and addresses of check payees.
D.   Cash disbursements are made directly out of cash receipts.

12-84   An auditor is planning the study and evaluation of internal control for purchasing and disbursement procedures. In planning this study and evaluation the auditor will be least influenced by

A.   The availability of a company manual describing purchasing and disbursement procedures.
B.   The scope and results of audit work by the company's internal auditor.
C.   The existence within the purchasing and disbursement area of internal control strengths that offset weaknesses.
D.   The strength or weakness of internal control in other areas, e.g., sales and accounts receivable.

12-85   Transaction authorization within an organization may be either specific or general. An example of specific transaction authorization is the

A.   Establishment of requirements to be met in determining a customer's credit limits.
B.   Setting of automatic reorder points for material or merchandise.
C.   Approval of a detailed construction budget for a warehouse.
D.   Establishment of sales prices for products to be sold to any customer.

12-86   Operating control over the check signature plate normally should be the responsibility of the

A.   Secretary.
B.   Chief accountant.
C.   Vice president of finance.
D.   Treasurer.

12-87   Based on observations made during an audit, the independent auditor should discuss with management the effectiveness of the company's internal procedures that protect against the purchase of

A.   Required supplies provided by a vendor who offers no trade or cash discounts.

B.   Inventory items acquired based on an economic order quantity (EOQ) inventory management concept.

C.   New equipment that is needed but does not qualify for investment tax credit treatment.

D.   Supplies individually ordered, without considering possible volume discounts.

12-88   In testing the payroll of a large company, the auditor wants to establish that the individuals included in a sample actually were employees of the company during the period under review. What will be the best source to determine this?

A.   Telephone contacts with the employees.

B.   Tracing from the payroll register to the employees' earnings records.

C.   Confirmation with the union or other independent organization.

D.   Examination of personnel department records.

12-89   A factory foreman at Steblecki Corporation discharged an hourly worker but did not notify the payroll department. The foreman then forged the worker's signature on time cards and work tickets and, when giving out the checks, diverted the payroll checks drawn for the discharged worker to his own use. The most effective procedure for preventing this activity is to

A.   Require written authorization for all employees added to or removed from the payroll.

B.   Have a paymaster who has no other payroll responsibility distribute the payroll checks.

C.   Have someone other than persons who prepare or distribute the payroll obtain custody of unclaimed payroll checks.

D.   From time to time, rotate persons distributing the payroll.

12-90   An auditor decides that it is important and necessary to observe a client's distribution of payroll checks on a particular audit. The client organization is so large that the auditor cannot conveniently observe the distribution of the entire payroll. In these circumstances, which of the following is most acceptable to the auditor?

A. Observation should be limited to one or more selected departments.

B. Observation should be made for all departments regardless of the inconvenience.

C. Observation should be eliminated and other alternative auditing procedures should be utilized to obtain satisfaction.

D. Observation should be limited to those departments where employees are readily available.

12-91 Effective internal control over purchases generally can be achieved in a well-planned organizational structure with a separate purchasing department that has

A. The ability to prepare payment vouchers based on the information on a vendor's invoice.

B. The responsibility of reviewing purchase orders issued by user departments.

C. The authority to make purchases of requisitioned materials and services.

D. A direct reporting responsibility to the controller of the organization.

12-92 A good system of internal accounting control over purchases will give proper evaluation to the time for ordering merchandise. When making this evaluation, the purchasing company should give primary consideration to

A. The price differences that exist between various vendors who can supply the merchandise at the required time.

B. The borrowing cost of money (interest) which the company must incur as a consequence of acquiring the merchandise.

C. The trade-off between cost of owning and storing excess merchandise and the risk of loss by not having merchandise on hand.

D. The flow of funds within the company which indicates when money is available to pay for merchandise.

12-93 Which of the following internal accounting control procedures is effective in preventing duplicate payment of vendor's invoices?

A. The invoices should be stamped, perforated, or otherwise effectively cancelled before submission for approval of the voucher.

B. Unused voucher forms should be prenumbered and accounted for.

C. Cancelled checks should be sent to persons other than the cashier or accounting department personnel.

D. Properly authorized and approved vouchers with appropriate documentation should be the basis for check preparation.

12-94 Which of the following is a standard internal accounting control for cash disbursements?

A. Checks should be signed by the controller and at least one other employee of the company.

B. Checks should be sequentially numbered and the numerical sequence should be accounted for by the person preparing bank reconciliations.

C. Checks and supporting documents should be marked "Paid" immediately after the check is returned with the bank statement.

D. Checks should be sent directly to the payee by the employee who prepares documents that authorize check preparation.

12-95 To avoid potential errors and irregularities, a well-designed system of internal accounting control in the accounts payable area should include a separation of which of the following functions?

A. Cash disbursements and invoice verification.

B. Invoice verification and merchandise ordering.

C. Physical handling of merchandise received and preparation of receiving reports.

D. Check signing and cancellation of payment documentation.

12-96 Which of the following is an internal control procedure that would prevent a paid disbursement voucher from being presented for payment a second time?

A. Vouchers should be prepared by individuals who are responsible for signing disbursement checks.

B. Disbursement vouchers should be approved by at least two responsible management officials.

C. The date on a disbursement voucher should be within a few days of the date the voucher is presented for payment.

D. The official signing the check should compare the check with the voucher and should deface the voucher documents.

12-97 Ball Company, which has no perpetual inventory records, takes a monthly physical inventory and reorders any item which is less than its reorder point. On February 5, 1984, Ball ordered 5,000 units of item

A. On February 6, 1984, Ball received 5,000 units of item A which had been ordered on January 3, 1984. To prevent this excess ordering, Ball should

A. Keep an adequate record of open purchases.
B. Use perpetual inventory records which indicate goods received, issued, and amounts on hand.
C. Use prenumbered purchase orders.
D. Prepare purchase orders only on the basis of purchase requisitions.

12-98   A CPA is engaged in the annual audit of a client for the year ended December 31, 1984. The client took a complete physical inventory under the CPA's observation on December 15 and adjusted its inventory control account and detailed perpetual inventory records to agree with the physical inventory. The client considers a sale to be made in the period that goods are shipped. Listed below are four items taken from the CPA's sales-cutoff-test worksheet. Which item does not require an adjusting entry on the client's books?

| | Date (Month/Day) | | |
	Shipped	Recorded as Sale	Credited to Inventory Control
A.	12/10	12/19	12/12
B.	12/14	12/16	12/16
C.	12/31	1/2	12/31
D.	1/2	12/31	12/31

12-99   An auditor obtains a magnetic tape that contains the dollar amounts of all client inventory items by style number. The information on the tape is in no particular sequence. The auditor can best ascertain that no consigned merchandise is included on the tape by using a computer program that

A. Statistically selects samples of all amounts.
B. Excludes all amounts for items with particular style numbers that indicate consigned merchandise.
C. Mathematically calculates the extension of each style quality by the unit price.
D. Prints on paper the information that is on the magnetic tape.

12-100   The cashier of Safir Company covered a shortage in the cash working fund with cash obtained on December 31 from a local bank by cashing but not recording a check drawn on the company's out-of-town bank. How would the auditor discover this manipulation?

A. Confirming all December 31 bank balances.
B. Counting the cash working fund at the close of business on December 31.
C. Preparing independent bank reconciliations as of December 31.
D. Investigating items returned with the bank-cutoff statements.

12-101   The standard bank cash confirmation form requests all of the following except

A. Maturity date of a direct liability.
B. The principal amount paid on a direct liability.
C. Description of collateral for a direct liability.
D. The interest rate of a direct liability.

12-102   Which of the following procedures would best detect the theft of valuable items from an inventory that consists of hundreds of different items selling for $1 to $10 and a few items selling for hundreds of dollars?

A. Maintain a perpetual inventory of only the more valuable items with frequent periodic verification of the validity of the perpetual inventory record.
B. Have an independent CPA firm prepare an internal control report on the effectiveness of the administrative and accounting controls over inventory.
C. Have separate warehouse space for the more valuable items with sequentially numbered tags.
D. Require an authorized officer's signature on all requisitions for the more valuable items.

12-103   A client's physical count of inventories was lower than the inventory quantities shown in its perpetual records. This situation could be the result of the failure to record

A. Sales.
B. Sales returns.
C. Purchases.
D. Purchase discounts.

12-104 The audit of a year-end physical inventory should include steps to verify that the client's purchases and sales cut-offs were adequate. The audit steps should be designed to detect whether merchandise included in the physical count at year-end was not recorded as a

A. Sale in the subsequent period.
B. Purchase in the current period.
C. Sale in the current period.
D. Purchase return in the subsequent period.

12-105 Purchase cut-off procedures should be designed to test that merchandise is included in the inventory of the client company, if the company

A. Has paid for the merchandise.
B. Has physical possession of the merchandise.
C. Holds legal title to the merchandise.
D. Holds the shipping documents for the merchandise issued in the company's name.

LEARNING OBJECTIVES

After studying this chapter, students should understand

1. The nature of financing and investing cycle.
2. The audit objectives for the financing and investing cycle.
3. The nature of compliance tests for the financing and investing cycle.
4. The substantive audit procedures which are usually applied in auditing marketable securities, long-term investments, prepaid expenses, property, plant and equipment, accumulated depreciation and amortization, and other assets.
5. The substantive audit procedures which are usually applied in auditing accounts payable, accrued liabilities, bonds payable, other liabilities, and shareholders equity accounts.

Chapter 13

Audit of the Financing and Investing Cycle

This chapter was written by
Wesley T. Andrews, Ph.D., C.P.A.,
Associate Professor of Accounting,
Florida Atlantic University

INTRODUCTION

For the majority of business firms, a substantial proportion of the total effort expended by a firm is directed at the production of revenue. Indeed, for such firms, many transactions that occur on a day-to-day basis involve revenue creation and collection, so that the revenue cycle and the expense and production cycle represent major segments of the firm's information processing system. Consideration of the audit of these two segments of the information processing system and of the accounts affected by those transactions has been discussed in Chapters 11 and 12, respectively. This chapter will discuss a third major activity of any firm, namely financing and investing for the firm. The chapter will discuss the information processing considerations concerning that activity and will deal with the procedural aspects of auditing the accounts related to the financing and investing activities of the firm. These matters will be discussed under the general heading of the financing and investing cycle.

OVERVIEW OF THE FINANCING AND INVESTING CYCLE

The activities of the financing and investing cycle are essentially two-fold: there are activities involving the generation of resources, either from debt or equity sources, to provide the initial resources for the conduct of business by the firm or the additional resources to enable the firm to expand its operations from time to time. In addition, the financing and investing cycle includes those non-operating activities of investing those resources in assets necessary to support the firm's ongoing operations. Hence, the accounts primarily affected by the activities of the financing and investing cycle include all of the liability and equity accounts, as well as those asset accounts that are not directly related to the other cycles of the firm, such as marketable securities; long-term investments; property, plant, and equipment; and other assets.

The foregoing distinction between activities of the revenue, expense, and production cycles and the financing and investing cycle is obviously not as clearcut as the preceding paragraph might suggest. Clearly, the sale of securities to the public involves the receipt of cash and the purchase of a new plant involves a cash disbursement. Therefore, one could argue that most of the transactions which are considered here under the general topic of the financing and investing cycle have already been covered in earlier discussions of the cash receipt and disbursement functions; indeed, that argument would be sound. On the other hand, it is convenient to separate transactions that are primarily of a non-operating nature for discussion purposes. Thus, this chapter considers those transactions that are concerned with the generation of resources from debt and equity sources, as well as those transactions that invest those resources in assets other than cash, accounts receivable, or inventory, to be part of the financing and investing cycle.

One characteristic of transactions in the financing and investing cycle is that such transactions are sometimes large infrequent transactions, as opposed to routine revenue and expense transactions which tend to be more numerous. As a result, transactions in the financing and investing cycle tend to require specific management authorization for each transaction, rather than a more general authorization, as is the case with transactions in the revenue and expense and production cycles. In addition, while there are relatively few transactions in the financing and investing cycle, a fair number of these transactions are recorded by general journal entry, rather than through the other segments of the client's information processing system.

Since the sales, purchases, cash receipts, and cash disbursements segments, as well as subsegments for payroll and perpetual inventory recordkeeping were discussed in Chapters 11 and 12, the only remaining segment of the client's information processing system to be discussed is the system for handling general journal entries.

Students will recall from the introductory accounting course that the general journal is used to record any journal entry that does not appropriately fit into one of the special journals, such as the cash receipts journal, the cash disbursements journal, the sales journal, or the voucher register. Therefore, since the general journal is appropriate only for a transaction other than a cash receipt, a cash disbursement, a purchase, a sale, or a sales return, general journal entries are relatively infrequent. Generally most journal entries require the specific authorization of someone within the client's organization.

In addition to being properly authorized, each general journal entry should be properly documented to provide evidence of the propriety of the entry. Even though most clients may maintain a general journal to record general entries, it is also fairly common to maintain a file of "journal vouchers" to support each journal entry. The journal voucher should contain properly approved documentary support, usually in the form of computational worksheets for the entry. Posting of the journal entry should be done by someone other than the preparer and/or authorizer of the entry.

After a brief discussion of the audit objectives of the financing and investing cycle and the procedures for compliance testing of general journal entries, the remainder of this chapter will be devoted to the procedures for gathering the substantive audit evidence needed to support the propriety of the transactions recorded in those accounts primarily affected by the financing and investing cycle.

AUDIT OBJECTIVES OF THE FINANCING AND INVESTING CYCLE

As was the case with the audit of the revenue and the expense and production cycles, the overall objectives of the audit of the elements and accounts of the financing and investing cycle are (1) to do the work necessary to furnish a reasonable basis for an opinion on the financial statements being audited, and (2) to plan and execute this work in accordance with the three standards of field work and to document the results.

More specifically with respect to the audit of the financing and investing cycle, these general audit objectives should be accomplished by planning and executing the work in a manner that will accomplish three specific objectives. First, as was the case when auditing the revenue cycle and the expense and production cycle, the audit process should begin with a review of the existing procedures and controls over the execution and recording of transactions. This work is undertaken in response to the requirement of the second standard of field work, which requires the auditor to review the system of internal control to provide a basis for making decisions concerning the nature, extent, and timing of substantive tests of balances that need to be conducted.

Second, the audit plan for the financing and investing cycle should include a review of the financial environment in which the client operates. Such a review should include both a summary of the financial environment in the client's business community and an analytical review of monthly or quarterly interim financial data, with particular emphasis on changes in the client's financial structure occurring during the year. In addition, specific authorization for all material changes in the company's financial plan should be documented, and controls over the issuance and processing of journal entries to record the resulting transactions should be reviewed and evaluated.

Third, substantive testing of the activity in those accounts affected by the financing and investing cycle should be conducted, including account analysis, reconciliation of activity in balance sheet accounts to recorded results in related income and expense accounts, confirmation, reference to authoritative documents, and so forth.

As noted earlier, several types of transactions involved in the financing and investing cycle are properly recorded through information processing segments that are related to the revenue cycle and/or the expense and production cycle. The specific objectives stated here are not intended to require additional compliance testing of the controls in the cash receipts, cash disbursements, and sales or purchase segments; rather, the discussion of compliance testing of internal controls in this chapter will be restricted to those controls over the processing of general journal entries.

DEVELOPING AUDIT PROGRAMS RELATED TO THE FINANCING AND INVESTING CYCLE

The following audit program steps connected with the financing and investing cycle can be essentially completed prior to year-end (with one minor exception) and accordingly may be characterized as being preliminary work.

1. Discuss with the client, prior to the end of the period, any significant changes or any plans for changes in the financial structure of the client company. If the client has prepared a written financial plan for the year being audited, obtain a copy of this plan and include the details of that plan in the discussion with the client. Document the results of this preliminary conference in the form of a memorandum for the working papers;

2. Prepare a memorandum for the working papers summarizing the probable impact of current economic and financial trends, both at the national and at the local level, on the client's financial plans for the period; and

3. Review and abstract minutes of any meetings of the following committees or groups within the client's organization:

    a. Stockholders,

    b. Board of directors and audit committee,

    c. Executive committee, and

    d. Finance committee.

With respect to this third step, the term "abstract" means to prepare abbreviated notes summarizing all items from the minutes that have accounting significance. For this purpose, it is not necessary to quote verbatim the entire text of the minutes and it is also not necessary to mention any items that are not of accounting significance, such as the reporting of deliberations over which advertising agency to employ for a particular advertising campaign. Each meeting's abstract is usually ended with a comment by the auditor that no other items of accounting significance were noted in the minutes.

It should also be noted that, if this is the first year that a company has been audited by the independent auditor, minutes of meetings should be reviewed and abstracted from the company's inception, in addition to the current year. In addition, the abstracts should be filed in the permanent file of the working papers and updated each year, so that continuous records of all such significant matters are maintained in the permanent file.

Finally, as will be discussed in Chapter 14 under the topic of subsequent events procedures, the review of minutes should not only be a preliminary procedure but should be updated through the date of completion of the audit field work.

> 4. Obtain interim financial data for the current year along with comparable interim and annual financial information for prior periods. Review this data analytically, particularly for changes in the financial structure of the company and for changes in the non-current assets of the company.

Note that the preliminary audit programs developed in Chapters 11 and 12 also called for analytical review of prior period and interim current period's financial information. This step, undertaken here to analytically review for significant changes in the financial structure of the company, can efficiently be performed at the same time as other analytical review procedures are performed in connection with the audit of the revenue cycle and the expense and production cycle.

The preceding four steps are designed to furnish the auditor with background information about the client and to identify potential areas where audit tests should be concentrated. Similar audit program steps were conducted in connection with the audit of the revenue cycle and the expense and production cycle. After this background information is accumulated, the auditor then undertakes to describe, test, and evaluate the internal accounting controls that exist in the information processing segments of the client's accounting system.

As mentioned earlier, the cash receipts, cash disbursements, purchase, and sales segments were compliance tested in connection with the audit of the revenue cycle and/or the audit of the expense and production cycle; the only remaining information processing segment to be tested then is the procedure for authorizing, executing, and recording general journal entries. The following two audit program steps are designed to compliance test the controls over this segment of the information processing system.

5. Discuss with the client the procedure for initiation and execution of transactions that are to be recorded through general journal entries. Specifically, determine what types of transactions these are, who in the client's organization has authority to initiate and approve such transactions, who prepares the journal entry to record such transactions (including the underlying documentation for the transaction), and how and by whom these journal entries are posted to the general ledger and filed; and

6. Scan the accounts in the general ledger, noting all postings from the general journal. Select a sample of these entries, trace the entries to the general journal, and examine the underlying documentary support for the entries selected.

It should be noted at this point that while scanning is an entirely appropriate audit procedure, and the formal selection of a sample of general journal entries for compliance testing, as specified in step six, may not be necessary. Whether to compliance test the process of preparing general journal entries depends primarily on the auditor's judgment about the most efficient way to achieve audit objectives. For example, if the ledger contains numerous general journal entries, the auditor may decide that the more efficient procedure would be to formally test the general journal process by selecting a sample of journal entries for test; if, on the other hand, general journal entries are relatively infrequent, it may be more efficient to scan the journal entries and examine documentation for only those journal entries that appear material when accounts are substantiated at year-end.

The remaining portion of this chapter will be devoted to the development of audit programs to substantively test and analyze those accounts that are primarily affected by transactions in the financing and investing cycle. In reviewing these audit programs, students should recognize that with the exception of accounts payable, the balance sheet accounts which are discussed are balance sheet accounts where the beginning and ending balances are closely related, as defined in Chapter 6. Thus, the substantive audit programs for the majority of the accounts parallel the minimum substantive audit procedures for balance sheet accounts for which the beginning and ending balances are closely related. Of course, the audit procedures for accounts payable parallel the minimum audit procedures for balance sheet accounts where the beginning and ending balances are not closely related.

Substantive Audit Program for Analysis of Marketable Securities and Long-Term Investments

Essentially, the audit of investments in securities, both short-term investments and long-term investments, involves two activities. First, it is necessary to have the client prepare an analysis of the investment account for the year, and second, the auditor should verify the existence of the securities at the end of the year by some appropriate substantive test. The following audit program steps are directed at accomplishing these two goals.

1. Have the client prepare (or prepare) an analysis of investments and investment activity for the period being audited. If the client prepares this analysis, foot and crossfoot the analysis. Also, trace the totals to the appropriate general ledger balances.

The analysis should be prepared on a columnar worksheet and should show the activity of each security that was either purchased, sold, or on hand as of the end of the period. Appropriate column headings for the analysis might be as follows:

Column	Column Heading
1	Balance per general ledger, beginning of the period (both number of shares or number of bonds and their cost)
2	Purchases during the period (both number of shares or number of bonds and their cost)
3	Sales during the year (both number of shares or number of bonds and the cost of securities sold)
4	Proceeds from sale of securities, net of sales fees paid
5	Gain (loss) on sale of securities
6	Balance per general ledger, end of the period (both number of shares or number of bonds and their cost)
7	End of period market value

Further, the auditor might prepare separate analyses for short-term investments in marketable securities and long-term investments in marketable securities, so that column totals for each balance sheet classification can be compared to the appropriate general ledger balances. Also, notice that the amounts on the schedule can be crossfooted as follows:

Column 1 + Column 2 − Column 3 = Column 6, and
Column 4 − Column 3 = Column 5.

On the same analyses, investments in bonds and notes (i.e., in interest earning securities) should be segregated from investments in common and preferred stocks (dividend-earning securities). In this manner, both interest income and accruals and dividend income and related accruals can be substantiated on the same working paper. This is accomplished by adding four additional columns to the analysis:

Column	Column Heading
8	Accrued interest receivable (or accrued dividends receivable), beginning of year
9	Interest (or dividends) collected during the year
10	Interest (or dividend) income
11	Accrued interest (or dividends) receivable, end of year

Again, column totals should crossfoot in the following manner:

Column 8 − Column 9 + Column 10 = Column 11

In addition, total dividend income and interest income, from column 10, should agree with the appropriate general ledger income accounts, and accrued interest (or dividends) receivable at both the beginning and the end of the year should agree with the appropriate general ledger balances.

An example of an eleven column worksheet for use in auditing marketable securities is shown in Exhibit 13-1. However, while a worksheet like the one shown may be useful in auditing marketable securities, other forms of worksheets may be used. For example, an alternative substantive audit working paper for marketable securities is shown in Exhibit 13-2. The point is that the auditor should specify the format for the worksheet which is efficient to prepare and still allows the auditor to adequately document the accounts.

Exhibit 13-1

Example of Eleven Column Worksheet for use in Auditing Marketable Securities

Bowler Lumber Co.
Investments in Marketable Securities
12/31/84

Prepared by: CLIENT 1-6-85
Date: P.T. ⨍.⨍. 1-15-85
Reviewed by:
Date:

(a) Short-Term Investment

	Securities						Dividends			
(1) Beginning Balance	(2) Purchases	(3) Sales	(4) Proceeds	(5) Gain	(6) Ending Balance	(7) Market Price 12/31/84	(8) Dividends Receivable 12/31/83	(9) Cash Received in 1984	(10) Dividends Income for 1984	(11) Dividends Receivable 12/31/84
$1,000 (100 shares Vepco) Ⓐ	2,500 (200 shares Vepco on 12/31/84) Ⓔ	500 (50 shares @ $10 share cost on 10/21/84) Ⓔ, Ⓣ	$600 Ⓣ	$100 Ⓡ, Ⓣ/ᴮ	$3,000 (250 shares) Ⓣ/ᴮ, Ⓘ	$4,000 Ⓥ	$100 Ⓐ	$100 Ⓣ	$100 Ⓜ	$100 Ⓜ

(b) Long-Term Investment

$2,000 (200 shares Johnson Rewriting Company of Athens, Georgia) Ⓐ					$2,000 (200 shares) Ⓣ/ᴮ, Ⓘ	$10,000 Ⓥ	$2,000 Ⓐ	$14,000 Ⓣ	$20,000 Ⓜ	$6,000 Ⓜ

The above securities were counted in my presence and returned to me intact.

Sara Bowler 12-31-84

Ⓐ Agrees with 1983 working paper #16.
Ⓔ Examined broker's advice.
Ⓣ Traced proceeds to cash receipts journal.
Ⓡ Recomputed.
Ⓣ/ᴮ Agrees with general ledger, trial balance and financial statements.
Ⓘ Inspected securities—see detail listing of securities, including serial numbers on working paper #6.
Ⓥ Verified by reference to Wall Street Journal.
Ⓜ Verified computation by reference to Moody's Dividend Record.

Exhibit 13-2
Example of Primary Substantive Audit Working Paper
for Marketable Securities

Prepared by: _J.J._
Date: _12-31-83_
Reviewed by: _P.T._
Date: _1-14-84_

Bowler Lumber Co.
Marketable Securities
12/31/83

Description	Balance 12/31/82	Additions	Disposals	Balance 12/31/83
100 shares Pepco	$2,000 ✓			$2,000 E
200 shares Georgia Power	2,500 ✓	___	$1,250 ①	1,250 E
	$4,500 ✓		$1,250	$3,250 ⊘
	✓✓	==	✓✓	✓✓

The above securities were examined in my presence
and returned to me intact on 12/31/83.

Sara Bowler
Treasurer

✓   Agrees with 1982 working paper #15.

✓✓   Footed.

⊘   Crossfooted.

①   Recomputed gain on sale. Examined broker's advice, and traced debit to Cash, credit to Gain on Sale of Marketable Securities, and credit to Marketable Securities accounts.

E   Examined securities and noted that, except for securities sold, the serial numbers on the securities agrees with 1982 count. See detailed listing of securities and serial numbers on working paper #43. Examined closing prices of securities in Wall Street Journal and noted that price per share exceeded cost per share for each security. Thus, no valuation allowance is needed for securities. Also, examined Moody's Dividend Record and no dividends were declared or paid on these securities in 1983.

Once the analyses have been completed and reconciled to the general ledger, the following audit program steps can be performed with respect to the information shown therein.

2. With respect to balances as of the beginning of the period, compare the detail of the information in columns 1 and 8 to last year's working papers.

Obviously, this step must be modified if this is the initial year that the auditor has done the audit for this client. In the case where this is the first year of operations for the client, the beginning of the year balances in all accounts will clearly be zero. If the client's financial statements for the previous year were audited by another auditor, the auditor may, after making a reasonable investigation of the competence of the predecessor auditor and after having secured permission of the client to discuss prior year's matters with the predecessor auditor, decide to rely on the predecessor auditor's work and simply compare beginning of the year information for the current year to the predecessor auditor's working papers.

The only other possible situation is that the client was in business last year but was not audited. In this circumstance, the auditor should examine sufficient documentary evidence, such as the securities, brokers' advices and cancelled checks, to determine the propriety of the beginning balances.

In all instances the following step should be carried out if the client has material purchases of investment securities.

3. With respect to securities purchased during the year, examine broker's advices for all material purchases of securities, noting that the description of the securities purchased, the date, and the net cost of the securities purchased agrees with the client's analysis. Also, trace the amounts paid for the transactions selected in this step to the cash disbursements journal.

If the number of purchases of securities during the year is large and if earlier compliance testing of the controls in the cash disbursements and voucher segments of the system indicated that those controls may be relied upon, the auditor may select a sample of purchases for verification rather than examining documents for all material purchases.

4. For all material sales of securities (or a sample, if appropriate), examine broker's advices to support the information on the client's

analysis regarding description of the securities sold, date of sale, and net proceeds. Trace the collection of the net proceeds to the cash disbursements journal. Check the accuracy of the computation of gain or loss on the sale and indicate on the analysis whether the gain or loss is long-term or short-term for federal income tax purposes.

Two additional observations are appropriate at this point. First, it is common for investors in securities to establish accounts with their brokers and have the broker hold cash as a part of that account. In such a case, the cash received when securities are sold would not be deposited in the client's bank account but rather held by the brokerage firm, pending another purchase of securities. In this event, the foregoing two audit program steps will need to be modified to require the auditor to examine monthly statements from the brokerage firm to determine that all cash held by the broker is properly accounted for during the year. Further, the auditor should determine that any cash held by the broker as of year-end is properly reflected as a receivable from the broker in the balance sheet.

Second, it is important to note the classification of gain or loss on sale of securities for two reasons: (1) the auditor may also be engaged to prepare the client's tax return, so that the information will be needed when the return is prepared, and (2) even if the auditor has not been engaged to prepare the tax return, it is necessary for the auditor to review the accrual of income taxes for the year, and the nature of such gains and losses, is important in estimating the proper income tax liability and income tax expense for the year.

5. Trace all material (or a sample of, if appropriate) collections of interest or dividends to the cash receipts journal. For publicly traded securities, examine a published dividend service (such as Standard and Poors), and determine the dividend declaration, record, and payment dates. Determine that all dividends have been properly accounted for as either collected or accrued as receivables. Likewise, check the computation of interest income and accrued interest receivable for each interest-bearing investment; and

6. For all securities on hand at the end of the year, plan to physically examine the securities, in the presence of client personnel, at or near year-end. Note that if marketable securities are negotiable, the timing of this examination of securities should be coordinated with the count of cash on hand and notes receivable, as required by audit programs discussed earlier in Chapters 11 and 12.

7. For all securities held by outside custodians (such as brokers), arrange for confirmation of details of securities as of year-end;

8. For all publicly traded securities held as of year-end, obtain closing market quotations from the financial press (for example, the Wall Street Journal for the first business day of each month will carry year-end closing quotations for all securities traded on most major exchanges and in the over-the-counter market). For all non-publicly traded securities, obtain audited financial statements of the issuers of the securities and obtain any other evidence available to estimate the market value of such securities as of year-end; and

9. Based upon the information and evidence gathered in steps 1 through 8 above, determine that marketable securities and related income and accrual accounts are fairly presented in accordance with generally accepted accounting principles.

Substantive Audit Program for the Audit of Prepaid Expenses

The analysis of all prepaid expenses is performed in a fashion that is very similar to the analysis of marketable securities and long-term investments just discussed. From a procedural point of view, a worksheet is developed that uses the same logical structure as the worksheet used in the analysis of investment accounts. Thus, a logical starting point in the analysis of prepaid expenses is as follows:

1. Have the client prepare (or prepare) an analysis of each prepaid expense account (prepaid rent, prepaid insurance, etc.) in a format that uses the following column headings:

Column	Column Heading
1	Prepaid balance, beginning of period
2	Paid during period
3	Expense for the period
4	Prepaid balance, end of period

Again, each analysis should crossfoot as follows:

Column 1 + Column 2 − Column 3 = Column 4

For each prepaid expense category, the details of supporting documents for the prepaid account can be itemized on the schedule. For example, in the analysis of prepaid insurance, each insurance policy can be listed, showing the name of the carrier, the coverage limits, the term of the policy and the policy number, as well as the premium amounts and dates of payment. Similarly, prepaid rent can be analyzed by rental unit. (Here, if the client is a lessee for leases that extend beyond the current period, copies of the lease agreements should be included in the permanent file of the working papers and cross-referenced to the analysis of prepaid rent.) A sample working paper for prepaid insurance is presented in Exhibit 13-3.

Other prepaid assets may be similarly analyzed and scheduled. Once the analysis of each prepaid expense account has been prepared (either by the auditor or the client), the following verification steps are appropriate.

2. Compare the total balance in column 1 of each analysis (prepaid balance, beginning of period) to last year's working papers.

Again, if this is the first year of business for the client, this step is inappropriate. In addition, if this is the first year the auditor has done the audit of this particular client, other appropriate measures, such as an examination of the predecessor's working papers, must be substituted in order for the auditor to determine the propriety of the opening balances in the prepaid accounts.

3. Trace all material (or a sample of, if numerous and otherwise appropriate) payments from column 2 to the cash disbursements journal; and

4. Refer to appropriate underlying documentary evidence to support the propriety of all information on the analysis, including the payments, that is pertinent to the calculation of the correct amount of period expense and/or the correct amount of prepaid expense as of the end of the period.

For example, in the audit of prepaid rent the auditor should review all material leases to determine the amount of rent to be paid, the dates that rent is due, and the amount of any security deposits that might be included in the prepaid rent amount. Similarly, insurance policies should be reviewed in connection with this step, and all pertinent information regarding the computation of prepaid insurance should be noted on the analysis.

In connection with the review of prepaid rent, the auditor should pay particular attention to new lease agreements made during the year being audited. Copies of these new leases should be included in the permanent

Exhibit 13-3
Sample Substantive Audit Working Paper
for Prepaid Insurance and Insurance Expense

Date: 1-15-84
Preparer: J.J.
Reviewer: F.J.

Bowler Lumber Company
Analysis of Prepaid Insurance and Insurance Expense
12/31/83

①, ∅ Description	① Period	Prepaid at 1/1/83	Premiums during 1983	Insurance expense	Prepaid at 12/31/83
Casualty Insurance on Buildings, Inventory, & Equipment ($1MM)	6/30/83 – 6/30/84	$12,000 ②	$24,000 ③	$24,000 ④ T/B	$12,000 ④ T/B

①   Examined policy—all details agree with policy.

②   Agrees with 1982 working paper #68.

③   Examined invoice.

④   Verified computation.

T/B   Agrees with financial statements and trial balance.

∅   The company has a policy of having its insurance coverage reviewed annually by Mike Dekel of State Farm. Examined Mike's report dated 6/18/83. He does not recommend any additional business coverage. However, he does recommend that the company purchase insurance on the lives of the officers. See WP #86 for analysis and management letter comment.

Working Paper #18

file of the working papers, and the terms of the leases should be carefully analyzed by the auditor to make sure that the client is properly treating the lease as an operating lease under current generally accepted accounting principles. If the auditor identifies any leases that, in his or her opinion, should be treated as capital leases, this information should be promptly discussed with the client so that appropriate adjustments to the books can be recorded in a timely manner.

5. Verify the computation of the amount of the expense for the period and the prepaid amount for the period, and trace the amount of the expense and the prepaid amount to the general ledger, trial balance, and financial statements.

Substantive Audit Program for Audit of Property, Plant and Equipment and Related Accumulated Depreciation or Amortization

In a similar fashion, the auditor conducts the test of balances in connection with property, plant, and equipment and related accumulated depreciation or amortization.

1. Have the client prepare (or prepare), an analysis of each account in the property, plant, and equipment category, in a format that uses the following column headings:

Column	Column Heading
1	Balance, beginning of year
2	Additions, at cost, during year
3	Investment credit on additions
4	Cost (or other carrying value) of retirements during year
5	Selling price (proceeds of sale) upon retirement
6	Gain (loss) on disposal
7	Investment credit to be recaptured, if any
8	Balance, end of year

In similar fashion, the accumulated depreciation and amortization accounts, as well as the related expense accounts, can be analyzed.

2. On the same analysis, have the client prepare (or prepare) an analysis of each of the accumulated depreciation and amortization accounts, using the following format:

Column	Column Heading
9	Accumulated depreciation, beginning of year
10	Depreciation expense
11	Accumulated depreciation on retirements or disposals
12	Accumulated depreciation, end-of-year

These last four column headings can be included on the analysis immediately to the right of the related asset accounts. Thus, for example, the analysis of office machines (or a particular office machine, if the analysis is to be prepared in detail) and the related depreciation expense and allowance will appear on the same horizontal line of the analysis. A sample substantive audit working paper for the audit of property, plant, and equipment, and related accumulated depreciation is shown in Exhibit 13-4.

In addition, the analyses of accumulated depreciation and depreciation expense should also reflect, for each asset or asset class, the method of depreciation, the estimated useful life of the asset, and the amount of any salvage value assigned to the asset. If this information is different for book and income tax purposes, both sets of information should be included, so that depreciation for tax purposes can be computed, if different, and so that information relevant to the proper computation of deferred income taxes is readily available. (The subject of review of tax accruals will be discussed later in this chapter.)

3. Foot and crossfoot (or, if the analyses are extensive, test the footing) of the analyses obtained in step 1. Trace the balances, by account, as of the end of the year (columns 8 and 12) to the appropriate general ledger accounts. Also trace total gain (loss) on disposal (column 6) and depreciation expense (column 10) to the appropriate expense accounts in the general ledger; and

4. Regarding beginning of the year balances in both asset and accumulated depreciation accounts (columns 1 and 9), trace detail and total amounts, by account, to the previous year's working papers.

Again, if this is the first year that the auditor has had the engagement, this step is not appropriate, since the auditor has no prior year working papers. In the case of a first year engagement, the auditor must evaluate the propriety of beginning of the year balances by the following method which is most practical in the circumstances.

a. If this is the first year the client has been in business, then the beginning balances will be zero and no further verification is necessary;

b. If the client has been in business for several years and was audited by another CPA last year, the auditor may, after determining that the prior auditor is qualified and may be relied upon (and after securing the permission of the client) trace the beginning of the year balances and details to the working papers of the predecessor auditor; or

c. If the client has been in business for several years but this is the initial year that the client's financial statements have been audited, the auditor must conduct additional tests to evaluate the propriety of the opening balances. This usually involves examination of documentary evidence from prior years, such as invoices, property tax records, titles, etc., which support the information contained in the opening balances for the current year.

Next, the audit program deals with additions to property, plant and equipment.

5. With respect to additions, trace all (or a sample of, if numerous) debits to property, plant, and equipment accounts to the cash disbursements records. Also, examine supporting documentation, such as invoices and contracts, for the addition; and

6. Inquire of management regarding the company's policy about capitalization vs. expensing of property items. Also, inquire regarding management's policy concerning specific authorization of large additions to property, plant and equipment. Prepare a memorandum for the working papers, indicating the results of these inquiries.

With respect to these last points, companies will typically adopt some policy for expensing small purchases of items that would normally be classified as property, plant, and equipment except for the fact that they are low dollar value items. For example, a company may adopt a policy to expense any item with a cost of less than $100, regardless of the nature of the item. Thus, a pencil sharpener, which may have a cost of $20 and an estimated useful life of 10 years, would be expensed rather than debited to Office Equipment. In addition, companies will usually have a policy requiring special authorization for larger property, plant, and equipment acquisitions. For example, company policy may require

Exhibit 13-4
Sample Substantive Audit Working Paper
for Property and Accumulated Depreciation

Bowler Lumber Co.
Property and Accumulated Depreciation
12/31/84

Asset

	(1)	(2)	(3)	(4)	(5)	(6)	(7)	(8)	
	Beginning Balance	Addition (at cost)	Investment Credit on Additions	Retirements (at cost)	Proceeds From Sale	Gain (loss)	Recaptured Credit	Ending Balance	
Machinery	$ 500,000 ✓	$10,000 E	$1,000 V	$5,000 T	$1,000 A	$(100) C	0 D	$ 505,000 ⊘	T/B
Land	100,000 ✓							100,000 ⊘	T/B
Building	800,000 ✓							800,000 ⊘	T/B
	$1,400,000 ✓	$10,000	$1,000	$5,000	$1,000	$(100)	0	$1,405,000	
		✓⁄	✓⁄	✓⁄	✓⁄	✓⁄	✓⁄	✓⁄	

✓   Traced to 12/31/83 working paper #52.

✓⁄   Footed.

⊘   Crossfooted.

E   Examined invoice.

V   Verified computation—machine has a ten year life and qualifies for full credit.

T   Traced to general ledger.

Prepared by: J.J.
Date: 1-15-85
Reviewed by: P.J.
Date: 1-20-85

Accumulated Depreciation

(9)	(10)	(11)	(12)
		Accumulated	
Beginning	*Depreciation*	*Depreciation*	*Ending*
Balance	*Expense*	*on Disposal*	*Balance*
$200,000 ✓	$20,000 C, S	$3,900 C	$216,100 (✓) T/B (✓) T/B
20,000 ✓	24,000 C, S		48,000 (✓) T/B
$220,000 ✓	$44,000	$3,900	$264,100 (✓)
	T/B, ✓	✓	✓

A   Traced to cash receipts journal.

C   Verified computation—depreciation properly recorded to date of sale.

D   Full credit has been earned (acquired 1976).

T/B Agrees with general ledger, trial balance, and financial statements.

S   Salvage values, depreciation method, and useful lives appear reasonable. See working paper #56 for the analysis of these items. As indicated on working paper #56, book and tax depreciation are the same.

a vice-president's approval for any addition to property, plant, and equipment of less than $10,000 and board of director's approval for any acquisition of $10,000 or more.

Thus, the auditor is interested in determining that all additions to property, plant and equipment are properly authorized and accounted for in accordance with company policy.

7. Determine that all material additions to property, plant and equipment are properly authorized and accounted for in accordance with management's policy, as determined in step 6;

8. Prepare an analysis of the repairs and maintenance expense account. Examine invoices for all (or a sample of, if numerous) material debits to repairs and maintenance expense, with particular attention to items that may have been expensed but should have been capitalized in accordance with management's policies. An example of an audit working paper which may be used in analyzing repairs and maintenance is shown in Exhibit 13-5; and

9. Review the reasonableness of estimated useful lives, salvage values, and depreciation methods for current year additions. Specifically, determine that the client has not changed its method of accounting for property, plant and equipment by using depreciation methods in the current period that are different from the methods used for similar assets in prior periods.

With respect to disposals of property, plant, and equipment, the following audit program steps are appropriate,

10. Trace the proceeds for all recorded disposals (or a sample, if numerous) of property, plant, and equipment to the cash receipts journal; and

11. For all disposals (or a sample, if numerous), determine that both the correct carrying value was removed from the asset account and that the correct accumulated depreciation, after recording the proper amount of depreciation expense on the disposed-of asset for the current year, was removed from the accumulated depreciation account. Check the computation of gain (loss) on the disposal. For assets disposed of by trade-in, determine that the carrying value of the acquired asset has been properly computed and that gain (loss) on the trade-in has been properly recorded in accordance with generally accepted accounting principles.

Exhibit 13-5
Sample Substantive Audit Working Paper
for Repairs and Maintenance

Prepared by: _J.K._
Date: _1-14-84_
Reviewed by: _P.T._
Date: _1-16-84_

Bowler Lumber Co.
Analysis of Repairs and Maintenance
12/31/83

Date	Description		Amount
3/14/83	Repairs to forklift	E	$ 600
5/16/83	Painting trucks	E	1,000
9/22/83	Repairs to building	E	200
	Total of amounts for less than $100.00 each	S	2,000
			$3,800
			T/B, ✓

E   Examined invoice and discussed work with client. All of these items are proper repairs and maintenance. None of these items should be capitalized.

✓   Footed.

S   Scanned general ledger for reasonableness of explanations and amounts. No exceptions noted.

T/B   Agrees with general ledger, trial balance, and financial statements.

Note that steps 10 and 11 are designed primarily to test the propriety of the details of disposals that were in fact recorded on the books. These procedures do not give the auditor any assurance that all disposals of property, plant, and equipment were recorded; the auditor relies on previously conducted tests of the system of internal accounting control to provide assurance that all disposals of property, plant, and equipment that took place during the year were recorded. If the results of these earlier compliance tests of the system indicate that the internal accounting controls in the cash receipts segment of the information processing system are weak, the auditor may wish to supplement his or her year-end test of balances in the property, plant, and equipment accounts by physically verifying the existence of recorded property, plant, and equipment as of year-end.

12. For all disposals during the year, determine from client records and prior year income tax returns the amount of investment tax credit claimed in prior years that is subject to recapture in the current year. In addition, prepare a schedule of investment tax credit to be claimed on additions to property, plant, and equipment during the current year. Based upon this information, prepare an analysis of the investment tax credit and carryover, if any, for use in preparation of the income tax return and/or for analysis of the federal income tax accrual.

With respect to accumulated depreciation and/or amortization and the related expense accounts, the propriety of the depreciation or amortization methods used for acquisitions during the year was reviewed in step 9 previously and the propriety of depreciation recorded on disposed-of items was reviewed in step 11. Therefore, the only remaining step is to review and test the computation of depreciation and amortization on items that were on hand at the beginning of the year and were not disposed of during the year.

13. Test the computation of depreciation and amortization of all items not tested in steps 9 and 11 above. For each item tested, determine that the accumulated depreciation and/or amortization as of the end of the period is properly computed.

14. If depreciation and/or amortization expense is computed for income tax purposes on a basis different than for book purposes, review and test the computation of depreciation and/or amortization for tax purposes and prepare a schedule computing the differences between book and taxable depreciation and/or amortization.

As discussed later, this latter schedule will be useful in analyzing the accrual of the income tax liability, including the deferred tax portion thereof.

Substantive Audit Program for the Audit of Other Assets

In a fashion similar to the procedures followed to analyze the above asset accounts, any other asset account can be audited and the balance therein can be supported by substantive evidence. Of course, the auditor must make some decisions as to what types of evidence will be acceptable to support the propriety of recorded debits and credits to such accounts; each account, by its nature, will suggest appropriate evidence. For example, in auditing intangible assets such as patents and copyrights, the auditor will wish to refer to copies of legal documents to indicate the existence of the patent or copyright. Also, the auditor will verify the appropriateness of the debits to the patent and copyright accounts by tracing these amounts to the cash disbursement records of the company. Likewise, in reviewing amounts recorded as leasehold improvements, the auditor will wish to obtain and review copies of the appropriate leases.

Finally, with respect to all asset accounts, the auditor will wish to discuss with the client any and all items that need to be disclosed in the financial statements in order to comply with the full disclosure requirements of generally accepted accounting principles. Also, items such as the nature of any agreements that pledge accounts receivable or inventory to secure loans, mortgage arrangements which use property, plant and equipment as collateral, and lease or purchase commitments that require disclosure in the financial statements should be included in the client's representation letter to the auditor. In addition to these specific representations, the client should indicate in the letter that all such matters that should be disclosed are in fact included in the notes to the financial statements. These matters will be discussed in more detail in Chapter 14, "Completing the Audit Engagement."

Substantive Audit Program for Audit of Accounts (Vouchers) Payable

In cases where the client has a formal voucher system in place, it is usually not customary to perform extensive tests of recorded vouchers payable as of year-end, although some CPA firms prefer to include a confirmation procedure of recorded vouchers payable in their audit programs. Instead, the auditing firm will rely on interim compliance tests of the voucher segment of the information processing system to provide assurance that the recorded liability for accounts (vouchers) payable is at least not overstated. Thus, the year-end procedure for accounts (vouchers) payable is primarily a test for understatement, called a "search for unrecorded liabilities." However, as indicated later, this test does provide some evidence about the reasonableness of accounts payable which are already recorded.

In cases where the client does not maintain a formal system for recording accounts payable upon receipt of invoice from suppliers, but rather records items on a cash basis and adjusts the accounts to reflect accounts payable only at year-end, preliminary testing of the information processing system by the auditor was restricted to compliance tests of the cash disbursements segment of the information processing system. In this case, the following audit program step as of year-end is appropriate.

1. Obtain from the client a listing of accounts payable as of year-end. For a sample of the items from the listing, examine supporting documentary evidence (supplier's invoice, receiving report, etc.) noting that the item is a proper account payable as of year-end and that the account distribution (i.e., the account to be debited) is appropriate. Trace the posting of the entry recording the accounts payable at year-end to the general ledger.

At this point, the auditor should be reasonably satisfied that the recorded accounts payable, as of year-end, are not overstated on the books, i.e., that the recorded accounts payable are all proper liabilities of the company at year-end. The remaining question is whether the recorded accounts payable are understated, i.e., are there any unrecorded liabilities at year-end? The next audit program step is designed to conduct a search for unrecorded liabilities.

2. Defining all cash disbursements in the subsequent period as a population, select a sample of cash disbursements for examination of underlying supporting documentation to determine that the disbursement is either for (a) a subsequent period expense or (b) a recorded liability as of year-end. As a result of the examination of supporting documentation for the sample items selected, reach a conclusion as to whether or not all material liabilities that should be recorded as of year-end are, in fact, included in accounts payable.

As indicated in detail in Chapter 14, the subsequent period begins the first day after the balance sheet date and extends to the date the auditor completes the field work for the audit; this is the same period of time for which the auditor is responsible for detection of subsequent events that require either adjustment to the accounts or disclosure in the financial statements being audited. A sample substantive audit working paper for accounts payable is shown in Exhibit 13-6.

Substantive Audit Program for Audit of Accrued Liabilities

Essentially, all accruals (such as accrued salaries and wages, accrued payroll and property taxes, and accrued interest payable) can be analyzed as follows:

Balance in accrual account, beginning of year..........		XXXXXX
Plus:	Expense for the year......................	XXXX
Minus:	Amount paid during the year..............	(XXXXX)
Balance in accrual account, end-of-year..............		XXXXXX

Using this format, accruals and related expense accounts can be analyzed in much the same fashion that asset accounts are analyzed, as described earlier. For example, the substantive audit working papers for accrued salaries and related tax liabilities might appear as shown in Exhibit 13-7. Thus, a generalized audit program for the analysis of any accrual would include the following steps.

1. Determine that the balance in the accrual account as of the beginning of the year is proper. This can be accomplished by tracing beginning of the year amounts in accrual accounts to the prior year's working papers, if this is not the initial year that the CPA has audited this client. In the case of an initial engagement, beginning balances will have to be verified by other appropriate means;

2. Trace payments of items accrued to the cash disbursements journal;

3. By reference to underlying supporting evidence and by computation, determine that the expense portion of the analysis is proper; and

4. Trace the total expense from the analysis to the appropriate expense account in the general ledger. Also, trace the balance in the accrual account as of the end of the year to the appropriate accrued liability account in the general ledger.

As was the case with the analysis of various asset accounts, the performance of step 1 previously is easy if prior year working papers are available. Also, in the case of a first-year engagement, however, the auditor may rely on the working papers of a predecessor auditor if one exists. If not, the auditor must gather evidence from the prior-year records of the company to determine the appropriateness of the begin-

Exhibit 13-6
Sample Substantive Audit Working Paper
for Accounts Payable

Date: 2-15-84

Preparer: J.J.

Reviewer: P.J.

Bowler Lumber Company
Listing of Accounts Payable
12/31/83

X

Vendor	Amount
Johnson Electric Company............................	$ 800.00
Gibson Lumber Company.............................	1,000.00
Vepco...	432.00
C&P Telephone......................................	318.00
Balance per general ledger............................	2,550.00
Adjusting entry #4 to accrue audit fee per Coopers and Lybrand WIP report dated 1/15/84................	1,000.00
	$3,550.00
	T/B, ✓

X Examined all cash disbursements and related invoices between 1/1/84 and 2/15/84 to verify that payables which should have been included on the list are in fact included and that bills which apply to 1984 are excluded from the list. No exceptions noted.

T/B Agrees with trial balance and financial statements.

✓ Footed.

Working Paper #19

Prepared by: _J.V._

Date: _1-14-85_

Reviewed by: _P.T._

Date: _1-18-85_

Bowler Lumber Co.
Accrued Salaries and Related Tax Liabilities
12/31/84

	Accrued Salaries	FICA Withheld	Federal Tax Withheld	State Tax Withheld	FICA Payable
Balances 12/31/83	$ 20,000 ✓	$1,400 ✓	$ 2,800 ✓	$2,000 ✓	$1,400 ✓
Expense for 1984	100,000 T,T/B	7,000 T	15,000 T	5,000 T	7,000 T,T/B
Payments during 1984	(95,000) C	(8,000) C	(16,000) C	(6,000) C	(8,000) C
Ending balance	$ 25,000	$ 400	$ 1,800	$1,000	$ 400
	ⱴ	ⱴ	ⱴ	ⱴ	ⱴ
	T/B	T/B	T/B	T/B	T/B

✓   Agrees with 1983 working paper #23.

T   Traced to adding machine tapes from monthly payroll journals. See working paper #46 for tapes.

C   Prepared adding machine tapes of checks used to pay payroll and taxes. Amounts agree with amounts paid. See working paper #46 for tapes. Also, reviewed payroll tax returns and determined that payments were properly computed.

ⱴ   Footed.

T/B   Agrees with trial balance, general ledger and financial statements.

ning balance in each accrual account. This latter procedure, of course, will increase the cost to the client of a first-year audit.

With respect to the performance of step 3 above, the supporting evidence available for verification of payroll expense, payroll tax expense, and other personal and real property tax expense is used to reconcile the recorded expense to the related tax returns for the taxes in question. For example, total salaries and wages *paid* for each quarter of the year should be summarized by employee on the individual earnings records maintained by the payroll department. The amount of earnings for the quarter, from these records, should not only be reconciled to the recorded amount of salaries and wages *expense* in the general ledger, but they should also be reconciled to the total amount of taxable wages reported to the Internal Revenue Service on the quarterly payroll withholding return (Form 941). Similarly, property and sales tax amounts, as well as recorded employer payroll tax expense, should be reconciled to appropriate returns filed with the various taxing authorities.

Analysis of the estimated liability for federal and state income taxes, the provision for income taxes, and the deferred tax accounts requires three steps that may be summarized as follows.

5. Review, for the past five years, federal and state income tax returns as filed. Inquire of the client regarding the status of any examinations of prior year tax returns by the taxing authorities and, if any such examinations have occurred, obtain copies of the revenue agent's reports which summarize any adjustments to prior years' tax liabilities;

6. Review the current year's federal and state income tax returns particularly with respect to differences between book income and taxable income. Prepare an analysis which identifies each difference as either a permanent or a timing difference; and

7. Using the information gathered in steps 5 and 6, prepare a cumulative analysis of the income tax provision, the income tax liability, and the details of the elements of deferred tax debits and credits for the preceding five years, as well as the current year. Trace the amounts computed for the current year's tax provision, the current year's tax liability, and the current year's balances in the deferred tax accounts to the appropriate general ledger balances.

An example of a working paper which might be used in auditing these income tax accounts is shown in Exhibit 13-8. Each year the auditor

Exhibit 13-8
Example of Substantive Audit Working Paper
for Income Tax Expense and Income Taxes Payable

Prepared by: J.J.
Date: 1-15-85
Reviewed by: P.T.
Date: 1-15-85

Bowler Lumber Co.
Income Tax Expense and Income Taxes Payable
12/31/84

	1984	✓ 1983	✓ 1982	✓ 1981	✓ 1980	✓ 1979
Accounting earnings	$500,000 T/B	$400,000	$500,000	$400,000	$300,000	$200,000
Add (subtract) permanent differences and timing differences:	None ①	None	None	None	None	None
Taxable income	$500,000	$400,000	$500,000	$400,000	$300,000	$200,000
Tax rate	.5	.5	.5	.5	.5	.5
Tax expense	$250,000 C	$200,000	$250,000	$200,000	$150,000	$100,000
Taxes payable beginning of year	Ⓐ $ 50,000	$ 25,000	$ 25,000	$ 25,000	$ 25,000	$ 25,000
Payments	(100,000) ②	(175,000)	(250,000)	(200,000)	(150,000)	(100,000)
Expense from above	250,000	200,000	250,000	200,000	150,000	100,000
Taxes payable end-of-year	$200,000 ✓ T/B	$ 50,000 Ⓐ	$ 25,000	$ 25,000	$ 25,000	$ 25,000

✓ All amounts for years prior to 1984 agree with 12/31/83 working paper #56. All returns prior to 1983 have been examined by the IRS. Examined agents report and noted that no adjustments to the client's tax were proposed.

T/B Agrees with trial balance, general ledger and financial statements.

C Verified computation.

① Based on my review of all of the working papers for client no timing or permanent differences were noted.

Ⓐ Beginning and ending balances agree.

② Examined checks for payment of estimated tax. Verified that no underpayment penalty applies for 1984.

✓ Footed.

adds the current year's data to the cumulative schedule and deletes the oldest year's data, i.e., the sixth previous year's data, from the schedule. A tax rate of 50 percent is assumed in the exhibit.

Substantive Audit Program for the Audit of Notes and Bond Payable

Unlike trade accounts payable, confirmation of notes and bonds payable is the usual procedure where material liabilities evidenced by note or bonds exist. The primary reason for this is that it is desirable to confirm not only that the liability exists as of the balance sheet date, but also that other aspects of such liabilities exist and are properly disclosed in the financial statements. Other aspects of the debt that should be confirmed include the interest rate, data for proper calculation of interest accrual, collateral agreements, and other restrictive covenants. Therefore, the following audit program steps are frequently appropriate for the audit of notes and/or bonds payable as of year-end.

1. Have the client prepare (or prepare) an analysis of notes payable for the year. For each note, the analysis should reflect:

    a. Balance, beginning of the year

    b. Notes issued during the year

    c. Payments (principal) during the year

    d. Balance, end-of-year

    e. Accrued interest payable, beginning of the year

    f. Interest paid during the year

    g. Interest expense

    h. Accrued interest payable, end-of-year

    For each note, the analysis should reflect the payee of the note, the date of the note, the interest rate, provisions regarding when interest is to be paid, and the details of any security or collateral arrangements, such as pledging of company assets or personal guarantees of officers or employees. Further, the analysis should segregate notes which should properly be classified as current liabilities in the balance sheet from those notes that should properly be classified as long-term.

As with the case with other such analyses, the analysis of notes payable should mechanically foot and crossfoot as follows:

Column A + Column B − Column C = Column D, and

Column E + Column G − Column F = Column H.

2. Foot and crossfoot the analysis and trace the column totals to the appropriate balances in the general ledger, as follows:

Total of Column D (both current and non-current portions) to appropriately classified note payable account,

Total of Column H to accrued interest payable, and

Total of Column G to interest expense account; and

3. Arrange for confirmation of all material note payable details as of year-end.

With respect to this last procedure, remember that confirmation of notes due to banks will already be arranged by requesting the standard bank confirmation form, in connection with the audit of cash (see Chapter 12). Confirmation request letters to other creditors will have to be prepared by the client sometime in advance of year-end. Of course, these letters will not be mailed, however, until the year-end, since the auditor is concerned with year-end data being confirmed.

4. With respect to new notes issued during the year, trace the proceeds of the notes to the cash receipts records. With respect to notes paid during the year, trace the payment to cash disbursements records. Also trace interest paid during the year to cash disbursements records; and

5. Check the computation of interest expense and accrued interest payable at year-end for each note.

With respect to the analysis of bonds payable, audit procedures similar to those outlined above for notes payable should be undertaken. One difference between bond payable and note payable procedures, however, is that if the bond issue uses the services of an independent registrar and transfer agent, the confirmation can be requested from this agent to cover the entire bond issue, eliminating the need to send confirmation requests to each bondholder. The registrar and transfer agents are usually banks. The registrar maintains independent records of the client's securities which have been registered for possible sale to the public and records of the securities which have been sold. The transfer agent maintains independent records of the individuals who own the securities and disburses dividends or interests.

In addition, bonds payable require two additional audit procedures, as follows.

6. Obtain a copy of the bond indenture from the permanent file and review the indenture to determine that (a) all disclosures that are required to be made in the financial statements are in fact made, and (b) none of the restrictive covenants required by the bond indenture have been violated.

A bond indenture agreement is a document which sets forth the rights and obligations of the issuing company and the bondholders. The bond indenture agreement contains basic information, such as the number of bonds authorized, the due dates of the bonds, and the interest rate on the bonds, which of course must be disclosed. Also, the bond indenture agreement may contain certain restrictions which the company is bound by and which must be disclosed. For example, the bond indenture agreement may contain a clause which prohibits the company from paying dividends to stockholders unless retained earnings are maintained at a certain level. Finally, the bond indenture agreement usually contains certain covenants which the company must keep or else be penalized. For example, if the bonds are secured by property, the company may agree that, unless the property is maintained and the taxes are paid on the property, the bonds payable are due and payable immediately. Of course, when this covenant is present, the auditor has to carefully review the covenant and the company's compliance to ensure that the bonds are in fact long-term debt.

7. Review the computation of bond premium or discount and amortization thereof (in connection with the computation of interest expense).

Finally, in connection with the verification of all liabilities as of year-end, the following general audit step is appropriate.

8. Obtain, by inclusion in the client's representation letter (to be signed by the client as of the date of the completion of the field work), a representation from the client that all liabilities of the company have been included in the financial statements and that all disclosures that the client believes necessary to make the statements in accordance with generally accepted accounting principles have been made in the statements.

A sample substantive audit working paper for notes payable is shown in Exhibit 13-9. Also, a sample substantive audit working paper for bonds payable is shown in Exhibit 13-10.

Substantive Audit Program for the Audit of Shareholder's Equity Accounts

With respect to the audit of the shareholders' equity accounts of a corporate client, it is appropriate to

1. Review the corporate charter (or other document issued by the state in which the corporation is domiciled) to determine that the corporation is authorized to do business and that shares of all classes of stock outstanding have been authorized as required by the corporate charter; and

2. For all classes of stock outstanding, review the capital stock records, determining that the number of shares, par values, etc., that are reflected as outstanding agree with the capital stock records.

Note that if the company is large enough to use the services of an external registrar and/or transfer agent for its stock, confirmation with the registrar/transfer agent is acceptable in lieu of actual examination of the capital stock records by the auditor.

3. If any outstanding stock has been reacquired during the year, examine supporting documentation for the entry recording the reacquisition and trace the authorization for the transaction to the minutes of the board of directors. If capital stock has been reacquired and not cancelled, determine that the transaction and the resulting treasury stock is properly accounted for in accordance with generally accepted accounting principles. If reacquired shares have been cancelled, examine the cancelled certificates;

4. For any new issues of securities during the year, determine that

   a. The issue is authorized in accordance with the client's corporate charter,

   b. The issue is authorized by appropriate action of the board of directors, and

   c. The issue is properly accounted for on the books of the company; and

5. Review the list of material security transactions during the year, noting transactions involving purchases and sales of client securities by officers and/or directors.

Exhibit 13-9
Sample Substantive Audit Working Paper
for Notes Payable

Prepared by: J.J.
Date: 1-14-85
Reviewed by: P.T.
Date: 1-16-85

Bowler Lumber Co.
Notes Payable
12/31/84

①	Balance 12/31/83	Notes		Balance 12/31/84	Balance 12/31/83	Accrued Interest		Balance 12/31/84
		Issues	Payments			Expense 1984	Payments in 1984	
12%, $10,000 note to Tibson Lumber Co. Issued 1/15/81 and due 1/15/86. Interest payable annually on 1/15.	$10,000 ✓			$10,000 T/B	$1,150 ✓	$1,200 T/B C	$1,200 T C	$1,150 T/B C

① Confirmed. All details agree with confirmation on working paper #92.

✓ Agrees with 1983 working paper #82.

T/B Agrees with trial balance, general ledger and financial statements.

T Traced to cash disbursements journal.

C Verified computation.

<hr>

Exhibit 13-10
Sample Substantive Audit Working Paper
for Bonds Payable

Prepared by: J.J.
Date: 1-14-85
Reviewed by: P.T.
Date: 1-16-85

Bowler Lumber Co.
Bonds Payable
12/31/84

① **Bonds**

12%, $1,000,000, 20-year bonds issued for 900,000
on 1/1/80. Interest due annually on 1/1

Face amount	$1,000,000
Original discount	$ 100,000
Amortization through 1984 (5 × 5,000)	25,000 ✓
Unamortized discount 12/31/84	$ 75,000
	✓✓, T/B

Interest Payable

Interest payable 12/31/83	$ 120,000 A
Payments in 1984	(120,000) T
Accrual in 1984 $1,000,000 × .12	120,000 ✓
Balance accrued 12/31/84	$ 120,000
	✓✓, T/B

Interest Expense

Accrual for 1984 from above	$ 120,000
Discount amortization	5,000 ✓
1984 expense	$ 125,000 T/B
	✓✓

① All details (interest rate and payment dates, face, time period, and
original discounts) confirmed with trustee, registrar, and transfer
agent. See working paper #56.

✓ Verified computation.

✓✓ Footed.

T/B Agrees with trial balance, general ledger, and financial statements.

A Traced to 1983 working paper #15.

T Traced to cash disbursements journal.

Events of Default

Examined indenture agreement. The only event of default occurs if
the company does not make interest payments on a timely basis.
Current and prior year's working paper indicate that all interest
payments have been made on a timely basis. Also, confirmed this
fact with the trustee. See confirmation on working paper #56.

This last step is particularly important in the audit of a publicly-traded company, subject to the Securities Exchange Act of 1934, which requires disclosure of such transactions in annual filings with the Securities and Exchange Commission.

6. Review the final draft of the client's financial statements to determine that all information, particularly with respect to the terms of any senior securities that may be outstanding, is properly disclosed in the financial statement.

Finally, with respect to the retained earnings account, the following audit program steps are appropriate.

7. Analyze the retained earnings account for the year. Obtain evidence to support the propriety of any entries to the account (for example, debits to retained earnings to record a stock dividend should be approved by the board of directors); and

8. With respect to dividends declared and/or paid during the year, trace the authorization for such dividends to minutes of the board of directors and trace payment of the dividends to the cash disbursements records.

One final note with respect to the audit of the stockholders' equity section of the balance sheet is in order. The foregoing audit program has been presented for a corporate audit client — obviously, these steps would be inappropriate for the audit of a partnership or proprietorship. In such a case, the audit program should be modified to include appropriate procedures, such as to review the partnership agreement, determine that the capital account balance of each of the partners has been calculated in accordance with that agreement, and that the distribution of income to the various partners has been reflected on the books in accordance with the partnership agreement.

Substantive Audit of the Revenue and Expense Accounts

Normally, very few explicit tests of balances in the revenue and expense accounts are conducted at the end of an audit engagement. Instead, the auditor will have made compliance tests of the various segments of the information processing system (cash receipts, cash disbursements, sales, purchases, etc.) and will have also gathered substantive evidence to support the propriety of revenue and expense information during the period. Also, the auditor will have performed analytic reviews of revenue and expense accounts and substantiated the balances in a number of these accounts as a by-product of the substantive audit work for the related asset and liability accounts. For example, as indicated earlier in this chapter and other chapters, the auditor typically substantiates the balances in each of the following revenue and expense accounts when he or she substantiates the balance in the related asset and liability accounts: interest expense and interest revenue, salaries expense, depreciation expense, insurance expense, tax expense, repairs and maintenance expense, and bad debts expense. Therefore, formal tests of the balances in the revenue and expense accounts are frequently not necessary at year-end.

There are perhaps two exceptions to this general rule. First, it is usually customary to analyze any miscellaneous expense or miscellaneous revenue because by definition classification problems are likely to occur with these accounts. Second, an analysis of the legal and audit expense account should reveal the names of legal firms with which the client has done business. This information may be useful in uncovering contingent liabilities that may exist. In addition, it furnishes the auditor with a list of legal firms from which an attorney's letter, as discussed in Chapter 14, should be requested at the conclusion of the field work.

SUMMARY

This chapter discussed the procedures involved in the audit of the financing and investing cycle. The activities of the financing and investing cycle are those involving the generation of resources, other than through operations, either from debt or equity sources, to provide funds for the conduct of business and those activities of a nonoperating nature involving the investment of resources not currently employed in the operation of the business. The accounts primarily affected by the activities of the financing cycle include all liability and equity accounts and those asset accounts that are not directly related to the operating cycle of the business (marketable securities; long-term investments; property, plant, and equipment; and other assets). One characteristic of transactions in the financing cycle is that such transactions are sometimes large and infrequent transactions. This chapter focused on audit objectives and procedures related to the handling of general journal entries. Audit programs were presented for marketable securities and long-term investments; prepaid expenses; property, plant, and equipment and related accumulated depreciation and amortization; other assets; accounts (vouchers) payable; accrued liabilities; notes and bonds payable; and shareholders' equity accounts.

REVIEW QUESTIONS

13-1   Identify the two sources from which resources are generated in the financing cycle of a business.

13-2   What type of authorization does a general journal entry normally require?

13-3   Why should each general journal entry be properly documented? Describe a common type of documentation for general journal entries.

13-4   Explain the purpose and significance of the auditor's review of all meetings of the stockholders, board of directors, and other committees.

13-5   Discuss the nature of the initial four audit steps in auditing the financial cycle of a client.

13-6   Describe the process of scanning the general ledger for postings from the general journal. Explain why an auditor carries out this procedure.

13-7   What are the two basic activities in auditing investments in securities?

13-8   What is the objective of tracing the total for short-term investments in marketable securities from the analysis worksheet to the general ledger account balance?

13-9   Discuss how the analyses of accrued interest receivable and accrued dividends receivable may be coordinated with the analyses of investment securities.

13-10   What is the purpose of tracing sales of investment securities to the cash receipts journal and purchases of investment securities to the cash disbursements journal?

13-11   Discuss why an auditor must ascertain the market value of investment securities as of the client's year-end.

13-12   When auditing prepaid expenses, under what circumstances should the auditor examine documentary evidence that a disbursement took place for that particular expense?

13-13   In auditing fixed assets the auditor will examine additions to fixed assets differently from beginning-of-the-year totals. Explain how and why the auditor treats these two items differently.

13-14   Why does the auditor have to ascertain and understand the client's policy regarding capitalization of property items?

13-15   Explain why the auditor analyzes the client's repairs and maintenance expense account.

13-16   The auditor must determine that the client uses and applies generally accepted accounting principles on a consistent basis. Discuss the relationship of this statement with the examination of depreciation expense and accumulated depreciation.

13-17   How does a weak system of internal accounting control over cash receipts affect the audit of fixed asset disposals?

13-18   What is the objective of examining legal documents and cash disbursements associated with patents and copyrights?

13-19   Does confirmation of accounts payable provide assurance as to understatement or overstatement of this liability account? Explain.

13-20   If the client does not maintain a formal vouchers payable system, describe year-end procedures that should be carried out to assure the auditor that accounts payable are not overstated.

13-21   Describe procedures that are carried out by the auditor on subsequent period's cash disbursements in searching for unrecorded liabilities as of the client's balance sheet date.

13-22   Describe the basic procedures for auditing accrued liabilities.

13-23   Explain the role that Form 941 (quarterly payroll withholding report sent to the Internal Revenue Service) plays in auditing accrued payroll and accrued payroll taxes.

13-24   Explain why the CPA should review the client's federal and state income tax returns in an audit engagement.

13-25   Why does the auditor prepare an analysis of permanent and timing differences between book and taxable incomes?

13-26   Discuss the primary reason for confirming notes and bonds payable.

13-27   Explain why the auditor reviews the corporate charter when auditing the financial statements of a corporation.

13-28   What type of authorization should the auditor expect to find when a corporation has reacquired its own stock?

13-29   Explain the types of evidence the auditor should examine when a corporation issues stock during the year under audit.

13-30   With respect to dividends declared and/or paid during the year under audit, explain how the auditor determines proper authorization and recording of the dividend.

13-31   What is the purpose of reviewing the partnership agreement when partnership financial statements are being audited?

13-32   Why is it important that the auditor analyze the legal and audit expense account?

DISCUSSION QUESTIONS AND PROBLEMS

13-33   In connection with his examination of the financial statements of Belasco Chemicals, Inc., Kenneth Mack, CPA, is considering the necessity of inspecting marketable securities on the balance-sheet date, May 31, 1973, or at some other date. The marketable securities held by Belasco include negotiable bearer bonds, which are kept in a safe in the treasurer's office, and miscellaneous stocks and bonds kept in a safe deposit box at The Merchants Bank. Both the negotiable bearer bonds and the miscellaneous stocks and bonds are material to proper presentation of Belasco's financial position.

Required:

a.   What are the factors that Mr. Mack should consider in determining the necessity for inspecting these securities on May 31, 1973, as opposed to other dates?

b.   Assume that Mr. Mack plans to send a member of his staff to Belasco's offices and The Merchants Bank on May 31, 1973, to make the security inspection. What instructions should he give to this staff member as to the conduct of the inspection and the evidence to be included in the audit working papers? (Note: Do not discuss the valuation of securities; the income from securities; or the examination of information contained in the books and records of the company.)

c. Assume that Mr. Mack finds it impracticable to send a member of his staff to Belasco's offices and The Merchants Bank on May 31, 1973. What alternative procedures may he employ to assure himself that the company had physical possession of its marketable securities on May 31, 1973, if the securities are inspected (1) May 28, 1973? (2) June 5, 1973?

(AICPA adapted)

13-34   As a result of highly profitable operations over a number of years, Eastern Manufacturing Corporation accumulated a substantial investment portfolio. In his examination of the financial statements for the year ended December 31, 19x0, the following information came to the attention of the Corporation's CPA:

1. The manufacturing operations of the corporation resulted in an operating loss for the year.
2. In 19x0, the corporation placed the securities making up the investment portfolio with a financial institution which will serve as custodian of the securities. Formerly, the securities were kept in the corporation's safe deposit box in the local bank.
3. On December 22, 19x0, the corporation sold and then repurchased on the same day a number of securities that had appreciated greatly in value. Management stated that the purpose of the sale and repurchases was to establish a higher cost and book value for the securities and to avoid the reporting of a loss for the year.

Required:

a. List the objectives of the CPA's examination of the investment account.
b. Under what conditions would the CPA accept a confirmation of the securities on hand from the custodian in lieu of inspecting and counting the securities himself?
c. What disclosure, if any, of the sale and repurchase of the securities would the CPA recommend for the financial statements?

(AICPA adapted)

13-35 In connection with a recurring examination of the financial statements of the Louis Manufacturing Company for the year ended December 31, you have been assigned the audit of the Manufacturing Equipment, Manufacturing Equipment—Accumulated Depreciation, and Repairs to Manufacturing Equipment accounts. Your review of Louis's policies and procedures has disclosed the following pertinent information:

1. The Manufacturing Equipment account includes the net invoice price plus related freight and installation costs for all of the equipment in Louis's manufacturing plant.
2. The Manufacturing Equipment and Accumulated Depreciation accounts are supported by a subsidiary ledger which shows the cost and accumulated depreciation for each piece of equipment.
3. An annual budget for capital expenditures of $1,000 or more is prepared by the budget committee and approved by the board of directors. Capital expenditures over $1,000 which are not included in this budget must be approved by the board of directors and variations of 20 percent or more must be explained to the board. Approval by the supervisor of production is required for capital expenditures under $1,000.
4. Company employees handle installation, removal, repair, and rebuilding of the machinery. Work orders are prepared for these activities and are subject to the same budgetary control as other expenditures. Work orders are not required for external expenditures.

Required:

a. List the major audit objectives that should be considered when examining the accounts for Manufacturing Equipment, Accumulated Depreciation—Manufacturing Equipment, and Repairs of Manufacturing Equipment.
b. Prepare an audit program applicable for current-year additions to the Manufacturing Equipment account.

13-36 In connection with the annual examination of Ramar Corporation, you have been assigned to audit the fixed assets. The company maintains a detailed property ledger for all fixed assets. You prepared an audit program for the balances of property, plant, and equipment but have yet to prepare one for accumulated depreciation and depreciation expense.

Required:

Prepare a separate comprehensive audit program for the accumulated depreciation and depreciation expense accounts.

(AICPA adapted)

13-37   Rivers, CPA, is the auditor for a manufacturing company with a balance sheet that includes the caption "Property, Plant and Equipment." Rivers has been asked by the company's management if audit adjustments or reclassifications are required for the following material items that have been included or excluded from "Property, Plant and Equipment."

1.   A tract of land was acquired during the year. The land is the future site of the client's new headquarters which will be constructed in the following year. Commissions were paid to the real estate agent used to acquire the land, and expenditures were made to relocate the previous owner's equipment. These commissions and expenditures were expensed and are excluded from "Property, Plant and Equipment."

2.   Clearing costs were incurred to make the land ready for construction. These costs were included in "Property, Plant and Equipment."

3.   During the land clearing process, timber and gravel were recovered and sold. The proceeds from the sale were recorded as other income and are excluded from "Property, Plant and Equipment."

4.   A group of machines was purchased under a royalty agreement which provides royalty payments based on units of production from the machines. The cost of the machines, freight costs, unloading charges, and royalty payments were capitalized and are included in "Property, Plant and Equipment."

Required:

a.   Describe the general characteristics of assets, such as land, buildings, improvements, machinery, equipment, fixtures, etc., that should normally be classified as "Property, Plant and Equipment," and identify audit objectives (i.e., how an auditor can obtain audit satisfaction) in connection with the examination of "Property, Plant and Equipment." Do not discuss specific audit procedures.

b.   Indicate whether each of the above items numbered 1 to 4 requires one or more audit adjustments or reclassifications, and explain why such adjustments or reclassifications are required or not required.

Organize your answer as follows:

Item Number	Is Audit Adjustment or Reclassification Required? Yes or No	Reasons Why Audit Adjustment or Reclassification is Required or Not Required

(AICPA adapted)

13-38   A properly designed audit program enables the auditor to determine conditions or establish relationships in more than one way.

Required:

Cite various procedures that an auditor could employ to detect unrecorded retirements of property, plant, and equipment.

13-39   You are engaged in the examination of the financial statements of the Ute Corporation for the year ended December 31, 19x8. The following schedules for the property, plant, and equipment and related allowance for depreciation accounts have been prepared by the client. You have checked your prior year's audit working papers.

Ute Corporation
Analysis of Property, Plant and Equipment and Related
Allowance for Depreciation Accounts
Year Ended December 31, 19x8

Assets

Description	Final 12/31/x7	Additions	Retirements	Per Books 12/31/x8
Land	$ 22,500	$ 5,000		$ 27,500
Buildings	120,000	17,500		137,500
Machinery and Equipment	385,000	40,400	$26,000	399,400
	$527,500	$62,900	$26,000	$564,400

Allowance for Depreciation

Description	Final 12/31/x7	Additions*	Retirements	Per Books 12/31/x8
Buildings	$ 60,000	$ 5,150		$ 65,150
Machinery and Equipment	173,250	39,220		212,470
	$233,250	$44,370		$277,620

*Depreciation expense for the year.

Your examination reveals the following information:

1. All equipment is depreciated on the straight line basis (no salvage value taken into consideration) based on the following estimated lives: buildings, 25 years; all other items, 10 years. The company's policy is to take one-half year's depreciation on all asset acquisitions and disposals during the year.

2. On April 1, the company entered into a ten-year lease contract for a die casting machine with annual rentals of $5,000 payable in advance every April 1. The lease is cancellable by either party (sixty days' written notice is required) and there is no option to renew the lease or buy the equipment at the end of the lease. The estimated useful life of the machine is ten years with no salvage value. The company recorded the die casting machine in the machinery and equipment account at $40,400, the present discounted value at the date of the lease, and $2,020, applicable to the machine has been included in depreciation expense for the year.

3. The company completed the construction of a wing on the plant building on June 30. The useful life of the building was not extended by this addition. The lowest construction bid received was $17,500, the amount recorded in the Buildings account. Company personnel were used to construct the addition at a cost of $16,000 (materials, $7,500; labor, $5,500; and overhead, $3,000).

4. On August 18, $5,000 was paid for paving and fencing a portion of land owned by the company and used as a parking lot for employees. The expenditure was charged to the Land account.

5. The amount shown in the machinery and equipment asset retirement column represents cash received on September 5 upon disposal of a machine purchased in July 19x6 for $48,000. The bookkeeper recorded depreciation expense of $3,500 on this machine in 19x8.

6. Crux City donated land and building appraised at $10,000 and $40,000, respectively, to the Ute Corporation for a plant. On September 1, the company began operating the plant. Since no costs were involved, the bookkeeper made no entry for the above transaction.

Required:

Prepare the formal adjusting journal entries with supporting computations that you would suggest at December 31, 19x8 to adjust the accounts for the above transactions. Disregard income tax implications. The books have not been closed. Computations should be rounded-off to the nearest dollar.

(AICPA adapted)

13-40   Mincin, CPA, is the auditor of the Raleigh Corporation. Mincin is considering the audit work to be performed in the accounts payable area for the current year's engagement.

The prior year's working papers show that confirmation requests were mailed to 100 of Raleigh's 1,000 suppliers. The selected suppliers were based on Mincin's sample that was designed to select accounts with large dollar balances. A substantial number of hours were spent by Raleigh and Mincin resolving relatively minor differences between the confirmation replies and Raleigh's accounting records. Alternate audit procedures were used for those suppliers who did not respond to the confirmation requests.

Required:

a.   Identify the accounts payable audit objectives that Mincin must consider in determining the audit procedures to be followed.

b.   Identify situations when Mincin should use accounts payable confirmations and discuss whether Mincin is required to use them.

c.   Discuss why the use of large dollar balances as the basis for selecting accounts payable for confirmation might not be the most efficient approach and indicate what more efficient procedures could be followed when selecting accounts payable for confirmation.

(AICPA adapted)

13-41   You were in the final stages of your examination of the financial statements of Ozine Corporation for the year ended December 31, 19x0, when you were consulted by the corporation's president who believes there is no point to your examining the 19x1 voucher register and testing data in support of 19x1 entries. He stated that (a) bills pertaining to 19x0 which were received too late to be included in the December voucher register were recorded as of the year-end by the corporation by journal entry, (b) the internal auditor made tests after the year-end, and (c) he would furnish you with a letter certifying that there were no unrecorded liabilities.

Required:

a.   Should a CPA's test for unrecorded liabilities be affected by the fact that the client made a journal entry to record 19x0 bills which were received late? Explain.

b.   Should a CPA's test for unrecorded liabilities be affected by the fact that a letter is obtained in which a responsible management official certifies that to the best of his knowledge all liabilities have been recorded? Explain.

c.   Should a CPA's test for unrecorded liabilities be eliminated or reduced because of the internal audit tests? Explain.

d.   Assume that the Corporation, which handled some government contracts, had no internal auditor but that an auditor for a federal agency spent three weeks auditing the records and was just completing his work at this time. How would the CPA's unrecorded liability test be affected by the work of the auditor for a federal agency?

e.   What sources in addition to the 19x1 voucher register should the CPA consider to locate possible unrecorded liabilities?

(AICPA adapted)

13-42   As part of his examination of the financial statements of the Marlborough Corporation for the year ended March 31, 19x1, Marion Romito, CPA, is reviewing the balance-sheet presentation of a $1.2 million advance to Franklin Olds, Marlborough's president. The advance, which represents 50 percent of current assets and 10 percent of total assets, was made during the year ended March 31, 19x1. It has been described in the balance sheet as "miscellaneous accounts receivable" and classified as a current asset.

Olds informs the CPA that he has used the proceeds of the advance to purchase 35,000 shares of Marlborough's common stock, in order to forestall a take-over raid on the company. He is reluctant to have his association with the advance described in the financial statements because he does not have voting control and fears that this will "just give the raiders ammunition."

Olds offers the following four-point program as an alternative to further disclosure:

1. Have the advance approved by the board of directors. (This can be done expeditiously because a majority of the board members are officers of the company.)
2. Prepare a demand note payable to the company with interest of 7.5 percent (the average bank rate paid by the company).
3. Furnish an endorsement of the stock to the company as collateral for the loan. (During the year under audit, despite the fact that earnings did not increase, the market price of Marlborough common rose from $20 to $40 per share. The stock has maintained its $40 per share market price subsequent to year-end.)
4. Obtain a written opinion from the company attorney supporting the legality of the company's advance and the use of the proceeds.

Required:

a. Discuss the proper balance-sheet classification of the advance to Olds' and other appropriate disclosures in the financial statements and footnotes.
b. Discuss each point of Olds' four-point program as to whether or not it is desirable and as to whether or not it is an alternative to further disclosure.
c. If Olds refuses to permit further disclosure, what action(s) should the CPA take? Discuss.
d. In his discussion with the CPA, Olds warns that the raiders, if successful, probably will appoint new auditors. What consideration should the CPA give to this factor? Explain.

(AICPA adapted)

13-43   You were engaged to examine the financial statements of Ronlyn Corporation for the year ended June 30.

On May 1, the Corporation borrowed $500,000 from Second National Bank to finance plant expansion. The long-term note agreement provided for the annual payment of principal and interest over five years. The existing plant was pledged as security for the loan.

Due to unexpected difficulties in acquiring the building site, the plant expansion had not begun at June 30. To make use of the borrowed funds, management decided to invest in stocks and bonds, and on May 16, the $500,000 was invested in securities.

Required:

a. What are the audit objectives in the examination of long-term debt?

b. Prepare an audit program for the examination of the long-term note agreement between Ronlyn and Second National Bank.

c. How could you verify the security position of Ronlyn at June 30?

d. In your audit of investments, how would you

1. Verify the dividend or interest income recorded?
2. Determine market value?
3. Establish the authority for security purchases?

(AICPA adapted)

13-44   The following covenants are extracted from the indenture of a bond issue. The indenture provides that failure to comply with its terms in any respect automatically advances the due date of the loan to the date of noncompliance (the regular due date is twenty years hence):

1. "The debtor company shall endeavor to maintain a working capital ratio of 2 to 1 at all times, and, in any fiscal year following a failure to maintain said ratio, the company shall restrict compensation of officers to a total of $100,000. Officers for this purpose shall include Chairman of the Board of Directors, President, all vice presidents, Secretary, and Treasurer."

2. "The debtor company shall keep all property which is security for this debt insured against loss by fire to the extent of 100 percent of its actual value. Policies of insurance comprising this protection shall be filed with the trustee."

3. "The debtor company shall pay all taxes legally assessed against property which is security for this debt within the time provided by law for payment without penalty, and shall deposit receipted tax bills or equally acceptable evidence of payment of same with the trustee."

4. "A sinking fund shall be deposited with the trustee by semiannual payments of $300,000, from which the trustee shall, in his discretion, purchase bonds of this issue."

Required:

a. Indicate the audit procedures you would perform for each covenant.

b. Comment on any disclosure requirements that you believe are necessary.

(AICPA adapted)

13-45 You are a CPA engaged in an examination of the financial statements of Pate Corporation for the year ended December 31, 19x3. The financial statements and records of Pate Corporation have not been audited by a CPA in prior years.

The stockholders' equity section of Pate Corporation's balance sheet at December 31, 19x3 follows:

Stockholders' Equity:

Capital stock—10,000 shares of $10 par value authorized; 5,000 shares issued and outstanding	$ 50,000
Capital contributed in excess of par value of capital stock	32,580
Retained earnings	47,320
Total stockholders' equity	$129,900

Pate Corporation was founded in 19x0. The corporation has ten stockholders and serves as its own registrar and transfer agent. There are no capital stock subscription contracts in effect.

Required:

a. Prepare the detailed audit program for the examination of the three accounts comprising the Stockholders' Equity section of Pate Corporation's balance sheet. (Do not include in the audit program the verification of the results of the current year's operations.)

b. After every other figure on the balance sheet has been audited by the CPA, it might appear that the retained earnings figure is a balancing figure and requires no further verification. Why does the CPA verify retained earnings as he does the other figures on the balance sheet? Discuss.

(AICPA adapted)

13-46 You are engaged in doing the audit of a corporation whose records have not previously been audited by you. The corporation has both an independent transfer agent and a registrar for its capital stock. The transfer agent maintains the record of stockholders and the registrar checks that there is no overissue of stock. Signatures of both are required to validate certificates.

It has been proposed that confirmations be obtained from both the transfer agent and the registrar as to stock outstanding at balance-sheet date. If such confirmations agree with the books, no additional work is to be performed as to capital stock.

Required:

If you agree that obtaining the confirmation as suggested would be sufficient in this case, give the justification for your position. If you do not agree, state specifically all additional steps you would take and explain your reason for taking them.

(AICPA adapted)

OBJECTIVE QUESTIONS*

13-47 If the auditor discovers that the carrying amount of a client's investments is overstated because of a loss in value which is *other than a temporary* decline in market value, the auditor should insist that

A. The approximate market value of the investments be shown on the face of the balance sheet.

B. The investments be classified as long term for balance sheet purposes with full disclosure in the footnotes.

C. The loss in value be recognized in the financial statements of the client.

D. The equity section of the balance sheet separately show a charge equal to the amount of the loss.

13-48 An auditor's client has violated a minor requirement of its bond indenture which could result in the trustee requiring immediate payment of the principal amount due. The client refuses to seek a waiver from the bond trustee. Request for immediate payment is *not* considered likely. Under these circumstances the auditor must

A. Require classification of bonds payable as a current liability.

B. Contact the bond trustee directly.

C. Disclose the situation in the auditor's report.

D. Obtain an opinion from the company's attorney as to the likelihood of the trustee's enforcement of the requirement.

13-49 Which of the following *best* describes the element of relative risk which underlies the application of generally accepted auditing standards, particularly the standards of field work and reporting?

Note: All questions in this section are AICPA adapted questions.

A. Cash audit work may have to be carried out in a more conclusive manner than inventory audit work.

B. Intercompany transactions are usually subject to less detailed scrutiny than arm's-length transactions with outside parties.

C. Inventories may require more attention by the auditor on an engagement for a merchandising enterprise than on an engagement for a public utility.

D. The scope of the examination need not be expanded if errors that arouse suspicion of fraud are of relatively insignificant amounts.

13-50 The first standard of field work requires, in part, that audit work be properly planned. Proper planning as intended by the first standard of field work would occur when the auditor

A. Eliminates the possibility of counting inventory items more than once by arranging to make extensive test counts.

B. Uses negative accounts receivable confirmations instead of positive confirmations because the latter require mailing of second requests and review of subsequent cash collections.

C. Compares all cash as of a particular date to avoid performing time consuming cash cut-off procedures.

D. Physically observes the movement of securities already counted to guard against the substitution of such securities for others which are not actually on hand.

13-51 With respect to an internal control measure that will assure accountability for fixed asset retirements, management should implement a system that includes

A. Continuous analysis of miscellaneous revenue to locate any cash proceeds from sale of plant assets.

B. Periodic inquiry of plant executives by internal auditors as to whether any plant assets have been retired.

C. Continuous utilization of serially numbered retirement work orders.

D. Periodic observation of plant assets by the internal auditors.

13-52 Where no independent stock transfer agents are employed and the corporation issues its own stocks and maintains stock records, cancelled stock certificates should

A. Be defaced to prevent reissuance and attached to their corresponding stubs.

B.   Not be defaced, but segregated from other stock certificates and retained in a cancelled certificates file.

C.   Be destroyed to prevent fraudulent reissuance.

D.   Be defaced and sent to the secretary of state.

13-53   Which of the following is an internal accounting control weakness related to factory equipment?

A.   Checks issued in payment of purchases of equipment are not signed by the controller.

B.   All purchases of factory equipment are required to be made by the department in need of the equipment.

C.   Factory equipment replacements are generally made when estimated useful lives, as indicated in depreciation schedules, have expired.

D.   Proceeds from sales of fully depreciated equipment are credited to other income.

13-54   Which of the following is the most important internal control procedure over acquisitions of property, plant and equipment?

A.   Establishing a written company policy distinguishing between capital and revenue expenditures.

B.   Using a budget to forecast and control acquisitions and retirements.

C.   Analyzing monthly variances between authorized expenditures and actual costs.

D.   Requiring acquisitions to be made by user departments.

13-55   In order to avoid the misappropriation of company-owned marketable securities, which of the following is the best course of action that can be taken by the management of a company with a large portfolio of marketable securities?

A.   Require that one trustworthy and bonded employee be responsible for access to the safekeeping area, where securities are kept.

B.   Require that employees who enter and leave the safekeeping area sign and record in a log the exact reason for their access.

C.   Require that employees involved in the safekeeping function maintain a subsidiary control ledger for securities on a current basis.

D.   Require that the safekeeping function for securities be assigned to a bank that will act as a custodial agent.

13-56   To achieve effective internal accounting control over fixed-asset additions, a company should establish procedures that require

A.   Capitalization of the cost of fixed-asset additions in excess of a specific dollar amount.
B.   Performance of recurring fixed-asset maintenance work solely by maintenance department employees.
C.   Classification as investments those fixed-asset additions that are not used in the business.
D.   Authorization and approval of major fixed-asset additions.

13-57   A company has additional temporary funds to invest. The board of directors decided to purchase marketable securities and assigned the future purchase and sale decisions to a responsible financial executive. The best person(s) to make periodic reviews of the investment activity should be

A.   The investment committee of the board of directors.
B.   The treasurer.
C.   The corporate controller.
D.   The chief operating officer.

13-58   All corporate capital stock transactions should ultimately be traced to the

A.   Minutes of the board of directors.
B.   Cash receipts journal.
C.   Cash disbursements journal.
D.   Numbered stock certificates.

13-59   An auditor would be least likely to use confirmations in connection with the examination of

A.   Inventories.
B.   Long-term debt.
C.   Property, plant and equipment.
D   Stockholders' equity.

13-60   Which of the following procedures is least likely to be performed before the balance sheet date?

A.   Observation of inventory.
B.   Review of internal control over cash disbursements.
C.   Search for unrecorded liabilities.
D.   Confirmation of receivables.

13-61 Which of the following is not one of the auditor's primary objectives in an examination of marketable securities?

A. To determine whether securities are authentic.
B. To determine whether securities are the property of the client.
C. To determine whether securities actually exist.
D. To determine whether securities are properly classified on the balance sheet.

13-62 Several years ago Conway, Inc., secured a conventional real estate mortgage loan. Which of the following audit procedures would be least likely to be performed by an auditor examining the mortgage balance?

A. Examine the current year's cancelled checks.
B. Review the mortgage amortization schedule.
C. Inspect public records of lien balances.
D. Recompute mortgage interest expense.

13-63 Which of the following audit procedures would be least likely to lead the auditor to find unrecorded fixed asset disposals?

A. Examination of insurance policies.
B. Review of repairs and maintenance expense.
C. Review of property tax files.
D. Scanning of invoices for fixed asset additions.

13-64 In the audit of a medium-sized manufacturing concern, which of the following areas would be expected to require the least amount of audit time?

A. Owners' equity.
B. Revenue.
C. Assets.
D. Liabilities.

13-65 The auditor can best verify a client's bond sinking fund transactions and year-end balance by

A. Confirmation with the bond trustee.
B. Confirmation with individual holders of retired bonds.
C. Recomputation of interest expense, interest payable, and amortization of bond discount or premium.
D. Examination and count of the bonds retired during the year.

13-66   Treetop Corporation acquired a building and arranged mortgage financing during the year. Verification of the related mortgage acquisition costs would be least likely to include an examination of the related

    A.   Deed.
    B.   Cancelled checks.
    C.   Closing statement.
    D.   Interest expense.

13-67   The auditor may conclude that depreciation charges are insufficient by noting

    A.   Insured values greatly in excess of book values.
    B.   Large amounts of fully depreciated assets.
    C.   Continuous trade-ins of relatively new assets.
    D.   Excessive recurring losses on assets retired.

13-68   The auditor is least likely to learn of retirements of equipment through which of the following?

    A.   Review of purchase return and allowance account.
    B.   Review of depreciation.
    C.   Analysis of the debits to the accumulated depreciation account.
    D.   Review of insurance policy riders.

13-69   Which of the following is the best evidence of real estate ownership at the balance sheet date?

    A.   Title insurance policy.
    B.   Original deed held in the client's safe.
    C.   Paid real estate tax bills.
    D.   Closing statement.

13-70   The auditor should insist that a representative of the client be present during the physical examination of securities in order to

    A.   Lend authority to the auditor's directives.
    B.   Detect forged securities.
    C.   Coordinate the return of all securities to proper locations.
    D.   Acknowledge the receipt of securities returned.

13-71   During an examination Wicks learns that the audit client was granted a three month waiver of the repayment of principal on the installment loan with Blank Bank without an extension of the maturity date. With respect to this loan, the audit program used by Wicks would be least likely to include a verification of the

A. Interest expense for the year.
B. Balloon payment.
C. Total liability at year-end.
D. Installment loan payments.

13-72 In connection with the audit of a current issue of long-term bonds payable, the auditor should

A. Determine whether bondholders are persons other than owners, directors, or officers of the company issuing the bond.
B. Calculate the effective interest rate to see if it is substantially the same as the rates for similar issues.
C. Decide whether the bond issue was made without violating state or local law.
D. Ascertain that the client has obtained the opinion of counsel on the legality of the issue.

13-73 Which of the following is the most important consideration of an auditor when examining the stockholders' equity section of a client's balance sheet?

A. Changes in the capital stock account are verified by an independent stock transfer agent.
B. Stock dividends and/or stock splits during the year under audit were approved by the stockholders.
C. Stock dividends are capitalized at par or stated value on the dividend declaration date.
D. Entries in the capital stock account can be traced to a resolution in the minutes of the board of directors' meetings.

13-74 Which of the following best describes the independent auditor's approach to obtaining satisfaction concerning depreciation expense in the income statement?

A. Verify the mathematical accuracy of the amounts charged to income as a result of depreciation expense.
B. Determine the method for computing depreciation expense and ascertain that it is in accordance with generally accepted accounting principles.
C. Reconcile the amount of depreciation expense to those amounts credited to accumulated depreciation accounts.

D. Establish the basis for depreciable assets and verify the depreciation expense.

13-75 During the year under audit, a company has completed a private placement of a substantial amount of bonds. Which of the following is the most important step in the auditor's program for the examination of bonds payable?

A. Confirming the amount issued with the bond trustee.
B. Tracing the cash received from the issue to the accounting records.
C. Examining the bond records maintained by the transfer agent.
D. Recomputing the annual interest cost and the effective yield.

13-76 During an examination of a publicly-held company, the auditor should obtain written confirmation regarding debenture transactions from the

A. Debenture holders.
B. Client's attorney.
C. Internal auditors.
D. Trustee.

13-77 An audit program for the examination of the retained earnings account should include a step that requires verification of the

A. Market value used to charge retained earnings to account for a two-for-one stock split.
B. Approval of the adjustment to the beginning balance as a result of a write-down of an account receivable.
C. Authorization for both cash and stock dividends.
D. Gain or loss resulting from disposition of treasury shares.

13-78 Patentex developed a new secret formula which is of great value because it resulted in a virtual monopoly. Patentex has capitalized all research and development costs associated with this formula. Greene, CPA, who is examining this account, will probably

A. Confer with management regarding transfer of the amount from the balance sheet to the income statement.
B. Confirm that the secret formula is registered and on file with the county clerk's office.
C. Confer with management regarding a change in the title of the account to "goodwill."

D.   Confer with management regarding ownership of the secret formula.

13-79   The auditor's program for the examination of long-term debt should include steps that require the

A.   Verification of the existence of the bondholders.
B.   Examination of any bond trust indenture.
C.   Inspection of the accounts payable subsidiary ledger.
D.   Investigation of credits to the bond interest income account.

13-80   Which of the following explanations might satisfy an auditor who discovers significant debits to an accumulated depreciation account?

A.   Extraordinary repairs have lengthened the life of an asset.
B.   Prior years' depreciation charges were erroneously understated.
C.   A reserve for possible loss on retirement has been recorded.
D.   An asset has been recorded at its fair value.

13-81   In a manufacturing company, which of the following audit procedures would give the least assurance of the validity of the general ledger balance of investment in stocks and bonds at the audit date?

A.   Confirmation from the broker.
B.   Inspection and count of stocks and bonds.
C.   Vouching all changes during the year to brokers' advices and statements.
D.   Examination of paid checks issued in payment of securities purchased.

13-82   An auditor determines that a client has properly capitalized a leased asset (and corresponding lease liability) as representing, in substance, an installment purchase. As part of the auditor's procedures, the auditor should

A.   Substantiate the cost of the property to the lessor and determine that this is the cost recorded by the client.
B.   Evaluate the propriety of the interest rate used in discounting the future lease payments.
C.   Determine that the leased property is being amortized over the life of the lease.
D.   Evaluate whether the total amount of lease payments represents the fair market value of the property.

13-83 The audit procedures used to verify accrued liabilities differ from those employed for the verification of accounts payable because

A. Accrued liabilities usually pertain to services of a continuing nature while accounts payable are the result of completed transactions.

B. Accrued liability balances are less material than accounts payable balances.

C. Evidence supporting accrued liabilities is nonexistent while evidence supporting accounts payable is readily available.

D. Accrued liabilities at year-end will become accounts payable during the following year.

13-84 Which of the following is the most efficient audit procedure for the detection of unrecorded liabilities?

A. Compare cash disbursements in the subsequent period with the accounts payable trial balance at year-end.

B. Confirm large accounts payable balances at the balance sheet date.

C. Examine purchase orders issued for several days prior to the close of the year.

D. Obtain a "liability certificate" from the client.

13-85 Which of the following is the best audit procedure for determining the existence of unrecorded liabilities?

A. Examine confirmation requests returned by creditors whose accounts appear on a subsidiary trial balance of accounts payable.

B. Examine a sample of cash disbursements in the period subsequent to year-end.

C. Examine a sample of invoices a few days prior to and subsequent to year-end to ascertain whether they have been properly recorded.

D. Examine unusual relationships between monthly accounts payable balances and recorded purchases.

13-86 The primary reason for preparing a reconciliation between interest-bearing obligations outstanding during the year and interest expense presented in the financial statements is to

A. Evaluate internal control over securities.

B. Determine the validity of prepaid interest expense.

C.   Ascertain the reasonableness of imputed interest.

D.   Detect unrecorded liabilities.

13-87   Tennessee Company violated company policy by erroneously capitalizing the cost of painting its warehouse. The CPA examining Tennessee's financial statements would most likely learn of this error by

A.   Discussing Tennessee's capitalization policies with its controller.

B.   Reviewing the titles and descriptions for all construction work orders issued during the year.

C.   Observing, during the physical inventory observation, that the warehouse has been painted.

D.   Examining in detail a sample of contruction work orders.

13-88   Which of the following audit procedures would be least likely to lead the auditor to find unrecorded fixed asset disposals?

A.   Examination of insurance policies.

B.   Review of repairs and maintenance expense.

C.   Review of property tax files.

D.   Scanning of invoice for fixed asset additions.

13-89   When a company has treasury stock certificates on hand, a year-end count of the certificates by the auditor is

A.   Required when the company classifies treasury stock with other assets.

B.   Not required if treasury stock is a deduction from stockholders' equity.

C.   Required when the company had treasury stock transactions during the year.

D.   Always required.

13-90   If a company employs a capital stock registrar and/or transfer agent, the registrar or agent, or both, should be requested to confirm directly to the auditor the number of shares of each class of stock

A.   Surrendered and cancelled during the year.

B.   Authorized at the balance sheet date.

C.   Issued and outstanding at the balance sheet date.

D.   Authorized, issued and outstanding during the year.

13-91   In connection with the examination of bonds payable, an auditor would expect to find in a trust indenture

    A.   The issue date and maturity date of the bond.

    B.   The names of the original subscribers to the bond issue.

    C.   The yield to maturity of the bonds issued.

    D.   The company's debt to equity ratio at the time of issuance.

13-92   Many of the Granada Corporation's convertible bondholders have converted their bonds into stock during the year under examination. The independent auditor should review the Granada Corporation's statement of changes in financial position to ascertain that it shows

    A.   Only financial resources used to reduce convertible debt.

    B.   Only financial resources provided by issuance of stock.

    C.   Financial resources provided by issuance of stock.

    D.   Nothing relating to the conversion because it does not affect net working capital.

13-93   During the course of an audit, a CPA observes that the recorded interest expense seems to be excessive in relation to the balance in the long-term debt account. This observation could lead the auditor to suspect that

    A.   Long-term debt is understated.

    B.   Discount on bonds payable is overstated.

    C.   Long-term debt is overstated.

    D.   Premium on bonds payable is understated.

13-94   The auditor is concerned with establishing that dividends are paid to stockholders of the client corporation owning stock as of the

    A.   Issue date.

    B.   Declaration date.

    C.   Record date.

    D.   Payment date.

13-95   Florida Corporation declared a 100% stock dividend during 1975. In connection with the examination of Florida's financial statements, Florida's auditor should determine that

    A.   The additional shares issued do not exceed the number of authorized but previously unissued shares.

    B.   Stockholders received their additional shares by confirming year-end holdings with them.

    C.   The stock dividend was properly recorded at fair market value.

D. Florida's stockholders have authorized the issuance of 100% stock dividends.

13-96   Which of the following is a customary audit procedure for the verification of the legal ownership of real property?

A. Examination of correspondence with the corporate counsel concerning acquisition matters.

B. Examination of ownership documents registered and on file at a public hall of records.

C. Examination of corporate minutes and resolutions concerning the approval to acquire property, plant and equipment.

D. Examination of deeds and title guaranty policies on hand.

13-97   Which of the following is an internal accounting control weakness related to factory equipment?

A. A policy exists requiring all purchases of factory equipment to be made by the department in need of the equipment.

B. Checks issued in payment of purchases of equipment are not signed by the controller.

C. Factory equipment replacements are generally made when estimated useful lives, as indicated in depreciation schedules, have expired.

D. Proceeds from sales of fully depreciated equipment are credited to other income.

13-98   During its fiscal year, a company issued, at a discount, a substantial amount of first-mortgage bonds. When performing audit work in connection with the bond issue, the independent auditor should

A. Confirm the existence of the bondholders.

B. Review the minutes for authorization.

C. Trace the net cash received from the issuance to the bond payable account.

D. Inspect the records maintained by the bond trustee.

After studying this chapter, students should understand

1. The financial statements which are considered basic financial statements.
2. The nature of required disclosures, and the way in which checklists are used to identify these disclosures.
3. The nature of audit review, includikng the use of checklists in this review.
4. The two types of subsequent events, the way these events are communicated to financial statement users, and procedures for identifying subsequent events.
5. The nature and forms of lawyer's letters.
6. The nature of management representation letters.

Completing the Audit Engagement

This chapter was written by
Thomas D. Hubbard, Ph.D., C.P.A.,
Nebraska CPAs Distinguished Professor of Accountancy and Director,
University of Nebraska, Lincoln

INTRODUCTION
The audit of the revenue cycle, expense and production cycle, and the financing and investing cycle were explained in the three preceding chapters. Developing an audit objective and an audit plan and performing procedures for gathering evidence were considered. This chapter discusses the procedures required to complete the audit engagement. Such procedures include preparing the financial statements, obtaining letters of representation from the client and its legal counsel, performing a subsequent events review and reviewing working papers for achievement of audit objectives. Writing an appropriate accountant's report is discussed in Chapters 15 and 16. Issuring a management letter reporting weaknesses in internal control was discussed in Chapter 7.

BASIC FINANCIAL STATEMENTS
If a complete financial report in conformity with generally accepted accounting principles is to be issued, the following constitutes what is referred to as the "basic financial statements."[1]

- Balance sheet
- Statement of income
- Statement of retained earnings or changes in stockholders' equity
- Statement of changes in financial position

Descriptions of accounting policies, notes to the financial statements, and schedules and explanatory material that are identified as being part of the basic financial statements are also considered necessary in a complete financial report. Because the notes and schedules accompanying the basic financial statements are considered an integral part of those statements, the statements should refer to the notes and schedules. For example, it is customary to include a reference on each page of the financial statements such as "see accompanying notes." The auditor's opinion will, of course, cover the basic financial statements and the related footnotes and schedules.

Generally accepted accounting principles require information to be disclosed in financial statements if its omission would tend to make the statements misleading. Information may be presented in financial statements in three ways:

---

[1] AICPA Professional Standards, Vol. 1, *SAS No. 29, Reporting on Information Accompanying the Basic Financial Statements in Auditor-Submitted Documents*, AU 551.02.

- Disclosure on the face of a financial statement by reporting a specific account and amount.

- Disclosure of additional information on the face of a financial statement by parenthetical notation or showing information short (that is, not including amounts in the totals reflected on the statements).

- Disclosure by a footnote or supplemental schedule accompanying the financial statements.

Generally, the information should be presented in financial statements in the fashion that most effectively communicates the information to the user of the statements. For example, presenting a parenthetical notation of the method of costing and pricing inventories along with the inventory accounts and amounts on the face of the balance sheet is usually considered more effective in communicating such information than footnote presentation. To ensure that audited financial statements reflect all of the disclosures required by GAAP, the auditor will usually employ a checklist that identifies the disclosures required by promulgated accounting pronouncements and those that are required because of common business practice. A disclosure checklist will typically include numerous brief statements in the form of inquiries which are accompanied by citations of authoritative pronouncements. Consider the following partial checklist for "Disclosures and Notes" reproduced from the *AICPA Audit and Accounting Manual* (AAM 8400.03):

Financial Statement Disclosure Checklist[2]

DISCLOSURES AND NOTES	YES	NO	N/A	REMARKS
Is a summary description of the significant accounting policies presented?				
Are related party transactions adequately disclosed in the financial statements and accompanying notes?				

---

[2] *AICPA Audit and Accounting Manual*, AAM 8400.03, Commerce Clearing House, Chicago, 1982.

Financial Statement Disclosure Checklist (Continued):

DISCLOSURES AND NOTES	YES	NO	N/A	REMARKS
Are subsequent events that provide evidence with respect to conditions that did not exist at the date of the balance sheet but arose subsequent to that date adequately disclosed to keep the financial statements from being misleading?				
For marketable equity securities, except if the equity basis is appropriate, (in statements for periods ending on or after 12/31/75) is there disclosure of the following:				
• For non-marketable securities FASB No. 16, paragraph 4				
a. Aggregate cost and market value (each segregated between current and non-current classifications if applicable) as of the date of each balance sheet presented?				
b. As of the date of the latest balance sheet presented, the gross unrealized gains and gross unrealized losses (segregated between current and non-current portfolios if applicable)?				
c. For each period in which an income statement is presented:				
(i) Net realized gain or loss included in the determination of net income?				
(ii) Basis on which cost was determined in computing realized gain or loss (i.e., average cost or other method used)?				
(iii) Change in the valuation allowance?				

AUDIT REVIEW

The first standard of field work states "The work is to be adequately planned and assistants, if any, are to be properly supervised."[3] Generally accepted auditing standards thus require supervision of audit work, which includes review. The auditor with the final responsibility for the examination (partner in charge) should direct the audit staff to bring to his or her attention accounting and auditing questions raised during the examination so that their significance may be assessed. The work of each audit assistant must be reviewed to determine whether it was adequately performed and to evaluate whether the audit objectives were attained and the results are consistent with the conclusions to be presented in the audit report.[4]

Thorough review of audit work is necessary to maintain quality control within a firm of independent auditors. A CPA firm must establish policies and procedures to provide it with reasonable assurance of conforming with GAAS in its audit engagements.[5] *Statement on Quality Control Standards No. 1* requires the establishment of policies and procedures at all organizational levels within a CPA firm to provide reasonable assurance that work performed meets quality control standards.[6]

Because of the professional nature of public accounting and the reliance placed on the work of the CPA, it is imperative that work be performed in a professional manner. The audit evidence obtained must be based on sound judgments and be in compliance with professional standards in order to provide support for the audit opinion. Review is the backbone of public accounting.

REVIEW PROCEDURES

Review procedures generally involve the work of the staff accountant being reviewed by the in-charge accountant (senior accountant), the work submitted by the in-charge accountant is reviewed by the manager and the partner in charge of the engagement. Often, an additional "horizontal" review of the engagement is performed by a manager or partner not working on the engagement to provide an objective assessment of compliance with firm standards in the performance of the engagement. For large multiple office CPA firms, it is

---

[3] *SAS No. 1, Codification of Auditing Standards and Procedures*, AU 310.01.
[4] *SAS No. 22, Planning and Supervision*, AU 311.10-11.
[5] *SAS No. 25, The Relationship of GAAS to Quality Control Standards*, AU 161.02.
[6] *Quality Control Standards 1, System of Quality Control for a CPA Firm*, QC 10.07.

common practice for review teams to visit the various offices periodically and review selected engagements with the objective of improving the quality of practice of the firm-wide operations. Also CPA firms are subject to quality control reviews by their peers (CPAs from other similar size firms) to determine whether quality control is being maintained in the firm and the profession.

Review procedures, of course, vary from firm to firm. In some firms one partner may review all reports issued by the firm or office. Other firms may fix review responsibility with the particular partner in charge of the engagement or a review department. Regardless of the review procedure followed in a particular CPA firm, certain functions must be performed. There must be a careful review of the audit work and a judgment decision made regarding the sufficiency and competency of evidence within each audit area. The financial statements, including disclosures, must be prepared in a form suitable for the client, considering its particular industry characteristics, and the final report must be typed and reproduced (although larger clients may type and reproduce their own reports, the CPA's review of the typing and reproduction is essentially the same as the review which is required when the typing and reproduction is done by the CPA firm). The flowchart on the next page reflects how these functions may be performed within a particular CPA firm.

The in-charge or senior accountant, before signing off on the audit work, must make sure that all phases of the work have been concluded in accordance with the engagement plan, applicable audit procedures have been satisfactorily completed, and the audit objectives have been satisfied. The in-charge or senior must also determine that the engagement has been conducted in accordance with generally accepted auditing standards and that the working papers reflect conclusions supporting the audit opinion. Some firms write a conclusion after the completion of each section of the audit. For example, the staff accountant completing the cash audit would write a conclusion as to whether or not cash is fairly presented. Other CPA firms follow the practice of drafting on overall memorandum (called a senior memorandum) at the conclusion of the engagement commenting on the fairness of presentation of each major financial statement category.

The in-charge or senior accountant must also obtain client approval for all proposed adjusting journal entries and reclassification journal entries before leaving the field. The proposed adjusting entries are approved by the manager before being submitted to the client for accep-

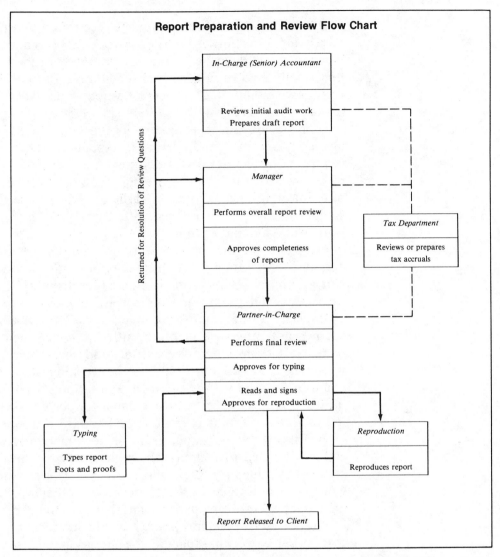

Report Preparation and Review Flow Chart

In-Charge (Senior) Accountant

Reviews initial audit work
Prepares draft report

Manager

Performs overall report review

Approves completeness
of report

Tax Department

Reviews or prepares
tax accruals

Partner-in-Charge

Performs final review

Approves for typing

Reads and signs
Approves for reproduction

Returned for Resolution of Review Questions

Typing

Types report
Foots and proofs

Reproduction

Reproduces report

Report Released to Client

tance. The in-charge or senior will also obtain the agreement of the
manager that the field work is complete before leaving the client's
premises. This will usually involve the manager and perhaps the partner
spending the last day or two of the field work at the client's offices
reviewing the working papers to determine that the audit programs are
complete and sufficient evidence has been obtained to support the opinion.

The overall report review performed by the manager, tax department
preparation of accruals, and partner review will generally be completed

at the CPA firm's office. It must be recognized that the final review is merely a completion of the review work that has already been done by the manager and partner during the final days of the field work and will not usually involve substantive procedures requiring reference to client records. Resolution of review questions raised at this point by the manager and partner will usually involve providing more extensive documentation and explanation in the working papers of the work already performed and, perhaps, explaining why certain audit procedures that were not performed were not applicable. This phase of the review will usually involve the completion of firm checklist, such as the disclosure checklist illustrated earlier, to determine that all reporting standards have been complied with in the preparation of the financial statements and audit report.

Presented on the next page is an example of a "vertical review checklist" used by a CPA firm to assure that the review of the audit work is thorough and complete and responsibility is fixed with those firm personnel performing the review. Following the vertical review checklist is a "horizontal review checklist" for use by a manager or partner not otherwise involved with the engagement. Each working paper should have identifying letters and/or numbers, generally in the upper right corner. For example, the working paper for cash-in-bank could be indexed with the following notation: CA-1. This notation indicates that it is the first working paper for current assets, and all working papers concerning current assets should be grouped together.

Identifying letters/numbers for all working papers form an indexing system designed to facilitate the review process. Indexing permits the reviewer to identify the source of information appearing on the workpaper and trace such information to other workpapers. To trace data from one working paper to another working paper, such data must be referenced by the appropriate indexing number. For instance, on the cash-in-bank working paper, the notation, $\frac{CA\text{-}1}{2}$, may be written beside a cash figure. This is called referencing because the notation refers to the index number of the working paper providing supporting documentation for that cash figure. The working paper with the notation $\frac{CA\text{-}1}{2}$ could be an AICPA Standard Bank Confirmation. Other cash figures on the cash-in-bank working paper may be referenced to petty cash counts, working trial balance, and so forth.

Each working paper should contain the name of the client and the audit period date—for example, Carter Company, Cash in Bank, December 31, 1985. The working paper also will show the initials of the

Johnson Grant & Co.
Vertical Review Questionnaire

Client _____

Closing Date _____

This questionnaire is to be completed by the person performing the comprehensive review of the working papers. If the engagement partner does not perform the review, he should inform himself about the examination and its results by reviewing the questions raised by the reviewer, by reviewing the report questionnaire, by reviewing this questionnaire, by reviewing the horizontal review questionnaire, and should bring his knowledge to bear on the problems which may exist.

The objective of a vertical review is to determine through a detailed and comprehensive review that audit procedures specified in the approved audit program were performed and documented, that all problems and exceptions noted in the course of the examination were properly resolved, that special procedures required as a result of our examination have been performed and that the financial statements and accompanying opinion conform in all respects with our conclusions.

Comments are required for all "No" answers.

	Yes	No	N/A

A. *General*

1. Have you reviewed workpaper files and do you concur with conclusions of the in-charge-accountant as documented in the Engagement Performance and Administration Review Questionnaire?

2. Have all exceptions noted on the Engagement Performance and Administration Review Questionnaire been resolved and Accountant's Report, Financial Statements and Notes Checklists been completed?

3. Are you satisfied that:
   a. The judgments and conclusions reached are supported by documented evidence?
   b. The workpaper files contain no unresolved statements which are prejudicial to the interests of the firm?
   c. Appropriate changes in the next examination, if any, have been summarized?

4. Do the workpapers include adequate documentation as to:
   a. Changes in accounting policies?
   b. Conformity with generally accepted accounting principles or another comprehensive basis of accounting, if appropriate?
   c. Conformity with generally accepted auditing standards?
   d. Adequacy of disclosure?

5. Have you reviewed the audit conclusions on all material items in the financial statements?

6. Based on your review and your knowledge of the client, do the financial statements fairly present the company's financial position, results of its operations and changes in its financial position?

7. Is the work performed consistent with the arrangements made with the client?

8. Does the work performed comply with the firm's policies in all material respects?

9. If the answer to Question No. 8 is "no," have you obtained and documented concurrence with the exceptions from the Director of Audit and Accounting?

	Yes	No	N/A

10. Are all applicable questionnaires completed and all review comments cleared with adequate documentation of disposition?

11. If computer-assisted audit techniques were used on this engagement, has the related documentation been reviewed by a qualified computer specialist (in the year of development and whenever significant modifications are made)?

12. Have required job evaluation forms been completed?

B. *Financial Statements*
1. Is the name of the company exact?
2. Are the dates of the balance sheet and period covered by statements of income, stockholders' equity and changes in financial position exact?
3. Are all material facts which are necessary to make the financial statements not misleading adequately disclosed? Have all material and/or extraordinary subsequent events been evaluated and properly treated and/or disclosed?
4. Is the nature of each financial statement caption clearly indicated by its title?
5. Is there adequate footnote disclosure? Does the footnote clearly communicate the facts?
6. Do the financial statements maintain a uniform manner of format, capitalization, headings and appearance in general within itself?
7. Are you satisfied that other information contained in the client's annual report or other document which contains our report is not materially misstated or inconsistent with the financial statements (*SAS No. 15)?*

C. *The Audit Report*
1. Is our audit report addressed to the proper party?
2. Does our opinion properly state the responsibility we wish to assume? Has an adequate examination been made to support the opinion we are rendering?
3. Is our opinion on the consistency of application of generally accepted accounting principles, or if applicable, another comprehensive basis of accounting proper?
4. Is the date of our report proper?
5. Is any date in the footnotes that requires special mention, with respect to the date of our report, appropriately reflected in the date of our report?
6. Is our opinion on the supplementary financial information proper and supported by our examination?
7. Are disclosures in the opinion, financial statements, and notes to financial statements adequate?

D. *Client Relations*
1. Have we performed the engagement in accordance with the arrangements (including any request by the client for extra services)?
2. Are you satisfied that the audit did not disclose any suspicions of irregularities or illegal acts?
3. Have arrangements been made:
   a. For the client's review and approval of the proposed adjustments?
   b. For the client to review a draft of the report?

	Yes	No	N/A
c. To communicate weaknesses in internal accounting control that we have observed?			
4. Have management advice suggestions been summarized for a management letter?			
5. Are we satisfied that no unusual client problem was noted during the audit?			

E. *Report Production*

	Yes	No	N/A
1. Are instructions as to processing specific, including the type of report, client number, number of copies required, due date, delivery instructions (when and how)?			
2. Do the report style and appearance conform appropriately with the standards we have established for all reports?			
3. Is the language of the report simple and concise?			

By (Audit Partner): _____

Date _____

Johnson Grant & Co.
Horizontal Review Questionnaire

Client _____

Closing Date _____

This questionnaire is to be completed by a partner, or designated person, not otherwise involved with the engagement. The objective of this review is to determine on an overall basis that all material items in the financial statements have been properly considered, that required disclosures have been made and that our opinion is appropriate in the circumstances.

Prior to commencing the horizontal review, a thorough and comprehensive vertical review of the entire working papers must have been completed. The report should be completed and the vertical review completed prior to the horizontal review. The scope of the horizontal review may vary somewhat from engagement to engagement.

The following questions should be used as a checklist in performing the horizontal review function. Comments are required for "No" answers.

	Yes	No	N/A
1. Have the following reviews been performed and the appropriate questionnaires completed and signed:			
a. In-Charge Engagement Performance and Administration Review?			
b. Vertical Review?			
2. Have all exceptions noted on the questionnaires discussed above been resolved?			
3. Have we obtained an appropriate engagement letter, legal representation letter and client representation letter?			
4. Have you reviewed the vertical review for completeness and unusual problems?			
5. Were an audit program, time budget and time summary prepared, approved and properly utilized?			
6. Were all problem areas adequately reviewed and conclusions properly documented?			

	Yes	No	N/A
7. Have you concurred with alternative procedures employed to satisfy ourselves when such procedures deviate from our firm's basic audit policies?			
8. Are the financial statements free from material errors of omission?			
9. Are the engagement files, to the extent reviewed, free from any evidence of material noncompliance with auditing standards or firm policies?			
10. Is our audit report appropriate?			
11. Does our audit report comply with generally accepted auditing standards?			
12. Do the report style and appearance conform appropriately with the standards we have established for all reports?			
13. Is the language of the report simple and concise?			
14. Have identified material weaknesses in internal accounting control been appropriately communicated?			
15. Have all conditions, that you are aware of, which require re-evaluation of our relationship with the client been appropriately considered?			
16. Have you reviewed the reference points raised in working paper review and noted the disposition thereof?			
17. Are you satisfied that there are no unresolved statements in the working paper files which are prejudicial? If there are any, they must be properly and adequately explained.			
18. Have you removed all queries from workpapers?			

By (Audit Partner): _____

Date _____

staff accountant performing the work and the date the working paper was completed as well as the initials of the senior who reviewed the work and the date the work was reviewed. The date the work was reviewed by the manager and the partner may be indicated on the working paper or on a review control sheet placed in the front of the working paper file. A control sheet would include information such as the following:

- Name of client and audit date
- Name of partner in charge
- Date the audit was started and completed
- Date report submitted for review
- Initials and dates of reviewers
- Date submitted for typing and reproduction
- Date released to client

The next page contains an illustrative control sheet from the *AICPA Audit and Accounting Manual*, AAM 9100.23.

Report Guide Sheet[7]
(To be bound with the — colored copy of report)

Engagement Information

Client _____   Date due _____

Assignment number _____   Assignment name _____

Account   administrator _____   Manager _____   In-charge accountant _____

☐   Compiled Financial Statements   Period _____

☐   Reviewed Financial Statements   Period _____

☐   Audited Statements   Period _____

☐   Review of Interim Financial Information   Period _____

☐   Other Unaudited Financial Statements   Period _____

☐   Special Reports —

     Description: Date _____

Delivery Instructions:

Name—attention of: _____   ☐   Mail

Address: _____   ☐   Delivery by:

_____   _____

Hold Items (describe):

	Cleared by	Date
_____	_____	_____
_____	_____	_____
_____	_____	_____
_____	_____	_____

Report Review:

	Signature	Date
In-charge	_____	_____
Acount Administrator	_____	_____
Review Department	_____	_____
Tax Department	_____	_____
Review Partner	_____	_____

Reporting Processing:

	Signature	Date
Typing Department	_____	_____
Comparing and Proofing	_____	_____
Final Reading	_____	_____

Final Release:

The report(s) described above were released by me after all hold items were cleared. All appropriate levels of review were signed off, and all processing steps completed.

_____   _____
(Signature)   (Date)

---

[7] *AICPA Audit and Accounting Manual*, AAM 9100.23.

SUBSEQUENT EVENTS

An important part of the work involved in winding up an audit is the performance of a subsequent events review. As further explained in Chapter 15, the date of the completion of the field work is the date used on the audit report. This date establishes the auditor's responsibility to perform a subsequent events review. That is, the auditor is responsible for a subsequent events review from the balance sheet date to the end of field work.

There are two types of subsequent events—those that require an adjusting journal entry because the subsequent event provides additional evidence regarding conditions that existed at the balance sheet date; and, second, events that provide evidence as to conditions that did not exist at the balance sheet date, but arose subsequent to that date. This type of subsequent event may require disclosure to make the financial statements fully informative.

All information that becomes available during the subsequent event period should be used by management and the auditor to evaluate the information presented in the financial statements. The statements may require adjustment and disclosure based on subsequent event information, or they may only require disclosure. Judgment is required to determine how events affect the statements. For example, a loss on an uncollectible trade account receivable as a result of a customer's deteriorating financial condition leading to bankruptcy subsequent to the balance-sheet date would be indicative of conditions existing at the balance-sheet date, thereby calling for an adjusting journal entry reflecting the loss.[8] A similar loss resulting from a customer's major casualty such as a fire or flood in the subsequent period would be an example of an event that may require disclosure, but would not result in adjustment of the financial statement amounts because the condition did not exist as of the balance-sheet date. Examples of events of the type that may require disclosure, but would not result in adjustment, include:

- Purchase of a business subsequent to the balance-sheet date.
- Settlement of litigation when the event giving rise to the claim took place subsequent to the balance-sheet date.
- Loss of plant or inventories as a result of fire or flood after the balance-sheet date.
- Losses on receivables resulting from conditions (such as a customer's major casualty) arising subsequent to the balance-sheet date.[9]

---

[8] *SAS No. 1, Codification of Auditing Standards and Procedures*, AU 560.04.
[9] *SAS No. 1, Codification of Auditing Standards and Procedures*, AU 560.06.

The auditor should apply certain procedures during the period following the date of the balance sheet up to the completion of the field work for the purpose of identifying subsequent events that may require adjustment or disclosure. These procedures generally include inquiry and review procedures, such as:

1. Read the latest available interim financial statements:

    a. Compare them with the financial statements being reported upon; and make any other comparisons considered appropriate in the circumstances.

    b. Inquire of officers and other executives having responsibility for financial and accounting matters as to whether the interim statements have been prepared on the same basis as that used for the statements under examination.

2. Inquire of and discuss with officers and other executives having responsibility for financial and accounting matters as to:

    a. Whether any substantial contingent liabilities or commitments existed at the date of the balance sheet being reported on or at the date of inquiry.

    b. Whether there was any significant change in the capital stock, long-term debt, or working capital to the date of inquiry.

    c. Whether there were any significant changes in estimates with respect to amounts included or disclosed in the financial statements being reported on.

    d. Whether any unusual adjustments had been made during the period from the balance-sheet date to the date of inquiry.

3. Read the available minutes of meetings of stockholders, directors, and appropriate committees; as to meetings for which minutes are not available, inquire about matters dealt with at such meetings.

4. Assemble pertinent findings resulting from response of client's legal counsel and other auditing procedures concerning litigation, claims, and assessments.

5. Obtain a letter of representation, dated as of the date of the auditor's report, from appropriate officials, generally the chief executive officer and chief financial officer.

6. Make such additional inquiries or perform such procedures deemed necessary and appropriate to dispose of questions that arise in carrying out the foregoing procedures, inquiries, and discussions.[10]

---

[10] *AICPA Audit and Accounting Manual*, AAM 5400.460.

LAWYERS' LETTERS

As stated above, a subsequent event review procedure requires the auditor to assemble pertinent findings resulting from response of client's legal counsel and other auditing procedures concerning litigation, claims, and assessments. Obtaining a lawyer's letter regarding contingent liabilities that may require reporting in the financial statements is a required subsequent events procedure (*SAS No. 12, Inquiry of a Client's Lawyer Concerning Litigation, Claims, and Assessments*, AU 337).

Contingencies and Accounting and Auditing Considerations[11]

Management is responsible for adopting policies and procedures to identify, evaluate, and account for litigation, claims, and assessments. FASB Statement No. 5, *Accounting for Contingencies*, outlines the procedures to be followed in accounting for loss contingencies, including those arising from legal considerations.[12] The auditor's responsibility is to obtain evidential matter relevant to:

- The existence of a condition, situation, or set of circumstances indicating an uncertainty as to the possible loss to an entity arising from litigation, claims, and assessments.
- The period in which the underlying cause for legal action occurred.
- The degree of probability of an unfavorable outcome.
- The amount or range of potential loss.

---

[11] The discussion of lawyers' letters is taken from *Readings and Cases in Auditing*, Hubbard, Ellison, and Strawser, Dame Publications, Inc., Houston, Texas, 1981, pp. 283-287.

[12] FASB No. 5 defines a contingency as an existing condition, situation, or set of circumstances involving uncertainty as to possible gain (a gain contingency) or loss (a loss contingency) to an enterprise that will ultimately be resolved when one or more future events occur or fail to occur. Resolution of the uncertainty may confirm the acquisition of an asset or the reduction of a liability or the loss or impairment of an asset or the incurrence of a liability. When a loss contingency exists, the likelihood that the future event or events will confirm the loss or impairment of an asset or the incurrence of a liability can range from *probable to remote*. *Probable* means the future event or events are likely to occur. *Reasonably possible* means the chance of the future event or events occurring is more than remote but less than likely. *Remote* means the chance of the future event or events occurring is slight.

FASB No. 5 requires an estimated loss from a loss contingency to be accrued by a charge to income if information available prior to issuance of the financial statements indicates that it is *probable* that an asset had been impaired or a liability had been incurred at the date of the financial statements and the amount of loss can be reasonably estimated. If accrual of a loss contingency is not made because the conditions for accrual are not met, disclosure of the contingency is required when there is at least a *reasonable possibility* that a loss may have been incurred. Disclosure is not required for a loss contingency involving an unasserted claim or assessment when there has been no manifestation by a potential claimant of an awareness of a possible claim or assessment unless it is considered *probable* that a claim will be asserted and there is a *reasonable possibility* that the outcome will be unfavorable.

An auditor looks primarily to management and its legal counsel as sources of information concerning litigation, claims, and assessments. Accordingly, the CPA's procedures should include the following:

- Inquire of and discuss with management the policies and procedures adopted for identifying, evaluating, and accounting for litigation, claims, and assessments.

- Obtain from management a description and evaluation of litigation, claims, and assessments that existed at the date of the balance sheet being reported on, and during the period from the balance date to the date the information is furnished, including an identification of those matters referred to legal counsel, and obtain assurances from management, ordinarily in writing, that they have disclosed all such matters required to be disclosed by FASB No. 5.

- Examine documents in the client's possession concerning litigation, claims, and assessments, including correspondence and invoices from lawyers.

- Obtain assurance from management, ordinarily in writing, that it has disclosed all unasserted claims that the lawyer has advised them are probable of assertion and must be disclosed in accordance with FASB No. 5. Also the auditor, with the client's permission, should inform the lawyer that the client has given the auditor this assurance. This client representation may be communicated by the client in the client's letter to the lawyer or by the auditor in a separate letter.

Procedures the auditor ordinarily performs as a regular part of every examination that may disclose pending or threatened litigation, claims against the client, or assessments made against the client as a result of legal action, include:

- Requesting that the client's management send a letter of inquiry to those lawyers with whom they consulted concerning litigation, claims, and assessments.

- Reviewing minutes of meetings of stockholders, directors, and appropriate committees held during and subsequent to the period being examined.

- Reviewing contracts, loan agreements, leases, and correspondence from taxing or other governmental agencies, and similar documents.

- Obtaining information concerning guarantees from bank confirmation forms.

- Inspecting other documents for possible guarantees by the client.

Inquiry of a Client's Lawyer

The auditor's role of evidence-gathering regarding litigation, claims, and assessments is primarily one of corroborating information provided by the client and information obtained from performing auditing procedures. A letter of inquiry to the client's lawyer is the CPA's primary means of corroboration of the information furnished by management. Evidential matter obtained from the client's inside general counsel or legal department may provide the necessary corroboration. However, the use of inside counsel is not considered a substitute for any information outside counsel refuses to furnish.

The matters that should be covered in a letter of audit inquiry include, but are not limited to, the following:

- Identification of the company (including subsidiaries) covered by the auditor's opinion and the date of examination.

- A list of pending or threatened litigation, claims, and assessments with respect to which the lawyer has been engaged and to which he or she has devoted substantive attention on behalf of the company in the form of legal consultation or representation. The list may be prepared by the client or the client may request the lawyer to prepare the list.

- A list, which must be prepared by the client, that describes and evaluates unasserted claims and assessments that management considers to be *probable* of assertion, and that, if asserted, would have at least a *reasonable possibility* of an unfavorable outcome. This list should include matters to which the lawyer has devoted substantive attention.

- As to each threatened or pending litigation, claim, or assessment listed in the letter, a request that the lawyer either furnish the following information or comment on those matters as to which his or her views differ from those stated by management:

  A description of the nature of the matter, the progress of the case to date, and the action the company intends to take.

  An evaluation of the likelihood of an unfavorable outcome and an estimate, if one can be made, of the amount or range of potential loss.

  With respect to a list prepared by management, an identification of the omission of any pending or threatened litigation, claims, and assessments or a statement that the list of such matters is complete.

- As to unasserted claims listed by management, a request that the lawyer comment on those matters as to which his or her views concerning the description or evaluation of the matter may differ from those stated by management.

- A statement by the client, that the client understands that the lawyer will advise him or her of unasserted possible claims or assessments that may require disclosure in accordance with the requirements of FASB No. 5. The letter should include a request that the lawyer confirm whether this understanding is correct.

- A request that the lawyer specifically identify the nature of and reasons for limitations on his or her response.

- The letter should request that the attorney's comments cover the current period and the subsequent period.

Inquiry need not be made of the client's legal counsel regarding items that are considered to be immaterial. However, the CPA, in requesting the lawyer to comment on material items, should come to an understanding with the client's lawyer concerning what the CPA considers to be material for financial statement presentation.

Illustrative Inquiry Letter

Presented on the next page is an illustrative lawyer's inquiry letter that incorporates the requirements of *SAS No. 12.*

In special situations, involving technical points of law, the CPA may obtain the information normally included in the inquiry letter in a conference with the client's attorney. In such cases, the conclusions reached concerning the need for accounting or for disclosure of litigations, claims, and assessments should be appropriately documented in the auditor's working papers.

When a client has terminated a relationship with an attorney, the CPA should consider inquiries as to the reasons for the termination of the relationship as it may affect financial statement disclosures.

Limitations on a Lawyer's Response

A lawyer may limit the response to a letter of inquiry to those matters to which he or she has given substantive attention. Also, the response may be limited for other reasons. For example, a lawyer may not be able to respond as to the outcome of a pending matter under litigation because there is insufficient experience in trying matters of this nature or because the client or other firms in the client's industry are not experienced with this kind of litigation. Such restrictions are not considered limitations on the scope of the auditor's examination. In such circumstances, the auditor ordinarily will conclude that the financial

MARA MANUFACTURING COMPANY

1537 West Atlantic Street, Springfield, Missouri 21304

December 31, 19x1

John Marshall, Attorney at Law
1600 Kearney Avenue
Springfield, Missouri 21304

Dear Sir:

Holdren & Co., 2140 Lee Street, Springfield, Missouri 21304, are making their usual annual examination of our accounts, and we will appreciate your furnishing them with information concerning the following matters as of December 31, 19x1 and as of the date of your reply:

1. A list of all open engagements you are now handling, including a description of the matter and its present status, the action the company intends to take, an evaluation of the likelihood of an unfavorable outcome and an estimate of the amount or range of potential loss, including court costs and legal fees.

2. Any explanation that you consider necessary to supplement our representations to Holdren & Co. that there are no unasserted claims against the company that are probable of assertion and, if asserted, would have at least a reasonable possibility of an unfavorable outcome.

   We understand that whenever, in the course of performing legal services for us with respect to a matter recognized to involve an unasserted possible claim or assessment that may call for financial statement disclosure, if you have formed a professional conclusion that we should disclose or consider disclosure concerning such possible claim or assessment, as a matter of professional responsibility to us, you will so advise us and will consult with us concerning the question of such disclosure and the applicable requirements of Statement of Financial Accounting Standards No. 5. Please specifically confirm to our auditors that our understanding is correct.

3. Any stock option agreements, subordination agreements, leases, guarantees of company debts by stockholders, officers or others, and any matters affecting title to assets of which you have knowledge.

4. A listing of companies of which you have knowledge, that may be deemed to be affiliates or related parties of the company.

5. Any amount due you for services and expenses.

Please specifically identify the nature of and reasons for any limitation on your response.

With respect to items (3) and (4), you need to report only items which have not previously been reported or which have been modified since your last letter replying to our request for this information.

The scheduled completion date of our auditors' examination is such that you should send your letter to Holdren & Co. on or about February 15, 19x2.

Sincerely,

Richard A. Mara
President

statements are affected by an uncertainty concerning the outcome of a future event which is not susceptible of reasonable estimation. If the effect of the matter is material, the CPA ordinarily will issue a qualified opinion.

When a lawyer has devoted substantive effort to matters covered in the inquiry letter and refuses to furnish the information requested in the letter, such limitation would be considered a limitation on the scope of the auditor's examination sufficient to prohibit the issuance of an unqualified opinion.

MANAGEMENT REPRESENTATION LETTERS[13]

As part of the subsequent event procedures performed in an audit of financial statements, the auditor obtains certain written representations from management (*SAS No. 19, Client Representations*, AU 333). Oral and written representations are made to the auditor during the course of the examination covering a variety of matters such as the overall fairness of the financial statements, the completeness of the minutes of meetings of the board of directors and company committees, the value and salability of the inventory, the adequacy of disclosures in the financial statements concerning related party transactions, legal matters, and so forth. Such representations are requested from management and provided because there are many matters regarding the financial statements that management alone has knowledge of and corroborating evidence is not ordinarily obtainable. Also, obtaining written representations impresses upon management its responsibility for the overall fairness of the financial statements, including disclosure.

SAS No. 19 requires the auditor to obtain written representations as part of the examination of financial statements in accordance with GAAS. Such representations confirm the continuing appropriateness of oral representations given to the auditor during the course of the engagement. Also, by emphasizing management's responsibility for the overall fairness of the financial statements, such representations may bring attention to information or evidence that the auditor otherwise would not be aware of. For example, attention may be called to an important subsequent event requiring disclosure in the financial statements such as a planned merger with another firm. Accordingly, written representations should be obtained by the auditor near the end

---

[13] The discussion of management representation letters is taken from *Readings and Cases in Auditing*, Hubbard, Ellison, and Strawser, Dame Publications, Inc., Houston, Texas, 1981, pp. 233-236.

of his or her field work (which is the date of the audit report) to cover the subsequent period.

Many representations obtained from management, as indicated, are not subject to corroboration. For example, criteria for classifying marketable equity securities as current assets is based on management's intent to use the securities for working capital purposes during the coming operating cycle if needed. By confirming the proper classification of marketable equity securities in the balance sheet, management is attesting to its intent to use the securities for working capital purposes, if needed. Unless audit evidence reveals conditions to the contrary, the auditor's reliance on truthfulness of management's representations is reasonable. This type of reliance should not be confused with the type of reliance placed on internal accounting controls. Management's representation letter cannot be relied upon as a basis to determine the extent, nature, and timing of substantive testing. In other words, generally accepted auditing standards require the auditor to obtain a management representation letter, but at the same time, the letter cannot be used to diminish the auditor's responsibility to gather sufficient competent evidence upon which to base an opinion on the financial statements.

Management's representations may be limited to matters that are considered material to the financial statements provided management and the auditor have reached an understanding as to the limits of materiality for such purposes.

Although the representation letter is ordinarily prepared by the auditor for the client's signature, it should be addressed to the auditor and signed by members of management with responsibility for company operations (usually the chief executive officer and the controller). Individuals responsible for specific functions may be requested to provide separate written representations regarding their function. For example, the individual responsible for maintaining the minutes of the corporation may be asked to represent that they are complete.

Management's refusal to furnish written representations that the auditor believes are necessary or the refusal to permit the auditor to perform procedures considered necessary regarding matters in a representation letter, is a scope limitation sufficient to preclude an unqualified opinion (probably a disclaimer of opinion would be called for).

The specific written representations obtained by the auditor will depend on the circumstances of the engagement and the nature and basis of presentation of the financial statements. According to *SAS No. 19*

(AU 333.04), the following matters ordinarily would be included in a representation letter:

1. Management's acknowledgement of its responsibility for the fair presentation in the financial statements of financial position, results of operations, and changes in financial position in conformity with generally accepted accounting principles or other comprehensive basis of accounting.

2. Availability of all financial records and related data.

3. Completeness and availability of all minutes of meetings of stockholders, directors, and committees of directors.

4. Absence of errors in the financial statements and unrecorded transactions.

5. Information concerning related party transactions and related amounts receivable or payable.

6. Noncompliance with aspects of contractual agreements that may affect the financial statements.

7. Information concerning subsequent events.

8. Irregularities involving management or employees.

9. Communications from regulatory agencies concerning noncompliance with, or deficiencies in, financial reporting practices.

10. Plans or intentions that may affect the carrying value or classification of assets or liabilities.

11. Disclosure of compensating balances or other arrangements involving restrictions on cash balances, and disclosure of line-of-credit or similar arrangements.

12. Reduction of excess or obsolete inventories to net realizable value.

13. Losses from sales commitments.

14. Satisfactory title to assets, liens on assets, and assets pledged as collateral.

15. Agreements to repurchase assets previously sold.

16. Losses from purchase commitments for inventory quantities in excess of requirements or at prices in excess of market.

17. Violations or possible violations of laws or regulations whose effects should be considered for disclosure in the financial statements or as a basis for recording a loss contingency.

18. Other liabilities and gain or loss contingencies that are required to be accrued or disclosed by FASB No. 5.

19. Unasserted claims or assessments that the client's lawyer has advised are probable of assertion and must be disclosed in accordance with FASB No. 5.

20. Capital stock repurchase options or agreements or capital stock reserved for options, warrants, conversions, or other requirements.

Following is an illustrative representation letter incorporating the above matters and other matters that could involve additions to the letter (note items 15 and 16 in the letter).

SUMMARY

Chapter 14 discusses the procedures necessary to complete the audit engagement, including preparation of financial statements, obtaining representation letters from the client and its legal counsel, and reviewing working papers and performing a subsequent events review.

The basic financial statements include the balance sheet, statement of income, statement of retained earnings or changes in stockholders' equity, and statement of changes in financial position. Descriptions of accounting policies and notes and schedules are also an integral part of the basic financial statements.

GAAP require information to be disclosed in financial statements if its omission would tend to make the statements misleading. There are several acceptable methods to disclose information in the financial statements. Information may be disclosed on the face of the financial statements by presenting an account and an amount, and by showing information parenthetically, or by showing information short. Also, disclosure can be in footnotes and schedules accompanying the statements. The presentation that is most effective in communicating the information to the reader should be used. Accountants frequently use a disclosure checklist to assure the completeness of the financial statement disclosures.

ABC Corporation
1000 Rosebud Ave.
Los Angeles, California 22233

January 29, 19x2

Anderson and Holdren
Certified Public Accountants
200 Life Building
Los Angeles, California 22244

Gentlemen:

In connection with your examination of the financial statements of ABC Corporation as of December 31, 19x1, and for the year then ended for the purpose of expressing an opinion as to whether the financial statements present fairly the financial position, results of operations, and changes in financial position of ABC Corporation, in conformity with generally accepted accounting principles, we confirm, to the best of our knowledge and belief, the following representations made to you during your examination.

1. We are responsible for the fair presentation in the statements of financial position, results of operations, and changes in financial position in conformity with generally accepted accounting principles.

2. We have made available to you, all —

   a. Financial records and related data.

   b. Minutes of the meetings of stockholders, directors, and committees of directors, or summaries of actions of recent meetings for which minutes have not yet been prepared.

3. There have been no —

   a. Irregularities involving management or employees who have significant roles in the system of internal accounting control.

   b. Irregularities involving other employees that could have a material effect on the financial statements.

4. We have no plans or intentions that may materially affect the carrying value or classification of assets and liabilities. (Except as stated in Item No. 15.)

5. The following have been properly recorded or disclosed in the financial statements:

   a. Related party transactions and related amounts receivable or payable, including sales, purchases, loans, transfers, leasing arrangements, and guarantees.

   b. Arrangements with financial institutions involving compensating balances or other arrangements involving restrictions on cash balances and line-of-credit or similar arrangements.

   c. Agreements to repurchase assets previously sold.

6. There are no —

   a. Violations or possible violations of laws or regulations whose effects should be considered for disclosure in the financial statements or as a basis for recording a loss contingency.

   b. Other material liabilities or gain or loss contingencies that are required to be accrued or disclosed by FASB Statement No. 5.

7. There are no unasserted claims or assessments that our lawyer has advised us are probable of assertion and must be disclosed in accordance with FASB Statement No. 5.

8. There are no material transactions that have not been properly recorded in the accounting records underlying the financial statements.

9. Provision, when material, has been made to reduce excess or obsolete inventories to their estimated net realizable value.

10. The company has satisfactory title to all owned assets, and there are no liens or encumbrances on such assets nor has any asset been pledged.

11. Provision has been made for any material loss to be sustained in the fulfillment of, or from inability to fulfill, any sales commitments.

12. Provision has been made for any material loss to be sustained as a result of purchase commitments for inventory quantities in excess of normal requirements or at prices in excess of the prevailing market prices.

13. We have complied with all aspects of contractual agreements that would have a material effect on the financial statements in the event of noncompliance.

14. No events have occurred subsequent to the balance sheet date that would require adjustment to, or disclosure in, the financial statements.

15. Short-term obligations have been excluded from current liabilities because it is the company's intention to refinance these obligations on a long-term basis and the company has demonstrated the ability to consummate such refinancing.

16. In the case of investments classified as marketable equity securities in the current asset section of the balance sheet, it is the company's intention to employ these securities as working capital during the next accounting period.

_____
President

_____
Controller

The first standard of field work requires a review of audit work. Thorough review of audit work is necessary to maintain quality control within a firm of independent auditors. Review procedures usually involve following checklists to assure completeness of audit working papers and to fix responsibility for review. The work of the staff accountant is reviewed by the in-charge accountant. The in-charge accountant's work is reviewed by the manager and partner in-charge of the audit engagement. A horizontal review may be performed involving a manager or partner that did not participate in the audit. Larger CPA firms often have review teams to provide uniformity in auditing and reporting on a firm-wide basis.

An important part of the completion of an audit engagement is the performance of a subsequent events review. There are two types of subsequent events—those that require adjustment of the financial statement amounts and those that require disclosure. The subsequent events review is applied during the period following the date of the financial statements to the completion of the field work and involves inquiry and review procedures.

A subsequent events review procedure requires obtaining a lawyer's letter. A letter of inquiry to the client's lawyer(s) is the auditor's primary means of corroborating information furnished by management. The letter will relate to litigation, claims, and assessments, and unasserted claims that may require accrual or disclosure in the financial statements in accordance with FASB No. 5, *Accounting for Contingencies*. The letter is frequently prepared by the CPA for the client's signature.

Obtaining a management representation letter is also a subsequent events procedure required in an audit examination. The purpose of the letter is to provide written representations to the auditor in support of oral representations made during the course of the examination. The letter also impresses upon management its responsibilities for the fairness of the financial statements and may bring to the attention of the auditor information he or she would not normally be aware of from performance of audit procedures other than the subsequent events review. The letter is usually prepared by the auditor for management's signature. The chief executive officer and the chief financial officer of the client should sign the letter. Individual representation letters may be obtained from other client personnel regarding their specific functions. For example, a letter as to the completeness of the minutes of the meetings of the board of directors and its committees may be obtained from the secretary of the corporation.

REVIEW QUESTIONS

14-1   What are the basic financial statements that must be issued when a complete financial report is being rendered in conformity with generally accepted accounting principles?

14-2   Does the auditor's opinion on financial statements prepared in accordance with generally accepted accounting principles cover related footnotes and schedules?

14-3   Identify three ways information can be presented in financial statements.

14-4   Discuss the importance of review of audit work.

14-5   What is the purpose of a horizontal review?

14-6   Discuss the criteria that should be used by an auditor to determine whether he or she should sign-off on audit work.

14-7   Briefly discuss vertical review procedures of a CPA firm.

14-8   What is the purpose of an indexing system used in working papers? Explain.

14-9   During what period of time does a subsequent events review take place?

14-10   Describe the nature of the two basic types of subsequent events.

14-11   Discuss the types of procedures the auditor should carry out for a subsequent events review. What is the nature of these procedures?

14-12   What is the purpose of obtaining a lawyer's letter from the client's legal counsel?

14-13   Information furnished by the client's attorney in a lawyer's letter concerning litigation, claims, and assessments should cover what period of time?

14-14   What is the nature of information furnished by the client's attorney in a lawyer's letter? Does this information include any agreements between stockholders, officers, and the corporation? Between the corporation and related parties?

14-15   There are two different types of limitations on a "Lawyer's Response." Describe both types of limitations and indicate the impact, if any, on the auditor's opinion.

14-16   When should the auditor obtain a management representation letter from the client? Who should sign the representation letter?

14-17   What impact does management's refusal to furnish a representation letter have on the auditor's opinion?

DISCUSSION QUESTIONS AND PROBLEMS

14-18   In connection with your examination of the financial statements of Olars Manufacturing Corporation for the year ended December 31, 19x0, your post-balance-sheet-date review disclosed the following items:

1.   January 3, 19x1:   The state government approved a plan for the construction of an express highway. The plan will result in the appropriation of a portion of the land area owned by Olars Manufacturing Corporation. Construction will begin in late 19x1. No estimate of the condemnation award is available.

2.   January 4, 19x1:   The funds for a $25,000 loan to the Corporation made by Mr. Olars on July 15, 19x0 were obtained by him by a loan on his personal life insurance policy. The loan was recorded in the account loan from officers. Mr. Olars' source of the funds was not disclosed in the Company records. The Corporation pays the premiums on the life insurance policy and Mrs. Olars, wife of the president, is the beneficiary of the policy.

3.   January 7, 19x1:   The mineral content of a shipment of ore enroute on December 31, 19x0 was determined to be 72%. The shipment was recorded at year-end at an estimated content of 50% by a debit to Raw Material Inventory and a credit to Accounts Payable in the amount of $20,600. The final liability to the vendor is based on the actual mineral content of the shipment.

4.   January 15, 19x1:   Culminating a series of personal disagreements between Mr. Olars, the president, and his brother-in-law, the treasurer, the latter resigned, effective immediately, under an agreement whereby the Corporation would purchase his 10% stock ownership at book value as of December 31, 19x0. Payment is to be made in two equal amounts in cash on April 1 and October 1, 19x1. In December the treasurer had obtained a divorce from his wife who was Mr. Olars' sister.

5.   January 31, 19x1:   As a result of reduced sales, production was curtailed in mid-January and some workers were laid off. On February 5, 19x1 all the remaining workers went on strike. To date the strike is unsettled.

6. February 10, 19x1: A contract was signed whereby Mammoth Enterprises purchased from Olars Manufacturing Corporation all of the latter's fixed assets (including rights to receive the proceeds of any property condemnation), inventories, and the right to conduct business under the name "Olars Manufacturing Division." The effective date of the transfer will be March 1, 19x1. The sale price was $500,000 subject to adjustment following the taking of a physical inventory. Important factors contributing to the decision to enter into the contract were the policy of the board of directors of Mammoth Industries to diversify the firm's activities and the report of a survey conducted by an independent market appraisal firm which revealed a declining market for Olars products.

Required:

Assume that the above items came to your attention prior to completion of your audit work on February 15, 19x1 and that you will render an audit report. For *each* of the above items:

a. Give the audit procedures, if any, that would have brought the item to your attention. Indicate other sources of information that may have revealed the item.
b. Discuss the disclosure that you would recommend for the item, listing all details that you would suggest should be disclosed. Indicate those items or details, if any, that should not be disclosed. Give your reasons for recommending or not recommending disclosure of the items or details.

(AICPA adapted)

14-19   During an audit engagement, Harper, CPA, has satisfactorily completed an examination of accounts payable and other liabilities and now plans to determine whether there are any loss contingencies arising from litigation, claims, or assessments.

Required:

What are the audit procedures that Harper should follow with respect to the existence of loss contingencies arising from litigation, claims, and assessments? Do not discuss reporting requirements.

(AICPA adapted)

14-20   In an examination of the Marco Corporation as at December 31, 1983, the following situations exist. No entries in respect thereto have been made in the accounting records.

1. The Marco Corporation has guaranteed the payment of interest on the 10-year, first-mortgage bonds of the Newart Company, an affiliate. Outstanding bonds of the Newart Company amount to $150,000 with interest payable at 5 percent per annum, due June 1 and December 1 of each year. The bonds were issued by the Newart Company on December 1, 1981, and all interest payments have been met by that company with the exception of the payment due December 1, 1983. The Marco Corporation states that it will pay the defaulted interest to the bondholders on January 15, 1984.

2. During the year 1983 the Marco Corporation was named as a defendant in a suit for damages by the Dalton Company for breach of contract. An adverse decision to the Marco Corporation was rendered and the Dalton Company was awarded $40,000 damages. At the time of the audit, the case was under appeal to a higher court.

3. On December 23, 1983, the Marco Corporation declared a common stock dividend of 1,000 shares, par $100,000, of its common stock, payable February 2, 1984, to the common stockholders of record December 30, 1983.

Required:

a. Define *contingent liability*.
b. Describe the audit procedures an auditor should use to learn about each situation above.
c. Describe the nature of the adjusting entries or disclosure, if any, the auditor should make for each situation.

(AICPA adapted)

14-21   Michael, CPA, is examining the financial statements of the Diannah Corporation as of and for the period ended September 30, 19x0. Michael plans to complete the field work and sign the auditor's report on November 15, 19x0. Michael's audit work is primarily designed to obtain evidence that will provide a reasonable degree of assurance that the Diannah Corporation's September 30, 19x0, financial statements present fairly the financial position, results of operations, and changes in financial position of that enterprise in accordance with generally accepted accounting principles consistently applied. Michael is concerned, however, about events and transactions of Diannah Corporation that occur after September 30, 19x0, since Michael does not have the same degree of assurance for such events as for those that occurred in the period ending September 30, 19x0.

Required:

a. Define what is commonly referred to in auditing as a "subsequent event" and describe the two general types of subsequent events that require consideration by the management of Diannah Corporation and evaluation by Michael.

b. Identify those auditing procedures that Michael should follow to obtain the necessary assurances concerning subsequent events.

(AICPA adapted)

14-22   In connection with his examination of Flowmeter, Inc., for the year ended December 31, 19x3, Hirsch, CPA, is aware that certain events and transactions that took place after December 31, 19x3, but before he issues his report dated February 28, 19x4, may affect the company's financial statements.

The following material events or transactions have come to his attention.

1. On January 3, 19x4, Flowmeter, Inc., received a shipment of raw materials from Canada. The materials had been ordered in October 19x3 and shipped FOB shipping point in November 19x3.

2. On January 15, 19x4, the company settled and paid a personal injury claim of a former employee as the result of an accident which occurred in March 19x3. The company had not previously recorded a liability for the claim.

3. On January 25, 19x4, the company agreed to purchase for cash the outstanding stock of Porter Electrical Co. The acquisition is likely to double the sales volume of Flowmeter, Inc.

4. On February 1, 19x4, a plant owned by Flowmeter, Inc. was damaged by a flood resulting in an uninsured loss of inventory.

5. On February 5, 19x4, Flowmeter, Inc., issued and sold to the general public $2,000,000 in convertible bonds.

Required:

For each of the above events or transactions, indicate the audit procedures that should have brought the item to the attention of the auditor, and the form of disclosure in the financial statements including the reasons for such disclosures.

Arrange your answer in the following format.

Item No.	Audit Procedures	Required Disclosure and Reasons

OBJECTIVE QUESTIONS

14-23 A limitation on the scope of the auditor's examination sufficient to preclude an unqualified opinion will *always* result when management

A. Engages an auditor after the year-end physical inventory count.
B. Refuses to furnish a representation letter.
C. Knows that direct confirmation of accounts receivable with debtors is not feasible.
D. Engages an auditor to examine only the balance sheet.

14-24 The date of the management representation letter should coincide with the

A. Date of the auditor's report.
B. Balance-sheet date.
C. Date of the latest subsequent event referred to in the notes to the financial statements.
D. Date of the engagement agreement.

14-25 When a contingency is resolved immediately subsequent to the issuance of a report which was qualified with respect to the contingency, the auditor should

A. Insist that the client issue revised financial statements.
B. Inform the audit committee that the report can*not* be relied upon.
C. Take *no* action regarding the event.
D. Inform the appropriate authorities that the report can*not* be relied upon.

14-26 Which event that occurred after the end of the fiscal year under audit but prior to issuance of the auditor's report would *not* require disclosure in the financial statements?

A. Sale of a bond or capital stock issue.

B. Loss of plant or inventories as a result of fire or flood.

C. A major drop in the quoted market price of the stock of the corporation.

D. Settlement of litigation when the event giving rise to the claim took place after the balance-sheet date.

14-27 A lawyer's response to a letter of audit inquiry may be limited to matters that are considered individually or collectively material to the financial statements if

A. The auditor has instructed the lawyer regarding the limits of materiality in financial statements.

B. The client and the auditor have agreed on the limits of materiality and the lawyer has been notified.

C. The lawyer and auditor have reached an understanding on the limits of materiality for this purpose.

D. The lawyer's response to the inquiry explains the legal meaning of materiality limits and establishes quantitative parameters.

14-28 Generally accepted auditing standards are applicable when an auditor examines and reports on any financial statement. For reporting purposes, the independent auditor should consider each of the following types of financial presentations to be a financial statement *except* a

A. Statement of assets and liabilities arising from cash transactions.

B. Statement of changes in owners' equity.

C. Statement of forecasted results of operations.

D. Statement of operations by product line.

14-29 If the auditor believes that required disclosures of a significant nature are omitted from the financial statements under examination, the auditor should decide between issuing

A. A qualified opinion or an adverse opinion.

B. A disclaimer of opinion or a qualified opinion.

C. An adverse opinion or a disclaimer of opinion.

D. An unqualified opinion or a qualified opinion.

14-30 Subsequent events affecting the realization of assets ordinarily will require adjustment of the financial statements under examination because such events typically represent

A. The culmination of conditions that existed at the balance sheet date.

B. The final estimates of losses relating to casualties occurring in the subsequent events period.

C. The discovery of new conditions occurring in the subsequent events period.

D. The preliminary estimate of losses relating to new events that occurred subsequent to the balance-sheet date.

14-31 An auditor must obtain written client representations that normally should be signed by

A. The president and the chairperson of the board.

B. The treasurer and the internal auditor.

C. The chief executive officer and the chief financial officer.

D. The corporate counsel and the audit committee chairperson.

14-32 Management furnishes the independent auditor with information concerning litigation, claims, and assessments. Which of the following is the auditor's primary means of initiating action to corroborate such information?

A. Request that client lawyers undertake a reconsideration of matters of litigation, claims, and assessments with which they were consulted during the period under examination.

B. Request that client management send a letter of audit inquiry to those lawyers with whom management consulted concerning litigation, claims, and assessments.

C. Request that client lawyers provide a legal opinion concerning the policies and procedures adopted by management to identify, evaluate, and account for litigation, claims, and assessments.

D. Request that client management engage outside attorneys to suggest wording for the text of a footnote explaining the nature and probable outcome of existing litigation, claims, and assessments.

14-33 In connection with the annual audit, which of the following is *not* a "subsequent events" procedure?

A. Review available interim financial statements.

B. Read available minutes of meetings of stockholders, directors, and committees and as to meetings for which minutes are *not* available inquire about matters dealt with at such meetings.

C. Make inquiries with respect to the financial statements covered by the auditor's previously issued report if new information has become available during the current examination that might affect that report.

D.   Discuss with officers the current status of items in the financial statements that were accounted for on the basis of tentative, preliminary or inconclusive data.

14-34   On January 28, 1977, a customer of Tom Corporation suffered a total loss as a result of a major casualty. On March 1, 1977, Tom wrote off as uncollectible a large receivable from this customer. The auditor's report on Tom's financial statements for the year ended December 31, 1976, has *not* yet been issued. The write-off in the subsequent period requires

A.   Disclosure in the 1976 financial statements.
B.   Adjustment to the 1976 financial statements.
C.   Presentation of the 1976 financial statements with a prior period adjustment.
D.   No adjustment or disclosure in the 1976 financial statements but disclosure in the 1977 financial statements.

14-35   An independent auditor has concluded that the client's records, procedures, and representations can be relied upon based on tests made during the year when internal control was found to be effective. The auditor should test the records, procedures, and representations again at year-end if

A.   Inquiries and observations lead the auditor to believe that conditions have changed significantly.
B.   Comparisons of year-end balances with like balances at prior dates revealed significant fluctuations.
C.   Unusual transactions occurred subsequent to the completion of the interim audit work.
D.   Client records are in a condition that facilitate effective and efficient testing.

14-36   Auditors often request that the audit client send a letter of inquiry to those attorneys who have been consulted with respect to litigation, claims, or assessments. The primary reason for this request is to provide the auditor with

A.   An estimate of the dollar amount of the probable loss.
B.   An expert opinion as to whether a loss is possible, probable or remote.
C.   Information concerning the progress of cases to date.
D.   Corroborative evidential matter.

14-37 When examining a client's statement of changes in financial position, for audit evidence, an auditor will rely primarily upon

A. Determination of the amount of working capital at year-end.
B. Cross-referencing to balances and transactions reviewed in connection with the examination of the other financial statements.
C. Analysis of significant ratios of prior years as compared to the current year.
D. The guidance provided by the APB Opinion on the statement of changes in financial position.

14-38 A CPA has received an attorney's letter in which no significant disagreements with the client's assessments of contingent liabilities were noted. The resignation of the client's lawyer shortly after receipt of the letter should alert the auditor that

A. Undisclosed unasserted claims may have arisen.
B. The attorney was unable to form a conclusion with respect to the significance of litigation, claims and assessments.
C. The auditor must begin a completely new examination of contingent liabilities.
D. An adverse opinion will be necessary.

14-39 Once satisfied that the balance sheet and income statement are fairly presented in accordance with generally accepted accounting principles, an auditor who is examining the statement of changes in financial position would be most concerned with details of transactions in

A. Cash.
B. Trade receivables.
C. Notes payable.
D. Dividends payable.

14-40 When an examination is made in accordance with generally accepted auditing standards, the independent auditor must

A. Utilize statistical sampling.
B. Employ analytical review procedures.
C. Obtain certain written representations from management.
D. Observe the taking of physical inventory on the balance-sheet date.

14-41 With respect to contingent liabilities, the Standard Bank Confirmation Inquiry form approved jointly by the AICPA and the Bank Administration Institute requests information regarding notes receivable

    A.   Held by the bank in a custodial account.

    B.   Held by the bank for collection.

    C.   Collected by the bank.

    D.   Discounted by the bank.

14-42   In connection with the third generally accepted auditing standard of field work, an auditor examines corroborating evidential matter which includes all of the following except

    A.   Client accounting manuals.

    B.   Written client representations.

    C.   Vendor invoices.

    D.   Minutes of board meetings.

14-43   Subsequent events affecting the realization of assets ordinarily will require adjustment of the financial statements under examination because such events typically represent

    A.   The culmination of conditions that existed at the balance-sheet date.

    B.   The final estimates of losses relating to casualties occurring in the subsequent events period.

    C.   The discovery of new conditions occurring in the subsequent events periods.

    D.   The preliminary estimate of losses relating to the balance-sheet date.

14-44   The primary responsibility for the adequacy of disclosure in the financial statements of a publicly held company rests with the

    A.   Partner assigned to the audit engagement.

    B.   Management of the company.

    C.   Auditor in charge of the field work.

    D.   Securities and Exchange Commission.

14-45   On January 15, 1974, before the Longview Co. released its financial statements for the year ended December 31, 1973, Agie Corp., a customer, declared bankruptcy. Agie has had a history of financial difficulty. Longview estimates that it will suffer a material loss on an account receivable from Agie. How should this loss be disclosed or recognized?

    A.   The loss should be disclosed in footnotes to the financial statements, but the financial statements themselves need not be adjusted.

    B.   The loss should be disclosed in an explanatory paragraph in the auditor's report.

    C.   No disclosure or recognition is required.

    D.   The financial statements should be adjusted to recognize the loss.

14-46   Harvey, CPA, is preparing an audit program for the purpose of ascertaining the occurrence of subsequent events that may require adjustment or disclosure essential to a fair presentation of the financial statements in conformity with generally accepted accounting procedures. Which one of the following procedures would be least appropriate for this purpose?

    A.   Confirm as of the completion of field work accounts receivable which have increased significantly from the year-end date.

    B.   Read the minutes of the board of directors.

    C.   Inquire of management concerning events which may have occurred.

    D.   Obtain a lawyer's letter as of the completion of field work.

14-47   As part of an audit, a CPA often requests a representation letter from his client. Which one of the following is not a valid purpose of such a letter?

    A.   To provide audit evidence.

    B.   To emphasize to the client his responsibility for the correctness of the financial statements.

    C.   To satisfy himself by means of other auditing procedures when certain customary auditing procedures are not performed.

    D.   To provide possible protection to the CPA against a charge of knowledge in cases where fraud is subsequently discovered to have existed in the accounts.

14-48   A client has a calendar year-end. Listed below are four events that occurred after December 31. Which one of these subsequent events might result in adjustment of the December 31, financial statements?

    A.   Adoption of accelerated depreciation methods.

    B.   Write-off of a substantial portion of inventory as obsolete.

    C.   Collection of 90% of the accounts receivable existing at December 31.

    D.   Sale of a major subsidiary.

14-49   A charge in the subsequent period to a notes receivable account from the cash disbursements journal should alert the auditor to the possibility that

A. A contingent asset has come into existence in the subsequent period.

B. A contingent liability has come into existence in the subsequent period.

C. A provision for contingencies is required.

D. A contingent liability has become a real liability and has been settled.

14-50 An auditor generally obtains from a client a formal written statement concerning the accuracy of inventory. This particular letter of presentation is used by the auditor to

A. Reduce the scope of the auditor's physical inventory work but not the other inventory audit work that is normally performed.

B. Confirm in writing the valuation basis used by the client to value the inventory at the lower of cost or market.

C. Lessen the auditor's responsibility for the fair presentation of balance sheet inventories.

D. Remind management that the primary responsibility for the overall fairness of the financial statements rests with management and not with the auditor.

14-51 Which of the following material events occurring subsequent to the balance-sheet date would require an adjustment to the financial statements before they could be issued?

A. Sale of long-term debt or capital stock.

B. Loss of a plant as a result of a flood.

C. Major purchase of a business which is expected to double the sales volume.

D. Settlement of litigation, in excess of the recorded liability.

14-52 The auditor's formal review of subsequent events normally should be extended through the date of the

A Auditor's report.

B. Next formal interim financial statements.

C. Delivery of the audit report to the client.

D. Mailing of the financial statements to the stockholders.

14-53 Which of the following audit procedures would be least effective for detecting contingent liabilities?

A. Abstracting the minutes of the meetings of the board of directors.

B. Reviewing the bank confirmation letters.

C. Examining confirmation letters from customers.

D. Confirming pending legal matters with the corporate attorney.

14-54 When auditing contingent liabilities, which of the following procedures would be least effective?

A. Abstracting the minutes of the board of directors.

B. Reviewing the bank confirmation letter.

C. Examining customer confirmation replies.

D. Examining invoices for professional services.

CONDUCT INDEPENDENCE EVIDENCE DUE CARE FAIR PRESENTATION ETHICAL CONDUCT INDEPENDENCE EVIDENCE DUE CARE FAIR PRESENTATION ETHICAL CONDUCT INDEPE
CAL CONDUCT INDEPENDENCE EVIDENCE DUE CARE FAIR PRESENTATION ETHICAL CONDUCT INDEPENDENCE EVIDENCE DUE CARE FAIR PRESENTATION ETHICAL CONDUCT INC
ETHICAL CONDUCT INDEPENDENCE EVIDENCE DUE CARE FAIR PRESENTATION ETHICAL CONDUCT INDEPENDENCE EVIDENCE DUE CARE FAIR PRESENTATION ETHICAL CONDUCT
ON ETHICAL CONDUCT INDEPENDENCE EVIDENCE DUE CARE FAIR PRESENTATION ETHICAL CONDUCT INDEPENDENCE EVIDENCE DUE CARE FAIR PRESENTATION ETHICAL COND
ATION ETHICAL CONDUCT INDEPENDENCE EVIDENCE DUE CARE FAIR PRESENTATION ETHICAL CONDUCT INDEPENDENCE EVIDENCE DUE CARE FAIR PRESENTATION ETHICAL C
SENTATION ETHICAL CONDUCT INDEPENDENCE EVIDENCE DUE CARE FAIR PRESENTATION ETHICAL CONDUCT INDEPENDENCE EVIDENCE DUE CARE FAIR PRESENTATION ETHICA
PRESENTATION ETHICAL CONDUCT INDEPENDENCE EVIDENCE DUE CARE FAIR PRESENTATION ETHICAL CONDUCT INDEPENDENCE EVIDENCE DUE CARE FAIR PRESENTATION ET
AIR PRESENTATION ETHICAL CONDUCT INDEPENDENCE EVIDENCE DUE CARE FAIR PRESENTATION ETHICAL CONDUCT INDEPENDENCE EVIDENCE DUE CARE FAIR PRESENTATION

DUE CARE FAIR PRESENTATION ETHICAL CONDUCT INDEPENDENCE EVIDENCE DUE CARE FAIR PRESENTATION ETHICAL CONDUCT INDEPENDENCE EVIDENCE DUE CARE FAIR PR
CE DUE CARE FAIR PRESENTATION ETHICAL CONDUCT INDEPENDENCE EVIDENCE DUE CARE FAIR PRESENTATION ETHICAL CONDUCT INDEPENDENCE EVIDENCE DUE CARE FAI
IDENCE DUE CARE FAIR PRESENTATION ETHICAL CONDUCT INDEPENDENCE EVIDENCE DUE CARE FAIR PRESENTATION ETHICAL CONDUCT INDEPENDENCE EVIDENCE DUE CARE
EVIDENCE DUE CARE FAIR PRESENTATION ETHICAL CONDUCT INDEPENDENCE EVIDENCE DUE CARE FAIR PRESENTATION ETHICAL CONDUCT INDEPENDENCE EVIDENCE DUE C
NCE EVIDENCE DUE CARE FAIR PRESENTATION ETHICAL CONDUCT INDEPENDENCE EVIDENCE DUE CARE FAIR PRESENTATION ETHICAL CONDUCT INDEPENDENCE EVIDENCE D
NDENCE EVIDENCE DUE CARE FAIR PRESENTATION ETHICAL CONDUCT INDEPENDENCE EVIDENCE DUE CARE FAIR PRESENTATION ETHICAL CONDUCT INDEPENDENCE EVIDENC
EPENDENCE EVIDENCE DUE CARE FAIR PRESENTATION ETHICAL CONDUCT INDEPENDENCE EVIDENCE DUE CARE FAIR PRESENTATION ETHICAL CONDUCT INDEPENDENCE EVID
INDEPENDENCE EVIDENCE DUE CARE FAIR PRESENTATION ETHICAL CONDUCT INDEPENDENCE EVIDENCE DUE CARE FAIR PRESENTATION ETHICAL CONDUCT INDEPENDENCE
UCT INDEPENDENCE EVIDENCE DUE CARE FAIR PRESENTATION ETHICAL CONDUCT INDEPENDENCE EVIDENCE DUE CARE FAIR PRESENTATION ETHICAL CONDUCT INDEPENDENC
ONDUCT INDEPENDENCE EVIDENCE DUE CARE FAIR PRESENTATION ETHICAL CONDUCT INDEPENDENCE EVIDENCE DUE CARE FAIR PRESENTATION ETHICAL CONDUCT INDEPENL
AL CONDUCT INDEPENDENCE EVIDENCE DUE CARE FAIR PRESENTATION ETHICAL CONDUCT INDEPENDENCE EVIDENCE DUE CARE FAIR PRESENTATION ETHICAL CONDUCT INDE
HICAL CONDUCT INDEPENDENCE EVIDENCE DUE CARE FAIR PRESENTATION ETHICAL CONDUCT INDEPENDENCE EVIDENCE DUE CARE FAIR PRESENTATION ETHICAL CONDUCT I
N ETHICAL CONDUCT INDEPENDENCE EVIDENCE DUE CARE FAIR PRESENTATION ETHICAL CONDUCT INDEPENDENCE EVIDENCE DUE CARE FAIR PRESENTATION ETHICAL CONDU
TION ETHICAL CONDUCT INDEPENDENCE EVIDENCE DUE CARE FAIR PRESENTATION ETHICAL CONDUCT INDEPENDENCE EVIDENCE DUE CARE FAIR PRESENTATION ETHICAL CON
ENTATION ETHICAL CONDUCT INDEPENDENCE EVIDENCE DUE CARE FAIR PRESENTATION ETHICAL CONDUCT INDEPENDENCE EVIDENCE DUE CARE FAIR PRESENTATION ETHICAL
RESENTATION ETHICAL CONDUCT INDEPENDENCE EVIDENCE DUE CARE FAIR PRESENTATION ETHICAL CONDUCT INDEPENDENCE EVIDENCE DUE CARE FAIR PRESENTATION ETH
IR PRESENTATION ETHICAL CONDUCT INDEPENDENCE EVIDENCE DUE CARE FAIR PRESENTATION ETHICAL CONDUCT INDEPENDENCE EVIDENCE DUE CARE FAIR PRESENTATION
FAIR PRESENTATION ETHICAL CONDUCT INDEPENDENCE EVIDENCE DUE CARE FAIR PRESENTATION ETHICAL CONDUCT INDEPENDENCE EVIDENCE DUE CARE FAIR PRESENTATI
CARE FAIR PRESENTATION ETHICAL CONDUCT INDEPENDENCE EVIDENCE DUE CARE FAIR PRESENTATION ETHICAL CONDUCT INDEPENDENCE EVIDENCE DUE CARE FAIR PRESEN
UE CARE FAIR PRESENTATION ETHICAL CONDUCT INDEPENDENCE EVIDENCE DUE CARE FAIR PRESENTATION ETHICAL CONDUCT INDEPENDENCE EVIDENCE DUE CARE FAIR PRE
E DUE CARE FAIR PRESENTATION ETHICAL CONDUCT INDEPENDENCE EVIDENCE DUE CARE FAIR PRESENTATION ETHICAL CONDUCT INDEPENDENCE EVIDENCE DUE CARE FAIR
ENCE DUE CARE FAIR PRESENTATION ETHICAL CONDUCT INDEPENDENCE EVIDENCE DUE CARE FAIR PRESENTATION ETHICAL CONDUCT INDEPENDENCE EVIDENCE DUE CARE F
EVIDENCE DUE CARE FAIR PRESENTATION ETHICAL CONDUCT INDEPENDENCE EVIDENCE DUE CARE FAIR PRESENTATION ETHICAL CONDUCT INDEPENDENCE EVIDENCE DUE CA
CE EVIDENCE DUE CARE FAIR PRESENTATION ETHICAL CONDUCT INDEPENDENCE EVIDENCE DUE CARE FAIR PRESENTATION ETHICAL CONDUCT INDEPENDENCE EVIDENCE DUE
DENCE EVIDENCE DUE CARE FAIR PRESENTATION ETHICAL CONDUCT INDEPENDENCE EVIDENCE DUE CARE FAIR PRESENTATION ETHICAL CONDUCT INDEPENDENCE EVIDENCE
EPENDENCE EVIDENCE DUE CARE FAIR PRESENTATION ETHICAL CONDUCT INDEPENDENCE EVIDENCE DUE CARE FAIR PRESENTATION ETHICAL CONDUCT INDEPENDENCE EVIDEN
INDEPENDENCE EVIDENCE DUE CARE FAIR PRESENTATION ETHICAL CONDUCT INDEPENDENCE EVIDENCE DUE CARE FAIR PRESENTATION ETHICAL CONDUCT INDEPENDENCE EV
CT INDEPENDENCE EVIDENCE DUE CARE FAIR PRESENTATION ETHICAL CONDUCT INDEPENDENCE EVIDENCE DUE CARE FAIR PRESENTATION ETHICAL CONDUCT INDEPENDENCE
NDUCT INDEPENDENCE EVIDENCE DUE CARE FAIR PRESENTATION ETHICAL CONDUCT INDEPENDENCE EVIDENCE DUE CARE FAIR PRESENTATION ETHICAL CONDUCT INDEPENDE
L CONDUCT INDEPENDENCE EVIDENCE DUE CARE FAIR PRESENTATION ETHICAL CONDUCT INDEPENDENCE EVIDENCE DUE CARE FAIR PRESENTATION ETHICAL CONDUCT INDEPE
ICAL CONDUCT INDEPENDENCE EVIDENCE DUE CARE FAIR PRESENTATION ETHICAL CONDUCT INDEPENDENCE EVIDENCE DUE CARE FAIR PRESENTATION ETHICAL CONDUCT INI
ETHICAL CONDUCT INDEPENDENCE EVIDENCE DUE CARE FAIR PRESENTATION ETHICAL CONDUCT INDEPENDENCE EVIDENCE DUE CARE FAIR PRESENTATION ETHICAL CONDUCT
ON ETHICAL CONDUCT INDEPENDENCE EVIDENCE DUE CARE FAIR PRESENTATION ETHICAL CONDUCT INDEPENDENCE EVIDENCE DUE CARE FAIR PRESENTATION ETHICAL COND
TATION ETHICAL CONDUCT INDEPENDENCE EVIDENCE DUE CARE FAIR PRESENTATION ETHICAL CONDUCT INDEPENDENCE EVIDENCE DUE CARE FAIR PRESENTATION ETHICAL C
SENTATION ETHICAL CONDUCT INDEPENDENCE EVIDENCE DUE CARE FAIR PRESENTATION ETHICAL CONDUCT INDEPENDENCE EVIDENCE DUE CARE FAIR PRESENTATION ETHIC
PRESENTATION ETHICAL CONDUCT INDEPENDENCE EVIDENCE DUE CARE FAIR PRESENTATION ETHICAL CONDUCT INDEPENDENCE EVIDENCE DUE CARE FAIR PRESENTATION ET

☐ REPORTING

FAIR PRESENTATION ETHICAL CONDUCT INDEPENDENCE EVIDENCE DUE CARE FAIR PRESENTATION ETHICAL CONDUCT INDEPENDENCE EVIDENCE DUE CARE FAIR PRESENTATIO
ARE FAIR PRESENTATION ETHICAL CONDUCT INDEPENDENCE EVIDENCE DUE CARE FAIR PRESENTATION ETHICAL CONDUCT INDEPENDENCE EVIDENCE DUE CARE FAIR PRESENT.
NE CARE FAIR PRESENTATION ETHICAL CONDUCT INDEPENDENCE EVIDENCE DUE CARE FAIR PRESENTATION ETHICAL CONDUCT INDEPENDENCE EVIDENCE DUE CARE FAIR PRES
E DUE CARE FAIR PRESENTATION ETHICAL CONDUCT INDEPENDENCE EVIDENCE DUE CARE FAIR PRESENTATION ETHICAL CONDUCT INDEPENDENCE EVIDENCE DUE CARE F
ENCE DUE CARE FAIR PRESENTATION ETHICAL CONDUCT INDEPENDENCE EVIDENCE DUE CARE FAIR PRESENTATION ETHICAL CONDUCT INDEPENDENCE EVIDENCE DUE CARE F.
EVIDENCE DUE CARE FAIR PRESENTATION ETHICAL CONDUCT INDEPENDENCE EVIDENCE DUE CARE FAIR PRESENTATION ETHICAL CONDUCT INDEPENDENCE EVIDENCE DUE CAR
CE EVIDENCE DUE CARE FAIR PRESENTATION ETHICAL CONDUCT INDEPENDENCE EVIDENCE DUE CARE FAIR PRESENTATION ETHICAL CONDUCT INDEPENDENCE EVIDENCE DUE
DENCE EVIDENCE DUE CARE FAIR PRESENTATION ETHICAL CONDUCT INDEPENDENCE EVIDENCE DUE CARE FAIR PRESENTATION ETHICAL CONDUCT INDEPENDENCE EVIDENCE

LEARNING OBJECTIVES

CT INDEPENDENCE EVIDENCE DUE CARE FAIR PRESENTATION ETHICAL CONDUCT INDEPENDENCE EVIDENCE DUE CARE FAIR PRESENTATION ETHICAL CONDUCT INDEPENDENCE
NDUCT INDEPENDENCE EVIDENCE DUE CARE FAIR PRESENTATION ETHICAL CONDUCT INDEPENDENCE EVIDENCE DUE CARE FAIR PRESENTATION ETHICAL CONDUCT INDEPENDE
L CONDUCT INDEPENDENCE EVIDENCE DUE CARE FAIR PRESENTATION ETHICAL CONDUCT INDEPENDENCE EVIDENCE DUE CARE FAIR PRESENTATION ETHICAL CONDUCT INDEPI
ICAL CONDUCT INDEPENDENCE EVIDENCE DUE CARE FAIR PRESENTATION ETHICAL CONDUCT INDEPENDENCE EVIDENCE DUE CARE FAIR PRESENTATION ETHICAL CONDUCT IN
ETHICAL CONDUCT INDEPENDENCE EVIDENCE DUE CARE FAIR PRESENTATION ETHICAL CONDUCT INDEPENDENCE EVIDENCE DUE CARE FAIR PRESENTATION ETHICAL CONDUCT

After studying this chapter, students should understand

1. The four reporting standards including the format and nature of an auditor's report.

2. The meaning of association with financial statements.

3. The nature and format of an auditor's report on unaudited financial statements.

4. The nature and format of an auditor's report when he or she is not independent.

5. The key elements in the auditor's standard audit report.

6. The meanings of present fairly in accordance with GAAP, including the sources of GAAP.

7. The meaning of the consistency expression, including the format of the auditor's report when the consistency standard is violated.

8. The types of audit opinions which can be issued, the nature of these opinions, and the format of these opinions.

9. The types of items an auditor may wish to emphasize, and the way an auditor emphasizes a matter in his or her report.

10. The auditor's reporting obligation when there is a departure from a promulgated accounting principle.

11. The predecessor and successor auditor's responsibility for updating audit opinions.

12. The nature and format of audit reports based in part on the work of a specialist.

13. The use of dual dating in the auditor's report and the auditor's responsibility for subsequent events.

14. The auditor's responsibility for other information, including segment information and long-form report type information.

ENCE DUE CARE FAIR PRESENTATION ETHICAL CONDUCT INDEPENDENCE EVIDENCE DUE CARE FAIR PRESENTATION ETHICAL CONDUCT INDEPENDENCE EVIDENCE DUE CARE FA
EVIDENCE DUE CARE FAIR PRESENTATION ETHICAL CONDUCT INDEPENDENCE EVIDENCE DUE CARE FAIR PRESENTATION ETHICAL CONDUCT INDEPENDENCE EVIDENCE DUE CAR
CE EVIDENCE DUE CARE FAIR PRESENTATION ETHICAL CONDUCT INDEPENDENCE EVIDENCE DUE CARE FAIR PRESENTATION ETHICAL CONDUCT INDEPENDENCE EVIDENCE DUE
DENCE EVIDENCE DUE CARE FAIR PRESENTATION ETHICAL CONDUCT INDEPENDENCE EVIDENCE DUE CARE FAIR PRESENTATION ETHICAL CONDUCT INDEPENDENCE EVIDENCE C

Chapter 15

Audit Reports

This chapter was written by
Thomas D. Hubbard, Ph.D., C.P.A.,
Nebraska CPAs Distinguished Professor of Accountancy and Director,
University of Nebraska, Lincoln

INTRODUCTION

This chapter considers the responsibilities of independent auditors to issue a report when they are associated with a client's financial statements. The audit report must be in accordance with professional standards, which means the report must explain the scope of the auditor's responsibilities regarding the financial statements or data examined and include either an expression of an opinion regarding the statements or data or state that an opinion cannot be expressed.

REPORTING STANDARDS

The auditor's reporting responsibilities are established by four generally accepted auditing standards. They are:

1. The report shall state whether the financial statements are presented in accordance with generally accepted accounting principles.[1]

2. The report shall state whether such principles have been consistently observed in the current period in relation to the preceding period.[2]

3. Informative disclosures in the financial statements are to be regarded as reasonably adequate unless otherwise stated in the report.[3]

4. The report shall either contain an expression of opinion regarding the financial statements, taken as a whole, or an assertion to the effect that an opinion cannot be expressed. When an overall opinion cannot be expressed, the reasons therefore should be stated. In all cases where an auditor's name is associated with financial statements, the report should contain a clear-cut indication of the character of the auditor's examination, if any, and the degree of responsibility he (or she) is taking.[4]

---

[1] AICPA Professional Standards, Volume 1, *Auditing, Management Advisory Services, Tax Practice, Accounting and Review Services*, 1982, Commerce Clearing House, Inc., Chicago, *SAS No. 1, Codification of Auditing Standards and Procedures*, AU 410.01. When expressing an opinion on financial statements prepared based on a comprehensive basis of accounting other than GAAP (cash basis or tax basis, for example) the auditor satisfies the first standard of reporting by stating in the opinion that the financial statements are not intended to be in conformity with GAAP.

[2] *SAS No. 1, Codification of Auditing Standards and Procedures*, AU 420.01.

[3] *SAS No. 1, Codification of Auditing Standards and Procedures*, AU 430.01.

[4] *SAS No. 26, Association with Financial Statements*, AU 504.01.

The first and second reporting standards require a declarative statement in the auditor's report. The auditor must say whether the financial statements are presented in conformity with GAAP and whether the financial statements are presented on a basis of accounting that is consistent with those followed in the previous period.

The third standard of reporting, relating to financial statement disclosures, does not require a declarative statement in the audit report. It requires exception reporting. When the auditor presents an unqualified opinion, asserting that the financial statements are presented fairly in conformity with GAAP, it is implied that the statements have adequate informative disclosure. The concept of adequate disclosure relates to the form, arrangement, and content of the statements, footnotes that expand on the basic statement elements, and the terminology used, detail presented, and classification of items in the statements. Matters that require disclosure and the manner of their presentation are determined by professional accounting standards and the exercise of audit judgment. A general rule is that disclosure should be made in the financial statements of information that would influence the decisions of an informed reader. The information should be presented in the manner that best achieves user understanding.

When financial statements lack adequate disclosure, a qualified opinion or an adverse opinion is required, depending on the effect of the disclosure deficiency on the overall fairness of the statements. An opinion that is modified because of disclosure deficiencies must present the needed disclosure information, if practicable. Practicable means that the information is reasonably obtainable and providing it would not require the auditor to become a preparer of financial statements or information. For example, the auditor would not be expected to prepare a basic financial statement (such as a statement of changes in financial position) that was omitted by the client.

Because of the confidential client relationship imposed by the AICPA Code of Ethics, information not required to be disclosed in financial statements by professional standards should not otherwise be presented without the client's permission.[5]

The fourth reporting standard requires the auditor to express an opinion or disclaim an opinion regarding a client's financial statements when the auditor is associated with such statements. The objective of

---

[5] *SAS No. 32, Adequacy of Disclosure in Financial Statements*, AU 431.

the fourth reporting standard is to prevent a misunderstanding of the degree of responsibility the auditor is assuming when his or her name is associated with a client's financial statements.

An accountant is associated with financial statements when he or she has consented to the use of his or her name in a report, document, or written communication containing the statements. Also, when an accountant submits to a client or a third party financial statements that he or she has prepared or has assisted in preparing, the accountant is deemed to be associated with the statements.[6] Accordingly, an accountant may be associated with audited or unaudited statements of a public company or with audited, compiled, or reviewed statements of a nonpublic company. (Reporting on financial statements of nonpublic companies is discussed in Chapter 18.)

A public company is defined as any company whose securities trade in a public market either on a stock exchange or in the over-the-counter market or a company that makes a filing with a regulatory agency such as the SEC in preparation for the sale of any class of its securities in a public market. When an auditor is associated with the unaudited financial statement of a *public* company, the fourth standard of reporting requires that the degree of responsibility assumed be explained. This means that the auditor will disclaim an opinion regarding the statements. The disclaimer is a one paragraph report that reads as follows:

Accountant's Report

(Address)

The accompanying balance sheet of X Company as of December 31, 19x1, and the related statements of income, retained earnings, and changes in financial position for the year then ended were not audited by us and, accordingly, we do not express an opinion on them.

(Signature and date)

Each page of the statements should be marked "unaudited." If the accountant is aware of departures from GAAP because of his or her

---

[6] *SAS No. 26, Association with Financial Statements*, AU 504.03.

association with the unaudited financial statements and the client refuses to revise the statements, a reservation paragraph would be added to the disclaimer explaining the deficiencies. The paragraph should state what GAAP requires and what the company has done. The paragraph should also provide the effect on the financial statements of the departure or state that the effect cannot be determined.

If an accountant is not independent regarding a client's financial statements, an examination in accordance with generally accepted auditing standards is not possible. If an accountant who is not independent is associated with financial statements he or she must, under the fourth standard of reporting, disclaim an opinion on the statements and give as the reason for the disclaimer the fact that the accountant is not independent regarding the statements. *Statements on Standards for Accounting and Review Services*, discussed in Chapter 18, explain the accountant's reporting responsibility when he or she is associated with a nonpublic company's financial statements and the accountant is not independent. The following disclaimer of opinion is appropriate when an accountant is associated with the financial statements of a public company and lacks independence under Rule 101 of the AICPA Code of Ethics.

Accountant's Report

(Address)

We are not independent with respect to XYZ Company, and the accompanying balance sheet as of December 31, 19x1, and the related statements of income, retained earnings, and changes in financial position for the year then ended were not audited by us and, accordingly, we do not express an opinion on them.

(Signature and date)

STANDARD AUDIT REPORT

The standard audit report is a two paragraph report (scope and opinion paragraphs) that contains certain key elements. The audit report of Mobile Corporation (reproduced from Chapter 1) presents an unqualified opinion.

Accountant's Report

February 17, 1985

Board of Directors and Shareholders
Mobile Corporation

We have examined the balance sheets of Mobile Corporation as of December 31, 1984 and 1983, and the related statements of income, retained earnings, and changes in financial position for the years then ended. Our examinations were made in accordance with generally accepted auditing standards and, accordingly, included such tests of the accounting records and such other auditing procedures as we considered necessary in the circumstances.

In our opinion, the financial statements referred to above present fairly the financial position of Mobile Corporation as of December 31, 1984 and 1983, and the results of its operations and the changes in its financial position for the years then ended, in conformity with generally accepted accounting principles applied on a consistent basis.

Bridges, Geisert & Vickery
Certified Public Accountants

The standard audit report contains the following key elements:

1. **Address.** The report may be addressed to the company whose statements are being audited or to its board of directors or stockholders (addressing the report to the board and stockholders emphasizes the auditor's independence from the company's management). A report on the statements of an unincorporated entity should be addressed to the owners (partners, for example).

2. **States that an examination (audit) was performed** (the scope paragraph states that the auditors have examined the financial statements of Mobile Corporation).

3. **Identifies the financial statements that were examined** (balance sheets, income statements, and statements of changes in financial position for the periods ended December 31, 1984 and 1983).

4. **Explains how the financial statements were examined** (the scope paragraph states that they were examined in accordance with generally accepted auditing standards and all procedures considered necessary were applied).

5. **Attests to the fairness of presentation of the financial statements** (the opinion paragraph states that, in the auditor's opinion, the statements are presented fairly in conformity with GAAP).

6. **Explains the basis upon which fairness was judged** (the opinion paragraph states that fairness is based on GAAP applied on a consistent basis).

7. **Signature.** The report should be signed in the firm's name.

The auditor is conveying to readers of the audit report certain specific information when he or she states that the examination of the financial statements was performed in accordance with generally accepted auditing standards and that the statements are presented fairly in conformity with GAAP applied on a consistent basis. Specifically, the auditor is telling the reader that generally accepted auditing standards were followed in conducting the audit. This means that the auditor has complied with the ten GAAS discussed in this text—the three general standards, the three standards of field work, and the four reporting standards—and that all other SASs applicable in the circumstances have been followed. Further, the auditor has performed other auditing procedures he or she considered necessary to provide a reasonable basis for expressing an opinion on the statements. In other words, the auditor has performed a professional service and is warranting to users of the audit report that the work that was done can be relied upon.

The term "generally accepted accounting principles" as used in the Mobile audit report, means that accounting principles and practices and the methods of applying them were considered in judging the fairness of the presentation of the financial statements.[7] GAAP constitutes the benchmark against which financial statements are compared to determine whether they are fair presentations.

The term "present fairly" has specific meaning in auditing. It is a technical accounting term encompassing the conventions, rules, and procedures necessary to define accepted accounting practice at a particular time. It includes not only broad guidelines of general application, but also detailed practices and procedures.[8]

The term GAAP includes promulgated accounting standards and accounting practice that is accepted because of general business usage.

---

[7] *SAS No. 1, Codification of Auditing Standards and Procedures*, AU 410.02.
[8] *SAS No. 1, Codification of Auditing Standards and Procedures*, AU 411.02.

The accounting pronouncements which are considered GAAP under Rule 203 of the AICPA *Code of Ethics* are:

- Accounting Research Bulletins (ARBs) issued by the AICPA Committee on Accounting Procedure.

- Opinions issued by the Accounting Principles Board of the AICPA (APB Opinions).

- Financial Accounting Standards (FASB Statements) issued by the Financial Accounting Standards Board.

- Interpretations (FASB Interpretations) issued by the Financial accounting Standards Board.

ARBs, APB Opinions, and FASB Statements and Interpretations are GAAP because they are (or were) issued by bodies designated by the AICPA with authority to issue such standards. Currently, the FASB is the authoritative body for issuing accounting standards. Authority for other accounting practices rests on their wide-spread usage and acceptance.

The auditor's opinion that financial statements are presented fairly must be based on his or her judgment as to the statements' compliance with GAAP. This means that the auditor, based on the examination of the financial statements, must judge fairness of presentation according to:

1. Whether the accounting principles selected and applied by the client have general acceptance,

2. Whether the accounting principles are appropriate in the circumstances,

3. Whether the statements contain adequate informative disclosure of information necessary to interpret them,

4. Whether the information presented in the statements is classified and summarized in a reasonable manner, that is, neither too detailed nor too condensed, and

5. Whether the financial statements reflect the underlying events and transactions in a manner that presents the financial position, results

of operations, and changes in financial position wthin a range of acceptable limits, that is, limits that are reasonable and practicable to attain in financial statements.[9]

THE CONSISTENCY EXPRESSION

Sometimes the expression is heard "figures don't lie, but liars figure." Because there are alternative generally accepted accounting principles that may be appropriately applied in given circumstances, it is important that readers of the financial statements and the auditor's report know the basis of accounting followed in preparing the statements and know that such procedures are consistent with those used in the previous period. Without consistent application of accounting principles, financial data would not be comparable. Financial statement results can be manipulated by merely changing accounting principles from one period to another. To prevent such manipulation, APB Opinion No. 22, *Disclosure of Accounting Policies*, requires that financial statements disclose the significant accounting principles and practices followed in their preparation. Further, APB No. 20, *Accounting Changes*, and the second standard of reporting require that such basis of accounting, once adopted, be followed consistently from period to period. When a change is made and properly reported in accordance with APB No. 20, the second standard of reporting requires that such basis of accounting, once adopted, be followed consistently from period to period. When a change is made and properly reported in accordance with APB No. 20, the second standard of reporting requires that the auditor clearly explain in the report the fact that the statements are not presented on a basis consistent with that of the prior period. In these circumstances, the audit report will contain a qualified opinion regarding consistency.

The objective of the consistency standard is two-fold:

1. To give assurance that the comparability of financial statements between periods has not been materially affected by changes in accounting principles, which include not only accounting principles and practices but also the methods of applying them, or

2. If comparability has been materially affected by such changes, to require appropriate reporting by the auditor regarding such changes.[10]

---

[9] *SAS No. 5, The Meaning of "Present Fairly in Conformity with GAAP" in the Independent Auditor's Report*, AU 411.04.

[10] *SAS No. 1, Codification of Auditing Standards Procedures*, AU 420.02.

Financial statement comparability between years may be affected by accounting changes, an error in previously issued statements, changes in classification, and events or transactions substantially different from those reflected in previously issued statements.[11] Changes in accounting principles having a material effect on the financial statements require recognition in the auditor's report. Other changes may require disclosure in the financial statements in order to make the statements sufficiently informative.

Accounting for a change in principle is specified by APB No.20, regarding annual statements and FASB Statement No. 3, *Reporting Accounting Changes in Interim Financial Statements*, regarding monthly or quarterly statements. Generally, the cumulative effect of the change on all prior periods must be reported in income in the year of change. There are also pro forma reporting requirements for net income and earnings per share and a requirement that the financial statements include a footnote explaining the nature of the change, its effect on the statements, and a financial accounting justification for the change.

A change in accounting principle includes, for example, a change from the straight-line method to an accelerated method of determining depreciation, or a change in the method of costing inventories, such as from the first-in, first-out to the last-in, first-out method.

A change in accounting principle may require restatement of prior-period statements presented for comparative purposes. For example, changing from the percentage-of-completion method in accounting for long-term construction contracts to the completed contract method or a change from the LIFO inventory valuation method to another valuation method requires such reporting.

When there has been a change in accounting principle, the auditor is required to modify his or her opinion as to consistency, indicating the nature of the change. Usually, when an audit opinion is other than unqualified, the reasons for the opinion must be explained in a middle paragraph(s) of the report. However, for consistency violations a descriptive paragraph is not required; the auditor will refer to the financial statement footnote that explains the reason for the change and the effect on the financial statements.

In a qualified opinion relating to inconsistency, the auditor's concurrence with the change is implicit unless he or she takes exception to the change in expressing an opinion regarding the fairness of the financial

---

[11] *SAS No. 1, Codification of Auditing Standards and Procedures*, AU 420.04.

statements. However, it is customary to make the auditor's concurrence with a change in principle explicit by using the expression "with which we concur" in referring to the change. The form of modification of the auditor's opinion regarding consistency depends on the method of accounting for the effect of the change.[12] Following are examples of appropriate language for qualified opinions for consistency violations:

Consistency violation requiring prior-period restatement:

(Standard scope paragraph)

(Opinion paragraph covering one year)

In our opinion, the financial statements referred to above present fairly the financial position of X Company as of (at) December 31, 19xx, and the results of its operations and changes in its financial position for the year then ended, in conformity with generally accepted accounting principles applied on a basis consistent with that of the preceding year after giving retroactive effect to the change, with which we concur, in the method of accounting for long-term construction contracts as described in Note X to the financial statements.

(Opinion paragraph covering two years)

In our opinion, the financial statements referred to above present fairly the financial position of X Company as of (at) December 31, 19xx and 19xx, and the results of its operations and the changes in its financial position for the years then ended, in conformity with generally accepted accounting principles applied on a consistent basis after restatement for the change, with which we concur, in the method of accounting for long-term construction contracts as described in Note X to the financial statements.[13]

Consistency violation requiring cumulative effect reporting:

If the auditor is reporting only on the year during which the change was made, the consistency qualification would read:

(Standard scope paragraph)

(Opinion paragraph)

. . . in conformity with generally accepted accounting principles which, except for the change, with which we concur, in the method of computing depreciation as described in Note X to the financial statements, have been applied on a basis consistent with that of the preceding year.

---

[12] *SAS No. 1, Codification of Auditing Standards and Procedures,* AU 546.01.

[13] *SAS No. 1, Codification of Auditing Standards and Procedures,* AU 546.02.

If the auditor is reporting on two or more years' statements, the auditor should make reference to an accounting principle change as long as the year of change is included in the years being reported upon. For example,

(Opinion paragraph, reporting on two or more years)

. . . in conformity with generally accepted accounting principles consistently applied during the period except for the change, with which we concur, in the method of computing depreciation as described in Note X to the financial statements.

If the year of change is the earliest year being reported upon, there is no inconsistency in the application of accounting principles during the current and preceding period. However, the auditor should refer to the change having been made in the year when the cumulative effect was reported. For example,

(Opinion paragraph)

. . . in conformity with generally accepted accounting principles consistently applied during the period subsequent to the change, with which we concur, made as of January 1, 19xx, in the method of computing depreciation as described in Note X to the financial statements.[14]

Beginning on the next page are exhibits of accounting principle changes from published annual reports. The exhibits include:

- Change in Accounting for Inventories—Longs Drug Stores, Inc.

- Change in Accounting for Compensated Absences—Toys "R" Us, Inc.

- Change in Reporting Entity—Sears, Roebuck and Co.

The exhibits present the qualifying language from the auditor's opinion paragraph, followed by the financial statement footnote. The exhibits are taken from *Principles and Presentation—Retailing, A Review of 1980 Annual Reports*, by Peat, Marwick, Mitchell & Co.

The auditor must judgmentally evaluate an accounting principle change to determine that the newly adopted principle is generally accepted and that the method of accounting for the effect of the change is in conformity with GAAP (APB No. 20). Also, management must have

---

[14] *SAS No. 1, Codification of Auditing Standards and Procedures*, AU 546.03

Exhibit 15-1
Longs Drug Stores, Inc.

. . . in conformity with generally accepted accounting principles consistently applied during the period except for the change, with which we concur, in 1981 in the method of accounting for merchandise as described in the summary of accounting policies in the notes to financial statements.

Notes to Financial Statements

Summary of Accounting Policies
The last-in, first-out (LIFO) method of valuing inventory was adopted by the company during 1981 because, in an inflationary period, it results in a better matching of current merchandise costs with current revenues. Previously, the company used the specific cost method. The effect of the change on the Statement of Income is summarized in the following supplementary information:

	1981 Specific Cost)	Effects of Change to LIFO	1981 (LIFO) Cost)
	(Thousands Except per Share)		
Net sales	$893,198		$893,198
Cost of merchandise	677,740	7,100	684,840
Gross profit	215,458	(7,100)	208,358
Other expenses	157,385		157,385
Income before taxes	58,073	(7,100)	50,973
Taxes on income	28,715	(3,604)	25,111
Net income	29,358	(3,496)	25,862
Earnings per common share	2.78	(.33)	2.45

The change also reduced merchandise inventory by $7,100,000. There is no cumulative effect on prior years since the ending inventory as previously reported (1980) is the beginning inventory for LIFO purposes. Accordingly, comparative results of operations for the prior year on a LIFO basis are not determinable.

Exhibit 15-2
Toys "R" Us, Inc.

. . . in conformity with generally accepted accounting principles consistently applied during the period, except for the change, with which we concur, made as of January 29, 1979, in the method of accounting for inventories and after restatement for the change, with which we concur, in the method of accounting for compensated absences, made as of February 4, 1980, as described in Notes 2 and 4, respectively, to the consolidated financial statements.

Change in Accounting for Compensated Absences

Effective for the year ended February 1, 1981, the company adopted the provisions of Financial Accounting Standards Board Statement No. 43, Accounting for Compensated Absences, and accrued vacation pay as earned. As a result of this change, the Statements of Consolidated Earnings for the years ended February 3, 1980, and January 28, 1979, were restated as follows:

| | Year ended | | | |
| | February 3, 1980 | | January 28, 1979 | |
(In thousands except per share information)	*Net earnings*	*Net earnings per common share*	*Net earnings*	*Net earnings per common share*
As previously reported	$26,897	$1.83(a)	$17,208	$1.22(a)
Effect of accruing vacation pay	(121)	(.01)	(61)	—
As restated	26,776	1.82	17,147	1.22

(a) Restated for the three-for-two stock split effected on July 28, 1980.

Exhibit 15-3
Sears, Roebuck and Co.

. . . in conformity with generally accepted accounting principles applied on a consistent basis after restatement for the change with which we concur, in the consolidation policy as described in Note 1 of Notes to Consolidated Financial Statements of the company.

Change in reporting entity

In 1980, Sears, Roebuck and Co. realigned its operations into three separate business groups. In connection with this organizational change, the company has changed its financial reporting. The basis of presentation of the accompanying financial statements has been changed to:

- Consolidate all domestic and significant international companies in which the company has more than a 50 percent equity ownership, except for manufacturing subsidiaries, to exhibit the extent of the company's operations; and

- Present financial statements for each of the company's business groups to provide financial data necessary to understand these operations.

The company believes that these changes provide financial statements that better reflect the company's organization and more clearly illustrate its results of operations and financial position.

Coincident with this change, the company modified its procedure for allocating its contribution to The Savings and Profit Sharing Fund of Sears Employees. The allocation is now based on the relative earnings of the respective groups, rather than employee contributions, to appropriately match the expense with the profit that gave rise to the company's contribution.

Prior periods have been restated to reflect these changes. The changes did not affect previously reported net income, although net income as previously reported by certain of the companies within the separate business groups was changed.

provided proper justification for the change which means including in the footnote an accounting reason for the change. If a change in accounting principles does not reflect these conditions, the auditor's opinion should be appropriately qualified to indicate that the new principle was adopted without proper justification. If a change in accounting principle involves changing from a generally accepted accounting principle to one that is not generally accepted, the auditor's opinion must recognize the lack of fairness, in addition to the consistency violation. If the departure is so serious as to require an adverse opinion, no mention of the consistency standard is made.

When an accountant's report is qualified (or an adverse opinion is given) for lack of fairness, a middle paragraph of the report must explain the reason for the opinion.

Following are examples of report terminology when the auditor's report is modified for both a consistency violation and lack of fairness in the application of accounting principles, and for reporting a principle change not properly justified:

The newly adopted principle is not generally accepted:

(Standard scope paragraph)

(Middle paragraph)

The company previously recorded its land at cost but adjusted the amounts to appraised values during the year, with a corresponding increase in stockholders' equity in the amount of (give amount). In our opinion, the new basis on which land is recorded is not in conformity with generally accepted accounting principles.

(Opinion paragraph)

In our opinion, except for the change to recording appraised values as described above, the aforementioned financial statements present fairly the financial position of X Company at December 31, 19xx, and the results of its operations and changes in its financial position for the year then ended, in conformity with generally accepted accounting principles applied on a basis consistent with that of the preceding year.

The newly adopted principle is not properly justified:

(Middle paragraph)

As disclosed in Note X to the financial statements, the company has adopted (description of newly adopted method), whereas it previously used (description of previous method). Although use of the (description of newly adopted method) is in conformity with generally accepted accounting principles, in our opinion the company has not provided reasonable justification for making a change as required by Opinion No. 20 of the Accounting Principles Board.

(Opinion paragraph)

In our opinion, except for the change in accounting principles as stated above, the aforementioned financial statements present fairly the financial position of X Company at December 31, 19xx, and the results of its operations and changes in its financial position for the year then ended, in conformity with generally accepted accounting principles applied on a basis consistent with that of the preceding year.[15]

The consistency standard applies to financial statements whether audited or unaudited. When an auditor has not examined the financial statements of a company for the preceding year (whether examined by other auditors or unaudited), he or she must adopt procedures that are practicable and reasonable in the circumstances to assure that accounting principles followed in the current period are consistent with those followed in the previous period. Such procedures will include examining invoices, contracts, official recorded deeds, journals and ledger amounts, and so forth, to obtain evidence supporting the beginning balances and past transactions in asset, liability, and owners' equity accounts. Also, evidence must support the consistent application of accounting principles and practices employed in the recognition of revenue and accounting for costs and expenses in the current period compared to the preceding period. Inadequate records may impose a scope restriction on the auditor's ability to obtain such evidence. In this event, the auditor would likely be unable to express an opinion on the current year's results of operations and changes in financial position. Following is an example of reporting when the records are not adequate to support an opinion on the results of operations and change in financial position or consistency between the current period and the preceding period:

Accountant's Report

(Address)

We have examined the balance sheet of X Company as of December 31, 19xx, and the related statement of income, retained earnings, and changes

---

[15] *SAS No. 1, Codification of Auditing Standards and Procedures,* AU 546.06.

in financial position for the year then ended. Our examination was made in accordance with generally accepted auditing standards and, accordingly, included such tests of the accounting records and such other auditing procedures as we considered necessary in the circumstances, except as indicated in the following paragraph.

Because of major inadequacies in the company's accounting records for the previous year, it was not practicable to extend our auditing procedures to enable us to express an opinion on results of operations and changes in financial position for the year ended (current year) or on the consistency of application of accounting principles with the preceding year.

In our opinion, the accompanying balance sheet presents fairly the financial position of X Company as of (current year-end) in conformity with generally accepted accounting principles.[16]

(Signature and date)

If accounting records have been kept on a basis of accounting other than GAAP (cash or income tax basis, for example) in prior periods and the current period's statements are to be audited on a GAAP basis, it may not be practicable or possible to restate the prior year's statements on a GAAP basis. When this circumstance exists, the auditor should omit from the report the reference to consistency. This type of report would read as follows:

(Standard scope paragraph)

(Middle paragraph)

The company has kept its records and has prepared its financial statements for previous years on the cash basis with no recognition having been accorded accounts receivable, accounts payable, or accrued expenses. At the beginning of the current year the company adopted the accrual basis of accounting. Although appropriate adjustments have been made to retained earnings as of the beginning of the year, it was not practicable to determine what adjustments would be necessary in the financial statements of the preceding year to restate results of operations and changes in financial position in conformity with the accounting principles used in the current year.

(Opinion paragraph)

In our opinion, the aforementioned financial statements present fairly the financial position of X Company as of October 31, 19xx, and the results of

---

[16] *SAS No. 1, Codification of Auditing Standards and Procedures*, AU 546.15.

its operations and the changes in its financial position for the year then ended, in conformity with generally accepted accounting principles.[17]

When an auditor is reporting on the first year of operations of a new
company, there is no reference to consistency in the report as there is no
previous period for comparison. The financial statements would, of
course, disclose in accordance with GAAP that they are the statements
of a newly organized company.

A change in reporting entity results in a violation of the consistency
standard. Such a change involves:

- Presenting consolidated or combined statements in place of statements of individual companies.

- Changing specific subsidiaries comprising the group of companies
  for which consolidated statements are prepared.

- Changing the companies included in combined financial statements.

- Changing among cost, equity, and consolidation methods of accounting for subsidiaries or other investments in common stock.[18]

A change in reporting entity is accounted for, in accordance with
APB No. 20, prior-period restatement. However, there is violation of
the consistency standard requiring recognition in the auditor's report.
The consistency expression, in this instance, (as previously illustrated in
the Sears report) states that the financial statements are presented on a
consistent basis "after restatement."

Sometimes a company will change an estimate and, at the same time,
change the principle followed in accounting for the item. For example,
a change in the estimated useful life of a depreciable asset may be made
at the same time that the method of depreciating the asset is changed.
That is, a "change in principle inseparable from a change in estimate" is
made. APB No. 20 requires such changes to be accounted for as
changes in estimates—they do not require cumulative type reporting or
restatement, but are accounted for currently and prospectively.
However, the auditor must recognize the inconsistency resulting from
the principle change by qualifying the audit report.

Changes in accounting estimates, corrections of errors in previously
issued financial statements not involving a principle change, and

---

[17] *SAS No. 1, Codification of Auditing Standards and Procedures*, AU 546.16.
[18] *SAS No. 1, Codification of Auditing Standards and Procedures*, AU 420.07.

changes in classification and statement format are examples of accounting changes that do not affect the consistency standard. Although such changes may require disclosure in the financial statements to make them sufficiently informative, the auditor's report would not be modified.

If an accounting change has no material effect on the financial statements of the current period, but is expected to have a substantial effect in later years, the change should be disclosed in the footnotes to the current statements. It would not, however, be reflected in the auditor's report.[19]

As previously illustrated, the auditor's consistency expression will vary depending on whether single year statements or comparative statements are covered by the audit report. When the auditor is expressing an opinion on financial statements of a single year the phrase "on a basis consistent with that of the preceding year" should be used. If the audit report relates to more than one year's statements, the phrase "on a consistent basis" is used. If the year preceding the earliest year being reported upon is presented, the consistency expression should be "consistently applied during the period and on a basis consistent with that of the preceding year."[20]

TYPES OF AUDIT OPINIONS

There are four basic types of audit reports that, under certain specific conditions, may be issued by auditors. They are "unqualified opinion," "qualified opinion," "adverse opinion," and "disclaimer of opinion." An auditor may issue an *unqualified* audit report (sometimes referred to as a "clean opinion") when he or she has reached the following conclusions, based upon an examination of the financial statements in accordance with generally accepted auditing standards:

1. The financial statements present fairly overall financial position, results of operations, and changes in financial position in conformity with GAAP or another comprehensive basis of accounting.

2. GAAP or the other comprehensive basis of accounting were applied on a basis consistent with that of the preceding period.

3. The financial statements have adequate informative disclosures.[21]

---

[19] *SAS No. 1, Codification of Auditing Standards and Procedures*, AU 420.18.
[20] *SAS No. 1, Codification of Auditing Standards and Procedures*, AU 420.21.
[21] *SAS No. 2, Reports on Audited Financial Statements*, AU 509.28.

An auditor may issue a *qualified* report when he or she has complied with applicable generally accepted auditing standards regarding an examination of financial statements and reached the conclusion that the financial statements present fairly overall in conformity with GAAP (or other comprehensive basis of accounting), but there is an exception regarding a material item(s), as follows:

1. The scope of the auditor's examination was restricted by the circumstances of the engagement, condition of the client's records, or for other reasons.

2. There is a material uncertainty regarding the statements (subject-to type qualified opinion).

3. Disclosure is lacking.

4. An accounting principle or the method of its application is not in conformity with GAAP.

5. Accounting principles followed in the current period are not consistent with those followed in the preceding period.[22]

With the exception of a consistency violation, the auditor's qualified report must disclose in a middle paragraph(s) all of the substantive reasons for the qualification. If the qualification results from a lack of fairness in the application of accounting principles or methods, the report must explain the effect of the departure on the financial statements. If the omission of a required statement disclosure is the basis of the qualification, the auditor must generally present the omitted disclosure information.

A qualified report will include the word "except" or "exception" in a phrase such as "except for" or "with the exception of" to indicate that the opinion contains a qualification. However, as discussed later, the qualifying phrase should be "subject to" when the qualification is due to a material uncertainty. Illustrated on the next page are examples of middle paragraph wording and opinion modifications appropriate for various types of auditor's qualified reports:

---

[22] *SAS No. 2, Reports on Audited Financial Statements*, AU 509.29.

Qualified opinion for GAAP violation (auditor has concluded that the qualification is not so serious as to warrant an adverse opinion):

(Standard scope paragraph)

(Middle paragraph)

The company has excluded from property and debt in the accompanying balance sheet certain lease obligations, which, in our opinion, should be capitalized in order to conform with generally accepted accounting principles. If these lease obligations were capitalized, property would be increased by (amount), long-term debt by (amount) and retained earnings by (amount) as of December 31, 19xx, and net income and earnings per share would be increased (decreased) by (amount) and (amount) respectively for the year then ended.

(Opinion paragraph)

In our opinion, except for the effects of not capitalizing lease obligations, as discussed in the preceding paragraph, the financial statements present fairly . . . .[23]

Qualified opinion for uncertainty (conditions of uncertainty are not such as to warrant a disclaimer of opinion):

(Standard scope paragraph)

(Middle paragraph)

As discussed in Note X to the financial statements, the company is defendant in a lawsuit alleging infringement of certain patent rights and claiming royalties and punitive damages. The company has filed a counter action, and preliminary hearings and discovery proceedings on both actions are in progress. Company offices and counsel believe the company has a good chance of prevailing, but the ultimate outcome of the lawsuits cannot presently be determined, and no provisions for any liability that may result has been made in the financial statements.

(Opinion paragraph)

In our opinion, subject to the effects, if any, on the financial statements of the ultimate resolution of the matter discussed in the preceding paragraph, the financial statements referred to above present fairly . . . .

or

---

[23] *SAS No. 2, Reports on Audited Financial Statements*, AU 509.37.

In our opinion, subject to the effects of such adjustments, if any, as might have been required had the outcome of the uncertainty referred to in the preceding paragraph been known, the financial statements referred to above present fairly . . . .[24]

An auditor may issue a subject-to qualified opinion when questions arise about a client's ability to continue in existence as a going concern. In these circumstances the auditor is concerned about the recoverability and classification of recorded asset amounts and the amounts and classification of liabilities. Going concern questions ordinarily relate to a company's ability to continue to meet current maturing obligations without substantial disposal of assets, restructuring of debt, externally forced revisions of its operations, or similar actions. When evidence contrary to the going concern assumption come to the attention of the auditor, he or she must consider any mitigating factors (factors or plans that management has that may overcome going concern problems) and make a judgment decision as to whether the financial statements require disclosure of the going concern problems and whether the opinion should be qualified subject-to the going concern contingency.

If the auditor determines that an opinion modification is required, along with footnote disclosure of the going concern problem, a subject-to qualified opinion will usually be issued covering only the current period statements (a disclaimer of opinion may be issued if the contingency regarding going concern is so pervasive that the scope of the examination is impaired). Following is an illustration of appropriate report language:

(Standard scope paragraph)

(Separate explanatory paragraph—following scope paragraph)

As shown in the financial statements, the company incurred a net loss of $ ____ during the year ended December 31, 19x1, and, as of that date, the company's current liabilities exceeded its current assets by $ _____ and its total liabilities exceeded its total assets by $ _____. These factors, among others, as discussed in Note X, indicate that the company may be unable to continue in existence. The financial statements do not include any adjustments relating to the recoverability and classification of recorded asset amounts or the amounts and classification of liabilities that might be necessary should the company be unable to continue in existence.

---

[24] *SAS No. 2, Reports on Audited Financial Statements*, AU 509.39. The first opinion paragraph should be used in those rare cases where the resolution of the uncertainty will be accounted for as a prior period adjustment. The second opinion paragraph (top of this page) should be used in all other cases where a subject to qualification is appropriate.

(Opinion paragraph)

In our opinion, subject to the effects on the financial statements of such adjustments, if any, as might have been required had the outcome of the uncertainty about the recoverability and classification of recorded asset amounts and the amounts and classification of liabilities referred to in the preceding paragraph been known, the financial statements referred to above present fairly the financial position of X Company as of December 31, 19x1, and the results of its operations and the changes in its financial position for the year then ended, in conformity with generally accepted accounting principles applied on a basis consistent with that of the preceding year.[25]

An *adverse* opinion states that the financial statements taken overall are not fair presentations. The auditor must have reached this opinion based on an examination in accordance with generally accepted auditing standards. An adverse opinion may result from lack of fairness in the application of accounting measurement or disclosure principles. The auditor's report must explain all of the substantive reasons for the opinion. Following is an example of report language appropriate for an adverse opinion:

(Standard scope paragraph)

(Middle paragraph)

As discussed in Note X to the financial statements, the company carries its property, plant and equipment accounts at appraisal values, and provides depreciation on the basis of such values. Further, the company does not provide for income taxes with respect to differences between financial income and taxable income arising because of the use, for income tax purposes, of the installment method of reporting gross profit from certain types of sales. Generally accepted accounting principles, in our opinion, require that property, plant and equipment be stated at an amount not in excess of cost, reduced by depreciation based on such amount, and that deferred income taxes be provided. Because of the departures from generally accepted accounting principles identified above, as of December 31, 19xx, inventories have been increased by (state amount) inclusion in manufacturing overhead of depreciation in excess of that based on cost; property, plant and equipment, less accumulated depreciation, is carried at (state amount) in excess of an amount based on the cost to the company; and allocated income tax of (amount) has not been recorded; resulting in

---

[25] *SAS No. 34, The Auditor's Considerations When a Question Arises About an Entity's Continued Existence,* AU 340.12.

an increase of (amount) in retained earnings and in appraisal capital of (amount). For the year ended December 31, 19xx, cost of goods sold has been increased (by amount) because of the effects of the depreciation accounting referred to above and deferred income taxes of (amount) have not been provided, resulting in an increase in net income and earnings per share of (amount) and (amount), respectively.

(Opinion paragraph)

In our opinion, because of the effects of the matters discussed in the preceding paragraph, the financial statements referred to above do not present fairly, in conformity with generally accepted accounting principles, the financial position of X Company as of December 31, 19xx, or the results of its operations and changes in its financial position for the year then ended.[26]

The adverse opinion and the qualified opinion are both issued in cases where the financial statements lack fairness of presentation in conformity with GAAP. The adverse is issued when the fairness violation is so pervasive that overall fairness is destroyed. A qualified opinion would be appropriate when a material item is not fairly presented, but overall fairness of the financial statements is not destroyed.

Issuance of an adverse opinion is a rare occurrence. Usually the auditor and the client are able to resolve the accounting problems that might mandate an adverse opinion through arbitration. The client cannot afford an adverse opinion if it sells its stock to the public—the stock exchanges and the SEC would suspend trading in the company's stock with resulting serious financial repercussions. Furthermore, if a nonpublic company needs an audit it means that particular users of the company's statements are demanding separate attestation as to the fairness of the company's financial condition and results of operations. An adverse would not satisfy these requirements. Consequently, the auditor and the client are usually able to implement accounting changes and provide needed information to avoid the issuance of an adverse opinion. It should be noted that because an opinion as to consistency implies the application of GAAP, no reference is made in an adverse opinion to consistent application of accounting principles.

A qualified opinion and a disclaimer are alternative opinions in situations involving scope restrictions. When the client, the timing of the

---

[26] *SAS No. 2, Reports on Audited Financial Statements*, AU 509.43.

engagement, the condition of the client's records, or other circumstances—such as the existence of material contingencies—impair the ability of the auditor to obtain sufficient competent evidential matter under the three standards of field work, the auditor must modify the opinion to reflect the restriction. A qualified opinion is issued for a scope restriction relating to a material item which is not so pervasive as to impair the ability to issue an overall opinion on the financial statements. If the restriction on the auditor's ability to gather evidence is so pervasive that the auditor cannot support an overall opinion on the financial statements, a disclaimer of opinion is warranted.

When a *disclaimer* of opinion is issued, the auditor's report must disclose all of the substantive reasons for the disclaimer. Disclaimers are issued for the following reasons:

- The auditor is unable to apply procedures deemed necessary in an audit engagement and the effect is so pervasive that a qualified opinion is not appropriate.

- An uncertainty regarding the financial statements is so pervasive that a qualified opinion is not appropriate.

- The accountant has not audited the financial statements:

  - Accountant is associated with a public company's unaudited financial statements.

  - The accountant is not independent regarding the financial statements of a public company with which he or she is associated.

  - The accountant has performed a review service for a nonpublic client (disclaim an audit opinion as the statements are unaudited).

  - An accountant is associated with complied statements of a nonpublic client (disclaim an audit opinion as the statements are unaudited).

Presented below is an example of appropriate wording for a disclaimer resulting from an audit engagement (other disclaimers were illustrated earlier in this chapter; accountant's reports on compiled and reviewed statements, that contain audit disclaimers, are illustrated in Chapter 18):

(Scope paragraph)

We have examined the balance sheet of X Company as of December 31, 19xx, and the related statements of income, retained earnings, and changes in financial position for the year then ended. Except as set forth in the following paragraph, our examination was made in accordance with generally accepted auditing standards and accordingly included such tests of the accounting records and such other auditing procedures as we considered necessary in the circumstances.

(Middle paragraph)

The company did not take a physical inventory of merchandise, stated at (amount) in the accompanying financial statements as of December 31, 19xx, and at (amount) as of January 1, 19xx. Further, evidence supporting the cost of property and equipment acquired prior to December 31, 19xx is no longer available. The company's records do not permit the application of adequate alternative procedures regarding the inventories or the cost of property and equipment.

(Disclaimer paragraph)

Since the company did not take physical inventories and we were unable to apply adequate alternative procedures regarding inventories and the cost of property and equipment, as noted in the preceding paragraph, the scope of our work was not sufficient to enable us to express, and we do not express, an opinion on the financial statements referred to above.[27]

EMPHASIS OF A MATTER

An auditor may depart from the standard unqualified report language by inserting a middle paragraph(s) in the report to emphasize a matter regarding the financial statements. The auditor's report, however, remains unqualified. This is a special form of disclosure made by the auditor to draw the report reader's attention to an item, already reported in the financial statements, that is extremely important in considering the overall significance of the financial statements. This type of disclosure in the audit report may, for example, refer to a matter discussed in the footnotes or to an item reported in the body of the financial statements.

Following is an example of an "unqualified" audit report that includes an emphasis paragraph referring to an important footnote:

---

[27] *SAS No. 2, Reports on Audited Financial Statements*, AU 509.47.

Accountant's Report

The Stockholders and Directors of
Rowan Companies, Inc.:

We have examined the consolidated balance sheets of Rowan Companies, Inc. and subsidiaries as of December 31, 19x2 and 19x1, and the related statements of consolidated income, changes in stockholders' equity, and changes in consolidated financial position for the years then ended. Our examination was made in accordance with generally accepted auditing standards, and accordingly included such tests of the accounting records and such other auditing procedures as we considered necessary in the circumstances.

As explained in Note 3, the company in 19x2 assigned salvage value to certain of its drilling equipment. Assigning salvage value to the equipment in our opinion does not represent a change in the consistent application of accounting principles but does affect the comparability of the financial statements.

In our opinion, the consolidated financial statements referred to above present fairly the financial position of the companies at December 31, 19x2 and 19x1, and the results of their operations and changes in their financial position for the years then ended, in conformity with generally accepted accounting principles applied on a consistent basis.

(Signature and date)

Note 3 to the financial statement reads:

3. Property and Depreciation

Estimated useful lives used to compute depreciation of property and equipment are as follows:

Drilling equipment...........................2 to 12 years
Aircraft and related equipment.................2 to 8 years
Other property and equipment.................2 to 33 years

In 19x2, the company, based on its operating experience assigned salvage value to certain of its drilling equipment. The effect of this change was to increase the company's consolidated net income for the year ended December 31, 19x2 by approximately $308,000 ($.14 per share).

OPINION BASED IN PART ON THE REPORT OF ANOTHER AUDITOR

SAS No. 1, Codification of Auditing Standards and Procedures, AU 543, provides guidance for reporting by a principle auditor who has used the work and report of another auditor (other auditors), for example, in reporting on the consolidated financial statements of a parent company and its subsidiaries. A principal auditor is an auditor who has examined a sufficient portion of the financial statements of the reporting entity to permit the expression of an overall opinion on such statements. A principal auditor may assume responsibility for the work of another auditor or he or she may refer to the other auditor's work and not assume responsibility for it.

Certain information must be disclosed in the principal auditor's report when he or she decides to make reference to the work of another auditor. The principal auditor's report should indicate, in the scope paragraph, the division of responsibility by stating the portion of the statements examined by the other auditor. This is usually done by presenting the dollar amounts or percentages of the financial statement items examined and reported on by the other auditor. The other auditor should not be named or his or her report should not be included in the consolidated statement's report without permission. Reference to the work of another auditor is not an opinion qualification, but rather a disclosure of the division of reporting responsibility.

If another auditor's report is used and it is qualified or an adverse opinion was issued, the principal auditor, in reporting on the consolidated financial statements, need not refer to the qualification or adverse opinion unless it is considered material to the financial statements of the reporting entity taken overall.

Presented below are examples of auditor's report language for a division of reporting responsibility relating to the annual reports of the Jewel Company and May Department Stores Co.:

Jewel Companies, Inc.

. . . necessary in the circumstances . . . . We have not examined the financial statements of Aurrera, S.A., a Mexican company in which Jewell has a 41.7% interest at January 31, 1981. The consolidated financial statements of Aurrera, S.A. for each of its three fiscal years in the period ended July 31, 1980 were examined by other independent auditors whose unqualified report thereon has been furnished to us.

In our opinion, which as to amounts with respect to Aurrera, S.A. for each of its three fiscal years in the period ended July 31, 1980 is based on the report of other independent auditors described above . . .

May Department Stores Co.

. . . necessary in the circumstances. . . . The financial statements of Volume Shoe Corporation which are included in the February 3, 1979 consolidated financial statements and which reflect total revenues and net earnings of 6% and 11%, respectively, of the consolidated totals, have been examined by other auditors whose report thereon has been furnished to us.

In our opinion, based upon our examinations and the report of other auditors as indicated in the preceding paragraph, the consolidated financial statements referred to above . . . .

It should be noted, as illustrated by both reports, that the scope and opinion paragraphs are modified to indicate the division of reporting responsibilities. The scope paragraphs above indicate the portion of the consolidated statements examined by the other accountants by stating the percent of consolidated interest represented by the other auditors' examinations. The opinion paragraphs both expressed an unqualified opinion that, as shown, is based on the opinion of the principal auditor and the report of the other auditors.

REPORTING A DEPARTURE FROM A PROMULGATED ACCOUNTING PRINCIPLE

A departure from GAAP involving measurement standards or disclosure standards will require the auditor to qualify his or her opinion or issue an adverse opinion, depending on the overall materiality and pervasiveness of the item(s) involved. In these cases, the auditor must disclose all the substantive reasons for the qualified or adverse opinion in a middle paragraph(s) of the audit report. The report must also include the effect of the departure on the financial statements or present the omitted disclosure information, if practical to do so.

A departure from a promulgated accounting principle covered by Rule 203 of the Code of Ethics will require disclosure in the auditor's report (if material) of the accounting principle requirement and the procedure followed by the client. As previously indicated, the promulgated accounting principles covered by Rule 203 are Accounting Research Bulletins, Accounting Principles Board Opinions, FASB Statements, and FASB Interpretations. An auditor, in rare circumstances, may give an unqualified opinion when the departure from a promulgated accounting principle occurs because the auditor determines that following the promulgated GAAP would result in misleading financial statements. In all cases, the auditor's report must disclose the procedure required by promulgated GAAP, the procedure followed by the client, and the effect on the financial statements.

PREDECESSOR AUDITOR— REPORTING RESPONSIBILITIES OF SUCCESSOR AUDITOR

When comparative financial statements are presented and the statements of the prior period have been examined by a predecessor auditor whose report is not presented (reissued), the successor auditor's report must disclose certain information regarding the predecessor's report. This is necessary to establish the successor auditor's reporting responsibility under the fourth reporting standard. The successor should indicate, in the scope paragraph of the report, the following information:

- That the financial statements of the prior period were examined by other auditors.

- The date of the other auditor's report.

- The type of opinion expressed by the predecessor.

- The substantive reasons for the predecessor auditor's report if it was other than unqualified.

If the financial statements of the prior period have been restated, the successor auditor should disclose, in the scope paragraph of the report, that the predecessor auditor reported on the statements of the prior period before restatement. Also, the successor, if he or she is able to become satisfied regarding the restatement, may include in the report an opinion as to the appropriateness of the restatement. Following is an example of an auditor's report on comparative statements involving a reference to a predecessor auditor:

Accountant's Report

(Address)

We have examined the balance sheet of ABC Company as of December 31, 19x2, and the related statements of income, retained earnings, and changes in financial position for the year then ended. Our examination was made in accordance with generally accepted auditing standards and, accordingly, included such tests of the accounting records and such other auditing procedures as we considered necessary in the circumstances. The financial statements of ABC Company for the year ended December 31, 19x1, were examined by other auditors whose report dated March 1, 19x2, expressed an unqualified opinion on those statements.

In our opinion, the 19x2 financial statements referred to above present fairly the financial position of ABC Company as of December 31, 19x2, and the results of its operations and the changes in its financial position for the year then ended, in conformity with generally accepted accounting principles applied on a basis consistent with that of the preceding year.

(Signature and date)

If the predecessor auditor's opinion was other than unqualified, the last sentence of the above scope paragraph would be modified to explain the nature of the opinion given. For example,

. . . were examined by other auditors whose opinion, dated March 1, 19x2, on those statements was qualified as being subject to the effects on the 19x1 financial statements of such adjustments, if any, as might have been required had the outcome of the litigation discussed in Note X to the financial statements been known.

If the statements reported on by the predecessor are restated based on currently developed information or, for example, the resolution of a contingency relating to those statements, the successor auditor should indicate that the predecessor auditor reported on the prior-period statements prior to their restatement. If the successor is able to satisfy himself or herself as to the appropriateness of the restatement, the following comment would be added to the scope paragraph.

We also reviewed the adjustments described in Note X that were applied to restate the 19xx financial statements. In our opinion, such adjustments are appropriate and have been properly applied to the 19xx financial statements.[28]

REPORTING ON UNAUDITED STATEMENTS IN COMPARATIVE FORM

When unaudited statements are presented in comparative form with audited statements, the auditor must explain the responsibility he or she is taking regarding the statements presented. This will usually involve expressing an opinion on the audited statements and including in the audit report an additional paragraph disclaiming an opinion regarding the unaudited statements. If the unaudited statements are included with audited statements in a document filed with the SEC, a registration statement, for example, it is required that the statements be marked as unaudited, but the auditor need not disclaim an opinion on the statements.

When the current period's statements are unaudited and the prior-period comparative statements are audited, the accountant may in-

---

[28] SAS No. 15, Reports on Comparative Financial Statements, AU 505.12.

clude a paragraph in his or her current disclaimer explaining the degree of responsibility assumed for the prior-period statements or the prior-period audit report can be reissued. An example of an accountant's report on comparative statements when the current period's statements are unaudited and the prior-period statements are audited follows:

Accountant's Report

(Address)

The accompanying balance sheet of X Company as of December 31, 19x2, and the related statements of income, retained earnings, and changes in financial position for the year then ended were not audited by us and, accordingly, we do not express an opinion on them.

The financial statements for the year ended December 31, 19x1, were examined by us (or other accountants if that is the case) and we (they) expressed an unqualified opinion on them in our (their) report dated March 1, 19x2, but we (they) have not performed any auditing procedures since that date.[29]

(Signature and date)

The disclaimer paragraph in the above report accomplishes the following:

1. It explains that the financial statements of the prior-period were audited.

2. It gives the date of the previous audit report.

3. It explains the type of opinion expressed previously.

4. It makes it clear to the reader that no auditing procedures have been performed since the date of the previous examination.

If the opinion on the prior year's statements had been other than unqualified, the reasons for the opinion would have had to have been included. If the prior-period statements were examined by other auditors, their names should not be mentioned unless permission is obtained from the other auditors.

---

[29] *SAS No. 26, Association with Financial Statements*, AU 504.17.

In lieu of adding a paragraph to the current accountant's report explaining the status of comparative statements, the previously issued accountant's report for the prior period may be reissued. A reissued report carries the original report date (dual-dating, explained later in this chapter, would be used for disclosures or adjustments made in the statements after their original issuance date). Before a predecessor accountant agrees to reissue his or her report on a prior-period's statements, the predecessor should perform procedures to assure that the presentation of the statements is appropriate. The predecessor may review the current working papers of the successor and may request a letter from the successor regarding any current matters that may impact on the prior-period statements. A predecessor, of course, is not required to reissue a prior-period report.

When the unaudited statements of a prior period presented for comparative purposes are those of a public company, the separate paragraph should include a disclaimer or a description of a review. If the statements are those of a nonpublic company the separate paragraph should contain a description of a compilation or review.

CONTINUING AUDITOR AND UPDATING

SAS No. 15, Reports on Comparative Financial Statements, AU 505, provides guidance for reporting when financial statements are presented in comparative form. *SAS No. 15* defines a continuing auditor as one who has audited the current period's financial statements and one or more immediately preceding period's statements. A continuing auditor is required to update his or her report on prior-periods' statements presented for comparative purposes. Updating means reissuing the same opinion as previously issued or revising the opinion as appropriate based on the current audit engagement. For example,

> If conditions are unchanged, as a result of the current examination, a prior-period unqualified, qualified, adverse, or disclaimer of opinion should be reexpressed using the current reporting date.

> If conditions have changed, based on the current examination, a prior-period opinion would be revised using the current reporting date. For example,

> > Subsequent resolution of an uncertainty relating to a prior period may result in updating a subject-to qualified opinion to unqualified.

Discovery of an uncertainty in a subsequent period that relates to prior statements may result in updating an unqualified opinion on the prior-period statements to a subject-to qualified opinion.

Subsequent restatement of prior-period statements to comply with GAAP may result in updating an adverse opinion or qualified opinion for lack of fairness to unqualified, after restatement.

Following is an example of an auditor's report (Baltimore Gas and Electric Company) that was updated because the auditors were continuing auditors. Furthermore, the opinion issued in the previous period was revised from an unqualified opinion to a subject-to qualified opinion due to the identification of a material uncertainty during the current period that also related to the preceding period's statements. When you read the report note the portion of the middle paragraph, which is in italics for emphasis, that states the following information required when an updated report includes a change in the type of opinion previously expressed:

1.   The date of the previous report.

2.   The type of opinion previously issued.

3.   The fact that the current opinion is different from that previously expressed.

Auditor's Report

To the Stockholders of
Baltimore Gas and Electric Company

We have examined the balance sheets of Baltimore Gas and Electric Company as of December 31, 19x3 and 19x2, and the related statements of income, retained earnings and changes in financial position for the years then ended. Our examinations were made in accordance with generally accepted auditing standards and, accordingly, included such tests of the accounting records and such other auditing procedures as we considered necessary in the circumstances.

As discussed in Note 9 to the financial statements, the Public Service Commission of Maryland on April 22, 19x3, ordered the company to refund previously collected revenue in the amount of $31,867,000, plus interest, to its electric customers, resulting from alleged overcollection of fuel rate adjustment revenues from February 19x1 through December 19x2. The company considered the Commission's order unlawful and appealed the order in the Circuit Court of Howard County which stayed the Commission's order and issued its final order in favor of the company stating that the Public Service Commission of Maryland did not have the power to order the refund. The Commission and People's Counsel subsequently appealed the Circuit Court's decision to the Court of Special Appeals of Maryland and the ultimate outcome is uncertain at this time. *In our report dated January 24, 19x3, our opinion on the balance sheet at December 31, 19x2 and the statements of income, retained earnings and changes in financial position for the year then ended was unqualified; however, in view of the possible refund referred to above, our present opinion on the balance sheet at December 31, 19x2, and the statements of income, retained earnings and changes in financial position for the year then ended, as presented herein, is different from that expressed in our previous report.*

In our opinion, subject to the effects, if any, on the balance sheet at December 31, 19x3 and 19x2 and the statements of income, retained earnings and changes in financial position for the year ended December 31, 19x2 of the ultimate resolution of the matter discussed in the preceding paragraph, the financial statements referred to above present fairly the financial position of Baltimore Gas and Electric Company at December 31, 19x3 and 19x2, and the results of its operations and changes in its financial position for the years then ended in conformity with generally accepted accounting principles applied on a consistent basis.

Baltimore Maryland
January 23, 19x4

REPORTS BASED IN PART ON THE WORK OF A SPECIALIST

SAS No. 11, Using the Work of a Specialist, AU 336, indicates the circumstances under which it would be appropriate for an independent auditor to rely on the findings of a specialist in reporting on the audited financial statements of an entity. For example, a specialist may be used in valuing inventory or in determining pension costs. Also, *SAS No. 11* identifies the procedures the auditor must follow before relying on the work of a specialist. Generally, the auditor must be satisfied that the specialist is a professional possessing expertise in the specialized area, has a license if such is required, understands the corroborative use the auditor intends to make of the specialist's findings, and will apply appropriate procedures and make assumptions that are consistent with those followed in prior periods.

An audit report based on the work of a specialist may be unqualified or appropriately qualified because of the specialist's findings. In an unqualified report, the specialist should not be referred to as a basis for the report. If the report is other than unqualified, reference to and identification of the specialist may be made in the auditor's report if he or she believes such reference will facilitate an understanding of the reason for the opinion modification.

DATING THE AUDIT REPORT

Generally, as indicated in Exhibit 15-4, the date of the completion of the auditor's field work should be used as the date of the audit report. Using the date of completion of the field work on the audit report fixes the auditor's responsibility for performing a subsequent event review concerning events and transactions occurring after the date of the financial statements that may require adjustment or disclosure in the statements.

The subsequent event period extends to the date the financial statements and audit report are released to the client and other users. However, as shown in the following exhibit, the auditor's responsibility for performing procedures designed to identify subsequent events must end with the completion of the field work.

Two types of subsequent events, as explained in Chapter 14, require consideration by the auditor—events that provide additional evidence with respect to conditions that existed at the date of the balance sheet and require an adjusting journal entry; and events that provide evidence as to conditions that did not exist at the date of the balance sheet being reported on but arose subsequent to that date and may require disclosure in the financial statements.

All information that becomes available during the subsequent event period should be used by management and the auditor to evaluate the information presented in the financial statements. The statements may require adjustment and disclosure based on subsequent event information or only disclosure.

When a subsequent event occurs after the date of the completion of the field work and comes to the attention of the auditor, it should be disclosed in a note to the financial statements or the statements should be adjusted, as appropriate. If the event is disclosed in a note or in the auditor's report, the auditor would date his or her report as follows:

> The auditor may use the date of the discovery of the subsequent event as the date of the report. In this case he or she would have to extend the subsequent event review procedures to that date.

> The auditor may use dual-dating. This would involve using the original report date (completion of the field work) except for the newly discovered date, which would be dated as of its discovery date.

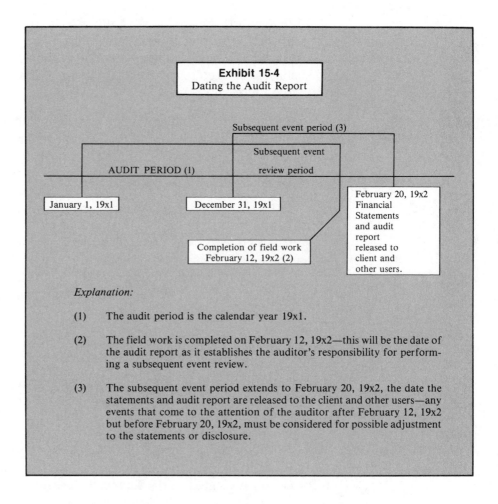

Exhibit 15-4
Dating the Audit Report

Subsequent event period (3)

Subsequent event review period

AUDIT PERIOD (1)

January 1, 19x1

December 31, 19x1

February 20, 19x2 Financial Statements and audit report released to client and other users.

Completion of field work February 12, 19x2 (2)

Explanation:

(1)   The audit period is the calendar year 19x1.

(2)   The field work is completed on February 12, 19x2—this will be the date of the audit report as it establishes the auditor's responsibility for performing a subsequent event review.

(3)   The subsequent event period extends to February 20, 19x2, the date the statements and audit report are released to the client and other users—any events that come to the attention of the auditor after February 12, 19x2 but before February 20, 19x2, must be considered for possible adjustment to the statements or disclosure.

Following is an example from the published report of Genesco Inc., illustrating dual-dating for a subsequent event:

To the Board of Directors and Stockholders of Genesco Inc.

In our opinion, the accompanying consolidated balance sheet and the related consolidated statements of earnings and accumulated deficit, of additional paid-in capital and of changes in financial position present fairly the financial position of Genesco Inc. and its subsidiaries at July 31, 1980 and 1979, and the results of their operations and the changes in their financial position for the years then ended, in conformity with generally accepted accounting principles consistently applied. Our examinations of these statements were made in accordance with generally accepted auditing standards and accordingly included such tests of the accounting records and such other auditing procedures as we considered necessary in the circumstances.[30]

August 26,1980 except as to Note 19, which is as of September 24, 1980.

Note 19 follows.

Post-Balance Sheet Event
Effective September 24, 1980, certain of the company's long-term loan agreements were amended to permit the company to pay fixed dividends on and to make mandatory redemptions of shares of its $4.50 Preferred Stock and its $4.25 Series A Preference Stock. The aggregate amount of such payments is limited to $800,000 during the fiscal year ending July 31, 1981 and $200,000 during any subsequent fiscal year.

On September 24, 1980 the board of directors declared dividends on the $4.50 Preferred Stock for all periods then in arrears and for the current quarter and authorized payment on November 17, 1980 of such dividends ($305,190) and of all redemption arrearages ($299,400) on the $4.50 Preferred Stock.

DISCOVERY OF INFORMATION AFTER RELEASING THE FINANCIAL STATEMENTS AND AUDIT REPORT

SAS No. 1, Codification of Auditing Standards and Procedures, AU 561, "Subsequent Discovery of Facts Existing at the Date of the Auditor's Report," specifies procedures to be followed by an auditor when information comes to his or her attention (after the statements and report have been issued) indicating that audited statements may be materially misleading or contain false information. Generally, the auditor must attempt to correct the situation and this may involve an investigation of the newly discovered information and revision of the statements and audit report. It also may only involve notifying regulatory authorities or others of the character of the information and the effect it may have on the statements and the audit report. The action taken will depend on the nature of the information and whether the client cooperates in investigating the matter and correcting the statements. Such information could come to the attention of the auditor as a result of other work performed for the client, through tax work or management advisory services, or the client might bring such informa-

---

[30] It should be noted that the scope and opinion paragraph have been combined by the auditors of Genesco into a single paragraph, with the opinion expressed first. The last sentence states the scope of the examination. This reporting format is used by some auditors.

tion to the auditor's attention. Section 561, in effect, takes up where Section 560—subsequent events leaves off—that is, the auditor's responsibility for the continuing appropriateness of the financial statements and audit report is expanded beyond the subsequent events period regarding information that comes to the attention of the auditor. Of course, the auditor does not perform any continuing procedures to identify such information.

When information comes to the auditor's attention that appears to be reliable and may materially affect the statements he or she has reported on, the auditor should notify the client and request permission to determine if the information does in fact exist and what the impact on the financial statements may be.

If the effect on the statements or on the auditor's report can promptly be determined, disclosure should consist of issuing, as soon as practicable, revised statements and auditor's report. The reasons for the revision usually should be described in a note and referred to in the auditor's report. Generally, only the most recently issued audited statements would need to be revised.

When issuance of statements accompanied by the auditor's report for a subsequent period is imminent, so that disclosure is not delayed, appropriate disclosure of the revision can be made in such statements.

When the effect on the statements cannot be determined without a prolonged investigation, appropriate disclosure would consist of notification by the client to persons who are known to be relying or who are likely to rely on the statements and the related report that they should not be relied upon, and that revised statements and auditor's report will be issued upon completion of an investigation.

If applicable, the client should be advised to discuss with the SEC, stock exchanges, and appropriate regulatory agencies, the disclosure to be made or other measures to be taken.

If the client does not cooperate in notifying persons known to be relying on the statements or who may rely on them, the action taken will depend on whether the auditor has been able to make a satisfactory investigation.

Unless the auditor's attorney recommends a different course of action, the auditor should notify the client that the report must no longer be associated with the statements, notify pertinent regulatory authorities, if any, of the situation, and notify each person known to the auditor to be relying on the statements that the audit report should no longer be relied upon.

If the auditor has been able to make a satisfactory investigation of the information and determined that the information is reliable, disclosure should describe the effect the information would have had on the auditor's report if it had been known to him or her at the date of the report and had not been reflected in the statements. The information disclosed should be as precise and factual as possible and should not go beyond that which is reasonably necessary to accomplish the disclosure. Comments concerning the conduct or motives of any person should be avoided.[31]

OTHER INFORMATION IN DOCUMENTS CONTAINING AUDITED STATEMENTS

Generally, an auditor has no obligation to corroborate information other than the financial statement information presented in a report. However, professional standards impose a responsibility on the auditor to consider other information included in a financial report and its effect on the fairness of the financial statements and the audit report. For example, *SAS No. 8, Other Information in Documents Containing Audited Financial Statements*, AU 550, requires the auditor to read other information (comments by management, financial analysis prepared by management, etc.) and consider whether such information or the manner of its presentation involves a material misstatement or is materially inconsistent with information or the manner of its presentation appearing in the financial statements. If, after reading the other information, the auditor concludes there is a material misstatement or inconsistency between the other information and the statements or the audit report, he or she must take action to remedy the matter. The statements, the report, or both may require revision.

The auditor must make a distinction between "other information" associated with audited financials and "supplementary information" required by the Financial Accounting Standards Board. For example, FASB Statement No. 33, *Financial Reporting and Changing Prices*, requires certain large public companies to disclose as supplemental information the effects of changing prices on the historically reported financial statement items. In audited reports, where this information is required or voluntarily presented, the auditor must consider whether the information is presented in conformity with the requirements of FASB No. 33. To help accomplish this objective, *SAS No. 27, Supplemen-*

---

[31] *SAS No. 1, Codification of Auditing Standards and Procedures*, AU 560.06-09.

tary Information Required by the Financial Accounting Standards Board, provides guidance to the auditor in carrying out procedures in determining whether the supplementary information conforms to FASB No. 33. The nature of the procedures as specified by *SAS No. 27* consists primarily of analytical tests and inquiries made to the appropriate client personnel.

The supplemental information would not normally be mentioned in the auditor's report since it is not required to be audited and is not considered a part of the basic financial statements. The auditor's report would, however, be expanded when the supplementary information is required and has been omitted, or the information is not presented in conformity with FASB No. 33, or the auditor is unable to complete required procedures relating to the supplementary information.

There is still another type of additional information that must be considered by the auditor. If additional information is presented to expand and support information contained in the financial statements, the audit report must be modified to recognize such additional information. This type of additional information may include details of items in the basic statements such as a breakdown of operating expenses, historical summaries, and statistical data and information of a non-accounting nature. Reports that include additional information of this nature have been referred to in the past as long-form reports, which are discussed in Chapter 16.

Since the fourth standard of reporting is applicable to additional information (long-form report type information), the auditor's report should establish the degree of responsibility he or she is taking regarding the additional information. The audit report, in this instance, should state that the examination has been made for the purpose of forming an opinion on the basic statements taken as a whole, that the additional information is presented for purposes of analysis only and is not necessary for a fair presentation of the basic statements in conformity with GAAP, and whether the additional information has been subjected to auditing procedures applied in the examination of the basic statements. In the latter case, the auditor should either express an opinion or disclaim an opinion on the additional information, as appropriate.

Since additional information is not required for a fair presentation it should be presented in a separate section of the financial report and labeled "additional information." The auditor's report on the additional information (opinion or disclaimer) may be placed with the additional information or presented as a separate paragraph of the standard audit report on the financial statements.

A paragraph expressing an opinion on accompanying information may read as follows:

(Standard scope and opinion paragraphs)

(Additional paragraph)

> Our examination was made for the purpose of forming an opinion on the basis financial statements taken as a whole. The (identify accompanying information) is presented for purposes of additional analysis and is not a required part of the basic financial statements. Such information has been subjected to the auditing procedures applied in the examination of the basic financial statements and, in our opinion, is fairly stated in all material respects in relation to the basic financial statements taken as a whole.

If the auditor has not audited the accompanying information he or she should disclaim an opinion on the information. If only part of the information has been audited, the additional paragraph should identify the audited and unaudited portions of the accompanying information. For example:

Disclaimer on All of the Information

> Our examination was made for the purpose of forming an opinion on the basic financial statements taken as a whole. The (identify the accompanying information) is presented for purposes of additional analysis and is not a required part of the basic financial statements. Such information has not been subjected to the auditing procedures applied in the examination of the basic financial statements, and, accordingly, we express no opinion on it.

Disclaimer on Part of the Information

> Our examination was made for the purpose of forming an opinion on the basic financial statements taken as a whole. The information on pages XX-XY is presented for purposes of additional analysis and is not a required part of the basic financial statements. Such information, except for that portion marked "unaudited," on which we express no opinion, has been subjected to the auditing procedures applied in the examination of the basic financial statements, and, in our opinion, the in-

formation is fairly stated in all material respects in relation to the basic financial statements taken as a whole.[32]

SEGMENT INFORMATION

A public company may present financial information disaggregated according to industry segments as required by FASB Statement No. 14, *Financial Reporting for Segments of a Business Enterprise*. If financial information is reported for segments in accordance with FASB No. 14, the auditor will apply procedures to determine if the information is appropriately presented. The auditor's report on financial statements applies to segment information included with the statements. However, the auditor would not refer in the report to the segment information unless his or her procedures revealed a misstatement or omission, or a change in accounting principle, relating to the segment information that is material in relation to the financial statements taken as a whole, or the auditor was unable to apply procedures considered necessary in the circumstances regarding the segment information.

Following are examples of auditor's reports qualified because of a misstatement and an omission of segment information and for a scope restriction relating to review of segment information to determining if it is properly presented.

Misstatement of segment information:

(Scope paragraph)

(Middle paragraph)

With respect to the segment information in Note X, $ _____ the operating expenses of Industry A were incurred jointly by Industries A and B. In our opinion, Statement No. 14 of the Financial Accounting Standards Board requires that those operating expenses be allocated between Industries A and B. The effect of the failure to allocate those operating expenses has been to understate the operating profit of Industry A and to overstate the operating profit of Industry B by an amount that has not been determined.

(Opinion paragraph)

In our opinion, except for the effects of not allocating certain common operating expenses between Industries A and B, as

---

[32] *SAS No. 29, Reporting on Information Accompanying the Basic Financial Statements in Auditor-Submitted Documents*, AU 551.12-13.

discussed in the preceding paragraph, the financial statements referred to above present fairly . . .

Omission of segment information:

(Scope paragraph)

(Middle paragraph)

The company declined to present segment information for the year ended December 31, 19xx. In our opinion, presentation of segment information concerning the company's operations in different industries, its foreign operations and export sales, and its major customers is required by Statement No. 14 of the Financial Accounting Standards Board. The omission of segment information results in an incomplete presentation of the company's financial statements.

(Opinion paragraph)

In our opinion, except for the omission of segment information, as discussed in the preceding paragraph, the financial statements referred to above present fairly . . .

Scope restriction:

(Scope paragraph)

. . . Except as explained in the following paragraph, our examination . . . and such other auditing procedures as we considered necessary in the circumstances.

(Middle paragraph)

In accordance with the company's request our examination of the financial statements did not include the segment information presented in Note X concerning the company's operations in different industries, its foreign operations and export sales, and its major customers.

(Opinion paragraph)

In our opinion, except for the effects of such adjustments or disclosures, if any, as might have been determined to be necessary had we applied to the segment information the procedures we considered necessary in the circumstances, the financial statements referred to above present fairly . . . [33]

[33] *SAS No. 21, Segment Information*, AU 435.08-.16.

SUMMARY

This chapter considers the responsibilities of auditors to issue an audit report when they are associated with a client's financial statements. The four standards of reporting were discussed—they require that the audit report state whether the financial statements are presented in accordance with GAAP; whether GAAP has been applied on a consistent basis; report any disclosure deficiencies; and express an opinion or disclaim an opinion when associated with financial statements.

The concept of adequate disclosure in financial statements relates to the form, arrangement, and content of the statements, footnotes that expand on the basic statements and other detail presented. When disclosure information is omitted, the auditor must present the information in his or her report unless its presentation would require the auditor to become a preparer of financial statements or data. The auditor's report is qualified for lack of fairness when disclosure is inadequate.

The objective of the fourth reporting standard is to prevent a misunderstanding of the degree of responsibility the auditor is assuming when his or her name is associated with a client's financial statements. An accountant may be associated with audited or unaudited statements of a public company, compiled or reviewed, or audited statements of a nonpublic company.

When an accountant is associated with unaudited statements, a disclaimer of opinion must be issued and each page of the statements must be marked as "unaudited." Also, if an accountant is not independent and is associated with a client's statements a disclaimer must be issued stating the lack of independence as the reason for the disclaimer.

The standard audit report has a scope and an opinion paragraph. It is addressed to the company whose statements are being examined or to its board of directors or stockholders (for unincorporated businesses, the report is addressed to the owners). The report states that an examination was performed, identifies the financial statements that were examined, explains how the financial statements were examined (in accordance with GAAS), attests to the fairness of presentation of the statements, explains the basis upon which fairness was judged (GAAP), and is signed by the audit firm.

The term GAAP, as used in the audit report, means the accounting principles and practices followed and the methods of applying them. Present fairly is a technical accounting term encompassing the conventions, rules, and procedures necessary to define accepted accounting practice at a particular time. It includes broad guidelines of general application and detailed practices and procedures. Promulgated accounting principles include Accounting Research Bulletins, APB Opinions, FASB Statements, and FASB Interpretations. These pronouncements derive their authority from Rule 203 of the AICPA Code of Ethics.

Comparability of financial statements between periods can be affected by a change in accounting principle, change in reporting entity, change in estimate, correction or an error in previously issued statements, and different events and circumstances. The consistency expression and APB Opinion No. 20 are designed to protect the reader of financial statements against artificial changes in accounting practices that may affect comparability. The consistency expression is intended to give assurance that comparability of financial statements between periods has not been materially affected by changes in accounting principles or, if comparability has been materially affected by such changes, to require appropriate reporting by the auditor regarding such changes.

A change in accounting principle or reporting entity requires a qualified opinion reflecting the inconsistency and referring to a financial statement footnote explaining the nature of the change and providing an accounting justification for the change. The effect of the change may require cumulative reporting or prior-period restatement. A change in estimate may require financial statement disclosure, but would not affect the auditor's opinion regarding consistency. A correction of an error requires restatement, but does not affect the consistency standard.

The auditor's consistency expression will vary depending on whether single year statements or comparative statements are covered by the audit report. "On a basis consistent with that of the preceding year" is the expression that should be used when reporting on single year statements. If the audit report relates to more than one year's statements, the phrase "on a consistent basis" is used. If the year preceding the earliest year being reported upon is presented, the phrase "consistently applied during the period and on a basis consistent with that of the preceding year" is used.

The various types of opinions an auditor may issue under certain conditions were discussed. They are the unqualified, qualified, adverse, and disclaimer of opinion.

An unqualified opinion is issued when an examination in accordance with GAAS has been completed and it has been determined that the financial statements present fairly in conformity with GAAP applied on a consistent basis.

A qualified opinion is issued when the financial statements present fairly in conformity with GAAP but there is a material item or items not fairly presented or the auditor's scope of examination has been limited, or there is a material uncertainty relating to the financial statements. An adverse opinion is issued for lack of overall fairness. When the auditor's opinion is qualified or adverse a middle paragraph(s) must explain all the substantive reasons for the opinion. A middle paragraph is not required, however, for an opinion that is qualified for a consistency violation. A disclaimer of opinion is appropriate in an audit engagement when the auditor's scope of examination has been restricted to the point where the auditor cannot obtain evidence to support an opinion; and where there is a material uncertainty regarding the statements that is so pervasive that an overall opinion is not warranted.

An auditor may insert a middle paragraph(s) in an unqualified opinion to emphasize a matter. The audit opinion remains unqualified. The matter emphasized is an item, already reported in the financial statements, that is considered extremely important in judging the fairness of the financial statements.

An auditor may base an opinion on his or her current examination of the financial statements and partly on the work of another auditor(s). A principal auditor in reporting on the consolidated statements of a client may, for example, base the opinion on work performed by another auditor regarding a subsidiary company included in the consolidated statements. In these circumstances, the principal auditor must have examined a sufficient portion of the consolidated group to express an overall opinion. Furthermore, the principal auditor must be satisfied with the work of the other auditor. The principal auditor's report must indicate the portion of the financial statements examined by the other auditor in dividing the reporting responsibility.

When there has been a departure from a promulgated accounting principle covered by Rule 203 of the Code of Ethics, and the effect is material, the auditor's report must state the departure. The auditor may then issue an unqualified opinion if he or she determines that following the promulgated accounting principle would have resulted in misleading financial statements. Such reporting is, of course, rare.

When comparative statements are presented and the prior-period statements were examined by a predecessor auditor, the successor auditor must explain this fact in the report. This is done by including an additional paragraph in the successor auditor's report stating that the prior-period statements were examined by other auditors, or, conversely, the predecessor auditor may be asked to reissue the prior-period audit report.

If audited and unaudited statements are presented in comparative form the current report must explain the nature of the service performed regarding the prior-period statements or the report for the prior-period must be reissued.

A continuing auditor must update his or her report when comparative statements are presented. Updating means expressing the same opinion as previously expressed with a current report date, or revising the previous opinion based on current information. A continuing auditor is an auditor who has examined the current period financial statements and the financial statements of one or more immediately preceding periods.

An auditor may rely on the work of a specialist in obtaining evidential matter in support of the fairness of financial statements. For example, an appraiser may be used to value merchandise inventory. An audit report based on the work of a specialist normally would not refer to the specialist. However, if the report is qualified or if an adverse opinion is issued because of the findings of a specialist it is appropriate to refer to the specialist as a basis for the opinion expressed. The auditor must be satisfied with the specialist's expertise and the nature of the work to be done by the specialist.

The audit report is dated as of the completion of the field work. The date of the report establishes the auditor's responsibility for performing a subsequent events review. The subsequent event period extends to the date the financial statements are released to the client and other users and certain events may require adjustment and disclosure or only disclosure. Dual-dating may be used for events discovered after the completion of the field work but before the statements are issued that require financial statement disclosure. The use of dual-dating avoids extending the subsequent events required review procedures to the date of the newly discovered event.

When the auditor becomes aware of information indicating that audited statements may be materially misleading or contain false information, the auditor must take action to prevent continued or future reliance on those statements and the related audit report. Discovery of such information after the financial statements and audit report have been released to the client and other users will require the auditor to perform specific procedures to prevent continued reliance. The financial statements and audit report may require revision, the client may be required to warn users that the statements are false or misleading and that revised statements will be issued, or the auditor may have to take action on his or her own if the client refuses to cooperate. For example, notify regulatory agencies of the potential problems involving the statements. The action the auditor is required to take will depend on how cooperative the client is in resolving the problem.

When information in addition to the basic financial statements is included in documents accompanying the auditor's opinion, the auditor must, under the fourth standard of reporting, explain the responsibility he or she is assuming for the other information. The auditor may only be required to read the other information and consider whether there are any inconsistencies or material misstatements in the other information when compared to the financial statements and audit report. The auditor may be required to express an opinion or disclaim an opinion on such information. For example, if long-form information is included with basic financial statements the auditor's report must explain whether the information is audited or unaudited.

A public company may be required to present segment information in its financial report. If so, the auditor must determine if the information is appropriately presented. If it is, there is no mention of the information in the audit report. If the information contains deficiencies, the auditor must expand the report to explain the deficiencies and the effect on the financial statements. The opinion would be qualified.

REVIEW QUESTIONS

15-1   Briefly discuss the two declarative statements the auditor must make in his or her report to satisfy the first and second standards of reporting.

15-2   Discuss the scope of financial statement disclosures in relation to the third standard of reporting.

15-3   What criteria should an auditor use to evaluate whether an item should be disclosed in the financial statements of a client?

15-4   Identify the types of opinions an auditor may render when the client fails to provide adequate financial statement disclosures.

15-5   If the client does not provide adequate financial statement disclosures, when is the auditor excused from providing such information in his or her report? Explain.

15-6 What is the objective of the fourth standard of reporting?

15-7 When is an accountant associated with financial statements?

15-8 Identify the type of report an auditor must render when he or she is associated with unaudited financial statements of a public company.

15-9 Is the accountant concerned with departures from GAAP when he or she is associated with unaudited financial statements of a public company? Explain why, or why not.

15-10 Identify the type of report an auditor must render when he or she lacks independence with respect to a client's financial statements.

15-11 State the seven key elements contained in the standard audit report. For each element indicate whether it is included in the scope paragraph or the opinion paragraph, or both.

15-12 What criteria does the auditor use in determining whether the financial statements are fairly presented? Identify the formal sources of such criteria.

15-13 Explain the two objectives of the consistency standard.

15-14 Describe in general terms how the auditor modifies the audit report when there has been a change in an accounting principle.

15-15 What is the impact upon the auditor's report when a client changes from a generally accepted accounting principle to a principle that is not generally accepted?

15-16 Can the auditor express an opinion on the current year's results of operations and changes in financial position when he or she has not examined the financial statements of the client for the preceding year?

15-17 Discuss the two situations where the auditor's report would not make reference to the consistent application of generally accepted accounting principles.

15-18 Explain how a change in the reporting entity is reflected in an auditor's report.

15-19 Should the auditor's report contain a consistency modification when the client has made a change in principle inseparable from a change in estimate?

15-20 Identify types of changes and situations that do not affect the consistency standard nor modify the auditor's report. Do these types of changes and situations need to be disclosed in the financial statements?

15-21 What is the impact upon an auditor's report of an accounting change which has no material effect on the current period's financials, but is expected to have a material impact upon financial statements of a subsequent period? Should the circumstances be disclosed in the current period's financials?

15-22 Under what conditions may the auditor issue an unqualified opinion? A qualified opinion?

15-23 Under what conditions should the auditor use the qualifying phrase, "subject to"? The qualifying phrase, "except for"?

15-24 What type of report may the auditor issue when the client's ability to continue in existence as a going concern is impaired?

15-25 Under what conditions does an auditor issue an adverse opinion?

15-26 Under what conditions does an auditor issue a disclaimer of opinion?

15-27 How does a principal auditor indicate that he or she is not assuming responsibility for the work of another auditor? Explain how the division of responsibility affects the scope and opinion paragraphs of the principal auditor's report.

15-28 Discuss in general terms the reporting responsibilities of a successor auditor when comparative financial statements are being presented and the statements of the prior period have been examined by a predecessor auditor whose report is not presented.

15-29 Explain the reporting responsibilities of an auditor when unaudited financial statements of a prior period are presented with current audited financials of a public company.

15-30 Define "updating" when a continuing auditor reports on comparative financial statements.

15-31 Identify the procedures an auditor must follow before relying on the work of a specialist.

15-32   Explain the relationship between the end of the auditor's field work, the audit report date, the auditor's subsequent events review, and the subsequent event period.

15-33   Explain the two alternative courses of action the auditor may take when a subsequent event occurs after the end of field work and comes to the attention of the auditor.

15-34   What is the auditor's responsibility when information comes to his or her attention after the statements and reports have been issued which indicate that the audited statements may be materially misleading?

15-35   Distinguish between the nature of the auditing procedures required by SAS No. 8, *Other Information in Documents Containing Audited Financial Statements*, and those procedures required by SAS No. 27, *Supplementary Information Required by the Financial Accounting Standards Board*.

15-36   Explain the auditor's reporting responsibility concerning additional information that expands information contained in the basic financial statements.

15-37   Under what conditions would the auditor modify his or her standard audit report issued in conjunction with segment information?

DISCUSSION QUESTIONS AND PROBLEMS

15-38   The CPA must comply with the GAAS of reporting when he prepares his opinion on the client's financial statements. One of the reporting standards relate to consistency.

Required:

a.   Discuss the statement regarding consistency that the CPA is required to include in his opinion. What is the objective of requiring the CPA to make this statement about consistency?

b.   Discuss what mention of consistency, if any, the CPA must make in his opinion relating to his first audit of the financial statements of the following companies:

1.   A newly organized company ending its first accounting period.

2.   A company established for a number of years.

    c.   Discuss whether the changes described in each of the cases below would require recognition in the CPA's opinion as to consistency. (Assume the amounts are material.)

        1.   The company disposed of one of its three subsidiaries that had been included in its consolidated statements for prior years.

        2.   After two years of computing depreciation under the declining balance method for income tax purposes and under the straight-line method for reporting purposes, the declining balance method was adopted for reporting purposes.

        3.   The estimated remaining useful life of plant property was reduced because of obsolescence.

(AICPA adapted)

15-39   Lando Corporation is a domestic company with two wholly-owned domestic subsidiaries. Michaels, CPA, has been engaged to examine the financial statements of the parent company and one of the subsidiaries and to act as the principal auditor. Thomas, CPA, has examined the financial statements of the other subsidiary whose operations are material in relation to the consolidated financial statement.

    The work performed by Michaels is sufficient for Michaels to serve as the principal auditor and to report as such on the financial statements. Michaels has not yet decided whether to make reference to the examination made by Thomas.

Required:

    a.   There are certain required audit procedures that Michaels should perform with respect to the examination made by Thomas, whether or not Michaels decides to make reference to Thomas in Michaels' auditor's report. What are these audit procedures?

    b.   What are the reporting requirements with which Michaels must comply if Michaels decides to name Thomas and make reference to the examination of Thomas?

(AICPA adapted)

15-40   Roscoe, CPA, has completed the examination of the financial statements of Excelsior Corporation as of and for the year ended December 31, 1975. Roscoe also examined and reported on the Excelsior financial statements for the prior year. Roscoe drafted the following report for 1975.

March 15, 1976

We have examined the balance sheet and statements of income and retained earnings of Excelsior Corporation as of December 31, 1975. Our examination was made in accordance with generally accepted accounting standards and accordingly included such tests of the accounting records as we considered necessary in the circumstances.

In our opinion, the above mentioned financial statements are accurately prepared and fairly presented in accordance with generally accepted accounting principles in effect at December 31, 1975.

Roscoe, CPA
(Signed)

Other information:

- Excelsior is presenting comparative financial statements.

- Excelsior does not wish to present a statement of changes in financial position for either year.

- During 1975 Excelsior changed its method of accounting for long-term construction contracts and properly reflected the effect of the change in the current year's financial statements and restated the prior-year's statements. Roscoe is satisfied with Excelsior's justification for making the change. The change is discussed in footnote number 12.

- Roscoe was unable to perform normal accounts receivable confirmation procedures but alternate procedures were used to satisfy Roscoe as to the validity of the receivables.

- Excelsior Corporation is the defendant in a litigation, the outcome of which is highly uncertain. If the case is settled in favor of the plaintiff, Excelsior will be required to pay a substantial amount of cash which might require the sale of certain fixed assets. The litigation and the possible effects have been properly disclosed in footnote number 11.

- Excelsior issued debentures on January 31, 1974, in the amount of $10,000,000. The funds obtained from the issuance were used to finance the expansion of plant facilities. The debenture agreement restricts the payment of future cash dividends to earnings after December 31, 1980. Excelsior declined to disclose this essential data in the footnotes to the financial statements.

Required:

Consider all facts given and rewrite the auditor's report in acceptable and complete format incorporating any necessary departures from the standard (short-form) report.

Do not discuss the draft of Roscoe's report but identify and explain any items included in *"Other Information"* that need not be part of the auditor's report.

(AICPA adapted)

15-41   Charles Burke, CPA, has completed field work for his examination of the Willingham Corporation for the year ended December 31, 1973, and now is in the process of determining whether to modify his report. Presented below are two, independent, unrelated situations which have arisen.

Situation I

In September 1973, a lawsuit was filed against Willingham to have the court order it to install pollution control equipment in one of its older plants. Willingham's legal counsel has informed Burke that it is not possible to forecast the outcome of this litigation; however, Willingham's management has informed Burke that the cost of the pollution-control equipment is not economically feasible and that the plant will be closed if the case is lost. In addition, Burke has been told by management that the plant and its production equipment would have only minimal resale values and that the production that would be lost could not be recovered at other plants.

Situation II

During 1973, Willingham purchased a franchise amounting to 20% of its assets for the exclusive right to produce and sell a newly patented product in the northeastern United States. There has been no production in marketable quantities of the product anywhere to date. Neither the franchisor nor any franchisee has conducted any market research with respect to the product.

Required:

In deciding the type-of-report modification, if any, Burke should take into account such considerations as follows:

Relative magnitude
Uncertainty of outcome
Likelihood of error
Expertise of the auditor
Pervasive impact on the financial statement
Inherent importance of the item

Discuss Burke's type-of-report decision for each situation in terms of the above and other appropriate considerations. Assume each situation is adequately disclosed in the notes to the financial statements. Each situation should be considered independently. In discussing each situation, ignore the other. It is not necessary for you to decide the type of report which should be issued.

(AICPA adapted)

15-42   Upon completion of all field work on September 23, 1975, the following "short-term" report was rendered by Timothy Ross to the Directors of The Rancho Corporation:

To the Directors of
The Rancho Corporation:

We have examined the balance sheet and the related statement of income and retained earnings of The Rancho Corporation as of July 31, 1975. In accordance with your instructions, a complete audit was conducted.

In many respects, this was an unusual year for The Rancho Corporation. The weakening of the economy in the early part of the year and the strike of plant employees in the summer of 1975 led to a decline in sales and net income. After making several tests of sales records, nothing came to our attention that would indicate that sales have not been properly recorded.

In our opinion, with the explanation given above, and with the exception of some minor errors that are considered immaterial, the aforementioned financial statements present fairly the financial position of The Rancho Corporation at July 31, 1975, and the results of its operations for the year then ended, in conformity with pronouncements of the Accounting Principles Board and the Financial Accounting Standards Board applied consistently throughout the period.

Timothy Ross, CPA
September 23, 1975

Required:

List and explain deficiencies and omissions in the auditor's report. The type of opinion (unqualified, qualified, adverse, or disclaimer) is of no consequence and need not be discussed.

Organize your answer sheet by paragraph (scope, explanatory, and opinion) of the auditor's report.

(AICPA adapted)

15-43 Presented below are three independent, unrelated auditor's reports. The corporation being reported on in each case, is profit oriented and publishes general-purpose financial statements for distribution to owners, creditors, potential investors, and the general public. Each of the following reports contains deficiencies.

Auditor's Report I

We have examined the consolidated balance sheet of Belasco Corporation and subsidiaries as of December 31 1973, and the related consolidated statements of income and retained earnings and changes in financial position for the year then ended. Our examination was made in accordance with generally accepted auditing standards and accordingly included such tests of the accounting records and such other auditing procedures as we considered necessary in the circumstances. We did not examine the financial statements of Seidel Company, a major consolidated subsidiary. These statements were examined by other auditors whose report thereon has been furnished to us, and our opinion expressed herein, insofar as it relates to Seidel Company, is based solely upon the report of the other auditors.

In our opinion, except for the report of the other auditors, the accompanying consolidated balance sheet and consolidated statements of income and retained earnings and changes in financial position present fairly the financial position of Belasco Corporation and subsidiaries at December 31, 1973, and the results of its operations and the changes in its financial position for the year then ended, in conformity with generally accepted accounting principles applied on a basis consistent with that of the preceding year.

Auditor's Report II

The accompanying balance sheet of Jones Corporation as of December 31, 1973, and the related statements of income and retained earnings and changes in financial position for the year then ended were not audited by us; however, we confirmed cash in the bank and performed a general review of the statements.

During the engagement, nothing came to our attention to indicate that the aforementioned financial statements do not present fairly the financial position of Jones Corporation at December 31, 1973, and the results of its operations and the changes in its financial position for the year then ended, in conformity with generally accepted accounting principles applied on a basis consistent with that of the preceding year; however, we do not express an opinion on them.

Auditor's Report III

I made my examination in accordance with generally accepted auditing standards. However, I am not independent with respect to Mavis Corporation because my wife owns 5% of the outstanding common stock of the company. The accompanying balance sheet as of December 31, 1973, and the related statements of income and retained earnings and changes in financial position for the year then ended were not audited by me; accordingly, I do not express an opinion on them.

Required:

For each auditor's report describe the reporting deficiencies, explain the reasons therefore, and briefly discuss how the report should be corrected. Each report should be considered separately. When discussing one report, ignore the other two. Do not discuss the addressee, signatures, and date. Also, do not rewrite any of the auditor's reports. Organize your answer sheet as follows:

Report No.	Deficiency	Reason	Correction

(AICPA adapted)

15-44   Various types of "accounting changes" can affect the second reporting standard of the generally accepted auditing standards. This standard reads, "The report shall state whether such principles have been consistently observed in the current period in relation to the preceding period."

Assume that the following list describes changes which have a material effect on a client's financial statements for the current year.

1. A change from the completed-contract method to the percentage-of-completion method of accounting for long-term construction contracts.
2. A change in the estimated useful life of previously recorded fixed assets based on newly acquired information.

3. Correction of a mathematical error in inventory pricing made in a prior period.

4. A change from prime costing to full absorption costing for inventory valuation.

5. A change from presentation of statements of individual companies to presentation of consolidated statements.

6. A change from deferring and amortizing preproduction costs to recording such costs as an expense when incurred because future benefits of the costs have become doubtful. The new accounting method was adopted in recognition of the change in estimated future benefits.

7. A change to including the employer share of FICA taxes as "retirement benefits" on the income statement from including it with "other taxes."

8. A change from the FIFO method of inventory pricing to the LIFO method of inventory pricing.

Required:

Identify the type of change which is described in each item above, state whether any modification is required in the auditor's report as it relates to the second standard of reporting, and state whether the prior year's financial statements should be restated when presented in comparative form with the current year's statements. Organize your answer sheet as shown below.

For example, a change of the LIFO method of inventory pricing to the FIFO method of inventory pricing would appear as shown below:

Item No.	Type of Change	Should Auditor's Report Be Modified?	Should Prior Year's Statements Be Restated?
Example	An accounting change from one generally accepted accounting principle to another generally accepted accounting principle.	Yes	Yes

(AICPA adapted)

15-45 Lancaster Electronics produces electronic components for sale to manufacturers of radios, television sets and phonographic systems. In connection with his examination of Lancaster's financial statements for the year ended December 31, 19x1, Don Olds, CPA, completed field work two weeks ago. Olds now is evaluating the significance of the following items prior to preparing his auditor's report. Except as noted none of these items have been disclosed in the financial statements or footnotes.

Item 1

Recently Lancaster interrupted its policy of paying cash dividends quarterly to its stockholders. Dividends were paid regularly through 19x0, discontinued for all of 19x1 in order to finance equipment for the company's new plant and resumed in the first quarter of 19x2. In the annual report dividend policy is to be discussed in the president's letter.

Item 2

A ten-year loan agreement, which the company entered into three years ago, provides that dividend payments may not exceed net income earned after taxes subsequent to the date of the agreement. The balance of retained earnings at the date of the loan agreement was $298,000. From that date through December 31, 19x1 net income after taxes has totaled $360,000 and cash dividends have totaled $130,000. Based upon these data the staff auditor assigned to this reveiw concluded that there was no retained earnings restriction at December 31, 19x1.

Item 3

The company's new manufacturing plant building, which cost $600,000 and has an estimated life of 25 years, is leased from the Sixth National Bank at an annual rental of $100,000. The company is obligated to pay property taxes, insurance and maintenance. At the conclusion of its ten-year noncancellable lease, the company has the option of purchasing the property for $1. In Lancaster's income statement the rental payment is reported on a separate line.

Item 4

A major electronics firm has introduced a line of products that will compete directly with Lancaster's primary line, now being produced in the specially designed new plant. Because of manufacturing innovations, the competitor's line will be of comparable quality but priced 50 percent below Lancaster's line. The competitor announced its new line during the week following completion of field work. Olds read the announcement in the newspaper and discussed the situation by telephone with Lancaster executives. Lancaster will meet the lower prices which are high enough to cover variable manufacturing and selling expenses but will permit recovery of only a portion of fixed costs.

Required:

For each item 1 to 4 above, discuss the following:

a. Any additional disclosure in the financial statements and footnotes that the CPA should recommend to his client.

b. The effect of this situation on the CPA's report upon Lancaster's financial statements. For this requirement assume that the client did not make the additional disclosure recommended in (a) above.

Complete your discussion of each item (both a and b above) before beginning discussion of the next item. The effects of each item on the financial statements and the CPA's report should be evaluated independently of the other items. The cumulative effects of the four items should not be considered.

(AICPA adapted)

15-46 Leer, CPA, has discussed various reporting considerations with three of Leer's audit clients. The three clients presented the following situations and asked how they would affect the audit report.

1. A client has changed its concept of "funds" on its statement of changes in financial position. Both Leer and the client agree that the new concept of "funds" is a more meaningful presentation. In prior years, when Leer issued an unqualified report on the client's comparative financial statements, this statement showed the net change in working capital, whereas in the current year the statement shows net change in cash balance. The client agrees with Leer that the change is material but believes the change is obvious to readers and need not be discussed in the footnotes to the financial statements or in Leer's report. The client is issuing comparative statements but wishes only to restate the prior year's statement to conform to the current format.

2. A client has a loan agreement that restricts the amount of cash dividends that can be paid and requires the maintenance of a particular current ratio. The client is in compliance with the terms of the agreement and it is not likely that there will be a

violation in the foreseeable future. The client believes there is no need to mention the restriction in the financial statements because such mention might mislead the readers.

3.   During the year, a client correctly accounted for the acquisition of a majority-owned domestic subsidiary but did not properly present the minority interest in retained earnings or net income of the subsidiary in the consolidated financial statements. The client agrees with Leer that the minority interest presented in the consolidated financial statements is materially misstated but takes the position that the minority shareholders of the subsidiary should look to that subsidiary's financial statements for information concerning their interest therein.

Required:

Each of the situations above relates to one of the four generally accepted auditing standards of reporting.

Identify and describe the applicable generally accepted auditing standard (GAAS) of reporting in each situation and discuss how the particular client situation relates to the standard and to Leer's report.

Organize your answer sheet as follows:

Situation No.	Applicable GAAS of Reporting	Discussion of Relationship of Client Situation to Standard of Report and to Leer's Report.

(AICPA adapted)

OBJECTIVE QUESTIONS*

15-47   A CPA's report on a client's balance sheet, income statement, and statement of changes in financial position was sent to the stockholders. The client now wishes to present only the balance sheet along with an appropriately modified auditor's report in a newspaper advertisement. The auditor may

A.   Permit the publication as requested.
B.   Permit only the publication of the orginially issued auditor's report and accompanying financial statements.
C.   Not permit publication of a modified auditor's report.
D.   Not permit publication of any auditor's report in connection with a newspaper advertisement.

15-48   After performing all necessary procedures, a predecessor auditor reissues a prior-period report on financial statements at the request of

*Note: All questions in this section are AICPA adapted questions.

the client without revising the original wording. The predecessor auditor should

A. Delete the date of the report.
B. Dual-date the report.
C. Use the reissue date.
D. Use the date of the previous report.

15-49 A change from cash to working capital in a statement of changes in financial position constitutes a change which requires

A. Only a disclosure in the auditor's report.
B. That the auditor's opinion contain a "subject to" qualification as to consistency.
C. That the auditor's opinion contain an exception as to conformity with generally accepted accounting principles.
D. That the auditor's opinion contain an exception as to consistency in the opinion paragraph.

15-50 If the auditor believes that financial statements which are prepared on a comprehensive basis of accounting other than generally accepted accounting principles are not suitably titled, the auditor should

A. Modify the auditor's report to disclose any reservations.
B. Consider the effects of the titles on the financial statements taken as a whole.
C. Issue a disclaimer of opinion.
D. Add a footnote to the financial statements which explains alternative terminology.

15-51 Jerome has completed an examination of the financial statements of Bold, Inc. Last year's financial statements were examined by Smith, CPA. Since last year's financial statements will be presented for comparative purposes without Smith's report, Jerome's report should

A. State that the prior year's financial statements were examined by another auditor.
B. State that the prior year's financial statements were examined by Smith.
C. Not refer to the prior year's examination.
D. Refer to Smith's report only if the opinion was other than unqualified.

15-52 The auditor who intends to express a qualified opinion should disclose all the substantive reasons in a separate explanatory paragraph of the report, *except* when the opinion paragraph

A. Makes reference to a note in the financial statements which discloses the pertinent facts.

B. Describes a limitation on the scope of the examination.

C. Describes an insufficiency in evidential matter.

D. Has been modified because of a change in accounting principle.

15-53 When financial statements are prepared on the basis of a going concern and the auditor believes that the client may not continue as a going concern, the auditor should issue

A. A "subject to" opinion.

B. An unqualified opinion with an explanatory middle paragraph.

C. An "except for" opinion.

D. An adverse opinion.

15-54 The principal auditor is satisfied with the independence and professional reputation of the other auditor who has audited a subsidiary but wants to indicate the division of responsibility. The principal auditor should

A. Modify the scope paragraph of the report.

B. Modify the scope and opinion paragraphs of the report.

C. Not modify the report except for inclusion of an explanatory middle paragraph.

D. Modify the opinion paragraph of the report.

15-55 A footnote to a company's financial statements includes an indication that the company's auditor performed certain procedures regarding the company's unaudited replacement cost information. The footnote does not indicate whether the auditor expresses an opinion on the replacement cost information. Which of the following is appropriate in these circumstances?

A. The auditor's report on the audited financial statements should be expanded to include a disclaimer of opinion on the replacement cost information.

B. A separate report on the unaudited replacement cost information should be rendered and should include a disclaimer of opinion on the replacement cost information.

C. The auditor's report on the audited financial statements should be qualified because of the replacement cost information.

D. A separate report on the replacement cost information should be rendered and should indicate whether the information is fairly presented in relation to the basic financial statements.

15-56   Which of the following circumstances would *not* be considered a departure from the auditor's standard report.

     A.   The auditor wishes to emphasize a particular matter regarding the financial statements.
     B.   The auditor's opinion is based in part on the report of another auditor.
     C.   The financial statements are affected by a departure from a generally accepted accounting principle.
     D.   The auditor is asked to report only on the balance sheet but has unlimited access to information underlying all the basic statements.

15-57   Which of the following material asset accounts would an auditor take exception to in the auditor's report?

     A.   Franchise fees paid.
     B.   Goodwill resulting from revaluation based on an objective appraisal by an expert.
     C.   Excess cost over the fair value of the assets of a significant subsidiary.
     D.   Research and development costs that will be billed to a customer at a subsequent date.

15-58   The consistency standard does not apply to an accounting change that results from a change in

     A.   An accounting principle that is not generally accepted.
     B.   An accounting estimate.
     C.   The reporting entity.
     D.   An accounting principle inseparable from a change in accounting estimate.

15-59   When comparative financial statements are presented, the fourth standard of reporting, which refers to financial statements "taken as a whole," should be considered to apply to the financial statements of the

     A.   Periods presented plus the one preceding period.
     B.   Current period only.
     C.   Current period and those of the other periods presented.
     D.   Current and immediately preceding period only.

15-60   With respect to consistency, which of the following should be done by an independent auditor, who has *not* examined a company's financial statements for the preceding year but is doing so in the current year?

    A.   Report on the financial statements of the current year without referring to consistency.

    B.   Consider the consistent application of principles within the year under examination but not between the current and preceding year.

    C.   Adopt procedures, that are practicable and reasonable in the circumstances, to obtain assurance that the principles employed are consistent between the current and preceding year.

    D.   Rely on the report of the prior year's auditors if such a report does not take exception as to consistency.

15-61   Addison Corporation is required to but does *not* wish to prepare and issue a statement of changes in financial position along with its other basic financial statements. In these circumstances the independent auditor's report on the Addison financial statements should include

    A.   A qualified opinion with a middle paragraph explaining that the company declined to present the required statement.

    B.   An unqualified opinion with an accurate and complete statement of changes in financial position prepared by the auditor and included in the auditor's report.

    C.   An adverse opinion stating that the financial statements, taken as a whole, are *not* fairly presented because of the omission of the required statement.

    D.   A disclaimer of opinion with a separate explanatory paragraph stating why the company declined to present the required statement.

15-62   If, during an audit examination, the successor auditor becomes aware of information that may indicate that financial statements reported on by the predecessor auditor may require revision, the successor auditor should

    A.   Ask the client to arrange a meeting among the three parties to discuss the information and attempt to resolve the matter.

    B.   Notify the client and the predecessor auditor of the matter and ask them to attempt to resolve it.

    C.   Notify the predecessor auditor who may be required to revise the previously issued financial statements and auditor's report.

    D.   Ask the predecessor auditor to arrange a meeting with the client to discuss and resolve the matter.

15-63   A CPA is associated with client-prepared financial statements, but is *not* independent. With respect to the CPA's lack of independence, which of the following actions by the CPA might confuse a reader of such financial statements?

A.   Stamping the word "unaudited" on each page of the financial statements.

B.   Disclaiming an opinion and stating that independence is lacking.

C.   Issuing a qualified auditor's report explaining the reason for the auditor's lack of independence.

D.   Preparing an auditor's report that included essential data that was *not* disclosed in the financial statements.

15-64   Morgan, CPA, is the principal auditor for a multinational corporation. Another CPA has examined and reported on the financial statements of a significant subsidiary of the corporation. Morgan is satisfied with the independence and professional reputation of the other auditor, as well as the quality of the other auditor's examination. With respect to Morgan's report on the financial statements, taken as a whole, Morgan

A.   Must not refer to the examination of the other auditor.

B.   Must refer to the examination of the other auditor.

C.   May refer to the examination of the other auditor.

D.   May refer to the examination of the other auditor, in which case Morgan must include in the auditor's report on the consolidated financial statements, a qualified opinion with respect to the examination of the other auditor.

15-65   When reporting on comparative financial statements, the auditor's report should include a consistency exception when the financial statements of the current year include

A.   A change in the format and presentation of the statement of changes in financial position from a cash concept to a working capital concept.

B.   A change in the estimated salvage value of several assets.

C.   A change in the income statement classification of an expense account from "Other Expenses" to "Selling Expenses."

D.   A change in the inventory pricing to correct a mathematical error in the total value of the opening inventory.

15-66   When a principal auditor decides to make reference to the examination of another auditor, the principal auditor's report should clearly indicate the

A. Principal auditor's qualification on the overall fairness of the financial statements, taken as a whole, "subject to" the work and report of the other auditor.

B. Procedures that were performed by the other auditor in connection with the other auditor's examination.

C. Division of responsibility between that portion of the financial statements covered by the examination of the principal auditor and that covered by the examination of the other auditor.

D. Procedures that were performed by the principal auditor to obtain satisfaction as to the reasonableness of the examination of the other auditor.

15-67 When the report of a principal auditor makes reference to the examination made by another auditor, the other auditor may be named if express permission to do so is given and

A. The report of the principal auditor names the other auditor in both the scope and opinion paragraphs.

B. The principal auditor accepts responsibility for the work of the other auditor.

C. The report of the other auditor is presented together with the report of the principal auditor.

D. The other auditor is not an associate or correspondent firm whose work is done at the request of the principal auditor.

15-68 Which of the following *best* describes the reference to the expression "taken as a whole" in the fourth generally accepted auditing standard of reporting?

A. It applies equally to a complete set of financial statements and to each individual financial statement.

B. It applies only to a complete set of financial statements.

C. It applies equally to each item in each financial statement.

D. It applies equally to each material item in each financial statement.

15-69 Which of the following publications does *not* qualify as a statement of generally accepted accounting principles under the AICPA Code of Professional Ethics?

A. Accounting interpretations issued by the FASB.

B. Accounting interpretations issued by the AICPA.

C. AICPA Accounting Research Bulletins.

D. Statements of Financial Standards issued by the FASB.

15-70   If the basic financial statements are accompanied by a separate statement of changes in stockholders' equity, this statement

A.   Should not be identified in the scope paragraph but should be reported on separately in the opinion paragraph.

B.   Should be excluded from both the scope and opinion paragraphs.

C.   Should be identified in the scope paragraph of the report but need not be reported on separately in the opinion paragraph.

D.   Should be identified in the scope paragraph of the report and must be reported on separately in the opinion paragraph.

15-71   Because an expression of opinion as to certain identified items in financial statements tends to overshadow or contradict a disclaimer of opinion or adverse opinion, it is inappropriate for an auditor to issue

A.   A piecemeal opinion.

B.   An unqualified opinion.

C.   An "except for" opinion.

D.   A "subject to" opinion.

15-72   It is *less* likely that a disclaimer of opinion would be issued when the auditor has reservations arising from

A.   Inability to apply necessary auditing procedures.

B.   Uncertainties.

C.   Inadequate internal control.

D.   Lack of independence.

15-73   Fox, CPA, is succeeding Tyrone, CPA, on the audit engagement of Genesis Corporation. Fox plans to consult Tyrone and to review Tyrone's prior-year working papers. Fox may do so if

A.   Tyrone and Genesis consent.

B.   Tyrone consents.

C.   Genesis consents.

D.   Tyrone and Fox consent.

15-74   When a principal auditor decides to make reference to the examination of another auditor, the principal auditor's report should indicate clearly the division of responsibility between the portions of the financial statements covered by each auditor. In which paragraph(s) of the report should the division of responsibility be stated?

A. Only the opinion paragraph.
B. Either the scope or opinion paragraph.
C. Only the scope paragraph.
D. Both the scope and opinion paragraphs.

15-75   In connection with the examination of the consolidated financial statements of Mott Industries, Frazier, CPA, plans to refer to another CPA's examination of the financial statements of a subsidiary company. Under these circumstances Frazier's report must disclose

    A. The name of the other CPA and the type of report issued by the other CPA.
    B. The magnitude of the portion of the financial statements examined by the other CPA.
    C. The nature of Frazier's review of the other CPA's work.
    D. In a footnote the portions of the financial statements that were covered by the examinations of both auditors.

15-76   Which of the following four events may be expected to result in a consistency exception in the auditor's report?

    A. The declining balance method of depreciation was adopted for newly acquired assets.
    B. A revision was made in the service lines and salvage values of depreciable assets.
    C. A mathematical error in computing the year-end LIFO inventory was corrected.
    D. The provision for bad debts increased considerably over the previous year.

15-77   When expressing a qualified opinion, the auditor generally should include a separate explanatory paragraph describing the effects of the qualification. The requirement for a separate explanatory paragraph does *not* apply when the opinion paragraph has been modified because of

    A. A change in accounting principle.
    B. Inability to apply necessary auditing procedures.
    C. Reclassification of an expense account.
    D. Uncertainties.

15-78   The auditor learned of the following situations subsequent to the issuance of his audit report on February 6, 1976. Each is considered important to users of the financial statements. For which one does the auditor have responsibility for appropriate disclosure of the newly discovered facts?

A. A major lawsuit against the company, which was the basis for a "subject to" auditor's opinion, was settled on unfavorable terms on March 1, 1976.

B. The client undertook merger negotiations on March 16, 1976, and concluded a tentative merger agreement on April 1, 1976.

C. On February 16, 1976 a fire destroyed the principal manufacturing plant.

D. A conflict of interest situation involving credit officers and a principal company supplier was discovered on March 3, 1976.

15-79   Halsey is the independent auditor examining the consolidated financial statements of Rex, Inc., a publicly-held corporation. Lincoln is the independent auditor who has examined and reported on the financial statements of a wholly-owned subsidiary of Rex, Inc. Halsey's *first* concern with respect to the Rex financial statements is to decide whether Halsey

A. Can serve as the principal auditor and report as such on the consolidated financial statements of Rex, Inc.

B. Can make reference to the work of Lincoln in Halsey's report on the consolidated financial statements.

C. Should review the workpapers of Lincoln with respect to the examination of the subsidiary's financial statements.

D. Should resign from the engagement since a qualified opinion is the only type that could be rendered on the consolidated financial statements.

15-80   In which of the following circumstances would an auditor be required to issue a qualified report with a separate explanatory paragraph?

A. The auditor satisfactorily performed alternative accounts receivable procedures because scope limitations prevented performance of normal procedures.

B. The financial statements reflect the effects of a change in accounting principles from one period to the next.

C. A particular note to the financial statements discloses a company accounting method which deviates from generally accepted accounting principles.

D. The financial statements of a significant subsidiary were examined by another auditor, and reference to the other auditor's report is to be made in the principal auditor's report.

15-81 Stone was asked to perform the first audit of a wholesale business that does not maintain perpetual inventory records. Stone has observed the current inventory but has not observed the physical inventory at the previous year-end date and concludes that the opening inventory balance, which is not auditable, is a material factor in the determination of cost of goods sold for the current year. Stone will probably

  A. Decline the engagement.
  B. Express an unqualified opinion on the balance sheet and income statement except for inventory.
  C. Express an unqualified opinion on the balance sheet and disclaim an opinion on the income statement.
  D. Disclaim an opinion on the balance sheet and income statement.

15-82 The annual report of a publicly held company presents the prior year's financial statements which are clearly marked "unaudited" in comparative form with current year audited financial statements. The auditor's report should

  A. Express an opinion on the audited financial statements and contain a separate paragraph describing the responsibility assumed for the financial statements of the prior period.
  B. Disclaim an opinion on the unaudited financial statements, modify the consistency phrase, and express an opinion on the current year's financial statements.
  C. State that the unaudited financial statements are presented solely for comparative purposes and express an opinion only on the current year's financial statements.
  D. Express an opinion on the audited financial statements and state whether the unaudited financial statements were compiled or reviewed.

15-83 When an independent CPA is associated with the financial statements of a publicly held entity, but has not audited or reviewed such statements, the appropriate form of report to be issued must include a(an)

  A. Negative assurance.
  B. Compilation opinion.
  C. Disclaimer of opinion.
  D. Explanatory paragraph.

15-84 A note to the financial statements of the First Security Bank indicates that all of the records relating to the bank's business operations are stored on magnetic discs, and that there are no emergency back-up systems or duplicate discs stored since the First Security Bank and their auditors consider the occurrence of a catastrophe to be remote. Based upon this, one would expect the auditor's report to express

A. A "subject to" opinion.
B. An "except for" opinion.
C. An unqualified opinion.
D. A qualified opinion.

15-85   Which of the following should be recognized in the auditor's report, whether or not the item is fully disclosed in the financial statements?

A. A change in accounting estimates.
B. Correction of an error not involving a change in accounting principle.
C. A change from a nonaccepted accounting principle to a generally accepted one.
D. A change in classification.

15-86   Which of the following statements with respect to an auditor's report expressing an opinion on a specific item on a financial statement is correct?

A. Materiality must be related to the specified item rather than to the financial statements taken as a whole.
B. Such a report can only be expressed if the auditor is also engaged to audit the entire set of financial statements.
C. The attention devoted to the specified item is usually less than it would be if the financial statements taken as a whole were being audited.
D. The auditor who has issued an adverse opinion on the financial statements taken as a whole can never express an opinion on a specified item in these financial statements.

15-87   A company issues audited financial statements under circumstances which require the presentation of a statement of changes in financial position. If the company refuses to present a statement of changes in financial position, the independent auditor should

A. Disclaim an opinion.
B. Prepare a statement of changes in financial position and note in a middle paragraph of the report that this statement is auditor-prepared.

C.   Prepare a statement of changes in financial position and disclose in a footnote that this statement is auditor-prepared.

D.   Qualify his opinion with an "except for" qualification and a description of the omission in a middle paragraph of the report.

15-88   The fourth reporting standard requires the auditor's report to either contain an expression of opinion regarding the financial statements, taken as a whole, or an assertion to the effect that an opinion cannot be expressed. The objective of the fourth standard is to prevent

A.   The CPA from reporting on one basic financial statement and not the others.

B.   The CPA from expressing different opinions on each of the basic financial statements.

C.   Misinterpretations regarding the degree of responsibility the auditor is assuming.

D.   Management from reducing its final responsibility for the basic financial statements.

15-89   Jones, CPA, is the principal auditor who is auditing the consolidated financial statements of his client. Jones plans to refer to another CPA's examination of the financial statements of a subsidiary company but does not wish to present the other CPA's audit report. Both Jones and the other CPA's audit reports have noted no exceptions to generally accepted accounting principles. Under these circumstances the opinion paragraph of Jones' consolidated audit report should express

A.   An unqualified opinion.

B.   A "subject to" opinion.

C.   An "except for" opinion.

D.   A principal opinion.

15-90   When an adverse opinion is expressed, the opinion paragraph should include a direct reference to

A.   A footnote to the financial statements which discusses the basis for the opinion.

B.   The scope paragraph which discusses the basis for the opinion rendered.

C.   A separate paragraph which discusses the basis for the opinion rendered.

D.   The consistency or lack of consistency in the application of generally accepted accounting principles.

15-91 An auditor need not mention consistency in the audit report if

    A. The client has acquired another company through a "pooling of interests."
    B. An adverse opinion is issued.
    C. This is the first year the client has had an audit.
    D. Comparative financial statements are issued.

15-92 With respect to issuance of an audit report which is dual dated for a subsequent event occurring after the completion of field work but before issuance of the auditor's report, the auditor's responsibility for events occurring subsequent to the completion of field work is

    A. Extended to include all events occurring until the date of the last subsequent event referred to.
    B. Limited to the specific event referred to.
    C. Limited to all events occurring through the date of issuance of the report.
    D. Extended to include all events occurring through the date of submission of the report to the client.

15-93 An auditor's report must state whether financial statements are presented in accordance with generally accepted accounting principles in each of the following situations except on an engagement involving

    A. A development-stage enterprise.
    B. A corporation in liquidation.
    C. A not-for-profit entity.
    D. A regulated company.

15-94 The auditor's opinion makes reference to generally accepted accounting principles (GAAP). Which of the following best describes GAAP?

    A. The interpretations of accounting rules and procedures by certified public accountants on audit engagements.
    B. The pronouncements made by the Financial Accounting Standards Board and its predecessor, the Accounting Principles Board.
    C. The guidelines set forth by various governmental agencies that derive their authority from Congress.
    D. The conventions, rules, and procedures which are necessary to define the accepted accounting practices at a particular time.

15-95 The fourth generally accepted auditing standard of reporting requires an auditor to render a report whenever an auditor's name is associated with financial statements. The overall purpose of the fourth standard of reporting is to require that reports

A. State that the examination of financial statements has been conducted in accordance with generally accepted auditing standards.
B. Indicate the character of the auditor's examination and the degree of responsibility assumed by the auditor.
C. Imply that the auditor is independent in fact as well as in appearance with respect to the financial statements under examination.
D. Express whether the accounting principles used in preparing the financial statements have been applied consistently in the period under examination.

15-96 On February 13, 1978, Fox, CPA, met with the audit committee of the Gem Corporation to review the draft of Fox's report on the company's financial statements as of and for the year ended December 31, 1977. On February 16, 1978, Fox completed all remaining field work at the Gem Corporation's headquarters. On February 17, 1978, Fox typed and signed the final version of the auditor's report. On February 18, 1978, the final report was mailed to Gem's audit committee. What date should have been used on Fox's report?

A. February 13, 1978.
B. February 16, 1978.
C. February 17, 1978.
D. February 18, 1978.

15-97 If the auditor believes that required disclosures of a significant nature are omitted from the financial statements under examination, the auditor should decide between issuing

A. A qualified opinion or an adverse opinion.
B. A disclaimer of opinion or a qualified opinion.
C. An adverse opinion or a disclaimer of opinion.
D. An unqualified opinion or a qualified opinion.

15-98 Nonaccounting data included in a long-form report have been subjected to auditing procedures. The auditor's report should state this fact and should explain that the nonaccounting data are presented for analysis purposes. In addition, the auditor's report should state whether the nonaccounting data are

A. Beyond the scope of the normal engagement and, therefore, not covered by the opinion on the financial statements.

B. Within the framework of generally accepted auditing standards, which apply to the financial statements, taken as a whole.

C. Audited, unaudited, or reviewed on a limited basis.

D. Fairly stated in all material respects in relation to the basic financial statements, taken as a whole.

15-99 When a client declines to make essential disclosures in the financial statements or in the footnotes, the independent auditor should

A. Provide the necessary disclosures in the auditor's report and appropriately modify the opinion.

B. Explain to the client that an adverse opinion must be issued.

C. Issue an unqualified report and inform the stockholders of the improper disclosure in an "unaudited" footnote.

D. Issue an opinion "subject to" the client's lack of disclosure of supplementary information as explained in a middle paragraph of the report.

15-100 Once the initial audit of a newly constructed industrial plant has been performed, with respect to consistency, which of the following is of least concern to the continuing auditor in the following year?

A. Prior years' capitalization policy.

B. Prior years' capitalized costs.

C. Prior years' depreciation methods.

D. Prior years' depreciable life.

15-101 Karr has examined the financial statements of Lurch Corporation for the year ended December 31, 1980. Although Karr's field work was completed on February 27, 1981, Karr's auditor's report was dated February 28, 1981, and was received by the management of Lurch on March 5, 1981. On April 4, 1981, the management of Lurch asked that Karr approve inclusion of this report in their annual report to stockholders which will include unaudited financial statements for the first quarter ended March 31, 1981. Karr approved of the inclusion of this auditor's report in the annual report to stockholders. Under the circumstances Karr is responsible for inquiring as to subsequent events occurring through

A. February 27, 1981.

B. February 28, 1981.

C. March 31, 1981.

D. April 4, 1981.

15-102   Which of the following consistency phrases would be contained in a continuing auditor's standard report on comparative financial statements?

A.   Applied on a consistent basis.
B.   Applied on a basis consistent with that of the preceding year.
C.   Applied consistently during interim periods.
D.   Applied consistently with previous years audited.

15-103   An auditor is confronted with an exception considered sufficiently material as to warrant some deviation from the standard unqualified auditor's report. If the exception relates to a departure from generally accepted accounting principles, the auditor must decide between expressing a(an)

A.   Adverse opinion and a "subject to" opinion.
B.   Adverse opinion and an "except for" opinion.
C.   Adverse opinion and a disclaimer of opinion.
D.   Disclaimer of opinion and a "subject to" opinion.

15-104   A continuing auditor would update his opinion on prior financial statements by issuing a "subject to" opinion for the

A.   Subsequent resolution of an uncertainty in the current period.
B.   Discovery of an uncertainty in the current period.
C.   Discovery of an uncertainty in the current period that relates to the prior-period statements being reported on.
D.   Restatement of prior-period statements in conformity with generally accepted accounting principles.

15-105   Thomas, CPA, has examined the consolidated financial statements of Kass Corporation. Jones, CPA, has examined the financial statements of the sole subsidiary which is material in relation to the total examined by Thomas. It would be appropriate for Thomas to serve as the principal auditor, but it is impractical for Thomas to review the work of Jones. Assuming an unqualified opinion is expressed by Jones, one would expect Thomas to

A.   Refuse to express an opinion on the consolidated financial statements.
B.   Express an unqualified opinion on the consolidated financial statements and not refer to the work of Jones.
C.   Express an unqualified opinion on the consolidated financial statements and refer to the work of Jones.

D.   Express an "except for" opinion on the consoldiated financial statements and refer to the work of Jones.

15-106   In a first audit of a new company the auditor's report will

A.   Remain silent with respect to consistency.
B.   State that the accounting principles have been applied on a consistent basis.
C.   State that accounting principles have been applied consistently during the period.
D.   State that the consistency standard does not apply because the current year is the first year of audit.

15-107   When a CPA has concluded that action should be taken to prevent future reliance on his report, he should

A.   Advise his client to make appropriate disclosure of the newly discovered facts and their impact on the financial statements to persons who are known to be currently relying or who are likely to rely on the financial statements and the related auditor's report.
B.   Recall the financial statements and issue revised statements and include an appropriate opinion.
C.   Advise the client and others not to rely on the financial statements and make appropriate disclosure of the correction in the statements of a subsequent period.
D.   Recall the financial statements and issue a disclaimer of opinion which should generally be followed by revised statements and a qualified opinion.

15-108   In reporting on the consolidated financial statements of a parent company and its subsidiaries, if the principal auditor decides to assume responsibility for the work of another CPA insofar as the other CPA's work relates to the principal auditor's expression of an opinion on the financial statements taken as a whole, the principal auditor should

A.   Make reference in his auditor's report to the other CPA's examination.
B.   Not make reference to the other CPA's examination.
C.   Make reference in his auditor's report to the other CPA's examination and responsibility and include the report of the other CPA.
D.   Not make reference to the other CPA's examination, but he should include the other CPA's report.

15-109 McPherson Corp. does not make an annual physical count of year-end inventories, but instead makes test counts on the basis of a statistical plan. During the year Mullins, CPA, observes such counts as he deems necessary and is able to satisfy himself as to the reliability of the client's procedures. In reporting on the results of his examination Mullins

    A.   Can issue an unqualified opinion without disclosing that he did not observe year-end inventories.

    B.   Must comment in the scope paragraph as to his inability to observe year-end inventories, but can nevertheless issue an unqualified opinion.

    C.   Is required, if the inventories were material, to disclaim an opinion on the financial statements taken as a whole.

    D.   Must, if the inventories were material, qualify his opinion.

15-110 Keller, CPA, was about to issue an unqualified opinion on the audit of Lupton Television Broadcasting Company when he received a letter from Lupton's independent counsel. The letter stated that the Federal Communications Commission has notified Lupton that its broadcasting license will not be renewed because of some alleged irregularities in its broadcasting practices. Lupton cannot continue to operate without this license. Keller has also learned that Lupton and its independent counsel plan to take all necessary legal action to retain the license. The letter from independent counsel, however, states that a favorable outcome of any legal action is highly uncertain. Based on this information what action should Keller take?

    A.   Issue a qualified opinion, subject to the outcome of the license dispute, with disclosure of the substantive reasons for the qualification in a separate explanatory paragraph of his report.

    B.   Issue an unqualified opinion if full disclosure is made of the license dispute in a footnote to the financial statements.

    C.   Issue an adverse opinion on the financial statements and disclose all reasons therefore.

    D.   Issue a piecemeal opinion with full disclosure made of the license dispute in a footnote to the financial statements.

LEARNING OBJECTIVES

After studying this chapter, students should understand

1. The nature of financial statements prepared in accordance with a comprehensive basis of accounting other than GAAP.
2. Auditing standards for other comprehensive basis of accounting statements.
3. The formats for the auditor's reports on other comprehensive basis of accounting statements.
4. The nature and format of the auditor's report on compliance with contractual and regulatory requirements.
5. The nature and format of the auditor's report on elements of a financial statement.
6. The auditor's responsibility for using or modifying prescribed report forms.
7. The nature and format of an auditor's report on internal control, including special-purpose reports of internal control for service organizations.
8. The nature and format of letters for underwriters.

INTRODUCTION

A large number of engagements conducted by independent accountants relate to reporting on financial statements prepared in accordance with generally accepted accounting principles (GAAP). There are a variety of situations where an accountant may be required to report on items other than financial statements taken as a whole or on financial information that is not a GAAP basis presentation. Generally accepted auditing standards (GAAS) and other reporting requirements apply in varying degrees in these cases. This chapter describes some of the more common types of engagements and reports in these areas.

FINANCIAL STATEMENTS PREPARED IN ACCORDANCE WITH A COMPREHENSIVE BASIS OF ACCOUNTING OTHER THAN GAAP

There is a general presumption that the product of financial accounting is a set of financial statements prepared in accordance with GAAP. This is expressed by *Accounting Principles Board Statement No. 4*, as Basic Feature No. 10 of financial accounting. The APB states that "General purpose financial statements are prepared by an enterprise under the presumption that users have common needs for information."[1]

While this presumption is valid in most cases, and, therefore, becomes the focus of the majority of accounting literature, there are areas where the user of financial information is better served by financial statements prepared on a basis of accounting other than GAAP. For example, a regulatory agency, such as the Federal Energy Regulator Commission, because of legal requirements may be better served by financial statements prepared on a basis of accounting which it determines. A person or organization making an investment with tax savings motives in mind might be better served by a set of financial statements prepared on the basis of income tax reporting as opposed to GAAP. Many small businesses and not-for-profit organizations find cash basis financial statements adequate since the management of cash is more important than the results of operations determined in conformity with GAAP.

This section relates to the Certified Public Accountants' role in auditing, preparing and reporting on financial statements prepared on a comprehensive basis of accounting other than GAAP. In this section the primary focus is on audited financial statements although the CPA

---

[1] Accounting Principles Board Statement No. 4, *Basic Concepts and Accounting Principles Underlying Financial Statements of Business Enterprises*, (New York, American Institute of Certified Public Accountants, 1970) AC 1021.12.

may have lesser association with these types of financial statements as discussed in Chapter 18.

Non-GAAP Criteria

SAS No. 14[2] establishes the criteria to be met in determining what constitutes a comprehensive basis of accounting other than GAAP. In practice, this terminology has been shortened to "other comprehensive basis of accounting" and has picked up the acronym OCBOA.

It is important to note that the determination of OCBOA must be made in conjunction with financial statement presentation, not merely based on a bookkeeping or accounting method employed by an entity. *SAS No. 14* defines a financial statement as "a presentation of financial data, including accompanying notes, derived from accounting records and intended to communicate an entity's economic resources or obligations at a point in time or the changes therein for a period of time in accordance with a comprehensive basis of accounting."[3] This definition goes beyond the common financial statements concept and includes such reports as statements of cash receipts and disbursements, statements of operation by product line, and summaries of operations.

OCBOA is a basis to which at least one of the following descriptions applies:

1. A basis of accounting that the reporting entity uses to comply with the requirements of financial reporting provisions of a government regulatory agency to whose jurisdiction the entity is subject. Examples are a basis of accounting prescribed in a uniform system of accounts that the Interstate Commerce Commission requires railroad companies to use and a basis of accounting insurance companies use pursuant to the rules of a state insurance commission.

2. A basis of accounting that the reporting entity uses or expects to use to file its income tax return for the period covered by the financial statements.

3. The cash receipts and disbursements basis of accounting, and modifications of the cash basis having substantial support, such as recording depreciation on fixed assets or accruing income taxes.

4. A definite set of criteria having substantial support that is applied to all material items appearing in financial statements, such as the price-level adjusted basis of accounting.[4]

---

[2] *SAS No. 14, Special Reports*, Auditing Standards Executive Committee, (New York, American Institute of Certified Public Accountants, 1976) AU 621.
[3] *SAS No. 14, Special Reports*, AU 621.02.
[4] *SAS No. 14, Special Reports*, AU 621.04.

If the client uses one of the above prescribed basis of accounting, the independent accountant must follow special reporting guidelines provided in *SAS No. 14*. These special reporting guidelines are outlined later in the chapter. Lacking one of the above prescribed basis of accounting, the auditor must consider his or her reporting requirements and alternatives under GAAS as they relate to GAAP basis presentations.

Disclosure in Non-GAAP Financial Statements

As pointed out on the previous page, most literature relates to GAAP basis presenttations. Under OCBOA, professional judgment is needed in many areas to determine whether adequate disclosure is contained in financial statements.

The auditor should consider the following in determining whether adequate, informative disclosure is present under OCBOA:

- Any disclosures which might be specifically required by OCBOA, such as requirements for disclosure issued by regulatory agencies.

- Disclosures which in the auditor's judgment are necessary to make the statements not misleading.

- When financial statements presented on OCBOA contain items that are the same as, or similar to, those in financial statements prepared in conformity with GAAP, the same degree of informative disclosure is generally appropriate. For example, statements prepared on an income tax basis or a modified cash basis usually reflect depreciation, long-term debt, and owners' equity. Thus, for tax basis statements, the informative disclosures for depreciation, long-term debt, and owners' equity in such statements should be comparable to those in statements prepared in conformity with GAAP.[5]

Reporting Under OCBOA

An independent auditor's report on financial statements prepared on OCBOA should include all of the following items:

1. A paragraph identifying the financial statements examined and stating whether the examination was made in accordance with GAAS.

2. A paragraph that—

    a. States, or preferably refers to the note to the financial statements that states, the basis of presentation of the financial statements on which the auditor is reporting.

---

[5] *SAS No. 14, Special Reports*, AU 9621.38.

b.   Refers to the note to the financial statements that describes how the basis of presentation differs from GAAP. (The monetary effect of such differences need not be stated.)

c.   States that the financial statements are not intended to be presented in conformity with GAAP.

3.   A paragraph that expresses the auditor's opinion (or disclaims an opinion) on whether—

a.   The financial statements are presented fairly in conformity with the basis of accounting described. If the auditor concludes that the financial statements are not presented fairly on the basis of accounting described, he or she should disclose all the substantive reasons for that conclusion in an additional explanatory paragraph(s) of the report and should include in the opinion paragraph appropriate modifying language and a reference to the explanatory paragraph(s).

b.   The disclosed basis of accounting used has been applied in a manner consistent with that of the preceding period.[6]

When reporting on a regulatory agency prescribed basis of accounting, the auditor's report must, in addition to the above, restrict the use of the statements to that agency unless other distribution is allowed by an American Institute of Certified Public Accountants (AICPA) accounting guide, audit guide or auditing interpretation. While this is a specific requirement, some practitioners include, as a regular part of their report, a restriction on use by only a designated party.

The auditor should also be satisfied that the title of the statements, in both his and her report and on the statements themselves, clearly indicates that the statements are prepared on a basis other than GAAP. Such terms as "balance sheet," "income statement" and "statement of changes in financial position" are not appropriate as they identify GAAP basis presentations. OCBOA statements must have more descriptive titles such as "statement of assets and liabilities" rather than "balance sheet." Examples of other titles are continued in the reporting examples presented later in this chapter.

---

[6] *SAS No. 14, Special Reports*, AU 621.05.

Auditing Standards in OCBOA Engagements

The general, field work and reporting standards apply to auditors' engagements involving OCBOA financial statements. This would include such standards as *SAS No. 19* which requires the auditor to obtain a representation letter from the client and *SAS No. 20* requiring communication of material weaknesses noted in internal accounting control. Other items which are not required but are a customary practice in audit engagements should be considered appropriate such as issuance of an engagement letter.

In addition, the planning and supervision requirements of the SASs must be met. Since presentation and disclosure requirements under OCBOA are not as pervasive as those under GAAP, it becomes increasingly important that the approach to the audit and the selection of procedures are well planned and documented.

In selecting an approach, the auditor should keep in mind the special purpose nature of the financial statements and, in many cases, be aware that smaller organizations may lack much of the internal accounting control present in larger organizations. This would indicate that the cycle approach dealt with earlier in this text may not be the most effective or efficient approach to be used. In such cases, there should generally be heavy reliance on substantive tests as opposed to compliance tests.

In designing specific procedures, the auditor may consider each line item of the financial statements separately. Procedures should be developed in the following sequence:

1. Determine the assertions made by each line item to an informed reader of the financial statements. This would include disclosure items.

2. State objectives of the audit of the line item that will ensure that the assertions in step one are determined to be valid in the circumstances.

3. Design detailed audit procedures to accomplish the audit objectives.

The format of the financial statements themselves should be kept as simple as possible while still remaining meaningful considering the basis of accounting being utilized. If the CPA is drafting the statements for his or her client, the format with which the client is most familiar should be considered as a starting point and revision made to conform with the required presentation. In other circumstances, statements may be drafted based on a GAAP presentation and modified for the OCBOA. In many cases trade associations and industry publications may be consulted for examples of a statement format.

Cash Basis Financial Statements

The most widely used OCBOA financial statements are probably those prepared on the cash basis. This is because of the relative simplicity of recordkeeping required and the ease of understanding the statements themselves. Depending on the nature of the reporting entity, cash basis statements may or may not be significantly different from GAAP basis statements.

It should be noted that cash basis means different things in different situations. Cash basis ranges from the most simple presentation to one which is virtually in conformity with GAAP. Exhibit 16-1 indicates some of the various stages of evolution of cash basis presentation. The areas identified in the exhibit are not clearly marked in practice and each column should be viewed as a sliding scale as opposed to rigid progression steps. The statement attributes are not intended as a complete listing, but as examples of the increasing complexity of cash basis statements.

The various possibilities shown above indicate the need for the exercise of the auditor's judgment in determining the title used for financial statements, the required disclosure items, and the appropriate wording of the audit report.

The auditor's typical report on cash basis financial statements including statements on financial position and results of operations reads as follows:

- We have examined the statement of income on a cash basis for the year ended December 31, 19x1 and the statement of certain assets and liabilities as of that date of the XYZ Company. Our examination was made in accordance with generally accepted auditing standards and, accordingly, included such tests of the accounting records and such other auditing procedures as we considered necessary in the circumstances.

- As described in Note 1 of the Notes to Financial Statements, the accompanying financial statements are prepared on the cash basis of accounting and, accordingly, they are not intended to present the results of operations and financial position in conformity with generally accepted accounting principles.

- In our opinion, the financial statements mentioned above present fairly the cash transactions of the XYZ Company for the year ended December 31, 19x1, and the individual assets and liabilities shown on the statement of certain assets and liabilities at December 31, 19x1, in conformity with the company's accounting policy, as described in Note 1 of the Notes to Financial Statements, applied on a basis consistent with the preceding year.

Exhibit 16-1
Stages of Cash Basis Presentation

Auditor's Report	Cash Basis Level	Statement Attributes		
		Balance Sheet	Income Statement	Statement of Changes in Financial Position*
• • • • • • • • • Special Purpose (OCBOA) • • • • • • • •	Strict cash basis	Cash = Equity	Receipts and disbursements only	Not applicable
	Simple cash basis	Cash includes cash equivalents (securities) depreciable assets recognized	Depreciation expense reported	Possible but seldom informative
	Complex cash basis	Assets and liabilities arising from cash transactions recorded	Affected by asset and liability recognition	Possibly applicable
	Modified cash basis	Certain prepaids and accruals, inventory and any related payables recognized	Income affected by inventory variations and prepaid and accrual recognition	Probably applicable
Qualified adverse or disclaimer relative to GAAP • •	Modified accrual basis	GAAP attributes with limited (cash basis income taxes, non-capitalized leases, prior period adjustments)	GAAP with modification related to balance sheet	Required
Unqualified related to GAAP	Accrual basis	GAAP	GAAP	GAAP (Required)

*APB Opinion No. 19, *Reporting Changes in Financial Position*, does not require a statement of changes in financial position unless both a balance sheet and an income statement are presented on a GAAP basis.

In the above case, Note 1 of the Notes to Financial Statements would be as follows:

Note 1. *Accounting Policy*

The accompanying financial statements are presented on a cash basis, reflecting only cash received and disbursed. Therefore, receivables and payables, inventories, accrued income and expenses, and equipment and depreciation, which may be material in amount, are not reflected in the statements and these statements do not intend to present the overall financial position or results of operations of the company in conformity with generally accepted accounting principles.

Minor additions and replacements of furniture and equipment intended to be paid out of normally recurring income are included in costs and expenses, in lieu of depreciation, on the statement of income on a cash basis.

In many situations, organizations using cash basis reporting may be small and not-for-profit in nature. This may cause an inherent limitation in internal control. In such situations, the scope paragraph of the auditor's report may be modified to indicate the restriction and an additional paragraph such as the following may be inserted in the report:

The organization's internal accounting control was not adequate to permit the application of auditing procedures to indicate whether all receipts from contributions were recorded.

The opinion paragraph would include the following modification:

In our opinion, except for the effects of any adjustments that might have been determined to be necessary had we been able to perform adequate auditing procedures in regard to the receipts referred to in the preceding paragraph, the accompanying financial statements present . . . .

Reports on Other Types to OCBOA Statements

The basic reporting considerations relative to OCBOA financial statements were identified above in discussing cash basis reporting. There are, however, two additional basic OCBOA reporting categories. Examples of these reports are as follows:

Financial Statements Prepared on a Basis Prescribed by a Regulatory Agency Solely for Filing With That Agency

We have examined the statement of admitted assets, liabilities, and surplus—statutory basis of Middletown Insurance Company as of December 31, 19x1, and the related statements of income—statutory basis and changes in surplus—statutory basis for the year then ended. Our examination was made in accordance with generally accepted auditing standards and, accordingly, included such tests of the accounting records and such other auditing procedures as we considered necessary in the circumstances.

As described in Note 1, the company's policy is to prepare its financial statements on the basis of accounting practices prescribed or permitted by the Insurance Department of Maryland. These practices differ in some respects from generally accepted accounting principles. Accordingly, the accompanying financial statements are not intended to present financial position and results of operations in conformity with generally accepted accounting principles. This report is intended solely for filing with regulatory agencies and is not intended for any other purpose.

In our opinion, the financial statements referred to above present fairly the admitted assets, liabilities and surplus of Middletown Insurance Company as of December 31, 19x1, and the results of its operations and changes in its surplus for the year then ended, on the basis of accounting described in Note 1, which basis has been applied in a manner consistent with that of the preceding year.

Financial Statements Prepared on the Entity's Income Tax Basis

We have examined the statement of assets, liabilities, and capital—income tax basis of SEK Partnership as of December 31, 19x1, and the related statements of revenue and expenses—income tax basis and of changes in partners' capital accounts—income tax basis for the year then ended. Our examination was made in accordance with generally accepted auditing standards and, accordingly, included such tests of the accounting records and such other auditing procedures as we considered necessary in the circumstances.

As described in Note 1, the Partnership's policy is to prepare its financial statements on the accounting basis used for income tax purposes; consequently, certain revenue and the related assets are recognized when received rather than when earned, and certain expenses are recognized when paid rather than when the obligation is incurred. Accordingly, the accompanying financial statements are not intended to present financial position and results of operations in conformity with generally accepted accounting principles.

In our opinion, the financial statements referred to above present fairly the assets, liabilities, and capital of SEK Partnership as of December 31, 19x1, and its revenue and expenses and changes in its partners' capital accounts for the year then ended, on the basis of accounting described in Note 1, which basis has been applied in a manner consistent with that of the preceding year.

REPORTS ON COMPLIANCE WITH CONTRACTUAL AND REGULATORY REQUIREMENTS

Nature of Restrictions

Business entities may enter into contracts of many different types or be subject to regulatory agencies that impose requirements that are financial in nature. If these requirements are not met or if covenants of contracts are violated, the financial status of the business entity may be affected. On occasion, auditors are required to submit a separate report giving assurance with respect to compliance with those restrictions.

It is common for loan agreements to contain covenants, or restrictions, that must be complied with if penalties are to be avoided. Some of the common restrictions are as follows:

- Limits on additional borrowing
- Maintaining a certain amount of working capital or a certain current ratio
- Limits on fixed asset additions
- Limits on salaries paid to key officers
- Limits on dividends that can be declared
- Maintaining a certain level of cash availability

In many cases, the penalty for violating a covenant is that the loan may become immediately due, interest rates may be increased, or other terms may be changed.

Regulatory agency requirements and restrictions might include:

- Limits on profits and charges
- Limits on investment in property or equipment
- Debt to equity ratios of a certain amount
- Prohibited transactions and business operations
- Geographical constants on operations

Penalties for violation might include monetary fines, additional restrictions, or increased regulatory agency control over total operations.

**Reporting on
Compliance**

In performing an examination in accordance with GAAS and issuing an opinion on financial statements, the auditor must consider compliance with various requirements and restrictions. This is necessary because if a restriction has been violated, the financial statements may have to be modified to reflect the revised status or additional disclosure might be necessary. For example, the total balance of a long-term note payable might become a current liability if a loan covenant is violated. Therefore, compliance with many covenants and restrictions is implied by the issuance of an unqualified opinion on financial statements.

On occasion, auditors are requested to issue a separate report commenting on compliance. Such a report should not be given unless the auditor has examined the client's financial statements in accordance with GAAS. The report is generally in the form of a negative assurance; that nothing came to the auditor's attention to indicate a restriction had been violated. In other cases, the auditor may add the negative assurance to the opinion on the financial statements.

If a separate report is issued, it should note that it is being given in connection with an examination of the financial statements and that the purpose of the examination was not primarily for compliance purposes and should indicate the date of the related opinion on the financial statements. Following is an example of such a report:

> We have examined the financial statements of ABC Company for the year ended May 31, 19x2 and our report thereon, dated July 25, 19x2, expressed an unqualified opinion on those statements. Our examination was made in accordance with generally accepted auditing standards and, accordingly, included such tests of the accounting records and such other auditing procedures as we considered necessary in the circumstances for the purpose of expressing our opinion on the financial statements for that year taken as a whole. In connection therewith, we have read the loan agreement with First National Bank and Trust Company of Hometown, State dated January 15, 19x0.

> In making our examination, we obtained no knowledge of any defaults during the year ended May 31, 19x2 by ABC Company in the observation, performance or fulfillment of any of the terms, covenants, provisions or conditions contained in the loan agreement mentioned above, and in the note executed thereunder, insofar as they pertain to accounting matters. However, it should be understood that our examination was not directed primarily toward obtaining knowledge of such non-compliance.

If the report on compliance is issued as part of the opinion on financial statements, the following paragraph should be added to the standard auditor's report:

In connection with our examination, nothing came to our attention that caused us to believe that the company was not in compliance with any of the terms, covenants, provisions or conditions of the loan agreement with First National Bank and Trust Company of Hometown, State dated January 15, 19x0. However, it should be noted that our examination was not directed primarily toward obtaining knowledge of such non-compliance.

The above report language would, of course, be modified to describe the specific regulation of an agency or law in reports dealing with regulatory compliance.

If the auditor finds that any covenants or restrictions have been violated, he or she should confer with the client and the client's legal counsel to determine if a waiver of non-compliance can be obtained. Failing that, the auditor must consider the impact on the financial statements and the opinion and modify any report on compliance accordingly.

Reporting on Financial Statements Prepared Pursuant to a Contractual Agreement

Some contractual agreements may specify the accounting and/or financial reporting necessary to indicate compliance with the terms of the agreement. When these requirements are not in agreement with GAAP, the auditor must issue an appropriate report on the special financial statements. It is unlikely that these requirements, in themselves, could constitute a comprehensive basis of accounting other than GAAP and allow related reporting since the requirements of "criteria having substantial support" would not be met.

In such cases, the auditor may issue a modified OCBOA report which contains an adverse or qualified opinion in relation to GAAP and an unqualified opinion as to the special financial statements. This may be done even when there is a separate opinion issued on separate financial statements prepared in conformity with GAAP.

In such cases, the auditor must quantify the departure from GAAP, if reasonably determinable. This may be done in the audit report on the special statements, by reference to a note to the special statements or by reference to coexisting audited statements, as of the same date and for the same period, presented in conformity with GAAP.

The following is an example of such a modified OCBOA report on special financial statements.

We have examined the special-purpose balance sheet of ABC Company as of December 31, 19x1, and the related special-purpose statements of income, retained earnings, and changes in financial position for the year then ended. Our examination was made in accordance with generally accepted auditing standards and, accordingly, included such tests of the accounting records and such other auditing procedures as we considered necessary in the circumstances.

The accompanying special-purpose financial statements have been prepared for the purpose of complying with, and on the basis of accounting practices specified in Section 4 of a loan agreement between DEF Bank and the company dated (date). These practices differ, as described in Note X, from generally accepted accounting principles. Accordingly, the financial statements are not intended to present and, in our opinion, do not present fairly the financial position, results of operations and changes in financial position of ABC Company in conformity with generally accepted accounting principles. The monetary effects of the departures from generally accepted accounting principles can be determined by comparing the special-purpose financial statements with the financial statements of ABC Company for the year ended December 31, 19x1, prepared in conformity with generally accepted accounting principles on which we issued our report dated February 14, 19x2.

In our opinion, however, the accompanying special purpose financial statements of ABC Company are presented fairly on the basis of accounting described in Note X, which basis has not been applied in a manner consistent with that of the preceding year.[7]

EXAMINATION OF FINANCIAL STATEMENT ELEMENTS AND REPORTING

On occasion, a certified public accountant may be called upon to conduct an engagement and issue a report relating to a specific element (line item) of a financial statement or perform certain procedures related to that element. These engagements might include issuance of an opinion on the specific element or describing the procedures performed without issuing an opinion.

Expressing an Opinion on Specified Elements, Accounts or Items of a Financial Statement

Engagements involving the issuance of an opinion on an element, account or line item of a financial statement should be conducted in accordance with GAAS, except that since an element in itself does not constitute a financial statement, the first standard of reporting does not apply. Also, if the item addressed is presented on a basis other than GAAP, the second standard of reporting relating to consistency may not be applicable.

---

[7] SAS No. 14, Special Reports, AU 9621.25.

In planning and conducting these engagements, the auditor should remember that the expression of an opinion on one item of a financial statement may be more difficult than it appears on the surface. This is because of the interrelationships of items contained in a set of financial statements. For example, there is a direct relationship between notes payable and interest expense or between investments and investment income. When these interrelationships and the financial statements as a whole cannot be addressed, many procedures related to system controls and analytical review may not be practical or cost beneficial. The auditor must consider the assertions made by the item being addressed and design his or her audit objectives and audit procedures carefully.

An engagement expressing an opinion on an item may be conducted in conjunction with an examination of the financial statements taken as a whole. If the total financial statement engagement results in a qualified or adverse opinion, care must be taken that the separate expression of an opinion on individual items does not constitute a prohibited piecemeal opinion. A piecemeal opinion involves expressing an overall adverse opinion or disclaimer of opinion on the financial statements and then stating that certain elements are presented fairly. In general, the number of items addressed and their relative significance should be considered in determining whether a piecemeal opinion is being given. Further, an opinion on an item or element of financial statements should not accompany the basic statements in any case.

The auditor's report setting forth an opinion on an item contained in a financial statement should:

1. Identify the specified elements, accounts, or items examined.

2. State whether the examination was made in accordance with GAAS and, if applicable, that it was made in conjunction with an examination of financial statements. (Also, if applicable, any modification of the auditor's standard report on those statements should be indicated.)

3. Identify the basis on which the specified elements, accounts, or items are presented and, when applicable, any agreements specifying such basis.

4. Describe and indicate the source of significant interpretations made by the client in the course of the engagement relating to the provisions of a relevant agreement.

5. Indicate whether in his or her opinion the specified elements, accounts, or items are presented fairly on the basis indicated.

6.   If applicable, indicate whether in his or her opinion the disclosed basis has been applied in a manner consistent with that of the preceding period.[8]

The following is an example of a report on an item contained in a financial statement.

We have examined the financial statements of ABC Company for the year ended December 31, 19x2 and our report thereon, dated March 3, 19x3 expresses an unqualified opinion on those statements. In connection with that examination, we have also examined certain accounting records of the company for the purpose of expressing an opinion on the amount of the gross sales during that year, as defined in the agreement dated June 30, 19x1 covering the lease of property in Clientown, U.S.A. to the company by Real Estate Investors, Inc. Our examination was made in accordance with generally accepted auditing standards and, accordingly, included such tests of the accounting records and such other auditing procedures as we considered necessary in the circumstances.

In our opinion, the gross sales of ABC Company for the year ended December 31, 19x2, on the basis specified in the lease referred to above, are fairly stated at $1,250,000.

Reporting on Agreed-Upon Procedures With Respect to Specified Elements, Accounts or Items of a Financial Statement

In engagements covered by the preceding section, the auditor was free to apply GAAS including other procedures considered necessary to the item which was the subject of his or her report. In some cases, however, the engagement may be restricted by the client, cost considerations, or other factors, to performing and reporting on agreed-upon procedures which are not adequate to allow expression of an opinion. In such engagements only the general and first field work standards are applicable. *SAS No. 35, Special Reports—Applying Agreed-Upon Procedures to Specified Elements, Accounts, or Items of a Financial Statement*, applies to these reporting situations.

Engagements of this type should be accepted only when the parties involved have a clear understanding of the procedures to be performed (including any inherent limitations) and the report distribution is restricted to those parties. The financial statements of the entity may, however, accompany the report. In such engagements, the issuance of an engagement letter outlining the scope of the engagement and an understanding of the needs of third parties who require and receive the

[8] *SAS No. 14, Special Reports*, AU 621.13.

report are extremely important on the part of the auditor. To be satisfied that the parties involved have a clear understanding of the procedures to be performed, the auditor should meet with the parties and discuss the procedures to be followed. A mere reading of a specific element, account, or item does not constitute a procedure sufficient to permit an accountant to report on the results of applying agreed-upon procedures. The accountant must apply substantive procedures. Discussion directly with the parties to receive the report as to the appropriateness of the procedures to be performed may not be feasible. If the accountant cannot discuss the procedures to be performed with the parties, other approaches, as described below, may be appropriate:

- Discussing the procedures to be applied with legal counsel or other appropriate representatives of the parties involved, such as a trustee, a receiver, or a creditors' committee.

- Reviewing relevant correspondence from the parties.

- Comparing the procedures to be applied to written requirements of a supervisory agency, such as a bank regulatory agency that receives a report in connection with a bank directors' examination.

- Distributing a draft of the report or a copy of the client's engagement letter to the parties involved with a request for their comments before the report is issued.[9]

A report issued as a result of an engagement based on the results of applying agreed-upon procedures should:

1. Indicate the specified elements, accounts, or items to which the agreed-upon procedures were applied.

2. Indicate the intended distribution of the report.

3. Enumerate the procedures performed.

4. State the accountant's findings.

5. Disclaim an opinion with respect to the specified elements, accounts, or items.

6. State that the report relates only to the elements, accounts, or items specified, and does not extend to the entity's financial statements taken as a whole.

---

[9] *SAS No. 35, Special Reports—Applying Agreed-Upon Procedures to Specified Elements, Accounts, or Items of a Financial Statement*, AU 622.02.

Following is an example of an appropriate report:

Trustee
XYZ Company

At your request, we have performed the procedures enumerated below with respect to the claims of creditors of XYZ Company as of May 31, 19xx, set forth in the accompanying schedules. Our review was made solely to assist you in evaluating the reasonableness of those claims, and our report is not to be used for any other purpose. The procedures we performed are summarized as follows:

a.   We compared the total of the trial balance of accounts payable at May 31, 19xx, prepared by the company, to the balance in the company's related general ledger account.

b.   We compared the claims received from creditors to the trial balance of accounts payable.

c.   We examined documentation submitted by the creditors in support of their claims and compared it to documentation in the company's files, including invoices, receiving records, and other evidence of receipt of goods or services.

Our findings are presented in the accompanying schedules. Schedule A lists claims that are in agreement with the company's records. Schedule B lists claims that are not in agreement with the company's records and sets forth the differences in amounts.

Because the above procedures do not constitute an examination made in accordance with generally accepted auditing standards, we do not express an opinion on the accounts payable balance as of May 31, 19xx. In connection with the procedures referred to above, except as set forth in Schedule B, no matters came to our attention that caused us to believe that the accounts payable balance might require adjustment. Had we performed additional procedures or had we made an examination of the financial statements in accordance with generally accepted auditing standards, other matters might have come to our attention that would have been reported to you. This report relates only to the accounts and items specified above and does not extend to any financial statements of XYZ Company, taken as a whole.[10]

PRESCRIBED FORM REPORTS

The term "prescribed form reports" generally describes one of two types of situations. In one case, the report or "opinion" to be signed by

---

[10] *SAS No. 25, Special Reports—Applying Agreed-Upon Procedures to Specified Elements, Accounts, or Items of a Financial Statement*, AU 622.04-06.

the auditor is preprinted or its required wording is specified by regulation. In the other case, the financial information is to be supplied on a preprinted form or in a format that is specified. It is common to find both of these situations existing in the same report.

Prescribed Auditor's Opinion

Regulatory agencies and other bodies that provide preprinted forms on which financial data is to be entered often preprint the report or "opinion" to be signed by the auditor. These preprinted opinions are often not acceptable to the auditor since they do not meet the standards of reporting or they include representations that the auditor cannot make.

In such cases, the preprinted opinion should be modified by inserting or deleting phrases. If this is not practical, a separate report should be written by the auditor and substituted for the printed report.[11]

Prescribed Financial Statement Format

There is a general presumption that an entity furnishing a printed form or describing the format of a financial statement wishes to obtain financial data in that designated format. Therefore, it is seldom appropriate to attempt to modify such a form to agree with conventional financial statements. The auditor must consider whether the form and the entity providing it constitute a "comprehensive basis of accounting other than GAAP." If so, the reporting standards described early in this chapter should be followed.

If the auditor decides that the authority for the report does not constitute another comprehensive basis of accounting, he or she must consider the alternatives related to GAAP basis reporting, including issuance of a qualified opinion, adverse opinion, or a disclaimer of opinion. For example, consider the following case:

> Under state law, corporations must file a form with the State Corporation Commission which purports to be financial statements. The form, however, does not have provisions that will assure adequate disclosure of all the necessary facts. The form also contains a statement which must be signed by the preparer which may not express the usual responsibility assumed by a CPA in such matters. Also, there is no space on the form for the CPA's disclaimer of opinion if an audit has not been performed. How should a CPA protect himself or herself on such unaudited "financial statements"?

---

[11] Reporting on prescribed forms based on a compilation engagement involving a nonpublic company is discussed in Chapter 18.

SAS No. 14 states in reference to such situations, "when a printed report form calls upon an independent auditor to make an assertion that he or she believes is not justified, the CPA should reword the form or attach a separate report."

On these forms, the CPA should type either an appropriate disclaimer or a reference such as, "See attached disclaimer of opinion." Such a disclaimer might read:

> This report has not been audited by us and accordingly we do not express an opinion on it. It has been prepared on a prescribed form for use by the State Corporation Commission, and does not necessarily include all disclosures required for fair presentation of the financial position of the company in accordance with generally accepted accounting principles.[12]

REPORTING ON INTERNAL ACCOUNTING CONTROL

There are several types of situations where the auditor reports on internal accounting control. As discussed in Chapter 8, *SAS No. 20* requires the auditor to inform an audit client of "material weaknesses" in internal control noted by the auditor during the conduct of his or her examination of the financial statements. This requirement is, therefore, part of GAAS and must be considered during audit engagements.[13] The current discussion covers auditors' reports on internal accounting control other than to satisfy the requirements of *SAS No. 20*.

SAS No. 30, Reporting on Internal Accounting Control, AU 642, describes procedures a CPA should apply in engagements to report on a client's system of internal accounting control and it describes the different forms of reports for such engagements.

A CPA may be engaged to:

- Express an opinion on a client's system of internal accounting control.

- Report on the client's system for the restricted use of management, specified regulatory agencies, or other specified third parties, based on a study and evaluation of internal accounting control made as part of an audit of the financial statements.

---

[12] *AICPA Technical Practice Aids*, TPA 9110.02, American Institute of CPAs, New York, 1982.

[13] *SAS No. 20, Required Communication of Material Weaknesses in Internal Accounting Control*, AU 323.

- Report on all or part of a client's system, for the restricted use of management or specified regulatory agencies, based on the regulatory agencies' preestablished criteria.

- Issue other special purpose reports on all or part of a client's system for the restricted use of management, specified regulatory agencies, or other specified third parties.

A CPA may also consult on improvement of a client's control system. In these circumstances, the CPA may communicate the results of his or her engagement by letters, memoranda, and other less formal means solely for the internal information of the client.

Expression of an Opinion on a Client's System of Accounting Control

When a CPA is expressing an opinion on a client's system of accounting control, he or she does not need to place any restrictions on the distribution of the report. An audit of a system of accounting control and an examination of financial statements in accordance with GAAS are two distinct services. An engagement to express an opinion on the accounting control system can be made as of a different date or by a different CPA as long as the CPA obtains the necessary understanding of the client's operations. Also, the purpose and scope of an audit of accounting control differs from the purpose and scope of the study and evaluation of internal control in an opinion audit of the financial statements. In an audit of the financial statements the CPA may decide not to rely on prescribed control procedures because he or she concludes either that the procedures are not satisfactory for the purpose of reliance or that the audit effort required to test compliance with the procedures to justify reliance would exceed the reduction in effort that could be achieved by such reliance. Accordingly, the study and evaluation of internal control in an audit of financial statements is generally more limited than in an audit of the control system itself.

Although the purpose and scope of the study and evaluation of accounting control differ in an audit of the financial statements and an audit of the control system, the procedures are similar in nature. Accordingly, the study and evaluation of internal control made for the purpose of expressing an opinion on the system may serve as a basis for reliance in an audit of the financial statements of the client.

Planning the Audit of Internal Control

Among the factors to be considered in determining the scope of an engagement to report on accounting control are:

- The nature of the client's operations

- The overall control environment, including

  - The client's organizational structure
  - The methods used to communicate responsibility and authority
  - The principal financial reports prepared for management planning and control purposes
  - Management's supervision of the system, including the internal audit function, if any

- The extent of recent changes, if any, in the client, its operations, or its control procedures

- Relative significance of the classes of transactions and related assets

- Knowledge obtained in auditing the client's financial statements and in past engagements to express an opinion on the client's control system

The work of internal auditors may have an important bearing on the CPA's procedures. If the CPA will be using the client's internal auditors, he or she should follow the guidance in *SAS No. 9, The Effect of an Internal Audit Function on the Scope of the Independent Auditor's Examination*, in considering their competence and objectivity and in evaluating their work.

The CPA must reach an understanding with the client regarding the system to be reported on and the form of the documentation of controls, including particularly the development of specific control objectives and the description of prescribed procedures to achieve those objectives. The specific control objectives and related procedures should be appropriately documented to serve as a basis for the accountant's report. The documentation of the system may take many forms—internal control manuals, accounting manuals, narrative memoranda, flowcharts, procedural write-ups, or answers to questionnaires.

Reviewing the Design of the Control System

The purpose of the review of the design of the control system is to obtain sufficient information to permit the CPA to reach a conclusion about whether the entity's control procedures are suitably designed to achieve the objectives of accounting control. For this purpose the CPA should obtain an understanding of

- The flow of transactions through the accounting system.
- The specific control objectives that relate to points in the flow of transactions and handling of assets where errors or irregularities could occur.

- The specific control procedures or techniques that the client has established to achieve the specific control objectives.

A CPA obtains an understanding of the accounting system to identify points in the processing of transactions and handling of assets where errors or irregularities may occur. His or her understanding must encompass each significant class of transactions processed through the system. The CPA's procedures in obtaining such an understanding may include inspection of written documentation, inquiries of client personnel, and observation of the processing of transactions and the handling of the related assets.

The objectives of internal control must be defined in terms of specific control objectives for classes of transactions and related assets. The CPA should determine whether management has identified the specific control objectives relating to points in the processing of transactions and the handling of assets where errors or irregularities could occur. An example of a specific control objective in a revenue cycle is that all goods shipped are billed.

Testing Compliance With Prescribed Procedures

The nature and extent of the CPA's tests of compliance with prescribed procedures in an audit of accounting control involves essentially the same considerations as tests of compliance made as part of an audit of financial statements (as discussed in Chapter 8). The CPA should test compliance with control procedures over a period that is adequate for him or her to determine whether the specific control procedures are being applied as prescribed as of the date specified in the audit report.

In evaluating a control system the CPA should identify weaknesses in the system and evaluate whether they are material, either individually or in combination. A weakness, as previously explained, is a condition in which the specific control procedures, or the degree of compliance with them, are not sufficient to achieve a specific control objective—that is, errors or irregularities may occur and not be detected within a timely period by employees in the normal courses of performing their assigned duties. A weakness is material if the condition results in more than a relatively low risk of such errors or irregularities in amounts that would be material in relation to the financial statements.

The evaluation of weaknesses in accounting control is a very subjective process that depends on factors such as the number and amount of transactions or assets exposed to weakness; the types of potential errors or irregularities that might result from the weakness; the number, competence and integrity of the individuals involved, the overall control environment; and the experience and judgment of those making the estimates. In estimating the amounts of errors and irregularities that might result, the accountant should consider any relevant historical data that are available or can reasonably be developed.

Historical data provide a more reasonable basis for estimating the risk of errors than they do for estimating the risk of irregularities. Errors are unintentional, and their underlying causes tend to result in a more recurring or predictable level of occurrence. Irregularities are intentional, and their underlying causes ordinarily involve a lack of integrity and motivation for personal gain, which are less predictable from historical experience. Accordingly, the accountant should presume a high risk of irregularities in those situations where inadequate segregation of duties places an individual in a position to perpetrate and to conceal irregularities in the normal course of that person's duties. The CPA should ordinarily obtain management's written representations, covering the following points:

- Acknowledging management's responsibility for establishing and maintaining the system of internal control.

- Stating that management has disclosed to the CPA all material weaknesses in the control system of which they are aware.

- Describing any irregularities involving management or employees who have significant roles in the control system.

- Stating whether there were any changes subsequent to the date being reported on that would significantly affect the control system, including any corrective action taken by management with regard to material weaknesses.

The CPA's Report

A CPA may express an opinion on a client's system of internal accounting control from which financial statements are prepared in conformity with GAAP or any other criteria applicable to such statements. The CPA's report should contain

1. A description of the scope of the engagement.

2. The date to which the opinion relates.

3. A statement that the establishment and maintenance of the system is the reponsibility of management.

4. A brief explanation of the broad objectives and inherent limitations of internal accounting control.

5. The CPA's opinion on whether the system taken as a whole was sufficient to meet the broad objectives of internal accounting control insofar as those objectives pertain to the prevention or detection of errors or irregularities in amounts that would be material in relation to financial statements.

The report should be dated as of the completion of the field work and addressed to the entity or its board of directors or stockholders. A standard report form is illustrated as follows:

Independent Accountant's Report on
Internal Accounting Control

We have made a study and evaluation of the system of internal accounting control of XYZ Company and subsidiaries in effect at (date). Our study and evaluation was conducted in accordance with standards established by the American Institute of Certified Public Accountants.

The management of XYZ Company is responsible for establishing and maintaining a system of internal accounting control. In fulfilling this responsibility, estimates and judgments by management are required to assess the expected benefits and related costs of control procedures. The objectives of a system are to provide management with reasonable, but not absolute, assurance that assets are safeguarded against loss from unauthorized use or disposition, and that transactions are executed in accordance with management's authorization and recorded properly to permit the preparation of financial statements in accordance with generally accepted accounting principles.

Because of inherent limitations in any system of internal accounting control, errors or irregularities may occur and not be detected. Also, projection of any evaluation of the system to future periods is subject to the risk that procedures may become inadequate because of changes in conditions, or that the degree of compliance with the procedures may deteriorate.

In our opinion, the system of internal accounting control of XYZ Company and subsidiaries in effect at (date), taken as a whole, was sufficient to meet the objectives stated above insofar as those objectives pertain to the prevention or detection of errors or irregularities in amounts that would be material in relation to the consolidated financial statements.

If the study and evaluation discloses one or more material weaknesses, the opinion paragraph of the accountant's report should be modified as follows:

> Our study and evaluation disclosed the following conditions in the system of internal accounting control of XYZ Company and subsidiaries in effect at (date), which, in our opinion, result in more than a relatively low risk that errors or irregularities in amounts that would be material in relation to the consolidated financial statements may occur and not be detected within a timely period.

The report should describe the material weaknesses, state whether they result from the absence of control procedures or the degree of compliance with them and describe the general nature of potential errors or irregularities that may occur as a result of the weaknesses.

If the opinion on the control system is issued in conjunction with an examination of the entity's financial statements, the following sentence should be included in the paragraph that describes the material weakness:

> These conditions were considered in determining the nature, timing, and extent of audit tests to be applied in our examination of the 19xx financial statements, and this report does not affect our report on these financial statements dated (date of report).

An unqualified opinion on an entity's system of accounting control can be expressed only if the accountant has been able to apply all the procedures he or she considers necessary in the circumstances. Restrictions on the scope of the engagement, whether imposed by the client or by the circumstances, may require the accountant to qualify or disclaim an opinion. When restrictions that significantly limit the scope of the study and evaluation are imposed by the client, the accountant generally should disclaim an opinion on the control system.

Report on Accounting Control Based on a Study and Evaluation Made as Part of an Audit

A CPA may be requested to report on accounting control based on a study and evaluation of the system as part of an audit engagement. The CPA may report in these circumstances provided that distribution of the report is restricted to management, a specified regulatory agency, or a specified third party and that the report describes the limited purpose of the accountant's review and evaluation of accounting control and disclaims an opinion on the system taken as a whole. The format and nature of this type of report was discussed in Chapter 8 and is not repeated here.

Special-Purpose Reports on Internal Accounting Control at Service Organizations

Some clients make use of service organizations to record transactions and process related accounting data. For example, some clients may provide a listing of their transactions to an EDP service center and have the center process the transactions and produce the client's general ledger and financial statements. Other clients may have the service center initiate and execute transactions and maintain the related accountability. For example, a bank trust department may be authorized to make investment decisions for the client and maintain the custody and accountability of the client's portfolio. In either case, the client's auditor is concerned with internal controls at the service center. Of course, the auditor could evaluate the controls at the service center by compliance testing these controls in the same way that he or she compliance tests the controls in the client's organization. However, it is often more efficient to obtain a report on internal control from the auditor of the service center and use this report as part of the audit evidence. Of course, before the client's auditor relys on the report of the service center auditor, the client's auditor must investigate the professional reputation of the auditor for the service center.

SAS No. 44 identifies three types of reports that a client's auditor may obtain from the auditor of a service center. One type of report is a report on the design of the service center's internal control. This report would be useful to the client's auditor in understanding the relationship of the client's controls to the controls of the service center. This report might be useful to the client's auditor in planning compliance tests at the client's organization. However, this report could not be used by the client's auditor for relying on the service center's controls, since the service center's auditor is reporting only on the design of the system and not compliance with the system.

A second type of report from the service center's auditor is a report on both the design and compliance tests of service center controls. Of course, the client's auditor could use this report as a basis for reliance on the service center controls.

A third type of report is a report on the specific controls of the service center over the processing of the client's transactions. This report differs from the second type of report in that it deals with specific controls of service center and not the overall controls of the service center. Of course, the client's auditor can use this report as a basis for relying on the specific controls of the service center which were tested by the service center's auditor.

In the final analysis, however, the client's auditor must understand that he or she, and not the service center auditor, is responsible for the opinion on the client's financial statements. In fact, the service center auditor's report cannot be mentioned in the auditor's report on the client's financial statements. However, if the client's auditor is performing an audit of the client's system of internal control (as described in the previous section) the client's auditor can indicate a division of responsibility between he or she and the service center's auditor for the client's overall system of internal control.

Reports Based on Criteria Established by Regulatory Agencies

Some governmental or other agencies that exercise regulatory, supervisory, or other public administrative functions may require reports on accounting control of organizations subject to their regulations. Such an agency may set forth specific criteria for the evaluation of the adequacy of accounting control procedures for their purposes and may require a report based on those criteria. For the CPA to be able to issue the report the criteria should be in reasonable detail and in terms susceptible to objective application. In these circumstances, the CPA's report should

1. Clearly identify the material covered by his or her study.

2. Indicate whether the study included tests of compliance with the procedures covered by his or her study.

3. Describe the objectives and limitations of accounting control and of CPA's evaluations of it.

4. State the CPA's conclusions based on the agency's criteria, concerning the adequacy of the procedures studied, with an exception regarding any material weaknesses, and

5. State that the report is intended for use in connection with the grant or other purpose to which the report refers and that it should not be used for any other purpose.

LETTERS FOR UNDERWRITERS

Financial statements and other schedules and data contained in filings with the Securities and Exchange Commission (SEC) under the Securities Act of 1933 are generally specific as to their format and content due to the regulations in the Act.

These statements are not to be regarded as "prescribed form reports" or "other comprehensive basis of accounting reports." Even though special requirements may exist, these statements should be reported upon the basis of GAAP. In such engagements, an auditor should closely follow the regulations and reference materials related to SEC filings and should consider the use of an SEC specialist.

The purpose of this section is to give a general introduction to one type of report that is usually present with certain types of SEC engagements.

The Auditor's Responsibility

When a company issues securities and offers them to the public either for cash or in exchange for other securities held by the public, a filing or registration statement, must be made with the SEC. The SEC does not approve or disapprove of the securities themselves but does comment on the adequacy of information made available to a prospective purchaser pursuant to the existing laws and regulations. Many of the SEC's pronouncements regarding required reporting are contained in a series of pronouncements issued by the SEC and called "Accounting Series Releases" or ASRs.

In such transactions, one or more security underwriting firms are involved to handle the sale of the securities and make the offer of sale to the public. Since there is a large financial exposure and the securities laws and regulations are quite technical, underwriters usually want an auditor to provide them with a letter addressing the completeness and accuracy of information contained in a registration statement, prospectus, or proxy material. Such letters are termed letters for underwriters or "comfort letters."

Auditors generally do not have problems in issuing comfort letters related to financial statements and data that have been audited. Underwriters, however, wish to obtain "comfort" on unaudited statements and data that might be included in the registration statement. In such cases, the auditor is limited by areas in which his or her expertise does not apply. Procedures short of an audit do not constitute a basis for issuance of positive assurance regarding data and it is not practical to develop a set of standards (short of an audit) to allow comfort to be given on such data. In such situations the auditor should meet with the underwriter and agree upon the procedures to be employed and the wording of the comfort letter early in the engagement. The auditor would be well advised to have his or her own legal counsel involved in engagements in which abnormal legal liability exposure and requirements exist.

Content of Comfort Letters

Comfort letters can be fairly long narrative reports which are tailored to the engagement and the related requirements. These letters usually address one or more of the following:

- Independence of the auditor
- Compliance of audited information with the requirements of law and regulations
- Unaudited information
- Changes in financial status since the date of the latest financial statement
- Tables, statistics, and other financial information

A typical comfort letter might include the following in its general format:

- Addressed to underwriter with a copy to client
- Identification of the financial statements which were audited and the registration statement in which they are included
- Statement of the auditor's independence regarding the client
- Assurance of the audited financial statements and data meeting the requirements of law
- Disclaimer on any unaudited financial statements included
- Listing of agreed-upon procedures performed such as reading minutes, reading interim financial statements, inquiries made of client personnel, and notation that these procedures do not constitute an audit
- Negative assurance on unaudited financial information
- Restriction on use of the comfort letter only by the underwriter

SUMMARY

This chapter discusses "special reports" or reports on financial statements presented in a form other than generally accepted accounting principles. The auditor's report may be based on an examination of the financial statements in accordance with GAAS or result from applying specified procedures to statements, control systems, or elements, items, or accounts of financial statements.

Auditors may report on the following:

- Cash basis statements
- Regulatory basis statements

- Income tax basis statements
- Price-level adjusted financial statements, or any other well defined basis of accounting
- Compliance with contractual and regulatory requirements
- Specified elements, accounts or items of a financial statement
- Agreed-upon procedures applied to specified elements, accounts or items of a financial statement
- Prescribed form reports and financial statements
- Internal accounting control
- Letters for underwriters—"comfort letters"

The chapter discusses the special procedures and report formats applicable to the above special types of auditors' reports.

REVIEW QUESTIONS

16-1   What are the requirements for a basis of accounting to qualify as "a comprehensive basis of accounting other than generally accepted accounting principles"?

16-2   Discuss the criteria an auditor may use to determine if there is adequate disclosure when financial statements are presented on a comprehensive basis of accounting other than GAAP (OCBOA).

16-3   List the basic items that should be contained in an auditor's report on a set of statements prepared on a comprehensive basis other than GAAP.

16-4   When financial statements are prepared on a comprehensive basis other than GAAP, the title of the statements should be descriptive of the basis so that a GAAP presentation will not be implied. For the cash basis, list several modified titles for a balance sheet and income statement.

16-5   Do the general, field work, and reporting standards apply to auditing engagements where the financial statements are prepared on a OCBOA?

16-6   What are the basic advantages and disadvantages of the cash basis of accounting and reporting?

16-7   Explain why an auditor wants to determine whether the client has violated any covenants of a loan agreement or has not complied with all regulatory requirements of a financial nature.

16-8 If an auditor issues a separate report setting forth a negative assurance with respect to a client's compliance with regulatory or contractual requirements, what items should be contained in this report?

16-9 Should the auditor follow *all* GAAS when asked to express an opinion on a specific financial statement account? Explain.

16-10 Distinguish between an opinion expressed on a specific financial statement account and a piecemeal opinion.

16-11 Identify the generally accepted auditing standards that are applicable to engagements which request auditors to report on the application of agreed-upon procedures to specified elements, accounts or items of a financial statement.

16-12 Under what conditions should an auditor accept an engagement to report on the application of agreed-upon procedures to specified elements, accounts or items of a financial statement?

16-13 Can an auditor express an opinion based on the application of agreed-upon procedures to specified elements, accounts or items of a financial statement? Explain.

16-14 Identify approaches an auditor may take when preprinted forms contain audit opinions that do not meet reporting standards or include representations the auditor cannot make.

16-15 Identify alternative courses of action an auditor may take when a prescribed financial statement format does not comply with GAAP or OCBOA.

16-16 Describe the different types of engagements in which the auditor would be asked to make a report on the client's system of internal accounting control.

16-17 Explain why the study and evaluation of internal accounting control made for the purpose of expressing an opinion on the system may serve as a basis for reliance in an audit of the financial statements of the client. Is the reverse situation appropriate?

16-18 List the different forms that can be used to document the client's system of internal accounting control.

16-19 Why does the auditor review the design of the client's internal accounting control system?

16-20   Identify the different points that should be covered in a management representation letter to the auditor in connection with an audit of the client's system of internal accounting control.

16-21   When an auditor is requested to report on a single element of a financial statement, may he or she do so in connection with a GAAS examination.

16-22   In Question 21, what concerns should the auditor have if his or her opinion on the basic financial statements is qualified or adverse?

16-23   What items should be considered when an auditor has to use a preprinted form for (a) the audit opinion, (b) the format of the financial statements?

16-24   Briefly discuss the five points that should be covered in the auditor's opinion concerning an audit of the client's system of internal accounting control. If a material weakness is found in the study and evaluation, to what extent should the auditor modify the report? If the opinion on the control system is issued in conjunction with an examination of the entity's financial statements, how should the auditor modify his or her report?

16-25   Refer to Chapter 8, and describe the reporting responsibilities of the auditor when he or she has been requested to report on the client's system of accounting control based on a study and evaluation of the system as part of an audit engagement.

16-26   Should financial statements and other schedules and data contained in filings with the SEC under the Securities Act of 1933 be considered as "prescribed form reports" or as "other comprehensive basis of accounting reports"? Discuss.

16-27   What type (or kind) of assurance may an auditor give an underwriter in a comfort letter concerning audited financial statements and data? Concerning unaudited financial statements and data?

16-28   What items or areas are normally addressed in an accountant's comfort letter prepared for an underwriter?

DISCUSSION QUESTIONS AND PROBLEMS

16-29   The financial statements of the Mountaineer Manufacturing Company have never been audited by an independent CPA. During the current year, Mountaineer's management asked Nancy Neat, CPA, to conduct a special study of Mountaineer's internal accounting controls for the purpose of expressing an opinion on the system. The study will not include an examination of Mountaineer's financial statements. Following completion of her special study, Nancy plans to prepare a report consistent with the requirements of SAS No. 30, *Reporting on Internal Accounting Control.*

Required:

a. Describe the responsibility of management for internal control and the broad objectives, and inherent limitations of internal accounting control as set forth in a report on internal accounting control.

b. Explain and contrast the study of internal accounting control that Nancy might make as part of an examination of financial statements with her engagement to express an opinion as to (1) objectives of review or study, (2) scope of review or study, and (3) nature and content of reports. Organize your answer for Part b as follows:

Examination of Financial Statements	*Special Study to Express an Opinion on the Internal Accounting Control System*
(1) Objective of review or study	(1) Objective of review or study
(2) Scope of review or study	(2) Scope of review or study
(3) Nature and content of report	(3) Nature and content of report

c. Write the first and fourth paragraphs of the auditor's report for the engagement to express an opinion on the client's system of internal accounting control.

d. Compare and contrast the differences between the first and fourth paragraphs of an internal accounting control report made in conjunction with the examination of financial statements and the report rendered in an engagement to express an opinion on the client's system of internal accounting control.

(AICPA adapted)

16-30 Jiffy Clerical Services is a corporation which furnishes temporary office help to its customers. Billings are rendered monthly based on predetermined hourly rates. You have examined the company's financial statements for several years. Following is an abbreviated statement of assets and liabilities on the modified cash basis as of December 31, 1983:

Assets:

Cash..	$20,000
Advances to employees......................................	1,000
Equipment and autos, less accumulated depreciation............	25,000
Total Assets...	$46,000

Liabilities:

Employees' payroll taxes withheld...........................	$ 8,000
Bank loan payable...	10,000
Estimated income taxes on cash basis profits..................	10,000
Total Liabilities......................................	$28,000
Net Assets..	$18,000

Represented by:

Common stock..	$ 3,000
Cash profits retained in the business........................	15,000
	$18,000

Unrecorded receivables were $55,000 and payables were $30,000.

Required:

a.   Prepare the report you would issue covering the statement of assets and liabilities as of December 31, 1983, as summarized above, and the related statement of cash revenue and expenses for the year ended that date.

b.   Briefly discuss and justify your modifications of the conventional report on accrual basis statements.

(AICPA adapted)

16-31   Indicate the general wording of the opinion paragraph in the auditor's *special report* on the statements for the two following cases.

1.   The financial statements of XYZ Market, a retail grocery operated as an individual proprietorship, are prepared on the basis of cash receipts and disbursements. These statements do not purport to present the financial position and results of operation of the company.

2.   The financial statements of the Raintree County Hospital, a private nonprofit organization, are prepared in accordance with the principles and practices of uniform accounting prescribed by a national hospital association. These statements purport to present the financial position and results of operation of the hospital.

(AICPA adapted)

OBJECTIVE QUESTIONS*

16-32   When asked to perform an examination in order to express an opinion on one or more specified elements, accounts or items of a financial statement, the auditor

A.   May not describe auditing procedures applied.

B.   Should advise the client that the opinion will result in a piecemeal opinion.

C.   May assume that the first standard of reporting with respect to generally accepted accounting principles does not apply.

D.   Should comply with the request only if they constitute a major portion of the financial statements on which an auditor has disclaimed an opinion based on an audit.

16-33   An auditor's report would be designated as a special report when it is issued in connection with which of the following?

A.   Financial statements for an interim period which are subjected to a limited review.

B.   Financial statements which are prepared in accordance with a comprehensive basis of accounting other than generally accepted accounting principles.

C.   Financial statements which purport to be in accordance with generally accepted accounting principles but do not include a presentation of the statement of changes in financial position.

D.   Financial statements which are unaudited and are prepared from a client's accounting records.

16-34   The term "special reports" may include all of the following except reports on financial statements

A.   Of an organization that has limited the scope of the auditor's examination.

B.   Prepared for limited purposes such as a report that relates to only certain aspects of financial statements.

C.   Of a not-for-profit organization which follows accounting practices differing in some respects from those followed by business enterprises organized for profit.

D.   Prepared in accordance with a cash basis of accounting.

Note: All questions in this section are AICPA adapted questions.

16-35   Whenever special reports, filed on a printed form designed by authorities, call upon the independent auditor to make an assertion that the auditor believes is *not* justified, the auditor should

     A.   Submit a short-form report with explanations.
     B.   Reword the form or attach a separate report.
     C.   Submit the form with questionable items clearly omitted.
     D.   Withdraw from the engagement.

16-36   One example of a "special report," as defined by Statements on Auditing Standards, is a report issued in connection with

     A.   A feasibility study.
     B.   A limited review of interim financial information.
     C.   Price-level basis financial statements.
     D.   Compliance with a contractual agreement not related to the financial statements.

16-37   An auditor is reporting on cash-basis financial statements. These statements are best referred to in his or her opinion by which one of the following descriptions?

     A.   Financial position and results of operations arising from cash transactions.
     B.   Assets and liabilities arising from cash transactions, and revenue collected and expenses paid.
     C.   Balance sheet and income statement resulting from cash transactions.
     D.   Cash balance sheet and the source and application of funds.

16-38   Which of the following reports is an indication of the changing role of the CPA that calls for an extension of the auditor's attest function?

     A.   Report on annual comparative financial statements.
     B.   Report on internal control based on an audit.
     C.   Report on separate balance sheet of a holding company.
     D.   Report on balance sheet and statements of income, retained earnings, and changes in financial position prepared from incomplete financial records.

16-39   If the auditor believes that financial statements which are prepared on a comprehensive basis of accounting other than generally accepted accounting principles are not suitably titled, the auditor should

A. Modify the auditor's report to disclose any reservations.

B. Consider the effects of the titles on the financial statements taken as whole.

C. Issue a disclaimer of opinion.

D. Add a footnote to the financial statements which explains alternative terminology.

16-40 A CPA should not normally refer to which one of the following subjects in a "comfort letter" to underwriters?

A. The independence of the CPA.

B. Changes in financial statement items during a period subsequent to the date and period of the latest financial statements in the registration statement.

C. Unaudited financial statements and schedules in the registration statement.

D. Management's determination of line of business classifications.

16-41 Which of the generally accepted auditing standards of reporting would not normally apply to special reports such as cash-basis statements?

A. First standard.

B. Second standard.

C. Third standard.

D. Fourth standard.

16-42 In a "comfort letter" to underwriters, the CPA should normally avoid using which of the following terms to describe the work performed?

A. Examined.

B. Read.

C. Made inquiries.

D. Made a limited review.

16-43 A CPA has been engaged to audit financial statements that were prepared on a cash basis. The CPA

A. Must ascertain that there is proper disclosure of the fact that the cash basis has been used, the general nature of material items omitted and the net effect of such omissions.

B. May not be associated with such statements which are not in accordance with generally accepted accounting principles.

C. Must render a qualified report explaining the departure from generally accepted accounting principles in the opinion paragraph.

D. Must restate the financial statements on an accrual basis and then render the standard (short-form) report.

16-44 Which of the following statements with respect to an auditor's report expressing an opinion on a specific item on a financial statement is correct?

A. Materiality must be related to the specified item rather than to the financial statements taken as a whole.

B. Such a report can only be expressed if the auditor is also engaged to audit the entire set of financial statements.

C. The attention devoted to the specified item is usually less than it would be if the financial statements taken as a whole were being audited.

D. The auditor who has issued an adverse opinion on the financial statements taken as a whole can never express an opinion on a specified item in these financial statements.

E FAIR PRESENTATION ETHICAL CONDUCT INDEPENDENCE EVIDENCE DUE CARE FAIR PRESENTATION ETHICAL CONDUCT INDEPENDENCE EVIDENCE DUE CARE FAIR PRESENTATI
CARE FAIR PRESENTATION ETHICAL CONDUCT INDEPENDENCE EVIDENCE DUE CARE FAIR PRESENTATION ETHICAL CONDUCT INDEPENDENCE EVIDENCE DUE CARE FAIR PRESEN
DUE CARE FAIR PRESENTATION ETHICAL CONDUCT INDEPENDENCE EVIDENCE DUE CARE FAIR PRESENTATION ETHICAL CONDUCT INDEPENDENCE EVIDENCE DUE CARE FAIR PRE
CE DUE CARE FAIR PRESENTATION ETHICAL CONDUCT INDEPENDENCE EVIDENCE DUE CARE FAIR PRESENTATION ETHICAL CONDUCT INDEPENDENCE EVIDENCE DUE CARE FAIR
DENCE DUE CARE FAIR PRESENTATION ETHICAL CONDUCT INDEPENDENCE EVIDENCE DUE CARE FAIR PRESENTATION ETHICAL CONDUCT INDEPENDENCE EVIDENCE DUE CARE
EVIDENCE DUE CARE FAIR PRESENTATION ETHICAL CONDUCT INDEPENDENCE EVIDENCE DUE CARE FAIR PRESENTATION ETHICAL CONDUCT INDEPENDENCE EVIDENCE DUE CA
NCE EVIDENCE DUE CARE FAIR PRESENTATION ETHICAL CONDUCT INDEPENDENCE EVIDENCE DUE CARE FAIR PRESENTATION ETHICAL CONDUCT INDEPENDENCE EVIDENCE DU
NDENCE EVIDENCE DUE CARE FAIR PRESENTATION ETHICAL CONDUCT INDEPENDENCE EVIDENCE DUE CARE FAIR PRESENTATION ETHICAL CONDUCT INDEPENDENCE EVIDENCE

LEARNING OBJECTIVES

After studying this chapter, students should understand

1. The CPA's legal liability under common law.
2. The CPA's legal liability under the Securities Acts of 1933 and 1934.
3. The nature of some of the most important cases filed against CPA firms.
4. The auditor's responsibility for the detection of errors or irregularities.
5. The auditor's responsibility for detecting illegal acts by clients.
6. The auditor's legal liability in connection with inadequate disclosure, the work of other auditors, subsequent events, subsequent discovery of facts existing at the report date, and unaudited statements.

PENDENCE EVIDENCE DUE CARE FAIR PRESENTATION ETHICAL CONDUCT INDEPENDENCE EVIDENCE DUE CARE FAIR PRESENTATION ETHICAL CONDUCT INDEPENDENCE EVIDEN
INDEPENDENCE EVIDENCE DUE CARE FAIR PRESENTATION ETHICAL CONDUCT INDEPENDENCE EVIDENCE DUE CARE FAIR PRESENTATION ETHICAL CONDUCT INDEPENDENCE EVI
CT INDEPENDENCE EVIDENCE DUE CARE FAIR PRESENTATION ETHICAL CONDUCT INDEPENDENCE EVIDENCE DUE CARE FAIR PRESENTATION ETHICAL CONDUCT INDEPENDENCE
NDUCT INDEPENDENCE EVIDENCE DUE CARE FAIR PRESENTATION ETHICAL CONDUCT INDEPENDENCE EVIDENCE DUE CARE FAIR PRESENTATION ETHICAL CONDUCT INDEPENDE
CONDUCT INDEPENDENCE EVIDENCE DUE CARE FAIR PRESENTATION ETHICAL CONDUCT INDEPENDENCE EVIDENCE DUE CARE FAIR PRESENTATION ETHICAL CONDUCT INDEPE
ICAL CONDUCT INDEPENDENCE EVIDENCE DUE CARE FAIR PRESENTATION ETHICAL CONDUCT INDEPENDENCE EVIDENCE DUE CARE FAIR PRESENTATION ETHICAL CONDUCT IND
ETHICAL CONDUCT INDEPENDENCE EVIDENCE DUE CARE FAIR PRESENTATION ETHICAL CONDUCT INDEPENDENCE EVIDENCE DUE CARE FAIR PRESENTATION ETHICAL CONDUCT
ION ETHICAL CONDUCT INDEPENDENCE EVIDENCE DUE CARE FAIR PRESENTATION ETHICAL CONDUCT INDEPENDENCE EVIDENCE DUE CARE FAIR PRESENTATION ETHICAL COND
ITATION ETHICAL CONDUCT INDEPENDENCE EVIDENCE DUE CARE FAIR PRESENTATION ETHICAL CONDUCT INDEPENDENCE EVIDENCE DUE CARE FAIR PRESENTATION ETHICAL C
ESENTATION ETHICAL CONDUCT INDEPENDENCE EVIDENCE DUE CARE FAIR PRESENTATION ETHICAL CONDUCT INDEPENDENCE EVIDENCE DUE CARE FAIR PRESENTATION ETHICA
R PRESENTATION ETHICAL CONDUCT INDEPENDENCE EVIDENCE DUE CARE FAIR PRESENTATION ETHICAL CONDUCT INDEPENDENCE EVIDENCE DUE CARE FAIR PRESENTATION ET
FAIR PRESENTATION ETHICAL CONDUCT INDEPENDENCE EVIDENCE DUE CARE FAIR PRESENTATION ETHICAL CONDUCT INDEPENDENCE EVIDENCE DUE CARE FAIR PRESENTATION
ARE FAIR PRESENTATION ETHICAL CONDUCT INDEPENDENCE EVIDENCE DUE CARE FAIR PRESENTATION ETHICAL CONDUCT INDEPENDENCE EVIDENCE DUE CARE FAIR PRESENTA
E CARE FAIR PRESENTATION ETHICAL CONDUCT INDEPENDENCE EVIDENCE DUE CARE FAIR PRESENTATION ETHICAL CONDUCT INDEPENDENCE EVIDENCE DUE CARE FAIR PRESE
DUE CARE FAIR PRESENTATION ETHICAL CONDUCT INDEPENDENCE EVIDENCE DUE CARE FAIR PRESENTATION ETHICAL CONDUCT INDEPENDENCE EVIDENCE DUE CARE FAIR PR
ENCE DUE CARE FAIR PRESENTATION ETHICAL CONDUCT INDEPENDENCE EVIDENCE DUE CARE FAIR PRESENTATION ETHICAL CONDUCT INDEPENDENCE EVIDENCE DUE CARE FA
VIDENCE DUE CARE FAIR PRESENTATION ETHICAL CONDUCT INDEPENDENCE EVIDENCE DUE CARE FAIR PRESENTATION ETHICAL CONDUCT INDEPENDENCE EVIDENCE DUE CARE
CE EVIDENCE DUE CARE FAIR PRESENTATION ETHICAL CONDUCT INDEPENDENCE EVIDENCE DUE CARE FAIR PRESENTATION ETHICAL CONDUCT INDEPENDENCE EVIDENCE DUE C
DENCE EVIDENCE DUE CARE FAIR PRESENTATION ETHICAL CONDUCT INDEPENDENCE EVIDENCE DUE CARE FAIR PRESENTATION ETHICAL CONDUCT INDEPENDENCE EVIDENCE D

Chapter 17

The Auditor's Professional Responsibility

This chapter was written by
Donna Lynn Welker, B.S., M. Acc., C.P.A.,
at
Texas A&M University

INTRODUCTION

In recent years, the volume of litigation brought against accountants has increased markedly. Disgruntled investors in bankrupt companies frequently seek to recover damages from a solvent party. Often, this party is the independent accounting firm. Class action suits, instigated by a group of many or all such investors, may involve the possibility of sizeable settlements, making these cases very attractive to an attorney, particularly on a contingent fee basis. Accountants are vulnerable to litigation, as certain recent court decisions have demonstrated.

Public accountants have been involved in numerous lawsuits over the years, particularly in the past two decades. These cases have all played a role (some more significant than others) in expanding the scope of the accountant's legal responsibility that is still evolving today. Although these cases have marked precedents which public accountants can follow, the courts have not provided definitive answers to many other questions and problems. Given the changing nature of the law and its interpretation, the liability of the auditor in the future may be much more encompassing than it is today.

Despite these uncertainties, the accountant, by being aware of the broad legal responsibilities of the profession and by performing his or her work well, should be able to avoid significant liability.

PROFESSIONAL LIABILITY OF THE PUBLIC ACCOUNTANT

Partners in accounting firms are liable for any and all fraudulent or negligent acts of firm employees that fall within the scope of employment. CPAs have a responsibility that extends beyond the client to creditors, investors and other interested parties relying on the audited financial statements.

The CPA has broad legal responsibilities for all services rendered, including auditing, management advisory services, write-up work, bookkeeping and tax services. These responsibilities are defined by both common law and statutory law.

Under *common law* (unwritten law based upon prior legal opinions in court cases), the following three general groups may bring civil action against the public accountant:

- Clients and subrogees[1] (party acquiring the rights of the client by substitution)

---

[1] For example, accountants purchase malpractice insurance to cover their negligence. Fidelity bonds protect the client by covering the loss resulting from negligence. After paying on the fidelity bond, the client's bonding company is *subrogated* to the client's rights for reimbursement from the auditor's malpractice insurance.

- Primary beneficiaries

- Known and unknown beneficiaries.

These parties (plaintiffs) under a civil proceeding may seek to recover damages in the form of monetary awards either for breach of contract or on a tort action (breach of duty other than contractual duty) for ordinary negligence, gross negligence or fraud.

Statutory law (written law) includes both state and federal statutes. The accountant may be held liable to the client and third parties for litigation filed under civil sections of statutes. The majority of cases brought against the accountant under statutory law involve investors under the Securities Act of 1933 and the Securities Exchange Act of 1934. Criminal action against CPAs must be instigated by the state or federal government or other governmental agency. The legal remedies in a criminal case include imprisonment and/or fines.

The law imposes a *standard of conduct* on the accountant similar to that required of other professional persons. As such, the accountant is expected to possess the *average degree of skill and ability* required of all accountants and to perform all duties with *reasonable care*. The law requires that the accountant meet the standards of competence and care that have developed within the profession. In the field of accounting, this means that the accountant must adhere to the Code of Professional Ethics, generally accepted accounting principles, and generally accepted auditing standards.

LIABILITY TO CLIENTS (or Subrogees)

The accountant forms a legal binding relationship with a client through either a verbal or written contract. When two or more parties form a contract, they are said to be in *privity of contract*, meaning that their relationship and rights are created by virtue of the contract. The concept of privity may also extend to a *third party beneficiary* when identified to the auditor as the party who is to receive the primary benefit of performance under the contract.

Generally, the services to be rendered and other terms agreed upon are set out in an engagement letter. When signed by the client, this letter serves as a contract. Therefore, it is essential that the accountant prepare a specific listing of all duties and liabilities assumed by the accountant to minimize the risk of any misunderstandings or disputes that may arise. The *1136 Tenants' Corporation* case (discussed later in this chapter) taught the profession a practical lesson of the importance of using an engagement letter.

The public accountant assumes the role of an independent contractor (not an employee), meaning that the CPA (not the client) controls the work to be done and holds legal title to all workpapers used in the audit engagement. The contract may not be delegated to others, but the accounting firm may assume the responsibility of work done for the firm by outside experts.

As mentioned above, a client may bring suit under common law for breach of contract. An accountant may be *held liable for breach of contract*, for example, for any of the following reasons:

- Nonfulfillment of terms in the contract, including late completion of an audit.
- Violation of privileged communications between the accountant and client.
- Failure to perform an audit engagement in accordance with GAAS (unless specifically agreed upon).

Although Rule 301 of the AICPA's Code of Professional Ethics expressly prohibits the disclosure of confidential client information, certain limited exceptions do exist. Prohibition is waived when complying with state statutes, court subpoenas or summons, voluntary firm quality control reviews, inquiries made by the ethics division or trial board of the AICPA or a state society or board of accountancy.

Privileged communications do not exist at common law, and only a few states have promulgated statutes preserving the accountant-client privilege. Therefore, in federal courts or state courts not recognizing such privilege, the auditor must testify or relinquish possession of working papers and other confidential information upon being served with an enforceable subpoena or summons. In these instances, the CPA cannot be held liable to the client for breach of duty for violating the confidental relationship.

If a breach of duty (other than contractual) occurs, the client may also bring suit under *tort law* for:

- **Ordinary Negligence** (Often referred to as negligence).   In the performance of his or her services, the auditor must exercise that degree of care which an average prudent member of his or her profession would exercise under the same or similar circumstances.
- **Gross Negligence.**   The auditor may be held liable for failure to use even slight care. This doctrine is also known as constructive (unintentional) fraud when reckless disregard for professional standards or the truth is evident.

- **Fraud.** Actual (intentional) fraud occurs when the auditor makes a material misrepresentation with the intent to deceive another.

In order to recover damages in a negligence or fraud action, a client often proceeds on the grounds that he or she incurred a loss because of his or her reliance upon the auditor's services in choosing a particular course of action or that a loss was sustained as a result of the auditor's failure to discover defalcations or other irregularities in the audit engagement.

Commonly sought *defenses* of the auditor for *malpractice suits* include the following:

- The auditor was not negligent.
- The loss was not incurred as a result of the auditor's negligence.
- The negligence of the plaintiff contributed to the loss (the doctrine of contributory negligence).
- The plaintiff was already indemnified for the loss from another party.

It is not sufficient for the plaintiff to substantiate that the auditor used poor judgment or that the accountant's work was inaccurate. To recover damages for malpractice, the client must prove that the auditor failed to use the standard of due care and the degree of competence required of all members of the accounting profession. The plaintiff must further *establish reliance* upon the auditor's work and demonstrate that the loss resulted as a proximate cause of such reliance.

The auditor may assert *contributory negligence* as a defense to an action brought by the client for negligence but not for breach of contract. For contributory negligence, the auditor will attempt to prove that the client's own negligence contributed to the inaccuracy or error. For example, the accountant may claim that the client restricted the audit investigation and that the nature of the error precluded its discovery. By asserting this defense, the auditor may be able to mitigate or avoid potential liability.

LIABILITY TO THIRD PARTIES UNDER COMMON LAW

In certain situations, the auditor may also be held civilly liable to persons, other than clients, who rely on the auditor's work. These third parties consist of primary beneficiaries and other beneficiaries.

As mentioned earlier, the auditor's contractual liability may extend to third parties when services rendered by the CPA are primarily for the benefit of the third party. For example, an accountant may have agreed to compile financial statements for the client for purposes of securing a loan from a certain bank. The bank is an intended third party beneficiary and as such is in privity of contract with the accountant. Other beneficiaries include third parties, such as investors, creditors, suppliers and customers, who have not been identified in the contract.

One of the earliest American cases concerning the CPA's liability to a third party was that of *Landell vs. Lybrand* (1919)[2]. The plaintiff (Landell) purchased stock, alleging reliance on an inaccurate report negligently prepared by the company's auditors (Lybrand). The Pennsylvania Supreme Court held that the auditors could not be held liable to the plaintiff for negligence in the absence of a contract.

In a subsequent case, *Glanzer vs. Shepard*[3] (1922), liability of the accountant to third parties was extended. Although this case did not actually involve an auditor, it was used as a precedent in establishing the liability of an expert (such as the CPA) to a primary beneficiary for ordinary negligence.

In the *Glanzer* case, a seller of goods commissioned public weighers to weigh the goods sold to the buyers (plaintiffs) and to furnish a weight certificate to the buyers. Later, it was discovered that the weight was inaccurately certified. The court ruled that the buyer was entitled to recovery from the public weigher due to negligence, emphasizing that the weigher was aware of the fact that the weighing was done "with the very end and aim of shaping the conduct of another."[4]

Generally, a CPA may be held liable for ordinary negligence only to third persons who are *known* to the accountant to be users or beneficiaries of the accountant's work. In the example cited previously, the CPA would be liable to the bank because the accountant knew that the unaudited statements requested by the client were required by a specific bank. However, if the CPA were not informed that the statements were to be prepared in order to secure a loan from the client's bank, then that bank could not hold the accountant liable.

The CPA may also be liable to third parties for gross negligence or fraud. The landmark case of *Ultramares vs. Touche*[5] (1931) has served as the dominant precedent throughout the years in defining the CPA's

[2] *Landell vs. Lybrand*, 264 Pa. 406, 107 Atl. 783 (1919).
[3] *Glanzer vs. Shepard*, 233 N.Y. 236, 135 N.E. 275 (1922).
[4] *Ibid.*
[5] *Ultramares Corp. vs. Touche*, 255 N.Y. 179, 174 N.E. 441 (1931).

liability under common law, limiting liability to third parties who are not in privity of contract to acts of gross negligence or fraud. In addition to developing the concept of gross negligence (constructive fraud), *Ultramares* promulgated the rule that public accountants cannot be held liable to unidentified third parties for ordinary negligence.

Although *Ultramares* is still used as a precedent in some states, many other jurisdictions have made inroads on this case by broadening the auditor's liability for negligence to foreseen third parties. That is, common law varies from state to state; thus, some jurisdictions apply the *Ultramares* rule, while others use the "foreseeability" rule.

One such case responsible for establishing the "foreseeability" trend was *Rusch Factors vs. Levin*[6] (1968). Rusch Factors (plaintiff) requested that the corporation's financial statements be certified as a precondition to obtaining a loan. The auditor was held liable to the third party plaintiff for the certification of financial statements which indicated that the corporation was solvent when in reality it was insolvent. The court held that:

> ". . . an accountant should be liable in negligence for careless financial misrepresentations relied upon by *actually foreseen and limited classes of persons*. According to the plaintiff's complaint in the instant case, the *defendant knew* that his *certification* was to be *used for*, and *had as its very aim and purpose*, the *reliance* of *potential financiers* of the Rhode Island Corporation."[7] (Emphasis added.)

The 1972 decision of *Rhode Island Hospital Trust National Bank vs. Swartz*[8] was based, in part, upon the *Rusch* case. It was concluded that Rhode Island law would hold auditors "liable in negligence for careless financial misrepresentations relied upon by actually foreseen and limited classes of persons."[9] Oddly enough, the *Rhode Island* case also held that an auditor may be liable for negligence to a third party, despite a disclaimer of opinion given by the auditor.

Under the foreseeability rule, a CPA who conducts an audit so that the client can obtain a loan from Bank Known can be held negligent by Bank Known or any Bank Unknown for negligence, provided reliance is established. However, an unforeseen trade creditor or investor could not assert ordinary negligence as a basis for action but would be re-

---

[6] *Rusch Factors, Inc. vs. Levin*, 284 F. Supp. 85 (D.R.I. 1968).
[7] *Ibid.*
[8] *Rhode Island Hospital Trust National Bank vs. Swartz*, 455 F.2d 847 (4th Cir. 1972).
[9] *Ibid.*

quired to prove gross negligence or fraud to reach the auditor. The *Restatement of Torts* provides that it is only necessary for the third party to be identified by class (e.g., bank credit), rather than as a specific person.

Several recent cases have embraced the foreseeability rule. In *Seedkem, Inc. vs. Safranek*[10] (1979) the third party plaintiff alleged that the defendant CPA foresaw or should have foreseen plaintiff's reliance on the CPA's work. Having concluded that Nebraska and Indiana would employ the foreseeability rule, the judge denied defendant's motion to dismiss on the grounds of privity. In *Coleco Industries, Inc. vs. Berman*[11] (1976), the trial court applying New Jersey and Pennsylvania law adjudged an accountant liable to a foreseeable third party for negligent audit work. Another case, *Merit Insurance Co. vs. Colao*[12] (1979) defined the CPA's liability to include a foreseen class of user and type of transaction. This case stated that CPAs under Illinois law are liable to third parties for negligence only when the CPAs know that one of a relatively small group of third parties will rely upon the accountants' work.

The court in *Stratton Group, Ltd. vs. Sprayregen*[13] (1979), however, dismissed the negligence claim because third party plaintiffs were not in privity with the accounting firm. Likewise, a number of Florida decisions have rejected the foreseeability rule in favor of the privity doctrine.

FEDERAL SECURITIES LAW

Securities Act of 1933

The Securities Act of 1933 (known as the Truth in Securities Law) was intended to provide the investing public with full and fair disclosure of the information necessary to adequately evaluate the merits of security[14] offerings and to prevent fraud or misrepresentation.

This Act requires that a *registration statement* be filed (in most cases[15]) with the Securities and Exchange Commission (SEC) before

---

[10] *Seedkem, Inc. vs. Safranek*, 466 F. Supp. 340 (D. Neb. 1979).

[11] *Coleco Industries, Inc. vs. Berman*, 423 F. Supp. 275 (E.D. Pa. 1976).

[12] *Merit Insurance Co. vs. Colao*, 603 F.2d 654 (7th Cir. 1979).

[13] *Stratton Group, Ltd. vs. Sprayregen*, 466 F. Supp. 1180 (S.D.N.Y. 1979).

[14] A security includes any stock, bond, note, investment contract or any interest or instrument commonly known as a security.

[15] Certain types of securities are exempt from registration requirements. Generally, these exemptions are allowed because public interest is not deemed to require protection (e.g., securities of charitable, not-for-profit organizations), or the securities are regulated by other governmental agencies. Certain transactions are also exempt from registration requirements, such as private offerings under Section 4(2) of the 1933 Act.

either a public sale or an offer to the public through the mail or an interstate sale or offer is made. The registration statement must include the corporation's financial statements, which have been audited by an independent public accountant. If sufficient time has elasped since the close of the previous fiscal year, interim statements for the period are also required, but need not be certified. However, the accountant is responsible for the review of these statements up to the effective date of the registration.

To provide the investing public with the information submitted to the SEC in the registration statement, a *prospectus* is to be furnished to potential investors with, or before, the sale or delivery of the securities. A prospectus is any circular, letter, notice or advertisement which offers a security for sale; it must also be filed with the SEC as part of the registration statement. Even if the securities are not required to be registered, failure to comply with these requirements or misrepresentation or fraud in the sale of securities may result in civil and criminal penalties.

Upon examination of the registration statement and prospectus, the SEC may issue a stop order, require amendments or allow registration to become effective on the 20th day after filing. In its examination, the SEC does not evaluate the "soundness" or value of the securities. The SEC merely mandates complete and fair disclosure so that the public can discern the merits of the security offerings.

State "Blue Sky" laws must also be complied with. These state statutes regulate the issuance and sale of securities and contain anti-fraud and registration provisions, as do the Federal Securities Laws. "Blue Sky" legislation was enacted to protect the public from fraudulent schemes involving worthless securities.

Section 11 of the 1933 Act states that an expert (such as an accountant) may be held liable by any purchaser of securities for any false and/or misleading statements of material facts or material omissions therein for that portion of the registration statement that is "*expertized*" (generally that portion of the financial statements covered by the CPA's opinion). The accountant is also liable for any false or misleading statements included in the prospectus. As the truth and accuracy of these statements are determined at the *date registration becomes effective* and not when the statements were prepared, the accountant is responsible for any errors which may result from changes occurring between the preparation date and the effective date of the statement.

The *burden of proof* under the 1933 Act rests upon the accountant.[16] The purchaser need not prove that the accountant acted negligently or fraudulently or that he or she had a contractual relationship with the accountant, nor must the purchaser prove reliance on the statement. The investor need only establish that the security(ies) he or she purchased were the ones offered through the registration statement and prove the existence of a false statement or material omission contained therein.

To counter the charges of the purchaser under this Act, the accountant may assert the *due diligence defense* to prove that he or she was not negligent or fraudulent. Under this defense, the accountant would prove that he or she had, after reasonable investigation, a *reasonable basis* to believe and did believe that the statements were accurate and that no material omissions occurred.

The accountant may also be able to avoid liability by proving (1) that the investor at the time of the acquisition knew of the untruth or omission, (2) that the investor's loss was not a proximate outcome of the misleading financial statement and either (3) that the statements were not materially misstated or (4) that before the effective date of the registration statement (or when first becoming aware of its effectiveness), the CPA had taken appropriate steps to sever his or her relationship with the client and had so advised both the client and the SEC.

Generally, the amount of recoverable damages is measured by the difference between the amount paid for the security and its market value at the time of the suit. The statute of limitations provides that the suit must be brought against the accountant within one year of the time when the error or omission was discovered or should have been discovered, not to exceed three years after the initial offering of the security.

Securities Exchange Act of 1934

The *Securities and Exchange Commission* (SEC) was established by the *Securities Exchange Act of 1934* to administer the 1933 and 1934 Acts and other related statutes. The SEC was granted the power to establish rules, conduct investigations, issue opinions and enforce its rules and laws.

Whereas the 1933 Act was established to regulate the *initial offerings* of securities, the 1934 Act (known as the Continuous Disclosure Act)

---

[16] A *possible exception* may shift the burden of proof to the purchaser under the 1933 Act. An investor must prove his or her reliance on the registration statement if an earnings statement covering at least a 12-month period after the registration statement was available to him or her before he or she purchased the security.

was created to regulate and control the *subsequent trading* of securities to prevent inequitable and unfair practices on securities exchanges and over-the-counter markets. The 1934 Act applies to *all* statements (not only registration statements) which have been filed in compliance with the Federal securities acts. Basically, the 1934 Act (in addition to the registration of securities) requires *annual reports* (Form 10-K) which contain financial statements that have been attested to by an independent public accountant and other periodic reports[17] to maintain a *current status* of the information already included in the files of the SEC.

Those required to register with the SEC under the 1934 Act[18] before trading of securities can occur include brokers and dealers involved in interstate commerce, national securities exchanges and companies transacting business in interstate commerce whose total assets are in excess of $1 million and which have a class of equity securities held by 500 or more shareholders.

The basis for action under the 1934 Act is basically the same as that of the 1933 Act. Section 18(a) imposes civil liability on the accountant or other persons who, in any SEC annual report, make a false or misleading statement as follows:

> Any person who shall make or cause to be made any statement in any application, report, or document filed pursuant to this title . . . which . . . was made false or misleading with respect to any material fact, shall be liable to any person (not knowing that such statement was false or misleading) who, in reliance upon such statement, shall have purchased or sold a security at a price which was affected by such statement, for damages caused by such reliance, *unless* the person sued shall *prove* that *he acted in good faith and had no knowledge that such statement was false or misleading.*[19] (Emphasis added.)

Section 18(a) states that a person (the accountant) can avoid liability if he or she proves he or she acted in good faith and had no knowledge that such statement was false or misleading. That is, the auditor may avoid liability by successfully asserting the due diligence doctrine.

---

[17] Although the certified financial statements included in Form 10-K create the principal source of liability for accountants, other reports, such as the 10-Q and 8-K (quarterly and monthly reports, respectively) also expose accountants to legal liability, as accountants are usually involved in the review of information contained in these other reports.

[18] As with the 1933 Act, certain securities and transactions are exempt under the 1934 Act.

[19] Securities Exchange Act of 1934, Section 18(a).

Section 10 of the 1934 Act pertains to the private trading of securities and to *both registered and unregistered* securities. Under Section 10(b), any buyer or seller of a security under the jurisdiction of the SEC may initiate the suit for fraudulent acts "in connection with the purchase or sale of a security."[20]

Section 10(b) reads as follows:

> It shall be unlawful for any person, directly or indirectly, by the use of any means or instrumentality of interstate commerce or of the mails, or of any facility of any national securities exchange . . . .
>
> (b) to use or employ, in connection with the purchase or sale of any security registered on a national securities exchange or any security not so registered, any manipulative or deceptive device or contrivance in contravention of such rules and regulations as the Commissioner may prescribe as necessary or appropriate in the public interest or for the protection of investors.[21]

As Section 10(b) deals specifically with *fraudulent acts*, the Section 18 defense of due diligence does not apply to suits filed under its provisions.

Rule 10(b)(5) also relates specifically to *fraudulent acts*. Rule 10(b)(5) states:

> It shall be unlawful for any person directly or indirectly, by the use of any means or instrumentality of *interstate commerce*, or of the *mails* or of any facility of any *national securities exchange*, (a) to employ any device, scheme, or artifice *to defraud*, (b) to make *any untrue statement* of a material fact or *omit* to state a material fact necessary in order to make the statements made, in the light of the circumstances under which they were made, not misleading, or (c) to engage in any act, practice, or course of business which operates or would operate as a *fraud* or *deceit* upon any person in connection with the purchase or sale of any security.[22] (Emphasis added.)

In sharp contrast to the 1933 Act, the Securities Exchange Act of 1934 severely broadens the range of third parties to whom the accountant may be held liable. Unlike the 1933 Act, though, the burden of proof in litigation brought under the 1934 Act is placed on the investor. The plaintiff must prove that:

---

[20] Securities Exchange Act of 1934, Section 10.

[21] *Ibid.*

[22] 17 C.F.R. § 240.10(b)(5).

- He or she bought or sold the security at a price that was affected by the false or misleading statement;

- He or she was not cognizant of the false or incorrect statement; and

- He or she relied on the statement.

Under Section 18, the plaintiff need not prove that the auditor acted with *scienter* (intent to deceive or defraud or with reckless disregard of the truth), but the investor must establish such proof under Section 10(b) and Rule 10(b)(5).

The statute of limitations for the 1934 Act parallels that of the 1933 Act (one year after discovery, not to exceed a maximum of three years) with the exception of Rule 10(b)(5). Generally, the statute of limitations under Rule 10(b)(5) can run as long as six years. Damages recoverable are those incurred by the purchaser or seller.

Criminal liability may also be imposed for any *willful violations* of the provision of these Acts. The offender may be subject to a maximum fine of $10,000 and/or 5 years imprisonment.

IMPORTANT CASES FILED UNDER THE PROVISIONS OF THE SECURITIES ACT

Escott vs. BarChris Construction Corp. (1968)[23]

The *BarChris* case is deemed significant because it was the first major case filed under Section 11 of the 1933 Act. It had the effect of alerting other potential litigants to this statutory provision and its application to accountants.

In order to issue convertible debentures, BarChris filed a registration statement, which included the audited financial statements for 1960 and unaudited statements for the interim period (referred to as the "stub period"). The industry (construction of bowling alleys) that BarChris was a part of later suffered a business letdown. BarChris filed for bankruptcy approximately a year after the registration statement became effective

The CPA firm, failing to establish due diligence, was found liable to third party investors for failure to make a reasonable investigation in an audit and for failure to perform a proper *S-1 review* (review of the period between the audit date and effective date of the registration statement). The following is a summary of conclusions reached by the trial judge:

---

[23] *Escott vs. BarChris Construction Corp.*, 283 F. Supp. 643, (S.D.N.Y. 1968).

- The audited balance sheet and income statement both contained errors, although only the balance sheet errors were considered material.

- Although the auditors' program for the stub period review was considered adequate, the senior accountant's review was judged negligent, mainly because the court felt the senior "was too easily satisfied with glib answers"[24] from management and because the senior did not read the registration statement (however, both the partner and manager did).

- The stub period statements were found to be materially in error, but the accountants not having "expertized" (reported on) them were not found liable on the basis of these statements alone. Rather, the judge held that the accountants should have discovered these errors and considered them in their report on the audited year-end statements.

- The auditor could be held liable to the underwriters but no other party on the basis of a comfort letter (normally issued by the auditor as a form of negative assurance for the stub period at the request of the underwriters).

- "Accountants should not be held to a higher standard than that recognized in their profession."[25]

United States vs. Simon (1969)[26]

In this case, commonly referred to as *Continental Vending*,[27] two partners and a manager of an accounting firm were convicted of criminal liability under Section 32 of the 1934 Act. The case focused on a footnote to the financial statements, which was deemed inadequate by the government, as certain significant transactions between Continental and one of its officers were not disclosed.

The judge declined to give the jury instructions requested by the defendants. The instructions would have relayed to the jury that the "defendant could be found guilty only if, according to generally accepted accounting principles, the financial statements as a whole did not fairly present the financial condition of Continental . . . and then only if his departure from accepted standards was due to willful disregard of these standards with knowledge of the falsity of the statements and an intent to deceive."[28] Instead, the judge determined "that the 'cricital

---

[24] *Ibid.*
[25] *Ibid.*
[26] *United States vs. Simon*, 425 F.2d 796 (2d Cir. 1969), cert. denied, 397 U.S. 1006 (1970.
[27] The interested reader is referred to an excellent article written about this case: "The Continental Vending Case: Lessons for the Profession," by David B. Isbell, *The Journal of Accountancy*, Aug., 1970.
[28] *United States vs. Simon*, 425 F.2d 796 (2d Cir. 1969).

test' was whether the financial statements as a whole fairly presented the financial position . . . and whether it accurately reported the operations . . . ."[29] The court further stated that proof of compliance with generally accepted standards was evidence which may be persuasive, though not conclusive, that an auditor acted in good faith.

Upholding an earlier conviction of the auditors, the appellate court commented that the government's burden "was not to show that defendants were wicked men with designs on anyone's purse, whichy they obviously were not, but rather that they had certified a statement knowing it to be false.[30]

Ernst & Ernst vs. Hochfelder[31]

The *Hochfelder* case was considered significant for two reasons: (1) it was the first case involving a CPA to reach the U.S. Supreme Court, and (2) it represented an important victory for the public accounting profession.

The opinion on the case states in part that:

> Respondents were customers of First Securities, who invested in a fraudulent securities scheme perpetrated by Leston B. Nay, president of the firm and owner of 92 percent of its stock. Nay induced the respondents to invest funds in "escrow" accounts that he represented would yield a high rate of return . . . . In fact, there were no escrow accounts as Nay converted respondents' funds to his own use immediately upon receipt . . . .

* * *

> This fraud came to light in 1968 when Nay committed suicide, leaving a note that described First Securities as bankrupt and the escrow accounts as "spurious."[32]

The defrauded customers subsequently filed an action for damages against Ernst & Ernst under the 1934 Act, charging that Nay's escrow scheme violated §10(b) and Rule 10(b)(5). The complaint alleged that Ernst & Ernst had "aided and abetted" Nay's violations by its "failure" to conduct proper audits of First Securities, which should have led them to uncover the "mail rule" and the fraud. However, no allegations were made accusing Ernst & Ernst of intentional fraud, only "inexcusable negligence." The "mail rule" involved a company rule that all

---

[29] *Ibid.*
[30] *Ibid.*
[31] *Ernst & Ernst vs. Hochfelder*, 425 U.S. 185 (1976).
[32] *Ibid.*

mail addressed to Nay was to be opened only by Nay. In his absence from the company, the mail was left unopened. Nay had established the mail rule, of course, to avoid detection of his escrow accounts scheme. Ernst & Ernst did indicate this weakness in internal control in their report to management.

The Supreme Court ruled *scienter* (intentional or willful misconduct) need be established or the accounting firm could not be held liable for aiding and abetting the broker's fraud. Thus, in effect, the court ruled that negligence cannot substantiate a Section 10(b) or Rule 10(b)(5) action.

The Supreme Court did not define the term "scienter." However, lower Federal Courts have held that "recklessness" is a sufficient cause of action under Section 10(b).[33]

PRACTICAL APPLICATIONS WHERE AUDITORS MAY INCUR LIABILITY

Auditor's Responsibility for the Detection of Errors and Irregularities

In making an examination of financial statements in accordance with GAAS, the auditor (with an attitude of professional skepticism) is required to plan the examination to search for errors or irregularities that would have a material effect on the financial statements.

The term errors refers to unintentional mistakes, which include mathematical or clerical mistakes, misinterpretations or mistakes in the application of accounting principles and oversight or misinterpretation of facts that existed at the time the financial statements were prepared. On the other hand, the term irregularities refers to intentional distortions, including management fraud (deliberate misrepresentations by management) and defalcations (misappropriation of assets).

The audit made in accordance with GAAS provides only reasonable, not absolute, assurance that statements are not materially affected by errors and irregularities. That is, the audit process is characterized by certain inherent limitations. Thus, the auditing procedures employed are influenced and restricted by the CPA's judgment of the integrity of management and the perceived strength of internal controls.

The auditor is not responsible for the discovery of all errors and irregularities. Rather, the CPA is expected to be aware of the possibility that errors and irregularities may occur and that management may have devised overriding controls which may preclude discovery by the audi-

---

[33] One such case was that of *Sharp vs. Coopers & Lybrand*, 457 F. Supp. 879 (E.D. Pa. 1978). The defendant accounting firm was held liable to third-party investors under Section 10(b) of the 1934 Act for recklessness in drafting a tax opinion letter.

tor. Bearing in mind conditions or circumstances that might predispose management (either intentionally or accidentally) to misstate its financial statements, the auditor should weigh the associated risk factors and plan the audit program accordingly.

Should the auditor encounter evidence that material errors or irregularities may exist, the CPA should consider their ramifications, and discuss the matter with an appropriate level of management. If such discussions do not alleviate the auditor's suspicions, then the board of directors or its audit committee should be made aware of the circumstances.

The CPA should attempt to obtain sufficient evidential matter as to the existence and effects of these abnormalities by extending his or her auditing procedures. However, it may not be practical or possible for the auditor to extend procedures search due to the nature of the errors or irregularities or because of a management-imposed scope limitation.

When the findings of the auditor indicate that errors or irregularities may exist and the auditor is unable to discern the effects they may have on the financial statements as a whole, then a qualified opinion or disclaimer of an opinion should be issued. Depending upon the circumstances, the auditor may also consider withdrawing from the engagement and communicating the reasons therefor in writing to the client board of directors.

Auditors' Responsibility for Illegal Client Acts

In the examination of financial statements made in accordance with GAAS, the auditor cannot be expected to provide assurance that illegal acts will be detected. Illegal acts include illegal political contributions, bribes to obtain business and other violations of laws and regulations. Although determining whether an act is illegal is usually beyond the professional competence of the auditor (a CPA is not an attorney), the CPA, by virtue of his or her training and experience, should be able to discern that certain client acts are in fact illegal.

During the course of an audit, the CPA should consider laws and regulations that may have a direct effect on the contents of the financial statements. Inquiries should be made of client's management concerning compliance with laws and regulations and preventive measures used by the client to circumvent illegal acts. Other audit procedures that may detect illegal acts include the evaluation of internal control, related tests of transactions and balances and inquiries of client's legal counsel and others. Despite the fact that the auditor does not have a responsibility to search for illegal acts, all of these procedures are usually employed because of the pervasive effects these acts may have on the statements.

When the auditor's examination provides evidence that illegal acts may have occurred, the auditor should (1) consider the implications of the act and its effect on the statements, (2) consult with the client's legal counsel, (3) report the incident to a sufficiently high level of management and (4) consider performing additional auditing procedures, if practical or possible.

A disclaimer of opinion or a qualified opinion would usually be issued by the auditor if the CPA is unable to obtain sufficient competent evidence regarding a possible illegal act. However, if the auditor concludes that an illegal act has occurred which is material and that disclosure should be made in the statements, a qualified or adverse opinion should be expressed if disclosure is not made (because of a departure from GAAP which requires adequate disclosure). A qualified opinion or disclaimer should be expressed if the auditor is unable to reasonably estimate the effect the illegal act has on the statements.

Even if an illegal act is not considered material by the CPA, the auditor should request that management take appropriate remedial action. If management refuses to do so, the auditor should consider withdrawing from the present engagement and possibly severing any future relationship with the client. It is the duty of management, not the auditor, to notify outside parties of illegal acts committed by the client.

Inadequate Disclosure

Auditors may incur liability for failure to disclose the existence of material items in the financial statements. For example, the CPA may fail to reveal the existence of loans made to officers, inadequate insurance or excessive political contributions. The CPA may avoid liability by issuing a qualified or adverse opinion, as appropriate in the circumstances.

Reliance Upon the Work of Another Auditor

Ordinarily, the auditor assumes responsibility for another auditor's work when no mention is made in the audit report of the other auditor and the respective responsibility undertaken by each auditor. A CPA cannot rely on the unaudited work of another auditor but must qualify or disclaim an opinion when material amounts have not been audited.

Subsequent Events and Subsequent Discovery of Facts Existing at the Report Date

Generally, an auditor is not responsible for events that occurred subsequent to the last day of the field work, unless the report is dated as of the date of the occurrence of the subsequent event. An exception to this rule exists for reports filed with the SEC. The auditor, in such cases, assumes liability up to the effective date of a registration statement.

The CPA may also incur liability for subsequently discovered facts that existed at the report date which indicate that the statements are misleading unless (1) an immediate investigation is proper, and (2) the statements are promptly corrected, or (3) the SEC and persons known to be relying on the statements are promptly notified.

The 1967 ruling in the case of *Yale Express* (*Fischer vs. Kletz*)[34] led to the issuance of Statement on Auditing Procedures No. 41, *Subsequent Discovery of Facts Existing at the Date of the Auditor's Report*[35] (now Section 516 of *SAS No. 1*). While performing a management services engagement for Yale, the accountants discovered that the audited figures in a prior annual report were in error. After the discovery but before the special study results were officially released, Yale issued erroneous interim financial statements.

Suit was then filed by the plaintiff for damages under Section 10(b), Rule 10(b)(5) and Section 18 of the 1934 Act. The plaintiff also argued that the failure to disclose the inaccuracies when discovered violated common law doctrines. The accountants felt they were in a precarious situation because the laws of most states and the AICPA Code of Professional Ethics prohibit the disclosure of confidential information between the client and auditor. In effect, the court ruled that an auditor has a duty to anyone still relying on the report to disclose subsequently discovered errors in the report, even when knowledge of the errors was obtained while performing a separate (and confidential) service for the client.

Unaudited Financial Statements

Financial statements are regarded as unaudited when no auditing procedures have been performed or when auditing procedures have been applied but are considered insufficient to warrant the expression of an opinion. Liability may arise from the failure to mark each page of the financial statements as "unaudited" and from failure to issue a disclaimer of opinion. As accountants have learned from the *1136*

---

[34] *Fischer vs. Kletz*, 266 F. Supp. 180 (S.D.N.Y. 1967).

[35] The reader is referred to *SAS No. 1*, AU§§561.01-.10.

Tenants' Corp. case, a CPA may also be held liable for not informing the client of defalcations or other suspicious circumstances the CPA encounters which may indicate the presence of errors or irregularities.

In the case of *1136 Tenants' Corp. vs. Max Rothenberg & Co.*,[36] the plaintiff charged the defendant accounting firm with breach of contract and negligence for failure to discover and report a defalcation, claiming that the defendant had been engaged for auditing services. Conversely, the defendant contended that they had been engaged to perform "write-up" work and prepare unaudited statements. (This case occurred before and eventually led to the establishment of separate reporting requirements for public and nonpublic companies—unaudited statements for public companies and compilation and review statements for nonpublic companies. The defendant's services were orally contracted for by conversations between Rothenberg, a partner in the CPA firm, and Riker, plaintiff's managing agent.

Both parties produced evidence to support their understanding of the oral retainer. The defendant submitted copies of financial statements containing the words "No independant verifications were undertaken thereon." However, the defendant's case was weakened when a senior partner of the defendant firm admitted in court that certain audit procedures were applied beyond the scope of a normal "write-up". Further damaging the accountant's case were working papers containing "audit notes" and other references which may have indicated that an audit had been conducted.

The court also placed great significance on a work sheet entitled "Missing Invoices 1/1/63-12/31/63" which totaled $44,000. Additionally, the disclaimer format suggested for unaudited statements was not used.

Thus, it was left to the court to settle the dispute of the oral retainer. The court construed that the defendant was engaged to perform an audit, further remarking:

> "... *even if* defendant were hired to perform only 'write-up' services, it is clear, beyond dispute, that it did *become aware* that material invoices purportedly paid by Riker were *missing*, and, accordingly, *had a duty to at least inform plaintiff of this.*"[37] (Emphasis added.)

---

[36] *1136 Tenants' Corp. vs. Max Rothenberg & Co.*, 36 App. Div. 2d 804, 319 N.Y.S. 2d 1007 (1971); 30 N.Y. 2d 585, 330 N.Y.S. 2d 800 (1972).
[37] *Ibid.*

It is clear that a written agreement (engagement letter) defining the scope of work and responsibility of the accountant would have avoided the dispute concerning whether the services rendered constituted an audit or a "write-up".

SUMMARY

Chapter 17 discusses the auditor's legal responsibility to clients and third parties under common law and statutory law. Under common law, these parties may seek to recover damages under civil proceedings either for breach of contract or on a tort action (breach of duty other than contractual duty) for ordinary negligence, gross negligence or fraud. The majority of cases brought against the accountant under statutory law involve the 1933 and 1934 Securities Acts. In these cases, the accountant may be held liable under civil and criminal sections of statutes.

Public accountants have been involved in a multitude of lawsuits over the years, particularly in the past two decades. These court decisions have all played a role (some more significant than others) in defining the accountant's legal liability. In this chapter, some of the more significant cases having an impact on the accountant's legal responsibility as it has evolved today are discussed. Additionally, practical situations in which the auditor may incur liability were illustrated, as well as guidelines for avoiding litigation.

Although litigation cases have marked precedents which public accountants can follow, the courts have failed to provide definitive answers to many other questions and problems. The liability of the auditor in the future may be much more encompassing than it is today because of the changing nature of the law and its interpretation. However, the accountant may be able to avoid liability by being cognizant of the broad legal responsibilities of the profession and by performing his or her work with the due care expected of all members of the accounting and auditing profession.

REVIEW QUESTIONS

17-1 How does common law differ from statutory law?

17-2 Under common law, identify the three general groups that may bring civil action against the public accountant.

17-3 What are the federal statutes under which the majority of cases are brought against accountants under statutory law?

17-4   Who must initiate criminal action against the CPA in a legal suit?

17-5   Describe the standard of conduct imposed on the accountant by law.

17-6   What is meant by the term "privity of contract"?

17-7   List several ways in which an accountant can be held liable for breach of contract.

17-8   When must the auditor, under Rule 301 of the AICPA's Code of Professional Ethics, disclose confidential client information?

17-9   Under what causes of action may a client bring suit against the accountant for breach of duty (including contractual duty)?

17-10   How does the doctrine of gross negligence differ from the doctrine of fraud?

17-11   List the commonly sought defenses of the auditor for a malpractice suits under common law.

17-12   Can the auditor be held liable for inaccurate work or poor judgment? Explain.

17-13   Describe the doctrine of contributory negligence, and explain when this doctrine may be used.

17-14   Name and give examples of the two classes of third parties that the accountant may be liable to under common law for ordinary negligence.

17-15   Why was the case of *Glanzer vs. Shepard* considered significant to accountants, even though the case did not involve an accountant?

17-16   Discuss the importance of the *Ultramares*, *Rusch Factors*, and *Rhode Island Hospital Trust* cases.

17-17   Will the CPA always be liable under common law to foreseen third parties for ordinary negligence?

17-18   What is the purpose of the Securities Act of 1933?

17-19   When must a business entity file a registration statement under the 1933 Act?

17-20   Discuss the auditor's legal responsibility under the 1933 Act.

17-21   Who has the burden of proof under the 1933 Act, the purchaser of securities or the auditor? Explain.

17-22   What is the statute of limitations under the 1933 Act?

17-23   Indicate the powers granted the Securities and Exchange Commission.

17-24   Cite the objective of the Securities Exchange Act of 1934.

17-25   Discuss the filing requirements of the 1934 Act.

17-26   Does the 1934 Act apply to anyone who publicy trades securities? Explain.

17-27   Who may bring suit against the auditor under the 1933 and 1934 Acts?

17-28   Distinguish between the liability of the auditor under Section 18 and Section 10(b) of the 1934 Act.

17-29   Who has the burden of proof under the 1934 Act? Explain.

17-30   What critical issues were decided in the cases of (a) *Escott vs. BarChris Construction Corp.*, (b) *United States vs. Simon (Continental Vending)* and (c) *Ernst & Ernst vs. Hochfelder*?

17-31   What was the significance of the *Yale Express* case *(Fischer vs. Kletz)*?

17-32   What lessons did the accounting profession learn from the *1136 Tenants' Corp. vs. Max Rothenberg & Co.* case?

17-33   Distinguish between errors and irregularities.

17-34   Is the auditor responsible for the discovery of all errors and irregularities? Explain.

17-35   Briefly discuss the courses of action the auditor should pursue when there is evidence that material errors or irregularities may exist.

17-36   Describe "illegal acts" which would be of concern for the auditor.

17-37   Discuss the auditor's responsibility for illegal acts.

**DISCUSSION
QUESTIONS
AND PROBLEMS**

17-38   *Part a.*

A CPA firm was engaged to examine the financial statements of Martin Manufacturing Corporation for the year ending December 31, 1977. The facts revealed that Martin was in need of cash to continue its operations and agreed to sell its common stock investment in a subsidiary through a private placement. The buyers insisted that the proceeds be placed in escrow because of the possibility of a major contingent tax liability that might result from a pending government claim. The payment in escrow was completed in late November 1977. The president of Martin told the audit partner that the proceeds from the sale of the subsidiary's common stock, held in escrow, should be shown on the balance sheet as an unrestricted current account receivable. The president was of the opinion that the government's claim was groundless and that Martin needed an "uncluttered" blanace sheet and a "clean" auditor's opinion to obtain additional working capital from lenders. The audit partner agreed with the president and issued an unqualified opinion on the Martin financial statements which did not refer to the contingent liability and did not properly describe the escrow arrangement.

The government's claim proved to be valid, and pursuant to the agreement with the buyers, the purchase price of the subsidiary was reduced by $450,000. This adverse development forced Martin into bankruptcy. The CPA firm is being sued for deceit (fraud) by several of Martin's unpaid creditors who extended credit in reliance upon the CPA firm's unqualified opinion on Martin's financial statements.

Required:

Answer the following, setting forth reasons for any conclusions stated.

Based on these facts, can Martin's unpaid creditors recover from the CPA firm?

Part b.

A CPA firm has been named as a defendant in a class action by purchasers of the shares of stock of the Newly Corporation. The offering was a public offering of securities within the meaning of the Securities Act of 1933. The plaintiffs allege that the firm was either negligent or fraudulent in connection with the preparation of the audited financial statements which accompanied the registration statement filed with the SEC. Specifically, they allege that the CPA firm either intentionally disregarded, or failed to exercise reasonable care to discover, materials facts which occurred subsequent to January 31, 1978, the date of the auditor's report. The securities were sold to the public on March 16, 1978. The plaintiffs have subpoenaed copies of the CPA firm's working papers. The CPA firm is considering refusing to relinquish the papers, asserting that they contain privileged communication between the CPA firm and its client. The CPA firm will, of course, defend on the merits irrespective of the questions regarding the working papers.

Required:

Answer the following, setting forth reasons for any conclusions stated.

1.   Can the CPA firm rightfully refuse to surrender its working papers?
2.   Discuss the liability of the CPA firm with respect to events which occur in the period between the date of the auditor's report and the effective date of the public offering of the securities.

(CPA adapted)

17-39   Brown, CPA, received a telephone call from Calhoun, the sole owner and manager of a small corporation. Calhoun asked Brown to prepare the financial statements for the corporation and told Brown that the statements were needed in two weeks for external financing purposes. Calhoun was vague when Brown inquired about the intended use of the statement's. Brown was convinced that Calhoun thought Brown's work would constitute an audit. To avoid confusion Brown decided not to explain to Calhoun that the engagement would only be to prepare the financial statements. Brown, with the understanding that a substantial fee would be paid if the work were completed in two weeks, accepted the engagement and started the work at once.

During the course of the work, Brown discovered an accrued expense account labeled "professional fees" and learned that the balance in the account represented an accrual for the cost of Brown's services. Brown suggested to Calhoun's bookkeeper that the account name be changed to "fees for limited audit engagement." Brown also reviewed several invoices to determine whether accounts were being properly classified. Some of the invoices were missing. Brown listed the missing invoice numbers in the working papers with a note indicating that there should be a follow-up on the next engagement. Brown also discovered that the available records included the fixed asset values at estimated current replacement costs. Based on the records available, Brown prepared a balance sheet, income statement and statement of stockholder's equity. In addition, Brown drafted the footnotes but decided that any mention of the replacement costs would only mislead the readers. Brown suggested to Calhoun that readers of the financial statements would be better informed if they received a separate letter from Calhoun explaining the meaning and effect of the estimated replacement costs of the fixed assets. Brown mailed the financial statements and footnotes to Calhoun with the following note included on each page:

> "The accompanying financial statements are submitted to you without complete audit verification."

Required:

Identify the inappropriate actions of Brown and indicate what Brown should have done to avoid each inappropriate action.

Organize your answer sheet as follows:

Inappropriate Action	What Brown Should Have Done to Avoid Inappropriate Action

(CPA adapted)

17-40   *Part a.*

Whitlow & Company is a brokerage firm registered under the Securities Exchange Act of 1934. The Act requires such a brokerage firm to file audited financial statements with the SEC annually. Mitchell & Moss, Whitlow's CPAs, performed the annual audit for the year ended December 31, 1979, and rendered an unqualified opinion, which was filed with the SEC along with Whitlow's financial statements. During 1979 Charles, the president of Whitlow & Company, engaged in a huge embezzlement scheme that eventually bankrupted the firm. As a result, substantial losses were suffered by customers and shareholders of Whitlow & Company, including Thaxton who had recently purchased several shares of stock of Whitlow & Company after reviewing the company's 1979 audit report. The Mitchell & Moss audit was deficient; if they had complied with generally accepted auditing standards, the embezzlement would have been discovered. However, Mitchell & Moss had no knowledge of the embezzlement nor could their conduct be categorized as reckless.

Required:

Answer the following, setting forth reasons for any conclusions stated.

1. What liability to Thaxton, if any, does Mitchell & Moss have under the Securities Exchange Act of 1934?
2. What theory or theories of liability, if any, are available to Whitlow & Company's customers and shareholders under common law?

Part b.

Jackson is a sophisticated investor. As such, she was initially a member of a small group who were going to participate in a private placement of $1 million of common stock of Clarion Corporation. Numerous meetings were held among management and the investor group. Detailed financial and other information was supplied to the participants. Upon the eve of completion of the placement, it was aborted when one major investor withdrew. Clarion then decided to offer $2.5 million of Clarion common stock to the public pursuant to the registration requirements of the Securities Act of 1933. Jackson subscribed to $300,000 of the Clarion public stock offering. Nine months later, Clarion's earnings dropped significantly and as a result the stock dropped 20% beneath the offering price. In addition, the Dow Jones Industrial Average was down 10% from the time of the offering.

Jackson has sold her shares at a loss of $60,000 and seeks to hold all parties liable who participated in the public offering including Allen, Dunn, and Rose, Clarion's CPA firm. Although the audit was performed in conformity with generally accepted auditing standards, there were some relatively minor irregularities. The financial statements of Clarion Corporation, which were part of the registration statement, contained minor misleading facts. It is believed by Clarion and Allen, Dunn and Rose, that Jackson's asserted claim is without merit.

Required:

Answer the following, setting forth reasons for any conclusions stated.

1. Assuming Jackson sues under the Securities Act of 1933, what will be the basis of her claim?
2. What are the probable defenses which might be asserted by Allen, Dunn, and Rose in light of these facts?

(CPA adapted)

17-41 The limitations on the CPA's professional responsibilities when he or she is associated with unaudited financial statements are often misunderstood. These misunderstandings can be substantially reduced by carefully following professional pronouncements in the course of the auditor's work, and taking other appropriate measures.

Required:

The following list describes seven situations a CPA may encounter, or contentions he or she may have to deal with in his or her association with and preparation of unaudited financial statements. Briefly discuss the extent of the CPA's responsibilities and, if appropriate, the actions he or she should take to minimize any misunderstandings. Number your answers to correspond with the numbering in the following list.

1. The CPA was engaged by telephone to perform write-up work including the preparation of financial statements. The client believes that the CPA has been engaged to audit the financial statements and examine the records accordingly.

2. A group of businessmen who own a farm which is managed by an independent agent engage a CPA to prepare (compile) quarterly unaudited financial statements for them. The CPA compiles the financial statements from information given to him by the independent agent. Subsequently, the businessmen find the statements were inaccurate because their independent agent was embezzling funds. The businessmen refuse to pay the CPA's fee and blame him for allowing the situation to go undetected contending that he should not have relied on representations from the independent agent.

3. In comparing the trial balance with the general ledger the CPA finds an account labeled "audit fees" in which the client has accumulated the CPA's quarterly billings for accounting services including the compilation of quarterly unaudited financial statements.

4. Unaudited financial statements were accompanied by the following letter of transmittal from the CPA.

   > "We are enclosing your company's balance sheet as of June 30, 19x4, and the related statements of income and retained earnings and changes in financial position for the six months then ended which we have reviewed."

5. To determine appropriate account classification, the CPA reviewed a number of the client's invoices. She noted in her

working papers that some invoices were missing but did nothing further because she felt they did not affect the unaudited financial statements she was preparing. When the client subsequently discovered that invoices were missing, he contended that the CPA should not have ignored the missing invoices when preparing the financial statements and had a responsibility to at least inform him that they were missing.

6. The CPA has prepared a draft of unaudited financial statements from the client's records. While reviewing this draft with her client, the CPA learns that the land and building were recorded at appraisal value.

7. The CPA is engaged to review without audit the financial statements prepared by the client's controller. During this review, the CPA learns of several items which by generally accepted accounting principles would require adjustment of the statements and footnote disclosure. The controller agrees to make the recommended adjustments to the statements but says that he is not going to add the footnotes because the statements are unaudited.

(CPA adapted)

17-42   *Part a.*

Ralph Sharp, CPA, has audited the Fargo Corporation for the last ten years. It was recently discovered that Fargo's top management has been engaged in some questionable financial activities since the last audited financial statements were issued.

Subsequently, Fargo was sued in state court by its major competitor, Nuggett, Inc. In addition, the SEC commenced an investigation against Fargo for possible violations of the federal securities laws.

Both Nuggett and the SEC have subpoenaed all of Sharp's workpapers relating to his audits of Fargo for the last ten years. There is no evidence either that Sharp did anything improper or that any questionable financial activities by Fargo occurred prior to this year.

Sharp estimates that the cost for his duplicate photocopying of all of the workpapers would be $25,000 (approximately one year's audit fee). Fargo has instructed Sharp not to turn over the workpapers to anyone.

Required:

Answer the following, setting forth reasons for any conclusions stated.

1. If Sharp practices in a state which has a statutory accountant-client privilege, may the state's accountant-client privilege be successfully asserted to avoid turning over the workpapers to the SEC?

2. Assuming Sharp, with Fargo's permission, turns over to Nuggett workpapers for the last two audit years, may the state's accountant-client privilege be successfully asserted to avoid producing the workpapers for the first eight years?

3. Other than asserting an accountant-client privilege, what major defenses might Sharp raise against the SEC and Nuggett in order to resist turning over the subpoenaed workpapers?

Part b.

Pelham & James, CPAs, were retained by Tom Stone, sole proprietor of Stone Housebuilders, to compile Stone's financial statements. Stone advised Pelham & James that the financial statements would be used in connection with a possible incorporation of the business and sale of stock to friends. Prior to undertaking the engagement, Pelham & James were also advised to pay particular attention to the trade accounts payable. They agreed to use every reasonable means to determine the correct amount.

At the time Pelham & James were engaged, the books and records were in total disarray. Pelham & James proceeded with the engagement applying all applicable procedures for compiling financial statements. They failed, however, to detect and disclose in the financial statements Stone's liability for certain unpaid bills. Documentation concerning those bills was available for Pelham & James' inspection had they looked. This omission led to a material understatement ($60,000) of the trade accounts payable.

Pelham & James delivered the compiled financial statements to Tom Stone with their compilation report which indicated that they did not express an opinion or any other assurance regarding the financial statements. Tom Stone met with two prospective investors, Dickerson and Nichols. At the meeting, Pelham & James stated that they were confident that the trade accounts payable balance was accurate to within $8,000.

Stone Housebuilders was incorporated. Dickerson and Nichols, relying on the financial statements, became stockholders along with Tom Stone. Shortly thereafter, the understatement of trade accounts payable was detected. As a result, Dickerson and Nichols discovered that they had paid substantially more for the stock than it was worth at the time of purchase.

Required:

Answer the following, setting forth reasons for any conclusions stated.

Will Pelham & James be found liable to Dickerson and Nichols in a common law action for their damages?

(CPA adapted)

17-43 Retail Corporation, a ten-store men's haberdashery chain, has a written company policy which states that company buyers may not have an investment in nor borrow money from an existing or potential supplier. Chan, the independent auditor, learns from a Retail employee that Williams, a buyer, is indebted to Park, a supplier, for a substantial amount of money. Retail's volume of business with Park increased significantly during the year. Chan believes the debtor-creditor relationship of Williams and Park constitutes a conflict of interest that might lead Williams to perpetrate a material fraud.

Required:

a. Discuss what immediate actions Chan should take upon discovery of the above facts.
b. Discuss what additional actions Chan should take to be satisfied that Retail has no significant inventory or cost of sales problems as a result of the weakness in internal control posed by the apparent conflict of interest. Identify and discuss in your answer the specific problems, such as overstocking, which Chan should consider.

(CPA adapted)

17-44 Gordon & Groton, CPAs, were the auditors of Bank & Company, a brokerage firm and member of a national stock exchange. Gordon & Groton examined and reported on the financial statements of Bank which were filed with the Securities and Exchange Commission.

Several of Bank's customers were swindled by a fraudulent scheme perpetrated by Bank's president who owned 90% of the voting stock of the company. The facts establish that Gordon & Groton were negligent but not reckless or grossly negligent in the conduct of the audit and neither participated in the fraudulent scheme nor knew of its existence.

The customers are suing Gordon & Groton under the antifraud provisions of Section 10(b) and Rule 10(b)(5) of the Securities Exchange

Act of 1934 for aiding and abetting the fraudulent scheme of the president. The customers' suit for fraud is predicated exclusively on the nonfeasance of the auditors in failing to conduct a proper audit, thereby failing to discover the fraudulent scheme.

Required:

Answer the following, setting forth reasons for any conclusions stated.

1.   What is the probable outcome of the lawsuit?
2.   What other theory of liability might the customers have asserted?

(CPA adapted)

17-45   The CPA firm of Martinson, Brinks & Sutherland, a partnership, was the auditor for Masco Corporation, a medium sized wholesaler. Masco leased warehouse facilities and sought financing for leasehold improvements to these facilities. Masco assured its bank that the leasehold improvements would result in a more efficient and profitable operation. Based on these assurances, the bank granted Masco a line of credit.

The loan agreement required annual audited financial statements. Masco submitted its 1975 audited financial statements to the bank which showed an operating profit of $75,000, leasehold improvements of $250,000, and net worth of $350,000. In reliance thereon, the bank loaned Masco $200,000. The audit report which accompanied the financial statements disclaimed an opinion because the cost of the leasehold improvements could not be determined from the company's records. The part of the audit report dealing with leasehold improvements reads as follows:

> Additions to fixed assets in 1975 were found to include principally warehouse improvements. Practically all of this work was done by company employees and the cost of materials and overhead was paid by Masco. Unfortunately, fully complete detailed cost records were not kept of these leasehold improvements and no exact determination could be made as to the actual cost of said improvements. The total amount capitalized is set forth in note 4.

In late 1976 Masco went out of business, at which time it was learned that the claimed leasehold improvements were totally fictitious. The labor expenses charged as leasehold improvements proved to be operating expenses. No item of building material cost had been recorded. No independent investigation of the existence of the leasehold improvements was made by the auditors.

If the $250,000 had not been capitalized, the income statement would have reflected a substantial loss from operations and the net worth would have been correspondingly decreased.

The bank has sustained a loss on its loan to Masco of $200,000 and now seeks to recover damages from the CPA firm, alleging that the accountants negligently audited the financial statements.

Required:

Answer the following, setting forth reasons for any conclusions stated.

a. Will the disclaimer of opinion absolve the CPA firm from liability?
b. Are the individual partners of Martinson, Brinks & Sutherland, who did not take part in the audit liable?
c. Briefly discuss the development of the common law regarding the liability of CPAs to third parties.

(CPA adapted)

OBJECTIVE QUESTIONS

17-46   As a consequence of his failure to adhere to generally accepted auditing standards in the course of his examination of the Lamp Corp., Harrison, CPA, did not detect the embezzlement of a material amount of funds by the company's controller. As a matter of common law, to what extent would Harrison be liable to the Lamp Corp. for losses attributable to the theft?

A. He would have no liability, since the ordinary examination cannot be relied upon to detect defalcations.
B. He would have no liability because privity of contract is lacking.
C. He would be liable for losses attributable to his negligence.
D. He would be liable only if it could be proven that he was grossly negligent.

17-47   In a "comfort letter" to underwriters, the CPA should normally avoid using which of the following terms to describe the work performed?

A. Examined.
B. Read.

C.   Made inquiries.

D.   Made a limited review.

17-48   Jackson Enterprises dismissed its auditors for cause. The CPA firm failed to complete its audit within the time stipulated due to its own inefficiency. Under the circumstances

A.   The client has the right to all of the CPA's working papers relating to the engagement which are retained by the CPA.

B.   The CPA firm is entitled to recover the full fee agreed upon less a per diem diminution of 5% for each day delayed.

C.   Recovery by the CPA firm in quasi-contract will not be available if as a result of the delay the audit is worthless to Jackson.

D.   If Jackson sues the CPA firm for damages for breach of contract, recovery will be denied because it is commonly recognized that unless the contract so stipulates, time is not of the essence.

17-49   The traditional common-law rules regarding accountants' liability to third parties for negligence

A.   Remain substantially unchanged since their inception.

B.   Were more stringent than the rules currently applicable.

C.   Are of relatively minor importance to the accountant.

D.   Have been substantially changed at both the federal and state levels.

17-50   Henry Lamb worked for several years for a major CPA firm which has offices in 37 states. He resigned his position with the CPA firm, then returned to his home state where he opened his own CPA practice. Under the circumstances

A.   Lamb will be liable for damages to his former employer if he engages in the practice of accounting in any state in which the firm has offices.

B.   Lamb will be liable for damages to his former employer if he accepts as his client any party, solicited or unsolicited, who had been a client of his former employer immediately prior to his being retained by said client.

C.   He must obtain permission of the state board of accountancy in the state in which he was previously employed in order to relocate.

D.   He must be licensed to practice as a CPA in his home state.

17-51   Walters & Whitlow, CPAs, failed to discover a fraudulent scheme used by Davis Corporation's head cashier to embezzle corporate funds during the past five years. Walters & Whitlow would have discovered the embezzlements promptly if they had not been negligent in their annual audits. Under the circumstances, Walters & Whitlow will normally not be liable for

A.   Punitive damages.
B.   The fees charged for the years in question.
C.   Lossess occurring after the time the fraudulent scheme should have been detected.
D.   Losses occurring prior to the time the fraudulent scheme should have been detected and which could have been recovered had it been so detected.

17-52   A registration statement filed with the Securities and Exchange Commission may contain the reports of two or more independent auditors on their examinations of the financial statements for different periods. What responsibility does the auditor who has not examined the most recent financial statements have relative to subsequent events which may affect the financial statements on which the auditor reported?

A.   The auditor has responsibility for events up to the subsequent fiscal year-end.
B.   The auditor has responsibility for events up to the date of the subsequent audit report.
C.   The auditor has responsibility for events up to the effective date of the registration statement.
D.   The auditor has no responsibility beyond the date of his original report.

17-53   When conducting an audit, errors that arouse suspicion of fraud should be given greater attention than other errors. This is an example of applying the criterion of

A.   Reliability of evidence.
B.   Materiality.
C.   Relative risk.
D.   Dual-purpose testing.

17-54   Which of the following best describes a trend in litigations involving CPAs?

A. A CPA cannot render an opinion on a company unless the CPA has audited all affiliates of that company.

B. A CPA may not successfully assert as a defense that the CPA had no motive to be part of a fraud.

C. A CPA may be exposed to criminal as well as civil liability.

D. A CPA is primarily responsible for a client's footnotes in an annual report filed with the SEC.

17-55 The 1136 Tenants' Corp. case was chiefly important because of its emphasis upon the legal liability of the CPA when associated with

A. A review of interim statements.

B. Unaudited financial statements.

C. An audit resulting in a disclaimer of opinion.

D. Letters for underwriters.

17-56 Martin Corporation orally engaged Humm & Dawson to audit its year-end financial statements. The engagement was to be completed within two months after the close of Martin's fiscal year for a fixed fee of $2,500. Under these circmstances what obligation is assumed by Humm & Dawson?

A. None, because the contract is unenforceable since it is not in writing.

B. An implied promise to exercise reasonable standards of competence and care.

C. An implied obligation to take extraordinary steps to discover all defalcations.

D. The obligation of an insurer of its work which is liable without fault.

17-57 Which of the following can a CPA firm legally do?

A. Accept a competing company in the same industry as another of its clients.

B. Establish an association of CPAs for the purpose of determining minimum fee schedules.

C. Effectively disclaim liability to third parties for any and all torts.

D. Effectively establish an absolute dollar limitation on its liability for a given engagement.

17-58 Winslow Manufacturing, Inc., sought a $200,000 loan from National Lending Corporation. National Lending insisted that audited financial statements be submitted before it would extend credit. Winslow agreed to this and also agreed to pay the audit fee. An audit was performed by an independent CPA who submitted his report to Winslow to be used solely for the purpose of negotiating a loan from National. National, upon reviewing the audited financial statements, decided in good faith not to extend the credit desired. Certain ratios, which as a matter of policy were used by National in reaching its decision, were deemed too low. Winslow used copies of the audited financial statements to obtain credit elsewhere. It was subsequently learned that the CPA, despite the exercise of reasonable care, had failed to discover a sophisticated embezzlement scheme by Winslow's chief accountant. Under these circumstances, what liability does the CPA have?

A. The CPA is liable to third parties who extended credit to Winslow based upon the audited financial statements.
B. The CPA is liable to Winslow to repay the audit fee because credit was not extended by National.
C. The CPA is liable to Winslow for any losses Winslow suffered as a result of failure to discover the embezzlement.
D. The CPA is not liable to any of the parties.

17-59 An investor seeking to recover stock market losses from a CPA firm, based upon an unqualified opinion on financial statements which accompanied a registration statement must establish that

A. There was a false statement or omission of material fact contained in the audited financial statements.
B. He relied upon the financial statements.
C. The CPA firm did not act in good faith.
D. The CPA firm would have discovered the false statement or omission if it had exercised due care in its examination.

17-60 After preliminary audit arrangements have been made, an engagement confirmation letter should be sent to the client. The letter usually would not include

A. A reference to the auditor's responsibility for the detection of errors or irregularities.
B. An estimate of the time to be spent on the audit work by audit staff and management.
C. A statement that management advisory services would be made available upon request.
D. A statement that a management letter will be issued outlining comments and suggestions as to any procedures requiring the client's attention.

17-61 A CPA is subject to criminal liability if the CPA

   A. Refuses to turn over the working papers to the client.
   B. Performs an audit in a negligent manner.
   C. Willfully omits a material fact required to be stated in a registration statement.
   D. Willfully breaches the contract with the client.

17-62 A CPA was engaged by Jackson & Wilcox, a small retail partnership, to examine its financial statements. The CPA discovered that due to other commitments, the engagement could not be completed on time. The CPA, therefore, unilaterally delegated the duty to Vincent, an equally competent CPA. Under these circumstances, which of the following is true?

   A. The duty to perform the audit engagement is delegable in that it is determined by an objective standard.
   B. If Jackson & Wilcox refuses to accept Vincent because of a personal dislike of Vincent by one of the partners, Jackson & Wilcox will be liable for breach of contract.
   C. Jackson & Wilcox must accept the delegation in that Vincent is equally competent.
   D. The duty to perform the audit engagement is nondelegable and Jackson & Wilcox need not accept Vincent as a substitute if they do not wish to do so.

17-63 Gaspard & Devlin, a medium sized CPA firm, employed Marshall as a staff accountant. Marshall was negligent in auditing several of the firm's clients. Under these circumstances which of the following statements is true?

   A. Gaspard & Devlin is not liable for Marshall's negligence because CPAs are generally considered to be independent contractors.
   B. Gaspard & Devlin would not be liable for Marshall's negligence if Marshall disobeyed specific instructions in the performance of the audits.
   C. Gaspard & Devlin can recover against its insurer on its malpractice policy even if one of the partners was also negligent in reviewing Marshall's work.
   D. Marshall would have no personal liability for negligence.

17-64 Sharp, CPA, was engaged by Peters & Sons, a partnership, to give an opinion on the financial statements which were to be submitted to several prospective partners as part of a planned expansion of the firm. Sharp's fee was fixed on a per diem basis. After a period of intensive work, Sharp completed about half of the necessary field work. Then due to unanticipated demands upon his time by other clients, Sharp was forced to abandon the work. The planned expansion of the firm failed to materialize because the prospective partners lost interest when the audit report was not promptly available. Sharp offers to complete the task at a later date. This offer was refused. Peters & Sons suffered damages of $4,000 as a result. Under the circumstances, what is the probable outcome of a lawsuit between Sharp and Peters & Sons?

A. Sharp will be compensated for the reasonable value of his services actually performed.
B. Peters & Sons will recover damages for breach of contract.
C. Peters & Sons will recover both punitive damages and damages for breach of contract.
D. Neither Sharp nor Peters & Sons will recover against the other.

17-65 Engagement letters are widely used in practice for professional engagements of all types. The primary purpose of the engagement letter is to

A. Remind management that the primary responsibility for the financial statements rests with management.
B. Satisfy the requirements of the CPA's liability insurance policy.
C. Provide a starting point for the auditor's preparation of the preliminary audit program.
D. Provide a written record of the agreement with the client as to the services to be provided.

17-66 When an independent auditor's examination of financial statements discloses special circumstances that make the auditor suspect that fraud may exist, the auditor's initial course of action should be to

A. Recommend that the client pursue the suspected fraud to a conclusion that is agreeable to the auditor.
B. Extend normal audit procedures in an attempt to detect full extent of the suspected fraud.
C. Reach an understanding with the proper client representative as to whether the auditor or the client is to make the investigation necessary to determine if a fraud has in fact occurred.
D. Decide whether the fraud, if in fact it should exist, might be of such a magnitude as to affect the auditor's report on the financial statements.

17-67   Preliminary arrangements agreed to by the auditor and the client should be reduced to writing by the auditor. The best place to set forth these arrangements is in

A.   A memorandum to be placed in the permanent section of the auditing working papers.
B.   An engagement letter.
C.   A client representation letter.
D.   A confirmation letter attached to the constructive services letter.

17-68   Magnus Enterprises engaged a CPA firm to perform the annual examination of its financial statements. Which of the following is a correct statement with respect to the CPA firm's liability to Magnus for negligence?

A.   Such liability cannot be varied by agreement of the parties.
B.   The CPA firm will be liable for any fraudulent scheme it does not detect.
C.   The CPA firm will not be liable if it can show that it exercised the ordinary care and skill of a reasonable man in the conduct of his own affairs.
D.   The CPA firm must not only exercise reasonable care in what it does, but also must possess at least that degree of accounting knowledge and skill expected of a CPA.

17-69   The Apex Surety Company wrote a general fidelity bond covering defalcations by the employees of Watson, Inc. Thereafter, Grand, an employee of Watson, embezzled $18,900 of company funds. When his activities were discovered, Apex paid Watson the full amount in accordance with the terms of the fidelity bond, and then sought recovery against Watson's auditors, Kane & Dobbs, CPAs. Which of the following would be Kane & Dobbs' best defense?

A.   Apex is not in privity of contract.
B.   The shortages were the result of clever forgeries and collusive fraud which would not be detected by an examination made in accordance with generally accepted auditing standards.
C.   Kane & Dobbs were not guilty either of gross negligence or fraud.
D.   Kane & Dobbs were not aware of the Apex-Watson surety relationship.

17-70   The CPA firm of Knox and Knox has been subpoenaed to testify and produce its correspondence and working papers in connection with a lawsuit brought against Johnson, one of its clients. Regarding the attempted resort to the privileged communication rule in seeking to avoid admission of such evidence in the lawsuit, which of the following is correct?

A. Federal law recognizes such a privilege if the accountant is a Certified Public Accountant.

B. The privilege is available regarding the working papers since the accountant is deemed to own them.

C. The privilege is as widely available as the attorney-client privilege.

D. In the absence of a specific statutory provision, the law does not recognize the existence of the privileged communication rule between an accountant and his client.

17-71 A CPA firm is being sued by a third party purchaser of securities sold in interstate commerce to the public. The third party is relying upon the Securities Act of 1933. The CPA firm had issued an unqualified opinion on incorrect financial statements. Which of the following represents the best defense available to the CPA firm?

A. The securities sold had not been registered with the SEC.

B. The CPA firm had returned the entire fee it charged with the engagement to the corporation.

C. The third party was not in privity of contract with the CPA firm.

D. The action had not been commenced within one year after the discovery of the material misrepresentation.

17-72 On July 25, 1978, Archer, the president of Post Corporation, with the approval of the board of directors, engaged Biggs, a CPA, to examine Post's July 31, 1978, financial statements and to issue a report in time for the annual stockholders' meeting to be held on September 5, 1978. Notwithstanding Bigg' reasonable efforts, the report was not ready until September 7 because of delays by Post's staff. Archer, acting on behalf of Post, refused to accept or to pay for the report since it no longer served its intended purpose. In the event Biggs brings legal action against Post, what is the probable outcome?

A. The case would be dismissed because it is unethical for a CPA to sue for his fee.

B. Biggs will be entitled to recover only in quasi-contract for the value of the services to the client.

C. Biggs will not recover since the completion by September 5th was a condition precedent to his recovery.

D. Biggs will recover because the delay by Post's staff prevented Biggs from performing on time and thereby eliminated the timely performance condition.

17-73 Tweed Manufacturing, Inc., plans to issue $5 million of common stock to the public in interstate commerce after its registration statement with the SEC becomes effective. What, if anything, must Tweed do in respect to those states in which the securities are to be sold?

A. Nothing, since approval by the SEC automatically constitutes satisfaction of any state requirements.
B. Make a filing in those states which have laws governing such offerings and obtain their approvals.
C. Simultaneously apply to the SEC for permission to market the securities in the various states without further clearance.
D. File in the appropriate state office of the state in which it maintains its principal office of business, obtain clearance, and forward a certified copy of that state's clearance to all other states.

17-74 Under the Securities Act of 1933, an accountant may be held liable for any materially false or misleading financial statements, including an omission of a material fact therefrom, provided the purchaser

A. Proves reliance on the registration statement or prospectus.
B. Proves negligence or fraud on the part of the accountant.
C. Brings suit within four years after the security is offered to the public.
D. Proves a false statement or omission existed and the specific securities were the ones offered through the registration statement.

17-75 If a CPA firm is being sued for common law fraud by a third party based upon materially false financial statements, which of the following is the best defense which the accountants could assert?

A. Lack of privity.
B. Lack of reliance.
C. A disclaimer contained in the engagement letter.
D. Contributory negligence on the part of the client.

17-76 Donalds & Company, CPAs, audited the financial statements included in the annual report submitted by Markum Securities, Inc., to the Securities and Exchange Commission. The audit was improper in several respects. Markum is now insolvent and unable to satisfy the claims of its customers. The customers have instituted legal action against Donalds based upon Section 10(b) and Rule 10(b)(5) of the Securities Exchange Act of 1934. Which of the following is likely to be Donalds' best defense?

A. They did not intentionally certify false financial statements.
B. Section 10(b) does not apply to them.
C. They were not in privity of contract with the creditors.
D. Their engagement letter specifically disclaimed any liability to any party which resulted from Markum's fraudulent conduct.

17-77 The understanding between the client and the auditor as to the degree of responsibilities to be assumed by each are normally set forth in a(an)

A. Representation letter.
B. Engagement letter.
C. Management letter.
D. Comfort letter.

17-78 DMO Enterprises, Inc., engaged the accounting firm of Martin, Seals and Anderson to perform its annual audit. The firm performed the audit in a competent, non-negligent manner and billed DMO for $16,000, the agreed fee. Shortly after delivery of the audited financial statements, Hightower, the assistant controller, disappeared, taking with him $28,000 of DMO's funds. It was then discovered that Hightower had been engaged in a highly sophisticated, novel defalcation scheme during the past year. He had previously embezzled $35,000 of DMO's funds. DMO has refused to pay the accounting firm's fee and is seeking to recover the $63,000 that was stolen by Hightower. Which of the following is correct?

A. The accountants cannot recover their fee and are liable for $63,000.
B. The accountants are entitled to collect their fee and are not liable for $63,000.
C. DMO is entitled to rescind the audit contract and thus is not liable for the $16,000 fee, but it cannot recover damages.
D. DMO is entitled to recover the $28,000 defalcation, and is not liable for the $16,000 fee.

17-79 The CPA firm of Knox and Knox has been subpoenaed to testify and produce its correspondence and workpapers in connection with a lawsuit brought by a third party against one of their clients. Knox considers the subpoenaed documents to be privileged communication and therefore seeks to avoid admission of such evidence in the lawsuit. Which of the following is correct?

A. Federal law recognizes such a privilege if the accountant is a Certified Public Accountant.
B. The privilege is available regarding the workpapers since the CPA is deemed to own them.
C. The privileged communication rule as it applies to a CPA-client relationship is the same as that of attorney-client.
D. In the absence of a specific statutory provision, the law does not recognize the existence of the privileged communication rule between a CPA and his client.

17-80   Major, Major & Sharpe, CPAs, are the auditors of MacLain Industries. In connection with the public offering of $10 million of MacLain securities, Major expressed an unqualified opinion as to the financial statements. Subsequent to the offering, certain misstatements and omissions were revealed. Major has been sued by the purchasers of the stock offered pursuant to the registration statement which included the financial statement audited by Major. In the ensuing lawsuit by the MacLain investors, Major will be able to avoid liability if

A. The errors and omissions were caused primarily by MacLain.
B. It can be shown that at least some of the investors did not actually read the audited financial statements.
C. It can prove due diligence in the audit of the financial statements of MacLain.
D. MacLain had expressly assumed any liability in connection with the public offering.

17-81   A CPA should not normally refer to which one of the following subjects in a "comfort letter" to underwriters?

A. The independence of the CPA.
B. Changes in financial-statement items during a period subsequent to the date and period of the latest financial statements in the registration statement.
C. Unaudited financial statements and schedules in the registration statement.
D. Management's determination of line of business classifications.

17-82   In connection with the examination of financial statements, an independent auditor could be responsible for failure to detect a material fraud if

A.   Statistical sampling techniques were not used on the audit engagement.
B.   The auditor planned the work in a hasty and inefficient manner.
C.   Accountants performing important parts of the work failed to discover a close relationship between the treasurer and the cashier.
D.   The fraud was perpetrated by one client employee, who circumvented the existing internal controls.

17-83   An auditor is unable to determine the amounts associated with certain illegal acts committed by a client. In these circumstances the auditor would most likely

A.   Issue either a qualified opinion or disclaimer of opinion.
B.   Issue only an adverse opinion.
C.   Issue either a qualified opinion or an adverse opinion.
D.   Issue only a disclaimer of opinion.

17-84   The most significant aspect of the Continental Vending case was that it

A.   Created a more general awareness of the auditor's exposure to criminal prosecution.
B.   Extended the auditor's responsibility for financial statements of subsidiaries.
C.   Extended the auditor's responsibility for events after the end of the audit period.
D.   Defined the auditor's common law responsibilities to third parties.

☐ SERVICES

After studying this chapter, students should understand

1. The definitions and objectives related to compilation and reviews.
2. The meaning of association with financial statements.
3. The general standards of performance.
4. The performance standards common to both compilation and reviews.
5. The performance standards which are unique to reviews.
6. The compilation reporting standards.
7. The review reporting standards.
8. The procedures for reporting on comparative financial statements.
9. The nature and form of communications between predecessor and successor accountants.
10. The CPA's responsibility when financial statements or the accountants report are required in prescribed form.
11. The nature of a review of interim financial information for a public or nonpublic company.

Chapter 18

Accountants' Compilation and Review Services

This chapter was written by
Louis G. Gutberlet, C.P.A.,
(formerly a member of the Accounting and Review Services Committee),
Kenneth Leventhal & Company, Certified Public Accountants

INTRODUCTION

This chapter discusses performance and reporting standards for nonauditing services associated with the financial statements of nonpublic companies. After presenting these standards, the chapter discusses the review of interim financial information for both public and nonpublic companies.

On December 4, 1978, the American Institute of Certified Public Accountants' (AICPA) Accounting and Review Services Committee (ARSC) approved the issuance of its first Statement on Standards for Accounting and Review Services (*SSARS No. 1*), entitled *Compilation and Review of Financial Statements* (AR 100). The ARSC is the senior technical committee of the AICPA designated to develop, on a continuing basis, standards and procedures for performing and reporting on the types of services an accountant may render in connection with the less-than-audited (unaudited) financial statements or other unaudited financial information of a *nonpublic entity*.

SSARS No. 1 defines two services an accountant may render in connection with the less-than-audited financial statements of nonpublic entities: the *compilation of financial statements* and the *review of financial statements* and, in addition, provides guidance concerning the standards and procedures applicable to such engagements. *SSARS No. 1* also provides guidance considered necessary to enable an accountant to comply with the general standards of the profession as set forth in Rule 201 of the rules of conduct of the AICPA's *Code of Professional Ethics* in the context of a compilation or review engagement.

SSARS No. 1 is written from the viewpoint of "the objectives of the engagement"; it describes in detail the differences between the objectives of a review and an audit. Therefore, the most important point to be remembered in determining the particular procedures to be employed and the type of report (compilation or review) an accountant should issue are the *terms and objectives of an engagement established at the time an understanding is reached with a client concerning the services to be rendered*. This understanding should obviously precede commencement of any field work. In other words, the *objectives of the service dictate the procedures and type of report, rather than having the procedures determine the report to be issued by an accountant*.

DEFINITIONS AND OBJECTIVES OF COMPILATIONS AND REVIEWS

The compilation of financial statements is defined as "a service resulting in the presentation of information in the form of financial statements that is the representation of the owners (management) of a nonpublic entity without undertaking to express any assurance on the statements for the benefit of the users (whoever they may be)."

The review of financial statements is defined as "a service which consists principally of inquiries of client personnel and analytical procedures applied to financial data, without corroboration, which should provide an accountant with a reasonable basis for expressing limited assurance that there are no material modifications that should be made to the financial statements in order for them to be in conformity with generally accepted accounting principles (GAAP) or, if applicable, with another comprehensive basis of accounting (OCBOA)."[1] Expressions of limited assurance indicate that nothing came to the attention of the accountant that would make one believe that the financial statements are not prepared in accordance with GAAP or OCBOA. The concept of limited assurance should further convey that the accountant did not actively carry out procedures for the purpose of expressing an opinion on whether the financial statements are fairly presented in accordance with GAAP.

The objective of a review of financial statements differs significantly from the objective of a compilation of financial statements. The inquiry and analytical procedures performed in a review should provide the accountant with a reasonable basis for achieving and expressing limited assurance that there are no material modifications that should be made to the financial statements in order for them to be in conformity with GAAP. *No expression of assurance is contemplated in a compilation.* This is not intended to imply that an accountant does not attain some level of assurance of confidence in a compilation engagement. It means that the objective of the engagement does not include the expression of any assurance to the users of the financial statements: hence, the phrase "without undertaking to express any assurance on the statements."

The objective of a review also differs significantly from that of an examination of financial statements in accordance with generally accepted auditing standards (GAAS). The objective of an audit is to provide a reasonable basis for expressing an opinion regarding the financial statements taken as a whole. A review, as defined above, does not provide a basis for the expression of such an opinion because a review does not contemplate the study, evaluation, or compliance testing of internal

---

[1] The term "other comprehensive basis of accounting" is defined in *SAS No. 14*, AU 621.04. Hereafter, reference to generally accepted accounting principles in this chapter includes, where applicable, another comprehensive basis of accounting, such as cash basis, income tax basis, or other appropriate basis of accounting.

accounting control, substantive auditing of account balances, and the subsequent evaluation of responses to inquiries of client personnel by obtaining corroborative evidential matter through inspection, observation, confirmation, or certain other procedures ordinarily performed during the course of an audit. Although a review may bring to an accountant's attention significant matters affecting the financial statements, it does not provide reasonable assurance that an accountant will become aware of all significant matters that might be disclosed in an audit.

SSARS No. 1 recognizes that accountants may perform other accounting services either in connection with the compilation or review of financial statements or as a separate service. Such services are distinguished from a compilation and from a review. The statement, however, does not establish standards or procedures for such other accounting services, examples of which include:

- Preparing a working trial balance.

- Assisting in adjusting the books of account.

- Consulting on accounting, tax, or similar matters.

- Preparing tax returns.

- Providing various manual or automated bookkeeping or data processing services, unless the output is in the form of financial statements.

- Processing financial data for clients of other accounting firms.

SSARS No. 1 implicitly recognizes that in many, if not most, cases the owners or management of a nonpublic entity will not be in a position to supply the necessary information for either the compilation or review of financial statements and that it might be necessary for the accountant to develop such data, including data or policies and practices for footnote disclosure.

Compilation and review engagements are rarely performed in the "pure" sense, which is how they are defined. That is, other accounting services are usually rendered by the accountant at approximately the same time that financial statements are compiled or reviewed. Accordingly, *SSARS No. 1* requires the exercise of professional judgment in determining the particular procedures necessary in order to comply with the common and unique standards of performance and the general standards of the profession.

ASSOCIATION WITH FINANCIAL STATEMENTS

Statement on Auditing Standards (*SAS No. 26*) defines "association with financial statements" as that term is used in the fourth reporting standard. The purpose of that section is to provide guidance to an accountant associated with the audited or less-than-audited financial statements of a *public entity* or with a *nonpublic entity's* financial statements that the accountant has been engaged to examine in accordance with GAAS.[2] The objective of the fourth reporting standard is to prevent misinterpretation of the degree of responsibility the accountant assumes when his or her name is associated with financial statements. Accordingly, the association concept may be described as follows:

> An accountant is associated with financial statements when he or she has consented to the use of his or her name in a report, document, or written communication containing the financial statements. Also, when an accountant submits to the client or others financial statements that he or she has prepared or assisted in preparing, the accountant is deemed to be associated even though the accountant does not append his or her name to the financial statements. Although the accountant may participate in the preparation of financial statements, the information contained therein is the representation of management, and the fairness of its presentation in conformity with GAAP or, if applicable, with OCBOA, is management's responsibility.

An accountant may be associated with audited or less-than-audited financial statements. When an accountant is associated with the financial statements of a public entity, but has not audited or reviewed (as previously defined) such statements, the form of report to be issued, as indicated in Chapter 15, is as follows:

> The accompanying balance sheet of ABC Company as of December 31, 19xx, and the related statements of operations and retained earnings and changes in financial position for the year then ended were not audited by us and, accordingly, we do not express an opinion on them.

This disclaimer of opinion is the means by which an accountant complies with the fourth standard of reporting when associated with less-

---

[2] A public entity may be defined as any entity (a) whose securities trade in a public market either on a stock exchange (domestic or foreign) or in the over-the-counter market, including securities quoted only locally or regionally, (b) that makes a filing with a regulatory agency in preparation for the sale of any class of its securities in a public market, or (c) a subsidiary, corporate joint venture, or other entity controlled by an entity covered by (a) or (b) above. A nonpublic entity would be the reciprocal of this definition.

than-audited financial statements of a public entity.[3] The disclaimer may accompany the less-than-audited financial statements or it may be placed directly on them. In addition, each page of the financial statements should be clearly and conspicuously marked as "unaudited." When an accountant issues this form of disclaimer of opinion, he or she has *no* responsibility to apply any procedures beyond reading the financial statements for obvious material errors. Any procedures that may have been performed should not be described, except in the limted circumstances set forth in Chapter 16, regarding special reports.

The ARSC decided to avoid the "association test" and the implications of that concept. It concluded that in the case of nonpublic entities, the great majority of users are well aware of the relationship between an issuer of financial statements and its accountant. As a result of this knowledge, users automatically associate, in the dictionary sense of the word, an accountant with a client's financial statements. Accordingly, it seemed more logical to explicitly address the accountant's relationship to financial statements by:

- Describing the nature of the services rendered, and

- Relating the services to the degree of responsibility assumed with respect to the statements, if any.

Therefore, *SSARS No. 1* sets forth the basic reporting framework for an accountant's involvement with less-than-audited financial statements of nonpublic entities by applying a "submission test."[4] The "submis-

---

[3] However, when a public entity does not have its annual financial statements audited, an accountant may be requested to review its annual or interim financial statements. In those circumstances, an accountant my conduct a review and look to the guidance in *SSARS No. 1* for the standards and procedures and form of report applicable to such an engagement. In addition, if an accountant becomes aware that his or her name is to be included in a client-prepared written communication of a public entity containing financial statements that have not been audited or reviewed, the accountant should request (a) that his or her name not be included in the communication or (b) that the financial statements be marked as "unaudited" and that there be a notation that the accountant does not express an opinion on them.

[4] For purposes of *SSARS No. 1*, financial statements of nonpublic entities are defined as the presentation of financial data, including accompanying footnotes, derived from accounting records and intended to communicate an entity's economic resources or obligations at a point in time or the changes therein for a period of time in accordance with GAAP or OCBOA. Financial forecasts, projections and similar presentations, and financial presentations included in tax returns are not financial statements for purposes of *SSARS No. 1*. A financial statement, therefore, may be that of a corporation, a combined group of affiliated entities, a nonprofit organization, a governmental unit, an estate or trust, a partnership, a proprietorship, a segment of any of the above, or an individual. The method of preparation (e.g., manual or computer preparation) is immaterial and irrelevant to the definition of financial statements.

sion test" requires compliance with either the compilation or review standards in performing the respective services and in reporting on them. The compilation standards are the minimum standards with which an accountant must comply when "submitting" financial statements. An accountant's reporting responsibility when "associated" with the financial statements of a nonpublic entity is summarized in Exhibit 18-1.

An accountant should not consent to the use of his or her name in a client-prepared document or written communication containing less-than-audited financial statements of a nonpublic entity unless (a) the accountant has compiled or reviewed the financial statements and his or

---

Exhibit 18-1
Nonpublic Association Standards

Submission Test

Anytime an accountant "submits" less-than-audited financial statements of a nonpublic entity to his or her client or others, the accountant must comply with the standards for a compilation or a review.

Plain Paper Prohibition

Anytime an accountant "completes" a compilation or a reveiw of a non-public entity, an appropriate report under the provisions of *SSARS No. 1* must accompany the financial statements submitted to the client or others. This precludes the accountant from merely typing or reproducing financial statements as an accommodation to the client.

Minimum Level of Service

When an accountant is involved with the financial statements of a non-public entity, the 'minimum" level of service he or she may render and report on is a compilation.

Pecking Order

When an independent accountant renders a compilation service in connection with financial statements which he or she also reviews, the accountant must issue a review report under the appropriate provisions of *SSARS No. 1.*

When an independent accountant renders a compilation service in connection with financial statements which he or she also audits, the accountant must issue an audit report under the appropriate provisions of GAAS.

her report accompanies them, or (b) the financial statements are accompanied by an indication, prepared by the client, that the accountant has not compiled or reviewed the financial statements and that the accountant assumes no responsibility for them. If an accountant becomes aware that his or her name has been used improperly in any client-prepared document containing less-than-audited financial statements, the accountant should advise the client that the use of his or her name is inappropriate and should consider what other actions might be appropriate, including consultation with an attorney.

GENERAL STANDARDS OF PERFORMANCE

SSARS No. 1 asserts that the statement has two specific purposes for the professional practice of public accountancy:

- Guidance in complying with the general standards of the profession (Rule 201 of the Institute's rules of conduct) as they apply to the compilation or review of financial statements.

- Establishment of the additional standards considered necessary for the proper performance of and reporting on compilation and review engagements.

Rule 201 of the AICPA's rules of conduct, entitled "General Standards," as it is presently written, was passed by the AICPA's membership and became effective on March 31, 1978. Its provisions are *applicable to all services rendered by the AICPA members for the benefit of clients, including services not covered by SSARS No. 1* (e.g., other accounting services). Rule 201 states that a member of the AICPA shall comply with the general standards of the profession and must justify any departure therefrom. The general standards, which were discussed in Chapter 3, are:

- **Professional competence.** A member shall undertake only those engagements which he (or she) or his (or her) firm can reasonably expect to complete with professional competence.

- **Due professional care.** A member shall exercise due professional care in the performance of an engagement.

- **Planning and supervision.** A member shall adequately plan and supervise an engagement.

- **Sufficient relevant data.** A member shall obtain sufficient relevant data to afford a reasonable basis for conclusions or recommendations in relation to an engagement.

- **Forecasts.** A member shall not permit his (or her) name to be used in conjunction with any forecast of future transactions in a manner which may lead to the belief that the member vouches for the achievability of the forecast.

The general standards of the profession are applicable to the performance of engagements in all major areas of professional practice. However, the general standard entitled "Forecasts" is not applicable to compilation or review engagements because the scope of *SSARS No. 1* does not include financial forecasts, projections, or similar presentations. Therefore, each provision of *SSARS No. 1* is designed to tie into one or more of the first four general standards, particularly due professional care. For example, when an accountant accepts a compilation or review engagement, the due care standard requires the accountant to consider whether it will be necessary to perform "other accounting services," such as assistance in adjusting the books of account or consultation on accounting matters. Also, the accountant may not close his or her eyes to information supplied by a client that is incorrect, incomplete, or otherwise unsatisfactory. In such circumstances, the accountant should obtain additional or revised information or perform whatever additional procedures he or she considers necessary under the circumstances to be satisfied as to the reasonableness of the data. If a client refuses to provide additional or revised information or if the accountant is not satisfied with respect to incorrect, incomplete, or otherwise "misleading" information, the accountant must withdraw from the engagement and refuse to be associated with the client's statements.

This standard should not be confused with the accountant's responsibilities when he or she becomes aware of simple departures from GAAP, which include adequate disclosure, that are material to the financial statements. In these circumstances (as opposed to incorrect, incomplete, or otherwise "misleading" information), if the accountant concludes that modification of his or her standard compilation or review report is adequate to indicate the deficiencies in the financial statements taken as a whole, the departure(s) should be disclosed in a separate paragraph(s) of the compilation or review report, including disclosure of the effects of the departure on the financial statements if such effects have been determined by the owners (management) or are known to the accountant as the result of other accounting services. The accountant, however, is not required to determine the effects of a departure if the owners (management) have not done so, provided the accountant states in his or her report that such determination has not been made.[5]

PERFORMANCE STANDARDS COMMON TO BOTH COMPILATIONS AND REVIEWS

The following performance standards are common to both compilations and reviews:

- Understanding with the client.

- Knowledge of the industry.

- Knowledge of the business.

- Reading the financial statements to consider whether they appear to be appropriate in form and free from obvious material error.

In addition, as previously discussed, the accountant must give consideration to the necessity of performing "other accounting services."

Understanding With the Client

An accountant should establish an understanding with the client, preferably in writing ("engagement letter" or "letter of understanding") concerning the services to be performed in connection with less-than-audited financial statements. This understanding should also provide that the engagement cannot be relied upon and is not designed to disclose errors,[6] irregularities, or illegal acts; but that the accountant will inform the client of any such matters that come to his or her attention.

---

[5] Some accountants believe that withdrawal from an engagement is mandated when the departures from GAAP are such that an adverse opinion might be required in an audit environment when, in fact, this is not necessarily the case. However, *SSARS No. 1* should have explicitly provided for reports which state that "the accompanying financial statements are not fairly presented in accordance with GAAP." The opinion expressed in this footnote is based on the belief that communication of such an "adverse conclusion" constitutes "modification of the accountant's standard report that is adequate to indicate the deficiencies in the financial statements taken as a whole."

[6] The term "errors" as used in this context refers to unintentional mistakes in financial statements and includes "mathematical or clerical mistakes in the underlying records and accounting data from which the financial statements were prepared" as that term is defined in *SAS No. 16* and discussed in Chapter 17, as opposed to "mistakes in the compilation of financial statements, including arithmetical or clerical mistakes, and mistakes in the application of accounting principles, including inadequate disclosure" as defined in *SSARS No. 1*, AR 100.13.

Knowledge of the Industry

An accountant should possess a degree of knowledge about the accounting principles and reporting practices of the industry in which a client operates that will enable him or her to compile financial statements that are appropriate in form and content for an entity operating in that industry. This standard does not prevent an accountant from accepting a compilation or review engagement for an entity in an industry with which the accountant has no previous experience. It does, however, place upon an accountant the responsibility to obtain the required level of knowledge. This may be accomplished by consulting AICPA industry and accounting guides, specialized industry publications, financial statements of other entities in that industry, textbooks and periodicals, or individuals knowledgeable about that industry. SSARS No. 1 does not indicate a deadline for obtaining the necessary knowledge of the industry. However, since the knowledge is necessary for the timely and proper judgments to be made during the "planning and supervision" phases of an engagement, it is reasonable to expect that this knowledge would be obtained early if the accountant does not already possess it at the start of an engagement.

Knowledge of the Business

In order to compile financial statements, the accountant should possess a general understanding of the nature of a client's business transactions, the form of its accounting records, the stated qualifications of its accounting personnel, the accounting basis on which the financial statements are to be presented, and the form and content of the financial statements. The accountant ordinarily acquires this level of knowledge through experience with the entity or inquiry of a client's personnel. It is important to note that an accountant is not required to make inquiries or perform other procedures designed to corroborate or otherwise check the accuracy of information supplied by a client unless he or she has reason to believe that the information is incorrect, incomplete, or otherwise unsatisfactory.

In order to review financial statements and express limited assurance, the accountant should obtain a level of knowledge of the accounting principles and reporting practices appropriate to the industry and an understanding of the entity's business, as opposed to an understanding of a client's business transactions as required for a compilation service. Therefore, to perform a review service, the understanding of a client's business must be such that the accountant is able to design and perform inquiry, analytical, and other procedures (including disclosure development procedures) considered necessary under the circumstances that will provide a reasonable basis for expressing limited assurance that there are no material modifications that should be made to the financial statements in order for them to be in conformity with GAAP. This understanding must encompass a client's organization, its operating characteristics, and the nature of its assets, liabilities, revenues, and expenses. This would ordinarily involve a general knowledge of the client's production, distribution, and compensation methods, types of products and services, operating locations, and material transactions with related parties.

While *SSARS No. 1* requires an accountant to have an understanding of the entity's business both to compile and review financial statements, the purpose of the knowledge is not the same in each instance. The basic purpose of the understanding of the business in a compilation is to determine the necessity for the accountant to perform "other accounting services," as previously discussed, in order to satisfactorily compile the financial statements. Accordingly, the level of knowledge necessary relates to the transactions and records of the entity. The purpose of the knowledge of the accounting principles and reporting practices of the industry is to enable the accountant to compile financial statements that are appropriate in form for an entity operating in that industry. On the other hand, in a review engagement the knowledge of the accounting principles and reporting practices of the industry and the understanding of the business are necessary to guide the accountant in determining the nature and extent of the inquiries and analytical procedures necessary to provide a reasonable basis for expressing limited assurance that there are no material modifications that should be made to the financial statements in order for the statements to be in conformity with GAAP.

Reading the Financial Statements

Before issuing a report on a compilation or a review, an accountant should read the financial statements and consider whether such statements appear to be appropriate in form and free from obvious material error and whether they conform with GAAP. In this context, the term "error" refers to mistakes in the preparation of financial statements, including arithmetical or clerical mistakes, and mistakes in the application of accounting principles, including the adequacy of disclosure. That is, the accountant should subject the financial statements to a "quality assurance review" to consider whether, in his or her professional judgment, there is anything in those statements materially inconsistent with the knowledge the accountant possesses of the entity's business, its industry, or applicable accounting principles, including the adequacy of disclosure.

Working Papers for a Compilation or Review

SSARS No. 1 does not contain explicit guidance on the planning or supervision of a compilation or review engagement. However, it is reasonable to assume that working papers resulting from such engagements will demonstrate that compilation and review engagements were properly planned; that assistants, if any, were adequately supervised; and that assistants' work was reviewed.

It is not possible to specify the exact procedures necessary to complete a compilation or review engagement because of the different circumstances of each individual engagement. Therefore, it is not possible to specify the form and content of the working papers that an accountant should prepare on such engagements. However, compilation working papers should contain sufficient documentation to support compliance with the general standards of the profession (professional competence, due professional care, and planning and supervision) and sufficient relevant data to afford a reasonable basis for conclusions reached by an accountant. In a review engagement, the accountant's working papers also should describe:

- The matters covered in the accountant's inquiry and analytical procedures.

- Unusual matters that the accountant considered during the performance of the review, including their disposition.

To comply with the general standards of the profession, the accountant's working papers for review engagements, in addition to documenting procedures performed in the preparation of financial statements, should document the fact that the engagement had been planned and that the work of any assistants had been supervised and reviewed. Furthermore, they should document (document, not corroborate) the accountant's understanding of a client's business, including a general understanding of the entity's organization, its operating characteristics, and the nature of its assets, liabilities, revenues, and expenses. This is necessary to enable the accountant to design and perform inquiry, analytical, and any other procedures considered necessary under the circumstances (including the development of sufficient information for footnote disclosures) that will provide the accountant with a reasonable basis for expressing limited assurance. In other words, the accountant should perform and document whatever procedures are necessary to accomplish the objectives of the engagement. These procedures only become audit procedures when performing an examination in accordance with GAAS. Otherwise, they are just "procedures" for the purpose of developing specific information necessary to compile or review financial statements or to accomplish the terms and objectives of the engagement.

PERFORMANCE STANDARDS UNIQUE TO REVIEWS

The performance of inquiry and anaytical procedures in a review engagement might include inquiry concerning, or the development of information about, a client's particular accounting principles and practices and its methods of application. Inquiries should be made concerning the entity's financial reporting cycle (i.e., the procedures for recording, classifying, and summarizing transactions, and accumulating information for disclosure in the financial statements) or, as is more likely in anything less than a "pure" review, the accountant will develop the information necessary for presentation and disclosure.

Analytical procedures, if applicable or appropriate, must be designed to identify relationships that would be expected to conform to a predictable pattern based on the entity's experience and any individual items that appear to be unusual. For purposes of *SSARS No. 1*, analytical procedures consist of the following:

- Comparison of the financial statements with statements for comparable prior periods.
- Comparison of the financial statements with anticipated results, if available (e.g., budgets and forecasts).
- A study of the relationships of the elements of the financial statements.

SSARS No. 1 indicates that the accountant should make inquiries concerning actions taken at meetings of stockholders, the board of directors, committees of the board of directors, or comparable meetings that may affect the financial statements. A direct approach in obtaining this information would be to read the minutes and extract information considered necessary for presentation in the financial statements. In those not-so-infrequent instances (in nonpublic corporations) where minutes are not maintained, it is incumbent upon the accountant to make inquiries concerning actions which should have been recorded in the minute book (e.g., executive salaries, pension or profit-sharing plan contributions, dividend declarations, etc.), particularly those actions which are intended to provide protection under the Internal Revenue Code.

Finally, the accountant should consider requesting the owners and/or management to sign a representation letter. This is desirable because *SSARS No. 1* requires that the accountant make inquiries of persons having responsibility for financial and accounting matters concerning:

- Whether the financial statements have been presented in conformity with GAAP, consistently applied.

- Changes in the entity's business activities or accounting principles and practices.

- Matters as to which questions have arisen during the course of applying other procedures.

- Events subsequent to the date of the financial statements that would have a material effect on the financial statements.

The accountant must consider the necessity of compiling the financial statements or of performing "other accounting services" to enable him or her to perform a review. In this connection, knowledge acquired in the performance of audits of the entity's financial statements, compilation of the financial statements, or "other accounting services" may result in modification of the review procedures discussed in the preceding paragraphs. However, such modification would *not* reduce the degree of responsibility the accountant assumes with respect to the financial statements reviewed.

Exhibit 18-2 presents a comparison of the performance standards for the compilation or review of financial statements of nonpublic entities.

ACCOUNTANT'S COMPILATION REPORTING STANDARDS

Reporting standards for compilation engagements have been set forth in *SSARS No. 1* and amended by *SSARS No. 5*, "Reporting on Compiled Financial Statements" which was issued in July of 1982. Financial statements compiled without audit or review by an accountant should be accompanied by a report disclosing that:

- A compilation has been performed in accordance with standards established by the American Institute of Certified Public Accountants.

- A compilation is limited to presenting information in the form of financial statements.

- All information in the financial statements is the representation of the management (owners) of the client.

<table>
<tr><td colspan="4" align="center">Exhibit 18-2
Nonpublic Performance Standards</td></tr>
</table>

	Standard	Compilation	Review
1.	Understanding with the client.	X	X
2.	Knowledge of the industry.	X	X
3.	Knowledge of the business.	X	X
4.	Consideration of the necessity to compile the financial statements.		X
5.	Consideration of the necessity to perform "other accounting services."	X	X
6.	Performing sufficient inquiry and analytical procedures to provide a reasonable basis for expressing limited assurance		X
7.	Reading the financial statements to consider whether they appear to be appropriate in form and free from obvious material error.	X	X
8.	If aware that information coming to the accountant's attention is incorrect, incomplete, or otherwise unsatisfactory:		
	a. Obtaining additional information or withdrawing.	X	
	b. Performing additional procedures necessary to achieve limited assurance or withdrawing.		X

- The financial statements have not been audited or reviewed and, accordingly, the accountant does not express an opinion or any other form of assurance on them.

In addition, the date of completion of the compilation should be used as the date of the accountant's report. Each page of the financial statements should include a cross-reference to the accountant's report (such as "See accountant's compilation report"). Any other procedures that the accountant might have performed before or during the compilation engagement should not be described in the report.

Compare the compilation report presented in Exhibit 18-3 with the disclaimer of opinion report presented earlier:

Exhibit 18-3
Standard Compilation Report

We have compiled the accompanying balance sheet of ABC Company as of December 31, 19xx, and the related statements of income and retained earnings, and changes in financial position for the year then ended, in accordance with standards established by the American Institute of Certified Public Accountants.

A compilation is limited to presenting in the form of financial statements information that is the representation of management (owners). We have not audited or reviewed the accompanying financial statements, and accordingly, do not express an opinion or any other form of assurance on them.

The concept of implicit assurance stemming from an accountant's merely being "associated" with a client's financial statements has been, and continues to be, a problem for the the accounting profession. Even though an accountant may not intend to communicate any assurance in a compilation report, most users would profess a higher degree of credibility in the financial statements simply because a CPA was "associated" with them. Empirical research suggests the following bankers' perceptions of less-than-audited financial statements with which a CPA is associated:

- Increased reliance on the financial statements.

- A belief that the statements are reasonably unlikely to be false or misleading.

- The opinion that the statements have an increased likelihood of conforming with GAAP.[7]

---

[7] A.J. Winters, "Banker Perceptions of Unaudited Financial Statements," *The CPA Journal* (August 1975), p. 32.

However, the standard compilation report presented in Exhibit 18-3 implicitly makes it clear that:

- The engagement was performed in accordance with professional standards.

- The terms and objectives of the engagement did not include the expression of an opinion or any other form of assurance.

- The accountant recognizes the concept of implicit assurance and its implications.

A client may request an accountant to compile financial statements that omit all or substantially all of the disclosures required by GAAP, including disclosures that might appear on the face of financial statements. *SSARS No. 1* addresses the additional reporting standards applicable to financial statements that omit all or substantially all disclosures. The following standard third paragraph must be added to the standard compilation report (presented in Exhibit 18-3) when compiled financial statements omit all or substantially all disclosures:

> Management has elected to omit substantially all of the disclosures (and the statement of changes in financial position) required by generally accepted accounting principles. If the omitted disclosures were included in the financial statements, they might influence the user's conclusions about the company's financial position, results of operations, and changes in financial position. Accordingly, these financial statements are not designed for those who are not informed about such matters.

An accountant may compile such financial statements provided three additional compilation reporting standards are considered. First, the accountant's compilation report must clearly indicate that the disclosures have been omitted. Under such circumstances, it would be difficult for a user to consider the omissions as an attempt to mislead or a misrepresentation of facts. Second, the omission must not be, to the accountant's knowledge, "undertaken with the intention of misleading those who might reasonably be expected to use such financial statements." Under normal circumstances, a recurring engagement to compile financial statements omitting all or substantially all disclosures would not be unusual, particularly where, from time to time, such as at year-end, the accountant audits or reviews a client's financial statements or compiles "full disclosure" financial statements. Finally, the accountant should take measures to ensure that the presence of some, but not all or substantially all, disclosures does not lead a user to believe that the financial statements are "complete" in all respects.

As a precaution against this unwarranted assumption, *SSARS No. 1* also requires that those disclosures which are included in the footnotes to such financial statements be labeled as "Selected Information — Substantially All Disclosures Required by Generally Accepted Accounting Principles Are Not Included." Of course, this labeling would be appropriately modified if the financial statements are presented on OCBOA. However, if financial statements are compiled in conformity with OCBOA and do not include disclosure of the basis of accounting used, the basis must be disclosed in the accountant's report.

ACCOUNTANT'S REVIEW REPORTING STANDARDS

Financial statements of nonpublic clients reviewed by an accountant should be accompanied by a report disclosing that:

- A review was performed in accordance with standards established by the American Institute of Certified Public Accountants.

- All information included in the financial statements is the representation of the management (owners) of the entity.

- A review consists principally of inquiries of company personnel and analytical procedures applied to financial data.

- A review is substantially less in scope than an audit, the objective of which is the expression of an opinion regarding the financial statements taken as a whole and, accordingly, no such opinion is expressed.

- The accountant is not aware of any material modifications that should be made to the financial statements in order for them to be in conformity with GAAP, other than those modifications, if any, indicated in his or her report.

The date of completion of the accountant's inquiry and analytical procedures should be used as the date of the report. Each page of the financial statements must include a cross-reference to the accountant's report (such as "See accountant's review report"). Any other procedures that the accountant might have performed before or during the review engagement, including those performed in connection with the compilation of the financial statements, should not be described in the report.

The standard review report presented in Exhibit 18-4 is in compliance with the review reporting standards:

Exhibit 18-4
Standard Review Report

We have reviewed the accompanying balance sheet of ABC Company as of December 31, 19xx, and the related statements of operations and retained earnings and changes in financial position for the year then ended, in accordance with standards established by the American Institute of Certified Public Accountants. All information included in these financial statements is the representation of the management (owners) of ABC Company.

A review consists principally of inquiries of company personnel and analytical procedures applied to financial data. It is substantially less in scope than an examination in accordance with generally accepted auditing standards, the objective of which is the expression of an opinion regarding the financial statements taken as a whole. Accordingly, we do not express such an opinion.

Based on our review, we are not aware of any material modifications that should be made to the accompanying financial statements in order for them to be in conformity with generally accepted accounting principles.

The first sentence of the second paragraph of the report in Exhibit 18-4 describes the "scope of a review," consisting "principally of inquiries of company personnel and analytical procedures applied to financial data." It was the ARSC's intent that the word "principally" would cover both the "other accounting services" and any other additional procedures the accountant deemed necessary if the accountant became aware that information coming to his or her attention was incorrect, incomplete, or otherwise unsatisfactory." Remember, a review does not contemplate a study and evaluation of internal accounting control, tests of accounting records, and the evaluation of responses to inquiries by obtaining corroborating evidential matter, or certain other procedures ordinarily performed during the course of an examination of financial statements in accordance with GAAS. It does, however, require the accountant to consider the necessity of performing "other accounting services," and it also requires that if the accountant becomes aware that information coming to his or her attention is incorrect, incomplete, or otherwise unsatisfactory, the accountant should perform the "additional procedures he or she deems necessary" to permit the expression of limited assurance that there are no material modifications that should be made to the financial statements in order for them to be in conformity with GAAP.

Whenever an accountant is unable, for whatever reason, to perform the inquiry and analytical procedures (or any other procedures) he or she considers necessary to achieve the limited assurance contemplated by a review, that review will be incomplete. *SSARS No. 1* does not provide for the issuance of a limited scope review report. If such a situation occurs, the accountant should consider whether the circumstances resulting in a limited scope review also preclude issuing a compilation report.

REPORTING ON COMPARATIVE FINANCIAL STATEMENTS

In October 1979, the ARSC issued *SSARS No. 2, Reporting on Comparative Financial Statements* (AR 200), which establishes standards for reporting on financial statements issued in comparative form by non-public companies. *SSARS No. 2* is applicable when statements of one or more periods presented in comparative form have been compiled or reviewed. If the comparative statements have been audited in accordance with GAAS, *SAS No. 15, Reporting on Comparative Financial Statements*, is applicable. However, both *SSARS No. 2* and *SAS No. 15* establish similar reporting standards. *SSARS No. 2* extends the submission test of association established in *SSARS No. 1* to comparative statements—requiring the accountant to issue a report explaining the degree of responsibility he or she is assuming regarding all comparative statements presented. A client may prepare financial statements and include them in a report (but not in comparative form) that also includes CPA prepared statements. If this happens, the CPA must require the client to include an indication that the accountant has not audited, reviewed, or compiled those statements and does not assume responsibility for them.

Continuing Accountant and Comparative Statements

SSARS No. 2 (AR 200.07) defines the terms "continuing accountant" and "updating." "A continuing accountant is an accountant who has been engaged to audit, review, or compile, and report on the financial statements of the current period and one or more consecutive periods immediately prior to the current period."

Updating means "taking into consideration information the accountant becomes aware of during his or her current engagement and re-expressing his or her previous conclusion (with a current report date) or depending on the circumstances, expressing different conclusions on the statements of a prior period (with a current report date)." An updated report differs from a reissued report in that a reissued report bears the same date as the original report and it is not based on a subsequent engagement. If a reissued report is revised, dual-dating must be used by the accountant.

A continuing accountant who performs the same or a higher level of service with respect to the financial statements of the current period should update his or her report on the prior-period statements that are presented for comparative purposes.

Standard reports on comparative financial statements, from *SSARS No. 2* (as amended by *SSARS No. 5*), for this type of situation are presented in Exhibit 18-5.

In cases where the continuing accountant performs a lower level of service with respect to the current-period statements he or she should report on the prior-period statements when they are presented for comparative purposes or the accountant should include an additional paragraph in the current period's report establishing the degree of responsibility he or she is taking regarding the prior-period statements. Such a paragraph would, of course, describe the previous engagement—review or audit. In either case, the accountant should state that he or she has not performed any procedures in connection with the prior-period review engagement or audit engagement since the date of his or her report. Following is an example of a paragraph that may be added to a current compilation report establishing responsibility for a prior-period review:

> The accompanying 19x1 financial statements of XYZ Company were previously reviewed by me (us) and my (our) report dated March 1, 19x2, stated that I was (we were) not aware of any material modifications that should be made to those statements in order for them to be in conformity with generally accepted accounting principles. I (we) have not performed any procedures in connection with that review engagement after the date of my (our) report on the 19x1 financial statements.

A continuing accountant is required to update his or her report on the prior-period statements presented for comparative purposes if information obtained in the current engagement so indicates. A changed reference may involve, for example, the addition of a reservation paragraph regarding a departure from GAAP discovered in the current

Exhibit 18-5

Compilation Each Period

I (we) have compiled the accompanying balance sheets of XYZ Company as of December 31, 19x2 and 19x1, and the related statements of income, retained earnings, and changes in financial position for the years then ended, in accordance with standards established by the American Institute of Certified Public Accountants.

A compilation is limited to presenting in the form of financial statements information that is the representation of management (owners). I (we) have not audited or reviewed the accompanying financial statements and, accordingly, do not express an opinion or any other form of assurance on them.

February 1, 19x3

Review Each Period

I (we) have reviewed the accompanying balance sheets of XYZ Company as of December 31, 19x2 and 19x1, and the related statements of income, retained earnings, and changes in financial position for the years then ended, in accordance with standards established by the American Institute of Certified Public Accountants. All information included in these financial statements is the representation of the management (owners) of XYZ Company.

A review consists principally of inquiries of company personnel and analytical procedures applied to financial data. It is substantially less in scope than an examination in accordance with generally accepted auditing standards, the objective of which is the expression of an opinion regarding the financial statements taken as a whole. Accordingly, I (we) do not express such an opinion.

Based on my (our) reviews, I am (we are) not aware of any material modifications that should be made to the accompanying financial statements in order for them to be in conformity with generally accepted accounting principles.

March 1, 19x3

Review in Current Period and Compilation in Prior Period

I (we) have reviewed the accompanying balance sheet of XYZ Company as of December 31, 19x2, and the related statements of income, retained earnings, any changes in financial position for the year then ended, in accordance with

> **Exhibit 18-5 (continued):**
>
> standards established by the American Institute of Certified Public Accountants. All information included in these financial statements is the representation of the management (owners) of XYZ Company.
>
> A review consists principally of inquiries of company personnel and analytical procedures applied to financial data. It is substantially less in scope than an examination in accordance with generally accepted auditing standards, the objective of which is the expression of an opinion regarding the financial statements taken as a whole. Accordingly, I (we) do not express such an opinion.
>
> Based on my (our) review, I am (we are) not aware of any material modifications that should be made to the 19x2 financial statements in order for them to be in conformity with generally accepted accounting principles.
>
> The accompanying 19x1 financial statements of XYZ Company were compiled by me (us) in accordance with standards established by the American Institute of Certified Public Accountants. A compilation is limited to presenting in the form of financial statements information that is the representation of management (owners). I (we) have not audited or reviewed the 19x1 financial statements and, accordingly, do not express an opinion or any other form of assurance on them.
>
> March 1, 19x3

period that also affects the prior-period statements. Conversely, a changed reference could involve deletion of a reservation paragraph regarding a departure from GAAP noted in the prior period that has been corrected by the client through restatement. When there is a changed reference to a departure from GAAP regarding the prior-period statements, the accountant's current report should include a separate explanatory paragraph indicating:

- The date of the accountant's previous report.
- The circumstances or events that caused the reference to be changed.
- When applicable, that the financial statements of the prior period have been changed.

Following is an example of such a paragraph:

> In my (our) previous (compilation) (review) report dated March 1, 19x2, on the 19x1 financial statements, I (we) referred to a departure from generally accepted accounting principles because the company carried its land at appraised values. However, as disclosed in Note X, the company has restated its 19x1 financial statements to reflect its land at cost in accordance with generally accepted accounting principles.

Predecessor Accountant and Comparative Statements

When the financial statements of a prior period or periods have been compiled, reviewed, or audited by a predecessor accountant and they are to be presented for comparative purposes with the current period statements, three reporting options exist. First, the predecessor accountant may be requested to reissue his or her report on the prior-period statements. Second, the successor accountant may make references to the report of the predecessor in his or her current report. And, third, the successor accountant may compile, review, or audit the prior-period statements and report accordingly.

Before agreeing to reissue the report on a prior-period's financial statements, a predecessor should consider whether his or her report is still appropriate. He or she should consider the current form and manner of presentation of the prior-period statements, subsequent events, and changes in the statements that would require an addition, deletion or modification to the standard report. Accordingly, the predecessor should read the current-period statements and the successor's report, compare the current-period statements with those he or she reported on, and obtain a letter of representation from the successor. The letter should indicate whether the successor is aware of any matter that may materially affect the prior-period statements. If the predecessor becomes aware of information that may affect the current presentation of the statements he or she reported upon, the predecessor should perform other procedures before reissuing the report. Such other procedures may include discussions with the successor and reviewing the working papers of the successor. A predecessor accountant who agrees to reissue his or her report is required to update that report for information learned from the successor that materially affects the statements reported upon. A predecessor who reissues a report on the prior-period statements should use the original reporting date. If the report is revised, based on information learned from the successor, dual-dating would be used.

A predecessor accountant, even though requested to do so, may decide, for various reasons, not to reissue his or her report. If the report of the predecessor is not reissued and the successor has not compiled, reviewed, or audited the prior-period statements, the successor should refer to the report of the predecessor in his or her current report. The following information should be included:

- A statement that the financial statements of the prior period, which are presented for comparative purposes, were compiled or reviewed by another accountant (other accountants) (the other accountants should not be named).

- The date of his or her (their) report.

- A description of the standard form of disclaimer or limited assurance, as applicable, included in the report.

- A description or a quotation of any modifications of the standard report and of any paragraphs emphasizing a matter regarding the financial statements.

When there is a successor-predecessor accountant relationship, the successor accountant should consider the guidance provided in *SSARS No. 4, Communications Between Predecessor and Successor Accountants*, discussed later in this Chapter.

Comparative Financial Statements Omitting Substantially All Disclosures

SSARS No. 2 prohibits the presentation in comparative form of financial statements that include full disclosure with those that omit substantially all of the disclosures required by GAAP. However, it is permissible to make such a statements comparable by omission of previously presented financial statement disclosures. For example, current-period "less than full-disclosure" compiled statements may be presented in comparative form with prior-period compiled or reviewed statements that included full disclosure providing the disclosures for the prior-period statements are omitted and the accountant's report on the comparative statements indicates the nature of the previous engagement. Following is an example of an appropriate report when prior-period statements that omit substantially all disclosures have been compiled from previously reviewed statements for the same period:

(Standard three paragraph compilation report in comparative form for "less-than-full-disclosure" statements)

(Fourth paragraph)

The accompanying 19x1 financial statements were compiled by me (us) from financial statements that did not omit substantially all of the disclosures required by generally accepted accounting principles and that I (we) previously reviewed as indicated in my (our) report dated March 1, 19x2.

February 1, 19x3

COMMUNICATIONS BETWEEN PREDECESSOR AND SUCCESSOR ACCOUNTANTS[8]

SSARS No. 4 provides guidance to a successor accountant who decides to communicate with a predecessor accountant in connection with the acceptance of an engagement to compile or review the financial statements of a nonpublic entity.

The Statement requires the predecessor to respond promptly and fully to appropriate inquiries of the succcessor, in ordinary circumstances.

A *successor accountant* is an accountant who has been invited to make a proposal for an engagement to compile or review statements or who has accepted such an engagement. A *predecessor accountant* is an accountant who has resigned or who has been notified that his or her services have been terminated and who, as a minimum, was engaged to compile the statements of the entity for the prior year or for a period ended within 12 months of the date of the statements to be compiled or reviewed by the successor.

When the successor decides to communicate with the predecessor, he or she should request that the client permit such inquiries of the predecessor and authorize the predecessor to respond fully. If the client refuses, the successor should consider the implications in making a decision on the acceptance of the new engagement.

The successor's inquiries may be oral or written and ordinarily should include matters concerning:

- Information that might bear on the integrity of management (owners).

- Disagreements with management (owners) about accounting principles or the necessity for the performance of certain procedures.

- The cooperation of management (owners) in providing additional information, if necessary.

- The predecessor's understanding of the reason for the change in accountants.

The predecessor should respond promptly and fully to inquirs of the type described above. If the predecessor decides,,due to unusual circumstances not to respond fully, he or she should indicate that the response is limited. The successor should consider the reasons for and implications of such a limited response in making the engagment decision.

---

[8] *SAS No. 7*, discussed in Chapter 4, provides guidance on communications between predecessor and successor auditors. *SSARS No. 4, Communication Between Predecessor and Successor Accountants* (AR 400), applies to nonpublic company clients only.

A successor may wish to make other inquiries of the predecessor to facilitate his or her compilation or review engagement. Such inquiries may be made before or after accepting the engagement and might involve such matters as review of the predecessor's working papers, questions about inadequacies in the entity's underlying financial data, the necessity to perform other accounting services, and so forth. It is customary for the predecessor to make himself or herself available to the successor for consultation and to make available certain of his or her working papers. However, valid business reasons may preclude such cooperation.

The successor should not make reference to the report or work of a predecessor in his or her own report, except as specifically permitted by *SSARS No. 2* or *SAS No. 26* (reporting on comparative statements) with respect to the financial statements of a prior period.

If the successor becomes aware of information that leads him or her to believe that the statements reported on by the predecessor may require revision, the successor should ask the client to communicate this information to the predecessor.[9] If the client refuses to communicate with the predecessor or if the successor is not satisfied with the predecessor's action, the successor would be well advised to consult with his or her attorney.

FINANCIAL STATEMENTS INCLUDED IN CERTAIN PRESCRIBED FORMS

SSARS No. 3, Compilation Reports on Financial Statements Included in Certain Prescribed Forms (AR 300), states that the requirements of *SSARS Nos. 1 and 2* are applicable when unaudited statements of a nonpublic entity are included in a prescribed form. However, *SSARS No. 3* provides for an alternative form of standard compilation report when the prescribed form or related instructions call for a departure from GAAP or OCBOA.

A prescribed form is any standard preprinted form designed or adopted by the body to which it is to be submitted. For example, preprinted forms may be used by:

---

[9] This requirement is similar to what is required in an audit engagement. The predecessor may have to take action to prevent continued reliance on the statements, such as requesting the client to notify current users of the financial statements that they contain errors and that revised statements will be issued.

- Industry trade associations.
- Credit agencies.
- Banks.
- Governmental and regulatory bodies other than those concerned with the sale or trading of securities.

SSARS No. 3 makes the presumption that information required by a prescribed form is sufficient to meet the needs of the body that designed or adopted the form and there is no need for the CPA to advise the entity of departures from GAAP or OCBOA required by the form or related instructions.

In the absence of a requirement or a request for a review report on financial statements included in a prescribed form, the following standard compilation report may be used when the unaudited statements of a nonpublic entity are included in a prescribed form that calls for departures from GAAP or OCBOA:

> I (we) have compiled the (identification of financial statements, including period covered and name of entity) included in the accompanying prescribed form, in accordance with standards established by the American Institute of Certified Public Accountants.
>
> My (our) compilation was limited to presenting in the form prescribed by (name of body) information that is the representation of management (owners). I (we) have not audited or reviewed the financial statements referred to above and, accordingly, do not express an opinion or any other form of assurance on them.
>
> These financial statements (including related disclosures) are presented in accordance with the requirements of (name of body) which differ from generally accepted accounting principles. Accordingly, these financial statements are not designed for those who are not informed about such differences.

If an accountant becomes aware of a departure from GAAP or OCBOA other than departures that may be called for by the prescribed form or related instructions, the accountant should add his or her reservations to the compilation report. For example, the following might be added to the report:

> However, I did become aware of a departure from generally accepted accounting principles that is not called for by the prescribed form or related instructions as described in the following paragraph.
>
> (Additional paragraph describing the departure)

An accountant should not sign a preprinted report form that does not conform with the guidance provided in *SSARS No. 3* or *SSARS No. 1*, whichever is applicable. In such circumstances, the accountant should append an appropriate report to the form.

REVIEW OF INTERIM FINANCIAL INFORMATION

Another type of service performed by CPA firms for public and non-public clients is a review of interim financial information. Interim financial *information*[10] may be presented as follows:

- Included with annual audited financial statements.
- Included in a note to annual audited financial statements.
- As a separate report.

In April, 1981, the Auditing Standards Board of the American Institute of Certified Public Accountants issued *SAS No. 36, Review of Interim Financial Information*, to provide guidance as to procedures and reporting responsibilities of the independent auditor in review engagements of interim financial information.

The objective of a review of interim financial data is to provide a basis for the accountant to express limited assurance that he or she is not aware of any material modifications that should be made to such data for it to conform with generally accepted accounting principles.

Procedures for a review of such interim statements consist primarily of inquiries of client personnel and analytical review procedures applied to the interim financial information. In these reviews, an accountant does not have to obtain corroborating evidence to substantiate client responses to inquiries. Nor does a review of interim data contemplate a study and evaluation of internal accounting control. Consequently, in a review of interim information, an accountant cannot be assured that all significant matters would come to his or her attention that would be discovered in an audit. Therefore, the accountant cannot express an overall opinion regarding the interim financial information.

With respect to reporting responsibilities specified by *SAS No. 36*, the following items should be included in the accountant's report to accompany the reviewed interim financial information:

---

[10] A review of interim financial statements of a nonpublic entity, as opposed to interim information, is covered by *SSARS No. 1*.

- A statement that the review of interim financial information was made in accordance with the standards for such reviews.

- An identification of the interim financial information reviewed.

- A description of the procedures for a review of interim financial information.

- A statement that a review of interim financial information is substantially less in scope than an examination in accordance with generally accepted auditing standards, the objective of which is an expression of opinion regarding the financial statements taken as a whole, and accordingly, no such opinion is expressed.

- A statement about whether the accountant is aware of any material modifications that should be made to the accompanying financial information so that it conforms with generally accepted accounting principles.

In addition to the above items, the review report should be addressed to the company, the board of directors, or the stockholders and each page of the interim financial data should be conspicuously marked as "UNAUDITED."

The following example of a review report is provided in paragraph 18 of *SAS No. 36*:

We have made a review of (describe the information reviewed) ABC Company and consolidated subsidiaries as of September 30, 19x1, and for the three-month and nine-month periods then ended, in accordance with standards established by the American Institute of Certified Public Accountants.

A review of interim financial information consists principally of obtaining an understanding of the system for the preparation of interim financial information, applying analytical review procedures to financial data, and making inquiries of persons responsible for financial and accounting matters. It is substantially less in scope than an examination in accordance with generally accepted auditing standards, the objective of which is the expression of an opinion regarding the financial statements taken as a whole. Accordingly, we do not express such an opinion.

Based on our review, we are not aware of any material modifications that should be made to the accompanying financial information for it to be in conformity with generally accepted accounting principles.

If interim financial information accompanies *audited* financial statements, the auditor should still apply review procedures to the interim information. Ordinarily, the auditor does not have to modify his or her audit report to refer to the review or interim information because such data is not required for financial statements to be in conformity with generally accepted accounting principles. However, if the client presents interim financial information on a *voluntary* basis, and if the auditor has not reviewed the interim information, the audit report may be expanded to state that the data has not been reviewed or the client may indicate that the interim information has not been reviewed.

On the other hand, if the client omits required interim financial information in annual reports (such as interim data required by the Security Exchange Commission), the auditor's report on the audited financial statements must be modified to indicate that the client has not presented such required data. If the required interim data is presented by the client but the auditor cannot review such data, the audit report must be expanded to indicate that the auditor did not perform an audit, or a review, on the interim financial information and, accordingly, does not express an opinion on that data.

SUMMARY

SSARS No. 1 defines two services an accountant may render with respect to the less-than-audited financial statements of nonpublic clients, the compilation of financial statements and the review of financial statements and, in addition, provides guidance concerning the standards and procedures applicable to such engagements.

SSARS No. 1 is written from the viewpoint of "the objectives of the engagement." It describes in detail the differences between the objectives of a compilation and those of a review and the differences between the objectives of a review and an audit.

Compilation and review engagements are rarely performed in the "pure" sense, which is how they are defined. That is, other accounting services are usually required during the compilation or review of financial statements. *SSARS No. 1* requires the accountant both to consider the necessity of performing "other accounting services" to properly complete the engagement and to apply his or her total knowledge of the client's business and operations in the decision to issue a report communicating an appropriate level of assurance.

SSARS No. 2 establishes standards for reporting on comparative financial statements for nonpublic companies. It applies when nonpublic companies issue in comparative form financial statements that have been compiled or reviewed.

SSARS No. 2 defines a "continuing accountant" and "updating" and requires a continuing accountant who has performed the same level of service or a higher level of service in the current period compared to the preceding period to update his or her report on comparative statements. A continuing accountant is an accountant who has been engaged to audit, review, or compile, and report on the financial statements of the current period and one or more consecutive periods immediately prior to the current period. Updating means taking into consideration information the accountant becomes aware of during his or her current engagement and re-expressing his or her previous conclusion (with a current report date) or depending on the circumstances, expressing different conclusions on the statements of the prior period.

A continuing accountant who performs a lower level service in the current period would reissue his or her report on the prior-period statements as opposed to updating that report.

SSARS No. 3 states that the provisions of *SSARS Nos. 1 and 2* are applicable when unaudited statements of a nonpublic entity are included in a prescribed form. *SSARS No. 3* provides for an alternative form of standard compilation report when the prescribed form or related instructions call for a departure from GAAP or OCBOA. A prescribed form is any standard preprinted form designed or adopted by the body to which it is to be submitted. There is a presumption that the information required on a prescribed form is sufficient to meet the needs of the body that designed or adopted the form and the accountant is not required to advise the entity of departures from GAAP or OCBOA required by the form or related instructions.

SSARS No. 4 provides guidance to a successor accountant who decides to communicate with a predecessor accountant in connection with acceptance of an engagement to compile or review the financial statements of a nonpublic company. The predecessor is required to respond to proper inquiries. Such inquiries may be oral or written and should cover information that might bear on the integrity of management (owners); disagreements with management (owners) about accounting principles or the necessity for the performance of certain procedures; the cooperation of management (owners) in providing additional information, if necessary; and the predecessor's understanding of the reason for the change in accountants. The successor may wish to make other inquiries to facilitate completion of his or her engagement.

The successor should carefully consider any response received from the predecessor in making his or her engagement decision.

SAS No. 36 establishes standards and procedures for reporting on reviews of interim financial information for both public and nonpublic companies. Basic procedures in a review consist of inquiries and analytical review procedures concerning the interim data to be reported upon. The objective of such a review is to provide a basis for the accountant to express limited assurance that he or she is not aware of any material modifications that should be made to such data for it to conform to generally accepted accounting principles.

REVIEW QUESTIONS

18-1   Define the two services an accountant may render in connection with the less-than-audited financial statements of nonpublic entities.

18-2   Explain the concept or point of view underlying the first Statement on Standards for Accounting and Review Services (*SSARS No. 1*).

18-3   Define and contrast the objectives of the compilation and review of financial statements.

18-4   Does *SSARS No. 1* establish standards for accounting services other than the compilation or review of financial statements? What does the phrase "other accounting services" mean?

18-5   Define the concept of association.

18-6   Describe the nonpublic association standards of "submission test," "plain paper prohibition," "minimum level of service," and "pecking order."

18-7   Name and describe the five general standards of the profession. Are all of these standards applicable to compilation or review engagements? What is the source of these standards?

18-8   Discuss the differences in the procedures an accountant should follow when a client's financials contain incorrect, incomplete, or otherwise "misleading" information as opposed to the impact upon the accountant's report when he or she becomes aware of simple departures from GAAP that are material to the financial statements.

18-9   List the six standards of performance applicable to compilation engagements.

18-10   Describe the nature of the necessary understanding of the business in a *compilation engagement* and contrast this understanding with the required knowledge of the business in a *review engagement*.

18-11   What are the *SSARS No. 1* working paper requirements for *compilations* and *reviews*?

18-12   List the eight standards of performance applicable to review engagements.

18-13   Why should an accountant seriously consider requesting client management to sign a representation letter even though *SSARS No. 1* does not require it?

18-14   Discuss the auditor's reporting responsibilities in a compilation engagement and identify the four compilation reporting standards.

18-15   Discuss the auditor's reporting responsibilities in a review engagement and identify the five review reporting standards.

18-16   Define "a continuing accountant" consistent with *SSARS No. 2*.

18-17   Describe and discuss the differences between an updated report and a reissued report.

18-18   When presenting comparative financial statements where the continuing accountant performs the same or a higher level of service with respect to the current-period statements, describe the reporting responsibility regarding the prior year's financials. Indicate the reporting alternatives concerning the prior year's financials when the continuing accountant performs a lower level of service with respect to the current-period statements.

18-19   List the 3 reporting options when financial statements of a prior period have been compiled, reviewed, or audited by a predecessor accountant and they are to be presented for comparative purposes with the current-period financials.

18-20   Discuss procedures that the predecessor accountant should carry out before agreeing to reissue the report on a prior-period's financial statements when presenting comparative statements with a successor accountant.

18-21   When the predecessor accountant agrees to reissue the report on a prior-period's financial statements, what are the reporting responsibilities of the predecessor accountant?

18-22   Discuss *SSARS No. 2* position concerning comparative financial statements which omit substantially all disclosures.

18-23   Discuss the reporting responsibilities of the accountant when unaudited financial statements of a nonpublic entity are included in a prescribed form that calls for departures from GAAP or OCBOA.

18-24   Is the predecessor accountant always required by *SSARS No. 4* to respond promptly and fully to inquiries made by the successor accountant? Explain.

18-25   What should be the nature of the inquiries made by the successor accountant to the predecessor accountant before accepting the unaudited engagement? After accepting the engagement?

18-26   What are the reporting responsibilities of a CPA who is associated with interim financial data that is included in a report with the annual audited financial statements of a public company? A nonpublic company?

DISCUSSION QUESTIONS AND PROBLEMS

18-27   Patsy Perfect, CPA, was engaged by Senuka Glass Company to assist in the preparation of financial statements without audit for the year ended December 31, 1983. From the accounting and other records Patsy learned the following information about Senuka Glass Company.

- Senuka Glass Company was incorporated in the State of West Virginia in 1952. All capital stock is currently held by two brothers and one aunt.

- The land on which the main warehouse sits was purchased on November 16, 1952 for a cost of $50,000.

- In 1982, the company controller wrote-up the land to an appraised value of $250,000 by recognizing additional paid-in capital of $200,000.

- Although Senuka had a controller, the accounting records were not properly adjusted to reflect expense and revenue accruals for the current year.

Required:

a. Describe the nonpublic performance standards that Patsy must adhere to in this compilation engagement.

b. Will Patsy have to consider rendering "other accounting services" for Senuka Glass? Explain.

c. Discuss the items that should be included in Patsy's report to be in compliance with reporting standards for a compilation engagement.

d. Since Senuka Glass has a material departure from GAAP, will Patsy have to consider such departure in writing the compilation report? How will the report be affected?

18-28 On March 3, 1983, Nancy Neat, CPA, was asked to review the financial statements of Mountaineer Mall, Incorporated for the year ended December 31, 1983. Mountaineer Mall is a closely held corporation without any stock being traded on any stock exchange or over-the-counter. Patsy Perfect, CPA, had been the corporation's accountant since incorporation by the State of West Virginia on August 2, 1972.

Required:

a. Discuss the procedures Nancy Neat should employ before accepting the review engagement. Should Nancy Neat communicate with Patsy Perfect, the predecessor auditor?

b. Assuming acceptance of the review engagement, describe the nonpublic performance standards that Nancy Neat should comply with in the review engagement.

c. Discuss the nature of and the type of inquiries and analytical procedures that Nancy Neat should carry out to provide a reasonable basis for expressing limited assurance on the financial statements.

d. Identify the items that should be included in Nancy Neat's report to be in compliance with reporting standards for a review engagement. Also, indicate any other reporting standards that Nancy should comply with.

18-29 Tom Tron, CPA, performed a review service for Electronic Games Incorporated for the year ended December 31, 1982. Electronic Games is a closely held corporation without any stock or securities being traded on an organized stock exchange. The corporation was formed January 2, 1982, for the purpose of developing and distributing electronic games packages and cassettes. The company did very well during its first year of operations. Since the president of the company hired a controller on May 5, 1983, Tron was asked if he could help the controller compile financial statements for the current year ended December 31, 1983, and to help prepare comparative financial statements for the first two years of operations.

Required:

a. Discuss Tron's reporting responsibilities concerning the comparative financial statements for the years ended December 31, 1982 and December 31, 1983.

b. If Tron had performed a review of the financial statements for the year ended December 31, 1983, would Tron's reporting responsibilities be different than for the situation described above? Explain.

18-30 Space Port, Incorporated is a closely held corporation. It was organized in 1978 to provide electronic game services to the northeastern section of the United States. The president of Space Port had engaged Nancy Neat, CPA, to review financial statements for the years ended December 31, 1978, through December 31, 1982. During the current year the president hired Tom Tron, CPA, to review the financial statements for the year ended December 31, 1983. Space Port, Incorporated also wanted to present comparative financial statements for the years ended December 31, 1982 and 1983.

After consulting Nancy Neat, Tom Tron accepted the review engagement for Space Port, Incorporated. Tom learned that in previous years Nancy's review reports were standard reports (without modification) as suggested by SSARS No. 1 and 2. Tom asked Nancy to reissue her prior year's review report to accompany the comparative statements for the years ended December 31, 1982 and 1983.

Required:

a. Discuss procedures and factors that Nancy Neat should carry out and consider before agreeing to reissue her prior year's report to accompany the current year's comparative financial statements.

b. Assuming that Nancy Neat agrees to reissue the review report, what are the reporting responsibilities of Nancy Neat concerning such reissued report?

18-31 Loman, CPA, who has examined the financial statements of the Broadwall Corporation, a publicly held company, for the year ended December 31, 1979, was asked to perform a limited review of the financial statements of Broadwall Corporation for the period ending March 31, 1980. The engagement letter stated that a limited review does not provide a basis for the expression of an opinion.

Required:

a. Explain why Loman's limited review will *not* provide a basis for the expression of an opinion.

b. What are the review procedures which Loman should perform, and what is the purpose of each procedure? Structure your response as follows:

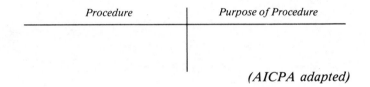

Procedure	*Purpose of Procedure*

(AICPA adapted)

18-32 Brown, CPA, received a telephone call from Calhoun, the sole owner and manager of a small corporation. Calhoun asked Brown to prepare the financial statements for the corporation and told Brown that the statements were needed in two weeks for external financing purposes. Calhoun was vague when Brown inquired about the intended use of the statements. Brown was convinced that Calhoun thought Brown's work would constitute an audit. To avoid confusion Brown decided not to explain to Calhoun that the engagement would only be to prepare the financial statements. Brown, with the understanding that a substantial fee would be paid if the work were completed in two weeks, accepted the engagement and started the work at once.

During the course of the work, Brown discovered an accrued expense account labeled "professional fees" and learned that the balance in the account represented an accrual for the cost of Brown's services. Brown suggested to Calhoun's bookkeeper that the account name be changed to "fees for limited audit engagement." Brown also reviewed several invoices to determine whether accounts were being properly classified. Some of the invoices were missing. Brown listed the missing invoice numbers in the working papers with a note indicating that there should be a follow-up on the next engagement.

Brown also discovered that the available records included the fixed asset values at estimated current replacement costs. Based on the records available, Brown prepared a balance sheet, income statement and statement of stockholder's equity. In addition, Brown drafted the footnotes but decided that any mention of the replacement costs would only mislead the readers. Brown suggested to Calhoun that readers of the financial statements would be better informed if they received a separate letter from Calhoun explaining the meaning and effect of the estimated replacement costs of the fixed assets. Brown mailed the financial statements and footnotes to Calhoun with the following note included on each page:

> "The accompanying financial statements are submitted to you without complete audit verification."

Required:

Identify the inappropriate actions of Brown and indicate what Brown should have done to avoid each inappropriate action.
    Organize your answer sheet as follows:

Inappropriate Action	What Brown Should Have Done to Avoid Inappropriate Action

(AICPA adapted)

18-33 The limitations on the CPA's professional responsibilities when he or she is associated with unaudited financial statements are often misunderstood. These misunderstandings can be substantially reduced by carefully following professional pronouncements in the course of his or her work, and taking other appropriate measures.

Required:

The following list describes seven situations the CPA may encounter, or contentions he or she may have to deal with in his or her association with and preparation of unaudited financial statements. Briefly discuss the extent of the CPA's responsibilities and, if appropriate, the actions he or she should take to minimize any misunderstandings. Number your answers to correspond with the numbering in the following list.

1. The CPA was engaged by telephone to perform write-up work including the preparation of financial statements of a nonpublic company. His client believes that the CPA has been engaged to audit the financial statements and examine the records accordingly.

2. A group of businessmen who own a farm which is managed by an independent agent engage a CPA to prepare quarterly unaudited financial statements for them. The CPA prepares the financial statements from information given to him by the independent agent. Subsequently, the businessmen find the statements were inaccurate because their independent agent was embezzling funds. The businessmen refuse to pay the CPA's fee and blame him for allowing the situation to go undetected contending that he should not have relied on representations from the independent agent.

3. In comparing the trial balance with the general ledger the CPA finds an account labeled "audit fees" in which the client has accumulated the CPA's quarterly billings for accounting services including the preparation of quarterly unaudited financial statements.

4. Unaudited financial statements of a nonpublic company were accompanied by the following letter of transmittal from the CPA.

    We are enclosing your company's balance sheet as of June 30, 19x0, and the related statements of income and retained earnings and changes in financial position for the twelve months then ended which we have reviewed.

5. To determine appropriate account classification, the CPA reviewed a number of the client's invoices. He noted in his working papers that some invoices were missing but did nothing further because he felt they did not affect the compilation of financial statements. When the client subsequently discovered that invoices were missing, he contended that the CPA should not have ignored the missing invoices when preparing the financial statements and had a responsibility to at least inform him that they were missing.

6. In a compilation engagement, the CPA prepared a draft of unaudited financial statements from the client's records. While reviewing this draft with his client, the CPA learns that the land and building were recorded at appraisal value.

7.   The CPA is engaged to review without audit the financial statements prepared by the client's controller. During this review, the CPA learns of several items which by generally accepted accounting principles would require adjustment of the statements and footnote disclosure. The controller agrees to make the recommended adjustments to the statements but says that he is not going to add the footnotes because the statements are unaudited.

(AICPA adapted)

OBJECTIVE QUESTIONS*

18-34   Which of the following would not be included in a CPA's report based upon a review of the financial statements of a nonpublic entity?

A.   A statement that the review was in accordance with generally accepted auditing standards.

B.   A statement that all information included in the financial statements are the representations of management.

C.   A statement describing the principal procedures performed.

D.   A statement describing the auditor's conclusions based upon the results of the review.

18-35   When making a limited review of interim financial information, the auditor's work consists primarily of

A.   Studying and evaluating limited amounts of documentation supporting the interim financial information.

B.   Scanning and reviewing client-prepared, internal financial statements.

C.   Making inquiries and performing analytical procedures concerning significant accounting matters.

D.   Confirming and verifying significant account balances at the interim date.

18-36   If, as a result of a limited review of interim financial information, a CPA concludes that such information does *not* conform with generally accepted accounting principles, the CPA should

A.   Insist that the management conform the information with generally accepted accounting principles and if this is not done, resign from the engagement.

B.   Adjust the financial information so that it conforms with generally accepted accounting principles.

Note: All questions in this section are AICPA adapted questions.

C. Prepare a qualified report that makes reference to the lack of conformity with generally accepted accounting principles.

D. Advise the board of directors of the respects in which the information does not conform with generally accepted principles.

18-37   A company includes selected interim financial information in a note to its annual financial statements. The independent auditor has made a limited review of the information and is satisfied with its presentation. Under these circumstances, the auditor's report on the annual financial statements.

A. Should be modified to make reference to the limited review and the selected interim financial information.

B. Need not be modified to make reference to the limited review but should be modified to make reference to the selected financial information.

C. Should be modified to make reference to the limited review but not the selected interim financial information.

D. Need not be modified to make reference to the limited review or the selected interim financial information.

18-38   Carolyn Burns, CPA, has been assisting Nestler Manufacturing Corporation (a public corporation) in the preparation of unaudited financial statements. It has come to the attention of Burns that Nestler is carrying a substantial investment in Salvemini, Inc., at cost, even though it is public knowledge that Salvemini is in bankruptcy and its stock is worthless. Burns' reporting responsibility is met by

A. Describing the deviation from generally accepted accounting principles in her disclaimer of opinion.

B. Issuing an adverse opinion.

C. Issuing the statements on plain paper without reference to Burns.

D. Stating in her disclaimer of opinion that Nestler's financial statements are unaudited.

(AICPA adapted)

18-39   Which of the following best describes the responsibility of the CPA when he or she prepares unaudited financial statements for a public client?

A. He or she should make a proper study and evaluation of the existing internal control as a basis for reliance thereon.

B. He or she is relieved of any responsibility to third parties.

C. He or she does not have responsibility to apply auditing procedures to the financial statements.

D. He or she has only to satisfy himself or herself that the financial statements were prepared in conformity with generally accepted accounting principles.

18-40 You are a CPA retained by the manager of a cooperative retirement village to do "write-up work." You are expected to prepare unaudited financial statements with each page marked "See accountant's compilation report." The report states that an audit or review was not made. In performing the work you discover that there are no invoices to support the $25,000 of the manager's claimed disbursements. The manager informs you that all the disbursements are proper. What should you do?

A. Submit the expected statements but omit the $25,000 of unsupported disbursements.

B. Include the unsupported disbursements in the statements since you are not expected to make an audit.

C. Obtain from the manager a written statement that you informed him of the missing invoices and his assurance that the disbursements are proper.

D. Notify the owners that some of the claimed disbursements are unsupported and withdraw if the situation is not satisfactorily resolved.

18-41 In the course of an engagement to prepare unaudited financial statements the client requests that the CPA perform normal accounts receivable audit confirmation procedures. The CPA agrees and performs such procedures. The confirmation procedures

A. Are a part of an auditing service that change the scope of the engagement to that of an audit in accordance with generally accepted auditing standards.

B. Are part of an accounting service and are *not* performed for the purpose of conducting an audit in accordance with generally accepted auditing standards.

C. Are *not* permitted when the purpose of the engagement is to prepare unaudited financial statements and work to be performed is *not* in accordance with generally accepted auditing standards.

D.   Would require the CPA to render a report that indicates that the examination was conducted in accordance with generally accepted auditing standards but was limited in scope.

18-42   When engaged to prepare unaudited financial statements the, CPA's responsibility to detect fraud

A.   Is limited to informing the client of any matters that come to the auditor's attention which cause the auditor to believe that an irregularity exists.
B.   Is the same as the responsibility that exists when the CPA is engaged to perform an audit of financial statements in accordance with generally accepted auditing standards.
C.   Arises out of the CPA's obligation to apply procedures which are designed to bring to light indications that a fraud or defalcation may have occurred.
D.   Does *not* exist unless an engagement letter is prepared.

18-43   Whenever negative assurance is provided by a CPA it is based upon

A.   An absence of nullifying evidence.
B.   A presence of substantiating evidence.
C.   An objective examination in accordance with generally accepted auditing standards.
D.   A judgmental determination in accordance with guidelines promulgated by the AICPA.

Index